Sams Teach Yourself C++ in One Hour a Day, Eighth Edition

Copyright © 2017 by Pearson Education, Inc.

ISBN-13: 978-0-7897-5774-6

ISBN-10: 0-7897-5774-5

Library of Congress Control Number: 2016958138

1   16

Trademarks

All terms mentioned in this book that are known to be trademarks or service marks have been appropriately capitalized. Sams Publishing cannot attest to the accuracy of this information. Use of a term in this book should not be regarded as affecting the validity of any trademark or service mark.

Warning and Disclaimer

Every effort has been made to make this book as complete and as accurate as possible, but no warranty or fitness is implied. The information provided is on an "as is" basis. The author and the publisher shall have neither liability nor responsibility to any person or entity with respect to any loss or damages arising from the information contained in this book.

Special Sales

For information about buying this title in bulk quantities, or for special sales opportunities (which may include electronic versions; custom cover designs; and content particular to your business, training goals, marketing focus, or branding interests), please contact our corporate sales department at corpsales@pearsoned.com or (800) 382-3419.

For government sales inquiries, please contact governmentsales@pearsoned.com.

For questions about sales outside the U.S., please contact intlcs@pearson.com.

Editor
Mark Taber

Senior Project Editor
Tonya Simpson

Copy Editor
Geneil Breeze

Indexer
Erika Millen

Proofreader
Sasirekha Durairajan

Technical Editor
Adrian Ngo

Compositor
codeMantra

Siddhartha Rao

Sams**TeachYourself**

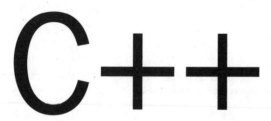

C++

in **One Hour** a Day

Eighth Edition

SAMS

800 East 96th Street, Indianapolis, Indiana 46240 USA

Contents

PART II: Fundamentals of Object-Oriented C++ Programming

LESSON 9: Classes and Objects   215

LESSON 12: Operator Types and Operator Overloading   335

LESSON 13: Casting Operators   377

Dedication

In memory of my father, who will continue to be my source of inspiration.

Acknowledgments

I am thankful to my family for the immense support, to my wife Clara, and to the editorial staff for their spirited engagement in getting this book to you!

About the Author

Siddhartha Rao is the Vice President in charge of Security Response at SAP SE, the world's leading supplier of enterprise software. The evolution of C++ convinces Siddhartha that you can program faster, simpler, and more powerful applications than ever before. He loves traveling and is a passionate mountain biker. He looks forward to your feedback on this effort!

We Want to Hear from You!

As the reader of this book, *you* are our most important critic and commentator. We value your opinion and want to know what we're doing right, what we could do better, what areas you'd like to see us publish in, and any other words of wisdom you're willing to pass our way.

We welcome your comments. You can email or write to let us know what you did or didn't like about this book—as well as what we can do to make our books better.

Please note that we cannot help you with technical problems related to the topic of this book.

When you write, please be sure to include this book's title and author as well as your name and email address. We will carefully review your comments and share them with the author and editors who worked on the book.

Email: feedback@samspublishing.com

Mail: Sams Publishing
           ATTN: Reader Feedback
           800 East 96th Street
           Indianapolis, IN 46240 USA

Reader Services

Visit the publisher's website and register this book at informit.com/register for convenient access to any updates, downloads, or errata that may be available for this book.

Introduction

2011 and 2014 were two special years for C++. While C++11 ushered in a dramatic improvement to C++, introducing new keywords and constructs that increased your programming efficiency, C++14 brought in incremental improvements that added finishing touches to the features introduced by C++11.

This book helps you learn C++ in tiny steps. It has been thoughtfully divided into lessons that teach you the fundamentals of this object-oriented programming language from a practical point of view. Depending on your proficiency level, you will be able to master C++ one hour at a time.

Learning C++ by doing is the best way—so try the rich variety of code samples in this book hands-on and help yourself improve your programming proficiency. These code snippets have been tested using the latest versions of the available compilers at the time of writing, namely the Microsoft Visual C++ compiler for C++ and GNU's C++ compiler, which both offer a rich coverage of C++14 features.

Who Should Read This Book?

The book starts with the very basics of C++. All that is needed is a desire to learn this language and curiosity to understand how stuff works. An existing knowledge of C++ programming can be an advantage but is not a prerequisite. This is also a book you might like to refer to if you already know C++ but want to learn additions that have been made to the language. If you are a professional programmer, Part III, "Learning the Standard Template Library (STL)," is bound to help you create better, more practical C++ applications.

NOTE

Visit the publisher's website and register this book at **informit.com/register** for convenient access to any updates, downloads, or errata that may be available for this book.

Organization of This Book

Depending on your current proficiency levels with C++, you can choose the section you would like to start with. Concepts introduced by C++11 and C++14 are sprinkled throughout the book, in the relevant lessons. This book has been organized into five parts:

- Part I, "The Basics," gets you started with writing simple C++ applications. In doing so, it introduces you to the keywords that you most frequently see in C++ code of a variable without compromising on type safety.

- Part II, "Fundamentals of Object-Oriented C++ Programming," teaches you the concept of classes. You learn how C++ supports the important object-oriented programming principles of encapsulation, abstraction, inheritance, and polymorphism. Lesson 9, "Classes and Objects," teaches you the concept of move constructor followed by the move assignment operator in Lesson 12, "Operator Types and Operator Overloading." These performance features help reduce unwanted and unnecessary copy steps, boosting the performance of your application. Lesson 14, "An Introduction to Macros and Templates," is your stepping stone to writing powerful generic C++ code.

- Part III, "Learning the Standard Template Library (STL)," helps you write efficient and practical C++ code using the STL `string` class and containers. You learn how `std::string` makes simple string concatenation operations safe and easy and how you don't need to use C-style `char*` strings anymore. You will be able to use STL dynamic arrays and linked lists instead of programming your own.

- Part IV, "More STL," focuses on algorithms. You learn to use `sort` on containers such as `vector` via iterators. In this part, you find out how keyword `auto` introduced by C++11 has made a significant reduction to the length of your iterator declarations. Lesson 22, "Lambda Expressions," presents a powerful new feature that results in significant code reduction when you use STL algorithms.

- Part V, "Advanced C++ Concepts," explains language capabilities such as smart pointers and exception handling, which are not a must in a C++ application but help make a significant contribution toward increasing its stability and quality. This part ends with a note on best practices in writing good C++ applications, and introduces you to the new features expected to make it to the next version of the ISO standard called C++17.

Conventions Used in This Book

Within the lessons, you find the following elements that provide additional information:

NOTE	These boxes provide additional information related to material you read.

CAUTION	These boxes alert your attention to problems or side effects that can occur in special situations.

TIP	These boxes give you best practices in writing your C++ programs.

DO	DON'T
DO use the "Do/Don't" boxes to find a quick summary of a fundamental principle in a lesson.	**DON'T** overlook the useful information offered in these boxes.

This book uses different typefaces to differentiate between code and plain English. Throughout the lessons, code, commands, and programming-related terms appear in a computer `typeface`.

Sample Code for This Book

The code samples in this book are available online for download from the publisher's website.

LESSON 1
Getting Started

Welcome to *Sams Teach Yourself C++ in One Hour a Day*! You're ready to get started on becoming a proficient C++ programmer.

In this lesson, you find out

- Why C++ is a standard in software development
- How to enter, compile, and link your first working C++ program
- What's new in C++

A Brief History of C++

The purpose of a programming language is to make consumption of computational resources easier. C++ is not a new language, yet one that is popularly adopted and continuously evolving. As of the time of writing this book, the newest version of C++ ratified by the International Organization for Standardization (ISO) is popularly called C++14, published in December 2014.

Connection to C

Initially developed by Bjarne Stroustroup at Bell Labs in 1979, C++ was designed to be a successor to C. In contrast to C, however, C++ was designed to be an object-oriented language that implements concepts such as inheritance, abstraction, polymorphism, and encapsulation. C++ features classes that are used to contain member data and member methods. These member methods operate using member data. The effect of this organization is that the programmer models data and actions he wants to perform using the same. Many popular C++ compilers have continued to support C programming too.

NOTE _____ | Knowledge or experience in C programming is not a prerequisite for learning C++. If your ultimate goal is to learn an object-oriented programming language like C++, then you don't need to start learning a procedural language like C.

Advantages of C++

C++ is considered an intermediate-level programming language, which means that it allows for high-level programming of applications as well as low-level programming of libraries that work close to the hardware. For many programmers, C++ provides the optimal mix of being a high-level language that lets one develop complex applications while supplying flexibility in allowing the developer to extract the best performance via accurate control of resource consumption and availability.

In spite of the presence of newer programming languages such as Java and others based on .NET, C++ has remained relevant and has also evolved. Newer languages provide certain features like memory management via garbage collection implemented in a runtime component that endear them to some programmers. Yet, C++ remains the language of choice for cases where accurate control over their application's resource consumption and performance is needed. A tiered architecture where a web server programmed in C++ serves other components programmed in HTML, Java, or .NET is common.

Evolution of the C++ Standard

Due to its popularity, years of evolution resulted in C++ being accepted and adopted on many different platforms, most using their own C++ compilers. This evolution caused compiler-specific deviations and, therefore, interoperability problems and porting issues. Hence, there emerged a need to standardize the language and provide compiler manufacturers with a standard language specification to work with.

In 1998, the first standard version of C++ was ratified by the ISO Committee in ISO/IEC 14882:1998. Since then the standard has undergone ambitious changes that have improved the usability of the language, and have extended the support of the standard library. As of the time of writing this book, the current ratified version of the standard is ISO/IEC 14882:2014, informally termed C++14.

NOTE

> The current standard may not be immediately or completely supported by all popular compilers. Therefore, while it may be good to know of the newest additions to the standard from an academic point of view, one must remember that these additions are not a prerequisite to writing good, functioning C++ applications.

Who Uses Programs Written in C++?

The list of applications, operating systems, web services, and database and enterprise software programmed in C++ is a long one. No matter who you are or what you do with a computer, chances are that you already are consuming software programmed in C++. In addition to software engineers, C++ is often a language of choice for research work by physicists and mathematicians.

Programming a C++ Application

When you start Notepad on Windows or the Terminal on Linux, you actually are telling the processor to run an executable of that program. The executable is the finished product that can be run and should do what the programmer intended to achieve.

Steps to Generating an Executable

Writing a C++ program is a first step towards creating an executable that can eventually run on your operating system. The basic steps in creating applications in C++ are the following:

1. Writing (or programming) C++ code using a text editor

2. Compiling code using a C++ compiler that converts it to a machine language version contained in "object files"

3. Linking the output of the compiler using a linker to get an executable (.exe in Windows, for example)

Compilation is the step where code in C++, contained typically in text files with the extension .cpp, is converted into byte code that the processor can execute. The compiler converts one code file at a time, generating an object file with a .o or .obj extension, ignoring dependencies that this CPP file may have on code in another file. The linker joins the dots and resolves these dependencies. In the event of successful linkage, it creates an executable for the programmer to execute and distribute. This entire process is also called building an executable.

Analyzing Errors and "Debugging"

Most applications rarely compile and execute as intended at the first run. A huge or complex application programmed in any language—C++ included—needs many runs as part of a testing effort to identify errors in code, called *bugs*. After the bugs are fixed, the executable is rebuilt, and the testing process continues. Thus, in addition to the three steps—programming, compiling, and linking—software development also involves a step called debugging in which the programmer analyzes errors in code and fixes them. Good development environments supply tools and features that help in debugging.

Integrated Development Environments

Many programmers prefer using an Integrated Development Environment (IDE) in which the programming, compiling, and linking steps are integrated within a unified user interface that also supplies debugging features that make it easier to detect errors and solve problems.

TIP

The fastest way to start writing, compiling, and executing C++ applications would be an online IDE that runs in your browser. Visit one such tool at http://www.tutorialspoint.com/compile_cpp_online.php.

In addition, install one of the many free C++ IDEs and compilers. The popular ones are Microsoft Visual Studio Express for Windows and the GNU C++ Compiler called g++ for Linux. If you're programming on Linux, you can install the free Eclipse IDE to develop C++ applications using the g++ compiler.

DO	DON'T
DO save your files with the .cpp extension. **DO** use a simple text editor or an Integrated Development Environment to write code.	**DON'T** use a .c extension for your C++ file because some compilers would compile these files as C programs instead of C++. **DON'T** use rich text editors like word processors to write code, because they often add their own markup in addition to the code you program.

Programming Your First C++ Application

Now that you know the tools and the steps involved, it is time to program your first C++ application that follows tradition and displays a "Hello World!" on your screen.

If you are programming on Linux, use a simple text editor (I used gedit on Ubuntu) to create a CPP file with contents as seen in Listing 1.1.

If you are on Windows and using Microsoft Visual Studio, you may follow these steps:

1. Invoke the New Project Wizard via the menu option File, New Project.

2. Under Visual C++, choose the type Win32 Console Application and name your project Hello. Click OK.

3. Under Application Settings, uncheck the Precompiled Header option. Click Finish.

4. Replace the automatically generated contents in Hello.cpp with the code snippet shown in Listing 1.1.

LISTING 1.1 Hello.cpp, the Hello World Program

```
1:  #include <iostream>
2:
3:  int main()
4:  {
5:     std::cout << "Hello World!" << std::endl;
6:     return 0;
7:  }
```

This simple application does nothing more than display a line on the screen using std::cout. std::endl instructs cout to end that line, and the application exits by returning 0 to the operating system.

NOTE

> To read a program to yourself, it might help if you know how to pronounce the special characters and keywords.
>
> For instance, you can call `#include` hash-include. Other versions are sharp-include or pound-include, depending on where you come from.
>
> Similarly, you can read `std::cout` as standard-c-out. `endl` is end-line.

CAUTION

> The devil is in the details, meaning that you need to be typing your code in exactly the same way as shown in the listings. Compilers are strict, and if you mistakenly put a `:` at the end of a statement where a `;` is required, you may expect a compilation failure accompanied by a long error report!

Building and Executing Your First C++ Application

If you're using Linux, open the terminal, navigate to the directory containing `Hello.cpp`, and invoke the g++ compiler and linker using the command line:

```
g++ -o hello Hello.cpp
```

This command instructs `g++` to create an executable named `hello` by compiling your C++ file `Hello.cpp`.

If you're using Microsoft Visual Studio on Windows, press Ctrl+F5 to run your program directly via the IDE. This compiles, links, and executes your application. Alternatively, perform the individual steps:

1. Right-click the project and select Build to generate the executable `Hello.exe`.
2. Navigate to the path of the executable using the command-prompt (typically under the Debug directory of the project folder).
3. Run it by typing the name of the executable.

Your program composed in Microsoft Visual Studio looks similar to that illustrated in Figure 1.1.

FIGURE 1.1
A simple "Hello World" C++ program edited in Microsoft Visual Studio Express.

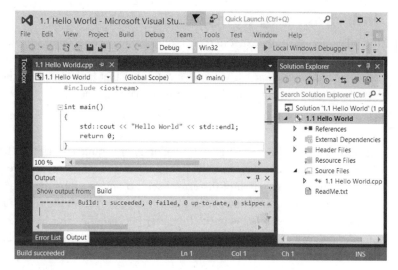

1

Executing ./hello on Linux or Hello.exe on Windows returns the following output:

```
Hello World!
```

Congratulations! You have started on your way to learning one of the most popular and powerful programming languages of all times!

Significance of the C++ ISO Standard

As you can see, standard compliance helps the code snippet in Listing 1.1 to be compiled and executed on multiple platforms or operating systems—the prerequisite being the availability of standard compliant C++ compilers. Thus, if you need to create a product that needs to be run by Windows as well as Linux users, for example, standard compliant programming practices (that don't use a compiler or platform-specific semantics) give you an inexpensive way to reach more users without needing to program specifically for every environment you need to be supporting. This, of course, works optimally for applications that don't need much interaction at an operating system level.

Understanding Compiler Errors

Compilers are painfully exact in their requirements, yet good ones make a decent effort at telling you where you have made mistakes. If you face a problem in compiling the application in Listing 1.1, you might get errors that look quite like the following (introduced deliberately by omitting the semicolon in Line 5):

```
hello.cpp(6): error C2143: syntax error : missing ';' before 'return'
```

This error message from the Visual C++ Compiler is quite descriptive: It tells the name of the file that contains the error, the line number (6, in this case) where you missed a semicolon, and a description of the error itself accompanied by the error number (C2143, in this case). Though the punctuation mark was deleted from the fifth line for this example, the error reported is in the line after because the error became apparent to the compiler only when it analyzed the return statement which indicated that the previous statement ought to have been terminated before the return. You can try to add the semicolon at the start of the sixth line and the program compiles just fine!

| NOTE | Line-breaks don't automatically terminate statements in C++ as they do in some languages such as VBScript. |
| | In C++, it is possible to have a statement spanning multiple lines. It is also possible to have multiple statements in a line with each statement terminated by a ;. |

What's New in C++?

If you are an experienced C++ programmer, you might have noticed that the basic C++ program in Listing 1.1 hasn't changed one bit. While it's true that C++ remains backward compliant with previous versions of C++, a lot of work has been done recently to make the language simpler to use and to program in.

The most recent major update in the language was released as a part of the ISO standard ratified in 2011, popularly called C++11. C++14 released in 2014 features minor improvements and corrections over C++11.

Features such as `auto` introduced first in C++11 allow you to define a variable whose type is deduced automatically by the compiler, compacting wordy declarations without compromising on type-safety. C++14 extends the same function to return types as well. *Lambda functions* are functions without a name. They allow you to write compact function objects without long class definitions, significantly reducing lines of code.

C++ promises programmers the ability to write portable, multithreaded, and yet standard-compliant C++ applications. These applications, when correctly built, support concurrent execution paradigms and are well positioned to scale in performance when the user boosts the capability of his hardware configuration by increasing the number of CPU cores. These are some of the many improvements featured in C++ that are discussed throughout this book.

1

New languages features expected in the next major revision, called C++17, are introduced at the end of the book in Lesson 29, "Going Forward."

Summary

In this lesson you learned how to program, compile, link, and execute your first C++ program. This lesson also gave you a brief overview on the evolution of C++ and demonstrated the effectiveness of a standard in showing that the same program can be compiled using different compilers on different operating systems.

Q&A

Q Can I ignore warning messages from my compiler?

A In certain cases, compilers issue warning messages. Warnings are different from errors in that the line in question is syntactically correct and compile-worthy. However, there possibly is a better way to write it, and good compilers issue a warning with a recommendation for a fix.

The suggested correction can mean a more secure way of programming or one that lets your application work with characters and symbols from non-Latin languages. You should heed these warnings and improve your program accordingly. Don't mask the warning messages, unless you are sure that they're false positives.

Q How does an interpreted language differ from a compiled language?

A Languages such as Windows Script are interpreted. There is no compilation step. An interpreted language uses an interpreter that directly reads the script text file (code) and performs the desired actions. Consequently, you need to have the interpreter installed on a machine where the script needs to be executed; consequently, performance usually takes a hit as the interpreter works as a runtime translator between the microprocessor and the code written.

Q What are runtime errors, and how are they different from compile-time errors?

A Errors that happen when you execute your application are called *runtime errors*. You might have experienced the infamous "Access Violation" on older versions of Windows, which is a runtime error. Compile-time errors don't reach the end-user and are an indication of syntactical problems; they keep the programmer from generating an executable.

Workshop

The Workshop provides quiz questions to help you solidify your understanding of the material covered and exercises to provide you with experience in using what you've learned. Try to answer the quiz and exercise questions before checking the answers in Appendix E, and be certain you understand the answers before continuing to the next lesson.

Quiz

1. What is the difference between an interpreter and a compiler?

2. What does the linker do?

3. What are the steps in the normal development cycle?

Exercises

1. Look at the following program and try to guess what it does without running it:

```
 1: #include <iostream>
 2: int main()
 3: {
 4:    int x = 8;
 5:    int y = 6;
 6:    std::cout << std::endl;
 7:    std::cout << x - y << " " << x * y << " " << x + y;
 8:    std::cout << std::endl;
 9:    return 0;
10: }
```

2. Type in the program from Exercise 1 and then compile and link it. What does it do? Does it do what you guessed?

3. What do you think is the error in this program:

```
1: include <iostream>
2: int main()
3: {
4:     std::cout << "Hello Buggy World \n";
5:     return 0;
6: }
```

4. Fix the error in the program in Exercise 3, compile, link, and run it. What does it do?

1

LESSON 2
The Anatomy of a
C++ Program

C++ programs are organized into classes comprising member functions and member variables. Most of this book is devoted to explaining these parts in depth, but to get a sense of how a program fits together, you must see a complete working program.

In this lesson, you learn

- The parts of a C++ program
- How the parts work together
- What a function is and what it does
- Basic input and output operations

Parts of the Hello World Program

Your first C++ program in Lesson 1, "Getting Started," did nothing more than write a simple "Hello World" statement to the screen. Yet this program contains some of the most important and basic building blocks of a C++ program. You use Listing 2.1 as a starting point to analyze components all C++ programs contain.

LISTING 2.1 `HelloWorldAnalysis.cpp`: Analyze a Simple C++ Program

```
 1: // Preprocessor directive that includes header iostream
 2: #include <iostream>
 3:
 4: // Start of your program: function block main()
 5: int main()
 6: {
 7:     /* Write to the screen */
 8:     std::cout << "Hello World" << std::endl;
 9:
10:     // Return a value to the OS
11:     return 0;
12: }
```

This C++ program can be broadly classified into two parts: the preprocessor directives that start with a # and the main body of the program that starts with `int main()`.

NOTE

Lines 1, 4, 7, and 10, which start with a `//` or with a `/*`, are called *comments* and are ignored by the compiler. These comments are for humans to read.

Comments are discussed in greater detail in the next section.

Preprocessor Directive `#include`

As the name suggests, a *preprocessor* is a tool that runs before the actual compilation starts. Preprocessor directives are commands to the preprocessor and always start with a pound sign #. In Line 2 of Listing 2.1, `#include <filename>` tells the preprocessor to take the contents of the file (`iostream`, in this case) and include them at the line where the directive is made. `iostream` is a standard header file that enables the usage of `std::cout` used in Line 8 to display "Hello World" on the screen. In other words, the compiler was able to compile Line 8 that contains `std::cout` because we instructed the preprocessor to include the definition of `std::cout` in Line 2.

NOTE

Professionally programmed C++ applications include standard headers supplied by the development environment and those created by the programmer. Complex applications are typically programmed in multiple files wherein some need to include others. So, if an artifact declared in FileA needs to be used in FileB, you need to include the former in the latter. You usually do that by inserting the following `include` statement in FileA:

```
#include "...relative path to FileB\FileB"
```

We use quotes in this case and not angle brackets in including a self-programmed header. <> brackets are typically used when including standard headers.

The Body of Your Program `main()`

Following the preprocessor directive(s) is the body of the program characterized by the function `main()`. The execution of a C++ program always starts here. It is a standardized convention that function `main()` is declared with an `int` preceding it. `int` is the return value type of the function `main()` and stands for integer.

NOTE

In many C++ applications, you find a variant of the `main()` function that looks like this:

```
int main (int argc, char* argv[])
```

This is also standard compliant and acceptable as main returns int. The contents of the parenthesis are "arguments" supplied to the program. This program possibly allows the user to start it with command-line arguments, such as

```
program.exe /DoSomethingSpecific
```

`/DoSomethingSpecific` is the argument for that program passed by the OS as a parameter to it, to be handled within `main (int argc, char* argv[])`.

Let's discuss Line 8 that fulfills the actual purpose of this program!

```
std::cout << "Hello World" << std::endl;
```

cout ("console-out", also pronounced see-out) is the statement that writes "Hello World" to the display console—that is, screen. cout is a *stream* defined in the standard std *namespace* (hence, std::cout), and what you are doing in this line is putting the text "Hello World" into this stream by using the stream insertion operator <<. std::endl is used to end a line, and inserting it into a stream is akin to inserting a carriage return. Note that the stream insertion operator << is used every time a new entity needs to be inserted into the stream.

The good thing about streams in C++ is that different stream types support similar stream semantics to perform a different operation with the same text. For example, insertion into a file instead of a console would use the same insertion operator << on an std::fstream instead of std::cout. Thus, working with streams gets intuitive, and when you are used to one stream (such as cout, which writes text to the console), you will find it easy to work with others (such as fstream, which helps save files to the disk).

Streams are discussed in greater detail in Lesson 27, "Using Streams for Input and Output."

NOTE	The actual text, including the quotes "Hello World", is called a *string literal*.

Returning a Value

Functions in C++ need to return a value unless explicitly specified otherwise. main() is a function, too, and always returns an integer. This integer value is returned to the operating system (OS) and, depending on the nature of your application, can be very useful as most OSes provide for an ability to query on the return value of an application that has terminated naturally. In many cases, one application is launched by another and the parent application (that launches) wants to know if the child application (that was launched) has completed its task successfully. The programmer can use the return value of main() to convey a success or error state to the parent application.

NOTE	Conventionally programmers return 0 in the event of success or −1 in the event of error. However, the return value is an integer, and the programmer has the flexibility to convey many different states of success or failure using the available range of integer return values.

CAUTION	C++ is case-sensitive. So, expect compilation to fail if you write Int instead of int and Std::Cout instead of std::cout.

The Concept of Namespaces

The reason you used `std::cout` in the program and not only `cout` is that the artifact (cout) that you want to invoke is in the standard (`std`) namespace.

So, what exactly are namespaces?

Assume that you didn't use the namespace qualifier in invoking `cout` and assume that cout existed in two locations known to the compiler—which one should the compiler invoke? This causes a conflict and the compilation fails, of course. This is where namespaces get useful. Namespaces are names given to parts of code that help in reducing the potential for a naming conflict. By invoking `std::cout`, you are telling the compiler to use that one unique `cout` that is available in the `std` namespace.

2

NOTE _____ You use the `std` (pronounced "standard") namespace to invoke functions, streams, and utilities that have been ratified by the ISO Standards Committee.

Many programmers find it tedious to repeatedly add the `std` namespace specifier to their code when using `cout` and other such features contained in the same. The `using namespace` declaration as demonstrated in Listing 2.2 helps you avoid this repetition.

LISTING 2.2   The `using namespace` Declaration

```
1: // Preprocessor directive
2: #include <iostream>
3:
4: // Start of your program
5: int main()
6: {
7:    // Tell the compiler what namespace to search in
8:    using namespace std;
9:
10:    /* Write to the screen using std::cout */
11:    cout << "Hello World" << endl;
12:
13:    // Return a value to the OS
14:    return 0;
15: }
```

Analysis ▼

Note Line 8. By telling the compiler that you are using the namespace `std`, you don't need to explicitly mention the namespace on Line 11 when using `std::cout` or `std::endl`.

A more restrictive variant of Listing 2.2 is shown in Listing 2.3 where you do not include a namespace in its entirety. You only include those artifacts that you wish to use.

LISTING 2.3 Another Demonstration of the `using` Keyword

```
1: // Preprocessor directive
2: #include <iostream>
3:
4: // Start of your program
5: int main()
6: {
7:     using std::cout;
8:     using std::endl;
9:
10:     /* Write to the screen using std::cout */
11:     cout << "Hello World" << endl;
12:
13:     // Return a value to the OS
14:     return 0;
15: }
```

Analysis ▼

Line 8 in Listing 2.2 has now been replaced by Lines 7 and 8 in Listing 2.3. The difference between `using namespace std` and `using std::cout` is that the former allows all artifacts in the `std` namespace (`cout`, `cin`, etc.) to be used without explicit inclusion of the namespace qualifier `std::`. With the latter, the convenience of not needing to disambiguate the namespace explicitly is restricted to only `std::cout` and `std::endl`.

Comments in C++ Code

Lines 1, 4, 10, and 13 in Listing 2.3 contain text in a spoken language (English, in this case) yet do not interfere with the ability of the program to compile. They also do not alter the output of the program. Such lines are called comments. Comments are ignored by the compiler and are popularly used by programmers to explain their code—hence, they are written in human-readable language.

C++ supports comments in two styles:

- `//` indicates the start of a comment, valid until the end of that line. For example:

  ```
  // This is a comment - won't be compiled
  ```

- `/*` followed by `*/` indicates that the contained text is a comment, even if it spans multiple lines:

  ```
  /* This is a comment
  and it spans two lines */
  ```

NOTE

It might seem strange that a programmer needs to explain his own code, but the bigger a program gets or the larger the number of programmers working on a particular module gets, the more important it is to write code that can be easily understood. Comments help a programmer document what is being done and why it is being done in that particular manner.

DO	DON'T
DO add comments explaining the working of complicated algorithms and complex parts of your program.	**DON'T** use comments to explain or repeat the obvious.
DO compose comments in a style that fellow programmers can understand.	**DON'T** forget that adding comments will not justify writing obscure code.
	DON'T forget that when code is modified, comments might need to be updated, too.

Functions in C++

Functions enable you to divide the content of your application into functional units that can be invoked in a sequence of your choosing. A function, when invoked, typically returns a value to the invoking/calling function. The most famous function is, of course, `int main()`. It is recognized by the compiler as the starting point of your C++ application and has to return an `int` (i.e., an integer).

You as a programmer have the choice and usually the need to compose your own functions. Listing 2.4 is a simple application that uses a function to display statements on the screen using `std::cout` with various parameters.

LISTING 2.4 Declaring, Defining, and Calling a Function That Demonstrates Capabilities of `std::cout`

```
 1: #include <iostream>
 2: using namespace std;
 3:
 4: // Declare a function
 5: int DemoConsoleOutput();
 6:
 7: int main()
 8: {
 9:     // Call i.e. invoke the function
10:     DemoConsoleOutput();
11:
12:     return 0;
13: }
14:
15: // Define i.e. implement the previously declared function
16: int DemoConsoleOutput()
17: {
18:     cout << "This is a simple string literal" << endl;
19:     cout << "Writing number five: " << 5 << endl;
20:     cout << "Performing division 10 / 5 = " << 10 / 5 << endl;
21:     cout << "Pi when approximated is 22 / 7 = " << 22 / 7 << endl;
22:     cout << "Pi is 22 / 7 = " << 22.0 / 7 << endl;
23:
24:     return 0;
25: }
```

Output ▼

```
This is a simple string literal
Writing number five: 5
Performing division 10 / 5 = 2
Pi when approximated is 22 / 7 = 3
Pi is 22 / 7 = 3.14286
```

Analysis ▼

Lines 5, 10, and 16 through 25 are those of interest. Line 5 is called a *function declaration*, which basically tells the compiler that you want to create a function called `DemoConsoleOutput()` that returns an `int` (integer). This declaration enables the

11/12

Hanna, F

Reserved Item

Branch: Canterbury Library
Date: 27/11/2023   Time: 12:34 PM
Name: Hanna, Frederick Keith
ID: ...2850

Item: Sams teach yourself C++ in
        one hour a day
        c334065582

Expires:11 Dec 2023

Instruction: Please process item

compiler to compile Line 10 where DemoConsoleOutput() is called inside main(). The compiler assumes that the *definition* (that is, the implementation of the function) is going to come up, which it does later in Lines 16 through 25.

This function actually demonstrates the capabilities of cout. Note how it not only prints text the same way as it displayed "Hello World" in previous examples, but also the result of simple arithmetic computations. Lines 21 and 22 both attempt to display the result of pi (22 / 7), but the latter is more accurate simply because by dividing 22.0 by 7, you tell the compiler to treat the result as a real number (a float in C++ terms) and not as an integer.

Note that your function is required to return an integer, as declared in Line 5, and returns 0. Similarly, main() returns 0, too. Given that main() has delegated all its activity to the function DemoConsoleOutput(), you would be wiser to use the return value of the function in returning from main() as seen in Listing 2.5.

LISTING 2.5 Using the Return Value of a Function

```
 1: #include <iostream>
 2: using namespace std;
 3:
 4: // Function declaration and definition
 5: int DemoConsoleOutput()
 6: {
 7:     cout << "This is a simple string literal" << endl;
 8:     cout << "Writing number five: " << 5 << endl;
 9:     cout << "Performing division 10 / 5 = " << 10 / 5 << endl;
10:     cout << "Pi when approximated is 22 / 7 = " << 22 / 7 << endl;
11:     cout << "Pi actually is 22 / 7 = " << 22.0 / 7 << endl;
12:
13:     return 0;
14: }
15:
16: int main()
17: {
18:     // Function call with return used to exit
19:     return DemoConsoleOutput();
20: }
```

Analysis ▼

The output of this application is the same as the output of the previous listing. Yet, there are slight changes in the way it is programmed. For one, as you have defined (i.e., implemented) the function before main() at Line 5, you don't need an extra declaration of the same. Modern C++ compilers take it as a function declaration and definition in one. `main()` is a bit shorter, too. Line 19 invokes the function `DemoConsoleOutput()` and simultaneously returns the return value of the function from the application.

> **NOTE**
>
> In cases such as this where a function is not required to make a decision, or return success or failure status, you can declare a function of return type `void`:
>
> `void DemoConsoleOutput()`
>
> This function cannot return a value.

Functions can take parameters, can be recursive, can contain multiple return statements, can be overloaded, can be expanded in-line by the compiler, and lots more. These concepts are introduced in greater detail in Lesson 7, "Organizing Code with Functions."

Basic Input Using `std::cin` and Output Using `std::cout`

Your computer enables you to interact with applications running on it in various forms and allows these applications to interact with you in many forms, too. You can interact with applications using the keyboard or the mouse. You can have information displayed on the screen as text, displayed in the form of complex graphics, printed on paper using a printer, or simply saved to the file system for later usage. This section discusses the very simplest form of input and output in C++—using the console to write and read information.

You use `std::cout` (pronounced "standard see-out") to write simple text data to the console and use `std::cin` ("standard see-in") to read text and numbers (entered using the keyboard) from the console. In fact, in displaying "Hello World" on the screen, you have already encountered `cout`, as seen in Listing 2.1:

```
8:    std::cout << "Hello World" << std::endl;
```

The statement shows `cout` followed by the insertion operator `<<` (that helps insert data into the output stream), followed by the string literal "Hello World" to be inserted, followed by a newline in the form of `std::endl` (pronounced "standard end-line").

The usage of `cin` is simple, too, and as `cin` is used for input, it is accompanied by the variable you want to be storing the input data in:

```
std::cin >> Variable;
```

Thus, `cin` is followed by the *extraction* operator `>>` (extracts data from the input stream), which is followed by the variable where the data needs to be stored. If the user input needs to be stored in two variables, each containing data separated by a space, then you can do so using one statement:

```
std::cin >> Variable1 >> Variable2;
```

Note that `cin` can be used for text as well as numeric inputs from the user, as shown in Listing 2.6.

LISTING 2.6 Use `cin` and `cout` to Display Number and Text Input by User

```
 1: #include <iostream>
 2: #include <string>
 3: using namespace std;
 4:
 5: int main()
 6: {
 7:     // Declare a variable to store an integer
 8:     int inputNumber;
 9:
10:     cout << "Enter an integer: ";
11:
12:     // store integer given user input
13:     cin >> inputNumber;
14:
15:     // The same with text i.e. string data
16:     cout << "Enter your name: ";
17:     string inputName;
18:     cin >> inputName;
19:
20:     cout << inputName << " entered " << inputNumber << endl;
21:
22:     return 0;
23: }
```

Output ▼

```
Enter an integer: 2017
Enter your name: Siddhartha
Siddhartha entered 2017
```

Analysis ▼

Line 8 shows how a variable of name `inputNumber` is declared to store data of type `int`. The user is requested to enter a number using `cout` in Line 10, and the entered number is stored in the integer variable using `cin` in Line 13. The same exercise is repeated with storing the user's name, which of course cannot be held in an integer but in a different type called `string` as seen in Lines 17 and 18. The reason you included `<string>` in Line 2 was to use type `string` later inside `main()`. Finally in Line 20, a `cout` statement is used to display the entered name with the number and an intermediate text to produce the output `Siddhartha entered 2017`.

This is a simple example of how basic input and output work in C++. Don't worry if the concept of variables is not clear to you as it is explained in good detail in the following Lesson 3, "Using Variables, Declaring Constants."

NOTE

> If I had entered a couple of words as my name (for example: Siddhartha Rao) while executing Listing 2.6, `cin` would've still stored only the first word, "Siddhartha," in the string. To be able to store entire lines, use the function `getline()`, discussed in Lesson 4, "Managing Arrays and Strings," in Listing 4.7.

Summary

This lesson introduced the basic parts of a simple C++ program. You understood what `main()` is, got an introduction to namespaces, and learned the basics of console input and output. You are able to use a lot of these in every program you write.

Q&A

Q What does `#include` do?

A This is a directive to the preprocessor that runs when you call your compiler. This specific directive causes the contents of the file named in `<>` after `#include` to be inserted at that line as if it were typed at that location in your source code.

Q What is the difference between `//` comments and `/*` comments?

A The double-slash comments (`//`) expire at the end of the line. Slash-star (`/*`) comments are in effect until there is a closing comment mark (`*/`). The double-slash comments are also referred to as *single-line comments*, and the slash-star comments are often referred to as *multiline comments*. Remember, not even the end of the function terminates a slash-star comment; you must put in the closing comment mark or you will receive a compile-time error.

Q When do you need to program command-line arguments?

A To supply options that allow the user to alter the behavior of a program. For example, the command `ls` in Linux or `dir` in Windows enables you to see the contents within the current directory or folder. To view files in another directory, you specify the path of the same using command-line arguments, as in `ls / ` or `dir \`.

Workshop

2

The Workshop provides quiz questions to help you solidify your understanding of the material covered and exercises to provide you with experience in using what you've learned. Try to answer the quiz and exercise questions before checking the answers in Appendix E, and be certain you understand the answers before continuing to the next lesson.

Quiz

1. What is the problem in declaring `Int main()`?

2. Can comments be longer than one line?

Exercises

1. BUG BUSTERS: Enter this program and compile it. Why does it fail? How can you fix it?

```
1: #include <iostream>
2: void main()
3: {
4:     std::Cout << Is there a bug here?";
5: }
```

2. Fix the bug in Exercise 1 and recompile, link, and run it.

3. Modify Listing 2.4 to demonstrate subtraction (using –) and multiplication (using *).

LESSON 3
Using Variables, Declaring Constants

Variables are tools that help the programmer temporarily store data for a finite amount of time. *Constants* are tools that help the programmer define artifacts that are not allowed to change or make changes.

In this lesson, you find out

- How to declare and define variables and constants
- How to assign values to variables and manipulate those values
- How to write the value of a variable to the screen
- How to use keywords `auto` and `constexpr`

What Is a Variable?

Before you actually explore the need and use of variables in a programming language, take a step back and first see what a computer contains and how it works.

Memory and Addressing in Brief

All computers, smart phones, and other programmable devices contain a microprocessor and a certain amount of memory for temporary storage called Random Access Memory (RAM). In addition, many devices also allow for data to be persisted on a storage device such as the hard disk. The microprocessor executes your application, and in doing so it works with the RAM to fetch the application binary code to be executed as well as the data associated with it, which includes that displayed on the screen and that entered by the user.

The RAM itself can be considered to be a storage area akin to a row of lockers in the dorms, each locker having a number—that is, an address. To access a location in memory, say location 578, the processor needs to be asked via an instruction to fetch a value from there or write a value to it.

Declaring Variables to Access and Use Memory

The following examples will help you understand what variables are. Assume you are writing a program to multiply two numbers supplied by the user. The user is asked to feed the multiplicand and the multiplier into your program, one after the other, and you need to store each of them so that you can use them later to multiply. Depending on what you want to be doing with the result of the multiplication, you might even want to store it for later use in your program. It would be slow and error-prone if you were to explicitly specify memory addresses (such as 578) to store the numbers, as you would need to worry about inadvertently overwriting existing data at the location or your data being overwritten at a later stage.

When programming in languages like C++, you define variables to store those values. Defining a variable is quite simple and follows this pattern:

```
VariableType VariableName;
```

or

```
VariableType VariableName = InitialValue;
```

The variable type attribute tells the compiler the nature of data the variable can store, and the compiler reserves the necessary space for it. The name chosen by the programmer is a friendly replacement for the address in the memory where the variable's value is stored.

Unless the initial value is assigned, you cannot be sure of the contents of that memory location, which can be bad for the program. Therefore, initialization is optional, but it's often a good programming practice. Listing 3.1 shows how variables are declared, initialized, and used in a program that multiplies two numbers supplied by the user.

LISTING 3.1 Using Variables to Store Numbers and the Result of Their Multiplication

```
1: #include <iostream>
2: using namespace std;
3:
4: int main ()
5: {
6:     cout << "This program will help you multiply two numbers" << endl;
7:
8:     cout << "Enter the first number: ";
9:     int firstNumber = 0;
10:    cin >> firstNumber;
11:
12:    cout << "Enter the second number: ";
13:    int secondNumber = 0;
14:    cin >> secondNumber;
15:
16:    // Multiply two numbers, store result in a variable
17:    int multiplicationResult = firstNumber * secondNumber;
18:
19:    // Display result
20:    cout << firstNumber << " x " << secondNumber;
21:    cout << " = " << multiplicationResult << endl;
22:
23:    return 0;
24: }
```

3

Output ▼

```
This program will help you multiply two numbers
Enter the first number: 51
Enter the second number: 24
51 x 24 = 1224
```

Analysis ▼

This application asks the user to enter two numbers, which the program multiplies and displays the result. To use numbers entered by the user, it needs to store them in the memory. Variables firstNumber and secondNumber declared in Lines 9 and 13 do the job of temporarily storing integer values entered by the user. You use std::cin in Lines 10 and 14 to accept input from the user and to store them in the two integer variables. The cout statement in Line 21 is used to display the result on the console.

Analyzing a variable declaration further:

```
9:    int firstNumber = 0;
```

What this line declares is a variable of type int, which indicates an integer, with a name called firstNumber. Zero is assigned to the variable as an initial value.

The compiler does the job of mapping this variable firstNumber to a location in memory and takes care of the associated memory-address bookkeeping for you for all the variables that you declare. The programmer thus works with human-friendly names, while the compiler manages memory-addressing and creates the instructions for the microprocessor to execute in working with the RAM.

CAUTION

> Naming variables appropriately is important for writing good, understandable, and maintainable code.
>
> Variable names in C++ can be alphanumeric, but they cannot start with a number. They cannot contain spaces and cannot contain arithmetic operators (such as +, -, and so on) within them. Variable names also cannot be reserved keywords. For example, a variable named return will cause compilation failure.
>
> Variable names can contain the underscore character_that often is used in descriptive variable naming.

Declaring and Initializing Multiple Variables of a Type

In Listing 3.1, firstNumber, secondNumber, and multiplicationResult are all of the same type—integers—and are declared in three separate lines. If you wanted to, you could condense the declaration of these three variables to one line of code that looks like this:

```
int firstNumber = 0, secondNumber = 0, multiplicationResult = 0;
```

NOTE

> As you can see, C++ makes it possible to declare multiple variables of a type at once and to declare variables at the beginning of a function. Yet, declaring a variable when it is first needed is often better as it makes the code readable—one notices the type of the variable when the declaration is close to its point of first use.

CAUTION

> Data stored in variables is data stored in RAM. This data is lost when the application terminates unless the programmer explicitly persists the data on a storage medium like a hard disk.
>
> Storing to a file on disk is discussed in Lesson 27, "Using Streams for Input and Output."

Understanding the Scope of a Variable

Ordinary variables like the ones we have declared this far have a well-defined scope within which they're valid and can be used. When used outside their scope, the variable names will not be recognized by the compiler and your program won't compile. Beyond its scope, a variable is an unidentified entity that the compiler knows nothing of.

To better understand the scope of a variable, reorganize the program in Listing 3.1 into a function `MultiplyNumbers()` that multiplies the two numbers and returns the result. See Listing 3.2.

3

LISTING 3.2 Demonstrating the Scope of the Variables

```
 1: #include <iostream>
 2: using namespace std;
 3:
 4: void MultiplyNumbers ()
 5: {
 6:     cout << "Enter the first number: ";
 7:     int firstNumber = 0;
 8:     cin >> firstNumber;
 9:
10:     cout << "Enter the second number: ";
11:     int secondNumber = 0;
12:     cin >> secondNumber;
13:
14:     // Multiply two numbers, store result in a variable
15:     int multiplicationResult = firstNumber * secondNumber;
16:
17:     // Display result
18:     cout << firstNumber << " x " << secondNumber;
19:     cout << " = " << multiplicationResult << endl;
20: }
21: int main ()
22: {
23:     cout << "This program will help you multiply two numbers" << endl;
24:
25:     // Call the function that does all the work
26:     MultiplyNumbers();
```

```
27:
28:     // cout << firstNumber << " x " << secondNumber;
29:     // cout << " = " << multiplicationResult << endl;
30:
31:     return 0;
32: }
```

Output ▼

```
This program will help you multiply two numbers
Enter the first number: 51
Enter the second number: 24
51 x 24 = 1224
```

Analysis ▼

Listing 3.2 does exactly the same activity as Listing 3.1 and produces the same output. The only difference is that the bulk of the work is delegated to a function called MultiplyNumbers() invoked by main(). Note that variables firstNumber and secondNumber cannot be used outside of MultiplyNumbers(). If you uncomment Lines 28 or 29 in main(), you experience compile failure of type undeclared identifier.

This is because the scope of the variables firstNumber and secondNumber is local, hence limited to the function they're declared in, in this case MultiplyNumbers(). A local variable can be used in a function after variable declaration till the end of the function. The curly brace (}) that indicates the end of a function also limits the scope of variables declared in the same. When a function ends, all local variables are destroyed and the memory they occupied returned.

When compiled, variables declared within MultiplyNumbers() perish when the function ends, and if they're used in main(), compilation fails as the variables have not been declared in there.

CAUTION

If you declare another set of variables with the same name in main(), then don't still expect them to carry a value that might have been assigned in MultiplyNumbers().

The compiler treats the variables in main() as independent entities even if they share their names with a variable declared in another function, as the two variables in question are limited by their scope.

Global Variables

If the variables used in function `MultiplyNumbers()` in Listing 3.2 were declared outside the scope of the function `MultiplyNumber()` instead of within it, then they would be usable in both `main()` and `MultiplyNumbers()`. Listing 3.3 demonstrates global variables, which are the variables with the widest scope in a program.

LISTING 3.3   Using Global Variables

```
 1: #include <iostream>
 2: using namespace std;
 3:
 4: // three global integers
 5: int firstNumber = 0;
 6: int secondNumber = 0;
 7: int multiplicationResult = 0;
 8:
 9: void MultiplyNumbers ()
10: {
11:     cout << "Enter the first number: ";
12:     cin >> firstNumber;
13:
14:     cout << "Enter the second number: ";
15:     cin >> secondNumber;
16:
17:     // Multiply two numbers, store result in a variable
18:     multiplicationResult = firstNumber * secondNumber;
19:
20:     // Display result
21:     cout << "Displaying from MultiplyNumbers(): ";
22:     cout << firstNumber << " x " << secondNumber;
23:     cout << " = " << multiplicationResult << endl;
24: }
25: int main ()
26: {
27:     cout << "This program will help you multiply two numbers" << endl;
28:
29:     // Call the function that does all the work
30:     MultiplyNumbers();
31:
32:     cout << "Displaying from main(): ";
33:
34:     // This line will now compile and work!
35:     cout << firstNumber << " x " << secondNumber;
36:     cout << " = " << multiplicationResult << endl;
37:
38:     return 0;
39: }
```

3

Output ▼

```
This program will help you multiply two numbers
Enter the first number: 51
Enter the second number: 19
Displaying from MultiplyNumbers(): 51 x 19 = 969
Displaying from main(): 51 x 19 = 969
```

Analysis ▼

Listing 3.3 displays the result of multiplication in two functions, neither of which has declared the variables firstNumber, secondNumber, and multiplicationResult. These variables are global as they have been declared in Lines 5–7, outside the scope of any function. Note Lines 23 and 36 that use these variables and display their values. Pay special attention to how multiplicationResult is first assigned in MultiplyNumbers() yet is effectively reused in main().

CAUTION

Indiscriminate use of global variables is considered poor programming practice. This is because global variables can be assigned values in any/every function and can contain an unpredictable state, especially when functions that modify them run in different threads or are programmed by different programmers in a team.

An elegant way of programming Listing 3.3 without using global variables would have the function MultiplyNumbers() return the integer result of the multiplication to main().

Naming Conventions

In case you haven't noticed, we named the function MultiplyNumbers() where every word in the function name starts with a capital letter (called *Pascal casing*), while variables firstNumber, secondNumber, and multiplicationResult were given names where the first word starts with a lowercase letter (called *camel casing*). This book follows a convention where variable names follow camel casing, while other artifacts such as function names follow Pascal casing.

You may come across C++ code wherein a variable name is prefixed with characters that explain the type of the variable. This convention is called the *Hungarian notation* and is frequently used in the programming of Windows applications. So, `firstNumber` in Hungarian notation would be `iFirstNumber`, where the prefix `i` stands for integer. A global integer would be called `g_iFirstNumber`. Hungarian notation has lost popularity in recent years in part due to improvements in Integrated Development Environments (IDEs) that display the type of a variable when required—on mouse hover, for instance.

Examples of commonly found bad variable names follow:

```
int i = 0;
bool b = false;
```

The name of the variable should indicate its purpose, and the two can be better declared as

```
int totalCash = 0;
bool isLampOn = false;
```

3

CAUTION

Naming conventions are used to make the code readable to programmers, not to compilers. So choose a convention that suits wisely and use it consistently.

When working in a team, it is a good idea to align on the convention to be used before starting a new project. When working on an existing project, adopt the used convention so that the new code remains readable to others.

Common Compiler-Supported C++ Variable Types

In most of the examples thus far, you have defined variables of type `int`—that is, integers. However, C++ programmers can choose from a variety of fundamental variable types supported directly by the compiler. Choosing the right variable type is as important as choosing the right tools for the job! A Phillips screwdriver won't work well with a regular screw head just like an unsigned integer can't be used to store values that are negative! Table 3.1 enlists the various variable types and the nature of data they can contain.

TABLE 3.1 Variable Types

Type	Values
`bool`	`true` or `false`
`char`	256 character values
`unsigned short int`	0 to 65,535
`short int`	–32,768 to 32,767
`unsigned long int`	0 to 4,294,967,295
`long int`	–2,147,483,648 to 2,147,483,647
`unsigned long long`	0 to 18,446,744,073,709,551,615
`long long`	–9,223,372,036,854,775,808 to 9,223,372,036,854,775,807
`int` (16 bit)	–32,768 to 32,767
`int` (32 bit)	–2,147,483,648 to 2,147,483,647
`unsigned int` (16 bit)	0 to 65,535
`unsigned int` (32 bit)	0 to 4,294,967,295
`float`	1.2e–38 to 3.4e38
`double`	2.2e–308 to 1.8e308

The following sections explain the important types in greater detail.

Using Type `bool` to Store Boolean Values

C++ provides a type that is specially created for containing Boolean values `true` or `false`, both of which are reserved C++ keywords. This type is particularly useful in storing settings and flags that can be ON or OFF, present or absent, available or unavailable, and the like.

A sample declaration of an initialized Boolean variable is

```
bool alwaysOnTop = false;
```

An expression that evaluates to a Boolean type is

```
bool deleteFile = (userSelection == "yes");
// evaluates to true if userSelection contains "yes", else to false
```

Conditional expressions are explained in Lesson 5, "Working with Expressions, Statements, and Operators."

Using Type `char` to Store Character Values

Use type `char` to store a single character. A sample declaration is

```
char userInput = 'Y'; // initialized char to 'Y'
```

Note that memory is comprised of bits and bytes. Bits can be either 0 or 1, and bytes can contain numeric representation using these bits. So, working or assigning character data as shown in the example, the compiler converts the character into a numeric representation that can be placed into memory. The numeric representation of Latin characters A–Z, a–z, numbers 0–9, some special keystrokes (for example, DEL), and special characters (such as backspace) has been standardized by the American Standard Code for Information Interchange, also called ASCII.

You can look up the table in Appendix D, "ASCII Codes," to see that the character Y assigned to variable `userInput` has the ASCII value 89 in decimal. Thus, what the compiler does is store 89 in the memory space allocated for `userInput`.

The Concept of Signed and Unsigned Integers

Sign implies positive or negative. All numbers you work with using a computer are stored in the memory in the form of bits and bytes. A memory location that is 1 byte large contains 8 bits. Each bit can either be a 0 or 1 (that is, carry one of these two values at best). Thus, a memory location that is 1 byte large can contain a maximum of 2 to the power 8 values—that is, 256 unique values. Similarly, a memory location that is 16 bits large can contain 2 to the power 16 values—that is, 65,536 unique values.

If these values were to be unsigned—assumed to be only positive—then one byte could contain integer values ranging from 0 through 255 and two bytes would contain values ranging from 0 through 65,535, respectively. Look at Table 3.1 and note that the `unsigned short` is the type that supports this range, as it is contained in 16 bits of memory. Thus, it is quite easy to model positive values in bits and bytes (see Figure 3.1).

FIGURE 3.1
Organization of bits in a 16-bit unsigned short integer.

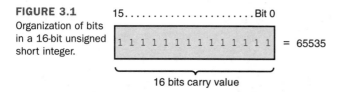

15 . . . . Bit 0

`1 1 1 1 1 1 1 1 1 1 1 1 1 1 1 1` = 65535

16 bits carry value

How to model negative numbers in this space? One way is to "sacrifice" a bit as the sign-bit that would indicate if the values contained in the other bits are positive or negative (see Figure 3.2). The sign-bit needs to be the most-significant-bit (MSB) as the least-significant-one would be required to model odd numbers. So, when the MSB contains sign-information, it is assumed that 0 would be positive and 1 would mean negative, and the other bytes contain the absolute value.

FIGURE 3.2
Organization of bits in a 16-bit signed short integer.

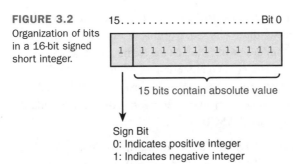

Thus, a signed number that occupies 8 bits can contain values ranging from –128 through 127, and one that occupies 16 bits can contain values ranging from –32,768 through 32,767. If you look at Table 3.1 again, note that the (signed) short is the type that supports positive and negative integer values in a 16-bit space.

Signed Integer Types `short`, `int`, `long`, and `long long`

These types differ in their sizes and thereby differ in the range of values they can contain. int is possibly the most used type and is 32 bits wide on most compilers. Use the right type depending on your projection of the maximum value that particular variable would be expected to hold.

Declaring a variable of a signed type is simple:

```
short int gradesInMath = -5; // not your best score
int moneyInBank = -70000; // overdraft
long populationChange = -85000; // reducing population
long long countryGDPChange = -70000000000;
```

Unsigned Integer Types `unsigned short`, `unsigned int`, `unsigned long`, and `unsigned long long`

Unlike their signed counterparts, unsigned integer variable types cannot contain sign information, and hence they can actually support twice as many positive values.

Declaring a variable of an unsigned type is as simple as this:

```
unsigned short int numColorsInRainbow = 7;
unsigned int numEggsInBasket = 24; // will always be positive
unsigned long   numCarsInNewYork = 700000;
unsigned long long countryMedicareExpense = 70000000000;
```

NOTE

You would use an unsigned variable type when you expect only positive values. So, if you're counting the number of apples, don't use `int`; use `unsigned int`. The latter can hold twice as many values in the positive range as the former can.

CAUTION

So, an unsigned type might not be suited for a variable in a banking application used to store the account balance as banks do allow some customers an overdraft facility. To see an example that demonstrates the differences between signed and unsigned types, visit Listing 5.3 in Lesson 5.

3

Avoid Overflow Errors by Selecting Correct Data Types

Data types such as `short`, `int`, `long`, `unsigned short`, `unsigned int`, `unsigned long`, and the like have a finite capacity for containing numbers. When you exceed the limit imposed by the type chosen in an arithmetic operation, you create an overflow.

Take `unsigned short` for an example. Data type `short` consumes 16 bits and can hence contain values from 0 through 65,535. When you add 1 to 65,535 in an `unsigned short`, the value overflows to 0. It's like the odometer of a car that suffers a mechanical overflow when it can support only five digits and the car has done 99,999 kilometers (or miles).

In this case, `unsigned short` was never the right type for such a counter. The programmer was better off using `unsigned int` to support numbers higher than 65,535.

In the case of a `signed short` integer, which has a range of –32,768 through 32,767, adding 1 to 32,767 may result in the `signed integer` taking the highest negative value. This behavior is compiler dependent.

Listing 3.4 demonstrates the overflow errors that you can inadvertently introduce via arithmetic operations.

LISTING 3.4   Demonstrating the Ill-Effects of Signed and Unsigned Integer Overflow Errors

```
0: #include <iostream>
1: using namespace std;
2:
3: int main()
4: {
5:     unsigned short uShortValue = 65535;
6:     cout << "Incrementing unsigned short " << uShortValue << " gives: ";
7:     cout << ++uShortValue << endl;
8:
9:     short signedShort = 32767;
10:     cout << "Incrementing signed short " << signedShort << " gives: ";
11:     cout << ++signedShort << endl;
12:
13:     return 0;
14: }
```

Output ▼

```
Incrementing unsigned  short 65535 gives: 0
Incrementing signed short 32767 gives: -32768
```

Analysis ▼

The output indicates that unintentional overflow situations result in unpredictable and unintuitive behavior for the application. Lines 7 and 11 increment an unsigned short and a signed short that have previously been initialized to their maximum supported values –65,535 and 32,767, respectively. The output demonstrates the value they hold after the increment operation, namely an overflow of 65,535 to zero in the unsigned short and an overflow of 32,767 to –32,768 in the signed short. One wouldn't expect the result of an increment operation to reduce the value in question, but that is exactly what happens when an integer type overflows. If you were using the values in question to allocate memory, then with the unsigned short, you can reach a point where you request zero bytes when your actual need is 65536 bytes.

NOTE

The operations `++uShortValue` and `++signedShort` seen in Listing 3.4 at lines 7 and 11 are prefix increment operations. These are explained in detail in Lesson 5.

Floating-Point Types `float` and `double`

Floating-point numbers are what you might have learned in school as real numbers. These are numbers that can be positive or negative. They can contain decimal values. So, if you want to store the value of pi (22 / 7 or 3.14) in a variable in C++, you would use a floating-point type.

Declaring variables of these types follows exactly the same pattern as the `int` in Listing 3.1. So, a `float` that allows you to store decimal values would be declared as the following:

```
float pi = 3.14;
```

And a double precision `float` (called simply a double) is defined as

```
double morePrecisePi = 22.0 / 7;
```

TIP

C++14 adds support for *chunking separators* in the form of a single quotation mark. This improves readability of code, as seen in the following initializations:

```
int moneyInBank = -70'000; // -70000
long populationChange = -85'000; // -85000
long long countryGDPChange = -70'000'000'000; // -70 billion
double pi = 3.141'592'653'59; // 3.14159265359
```

NOTE

The data types mentioned thus far are often referred to as POD (Plain Old Data). The category POD contains these as well as aggregations (structs, enums, unions, or classes) thereof.

3

Determining the Size of a Variable Using `sizeof`

Size is the amount of memory that the compiler reserves when the programmer declares a variable to hold the data assigned to it. The size of a variable depends on its type, and C++ has a very convenient operator called `sizeof` that tells you the size in bytes of a variable or a type.

The usage of `sizeof` is simple. To determine the size of an integer, you invoke `sizeof` with parameter `int` (the type) as demonstrated by Listing 3.5.

```
cout << "Size of an int: " << sizeof (int);
```

LISTING 3.5   Finding the Size of Standard C++ Variable Types

```
 1: #include <iostream>
 2:
 3: int main()
 4: {
 5:    using namespace std;
 6:    cout << "Computing the size of some C++ inbuilt variable types" << endl;
 7:
 8:    cout << "Size of bool: " << sizeof(bool) << endl;
 9:    cout << "Size of char: " << sizeof(char) << endl;
10:    cout << "Size of unsigned short int: " << sizeof(unsigned short) << endl;
11:    cout << "Size of short int: " << sizeof(short) << endl;
12:    cout << "Size of unsigned long int: " << sizeof(unsigned long) << endl;
13:    cout << "Size of long: " << sizeof(long) << endl;
14:    cout << "Size of int: " << sizeof(int) << endl;
15:    cout << "Size of unsigned long long: "<< sizeof(unsigned long long)<<
endl;
16:    cout << "Size of long long: " << sizeof(long long) << endl;
17:    cout << "Size of unsigned int: " << sizeof(unsigned int) << endl;
18:    cout << "Size of float: " << sizeof(float) << endl;
19:    cout << "Size of double: " << sizeof(double) << endl;
20:
21:    cout << "The output changes with compiler, hardware and OS" << endl;
22:
23:    return 0;
24: }
```

Output ▼

```
Computing the size of some C++ inbuilt variable types
Size of bool: 1
Size of char: 1
Size of unsigned short int: 2
Size of short int: 2
Size of unsigned long int: 4
Size of long: 4
Size of int: 4
Size of unsigned long long: 8
Size of long long: 8
Size of unsigned int: 4
Size of float: 4
Size of double: 8
The output changes with compiler, hardware and OS
```

Analysis ▼

3

The output of Listing 3.5 reveals sizes of various types in bytes and is specific to my platform: compiler, OS, and hardware. This output in particular is a result of running the program in 32-bit mode (compiled by a 32-bit compiler) on a 64-bit operating system. Note that a 64-bit compiler probably creates different results, and the reason I chose a 32-bit compiler was to be able to run the application on 32-bit as well as 64-bit systems. The output tells that the `sizeof` a variable doesn't change between an unsigned or signed type; the only difference in the two is the MSB that carries sign information in the former.

NOTE

All sizes seen in the output are in bytes. The size of a type is an important parameter to be considered, especially for types used to hold numbers. A `short int` can hold a smaller range than a `long long`. You therefore wouldn't use a `short int` to hold the population of a country, for example.

TIP

C++11 introduced fixed-width integer types that allow you to specify the exact width of the integer in bits. These are `int8_t` or `uint8_t` for 8-bit signed and unsigned integers, respectively. You may also use 16-bit (`int16_t`, `uint16_t`), 32-bit (`int32_t`, `uint32_t`), and 64-bit (`int64_t`, `uint64_t`) integer types. To use these types, remember to include header `<cstdint>`.

Avoid Narrowing Conversion Errors by Using List Initialization

When you initialize a variable of a smaller integer type (say, `short`) using another of a larger type (say, an `int`), you are risking a narrowing conversion error, because the compiler has to fit data stored in a type that can potentially hold much larger numbers into a type that doesn't have the same capacity (that is, is narrower). Here's an example:

```
int largeNum = 5000000;
short smallNum = largeNum; // compiles OK, yet narrowing error
```

Narrowing isn't restricted to conversions between integer types only. You may face narrowing errors if you initialize a `float` using a `double`, a `float` (or `double`) using an `int`, or an `int` using a `float`. Some compilers may warn, but this warning will not cause an error that stops compilation. In such cases, you may be confronted by bugs that occur infrequently and at execution time.

To avoid this problem, C++11 recommends *list initialization* techniques that prevent narrowing. To use this feature, insert initialization values/variables within braces {...}. The list initialization syntax is as follows:

```
int largeNum = 5000000;
short anotherNum{ largeNum }; // error! Amend types
int anotherNum{ largeNum }; // OK!
float someFloat{ largeNum }; // error! An int may be narrowed
float someFloat{ 5000000 }; // OK! 5000000 can be accomodated
```

It may not be immediately apparent, but this feature has the potential to spare bugs that occur when data stored in a type undergoes a narrowing conversion at execution time—these occur implicitly during an initialization and are tough to solve.

Automatic Type Inference Using `auto`

There are cases where the type of a variable is apparent given the initialization value being assigned to it. For example, if a variable is being initialized with the value `true`, the type of the variable can be best estimated as `bool`. Compilers supporting C++11 and beyond give you the option of not having to explicitly specify the variable type when using the keyword `auto`.

```
auto coinFlippedHeads = true;
```

We have left the task of defining an exact type for variable coinFlippedHeads to the compiler. The compiler checks the nature of the value the variable is being initialized to and then decides on the best possible type that suits this variable. In this particular case, it is clear that an initialization value of true best suits a variable that is of type bool. The compiler thus determines bool as the type that suits variable coinFlipped-Heads best and internally treats coinFlippedHeads as a bool, as also demonstrated by Listing 3.6.

LISTING 3.6   Using the auto Keyword and Relying on the Compiler's Type-Inference Capabilities

```
 1: #include <iostream>
 2: using namespace std;
 3:
 4: int main()
 5: {
 6:     auto coinFlippedHeads = true;
 7:     auto largeNumber = 2500000000000;
 8:
 9:     cout << "coinFlippedHeads = " << coinFlippedHeads;
10:     cout << " , sizeof(coinFlippedHeads) = " << sizeof(coinFlippedHeads) <<
endl;
11:     cout << "largeNumber = " << largeNumber;
12:     cout << " , sizeof(largeNumber) = " << sizeof(largeNumber) << endl;
13:
14:     return 0;
15: }
```

Output ▼

```
coinFlippedHeads = 1 , sizeof(coinFlippedHeads) = 1
largeNumber = 2500000000000 , sizeof(largeNumber) = 8
```

Analysis ▼

See how instead of deciding that coinFlippedHeads should be of type bool or that largeNumber should be a long long, you have used the auto keyword in Lines 6 and 7 where the two variables have been declared. This delegates the decision on the type of variable to the compiler, which uses the initialization value as a ballpark. You have used sizeof to actually check whether the compiler created the types you suspected it would, and you can check against the output produced by your code to verify that it really did.

NOTE

> Using `auto` requires you to initialize the variable for the compiler
> that uses this initial value in deciding what the variable type
> can be.
>
> When you don't initialize a variable of type `auto`, you get a
> compile error.

Even if `auto` seems to be a trivial feature at first sight, it makes programming a lot easier in those cases where the type variable is a complex type. The role of `auto` in writing simpler, yet type-safe code is revisited in Lesson 15, "An Introduction to the Standard Template Library," and beyond.

Using `typedef` to Substitute a Variable's Type

C++ allows you to substitute variable types to something that you might find convenient. You use the keyword `typedef` for that. Here is an example where a programmer wants to call an `unsigned int` a descriptive `STRICTLY_POSITIVE_INTEGER`.

```
typedef unsigned int STRICTLY_POSITIVE_INTEGER;
STRICTLY_POSITIVE_INTEGER numEggsInBasket = 4532;
```

When compiled, the first line tells the compiler that a `STRICTLY_POSITIVE_INTEGER` is nothing but an unsigned int. At later stages when the compiler encounters the already defined type `STRICTLY_POSITIVE_INTEGER`, it substitutes it for unsigned `int` and continues compilation.

NOTE

> `typedef` or type substitution is particularly convenient when
> dealing with complex types that can have a cumbersome syntax,
> for example, types that use templates. Templates are discussed
> later in Lesson 14, "An Introduction to Macros and Templates."

What Is a Constant?

Imagine you are writing a program to calculate the area and the circumference of a circle. The formulas are

```
Area = pi * Radius * Radius;
Circumference = 2 * pi * Radius
```

In this formula, `pi` is the constant of value 22 / 7. You don't want the value of `pi` to change anywhere in your program. You also want to avoid any accidental assignments of possibly incorrect values to `pi`. C++ enables you to define `pi` as a constant that cannot be changed after declaration. In other words, after it's defined, the value of a constant cannot be altered. Assignments to a constant in C++ cause compilation errors.

Thus, constants are like variables in C++ except that these cannot be changed. Similar to variables, constants also occupy space in the memory and have a name to identify the address where the space is reserved. However, the content of this space cannot be overwritten. Constants in C++ can be

- Literal constants
- Declared constants using the `const` keyword
- Constant expressions using the `constexpr` keyword (new since C++11)
- Enumerated constants using the `enum` keyword
- Defined constants that are not recommended and deprecated

Literal Constants

Literal constants can be of many types—integer, string, and so on. In your first C++ program in Listing 1.1, you displayed "Hello World" using the following statement:

```
std::cout << "Hello World" << std::endl;
```

In here, "Hello World" is a string literal constant. You literally have been using literal constants all the while! When you declare an integer `someNumber`, like this:

```
int someNumber = 10;
```

The integer variable `someNumber` is assigned an initial value of ten. Here decimal ten is a part of the code, gets compiled into the application, is unchangeable, and is a literal constant too. You may initialize the integer using a literal in octal notation, like this:

```
int someNumber = 012 // octal 12 evaluates to decimal 10
```

Starting in C++14, you may also use binary literals, like this:

```
int someNumber = 0b1010; // binary 1010 evaluates to decimal 10
```

TIP

C++ also allows you to define your own literals. For example, temperature as `32.0_F` (Fahrenheit) or `0.0_C` (Centigrade), distance as `16_m` (Miles) or `10_km` (Kilometers), and so on.

These suffixes `_F`, `_C`, `_m`, and `_km` are called user-defined literals and are explained in Lesson 12, "Operator Types and Operator Overloading," after the prerequisite concepts are explained.

Declaring Variables as Constants Using `const`

The most important type of constants in C++ from a practical and programmatic point of view are declared by using keyword `const` before the variable type. The generic declaration looks like the following:

```
const type-name constant-name = value;
```

Let's see a simple application that displays the value of a constant called pi (see Listing 3.7).

LISTING 3.7 Declaring a Constant Called `pi`

```
 1: #include <iostream>
 2:
 3: int main()
 4: {
 5:    using namespace std;
 6:
 7:    const double pi = 22.0 / 7;
 8:    cout << "The value of constant pi is: " << pi << endl;
 9:
10:    // Uncomment next line to view compile failure
11:    // pi = 345;
12:
13:    return 0;
14: }
```

Output ▼

```
The value of constant pi is: 3.14286
```

Analysis ▼

Note the declaration of constant pi in Line 7. We use the `const` keyword to tell the compiler that pi is a constant of type `double`. If you uncomment Line 11 where the programmer tries to assign a value to a variable you have defined as a constant, you see a compile failure that says something similar to, "You cannot assign to a variable that is const." Thus, constants are a powerful way to ensure that certain data cannot be modified.

> **NOTE**
> It is good programming practice to define variables that are not supposed to change their values as const. The usage of the const keyword indicates that the programmer has thought about ensuring the constantness of data where required and protects his application from inadvertent changes to this constant.
>
> This is particularly useful in a multiprogrammer environment.

Constants are useful when declaring the length of static arrays, which are fixed at compile time. Listing 4.2 in Lesson 4, "Managing Arrays and Strings," includes a sample that demonstrates the use of a const int to define the length of an array.

Constant Expressions Using constexpr

Keyword constexpr allows function-like declaration of constants:

```
constexpr double GetPi() {return 22.0 / 7;}
```

One constexpr can use another:

```
constexpr double TwicePi() {return 2 * GetPi();}
```

constexpr may look like a function, however, allows for optimization possibilities from the compiler's and application's point of view. So long as a compiler is capable of evaluating a constant expression to a constant, it can be used in statements and expressions at places where a constant is expected. In the preceding example, TwicePi() is a constexpr that uses a constant expression GetPi(). This will possibly trigger a compile-time optimization wherein every usage of TwicePi() is simply replaced by 6.28571 by the compiler, and not the code that would calculate 2 x 22 / 7 when executed.

Listing 3.8 demonstrates the usage of constexpr.

LISTING 3.8   Using constexpr to Calculate Pi

```
1: #include <iostream>
2: constexpr double GetPi() { return 22.0 / 7; }
3: constexpr double TwicePi() { return 2 * GetPi(); }
4:
5: int main()
```

```
6: {
7:     using namespace std;
8:     const double pi = 22.0 / 7;
9:
10:     cout << "constant pi contains value " << pi << endl;
11:     cout << "constexpr GetPi() returns value " << GetPi() << endl;
12:     cout << "constexpr TwicePi() returns value " << TwicePi() << endl;

13:     return 0;
14: }
```

Output ▼

```
constant pi contains value 3.14286
constexpr GetPi() returns value 3.14286
constexpr TwicePi() returns value 6.28571
```

Analysis ▼

The program demonstrates two methods of deriving the value of pi—one as a constant variable pi as declared in Line 8 and another as a constant expression GetPi() declared in Line 2. GetPi() and TwicePi() may look like functions, but they are not exactly. Functions are invoked at program execution time. But, these are constant expressions and the compiler had already substituted every usage of GetPi() by 3.14286 and every usage of TwicePi() by 6.28571. Compile-time resolution of TwicePi() increases the speed of program execution when compared to the same calculation being contained in a function.

NOTE

Constant expressions need to contain simple implementations that return simple types like integer, double, and so on. C++14 allows constexpr to contain decision-making constructs such as if and switch statements. These conditional statements are discussed in detail in Lesson 6, "Controlling Program Flow."

The usage of constexpr will not guarantee compile-time optimization—for example, if you use a constexpr expression to double a user provided number. The outcome of such an expression cannot be calculated by the compiler, which may ignore the usage of constexpr and compile as a regular function.

To see a demonstration of how a constant expression is used in places where the compiler expects a constant, see the code sample in Listing 4.2 in Lesson 4.

3

TIP

> In the previous code samples, we defined our own constant `pi` as an exercise in learning the syntax of declaring constants and `constexpr`. Yet, most popular C++ compilers already supply you with a reasonably precise value of `pi` in the constant `M_PI`. You may use this constant in your programs after including header file `<cmath>`.

Enumerations

There are situations where a particular variable should be allowed to accept only a certain set of values. These are situations where you don't want the colors in the rainbow to contain Turquoise or the directions on a compass to contain Left. In both these cases, you need a type of variable whose values are restricted to a certain set defined by you. *Enumerations* are exactly the tool you need in this situation and are characterized by the keyword enum. Enumerations comprise a set of constants called *enumerators*.

In the following example, the enumeration `RainbowColors` contains individual colors such as `Violet` as enumerators:

```
enum RainbowColors
{
    Violet = 0,
    Indigo,
    Blue,
    Green,
    Yellow,
    Orange,
    Red
};
```

Here's another enumeration for the cardinal directions:

```
enum CardinalDirections
{
    North,
    South,
    East,
    West
};
```

Enumerations are used as user-defined types. Variables of this type can be assigned a range of values restricted to the enumerators contained in the enumeration. So, if defining a variable that contains the colors of a rainbow, you declare the variable like this:

```
RainbowColors MyFavoriteColor = Blue; // Initial value
```

In the preceding line of code, you declared an enumerated constant `MyFavoriteColor` of type `RainbowColors`. This enumerated constant variable is restricted to contain any of the legal **VIBGYOR** colors and no other value.

NOTE _____ | The compiler converts the enumerator such as `Violet` and so on into integers. Each enumerated value specified is one more than the previous value. You have the choice of specifying a starting value, and if this is not specified, the compiler takes it as 0. So, `North` is evaluated as value 0.
| If you want, you can also specify an explicit value against each of the enumerated constants by initializing them.

Listing 3.9 demonstrates how enumerated constants are used to hold the four cardinal directions, with an initializing value supplied to the first one.

LISTING 3.9 Using Enumerated Values to Indicate Cardinal Wind Directions

```
 1: #include <iostream>
 2: using namespace std;
 3:
 4: enum CardinalDirections
 5: {
 6:     North = 25,
 7:     South,
 8:     East,
 9:     West
10: };
11:
12: int main()
13: {
14:     cout << "Displaying directions and their symbolic values" << endl;
15:     cout << "North: " << North << endl;
16:     cout << "South: " << South << endl;
17:     cout << "East: " << East << endl;
18:     cout << "West: " << West << endl;
19:
20:     CardinalDirections windDirection = South;
21:     cout << "Variable windDirection = " << windDirection << endl;
22:
23:     return 0;
24: }
```

Output ▼

```
Displaying directions and their symbolic values
North: 25
South: 26
East: 27
West: 28
Variable windDirection = 26
```

Analysis ▼

Note how we have enumerated the four cardinal directions but have given the first `North` an initial value of 25 (see Line 6). This automatically ensures that the following constants are assigned values 26, 27, and 28 by the compiler as demonstrated in the output. In Line 20 you create a variable of type `CardinalDirections` that is assigned an initial value `South`. When displayed on the screen in Line 21, the compiler dispatches the integer value associated with South, which is 26.

3

> **TIP**
>
> You may want to take a look at Listings 6.4 and 6.5 in Lesson 6. They use `enum` to enumerate the days of the week and conditional processing to tell what the day of the user's choosing is named after.

Defining Constants Using `#define`

First and foremost, don't use this if you are writing a program anew. The only reason this book analyzes the definition of constants using `#define` is to help you understand certain legacy programs that do define constants such as `pi` using this syntax:

```
#define pi 3.14286
```

`#define` is a preprocessor macro, and what is done here is that all mentions of `pi` henceforth are replaced by 3.14286 for the compiler to process. Note that this is a text replacement (read: non-intelligent replacement) done by the preprocessor. The compiler neither knows nor cares about the actual type of the constant in question.

> **CAUTION**
>
> Defining constants using the preprocessor via `#define` is deprecated and should not be used.

Keywords You Cannot Use as Variable or Constant Names

Some words are reserved by C++, and you cannot use them as variable names. These keywords have special meaning to the C++ compiler. Keywords include if, while, for, and main. A list of keywords defined by C++ is presented in Table 3.2 as well as in Appendix B, "C++ Keywords." Your compiler might have additional reserved words, so you should check its manual for a complete list.

TABLE 3.2 Major C++ Keywords

asm	else	new	this
auto	enum	operator	throw
bool	explicit	private	true
break	export	protected	try
case	extern	public	typedef
catch	false	register	typeid
char	float	reinterpret_cast	typename
class	for	return	union
const	friend	short	unsigned
constexpr	goto	signed	using
continue	if	sizeof	virtual
default	inline	static	void
delete	int	static_cast	volatile
do	long	struct	wchar_t
double	mutable	switch	while
dynamic_cast	namespace	template	

In addition, the following words are reserved:

and	bitor	not_eq	xor
and_eq	compl	or	xor_eq
bitand	not	or_eq	

DO	DON'T
DO give variables descriptive names, even if that makes them long.	**DON'T** give names that are too short or contain just a character.
DO initialize variables, and use list initialization to avoid narrowing conversion errors.	**DON'T** give names that use exotic acronyms known only to you.
DO ensure that the name of the variable explains its purpose.	**DON'T** give names that are reserved C++ keywords as these won't compile.
DO put yourself into the shoes of one who hasn't seen your code yet and think whether the name would make sense to him or her.	
DO check whether your team is following certain naming conventions and follow them.	

3

Summary

In this lesson you learned about using memory to store values temporarily in variables and constants. You learned that variables have a size determined by their type and that the operator `sizeof` can be used to determine the size of one. You got to know of different types of variables such as `bool`, `int`, and so on and that they are to be used to contain different types of data. The right choice of a variable type is important in effective programming, and the choice of a variable that's too small for the purpose can result in a wrapping error or an overflow situation. You learned about the keyword `auto`, where you let the compiler decide the data-type for you on the basis of the initialization value of the variable.

You also learned about the different types of constants and usage of the most important ones among them using the keywords `const`, `constexpr`, and `enum`.

Q&A

Q Why define constants at all if you can use regular variables instead of them?

A Constants, especially those declared using the keyword `const`, are your way of telling the compiler that the value of a particular variable be fixed and not allowed to change. Consequently, the compiler always ensures that the constant variable is never assigned another value, not even if another programmer was to take up your work and inadvertently try to overwrite the value. So, declaring constants where you know the value of a variable should not change is a good programming practice and increases the quality of your application.

Q Why should I initialize the value of a variable?

A If you don't initialize, you don't know what the variable contains for a starting value. The starting value is just the contents of the location in the memory that are reserved for the variable. Initialization such as that seen here:

```
int myFavoriteNumber = 0;
```

writes the initial value of your choosing, in this case 0, to the memory location reserved for the variable `myFavoriteNumber` as soon as it is created. There are situations where you do conditional processing depending on the value of a variable (often checked against nonzero). Such logic does not work reliably without initialization because an unassigned or initiated variable contains junk that is often nonzero and random.

Q Why does C++ give me the option of using `short int` and `int` and `long int`? Why not just always use the integer that always allows for the highest number to be stored within?

A C++ is a programming language that is used to program for a variety of applications, many running on devices with little computing capacity or memory resources. The simple old cell phone is one example where processing capacity and available memory are both limited. In this case, the programmer can often save memory or speed or both by choosing the right kind of variable if he doesn't need high values. If you are programming on a regular desktop or a high-end smartphone, chances are that the performance gained or memory saved in choosing one integer type over another is going to be insignificant and in some cases even absent.

Q Why should I not use global variables frequently? Isn't it true that they're usable throughout my application and I can save some time otherwise lost to passing values around functions?

A Global variables can be read and assigned globally. The latter is the problem as they can be changed globally. Assume you are working on a project with a few other programmers in a team. You have declared your integers and other variables to be global. If any programmer in your team changes the value of your integer inadvertently in his code—which even might be a different .CPP file than the one you are using—the reliability of your code is affected. So, sparing a few seconds or minutes should not be criteria, and you should not use global variables indiscriminately to ensure the stability of your code.

Q C++ is giving me the option of declaring unsigned integers that are supposed to contain only positive integer values and zero. What happens if I decrement a zero value contained in an `unsigned int`?

A You see a wrapping effect. Decrementing an unsigned integer that contains 0 by 1 means that it wraps to the highest value it can hold! Check Table 3.1—you see that an `unsigned short` can contain values from 0 to 65,535. So, declare an `unsigned short` and decrement it to see the unexpected:

```
unsigned short myShortInt = 0;   // Initial Value
myShortInt = myShortInt - 1; // Decrement by 1
std::cout << myShortInt << std::endl; // Output: 65535!
```

Note that this is not a problem with the `unsigned short`, rather with your usage of the same. An unsigned integer (or short or long) is not to be used when negative values are within the specifications. If the contents of `myShortInt` are to be used to dynamically allocate those many number of bytes, a little bug that allows a zero value to be decremented would result in 64KB being allocated! Worse, if `myShortInt` were to be used as an index in accessing a location of memory, chances are high that your application would access an external location and would crash!

Workshop

The Workshop provides quiz questions to help you solidify your understanding of the material covered and exercises to provide you with experience in using what you've learned. Try to answer the quiz and exercise questions before checking the answers in Appendix E, and be certain that you understand the answers before continuing to the next lesson.

Quiz

1. What is the difference between a signed and an unsigned integer?
2. Why should you not use `#define` to declare a constant?
3. Why would you initialize a variable?
4. Consider the `enum` below. What is the value of `Queen`?

   ```
   enum YourCards {Ace, Jack, Queen, King};
   ```

5. What is wrong with this variable name?

   ```
   int Integer = 0;
   ```

Exercises

1. Modify `enum YourCards` in quiz question 4 to demonstrate that the value of `Queen` can be 45.

2. Write a program that demonstrates that the size of an unsigned integer and a normal integer are the same, and that both are smaller in size than a long integer.

3. Write a program to calculate the area and circumference of a circle where the radius is fed by the user.

4. In Exercise 3, if the area and circumference were to be stored in integers, how would the output be any different?

5. BUGBUSTERS: What is wrong in the following initialization:

```
auto Integer;
```

LESSON 4
Managing Arrays and Strings

In previous lessons, you declared variables used to contain a single `int`, `char`, or `string` to mention a few instances. However, you may want to declare a collection of objects, such as 20 `int`s or a string of characters to hold a name.

In this lesson, you learn

- What arrays are and how to declare and use them
- What strings are and how to use character arrays to make them
- A brief introduction to `std::string`

What Is an Array?

The dictionary definition of an *array* gets really close to what we want to be understanding. According to Merriam Webster, an *array* is "a group of elements forming a complete unit, for example an array of solar panels."

The following are characteristics of an array:

- An array is a collection of elements.
- All elements contained in an array are of the same kind.
- This collection forms a complete set.

In C++, arrays enable you to store data elements of a type in the memory, in a sequential and ordered fashion.

The Need for Arrays

Imagine that you are writing a program where the user can type in five integers and you display them back to him. One way would be to have your program declare five distinct and unique integer variables and use them to store and display values. The declarations would look like this:

```
int firstNumber = 0;
int secondNumber = 0;
int thirdNumber = 0;
int fourthNumber = 0;
int fifthNumber = 0;
```

If your user wants this program to store and display 500 integers at a later stage, you need to declare 500 such integers using the preceding system. This still is doable given generous amounts of patience and time. However, imagine the user asks you to support 500,000 integers instead of 5—what would you do?

You would do it right and do it smart from the point go by declaring an array of five integers each initialized to zero, like this:

```
int myNumbers [5] = {0};
```

Thus, if you were asked to support 500,000 integers, your array would scale up quite quickly, like this:

```
int manyNumbers [500000] = {0};
```

An array of five characters would be defined as

```
char myCharacters [5];
```

Such arrays are called *static arrays* because the number of elements they contain as well as the memory the array consumes is fixed at the time of compilation.

Declaring and Initializing Static Arrays

In the preceding lines of code, you declared an array called `myNumbers` that contains five elements of type `int`—that is, integer—all initialized to a value 0. Thus, array declaration in C++ follows a simple syntax:

```
ElementType ArrayName [constant_number of elements] = {optional initial values};
```

You can even declare an array and initialize its contents on a per-element basis, like this integer array where each of the five integers is initialized to five different integer values:

```
int myNumbers [5] = {34, 56, -21, 5002, 365};
```

You can have all elements in an array initialized to zero (the default supplied by the compiler to numerical types), like this:

```
int myNumbers [5] = {}; // initializes all integers to 0
```

You can also partially initialize elements in an array, like this:

```
int myNumbers [5] = {34, 56};
// initialize first two elements to 34 and 56 and the rest to 0
```

You can define the length of an array (that is, the number of elements in one) as a constant and use that constant in your array definition:

```
const int ARRAY_LENGTH = 5;
int myNumbers [ARRAY_LENGTH] = {34, 56, -21, 5002, 365};
```

This is particularly useful when you need to access and use the length of the array at multiple places, such as when iterating elements in one, and then instead of having to change the length at each of those places, you just correct the initialization value at the `const int` declaration.

You can opt to leave out the number of elements in an array if you know the initial values of the elements in the array:

```
int myNumbers [] = {2016, 2052, -525}; // array of 3 elements
```

The preceding code creates an array of three integers with the initial values `2016`, `2052`, and `-525`.

4

Arrays declared thus far are called *static arrays* as the length of the array is a constant and fixed by the programmer at compile-time. This array cannot take more data than what the programmer has specified. It also does not consume any less memory if left half-used or unused. Arrays where the length is decided at execution-time are called *dynamic arrays*. Dynamic arrays are briefly introduced later in this lesson and are discussed in detail in Lesson 17, "STL Dynamic Array Classes."

How Data Is Stored in an Array

Think of books placed on a shelf, one next to the other. This is an example of a one-dimensional array, as it expands in only one dimension, that is the number of books on it. Each book is an element in the array, and the rack is akin to the memory that has been reserved to store this collection of books as shown in Figure 4.1.

FIGURE 4.1
Books on a shelf: a one-dimensional array.

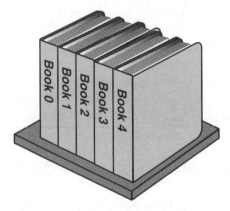

It is not an error that we started numbering the books with 0. As you later see, indexes in C++ start at 0 and not at 1. Similar to the five books on a shelf, the array myNumbers containing five integers looks similar to Figure 4.2.

FIGURE 4.2
Organization of an
array of five integers,
myNumbers, in
memory.

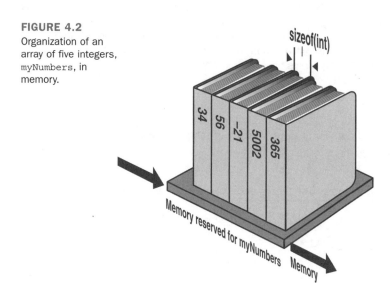

Note that the memory space occupied by the array is comprised of five blocks, each of equal size, that is defined by the type of data to be held in the array, in this case integer. If you remember, you studied the size of an integer in Lesson 3, "Using Variables, Declaring Constants." The amount of memory reserved by the compiler for the array myNumbers is hence sizeof(int) * 5. In general, the amount of memory reserved by the compiler for an array in bytes is

```
Bytes consumed by an array = sizeof(element-type) * Number of Elements
```

Accessing Data Stored in an Array

Elements in an array can be accessed using their zero-based index. These indexes are called zero-based because the first element in an array is at index 0. So, the first integer value stored in the array myNumbers is myNumbers[0], the second is myNumbers[1], and so on. The fifth is myNumbers[4]. In other words, the index of the last element in an array is always (Length of Array – 1).

When asked to access element at index N, the compiler uses the memory address of the first element (positioned at index zero) as the starting point and then skips *N* elements by adding the offset computed as N*sizeof(element) to reach the address containing the (N+1)th element. The C++ compiler does not check if the index is within the actual defined bounds of the array. You can try fetching the element at index 1001 in an array of only 10 elements, putting the security and stability of your program at risk. The onus of ensuring that the array is not accessed beyond its bounds lies solely on the programmer.

4

CAUTION ⎯⎯

> Accessing an array beyond its bounds results in unpredictable behavior. In many cases this causes your program to crash. Accessing arrays beyond their bounds should be avoided at all costs.

Listing 4.1 demonstrates how you declare an array of integers, initialize its elements to integer values, and access them to display them on the screen.

LISTING 4.1   Declaring an Array of Integers and Accessing Its Elements

```
 0:   #include <iostream>
 1:
 2:   using namespace std;
 3:
 4:   int main ()
 5:   {
 6:      int myNumbers [5] = {34, 56, -21, 5002, 365};
 7:
 8:      cout << "First element at index 0: " << myNumbers [0] << endl;
 9:      cout << "Second element at index 1: " << myNumbers [1] << endl;
10:      cout << "Third element at index 2: " << myNumbers [2] << endl;
11:      cout << "Fourth element at index 3: " << myNumbers [3] << endl;
12:      cout << "Fifth element at index 4: " << myNumbers [4] << endl;
13:
14:      return 0;
15:   }
```

Output ▼

```
First element at index 0: 34
Second element at index 1: 56
Third element at index 2: -21
Fourth element at index 3: 5002
Fifth element at index 4: 365
```

Analysis ▼

Line 6 declares an array of five integers with initial values specified for each of them. The subsequent lines simply display the integers using cout and using the array variable myNumbers with an appropriate index.

NOTE   To familiarize you with the concept of zero-based indexes used to access elements in arrays, we started numbering lines of code in Listing 4.1 and beyond with the first line being numbered as Line 0.

Modifying Data Stored in an Array

In the previous code listing, you did not enter user-defined data into the array. The syntax for assigning an integer to an element in that array is quite similar to assigning an integer value to an integer variable.

For example, assigning a value 2016 to an integer is like the following:

```
int thisYear;
thisYear = 2016;
```

Assigning a value 2016 to the fourth element in your array is like this:

```
myNumbers [3] = 2016; // Assign 2016 to the fourth element
```

Listing 4.2 demonstrates the use of constants in declaring the length of an array and shows how individual array elements can be assigned values during the execution of the program.

4

LISTING 4.2 Assigning Values to Elements in an Array

```
0: #include <iostream>
1: using namespace std;
2: constexpr int Square(int number) { return number*number; }
3:
4: int main()
5: {
6:   const int ARRAY_LENGTH = 5;
7:
8:     // Array of 5 integers, initialized using a const
9:     int myNumbers [ARRAY_LENGTH] = {5, 10, 0, -101, 20};
10:
11:    // Using a constexpr for array of 25 integers
12:    int moreNumbers [Square(ARRAY_LENGTH)];
13:
14:    cout << "Enter index of the element to be changed: ";
15:    int elementIndex = 0;
16:    cin >> elementIndex;
17:
18:    cout << "Enter new value: ";
19:    int newValue = 0;
20:    cin >> newValue;
21:
```

```
22:     myNumbers[elementIndex] = newValue;
23:     moreNumbers[elementIndex] = newValue;
24:
25:     cout << "Element " << elementIndex << " in array myNumbers is: ";
26:     cout << myNumbers[elementIndex] << endl;
27:
28:     cout << "Element " << elementIndex << " in array moreNumbers is: ";
29:     cout << moreNumbers[elementIndex] << endl;
30:
31:     return 0;
32: }
```

Output ▼

```
Enter index of the element to be changed: 3
Enter new value: 101
Element 3 in array myNumbers is: 101
Element 3 in array moreNumbers is: 101
```

Analysis ▼

Array length needs to be a constant integer. This can therefore also be specified in a constant ARRAY_LENGTH used in Line 9 or a constant expression Square() used in Line 12. Thus, the array myNumbers is declared to be 5 elements in length, while the array moreNumbers to be 25. Lines 14–20 ask the user to enter the index in the array of the element he wants to modify and the new value to be stored at that index. Lines 22 and 23 demonstrate how to modify a specific element in an array given that index. Lines 26–29 demonstrate how to access elements in an array given an index. Note that modifying the element at index 3 actually modifies the fourth element in the array, as indexes are zero-based entities. You have to get used to this.

NOTE

Many novice C++ programmers assign the fifth value at index five in an array of five integers. Note that this exceeds the bound of the array as the compiled code tries accessing the sixth element in the array which is beyond its defined bounds.

This kind of error is called a fence-post error. It's named after the fact that the number of posts needed to build a fence is always one more than the number of sections in the fence.

CAUTION

Something fundamental is missing in Listing 4.2: It does not check whether the index entered by the user is within the bounds of the array. The previous program should actually verify whether `elementIndex` is within 0 and 4 for array `myNumbers` and within 0 and 24 for array `moreNumbers` and reject all other entries. This missing check allows the user to potentially assign and access a value beyond the bounds of the array. This can potentially cause the application—and the system, in a worst-case scenario—to crash.

Performing checks is explained in Lesson 6, "Controlling Program Flow."

Using Loops to Access Array Elements

When working with arrays and their elements in serial order, you should access them (in other words, iterate) using loops. See Lesson 6, and Listing 6.10 in particular, to quickly learn how elements in an array can be efficiently inserted or accessed using a `for` loop.

4

DO	DON'T
DO always initialize arrays, or else they will contain junk values.	**DON'T** ever access the Nth element using index N, in an array of N elements. Use index (N–1).
DO always ensure that your arrays are used within their defined boundaries.	**DON'T** forget that the first element in an array is accessed using index 0.

Multidimensional Arrays

The arrays that we have seen thus far have been akin to books on a shelf. There can be more books on a longer shelf and fewer books on a shorter one. That is, the length of the shelf is the only dimension defining the capacity of the shelf, hence it is one-dimensional. Now, what if we were to use arrays to model an array of solar panels as shown in Figure 4.3? Solar panels, unlike bookshelves, expand in two dimensions: in length and in breadth.

FIGURE 4.3
Array of solar panels on a roof.

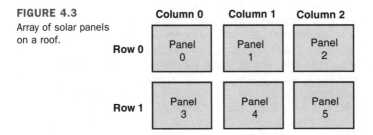

As you see in Figure 4.3, six solar panels are placed in a two-dimensional arrangement comprised of two rows and three columns. From one perspective, you can see this arrangement as an array of two elements, each element itself being an array of three panels—in other words, an array of arrays. In C++, you can model two-dimensional arrays, but you are not restricted to just two dimensions. Depending on your need and the nature of the application, you can model multidimensional arrays in memory, too.

Declaring and Initializing Multidimensional Arrays

C++ enables you to declare multidimensional arrays by indicating the number of elements you want to reserve in each dimension. So, a two-dimensional array of integers representing the solar panels in Figure 4.3 is

```
int solarPanels [2][3];
```

Note that in Figure 4.3, you have also assigned each panel an ID ranging from 0 through 5 for the six panels in the solar array. If you were to initialize the integer array in the same order, it would look like the following:

```
int solarPanels [2][3] = {{0, 1, 2}, {3, 4, 5}};
```

As you see, the initialization syntax used is actually similar to one where we initialize two one-dimensional arrays. An array comprising of three rows and three columns would look like this:

```
int threeRowsThreeColumns [3][3] = {{-501, 206, 2016}, {989, 101, 206}, {303, 456, 596}};
```

NOTE

> Even though C++ enables us to model multidimensional arrays, the memory where the array is contained is one-dimensional. So, the compiler maps the multidimensional array into the memory space, which expands only in one direction.
>
> If you wanted to, you could also initialize the array called `solarPanels` like the following, and it would still contain the same values in the respective elements:
>
> `int solarPanels [2][3] = {0, 1, 2, 3, 4, 5};`
>
> However, the earlier method makes a better example because it's easier to imagine and understand a multidimensional array as an array of arrays.

Accessing Elements in a Multidimensional Array

Think of a multidimensional array as an array comprising elements that are arrays. So, when dealing with a two-dimensional array comprising three rows and three columns, each containing integers, visualize it as handling an array comprising three elements, where each element is an array comprising three integers.

When you need to access an integer in this array, you would need to use a first subscript to address the array where the integer is and the second subscript to address that integer in this array. Consider this array:

```
int threeRowsThreeColumns [3][3] = {{-501, 205, 2016}, {989, 101, 206}, {303, 456, 596}};
```

It has been initialized in a way you can visualize three arrays, each containing three integers. Here, the integer element with value `205` is at position `[0][1]`. The element with value `456` is at position `[2][1]`. Listing 4.3 explains how integer elements in this array can be accessed.

LISTING 4.3 Accessing Elements in a Multidimensional Array

```cpp
0: #include <iostream>
1: using namespace std;
2:
3: int main()
4: {
5:     int threeRowsThreeColumns [3][3] = \
6:     {{-501, 205, 2016}, {989, 101, 206}, {303, 456, 596}};
7:
8:     cout << "Row 0: " << threeRowsThreeColumns [0][0] << " " \
9:                       << threeRowsThreeColumns [0][1] << " " \
```

4

```
10:                       << threeRowsThreeColumns [0][2] << endl;
11:
12:
13:     cout << "Row 1: " << threeRowsThreeColumns [1][0] << " " \
14:                       << threeRowsThreeColumns [1][1] << " " \
15:                       << threeRowsThreeColumns [1][2] << endl;
16:
17:     cout << "Row 2: " << threeRowsThreeColumns [2][0] << " "\
18:                       << threeRowsThreeColumns [2][1] << " " \
19:                       << threeRowsThreeColumns [2][2] << endl;
20:
21:     return 0;
22: }
```

Output ▼

```
Row 0: -501 205 2016
Row 1: 989 101 206
Row 2: 303 456 596
```

Analysis ▼

Note how you have accessed elements in the array row-wise, starting with the array that is Row 0 (the first row, with index 0) and ending with the array that is Row 2 (third row, with index 2). As each of the rows is an array, the syntax for addressing the third element in the first row (row index 0, element index 2) is seen in Line 10.

NOTE

> In Listing 4.3 the length of the code increases dramatically with the increase in the number of elements in the array or dimensions thereof. This code is actually unsustainable in a professional development environment.
>
> You can see a more efficient way to program accessing elements in a multidimensional array in Listing 6.14 in Lesson 6, in which you use a nested `for` loop to access all elements in such an array. Using `for` loops is actually shorter and less error-prone, and the length of the program is not affected by changing the number of elements in the array.

Dynamic Arrays

Consider an application that stores medical records for hospitals. There is no good way for the programmer to know what the upper limits of the number of records his application might need to handle are. He can make an assumption that is way more than the reasonable limit for a small hospital to err on the safe side. In those cases, he is reserving huge amounts of memory without reason and reducing the performance of the system.

The key is to not use static arrays like the ones we have seen thus far, rather to choose dynamic arrays that optimize memory consumption and scale up depending on the demand for resources and memory at execution-time. C++ provides you with convenient and easy-to-use dynamic arrays in the form of `std::vector` as shown in Listing 4.4.

LISTING 4.4   Creating a Dynamic Array of Integers and Inserting Values Dynamically

```
 0: #include <iostream>
 1: #include <vector>
 2:
 3: using namespace std;
 4:
 5: int main()
 6: {
 7:     vector<int> dynArray (3); // dynamic array of int
 8:
 9:     dynArray[0] = 365;
10:     dynArray[1] = -421;
11:     dynArray[2]= 789;
12:
13:     cout << "Number of integers in array: " << dynArray.size() << endl;
14:
15:     cout << "Enter another element to insert" << endl;
16:     int newValue = 0;
17:     cin >> newValue;
18:     dynArray.push_back(newValue);
19:
20:     cout << "Number of integers in array: " << dynArray.size() << endl;
21:     cout << "Last element in array: ";
22:     cout << dynArray[dynArray.size() - 1] << endl;
23:     return 0;
24:
25: }
```

Output ▼

```
Number of integers in array: 3
Enter another element to insert
2017
Number of integers in array: 4
Last element in array: 2017
```

Analysis ▼

Don't worry about the syntax in Listing 4.4 as vector and templates have not been explained as yet. Try to observe the output and correlate it to the code. The initial size of the array according to the output is 3, consistent with the declaration of the array (`std::vector`) at Line 7. Knowing this, you still ask the user to enter a fourth number at Line 15, and, interestingly enough, you are able to insert this number into the back of the array using `push_back()` at Line 18. The `vector` dynamically resizes itself to accommodate more data. This can be then seen in the size of the array that increases to 4. Note the usage of the familiar static array syntax to access data in the vector. Line 22 accesses the last element (wherever that might be, given a position calculated at run-time) using the zero-based index, where the last element is at index "`size() - 1`". `size()` being the function that returns the total number of elements (integers) contained in the `vector`.

NOTE

> To use the dynamic array class `std::vector`, you need to include header vector, which is also shown in Line 1 of Listing 4.4.
>
> `#include <vector>`
>
> Vectors are explained in greater detail in Lesson 17.

C-style Character Strings

C-style strings are a special case of an array of characters. You have already seen some examples of C-style strings in the form of string literals that you have been writing into your code:

```
std::cout << "Hello World";
```

This is equivalent to using the array declaration:

```
char sayHello[] = {'H', 'e', 'l', 'l', 'o', ' ', 'W', 'o', 'r', 'l', 'd', '\0'};
std::cout << sayHello << std::endl;
```

Note that the last character in the array is a null character '\0'. This is also called the string-terminating character because it tells the compiler that the string has ended. Such C-style strings are a special case of character arrays in that the last character always precedes the null-terminator '\0'. When you embed a string literal in your code, the compiler does the job of adding a '\0' after it.

If you inserted '\0' anywhere in the middle of the array, it would not change the size of the array; it would only mean that string-processing using the array as input would stop at that point. Listing 4.5 demonstrates this point.

> **NOTE**
>
> '\0' might look like two characters to you, and it indeed is two characters typed using the keyboard. Yet, the backslash is a special escape code that the compiler understands and \0 means null—that is, it asks the compiler to insert a null or zero in there.
>
> You could not write '0' directly because that would be accepted as character zero, which has the nonzero ASCII code 48.
>
> Check the table in Appendix D, "ASCII Codes," to see this and other ASCII values.

LISTING 4.5 Analyzing the Null-Terminator in a C-style String

```
0: #include <iostream>
1: using namespace std;
2:
3: int main()
4: {
5:     char sayHello[] = {'H','e','l','l','o',' ','W','o','r','l','d','\0'};
6:     cout << sayHello << endl;
7:     cout << "Size of array: " << sizeof(sayHello) << endl;
8:
9:     cout << "Replacing space with null" << endl;
10:     sayHello[5] = '\0';
11:     cout << sayHello << endl;
12:     cout << "Size of array: " << sizeof(sayHello) << endl;
13:
14:     return 0;
15: }
```

Output ▼

```
Hello World
Size of array: 12
Replacing space with null
Hello
Size of array: 12
```

Analysis ▼

Line 10 is where we replace the space in "Hello World" by the null-terminating character. Note that the array now has two null-terminators, but it's the first one that results in the display of the string in Line 11 being truncated to just "Hello". `sizeof()` at Lines 7 and 12 indicates that the size of the array has not changed, even if the displayed data changed a lot.

CAUTION

> If you forget to add the `'\0'` when declaring and initializing the character array in Listing 4.5 at Line 5, then expect the output to contain garbled characters after printing "Hello World"; this is because `std::cout` does not stop with printing the array until it reaches a null character, even if it means exceeding the bounds of the array.
>
> This mistake can cause your program to crash and, in some cases, compromise the stability of the system.

C-style strings are fraught with danger. Listing 4.6 demonstrates the risks involved in using one.

LISTING 4.6   A Risky Application Using C-style Strings and User Input

```
0: #include<iostream>
1: #include<string.h>
2: using namespace std;
3: int main()
4: {
5:    cout << "Enter a word NOT longer than 20 characters:" << endl;
6:
7:    char userInput [21] = {'\0'};
8:    cin >> userInput;
9:
10:    cout << "Length of your input was: " << strlen (userInput) << endl;
11:
12:    return 0;
13: }
```

Output ▼

```
Enter a word NOT longer than 20 characters:
Don'tUseThisProgram
Length of your input was: 19
```

Analysis ▼

The danger is visible in the output. The program is begging the user to not enter data longer than 20 characters. The reason it does so is that the character buffer declared in Line 7 meant to store user input has a fixed—static—length of 21 characters. As the last character in the string needs to be a null-terminator `'\0'`, the maximum length of text stored by the buffer is limited to 20. Note the usage of `strlen()` in Line 10 to compute the length of the string. `Strlen()` walks the character buffer and counts the number of characters crossed until it reaches the null-terminator that indicates the end of the string. This null-terminator has been inserted by `cin` at the end of the user's input. This behavior of `strlen` makes it dangerous as it can easily walk past the bounds of the character array if the user has supplied text longer than the mentioned limit. See Listing 6.2 in Lesson 6 to learn how to implement a check that ensures an array is not written beyond its bounds.

> **CAUTION**
>
> Applications programmed in C (or in C++ by programmers who have a strong C background) often use string copy functions such as `strcpy()`, concatenation functions such as `strcat()`, and `strlen()` to determine the length of a string, in addition to others of this kind.
>
> These functions take C-style strings as input and are dangerous as they seek the null-terminator and can exceed the boundaries of the character array they're using if the programmer has not ensured the presence of the terminating null.

4

C++ Strings: Using `std::string`

C++ standard strings are an efficient and safer way to deal with text input—and to perform string manipulations like concatenations. `std::string` is not static in size like a `char` array implementation of a C-style string is and can scale up when more data needs to be stored in it. Using `std::string` to manipulate string data is shown in Listing 4.7.

LISTING 4.7   Using `std::string` to Initialize, Store User Input, Copy, Concatenate, and Determine the Length of a String

```
0: #include <iostream>
1: #include <string>
2:
3: using namespace std;
4:
```

```
 5: int main()
 6: {
 7:     string greetString ("Hello std::string!");
 8:     cout << greetString << endl;
 9:
10:     cout << "Enter a line of text: " << endl;
11:     string firstLine;
12:     getline(cin, firstLine);
13:
14:     cout << "Enter another: " << endl;
15:     string secondLine;
16:     getline(cin, secondLine);
17:
18:     cout << "Result of concatenation: " << endl;
19:     string concatString = firstLine + " " + secondLine;
20:     cout << concatString << endl;
21:
22:     cout << "Copy of concatenated string: " << endl;
23:     string aCopy;
24:     aCopy = concatString;
25:     cout << aCopy << endl;
26:
27:     cout << "Length of concat string: " << concatString.length() << endl;
28:
29:     return 0;
30: }
```

Output ▼

```
Hello std::string!
Enter a line of text:
I love
Enter another:
C++ strings
Result of concatenation:
I love C++ strings
Copy of concatenated string:
I love C++ strings
Length of concat string: 18
```

Analysis ▼

Try to understand the output and correlate it to the various elements in code. Don't let new syntax features bother you at this stage. The program starts with displaying a string that has been initialized in Line 7 to "Hello std::string". It then asks the user to enter two lines of text, which are stored in variables firstLine and secondLine in Lines 12 and 16. The actual concatenation is simple and looks like an arithmetic addition in Line 19, where even a space has been added to the first line. The act of copying is a simple act of assigning in Line 24. Determining the length of the string is done by invoking `length()` on it in Line 27.

> **NOTE**
>
> To use a C++ string, you need to include the header `string`:
>
> `#include <string>`
>
> This is also visible in Line 1 in Listing 4.7.

To learn the various functions of `std::string` in detail, take a quick look at Lesson 16, "The STL `string` Class." Because you have not learned about classes and templates yet, ignore sections that seem unfamiliar in that lesson and concentrate on understanding the gist of the samples.

Summary

This lesson taught you about the basics of arrays, what they are, and where they can be used. You learned how to declare them, initialize them, access elements in an array, and write values to elements in an array. You learned how important it is to not exceed the bounds of an array. That is called a *buffer overflow*, and ensuring that input is checked before using to index elements helps ensure that the limits of an array are not crossed.

Dynamic arrays are those where the programmer doesn't need to worry about fixing the max length of an array at compile-time, and they allow for better memory management in the event of usage that is lesser than the expected maximum.

You also learned that C-style strings are a special case of `char` arrays where the end of the string is marked by a null-terminating character `'\0'`. More importantly, though, you learned that C++ offers a far better option in the `std::string`, which provides convenient utility functions that enable you to determine the length, concatenate, and perform similar actions.

Q&A

Q Why take the trouble to initialize a static array's elements?

A Unless initialized, the array, unlike a variable of any other type, contains junk and unpredictable values as the memory at that location was left untouched after the last operations. Initializing arrays ensures that the information therein has a distinct and predictable initial state.

Q Would you need to initialize the elements in a dynamic array for the same reasons as mentioned in the first question?

A Actually, no. A dynamic array is quite a smart array. Elements in the array don't need to be initialized to a default value unless there is a specific reason related to the application that needs you to have certain initial values in the array.

Q Given a choice, would you use C-style strings that need a null-terminator?

A Yes, but only if someone places a gun to your head. C++ `std::string` is a lot safer and supplies features that should make any good programmer stay away from using C-style strings.

Q Does the length of the string include the null-terminator at the end of it?

A No, it doesn't. The length of string "Hello World" is 11, including the space and excluding the null character at the end of it.

Q Well, I still want to use C-style strings in `char` arrays defined by myself. What should be the size of the array I am using?

A Here you go with one of the complications of using C-style strings. The size of the array should be one greater than the size of the largest string it will ever contain. This is essential so that it can accommodate for the null character at the end of the largest string. If "Hello World" was to be the largest string your `char` array would ever hold, then the length of the array needs to be 11 + 1 = 12 characters.

Workshop

The Workshop provides quiz questions to help you solidify your understanding of the material covered and exercises to provide you with experience in using what you've learned. Try to answer the quiz and exercise questions before checking the answers in Appendix E, and be certain you understand the answers before continuing to the next lesson.

Quiz

1. Check the array `myNumbers` in Listing 4.1. What are the indexes of the first and last elements in that array?

2. If you need to allow the user to input strings, would you use C-style strings?

3. How many characters are in `'\0'` as seen by the compiler?

4. You forget to end your C-style string with a null-terminator. What happens when you use it?

5. See the declaration of vector in Listing 4.4 and try composing a dynamic array that contains elements of the type `char`.

Exercises

1. Declare an array that represents the squares on the chessboard; the type of the array being an `enum` that defines the pieces that may possibly occupy the squares.

   HINT: The `enum` will contain enumerators (`Rook`, `Bishop`, and so on), thereby limiting the range of possible values that the elements in the array can hold. Don't forget that a cell may also be empty!

2. **BUG BUSTERS:** What is wrong with this code fragment?

```
int myNumbers[5] = {0};
myNumbers[5] = 450; // Setting the 5th element to value 450
```

3. **BUG BUSTERS:** What is wrong with this code fragment?

```
int myNumbers[5];
cout << myNumbers[3];
```

4

LESSON 5
Working with Expressions, Statements, and Operators

At its heart, a program is a set of commands executed in sequence. These commands are programmed into expressions and statements and use operators to perform specific calculations or actions.

In this lesson, you learn

- What statements are
- What blocks or compound statements are
- What operators are
- How to perform simple arithmetic and logical operations

Statements

Languages—spoken or programmed—are composed of statements that are executed one after another. Let's analyze the first important statement you learned:

```
cout << "Hello World" << endl;
```

A statement using `cout` displays text using the console on the screen. All statements in C++ end with a semicolon (;), which defines the boundary of a statement. This is similar to the period (.) you add when ending a sentence in English. The next statement can start immediately after the semicolon, but for convenience and readability you often program successive statements on successive lines. In other words, this is actually a set of two statements in a line:

```
cout << "Hello World" << endl; cout << "Another hello" << endl;
```

NOTE

> Whitespaces typically are not visible to the compiler. This includes spaces, tabs, line feeds, carriage returns, and so on. Whitespaces within string literals, though, make a difference to the output.

The following would be invalid:

```
cout << "Hello
    World" << endl; // new line in string literal not allowed
```

Such code typically results in an error indicating that the compiler is missing a closing quote (") and a statement-terminating semicolon (;) in the first line. If you need to spread a statement over two lines for some reason, you can do it by inserting a backslash (\) at the end:

```
cout << "Hello \
    World" << endl; // split to two lines is OK
```

Another way of writing the preceding statement in two lines is to write two string literals instead of just one:

```
cout << "Hello "
   "World" << endl; // two string literals is also OK
```

In the preceding example, the compiler notices two adjacent string literals and concatenates them for you.

NOTE

> Splitting a statement into many lines can be useful when you have long text elements or complex expressions comprised of many variables that make a statement much longer than what most displays can allow.

Compound Statements or Blocks

When you group statements together within braces {...}, you create a compound statement or a block.

```
{
    int daysInYear = 365;
    cout << "Block contains an int and a cout statement" << endl;
}
```

A block typically groups many statements to indicate that they belong together. Blocks are particularly useful when programming conditional if statements or loops, which are explained in Lesson 6, "Controlling Program Flow."

Using Operators

Operators are tools that C++ provides for you to be able to work with data, transform it, process it, and possibly make decisions on the basis of it.

The Assignment Operator (=)

The assignment operator is one that you already have been using intuitively in this book:

```
int daysInYear = 365;
```

The preceding statement uses the assignment operator in initializing the integer to 365. The assignment operator replaces the value contained by the operand to the left (unimaginatively called l-value) by that on the right (called r-value).

Understanding L-values and R-values

L-values often refer to locations in memory. A variable such as daysInYear from the preceding example is actually a handle to a memory location and is an l-value. R-values, on the other hand, can be the very content of a memory location.

So, all l-values can be r-values, but not all r-values can be l-values. To understand it better, look at the following example, which doesn't make any sense and therefore won't compile:

```
365 = daysInYear;
```

Operators to Add (+), Subtract (-), Multiply (*), Divide (/), and Modulo Divide (%)

You can perform an arithmetic operation between two operands by using + for addition, - for subtraction, * for multiplication, / for division, and % for modulo operation:

```
int num1 = 22;
int num2 = 5;
int addNums = num1 + num2; // 27
int subtractNums = num1 - num2; // 17
int multiplyNums = num1 * num2; // 110
int divideNums = num1 / num2; // 4
int moduloNums = num1 % num2; // 2
```

Note that the division operator (/) returns the result of division between two operands. In the case of integers, however, the result contains no decimals as integers by definition cannot hold decimal data. The modulo operator (%) returns the remainder of a division operator, and it is applicable only on integer values. Listing 5.1 is a simple program that demonstrates an application to perform arithmetic functions on two numbers input by the user.

LISTING 5.1 Demonstrate Arithmetic Operators on Integers Input by the User

```
 0: #include <iostream>
 1: using namespace std;
 2:
 3: int main()
 4: {
 5:     cout << "Enter two integers:" << endl;
 6:     int num1 = 0, num2 = 0;
 7:     cin >> num1;
 8:     cin >> num2;
 9:
10:     cout << num1 << " + " << num2 << " = " << num1 + num2 << endl;
11:     cout << num1 << " - " << num2 << " = " << num1 - num2 << endl;
12:     cout << num1 << " * " << num2 << " = " << num1 * num2 << endl;
```

```
13:    cout << num1 << " / " << num2 << " = " << num1 / num2 << endl;
14:    cout << num1 << " % " << num2 << " = " << num1 % num2 << endl;
15:
16:  return 0;
17: }
```

Output ▼

```
Enter two integers:
365
25
365 + 25 = 390
365 - 25 = 340
365 * 25 = 9125
365 / 25 = 14
365 % 25 = 15
```

Analysis ▼

Most of the program is self-explanatory. The line of most interest is possibly the one that uses the % modulo operator. This returns the remainder that is the result of dividing num1 (365) by num2 (25).

Operators to Increment (++) and Decrement (--)

Sometimes you need to count in increments of one. This is particularly required in variables that control loops where the value of the variable needs to be incremented or decremented every time a loop has been executed.

C++ includes the ++ (increment) and -- (decrement) operators to help you with this task.

The syntax for using these is the following:

```
int num1 = 101;
int num2 = num1++; // Postfix increment operator
int num2 = ++num1; // Prefix increment operator
int num2 = num1--; // Postfix decrement operator
int num2 = --num1; // Prefix decrement operator
```

As the code sample indicates, there are two different ways of using the incrementing and decrementing operators: before and after the operand. Operators that are placed before the operand are called prefix increment or decrement operators, and those that are placed after are called postfix increment or decrement operators.

5

To Postfix or to Prefix?

It's important to first understand the difference between prefix and postfix and then use the one that works for you. The result of execution of the postfix operators is that the l-value is first assigned the r-value and after that assignment the r-value is incremented (or decremented). This means that in all cases where a postfix operator has been used, the value of num2 is the old value of num1 (the value before the increment or decrement operation).

Prefix operators have exactly the opposite in behavior. The r-value is first incremented and then assigned to the l-value. In these cases, num2 and num1 carry the same value. Listing 5.2 demonstrates the effect of prefix and postfix increment and decrement operators on a sample integer.

LISTING 5.2 Demonstrate the Difference Between Postfix and Prefix Operators

```
 0: #include <iostream>
 1: using namespace std;
 2:
 3: int main()
 4: {
 5:     int startValue = 101;
 6:     cout << "Start value of integer being operated: " << startValue << endl;
 7:
 8:     int postfixIncrement = startValue++;
 9:     cout << "Result of Postfix Increment = " << postfixIncrement << endl;
10:     cout << "After Postfix Increment, startValue = " << startValue << endl;
11:
12:     startValue = 101; // Reset
13:     int prefixIncrement = ++startValue;
14:     cout << "Result of Prefix Increment = " << prefixIncrement << endl;
15:     cout << "After Prefix Increment, startValue = " << startValue << endl;
16:
17:     startValue = 101; // Reset
18:     int postfixDecrement = startValue--;
19:     cout << "Result of Postfix Decrement = " << postfixDecrement << endl;
20:     cout << "After Postfix Decrement, startValue = " << startValue << endl;
21:
22:     startValue = 101; // Reset
23:     int prefixDecrement = --startValue;
24:     cout << "Result of Prefix Decrement = " << prefixDecrement << endl;
25:     cout << "After Prefix Decrement, startValue = " << startValue << endl;
26:
27:     return 0;
28: }
```

Output ▼

```
Start value of integer being operated: 101
Result of Postfix Increment = 101
After Postfix Increment, startValue = 102
Result of Prefix Increment = 102
After Prefix Increment, startValue = 102
Result of Postfix Decrement = 101
After Postfix Decrement, startValue = 100
Result of Prefix Decrement = 100
After Prefix Decrement, startValue = 100
```

Analysis ▼

The results show that the postfix operators were different from the prefix ones in that the l-values being assigned in Lines 8 and 18 contain the original values of the integer before the actual increment or decrement operations. The prefix operations in Lines 13 and 23, on the other hand, result in the l-value being assigned the incremented or decremented value. This is the most important difference that needs to be kept in perspective when choosing the right operator type.

Note that in the following statements, the prefix or postfix operators make no difference to the output of the program:

```
startValue++; // Is the same as…
++startValue;
```

This is because there is no assignment of an initial value, and the end result in both cases is just that the integer startValue is incremented.

5

NOTE

You often hear of cases where prefix increment or decrement operators are preferred on grounds of better performance. That is, ++startValue is preferred over startValue++.

This is true at least theoretically because with the postfix operators, the compiler needs to store the initial value temporarily in the event of it needing to be assigned. The effect on performance in these cases is negligible with respect to integers, but in the case of certain classes there might be a point in this argument. Smart compilers may optimize away the differences.

Equality Operators (==) and (!=)

Often you need to check for a certain condition being fulfilled or not being fulfilled before you proceed to take an action. Equality operators == (operands are equal) and != (operands are unequal) help you with exactly that.

The result of an equality check is a bool—that is, true or false.

```
int personAge = 20;
bool checkEquality = (personAge == 20); // true
bool checkInequality = (personAge != 100); // true

bool checkEqualityAgain = (personAge == 200); // false
bool checkInequalityAgain = (personAge != 20); // false
```

Relational Operators

In addition to equality checks, you might want to check for inequality of a certain variable against a value. To assist you with that, C++ includes relational operators (see Table 5.1).

TABLE 5.1 Relational Operators

Operator Name	Description
Less than (<)	Evaluates to true if one operand is less than the other (op1 < op2), else evaluates to false
Greater than (>)	Evaluates to true if one operand is greater than the other (op1 > op2), else evaluates to false
Less than or equal to (<=)	Evaluates to true if one operand is less than or equal to another, else evaluates to false
Greater than or equal to (>=)	Evaluates to true if one operand is greater than or equal to another, else evaluates to false

As Table 5.1 indicates, the result of a comparison operation is always true or false, in other words a bool. The following sample code indicates how the relational operators introduced in Table 5.1 can be put to use:

```
int personAge = 20;
bool checkLessThan = (personAge < 100);   // true
bool checkGreaterThan = (personAge > 100); // false
bool checkLessThanEqualTo = (personAge <= 20); // true
```

```
bool checkGreaterThanEqualTo = (personAge >= 20); // true
bool checkGreaterThanEqualToAgain = (personAge >= 100); // false
```

Listing 5.3 is a program that demonstrates the effect of using these operators by displaying the result on the screen.

LISTING 5.3 Demonstrating Equality and Relational Operators

```
0: #include <iostream>
1: using namespace std;
2:
3: int main()
4: {
5:     cout << "Enter two integers:" << endl;
6:     int num1 = 0, num2 = 0;
7:     cin >> num1;
8:     cin >> num2;
9:
10:    bool isEqual = (num1 == num2);
11:    cout << "Result of equality test: " << isEqual << endl;
12:
13:    bool isUnequal = (num1 != num2);
14:    cout << "Result of inequality test: " << isUnequal << endl;
15:
16:    bool isGreaterThan = (num1 > num2);
17:    cout << "Result of " << num1 << " > " << num2;
18:    cout << " test: " << isGreaterThan << endl;
19:
20:    bool isLessThan = (num1 < num2);
21:    cout << "Result of " << num1 << " < " << num2 << " test:
" << isLessThan << endl;
22:
23:    bool isGreaterThanEquals = (num1 >= num2);
24:    cout << "Result of " << num1 << " >= " << num2;
25:    cout << " test: " << isGreaterThanEquals << endl;
26:
27:    bool isLessThanEquals = (num1 <= num2);
28:    cout << "Result of " << num1 << " <= " << num2;
29:    cout << " test: " << isLessThanEquals << endl;
30:
31:    return 0;
32: }
```

5

Output ▼

```
Enter two integers:
365
-24
Result of equality test: 0
Result of inequality test: 1
Result of 365 > -24 test: 1
Result of 365 < -24 test: 0
Result of 365 >= -24 test: 1
Result of 365 <= -24 test: 0
```

Next run:

```
Enter two integers:
101
101
Result of equality test: 1
Result of inequality test: 0
Result of 101 > 101 test: 0
Result of 101 < 101 test: 0
Result of 101 >= 101 test: 1
Result of 101 <= 101 test: 1
```

Analysis ▼

The program displays the binary result of the various operations. Interesting is to note the output in the event the two supplied integers are identical. The operators ==, >=, and <= produce identical results too.

The fact that the output of equality and relational operators is binary makes these perfectly suited to using them in statements that help in decision-making and as loop condition expressions that ensure a loop executes only so long as the condition evaluates to true. You can learn more about conditional execution and loops in Lesson 6.

NOTE

The output of Listing 5.3 displayed Boolean values containing false as 0. Those containing true were displayed as 1. From a compiler's point of view, an expression evaluates false when it evaluates to zero. A check against false is a check against zero. An expression that evaluates to a non-zero value is evaluated as true.

Logical Operations NOT, AND, OR, and XOR

Logical NOT operation is supported by the operator ! and works on a single operand. Table 5.2 is the truth table for a logical NOT operation, which, as expected, simply inverses the supplied Boolean flag.

TABLE 5.2 Truth Table of Logical NOT Operation

Operand	Result of NOT (Operand)
False	True
True	False

Other operators such as AND, OR, and XOR need two operands. Logical AND operation evaluates to true only when each operand evaluates to true. Table 5.3 demonstrates the functioning of a logical AND operation.

TABLE 5.3 Truth Table of Logical AND Operation

Operand 1	Operand 2	Result of Operand1 AND Operand2
False	False	False
True	False	False
False	True	False
True	True	True

Logical AND operation is supported by operator &&.

Logical OR evaluates to true when at least one of the operands evaluates to true, as demonstrated by Table 5.4.

TABLE 5.4 Truth Table of Logical OR Operation

Operand 1	Operand 2	Result of Operand1 OR Operand2
False	False	False
True	False	True
False	True	True
True	True	True

5

Logical OR operation is supported by operator ||.

The exclusive OR (abbreviated to XOR) operation is slightly different than the logical OR for it evaluates to true when any one operand is `true` but not both, as demonstrated by Table 5.5.

TABLE 5.5   Truth Table of Logical XOR Operation

Operand 1	Operand 2	Result of Operand1 OR Operand2
False	False	False
True	False	True
False	True	True
True	True	False

C++ provides a bitwise XOR in the form of operator ^. This operator helps evaluate a result that is generated via an XOR operation on the operand's bits.

Using C++ Logical Operators NOT (!), AND (&&), and OR (||)

Consider these statements:

- "If it is raining AND if there are no buses, I cannot go to work."
- "If there is a deep discount OR if I am awarded a record bonus, I can buy that car."

You need such logical constructs in programming where the result of two operations is used in a logical context in deciding the future flow of your program. C++ provides logical AND and OR operators that you can use in conditional statements, hence conditionally changing the flow of your program.

Listing 5.4 demonstrates the workings of logical AND and logical OR operators.

LISTING 5.4   Analyzing C++ Logical Operators && and ||

```
0: #include <iostream>
1: using namespace std;
2:
3: int main()
4: {
5:     cout << "Enter true(1) or false(0) for two operands:" << endl;
6:     bool op1 = false, op2 = false;
```

```
 7:      cin >> op1;
 8:      cin >> op2;
 9:
10:      cout << op1 << " AND " << op2 << " = " << (op1 && op2) << endl;
11:      cout << op1 << " OR " << op2 << " = " << (op1 || op2) << endl;
12:
13:      return 0;
14: }
```

Output ▼

```
Enter true(1) or false(0) for two operands:
1
0
1 AND 0 = 0
1 OR 0 = 1
```

Next run:

```
Enter true(1) or false(0) for two operands:
1
1
1 AND 1 = 1
1 OR 1 = 1
```

Analysis ▼

The program actually indicates how the operators supply logical AND and OR functions to you. What the program doesn't do is show you how to use them in making decisions.

Listing 5.5 demonstrates a program that executes different lines of code depending on the values contained in variables using conditional statement processing and logical operators.

LISTING 5.5 Using Logical NOT (!) and Logical AND (&&) Operators in `if` Statements for Conditional Processing

```
0: #include <iostream>
1: using namespace std;
2:
3: int main()
4: {
5:     cout << "Use boolean values(0 / 1) to answer the questions" << endl;
6:     cout << "Is it raining? ";
7:     bool isRaining = false;
8:     cin >> isRaining;
```

5

```
 9:
10:     cout << "Do you have buses on the streets? ";
11:     bool busesPly = false;
12:     cin >> busesPly;
13:
14:     // Conditional statement uses logical AND and NOT
15:     if (isRaining && !busesPly)
16:        cout << "You cannot go to work" << endl;
17:     else
18:        cout << "You can go to work" << endl;
19:
20:     if (isRaining && busesPly)
21:        cout << "Take an umbrella" << endl;
22:
23:     if ((!isRaining) && busesPly)
24:         cout << "Enjoy the sun and have a nice day" << endl;
25:
26:     return 0;
27: }
```

Output ▼

```
Use boolean values(0 / 1) to answer the questions
Is it raining? 1
Do you have buses on the streets? 1
You can go to work
Take an umbrella
```

Next run:

```
Use boolean values(0 / 1) to answer the questions
Is it raining? 1
Do you have buses on the streets? 0
You cannot go to work
```

Last run:

```
Use boolean values(0 / 1) to answer the questions
Is it raining? 0
Do you have buses on the streets? 1
You can go to work
Enjoy the sun and have a nice day
```

Analysis ▼

The program in Listing 5.5 uses conditional statements in the form of the `if` construct that has not been introduced to you. Yet, try to understand the behavior of this construct by correlating it against the output. Line 15 contains the logical expression (`isRaining && !busesPly`) that can be read as "Raining AND NO buses." This uses the logical AND operator to connect the absence of buses (indicated by the logical NOT on presence of buses) to the presence of rain.

> **NOTE**
>
> If you want to read a little about the `if` construct that helps in conditional execution, you can quickly visit Lesson 6.

Listing 5.6 uses logical NOT (!) and OR (||) operators in a demonstration of conditional processing.

LISTING 5.6   Using Logical NOT and Logical OR Operators to Help You Decide If You Can Buy That Dream Car

```
0: #include <iostream>
1: using namespace std;
2:
3: int main()
4: {
5:     cout << "Answer questions with 0 or 1" << endl;
6:     cout << "Is there a discount on your favorite car? ";
7:     bool onDiscount = false;
8:     cin >> onDiscount;
9:
10:     cout << "Did you get a fantastic bonus? ";
11:     bool fantasticBonus = false;
12:     cin >> fantasticBonus;
13:
14:     if (onDiscount || fantasticBonus)
15:         cout << "Congratulations, you can buy that car!" << endl;
16:     else
17:         cout << "Sorry, waiting a while is a good idea" << endl;
18:
19:     if (!onDiscount)
20:         cout << "Car not on discount" << endl;
21:
22:     return 0;
23: }
```

5

Output ▼

```
Answer questions with 0 or 1
Is there a discount on your favorite car? 0
Did you get a fantastic bonus? 1
Congratulations, you can buy that car!
Car not on discount
```

Next run:

```
Answer questions with 0 or 1
Is there a discount on your favorite car? 0
Did you get a fantastic bonus? 0
Sorry, waiting a while is a good idea
Car not on discount
```

Last run:

```
Answer questions with 0 or 1
Is there a discount on your favorite car? 1
Did you get a fantastic bonus? 1
Congratulations, you can buy that car!
```

Analysis ▼

The program recommends buying a car if you get a discount or if you got a fantastic bonus (or both). If not, it recommends waiting. It also uses the logical not operation in Line 19 to remind you that the car is not on discount. Line 14 uses the `if` construct followed by an accompanying `else` in Line 16. The `if` construct executes the following statement in Line 15 when the condition (`onDiscount || fantasticBonus`) evaluates to `true`. This expression contains the logical OR operator and evaluates to `true` when there is a discount on your favorite car or if you have received a fantastic bonus. When the expression evaluates to `false`, the statement following `else` in Line 17 is executed.

Bitwise NOT (~), AND (&), OR (|), and XOR (^) Operators

The difference between the logical and the bitwise operators is that bitwise operators don't return a boolean result. Instead, they supply a result in which individual bits are governed by executing the operator on the operands' bits. C++ allows you to perform operations such as NOT, OR, AND, and exclusive OR (that is, XOR) operations on a bitwise mode where you can manipulate individual bits by negating them using ~, ORring them using |, ANDing them using &, and XORring them using ^. The latter three are performed against a number (typically a bit mask) of your choosing.

Some bitwise operations are useful in those situations where bits contained in an integer—for example, each specify the state of a certain flag. Thus, an integer with 32 bits can be used to carry 32 Boolean flags. Listing 5.7 demonstrates the use of bitwise operators.

LISTING 5.7 Demonstrating the Use of Bitwise Operators to Perform NOT, AND, OR, and XOR on Individual Bits in an Integer

```
0: #include <iostream>
1: #include <bitset>
2: using namespace std;
3:
4: int main()
5: {
6:     cout << "Enter a number (0 - 255): ";
7:     unsigned short inputNum = 0;
8:     cin >> inputNum;
9:
10:     bitset<8> inputBits (inputNum);
11:     cout << inputNum << " in binary is " << inputBits << endl;
12:
13:     bitset<8> bitwiseNOT = (~inputNum);
14:     cout << "Logical NOT ~" << endl;
15:     cout << "~" << inputBits  << " = " << bitwiseNOT << endl;
16:
17:     cout << "Logical AND, & with 00001111" << endl;
18:     bitset<8> bitwiseAND = (0x0F & inputNum);// 0x0F is hex for 0001111
19:     cout << "0001111 & " << inputBits  << " = " << bitwiseAND << endl;
20:
21:     cout << "Logical OR, | with 00001111" << endl;
22:     bitset<8> bitwiseOR = (0x0F | inputNum);
23:     cout << "00001111 | " << inputBits  << " = " << bitwiseOR << endl;
24:
25:     cout << "Logical XOR, ^ with 00001111" << endl;
26:     bitset<8> bitwiseXOR = (0x0F ^ inputNum);
27:     cout << "00001111 ^ " << inputBits  << " = " << bitwiseXOR << endl;
28:
29:     return 0;
30: }
```

5

Output ▼

```
Enter a number (0 - 255): 181
181 in binary is 10110101
Logical NOT ~
~10110101 = 01001010
Logical AND, & with 00001111
0001111 & 10110101 = 00000101
Logical OR, | with 00001111
00001111 | 10110101 = 10111111
Logical XOR, ^ with 00001111
00001111 ^ 10110101 = 10111010
```

Analysis ▼

This program uses `bitset`—a type you have not seen yet—to make displaying binary data easier. The role of `std::bitset` here is purely to help with displaying and nothing more. In Lines 10, 13, 18, and 22 you actually assign an integer to a bitset object, which is used to display that same integer data in binary mode. The operations are done on integers. For a start, focus on the output, which shows you the original integer 181 fed by the user in binary and then proceeds to demonstrate the effect of the various bitwise operators ~, &, |, and ^ on this integer. You see that the bitwise NOT used in Line 14 toggles the individual bits. The program also demonstrates how the operators &, |, and ^ work, performing the operations using each bit in the two operands to create the result. Correlate this result with the truth tables introduced earlier, and the workings should become clearer to you.

NOTE

> If you want to learn more about manipulating bit flags in C++, take a look at Lesson 25, "Working with Bit Flags Using STL." It discusses the `std::bitset` in detail.

Bitwise Right Shift (>>) and Left Shift (<<) Operators

Shift operators move the entire bit sequence to the right or to the left, and thus can help with multiplication or division by multiples of two, apart from having other uses in an application.

A sample use of a shift operator used to multiply by two is the following:

```
int doubledValue = num << 1; // shift bits one position left to double value
```

A sample use of a shift operator used to halve is the following:

```
int halvedValue = num >> 1; // shift bits one position right to halve value
```

Listing 5.8 demonstrates how you can use shift operators to effectively multiply or divide an integer value.

LISTING 5.8 Using Bitwise Right Shift Operator (>>) to Quarter and Half and Left Shift (<<) to Double and Quadruple an Input Integer

```
0: #include <iostream>
1: using namespace std;
2:
3: int main()
4: {
5:     cout << "Enter a number: ";
6:     int inputNum = 0;
7:     cin >> inputNum;
8:
9:     int halfNum = inputNum >> 1;
10:    int quarterNum = inputNum >> 2;
11:    int doubleNum = inputNum << 1;
12:    int quadrupleNum = inputNum << 2;
13:
14:    cout << "Quarter: " << quarterNum << endl;
15:    cout << "Half: " << halfNum << endl;
16:    cout << "Double: " << doubleNum << endl;
17:    cout << "Quadruple: " << quadrupleNum << endl;
18:
19:    return 0;
20: }
```

5

Output ▼

```
Enter a number: 16
Quarter: 4
Half: 8
Double: 32
Quadruple: 64
```

10000 ½b

Analysis ▼

The input number is 16, which in binary terms is 1000. In Line 9, you move it one bit right to change it to 0100, which is 8, effectively halving it. In Line 10, you move it two bits right changing 1000 to 00100, which is 4. Similarly the effect of the left shift operators in Lines 11 and 12 are exactly the opposite. You move it one bit left to get 10000,

←1,000,000 ?????

which is 32 and two bits left to get 100000, which is 64, effectively doubling and quadrupling the number!

NOTE	Bitwise shift operators don't rotate values. Additionally, the result of shifting signed numbers is implementation dependent. On some compilers, most-significant-bit when shifted left is not assigned to the least-significant-bit; rather the latter is zero.

Compound Assignment Operators

Compound assignment operators are assignment operators where the operand to the left is assigned the value resulting from the operation.

Consider the following code:

```
int num1 = 22;
int num2 = 5;
num1 += num2; // num1 contains 27 after the operation
```

This is similar to what's expressed in the following line of code:

```
num1 = num1 + num2;
```

Thus, the effect of the += operator is that the sum of the two operands is calculated and then assigned to the operand on the left (which is num1). Table 5.6 is a quick reference on the many compound assignment operators and explains their working.

TABLE 5.6   Compound Assignment Operators

Operator	Usage	Equivalent
Addition Assignment	num1 += num2;	num1 = num1 + num2;
Subtraction Assignment	num1 -= num2;	num1 = num1 - num2;
Multiplication Assignment	num1 *= num2;	num1 = num1 * num2;
Division Assignment	num1 /= num2;	num1 = num1 / num2;
Modulo Assignment	num1 %= num2;	num1 = num1 % num2;
Bitwise Left-Shift Assignment	num1 <<= num2;	num1 = num1 << num2;

Operator	Usage	Equivalent
Bitwise Right-Shift Assignment	num1 >>= num2;	num1 = num1 >> num2;
Bitwise AND Assignment	num1 &= num2;	num1 = num1 & num2;
Bitwise OR Assignment	num1 |= num2;	num1 = num1 | num2;
Bitwise XOR Assignment	num1 ^= num2;	num1 = num1 ^ num2;

Listing 5.9 demonstrates the effect of using these operators.

LISTING 5.9   Using Compound Assignment Operators to Add; Subtract; Divide; Perform Modulus; Shift; and Perform Bitwise OR, AND, and XOR

```
0: #include <iostream>
1: using namespace std;
2:
3: int main()
4: {
5:     cout << "Enter a number: ";
6:     int value = 0;
7:     cin >> value;
8:
9:     value += 8;
10:    cout << "After += 8, value = " << value << endl;
11:    value -= 2;
12:    cout << "After -= 2, value = " << value << endl;
13:    value /= 4;
14:    cout << "After /= 4, value = " << value << endl;
15:    value *= 4;
16:    cout << "After *= 4, value = " << value << endl;
17:    value %= 1000;
18:    cout << "After %= 1000, value = " << value << endl;
19:
20:    // Note: henceforth assignment happens within cout
21:    cout << "After <<= 1, value = " << (value <<= 1) << endl;
22:    cout << "After >>= 2, value = " << (value >>= 2) << endl;
23:
24:    cout << "After |= 0x55, value = " << (value |= 0x55) << endl;
25:    cout << "After ^= 0x55, value = " << (value ^= 0x55) << endl;
26:    cout << "After &= 0x0F, value = " << (value &= 0x0F) << endl;
27:
28:    return 0;
29: }
```

5

Output ▼

```
Enter a number: 440
After += 8, value = 448
After -= 2, value = 446
After /= 4, value = 111
After *= 4, value = 444
After %= 1000, value = 444
After <<= 1, value = 888
After >>= 2, value = 222
After |= 0x55, value = 223
After ^= 0x55, value = 138
After &= 0x0F, value = 10
```

Analysis ▼

Note that `value` is continually modified throughout the program via the various assignment operators. Each operation is performed using `value`, and the result of the operation is assigned back to it. Hence, at Line 9, the user input 440 is added to 8, which results in 448 and is assigned back to `value`. In the subsequent operation at Line 11, 2 is subtracted from 448, resulting in 446, which is assigned back to `value`, and so on.

Using Operator `sizeof` to Determine the Memory Occupied by a Variable

This operator tells you the amount of memory in bytes consumed by a particular type or a variable. The usage of `sizeof` is the following:

```
sizeof (variable);
```

or

```
sizeof (type);
```

NOTE

> `sizeof(...)` might look like a function call, but it is not a function. `sizeof` is an operator. Interestingly, this operator cannot be defined by the programmer and hence cannot be overloaded.
>
> You learn more about defining your own operators in Lesson 12, "Operator Types and Operator Overloading."

Listing 5.10 demonstrates the use of `sizeof` in determining memory space occupied by an array. Additionally, you might want to revisit Listing 3.4 to analyze the usage of `sizeof` in determining memory consumed by the most familiar variable types.

LISTING 5.10 Using `sizeof` to Determine the Number of Bytes Occupied by an Array of 100 Integers, and That by Each Element Therein

```
 0: #include <iostream>
 1: using namespace std;
 2:
 3: int main()
 4: {
 5:     cout << "Use sizeof to determine memory used by arrays" << endl;
 6:     int myNumbers [100] = {0};
 7:
 8:     cout << "Bytes used by an int: " << sizeof(int) << endl;
 9:     cout << "Bytes used by myNumbers: " << sizeof(myNumbers) << endl;
10:     cout << "Bytes used by an element: " << sizeof(myNumbers[0]) << endl;
11:
12:     return 0;
13: }
```

Output ▼

```
Use sizeof to determine memory used by arrays
Bytes used by an int: 4
Bytes used by myNumbers: 400
Bytes used by an element: 4
```

Analysis ▼

The program demonstrates how `sizeof` is capable of returning the size of an array of 100 integers in bytes, which is 400 bytes. The program also demonstrates that the size of each element is 4 bytes.

`sizeof` can be useful when you need to dynamically allocate memory for *N* objects, especially of a type created by yourself. You would use the result of the `sizeof` operation in determining the amount of memory occupied by each object and then dynamically allocate using the operator `new`.

Dynamic memory allocation is explained in detail in Lesson 8, "Pointers and References Explained."

5

Operator Precedence

You possibly learned something in school on the order of arithmetic operations called BODMAS (Brackets Orders Division Multiplication Addition Subtraction), indicating the order in which a complex arithmetical expression should be evaluated.

In C++, you use operators and expressions such as the following:

```
int myNumber = 10 * 30 + 20 - 5 * 5 << 2;
```

The question is, what value would `myNumber` contain? This is not left to guesswork of any kind. The order in which the various operators are invoked is very strictly specified by the C++ standard. This order is what is meant by operator precedence. See Table 5.7.

TABLE 5.7 The Precedence of Operators

Rank	Name	Operator
1	Scope resolution	`::`
2	Member selection, subscripting, increment, and decrement	`.  ->`
		`()`
		`++  --`
3	`sizeof`, prefix increment and decrement, complement, and, not, unary minus and plus, address-of and dereference, `new`, `new[]`, `delete`, `delete[]`, casting, `sizeof()`	`++  --`
		`^  !`
		`-  +`
		`&  *`
		`()`
4	Member selection for pointer	`.*  ->*`
5	Multiply, divide, modulo	`*  /  %`
6	Add, subtract	`+  -`
7	Shift (shift left, shift right)	`<<  >>`
8	Inequality relational	`<<  =  >>=`
9	Equality, inequality	`==  !=`
10	Bitwise AND	`&`
11	Bitwise exclusive OR	`^`
12	Bitwise OR	`|`

Rank	Name	Operator
13	Logical AND	&&
14	Logical OR	||
15	Conditional	? :
16	Assignment operators	= *= /= %=
		+= -= <<=
		>>=
		&= |= ^=
17	Comma	,

Have another look at the complicated expression used as the earlier example:

```
int myNumber = 10 * 30 + 20 - 5 * 5 << 2;
```

In evaluating the result of this expression, you need to use the rules related to operator precedence as shown in Table 5.7 to understand what value the compiler assigns it. As multiply and divide have priority over add and subtract, which in turn have priority over shift, you simplify it to the following:

```
int myNumber = 300 + 20 - 25 << 2;
```

As add and subtract have priority over shift, this gets simplified to:

```
int myNumber = 295 << 2;
```

Finally, you perform the shift operation. Knowing that one bit left shift doubles, and hence two bits left shift quadruples, you can say that the expression evaluates to 295 * 4, which is 1180.

5

CAUTION

Use parentheses to make reading code easy.

The expression used earlier is deliberately composed poorly for explaining operator precedence. It is easy for the compiler to understand, but you should write code that humans can understand, too.

So, the same expression is much better written this way:

```
int myNumber = ((10 * 30) - (5 * 5) + 20) << 2; //
1180
```

DO	DON'T
DO use parentheses to make your code and expressions readable.	**DON'T** program complicated expressions relying on the operator precedence table; your code needs to be human readable, too.
DO use the right variable types and ensure that it will never reach overflow situations.	**DON'T** confuse `++Variable` and `Variable++` thinking they're the same. They're different when used in an assignment.
DO understand that all l-values (for example, variables) can be r-values, but not all r-values (for example, "Hello World") can be l-values.	

Summary

In this lesson you learned what C++ statements, expressions, and operators are. You learned how to perform basic arithmetic operations such as addition, subtraction, multiplication, and division in C++. You also had an overview on logical operations such as NOT, AND, OR, and xOR. You learned of the C++ logical operators !, &&, and || that help you in conditional statements and the bitwise operators such as ~, &, |, and ^ that help you manipulate data, one bit at a time.

You learned about operator precedence and how important it is to use parenthesis to write code that can also be understood by fellow programmers. You were given an overview on integer overflow and how important avoiding it actually is.

Q&A

Q Why do some programs use `unsigned int` if `unsigned short` takes less memory and compiles, too?

A `unsigned short` typically has a limit of 65535, and if incremented, overflows to zero. To avoid this behavior, well-programmed applications choose `unsigned int` when it is not certain that the value will stay well below this limit.

Q I need to calculate the double of a number after it's divided by three. So, do you see any problem in the following code:

```
int result = Number / 3 << 1;
```

A Yes! Why didn't you simply use parenthesis to make this line simpler to read to fellow programmers? Adding a comment or two won't hurt either.

Q **My application divides two integer values 5 and 2:**

```
int num1 = 5, num2 = 2;
int result = num1 / num2;
```

On execution, the result contains value 2. Isn't this wrong?

A Not at all. Integers are not meant to contain decimal data. The result of this operation is hence 2 and not 2.5. If 2.5 is the result you expect, change all data types to `float` or `double`. These are meant to handle floating-point (decimal) operations.

Workshop

The Workshop provides quiz questions to help you solidify your understanding of the material covered and exercises to provide you with experience in using what you've learned. Try to answer the quiz and exercise questions before checking the answers in Appendix E, and be certain that you understand the answers before continuing to the next lesson.

Quiz

1. I am writing an application to divide numbers. What's a better suited data type: `int` or `float`?

2. What is the value of 32 / 7?

3. What is the value of 32.0/7?

4. Is `sizeof(...)` a function?

5. I need to compute the double of a number, add 5 to it, and then double it again. Is this correct?

```
int result = number << 1 + 5 << 1;
```

6. What is the result of XOR operation where the XOR operands both evaluate to true?

Exercises

1. Improve on the code in quiz question 5, using parenthesis to create clarity.

2. What is the value of `result` stored by this expression:

```
int result = number << 1 + 5 << 1;
```

3. Write a program that asks the user to input two Boolean values and demonstrates the result of various bitwise operators on them.

5

LESSON 6
Controlling Program Flow

Most applications behave differently given a new situation or different user input. To enable your application to react differently, you need to program conditional statements that execute different code segments in different situations.

In this lesson, you find out

- How to make your program behave differently in certain conditions
- How to execute a section of code repeatedly in a loop
- How to better control the flow of execution in a loop

Conditional Execution Using `if ... else`

Programs you have seen and composed thus far have a serial order of execution—from top-down. Every line was executed and no line was ever ignored. But, serial execution of all lines of code in a top-down fashion rarely happens in most applications.

Imagine you want a program that multiplies two numbers if the user presses *m* or adds the numbers if he presses anything else.

As you can see in Figure 6.1, not all code paths are executed in every run. If the user presses *m*, the code that multiplies the two numbers is executed. If he enters anything other than *m*, the code that performs addition is executed. There is never a situation where both are executed.

FIGURE 6.1
Example of conditional processing required on the basis of user input.

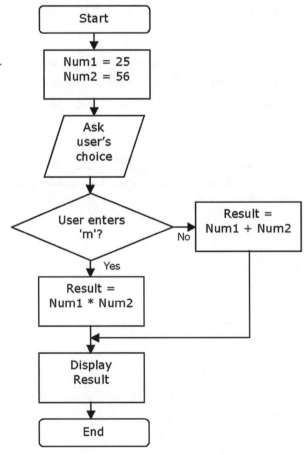

Conditional Programming Using `if … else`

Conditional execution of code is implemented in C++ using the `if … else` construct that looks like this:

```
if (conditional expression)
    Do something when expression evaluates true;
else     // Optional
    Do something else when condition evaluates false;
```

So, an `if … else` construct that lets a program multiply if the user enters *m* and adds otherwise looks like this:

```
if (userSelection == 'm')
    result = num1 * num2;  // multiply
else
    result = num1 + num2;  // add
```

NOTE

> Note that evaluation of an expression to `true` in C++ essentially means that the expression does not evaluate to `false`, `false` being zero. So, an expression that evaluates to any non-zero number—negative or positive—is essentially considered to be evaluating to `true` when used in a conditional statement.

Let's analyze this construct in Listing 6.1, which enables the user to decide whether he wants to either multiply or divide two numbers, hence using conditional processing to generate the desired output.

LISTING 6.1   Multiplying or Adding Two Integers on the Basis of User Input

```
 0: #include <iostream>
 1: using namespace std;
 2:
 3: int main()
 4: {
 5:     cout << "Enter two integers: " << endl;
 6:     int num1 = 0, num2 = 0;
 7:     cin >> num1;
 8:     cin >> num2;
 9:
10:     cout << "Enter \'m\' to multiply, anything else to add: ";
11:     char userSelection = '\0';
12:     cin >> userSelection;
13:
```

6

```
14:     int result = 0;
15:     if (userSelection == 'm')
16:         result = num1 * num2;
17:     else
18:         result = num1 + num2;
19:
20:     cout << "result is: " << result << endl;
21:
22:     return 0;
23: }
```

Output ▼

```
Enter two integers:
25
56
Enter 'm' to multiply, anything else to add: m
result is: 1400
```

Next run:

```
Enter two integers:
25
56
Enter 'm' to multiply, anything else to add: a
result is: 81
```

Analysis ▼

Note the use of `if` in Line 15 and `else` in Line 17. We are instructing the compiler to execute multiplication in Line 15 when the expression (`userSelection == 'm'`) that follows `if` evaluates to `true` or to execute addition if the expression evaluates to `false`. (`userSelection == 'm'`) is an expression that evaluates to `true` when the user has entered character *m* (case-sensitive), else it evaluates to `false`. Thus, this simple program models the flowchart in Figure 6.1 and demonstrates how your application can behave differently in different situations.

NOTE	The `else` part of the `if … else` construct is optional and doesn't need to be used in those situations where there is nothing to be executed in event of failure.

6

CAUTION

> If in Listing 6.1, Line 15 is
>
> ```
> 15:     if (userSelection == 'm');
> ```
>
> then the `if` construct is meaningless as it has been terminated in the same line by an empty statement (the semicolon). Be careful and avoid this situation as you won't get a compile error in such cases.
>
> Some good compilers may warn you of an "empty control statement" in this situation.

Executing Multiple Statements Conditionally

If you want to execute multiple statements in event of a condition succeeding or failing, you need to enclose them within statement blocks. These are essentially braces {...} enclosing multiple statements to be executed as a block. For example:

```
if (condition)
{
   // condition success block
   Statement 1;
   Statement 2;
}
else
{
   // condition failure block
   Statement 3;
   Statement 4;
}
```

Such blocks are also called *compound statements*.

Listing 6.2 is a safer version of Listing 4.6 in Lesson 4, "Managing Array and Strings." It uses a compound statement that copies user input into a static character array `if` the length of user input is within the bounds of the array.

LISTING 6.2 Check for Bounds Before Copying a String into a `char` Array

```
0: #include <iostream>
1: #include <string>
2: #include <string.h>
3: using namespace std;
4: int main()
5: {
```

```
6:       cout << "Enter a line of text: " << endl;
7:       string userInput;
8:       getline (cin, userInput);
9:
10:      char copyInput[20] = { '\0' };
11:      if (userInput.length() < 20) // check bounds
12:      {
13:          strcpy(copyInput, userInput.c_str());
14:          cout << "copyInput contains: " << copyInput << endl;
15:      }
16:      else
17:        cout << "Bounds exceeded: won't copy!" << endl;
18:
19:      return 0;
20: }
```

Output ▼

```
Enter a line of text:
This fits buffer!
copyInput contains: This fits buffer!
```

Next run:

```
Enter a line of text:
This doesn't fit the buffer!
Bounds exceeded: won't copy!
```

Analysis ▼

Note how the length of the string is checked against the length of the buffer in Line 11 before copying into it. What is also special about this if check is the presence of a statement block in Lines 12 through 15 (also called compound statement) in the event of the check evaluating to true.

Nested if Statements

Often you have situations where you need to validate against a host of different conditions, many of which are dependent on the evaluation of a previous condition. C++ allows you to nest if statements to handle such requirements.

Nested if statements are similar to this:

```
if (expression1)
{
```

```
        DoSomething1;
        if (expression2)
            DoSomething2;
        else
            DoSomethingElse2;
    }
else
        DoSomethingElse1;
```

Consider an application similar to Listing 6.1, in which the user can instruct the application to divide or multiply by pressing a command character *d* or *m*. Now, division should be permitted only when the divisor is non-zero. So, in addition to checking the user input for the intended command, it is also important to check if the divisor is non-zero when the user instructs the program to divide. Listing 6.3 uses a nested `if` construct.

LISTING 6.3   Using Nested `if` Statements in Multiplying or Dividing a Number

```cpp
 0: #include <iostream>
 1: using namespace std;
 2:
 3: int main()
 4: {
 5:     cout << "Enter two numbers: " << endl;
 6:     float num1 = 0, num2 = 0;
 7:     cin >> num1;
 8:     cin >> num2;
 9:
10:     cout << "Enter 'd' to divide, anything else to multiply: ";
11:     char userSelection = '\0';
12:     cin >> userSelection;
13:
14:     if (userSelection == 'd')
15:     {
16:         cout << "You wish to divide!" << endl;
17:         if (num2 != 0)
18:             cout << num1 << " / " << num2 << " = " << num1 / num2 << endl;
19:         else
20:             cout << "Division by zero is not allowed" << endl;
21:     }
22:     else
23:     {
24:         cout << "You wish to multiply!" << endl;
25:         cout << num1 << " x " << num2 << " = " << num1 * num2 << endl;
26:     }
27:
28:     return 0;
29: }
```

6

Output ▼

```
Enter two numbers:
45
9
Enter 'd' to divide, anything else to multiply: m
You wish to multiply!
45 x 9 = 405
```

Next run:

```
Enter two numbers:
22
7
Enter 'd' to divide, anything else to multiply: d
You wish to divide!
22 / 7 = 3.14286
```

Last run:

```
Enter two numbers:
365
0
Enter 'd' to divide, anything else to multiply: d
You wish to divide!
Division by zero is not allowed
```

Analysis ▼

The output is the result of running the program three times with three different sets of input, and as you can see, the program has executed different code paths for each of these three runs. This program has a few changes over Listing 6.1:

- The numbers are accepted as floating-point variables, to better handle decimals, which are important when dividing numbers.

- The if condition is different than in Listing 6.1. You no longer check whether the user has pressed *m*; rather, Line 14 contains an expression (userSelection == 'd') that evaluates to true when the user enters character 'd'. If so, you proceed with division.

- Given that this program divides two numbers and the divisor is entered by the user, it is important to check if the divisor is non-zero. This is done using the nested if in Line 17.

Thus, what this program demonstrates is how nested if constructs can be very useful in performing different tasks depending on the evaluation of multiple parameters.

TIP

> The nested tabs (white spaces) that you inserted in the code are optional, but they make a significant contribution to the readability of the nested if constructs. Many modern IDEs indent code automatically.

Note that if...else constructs can also be grouped together. Listing 6.4 is a program that asks the user for the day of the week and then tells what that day is named after using grouped if...else constructs.

LISTING 6.4   Using a Grouped if...else Construct

```
0: #include <iostream>
1: using namespace std;
2:
3: int main()
4: {
5:     enum DaysOfWeek
6:     {
7:         Sunday = 0,
8:         Monday,
9:         Tuesday,
10:        Wednesday,
11:        Thursday,
12:        Friday,
13:        Saturday
14:    };
15:
16:    cout << "Find what days of the week are named after!" << endl;
17:    cout << "Enter a number for a day (Sunday = 0): ";
18:
19:    int dayInput = Sunday;    // Initialize to Sunday
20:    cin >> dayInput;
21:
22:    if (dayInput == Sunday)
23:        cout << "Sunday was named after the Sun" << endl;
24:    else if (dayInput == Monday)
25:        cout << "Monday was named after the Moon" << endl;
26:    else if (dayInput == Tuesday)
27:        cout << "Tuesday was named after Mars" << endl;
28:    else if (dayInput == Wednesday)
29:        cout << "Wednesday was named after Mercury" << endl;
30:    else if (dayInput == Thursday)
31:        cout << "Thursday was named after Jupiter" << endl;
```

6

```
32:    else if (dayInput == Friday)
33:        cout << "Friday was named after Venus" << endl;
34:    else if (dayInput == Saturday)
35:        cout << "Saturday was named after Saturn" << endl;
36:    else
37:        cout << "Wrong input, execute again" << endl;
38:
39:    return 0;
40: }
```

Output ▼

```
Find what days of the week are named after!
Enter a number for a day (Sunday = 0): 5
Friday was named after Venus
```

Next run:

```
Find what days of the week are named after!
Enter a number for a day (Sunday = 0): 9
Wrong input, execute again
```

Analysis ▼

Note the `if-else-if` construct used in Lines 22 through 37 to check user input and produce the corresponding output. The output in the second run indicates that the program is able to tell the user when he enters a number that is outside the expected range 0–6, and hence does not correspond to any day of the week. The advantage of this construct is that it is perfectly suited to validating conditions that are mutually exclusive, that is, Monday can never be a Tuesday and an invalid input cannot be any day of the week. Another interesting thing to note in this program is the use of the enumeration called `DaysOfWeek` declared in Line 5 and used throughout the `if` statements. You could've simply compared user input against integer values such as 0 for Sunday and so on. However, the use of the enumerator `Sunday` makes the code more readable.

Conditional Processing Using `switch-case`

The objective of `switch-case` is to enable you to check a particular expression against a host of possible constants and possibly perform a different action for each of those different values. The new C++ keywords you would often find in such a construct are `switch` `case`, `default`, and `break`.

The following is the syntax of a `switch-case` construct:

```
switch(expression)
{
case LabelA:
   DoSomething;
   break;

case LabelB:
   DoSomethingElse;
   break;

// And so on...
default:
   DoStuffWhenExpressionIsNotHandledAbove;
   break;
}
```

What happens is that the resulting code evaluates the expression and checks against each of the case labels following it for equality. Each case label needs to be a constant. It then executes the code following that label. When the `expression` does not evaluate to `LabelA`, it checks against `LabelB`. If that check evaluates to `true`, it executes `DoSomethingElse`. This check continues until it encounters a `break`. This is the first time we are using the keyword `break`. `break` causes execution to exit the code block. `break`s are not compulsory; however, without a `break` the execution simply continues checking against the next labels and so on, which is what you want to avoid in this case. `default` is optional, too, and is the case that is executed when the expression does not equate to any of the labels in the `switch-case` construct.

TIP

> `switch-case` constructs are well-suited to being used with enumerators. The keyword `enum` was introduced in Lesson 3, "Using Variables, Declaring Constants."

6

Listing 6.5 is the `switch-case` equivalent of the program in Listing 6.4 that tells what the days of the week are named after and also uses enumerated constants.

LISTING 6.5 Tell What Days of the Week Are Named After Using `switch-case`, `break`, and `default`

```
0: #include <iostream>
1: using namespace std;
2:
3: int main()
4: {
5:     enum DaysOfWeek
6:     {
7:         Sunday = 0,
8:         Monday,
9:         Tuesday,
10:        Wednesday,
11:        Thursday,
12:        Friday,
13:        Saturday
14:    };
15:
16:    cout << "Find what days of the week are named after!" << endl;
17:    cout << "Enter a number for a day (Sunday = 0): ";
18:
19:    int dayInput = Sunday;    // Initialize to Sunday
20:    cin >> dayInput;
21:
22:    switch(dayInput)
23:    {
24:    case Sunday:
25:        cout << "Sunday was named after the Sun" << endl;
26:        break;
27:
28:    case Monday:
29:        cout << "Monday was named after the Moon" << endl;
30:        break;
31:
32:    case Tuesday:
33:        cout << "Tuesday was named after Mars" << endl;
34:        break;
35:
36:    case Wednesday:
37:        cout << "Wednesday was named after Mercury" << endl;
38:        break;
39:
40:    case Thursday:
41:        cout << "Thursday was named after Jupiter" << endl;
42:        break;
43:
44:    case Friday:
45:        cout << "Friday was named after Venus" << endl;
46:        break;
```

```
47:
48:    case Saturday:
49:        cout << "Saturday was named after Saturn" << endl;
50:        break;
51:
52:    default:
53:        cout << "Wrong input, execute again" << endl;
54:        break;
55:    }
56:
57:    return 0;
58: }
```

Output ▼

```
Find what days of the week are named after!
Enter a number for a day (Sunday = 0): 5
Friday was named after Venus
```

Next run:

```
Find what days of the week are named after!
Enter a number for a day (Sunday = 0): 9
Wrong input, execute again
```

Analysis ▼

Lines 22–55 contain the `switch-case` construct that produces different output depending on the integer contained in `dayInput` as entered by the user. When the user enters the number 5, the application checks the `switch` expression `dayInput` that evaluates to 5 against the first four labels that are enumerators `Sunday` (value 0) through Thursday (value 4), skipping the code below each of them as none of them are equal to 5. It reaches label `Friday` where the expression evaluating to 5 equals enumerated constant `Friday`. Thus, it executes the code under `Friday` until it reaches `break` in Line 46 and exits the `switch` construct. In the second run, when an invalid value is entered, the execution reaches `default` and runs the code under it, displaying the message asking the user to execute again.

6

This program using `switch-case` produces exactly the same output as Listing 6.4 using the `if-else-if` construct. Yet, the `switch-case` version looks a little more structured and is possibly well-suited to situations where you want to be doing more than just writing a line to the screen (in which case you would also include code within a case within braces, creating blocks).

Conditional Execution Using Operator (?:)

C++ has an interesting and powerful operator called the conditional operator that is similar to a compacted `if-else` construct.

The conditional operator is also called a ternary operator as it takes three operands:

```
(conditional expression evaluated to bool) ? expression1 if true : expression2
if false;
```

Such an operator can be used in compactly evaluating the greater of two given numbers, as seen here:

```
int max = (num1 > num2)? num1 : num2; // max contains greater of num1 and num2
```

Listing 6.6 is a demonstration of conditional processing using operator (?:).

LISTING 6.6   Using the Conditional Operator (?:) to Find the Max of Two Numbers

```
0: #include <iostream>
1: using namespace std;
2:
3: int main()
4: {
5:     cout << "Enter two numbers" << endl;
6:     int num1 = 0, num2 = 0;
7:     cin >> num1;
8:     cin >> num2;
9:
10:     int max = (num1 > num2)? num1 : num2;
11:     cout << "The greater of " << num1 << " and " \
12:         << num2 << " is: " << max << endl;
13:
14:     return 0;
15: }
```

Output ▼

```
Enter two numbers
365
-1
The greater of 365 and -1 is: 365
```

Analysis ▼

Line 10 is the code of interest. It contains a compact statement that makes a decision on which of the two numbers input is larger. This line is another way to code the following using `if-else`:

```
int max;
if (num1 > num2)
    max = num1;
else
    max = num2;
```

Thus, conditional operators saved a few lines! Saving lines of code, however, should not be a priority. There are programmers who prefer conditional operators and those that don't. It is important to code conditional operators in a way that can be easily understood.

DO	DON'T
DO use enumerators in switch expressions to make code readable.	**DON'T** add two cases with the same label—it won't make sense and won't compile.
DO remember to handle `default`, unless deemed totally unnecessary.	**DON'T** complicate your `case` statements by including `cases` without `break` and relying on sequence. This will break functionality in the future when you move the `case` statements without paying adequate attention to sequence.
DO check whether you inadvertently forgot to insert `break` in each case statement.	**DON'T** use complicated conditions or expressions when using conditional operators (`? :`).

6

TIP

C++17 is expected to introduce conditional compilation using `if constexpr`, and initializers within `if` and `switch` constructs. Learn more about these features in Lesson 29, "Going Forward."

Getting Code to Execute in Loops

So far you have seen how to make your program behave differently when certain variables contain different values—for example, in Listing 6.1 where you multiplied when the user pressed *m*; otherwise, you added. However, what if the user doesn't want the program to just end? What if he wants to perform another add or multiply operation, or maybe five more? This is when you need to repeat the execution of already existing code.

This is when you need to program a loop.

A Rudimentary Loop Using goto

As the name suggests, goto instructs execution to continue from a particular, labeled, point in code. You can use it to go backward and re-execute certain statements.

The syntax for the goto statement is

```
SomeFunction()
{
Start: // Called a label
    CodeThatRepeats;

    goto Start;
}
```

You declare a label called Start and use goto to repeat execution from this point on, as demonstrated in Listing 6.7. Unless you invoke goto given a condition that can evaluate to false under certain circumstances, or unless the code that repeats contains a return statement executed under certain conditions, the piece of code between the goto command and label will repeat endlessly and keep the program from ending.

LISTING 6.7 Asking the User Whether He Wants to Repeat Calculations Using goto

```
0: #include <iostream>
1: using namespace std;
2:
3: int main()
4: {
5: Start:
6:     int num1 = 0, num2 = 0;
7:
8:     cout << "Enter two integers: " << endl;
9:     cin >> num1;
10:    cin >> num2;
11:
```

```
12:     cout << num1 << " x " << num2 << " = " << num1 * num2 << endl;
13:     cout << num1 << " + " << num2 << " = " << num1 + num2 << endl;
14:
15:     cout << "Do you wish to perform another operation (y/n)?" << endl;
16:     char repeat = 'y';
17:     cin >> repeat;
18:
19:     if (repeat == 'y')
20:         goto Start;
21:
22:     cout << "Goodbye!" << endl;
23:
24:     return 0;
25: }
```

Output ▼

```
Enter two integers:
56
25
56 x 25 = 1400
56 + 25 = 81
Do you wish to perform another operation (y/n)?
y
Enter two integers:
95
-47
95 x -47 = -4465
95 + -47 = 48
Do you wish to perform another operation (y/n)?
n
Goodbye!
```

Analysis ▼

Note that the primary difference between Listing 6.7 and Listing 6.1 is that 6.1 needs two runs (two separate executions) to enable the user to enter a new set of numbers and see the result of her addition and multiplication. Listing 6.7 does that in one execution cycle by asking the user if she wishes to perform another operation. The code that actually enables this repetition is in Line 20, where goto is invoked if the user enters character 'y' for yes. Execution of goto in Line 20 results in the program jumping to the label Start declared in Line 5, which effectively restarts the program.

6

CAUTION

> goto is not the recommended form of programming loops because the prolific usage of goto can result in unpredictable flow of code where execution can jump from one line to another in no particular order or sequence, in some cases leaving variables in unpredictable states, too.
>
> A bad case of programming using goto results in what is called *spaghetti code*. You can avoid goto by using while, do...while, and for loops that are explained in the following pages.
>
> The only reason you were taught goto is so that you understand code that uses one.

The while Loop

C++ keyword while can help do what goto did in Listing 6.7, but in a refined manner. Its usage syntax is

```
while(expression)
{
    // Expression evaluates to true
    StatementBlock;
}
```

The statement block is executed repeatedly so long as the expression evaluates to true. It is hence important to code in a way that there are situations where the expression would also evaluate to false, else the while loop would never end.

Listing 6.8 is an equivalent of Listing 6.7 but uses while instead of goto in allowing the user to repeat a calculation cycle.

LISTING 6.8   Using a while Loop to Help the User Rerun Calculations

```
 0: #include <iostream>
 1: using namespace std;
 2:
 3: int main()
 4: {
 5:    char userSelection = 'm';   // initial value
 6:
 7:    while (userSelection != 'x')
 8:    {
 9:       cout << "Enter the two integers: " << endl;
10:       int num1 = 0, num2 = 0;
11:       cin >> num1;
```

```
12:        cin >> num2;
13:
14:        cout << num1 << " x " << num2 << " = " << num1 * num2 << endl;
15:        cout << num1 << " + " << num2 << " = " << num1 + num2 << endl;
16:
17:        cout << "Press x to exit(x) or any other key to recalculate" << endl;
18:        cin >> userSelection;
19:    }
20:
21:    cout << "Goodbye!" << endl;
22:
23:    return 0;
24: }
```

Output ▼

```
Enter the two integers:
56
25
56 x 25 = 1400
56 + 25 = 81
Press x to exit(x) or any other key to recalculate
r
Enter the two integers:
365
-5
365 x -5 = -1825
365 + -5 = 360
Press x to exit(x) or any other key to recalculate
x
Goodbye!
```

Analysis ▼

The while loop in Lines 7–19 contains most of the logic in this program. Note how the while checks the expression (userSelection != 'x'), proceeding only if this expression evaluates to true. To enable a first run, you initialized the char variable userSelection to 'm' in Line 5. This needed to be any value that is not 'x' (else the condition would fail at the very first loop and the application would exit without letting the user do anything constructive). The first run is very simple, but the user is asked in Line 17 if he wishes to perform another set of calculations. Line 18 containing the user's input is where you modify the expression that while evaluates, giving the program a chance to continue or to terminate. When the first loop is done, execution returns to evaluating the expression in the while statement at Line 7 and repeats if the user has not pressed x. When the user presses x at the end of a loop, the next evaluation of the expression at

6

Line 7 results in a `false`, and the execution exits the `while` loop, eventually ending the application after displaying a goodbye statement.

NOTE	A loop is also called an *iteration*. Statements involving `while`, `do...while`, and `for` are also called *iterative statements*.

The `do...while` Loop

There are cases (like the one in Listing 6.8) where you need to ensure that a certain segment of code repeats in a loop and that it executes at least once. This is where the `do...while` loop is useful.

The syntax of the `do...while` loop is

```
do
{
    StatementBlock; // executed at least once
} while(condition); // ends loop if condition evaluates to false
```

Note how the line containing the `while(expression)` terminates with a semicolon. This is different from the previous `while` loop in which a semicolon following `while` would've effectively terminated the loop in the very line, resulting in an empty statement.

Listing 6.9 demonstrates how `do...while` loops can be implemented in executing statements at least once.

LISTING 6.9   Using `do...while` to Repeat Execution of a Block of Code

```
 0: #include <iostream>
 1: using namespace std;
 2:
 3: int main()
 4: {
 5:     char userSelection = 'x';    // initial value
 6:     do
 7:     {
 8:         cout << "Enter the two integers: " << endl;
 9:         int num1 = 0, num2 = 0;
10:         cin >> num1;
11:         cin >> num2;
12:
13:         cout << num1 << " x " << num2 << " = " << num1 * num2 << endl;
14:         cout << num1 << " + " << num2 << " = " << num1 + num2 << endl;
15:
```

```
16:         cout << "Press x to exit(x) or any other key to recalculate" << endl;
17:         cin >> userSelection;
18:     } while (userSelection != 'x');
19:
20:     cout << "Goodbye!" << endl;
21:
22:     return 0;
23: }
```

Output ▼

```
Enter the two integers:
654
-25
654 x -25 = -16350
654 + -25 = 629
Press x to exit(x) or any other key to recalculate
m
Enter the two integers:
909
101
909 x 101 = 91809
909 + 101 = 1010
Press x to exit(x) or any other key to recalculate
x
Goodbye!
```

Analysis ▼

This program is similar in behavior and output to Listing 6.8. Indeed the only difference is the do keyword at Line 6 and the usage of while later at Line 18. The execution of code happens serially, one line after another until the while is reached at Line 18. This is where while evaluates the expression (userSelection != 'x'). When the expression evaluates to true (that is, the user doesn't press character 'x' to exit), execution of the loop repeats. When the expression evaluates to false (that is, the user presses 'x'), execution quits the loop and continues with wishing goodbye and ending the application.

The for Loop

The for statement is a more sophisticated loop in that it allows for an initialization statement executed once (typically used to initialize a counter), checking for an exit condition (typically using this counter), and performing an action at the end of every loop (typically incrementing or modifying this counter).

6

The syntax of the `for` loop is

```
for (initial expression executed only once;
     exit condition executed at the beginning of every loop;
     loop expression executed at the end of every loop)
{

    DoSomething;

}
```

The `for` loop is a feature that enables the programmer to define a counter variable with an initial value, check the value against an exit condition at the beginning of every loop, and change the value of the variable at the end of a loop.

Listing 6.10 demonstrates an effective way to access elements in an array using a `for` loop.

LISTING 6.10 Using `for` Loops to Enter Elements in a Static Array and Displaying It

```
 0: #include <iostream>
 1: using namespace std;
 2:
 3: int main()
 4: {
 5:     const int ARRAY_LENGTH = 5;
 6:     int myNums[ARRAY_LENGTH] = {0};
 7:
 8:     cout << "Populate array of " << ARRAY_LENGTH << " integers" << endl;
 9:
10:     for (int counter = 0; counter < ARRAY_LENGTH; ++counter)
11:     {
12:         cout << "Enter an integer for element " << counter << ": ";
13:         cin >> myNums[counter];
14:     }
15:
16:     cout << "Displaying contents of the array: " << endl;
17:
18:     for (int counter = 0; counter < ARRAY_LENGTH; ++counter)
19:         cout << "Element " << counter << " = " << myNums[counter] << endl;
20:
21:     return 0;
22: }
```

Output ▼

```
Populate array of 5 integers
Enter an integer for element 0: 365
Enter an integer for element 1: 31
Enter an integer for element 2: 24
Enter an integer for element 3: -59
Enter an integer for element 4: 65536
Displaying contents of the array:
Element 0 = 365
Element 1 = 31
Element 2 = 24
Element 3 = -59
Element 4 = 65536
```

Analysis ▼

There are two for loops in Listing 6.10—at Lines 10 and 18. The first helps enter elements into an array of integers and the other to display. Both for loops are identical in syntax. Both declare an index variable counter to access elements the array. This variable is incremented at the end of every loop; therefore, it helps access the next element in the next run of the loop. The middle expression in the for loop is the exit condition. It checks whether counter that is incremented at the end of every loop is still within the bounds of the array by comparing it against ARRAY_LENGTH. This way, it is also ensured that the for loop never exceeds the length of the array.

NOTE

> A variable such as counter from Listing 6.10 that helps access elements in a collection such as an array is also called an *iterator*.
>
> The scope of this iterator declared within the for construct is limited to the for loop. Thus, in the second for loop in Listing 6.10, this variable that has been re-declared is effectively a new variable.

6

The usage of the initialization, conditional expression, and the expression to be evaluated at the end of every loop is optional. It is possible to have a for loop without some or any of these, as shown in Listing 6.11.

LISTING 6.11 Using a `for` Loop, Omitting Loop Expression, to Repeat Calculations on User Request

```
0: #include <iostream>
1: using namespace std;
2:
3: int main()
4: {
5:    // without loop expression (third expression missing)
6:    for(char userSelection = 'm'; (userSelection != 'x');)
7:    {
8:       cout << "Enter the two integers: " << endl;
9:       int num1 = 0, num2 = 0;
10:       cin >> num1;
11:       cin >> num2;
12:
13:       cout << num1 << " x " << num2 << " = " << num1 * num2 << endl;
14:       cout << num1 << " + " << num2 << " = " << num1 + num2 << endl;
15:
16:       cout << "Press x to exit or any other key to recalculate" << endl;
17:       cin >> userSelection;
18:    }
19:
20:    cout << "Goodbye!" << endl;
21:
22:    return 0;
23: }
```

Output ▼

```
Enter the two integers:
56
25
56 x 25 = 1400
56 + 25 = 81
Press x to exit or any other key to recalculate
m
Enter the two integers:
789
-36
789 x -36 = -28404
789 + -36 = 753
Press x to exit or any other key to recalculate
x
Goodbye!
```

Analysis ▼

This program is identical to Listing 6.8 that used the `while` loop; the only difference is that this one uses the `for` construct in Line 6. The interesting thing about this `for` loop is that it contains only the initialization expression and the conditional expression, ignoring the option to change a variable at the end of each loop.

NOTE

> You can initialize multiple variables in a `for` loop within the first initialization expression that is executed once. A `for` loop in Listing 6.11 with multiple initializations looks like the following:
>
> ```
> for (int counter1 = 0, counter2 = 5; // initialize
>         counter1 < ARRAY_LENGTH;    // check
>             ++counter1, --counter2)   // increment, decrement
> ```
>
> Note the new addition called `counter2` that is initialized to 5.
>
> Interestingly, we also are able to decrement it in the loop expression, once per loop.

The Range-Based `for` Loop

C++11 introduced a new variant of the `for` loop that makes operating over a range of values, such as those contained in an array, simpler to code and to read.

The syntax of the range-based `for` loop also uses the same keyword `for`:

```
for (VarType varName : sequence)
{
    // Use varName that contains an element from sequence
}
```

For example, given an array of integers `someNums`, you would use a range-based `for` to read elements contained in the array, like this:

```
int someNums[] = { 1, 101, -1, 40, 2040 };

for (int aNum : someNums) // range based for
    cout << "The array elements are " << aNum << endl;
```

6

> **TIP**
>
> You may simplify this `for` statement further by using automatic variable type deduction feature via keyword `auto` to compose a generic `for` loop that will work for an array `elements` of any type:
>
> ```
> for (auto anElement : elements) // range based for
>     cout << "Array elements are " << anElement << endl;
> ```
>
> Keyword `auto` and the automatic variable type inferencing feature was introduced in Lesson 3.

Listing 6.12 demonstrates the range-based `for` on ranges of different types.

LISTING 6.12   Using Range-Based `for` Loop Over Arrays and a `std::string`

```
 0: #include<iostream>
 1: #include <string>
 2: using namespace std;
 3:
 4: int main()
 5: {
 6:     int someNums[] = { 1, 101, -1, 40, 2040 };
 7:
 8:     for (const int& aNum : someNums)
 9:         cout << aNum << ' ';
10:     cout << endl;
11:
12:     for (auto anElement : { 5, 222, 110, -45, 2017 })
13:         cout << anElement << ' ';
14:     cout << endl;
15:
16:     char charArray[] = { 'h', 'e', 'l', 'l', 'o' };
17:     for (auto aChar : charArray)
18:         cout << aChar << ' ';
19:     cout << endl;
20:
21:     double moreNums[] = { 3.14, -1.3, 22, 10101 };
22:     for (auto anElement : moreNums)
23:         cout << anElement << ' ';
24:     cout << endl;
25:
26:     string sayHello{ "Hello World!" };
27:     for (auto anElement : sayHello)
28:         cout << anElement << ' ';
29:     cout << endl;
30:
31:     return 0;
32: }
```

Output ▼

```
1 101 -1 40 2040
5 222 110 -45 2017
h e l l o
3.14 -1.3 22 10101
H e l l o   W o r l d !
```

Analysis ▼

The code sample contains multiple implementations of the range-based `for`, as seen in Lines 8, 12, 17, 22, and 27, respectively. Each of these instances uses the loop to display the contents of a range on the screen, one element at a time. What's interesting is that, while the nature of the range changes from being an array of integers `someNums` in Line 8 to an unspecified range in Line 12 to an array of `char charArray` in Line 17, and even a `std::string` in Line 27, the syntax of the range-based `for` loop remains consistent.

This simplicity of implementation makes the range-based `for` one of the more popular features recently introduced by C++.

Modifying Loop Behavior Using `continue` and `break`

There are a few cases—especially in complicated loops handling many parameters with many conditions—where you are not able to program the loop condition efficiently and need to modify program behavior even within the loop. This is where `continue` and `break` can help you.

`continue` lets you resume execution from the top of the loop. The code following it within the block is skipped. Thus, the effect of `continue` in a `while`, `do...while`, or `for` loop is that it results in the loop condition being reevaluated and the loop block being reentered if the condition evaluates to `true`.

NOTE

> In case of a `continue` within a `for` loop, the loop expression (the third expression within the `for` statement typically used to increment the counter) is evaluated before the condition is reevaluated.

6

On the other hand, break exits the loop's block, thereby ending the loop when invoked.

Loops That Don't End—That Is, Infinite Loops

Remember that while, do...while, and for loops have a condition expression that results in the loop terminating when the condition evaluates to false. If you program a condition that always evaluates to true, the loop never ends.

An infinite while loop looks like this:

```
while(true)    // while expression fixed to true
{
    DoSomethingRepeatedly;
}
```

An infinite do...while loop would be

```
do
{
    DoSomethingRepeatedly;
} while(true);    // do…while expression never evaluates to false
```

An infinite for loop can be programmed the following way:

```
for (;;)    // no condition supplied = unending for
{
    DoSomethingRepeatedly;
}
```

Strange as it may seem, such loops do have a purpose. Imagine an operating system that needs to continually check whether you have connected a device such as a USB stick to the USB port. This is an activity that should not stop for so long as the OS is running. Such cases warrant the use of loops that never end. Such loops are also called infinite loops as they execute forever, to eternity.

Controlling Infinite Loops

If you want to end an `infinite loop` (say the OS in the preceding example needs to shut down), you do so by inserting a `break` (typically used within an `if (condition)` block).

The following is an example of using `break` to exit an infinite `while`:

```
while(true)    // while condition fixed to true
{
   DoSomethingRepeatedly;
   if(expression)
      break;  // exit loop when expression evaluates to true
}
```

Using break inside an infinite `do...while`:

```
do
{
   DoSomethingRepeatedly;
   if(expression)
      break;  // exit loop when expression evaluates to true
} while(true);
```

Using break inside an infinite `for` loop:

```
for (;;)    // no condition supplied = unending for
{
   DoSomethingRepeatedly;
   if(expression)
      break;  // exit loop when expression evaluates to true
}
```

Listing 6.13 shows how to program infinite loops using `continue` and `break` to control the exit criteria.

6

LISTING 6.13   Using `continue` to Restart and `break` to Exit an Infinite `for` Loop

```
0: #include <iostream>
1: using namespace std;
2:
3: int main()
4: {
5:    for(;;)    // an infinite loop
6:    {
7:       cout << "Enter two integers: " << endl;
```

```
 8:        int num1 = 0, num2 = 0;
 9:        cin >> num1;
10:        cin >> num2;
11:
12:        cout << "Do you wish to correct the numbers? (y/n): ";
13:        char changeNumbers = '\0';
14:        cin >> changeNumbers;
15:
16:        if (changeNumbers == 'y')
17:           continue;   // restart the loop!
18:
19:        cout << num1 << " x " << num2 << " = " << num1 * num2 << endl;
20:        cout << num1 << " + " << num2 << " = " << num1 + num2 << endl;
21:
22:        cout << "Press x to exit or any other key to recalculate" << endl;
23:        char userSelection = '\0';
24:        cin >> userSelection;
25:
26:        if (userSelection == 'x')
27:           break;    // exit the infinite loop
28:     }
29:
30:     cout << "Goodbye!" << endl;
31:
32:     return 0;
33: }
```

Output ▼

```
Enter two integers:
560
25
Do you wish to correct the numbers? (y/n): y
Enter two integers:
56
25
Do you wish to correct the numbers? (y/n): n
56 x 25 = 1400
56 + 25 = 81
Press x to exit or any other key to recalculate
r
Enter two integers:
95
-1
Do you wish to correct the numbers? (y/n): n
95 x -1 = -95
95 + -1 = 94
Press x to exit or any other key to recalculate
x
Goodbye!
```

Analysis ▼

The `for` loop in Line 5 is different from the one in Listing 6.11 in that this is an infinite `for` loop containing no condition expression that is evaluated on every iteration of the loop. In other words, without the execution of a `break` statement, this loop (and hence this application) never exits. Note the output, which is different from the other output you have seen so far in that it allows the user to make a correction to his input before the program proceeds to calculate the sum and multiplication. This logic is implemented using a `continue` given the evaluation of a certain condition in Lines 16 and 17. When the user presses character `'y'` on being asked whether he wants to correct the numbers, the condition in Line 16 evaluates to `true`, hence executing the following `continue`. When `continue` is encountered, execution jumps to the top of the loop, asking the user again whether he wants to enter two integers. Similarly, at the end of the loop when the user is asked whether he wants to exit, his input is checked against `'x'` in Line 26, and if so, the following `break` is executed, ending the infinite loop.

NOTE

> Listing 6.13 uses an empty `for(;;)` statement to create an infinite loop. You can replace that with `while(true)` or a `do...while(true);` to generate the same output using a different loop type.

DO	DON'T
DO use do...while when the logic in the loop needs to be executed at least once.	**DON'T** use `goto`.
	DON'T use `continue` and `break` indiscriminately.
DO use `while`, `do...while`, or `for` loops with well-defined condition expressions.	**DON'T** program infinite loops terminated using `break` unless absolutely necessary.
DO indent code in a statement block contained in a loop to improve readability.	

6

Programming Nested Loops

Just as you saw nested `if` statements in the beginning of this lesson, often you do need to nest one loop under another. Imagine two arrays of integers. If you want to find the multiple of each number in `array1` against each in `array2`, you use a nested loop to make programming this easy. The first loop iterates `array1`, while the second iterates `array2` under the first.

Listing 6.14 demonstrates the usage of nested loops.

LISTING 6.14   Using Nested Loops to Multiply Each Element in an Array by Each in Another

```
0: #include <iostream>
1: using namespace std;
2:
3: int main()
4: {
5:     const int ARRAY1_LEN = 3;
6:     const int ARRAY2_LEN = 2;
7:
8:     int myNums1[ARRAY1_LEN] = {35, -3, 0};
9:     int myNums2[ARRAY2_LEN] = {20, -1};
10:
11:     cout << "Multiplying each int in myNums1 by each in myNums2:" << endl;
12:
13:     for(int index1 = 0; index1 < ARRAY1_LEN; ++index1)
14:         for(int index2 = 0; index2 < ARRAY2_LEN; ++index2)
15:             cout << myNums1[index1] << " x " << myNums2[index2] \
16:                 << " = " << myNums1[index1] * myNums2[index2] << endl;
17:
18:     return 0;
19: }
```

Output ▼

```
Multiplying each int in myNums1 by each in myNums2:
35 x 20 = 700
35 x -1 = -35
-3 x 20 = -60
-3 x -1 = 3
0 x 20 = 0
0 x -1 = 0
```

Analysis ▼

The two nested `for` loops in question are in Lines 13 and 14. The first `for` loop iterates the array `myNums1`, whereas the second `for` loop iterates the other array `myNums2`. The first `for` loop executes the second `for` loop within each iteration. The second `for` loop iterates over all elements in `myNums2` and in each iteration multiplies that element with the element indexed via `index1` from the first loop above it. So, for every element in `myNums1`, the second loop iterates over all elements in `myNums2`, resulting in the first element in `myNums1` at offset 0 being multiplied with all elements in `myNums2`. Then the second element in `myNums1` is multiplied with all elements in `myNums2`. Finally, the third element in `myNums1` is multiplied with all elements in `myNums2`.

NOTE

> For convenience and for keeping focus on the loops, the contents of the array in Listing 6.14 are initialized. You should feel free to derive from previous examples, such as Listing 6.10, to get the user to enter numbers into the integer array.

Using Nested Loops to Walk a Multidimensional Array

In Lesson 4, you learned of multidimensional arrays. Indeed in Listing 4.3 you access elements in a two-dimensional array of three rows and three columns. What you did there was to individually access each element in the array, one element per line. There was no automation, and, if the array was to be made larger, you would need to code a lot more, in addition to changing the array's dimensions to access its elements. However, using loops can change all that, as demonstrated by Listing 6.15.

LISTING 6.15   Using Nested Loops to Iterate Elements in a Two-dimensional Array of Integers

```
0: #include <iostream>
1: using namespace std;
2:
3: int main()
4: {
5:     const int NUM_ROWS = 3;
6:     const int NUM_COLUMNS = 4;
7:
8:     // 2D array of integers
9:     int MyInts[NUM_ROWS][NUM_COLUMNS] = { {34, -1, 879, 22},
10:                                           {24, 365, -101, -1},
11:                                           {-20, 40, 90, 97} };
12:
13:     // iterate rows, each array of int
```

6

```
14:    for (int row = 0; row < NUM_ROWS; ++row)
15:    {
16:        // iterate integers in each row (columns)
17:        for (int column = 0; column < NUM_COLUMNS; ++column)
18:        {
19:            cout << "Integer[" << row << "][" << column \
20:                << "] = " << MyInts[row][column] << endl;
21:        }
22:    }
23:
24:    return 0;
25: }
```

Output ▼

```
Integer[0][0] = 34
Integer[0][1] = -1
Integer[0][2] = 879
Integer[0][3] = 22
Integer[1][0] = 24
Integer[1][1] = 365
Integer[1][2] = -101
Integer[1][3] = -1
Integer[2][0] = -20
Integer[2][1] = 40
Integer[2][2] = 90
Integer[2][3] = 97
```

Analysis ▼

Lines 14–22 contain two `for` loops that you need to access and iterate through a two-dimensional array of integers. A two-dimensional array is in effect an array of an array of integers. Note how the first `for` loop accesses the rows (each being an array of integers), whereas the second accesses each element in this array—that is, accesses columns therein.

NOTE

Listing 6.15 uses braces to enclose the nested `for` only to improve readability. This nested loop works just fine without the braces, too, as the loop statement is just a single statement to be executed (and not a compound statement that necessitates the use of enclosing braces).

Using Nested Loops to Calculate Fibonacci Numbers

The famed Fibonacci series is a set of numbers starting with 0 and 1, where every following number in the series is the sum of the previous two. So, a Fibonacci series starts with a sequence like this:

0, 1, 1, 2, 3, 5, 8, ... and so on

Listing 6.16 demonstrates how to create a Fibonacci series comprised of as many numbers as you want (limited by the data-bearing capacity of the integer holding the final number).

LISTING 6.16   Using Nested Loops to Calculate a Fibonacci Series

```
0: #include <iostream>
1: using namespace std;
2:
3: int main()
4: {
5:     const int numsToCalculate = 5;
6:     cout << "This program will calculate " << numsToCalculate \
7:          << " Fibonacci Numbers at a time" << endl;
8:
9:     int num1 = 0, num2 = 1;
10:     char wantMore = '\0';
11:     cout << num1 << " " << num2 << " ";
12:
13:     do
14:     {
15:         for (int counter = 0; counter < numsToCalculate; ++counter)
16:         {
17:             cout << num1 + num2 << " ";
18:
19:             int num2Temp = num2;
20:             num2 = num1 + num2;
21:             num1 = num2Temp;
22:         }
23:
24:         cout << endl << "Do you want more numbers (y/n)? ";
25:         cin >> wantMore;
26:     }while (wantMore == 'y');
27:
28:     cout << "Goodbye!" << endl;
29:
30:     return 0;
31: }
```

6

Output ▼

```
This program will calculate 5 Fibonacci Numbers at a time
0 1 1 2 3 5 8
Do you want more numbers (y/n)? y
13 21 34 55 89
Do you want more numbers (y/n)? y
144 233 377 610 987
Do you want more numbers (y/n)? y
1597 2584 4181 6765 10946
Do you want more numbers (y/n)? n
Goodbye!
```

Analysis ▼

The outer `do...while` at Line 13 is basically the query loop that repeats if the user wants to see more numbers. The inner `for` loop at Line 15 does the job of calculating the next Fibonacci number and displays five numbers at a time. In Line 19 you hold the value in `num2` in a temporary variable `num2Temp` to be able to reuse it at Line 21. Note that if you hadn't stored this temp value, you would be assigning the modified value in Line 20 directly to `num1`, which is not what you want. When the user presses 'y' to get more numbers, the `do...while` loop executes once more, thereby executing the nested `for` loop that generates five more Fibonacci numbers.

Summary

This lesson taught you how to code conditional statements that create alternative execution paths and make code blocks repeat in a loop. You learned the `if...else` construct and using `switch-case` statements to handle different situations in the event of variables containing different values.

In understanding loops, you were taught `goto`—but you were simultaneously warned against using it due to its ability to create code that cannot be understood. You learned programming loops in C++ using `while`, `do...while`, and `for` constructs. You learned how to make the loops iterate endlessly to create infinite loops and to use `continue` and `break` to better control them.

Q&A

Q What happens if I omit a `break` in a `switch-case` statement?

A The `break` statement enables program execution to exit the `switch` construct. Without it, execution continues evaluating the following `case` statements.

Q How do I exit an infinite loop?

A Use `break` to exit any loop containing it. Using `return` exits the function module, too.

Q My `while` loop looks like `while(Integer)`. Does the `while` loop execute when `Integer` evaluates to -1?

A Ideally a `while` expression should evaluate to a Boolean value `true` or `false`. `false` is zero. A condition that does not evaluate to zero is considered to evaluate to `true`. Because -1 is not zero, the `while` condition evaluates to `true` and the loop is executed. If you want the loop to be executed only for positive numbers, write an expression `while(Integer>0)`. This rule is true for all conditional statements and loops.

Q Is there an empty `while` loop equivalent of `for(;;)`?

A No, `while` always needs an accompanying conditional expression.

Q I changed a `do…while(exp);` to a `while(exp);` by copying and pasting. Should I anticipate any problems?

A Yes, big ones! `while(exp);` is already a valid yet empty `while` loop due to the null statement (the semicolon) following the `while`, even if it is followed by a statement block. The statement block in question is executed once, but outside of the loop. Exercise caution when copying and pasting code.

Workshop

The Workshop provides quiz questions to help you solidify your understanding of the material covered as well as exercises to provide you with experience in using what you've learned. Try to answer the quiz and exercise questions before checking the answers in Appendix E, and be certain you understand the answers before continuing to the next lesson.

6

Quiz

1. Why bother to indent code within statement blocks, nested `if`s, and nested loops when it compiles even without indentation?

2. You can implement a quick fix using `goto`. Why would you still avoid it?

3. Is it possible to write a `for` loop where the counter decrements? How would it look?

4. What is the problem with the following loop?

```
for (int counter=0; counter==10; ++counter)
    cout << counter << " ";
```

Exercises

1. Write a `for` loop to access elements in an array in the reverse order.

2. Write a nested loop equivalent of Listing 6.14 that adds elements in two arrays, but in reverse order.

3. Write a program that displays Fibonacci numbers similar to Listing 6.16 but asks the user how many numbers she wants to compute.

4. Write a `switch-case` construct that tells if a color is in the rainbow or otherwise. Use enumerated constants.

5. BUG BUSTERS: What is wrong with this code?

```
for (int counter=0; counter=10; ++counter)
    cout << counter << " ";
```

6. BUG BUSTERS: What is wrong with this code?

```
int loopCounter = 0;
while(loopCounter <5);
{
    cout << loopCounter << " ";
    loopCounter++;
}
```

7. BUG BUSTERS: What is wrong with this code?

```
cout << "Enter a number between 0 and 4" << endl;
int input = 0;
cin >> input;
switch (input)
{
case 0:
case 1:
case 2:
case 3:
case 4:
cout << "Valid input" << endl;
default:
    cout << "Invalid input" << endl;
}
```

LESSON 7
Organizing Code with Functions

So far in this book you have seen simple programs where all programming effort is contained in `main()`. This works well for really small programs and applications. The larger and more complex your program gets, the longer the contents of `main()` become, unless you choose to structure your program using functions.

Functions give you a way to compartmentalize and organize your program's execution logic. They enable you to split the contents of your application into logical blocks that are invoked sequentially.

A function is hence a subprogram that optionally takes parameters and returns a value, and it needs to be invoked to perform its task. In this lesson you learn

- The need for programming functions
- Function prototypes and function definition
- Passing parameters to functions and returning values from them
- Overloading functions
- Recursive functions
- C++11 lambda functions

The Need for Functions

Think of an application that asks the user to enter the radius of a circle and then computes the circumference and area. One way to do this is to have it all inside main(). Another way is to break this application into logical blocks: in particular two that compute area and circumference given radius, respectively. See Listing 7.1.

LISTING 7.1 Two Functions That Compute the Area and Circumference of a Circle Given Radius

```
0: #include <iostream>
1: using namespace std;
2:
3: const double Pi = 3.14159265;
4:
5: // Function Declarations (Prototypes)
6: double Area(double radius);
7: double Circumference(double radius);
8:
9: int main()
10: {
11:    cout << "Enter radius: ";
12:    double radius = 0;
13:    cin >> radius;
14:
15:    // Call function "Area"
16:    cout << "Area is: " << Area(radius) << endl;
17:
18:    // Call function "Circumference"
19:    cout << "Circumference is: " << Circumference(radius) << endl;
20:
21:    return 0;
22: }
23:
24: // Function definitions (implementations)
25: double Area(double radius)
26: {
27:    return Pi * radius * radius;
28: }
29:
30: double Circumference(double radius)
31: {
32:    return 2 * Pi * radius;
33: }
```

Output ▼

```
Enter radius: 6.5
Area is: 132.732
Circumference is: 40.8407
```

Analysis ▼

main(), which is also a function, is compact and delegates activity to functions such as Area() and Circumference() that are invoked in Lines 16 and 19, respectively.

The program demonstrates the following artifacts involved in programming using functions:

- Function prototypes are *declared* in Lines 6 and 7, so the compiler knows what the terms Area and Circumference are when used in main() mean.

- Functions Area() and Circumference() are *invoked* in main() in Lines 16 and 19.

- Function Area() is defined in Lines 25–28, Circumference() in Lines 30–33.

Compartmentalizing the computation of area and circumference into different functions can potentially help reuse as the functions can be invoked repeatedly, as and when required.

What Is a Function Prototype?

Let's take a look at Listing 7.1 again—Lines 6 and 7 in particular:

```
double Area(double radius);
double Circumference(double radius);
```

Figure 7.1 shows what a function prototype is comprised of.

FIGURE 7.1
Parts of a function prototype.

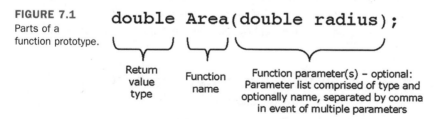

```
double Area(double radius);
```

Return value type

Function name

Function parameter(s) – optional: Parameter list comprised of type and optionally name, separated by comma in event of multiple parameters

7

The function prototype basically tells what a function is called (the name, `Area`), the list of parameters the function accepts (one parameter, a `double` called `radius`), and the return type of the function (a `double`).

Without the function prototype, on reaching Lines 16 and 19 in `main()` the compiler wouldn't know what the terms `Area` and `Circumference` are. The function prototypes tell the compiler that `Area` and `Circumference` are functions; they take one parameter of type `double` and return a value of type `double`. The compiler then recognizes these statements as valid and the job of linking the function call to its implementation and ensuring that the program execution actually triggers them is that of the linker.

NOTE

> A function can have multiple parameters separated by commas, but it can have only one return type.
>
> When programming a function that does not need to return any value, specify the return type as `void`.

What Is a Function Definition?

The actual meat and potatoes—the implementation of a function—is what is called the *definition*. Analyze the definition of function `Area()`:

```
25: double Area(double radius)
26: {
27:     return Pi * radius * radius;
28: }
```

A function definition is always comprised of a statement block. A return statement is necessary unless the function is declared with return type `void`. In this case, `Area()` needs to `return` a value because the function has been declared as one that returns as `double`. The statement block contains statements within open and closed braces ({...}) that are executed when the function is called. `Area()` uses the input parameter `radius` that contains the radius as an *argument* sent by the caller to compute the area of the circle.

What Is a Function Call, and What Are Arguments?

Calling a function is the same as invoking one. When a function declaration contains parameters, the function call needs to send *arguments*. Arguments are values the function requests within its parameter list. Let's analyze a call to `Area()` in Listing 7.1:

```
16:     cout << "Area is: " << Area(radius) << endl;
```

Here, `Area(radius)` is the function call, wherein `radius` is the argument sent to the function `Area()`. When invoked, execution jumps to function `Area()` that uses the radius sent to compute the area of the circle.

Programming a Function with Multiple Parameters

Assume you were writing a program that computes the surface area of a cylinder, as shown in Figure 7.2.

FIGURE 7.2
A cylinder.

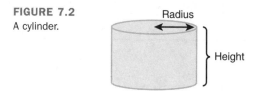

The formula you use would be the following:

```
Area of Cylinder = Area of top circle + Area of bottom circle + Area of Side
                 = Pi *  radius^2 + Pi * radius ^2 + 2 * Pi * radius * height
                 = 2 * Pi * radius^2 + 2 * Pi * radius * height
```

Thus, you need to work with two variables, the radius and the height, in computing the area of the cylinder. In such cases, when writing a function that computes the surface area of the cylinder, you specify at least two parameters in the parameter list, within the function declaration. You do this by separating individual parameters by a comma as shown in Listing 7.2.

LISTING 7.2   Function That Accepts Two Parameters to Compute the Surface Area of a Cylinder

```cpp
0: #include <iostream>
1: using namespace std;
2:
3: const double Pi = 3.14159265;
4:
5: // Declaration contains two parameters
6: double SurfaceArea(double radius, double height);
7:
8: int main()
9: {
10:    cout << "Enter the radius of the cylinder: ";
11:    double radius = 0;
12:    cin >> radius;
13:    cout << "Enter the height of the cylinder: ";
```

7

```
14:     double height = 0;
15:     cin >> height;
16:
17:     cout << "Surface area: " << SurfaceArea(radius, height) << endl;
18:
19:     return 0;
20: }
21:
22: double SurfaceArea(double radius, double height)
23: {
24:     double area = 2 * Pi * radius * radius + 2 * Pi * radius * height;
25:     return area;
26: }
```

Output ▼

```
Enter the radius of the cylinder: 3
Enter the height of the cylinder: 6.5
Surface Area: 179.071
```

Analysis ▼

Line 6 contains the declaration of the function SurfaceArea() with two parameters: radius and height, both of type double, separated by a comma. Lines 22–26 show the definition—that is, the implementation of SurfaceArea(). As you can see, the input parameters radius and height are used to compute the value stored in the local variable area that is then returned to the caller.

NOTE | Function parameters are like local variables. They are valid within the scope of the function only. So in Listing 7.2, parameters radius and height within function SurfaceArea() are copies of variables with similar names within main().

Programming Functions with No Parameters or No Return Values

If you delegate the task of saying "Hello World" to a function that does only that and nothing else, you could do it with one that doesn't need any parameters (as it doesn't need to do anything apart from say "Hello"), and possibly one that doesn't return any value (because you don't expect anything from such a function that would be useful elsewhere). Listing 7.3 demonstrates one such function.

LISTING 7.3   A Function with No Parameters and No Return Values

```
0: #include <iostream>
1: using namespace std;
2:
3: void SayHello();
4:
5: int main()
6: {
7:     SayHello();
8:     return 0;
9: }
10:
11: void SayHello()
12: {
13:     cout << "Hello World" << endl;
14: }
```

Output ▼

```
Hello World
```

Analysis ▼

Note that the function prototype in Line 3 declares function SayHello() as one with return value of type void—that is, SayHello() doesn't return a value. Consequently, in the function definition in Lines 11–14, there is no return statement. Some programmers prefer to insert a symbolic empty return statement at the end:

```
void SayHello()
{
    cout << "Hello World" << endl;
    return; // an empty return
}
```

Function Parameters with Default Values

In samples thus far, you assumed the value of Pi, fixed it as a constant, and never gave the user an opportunity to change it. However, the user may be interested in a less or more accurate reading. How do you program a function that would use a default value of Pi of your choosing unless another one is supplied?

One way of solving this problem is to supply an additional parameter in function Area() for Pi and supply a value chosen by you as a default one. Such an adaptation of function Area() from Listing 7.1 would look like the following:

```
double Area(double radius, double pi = 3.14);
```

7

Note the second parameter `pi` is assigned a default value of 3.14. This second parameter is therefore an optional parameter for the caller. The function `Area()` can be invoked as if the second parameter didn't exist:

```
Area(radius);
```

In this case, the second parameter defaults to the value of 3.14. However, when required, the same function can be invoked using two arguments:

```
Area(radius, 3.14159); // more precise pi
```

Listing 7.4 demonstrates how you can program functions that contain default values for parameters that can be overridden with a user-supplied value, if available and desired.

LISTING 7.4   Function That Computes the Area of a Circle, Using Pi as a Second Parameter with Default Value 3.14

```
 0: #include <iostream>
 1: using namespace std;
 2:
 3: // Function Declarations (Prototypes)
 4: double Area(double radius, double pi = 3.14);
 5:
 6: int main()
 7: {
 8:     cout << "Enter radius: ";
 9:     double radius = 0;
10:     cin >> radius;
11:
12:     cout << "pi is 3.14, do you wish to change this (y / n)? ";
13:     char changePi = 'n';
14:     cin >> changePi;
15:
16:     double circleArea = 0;
17:     if (changePi == 'y')
18:     {
19:        cout << "Enter new pi: ";
20:        double newPi = 3.14;
21:        cin >> newPi;
22:        circleArea = Area (radius, newPi);
23:     }
24:     else
25:        circleArea = Area(radius); // Ignore 2nd param, use default value
26:
27:     // Call function "Area"
28:     cout << "Area is: " << circleArea << endl;
29:
30:     return 0;
31: }
```

```
32:
33: // Function definitions (implementations)
34: double Area(double radius, double pi)
35: {
36:     return pi * radius * radius;
37: }
```

Output ▼

```
Enter radius: 1
Pi is 3.14, do you wish to change this (y / n)? n
Area is: 3.14
```

Next run:

```
Enter radius: 1
Pi is 3.14, do you wish to change this (y / n)? y
Enter new Pi: 3.1416
Area is: 3.1416
```

Analysis ▼

In the two runs, the radius entered by the user was the same—1. In the second run, however, the user opted for the choice to change the precision of Pi, and hence the area computed is slightly different. Note that in both cases, as seen in Lines 22 and 25, you invoke the same function. Line 25 invokes Area() without the second parameter pi. In this case, the parameter pi in Area() contains value 3.14, supplied as default in the declaration in Line 4.

NOTE | You can have multiple parameters with default values; however, these should all be at the tail end of the parameter list.

Recursion—Functions That Invoke Themselves

In certain cases, you can actually have a function call itself. Such a function is called a *recursive function*. Note that a recursive function should have a very clearly defined exit condition where it returns without invoking itself again.

CAUTION | In the absence of an exit condition or in the event of a bug in the same, your program execution gets stuck at the recursive function that won't stop invoking itself, and this eventually stops when the "stack overflows," causing an application crash.

7

Recursive functions can be useful when determining a number in the Fibonacci series as shown in Listing 7.5. This series starts with two numbers, 0 and 1:

```
F(0) = 0
F(1) = 1
```

And the value of a subsequent number in the series is the sum of the previous two numbers. So, the *n*th value (for n > 1) is determined by the (recursive) formula:

```
Fibonacci(n) = Fibonacci(n - 1) + Fibonacci(n - 2)
```

As a result the Fibonacci series expands to

```
F(2) = 1
F(3) = 2
F(4) = 3
F(5) = 5
F(6) = 8, and so on.
```

LISTING 7.5   Using Recursive Functions to Calculate a Number in the Fibonacci Series

```cpp
 0: #include <iostream>
 1: using namespace std;
 2:
 3: int GetFibNumber(int fibIndex)
 4: {
 5:    if (fibIndex < 2)
 6:       return fibIndex;
 7:    else // recursion if fibIndex >= 2
 8:       return GetFibNumber(fibIndex - 1) + GetFibNumber(fibIndex - 2);
 9: }
10:
11: int main()
12: {
13:    cout << "Enter 0-based index of desired Fibonacci Number: ";
14:    int index = 0;
15:    cin >> index;
16:
17:    cout << "Fibonacci number is: " << GetFibNumber(index) << endl;
18:    return 0;
19: }
```

Output ▼

```
Enter 0-based index of desired Fibonacci Number: 6
Fibonacci number is: 8
```

Analysis ▼

The function GetFibNumber() defined in Lines 3–9 is recursive as it invokes itself at Line 8. The exit condition programmed in Lines 5 and 6 ensures that the function will return without recursion if fibIndex is less than two. Thus, GetFibNumber() invokes itself recursively with ever reducing values of fibIndex. It ultimately reaches a state where the exit condition is satisfied, the recursion ends, and a Fibonacci value is determined and returned to main().

Functions with Multiple Return Statements

You are not restricted to having only one return statement in your function definition. You can return from any point in the function, and multiple times if you want, as shown in Listing 7.6. Depending on the logic and the need of the application, this might or might not be poor programming practice.

LISTING 7.6   Using Multiple Return Statements in One Function

```
0: #include <iostream>
1: using namespace std;
2: const double Pi = 3.14159265;
3:
4: void QueryAndCalculate()
5: {
6:    cout << "Enter radius: ";
7:    double radius = 0;
8:    cin >> radius;
9:
10:    cout << "Area: " << Pi * radius * radius << endl;
11:
12:    cout << "Do you wish to calculate circumference (y/n)? ";
13:    char calcCircum = 'n';
14:    cin >> calcCircum;
15:
16:    if (calcCircum == 'n')
17:        return;
18:
19:    cout << "Circumference: " << 2 * Pi * radius << endl;
20:    return;
21: }
22:
23: int main()
24: {
25:    QueryAndCalculate ();
26:
27:    return 0;
28: }
```

7

Output ▼

```
Enter radius: 1
Area: 3.14159
Do you wish to calculate circumference (y/n)? y
Circumference: 6.28319
```

Next run:

```
Enter radius: 1
Area: 3.14159
Do you wish to calculate circumference (y/n)? n
```

Analysis ▼

The function `QueryAndCalculate()` contains multiple `return` statements: one at Line 17 and the next one at Line 20. If the user presses `'n'` for calculating circumference, the program quits by using the `return` statement. For all other values, it continues with calculating the circumference and then returning.

CAUTION

> Use multiple returns in a function with caution. It is a lot easier to understand and follow a function that starts at the top and returns at the bottom than one that returns at multiple points in-between.
>
> In Listing 7.6, use of multiple returns could've been avoided simply by changing the `if` condition to testing for `'y'` or yes:
>
> ```
> if (calcCircum == 'y')
>     cout << "Circumference: " << 2*Pi*radius << endl;
> ```

Using Functions to Work with Different Forms of Data

Functions don't restrict you to passing values one at a time; you can pass an array of values to a function. You can create two functions with the same name and return value but different parameters. You can program a function such that its parameters are not created and destroyed within the function call; instead, you use references that are valid even after the function has exited so as to allow you to manipulate more data or parameters in a function call. In this section you learn about passing arrays to functions, function overloading, and passing arguments by reference to functions.

Overloading Functions

Functions with the same name and return type but with different parameters or set of parameters are said to be overloaded functions. Overloaded functions can be quite useful in applications where a function with a particular name that produces a certain type of output might need to be invoked with different sets of parameters. Say you need to be writing an application that computes the area of a circle and the area of a cylinder. The function that computes the area of a circle needs a parameter—the radius. The other function that computes the area of the cylinder needs the height of the cylinder in addition to the radius of the cylinder. Both functions need to return the data of the same type, containing the area. So, C++ enables you to define two overloaded functions, both called `Area`, both returning `double`, but one that takes only the radius as input and another that takes the height and the radius as input parameters as shown in Listing 7.7.

LISTING 7.7   Using an Overloaded Function to Calculate the Area of a Circle or a Cylinder

```
0: #include <iostream>
1: using namespace std;
2:
3: const double Pi = 3.14159265;
4:
5: double Area(double radius);    // for circle
6: double Area(double radius, double height); // for cylinder
7:
8: int main()
9: {
10:    cout << "Enter z for Cylinder, c for Circle: ";
11:    char userSelection = 'z';
12:    cin >> userSelection;
13:
14:    cout << "Enter radius: ";
15:    double radius = 0;
16:    cin >> radius;
17:
18:    if (userSelection == 'z')
19:    {
20:       cout << "Enter height: ";
21:       double height = 0;
22:       cin >> height;
23:
24:       // Invoke overloaded variant of Area for Cyclinder
25:       cout << "Area of cylinder is: " << Area (radius, height) << endl;
26:    }
27:    else
28:       cout << "Area of cylinder is: " << Area (radius) << endl;
29:
```

7

```
30:    return 0;
31: }
32:
33: // for circle
34: double Area(double radius)
35: {
36:    return Pi * radius * radius;
37: }
38:
39: // overloaded for cylinder
40: double Area(double radius, double height)
41: {
42:    // reuse the area of circle
43:    return 2 * Area (radius) + 2 * Pi * radius * height;
44: }
```

Output ▼

```
Enter z for Cylinder, c for Circle: z
Enter radius: 2
Enter height: 5
Area of cylinder is: 87.9646
```

Next run:

```
Enter z for Cylinder, c for Circle: c
Enter radius: 1
Area of cylinder is: 3.14159
```

Analysis ▼

Lines 5 and 6 declare the prototype for the overloaded forms of Area(): The first overloaded variant accepts a single parameter—radius of a circle. The next one accepts two parameters—radius and height of a cylinder. The function is called overloaded because there are two prototypes with the same name, Area(); same return types, double; and different sets of parameters. The definitions of the overloaded functions are in Lines 34–44, where the two functions determine the area of a circle given the radius and the area of a cylinder given the radius and height, respectively. Interestingly, as the area of a cylinder is comprised of the area of the two circles it contains (one on top and the other on the bottom) in addition to the area of the sides, the overloaded version for cylinder was able to reuse Area() for the circle, as shown in Line 43.

Passing an Array of Values to a Function

A function that displays an integer can be represented like this:

```
void DisplayInteger(int Number);
```

A function that can display an array of integers has a slightly different prototype:

```
void DisplayIntegers(int[] numbers, int Length);
```

The first parameter tells the function that the data being input is an array, whereas the second parameter supplies the length of the array such that you can use the array without crossing its boundaries. See Listing 7.8.

LISTING 7.8 Function That Takes an Array as a Parameter

```
 0: #include <iostream>
 1: using namespace std;
 2:
 3: void DisplayArray(int numbers[], int length)
 4: {
 5:    for (int index = 0; index < length; ++index)
 6:       cout << numbers[index] << " ";
 7:
 8:    cout << endl;
 9: }
10:
11: void DisplayArray(char characters[], int length)
12: {
13:    for (int index = 0; index < length; ++index)
14:       cout << characters[index] << " ";
15:
16:    cout << endl;
17: }
18:
19: int main()
20: {
21:    int myNums[4] = {24, 58, -1, 245};
22:    DisplayArray(myNums, 4);
23:
24:    char myStatement[7] = {'H', 'e', 'l', 'l', 'o', '!', '\0'};
25:    DisplayArray(myStatement, 7);
26:
27:    return 0;
28: }
```

7

Output ▼

```
24 58 -1 245
H e l l o !
```

Analysis ▼

There are two overloaded functions called `DisplayArray()` here: one that displays the contents of elements in an array of integers and another that displays the contents of an array of characters. In Lines 22 and 25, the two functions are invoked using an array of integers and an array of characters, respectively, as input. Note that in declaring and initializing the array of characters in Line 24, you have intentionally included the null character—as a best practice and a good habit—even though the array is not used as a string in a `cout` statement or the like (`cout << myStatement;`) in this application.

Passing Arguments by Reference

Take another look at the function in Listing 7.1 that computed the area of a circle given the radius:

```
24: // Function definitions (implementations)
25: double Area(double radius)
26: {
27:     return Pi * radius * radius;
28: }
```

Here, the parameter `radius` contains a value that is copied into it when the function is invoked in `main()`:

```
15:     // Call function "Area"
16:     cout << "Area is: " << Area(radius) << endl;
```

This means that the variable `radius` in `main()` is unaffected by the function call, as `Area()` works on a copy of the value `radius` contains, held in `radius`. There are cases where you might need a function to work on a variable that modifies a value that is available outside the function, too, say in the calling function. This is when you declare a parameter that takes an argument *by reference*. A form of the function `Area()` that computes and returns the area as a parameter by reference looks like this:

```
// output parameter result by reference
void Area(double radius, double& result)
{
    result = Pi * radius * radius;
}
```

Note how `Area()` in this form takes two parameters. Don't miss the ampersand (&) next to the second parameter `result`. This sign indicates to the compiler that the second argument should NOT be copied to the function; instead, it is a reference to the variable being passed. The return type has been changed to void as the function no longer supplies the area computed as a return value, rather as an output parameter by reference. Returning values by references is demonstrated in Listing 7.9, which computes the area of a circle.

LISTING 7.9   Fetching the Area of a Circle as a Reference Parameter and Not as a Return Value

```
0: #include <iostream>
1: using namespace std;
2:
3: const double Pi = 3.1416;
4:
5: // output parameter result by reference
6: void Area(double radius, double& result)
7: {
8:     result = Pi * radius * radius;
9: }
10:
11: int main()
12: {
13:     cout << "Enter radius: ";
14:     double radius = 0;
15:     cin >> radius;
16:
17:     double areaFetched = 0;
18:     Area(radius, areaFetched);
19:
20:     cout << "The area is: " << areaFetched << endl;
21:     return 0;
22: }
```

Output ▼

```
Enter radius: 2
The area is: 12.5664
```

7

Analysis ▼

Note Lines 17 and 18 where the function `Area()` is invoked with two parameters; the second is one that should contain the result. As `Area()` takes the second parameter by reference, the variable `result` used in Line 8 within `Area` points to the same memory location as the `double areaFetched` declared in Line 17 within the caller `main()`. Thus, the result computed in function `Area()` at Line 8 is available in `main()` and displayed on the screen in Line 20.

NOTE

> A function can return only one value using the `return` statement. So, if your function needs to perform operations that affect many values required at the caller, passing arguments by reference is one way to get a function to supply those many modifications back to the calling module.

How Function Calls Are Handled by the Microprocessor

Although it is not extremely important to know exactly how a function call is implemented on a microprocessor level, you might find it interesting. Understanding this helps you understand why C++ gives you the option of programming inline functions, which are explained later in this section.

A function call essentially means that the microprocessor jumps to executing the next instruction belonging to the called function at a nonsequential memory location. After it is done with executing the instructions in the function, it returns to where it left off. To implement this logic, the compiler converts your function call into a CALL instruction for the microprocessor. This instruction is accompanied by the address in memory the next instruction needs to be taken from—this address belongs to your function routine. When the microprocessor encounters CALL, it saves the position of the instruction to be executed after the function call on the stack and jumps to the memory location contained in the CALL instruction.

Understanding the Stack

The stack is a Last-In-First-Out memory structure, quite like a stack of plates where you pick the plate on top, which was the last one to be placed on the stack. Putting data onto the stack is called a *push* operation. Getting data out of the stack is called a *pop* operation. As the stack grows upward, the stack pointer always increments as it grows and points to the top of the stack. See Figure 7.3.

FIGURE 7.3
A visual representation of a stack containing three integers.

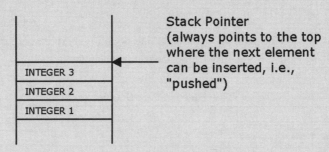

**Stack Pointer
(always points to the top
where the next element
can be inserted, i.e.,
"pushed")**

The nature of the stack makes it optimal for handling function calls. When a function is called, all local variables are instantiated on the stack—that is, pushed onto the stack. When the function ends, they're simply popped off it, and the stack pointer returns to where it originally was.

This memory location contains instructions belonging to the function. The microprocessor executes them until it reaches the RET statement (the microprocessor's code for return programmed by you). The RET statement results in the microprocessor popping that address from the stack stored during the CALL instruction. This address contains the location in the calling function where the execution needs to continue from. Thus, the microprocessor is back to the caller and continues where it left off.

Inline Functions

A regular function call is translated into a CALL instruction, which results in stack operations and microprocessor execution shift to the function and so on. This might sound like a lot of stuff happening under the hood, but it happens quite quickly—for most of the cases. However, what if your function is a very simple one like the following?

```
double GetPi()
{
    return 3.14159;
}
```

7

The overhead of performing an actual function call on this might be quite high for the amount of time spent actually executing `GetPi()`. This is why C++ compilers enable the programmer to declare such functions as inline. Keyword inline is the programmers' request that these functions be expanded inline where called.

```cpp
inline double GetPi()
{
    return 3.14159;
}
```

Functions that perform simple operations like doubling a number are good candidates for being inlined, too. Listing 7.10 demonstrates one such case.

LISTING 7.10 Using an Inline Function That Doubles an Integer

```cpp
 0: #include <iostream>
 1: using namespace std;
 2:
 3: // define an inline function that doubles
 4: inline long DoubleNum (int inputNum)
 5: {
 6:    return inputNum * 2;
 7: }
 8:
 9: int main()
10: {
11:    cout << "Enter an integer: ";
12:    int inputNum = 0;
13:    cin >> inputNum;
14:
15:    // Call inline function
16:    cout << "Double is: " << DoubleNum(inputNum) << endl;
17:
18:    return 0;
19: }
```

Output ▼

```
Enter an integer: 35
Double is: 70
```

Analysis ▼

The keyword in question is `inline` used in Line 4. Compilers typically see this keyword as a request to place the contents of the function `DoubleNum()` directly where the function has been invoked—in Line 16—which increases the execution speed of the code.

Classifying functions as inline can also result in a lot of code bloat, especially if the function being inline does a lot of sophisticated processing. Using the `inline` keyword should be kept to a minimum and reserved for only those functions that do very little and need to do it with minimal overhead, as demonstrated earlier.

> **NOTE**
>
> Most modern C++ compilers offer various performance optimization options. Some, such as the Microsoft C++ Compiler, offer you to optimize for size or speed. Optimizing for size may help in developing software for devices and peripherals where memory may be at a premium. When optimizing for size, the compiler might often reject many inline requests as that might bloat code.
>
> When optimizing for speed, the compiler typically sees and utilizes opportunities to inline code where it would make sense and does it for you—sometimes even in those cases where you have not explicitly requested it.

Automatic Return Type Deduction

You learned about the keyword `auto` in Lesson 3, "Using Variables, Declaring Constants." It lets you leave variable type deduction to the compiler that does so on the basis of the initialization value assigned to the variable. Starting with C++14, the same applies also to functions. Instead of specifying the return type, you would use `auto` and let the compiler deduce the return type for you on the basis of return values you program.

Listing 7.11 demonstrates the usage of `auto` in a function that computes the area of a circle.

LISTING 7.11   Using `auto` as Return Type of Function `Area()`

```
0: #include <iostream>
1: using namespace std;
2:
3: const double Pi = 3.14159265;
4:
5: auto Area(double radius)
6: {
7:     return Pi * radius * radius;
8: }
9:
10: int main()
11: {
12:     cout << "Enter radius: ";
13:     double radius = 0;
```

7

```
14:     cin >> radius;
15:
16:     // Call function "Area"
17:     cout << "Area is: " << Area(radius) << endl;
18:
19:     return 0;
20: }
```

Output ▼

```
Enter radius: 2
Area is: 12.5664
```

Analysis ▼

The line of interest is Line 5, which uses `auto` as the return type of function `Area()`. The compiler deduces the return type on the basis of the return expression that uses double. Thus, in spite of using `auto`, `Area()` in Listing 7.11 compiles to no different code than `Area()` in Listing 7.1 with return type double.

NOTE ———— | Functions that rely on automatic return type deduction need to be defined (i.e., implemented) before they're invoked. This is because the compiler needs to know a function's return type at the point where it is used. If such a function has multiple return statements, they need to all deduce to the same type. Recursive calls need to follow at least one return statement.

Lambda Functions

This section is just an introduction to a concept that's not exactly easy for beginners. So, skim through it and try to learn the concept without being disappointed if you don't grasp it all. Lambda functions are discussed in depth in Lesson 22, "Lambda Expressions."

Lambda functions were introduced in C++11 and help in the usage of STL algorithms to sort or process data. Typically, a sort function requires you to supply a binary predicate. This is a function that compares two arguments and returns `true` if one is less than the other, else `false`, thereby helping in deciding the order of elements in a sort operation. Such predicates are typically implemented as operators in a class, leading to a tedious bit of coding. Lambda functions can compact predicate definitions as shown in Listing 7.12.

LISTING 7.12   Using Lambda Functions to Display Elements in an Array and to Sort Them

```
 0: #include <iostream>
 1: #include <algorithm>
 2: #include <vector>
 3: using namespace std;
 4:
 5: void DisplayNums(vector<int>& dynArray)
 6: {
 7:    for_each (dynArray.begin(), dynArray.end(), \
 8:             [](int Element) {cout << Element << " ";} );
 9:
10:    cout << endl;
11: }
12:
13: int main()
14: {
15:    vector<int> myNums;
16:    myNums.push_back(501);
17:    myNums.push_back(-1);
18:    myNums.push_back(25);
19:    myNums.push_back(-35);
20:
21:    DisplayNums(myNums);
22:
23:    cout << "Sorting them in descending order" << endl;
24:
25:    sort (myNums.begin(), myNums.end(), \
26:          [](int Num1, int Num2) {return (Num2 < Num1); } );
27:
28:    DisplayNums(myNums);
29:
30:    return 0;
31: }
```

Output ▼

```
501 -1 25 -35
Sorting them in descending order
501 25 -1 -35
```

Analysis ▼

The program contains integers pushed into a dynamic array provided by the C++ Standard Library in the form of a `std::vector` in Lines 15–19. The function `DisplayNums()` uses the STL algorithm `for_each` to iterate through each element in the array and display its value. In doing so, it uses a lambda function in Line 8. `std::sort` used in Line 25 also uses a binary predicate (Line 26) in the form of

7

a lambda function that returns `true` if the second number is smaller than the first, effectively sorting the collection in an ascending order.

The syntax of a lambda function is the following:

```
[optional parameters](parameter list){ statements; }
```

NOTE ───────── Predicates and their use in algorithms such as sort are discussed at length in Lesson 23, "STL Algorithms." Listing 23.6 in particular is a code sample that uses a lambda and a non-lambda variant in an algorithm, thereby allowing you to compare the programming efficiency introduced by lambda functions.

Summary

In this lesson, you learned the basics of modular programming. You learned how functions can help you structure your code better and also help you reuse algorithms you write. You learned that functions can take parameters and return values, parameters can have default values that the caller can override, and parameters can also contain arguments passed by reference. You learned how to pass arrays, and you also learned how to program overloaded functions that have the same name and return type but different parameter lists.

Last but not the least, you got a sneak preview into what lambda functions are. Completely new as of C++11, lambda functions have the potential to change how C++ applications will be programmed henceforth, especially when using STL.

Q&A

Q What happens if I program a recursive function that doesn't end?

A Program execution doesn't end. That might not be bad, per se, for there are `while(true)` and `for(;;)` loops that do the same; however, a recursive function call consumes more and more stack space, which is finite and runs out, eventually causing an application crash due to a stack overflow.

Q Why not inline every function? It increases execution speed, right?

A That really depends. However, inlining every function results in functions that are used in multiple places to be placed at the point where they're called, and this results in code bloat. That apart, most modern compilers are better judges of what calls can be inlined and do so for the programmer, depending on the compiler's performance settings.

Q Can I supply default parameter values to all parameters in a function?

A Yes, that is definitely possible and recommended when that makes sense.

Q I have two functions, both called `Area`. One takes a radius and the other takes height. I want one to return `float` and the other to return `double`. Will this work?

A Function overloading needs both functions with the same name to also have the same return types. In this case, your compiler shows an error as the name has been used twice in what it expects to be two functions of different names.

Workshop

The Workshop provides quiz questions to help you solidify your understanding of the material covered and exercises to provide you with experience in using what you've learned. Try to answer the quiz and exercise questions before checking the answers in Appendix E, and be certain that you understand the answers before continuing to the next lesson.

Quiz

1. What is the scope of variables declared in a function's prototype?

2. What is the nature of the value passed to this function?

```
int Func(int &someNumber);
```

3. I have a function that invokes itself. What is such a function called?

4. I have declared two functions, both with the same name and return type but different parameter lists. What are these called?

5. Does the stack pointer point to the top, middle, or bottom of the stack?

Exercises

1. Write overloaded functions that calculate the volume of a sphere and a cylinder. The formulas are the following:

```
Volume of sphere = (4 * Pi * radius * radius * radius) / 3
Volume of a cylinder = Pi * radius * radius * height
```

7

2. Write a function that accepts an array of double as input.

3. BUG BUSTERS: What is wrong with the following code?

```
#include <iostream>
using namespace std;
const double Pi = 3.1416;

void Area(double radius, double result)
{
    result = Pi * radius * radius;
}

int main()
{
    cout << "Enter radius: ";
    double radius = 0;
    cin >> radius;

    double areaFetched = 0;
    Area(radius, areaFetched);

    cout << "The area is: " << areaFetched << endl;
    return 0;
}
```

4. BUG BUSTERS: What is wrong with the following function declaration?

```
double Area(double Pi = 3.14, double radius);
```

5. Write a function with return type void that still helps the caller calculate the area and circumference of a circle when supplied the radius.

LESSON 8
Pointers and References Explained

One of the biggest advantages of C++ is that it enables you to write high-level applications that are abstracted from the machine as well as those that work close to the hardware. Indeed, C++ enables you to tweak the performance of your application on a bytes and bits level. Understanding how pointers and references work is one step toward being able to write programs that are effective in their consumption of system resources.

In this lesson, you find out

- What pointers are
- What the free store is
- How to use operators `new` and `delete` to allocate and free memory
- How to write stable applications using pointers and dynamic allocation
- What references are
- Differences between pointers and references
- When to use a pointer and when to use references

What Is a Pointer?

A *pointer* is also a variable—one that stores an address in memory. Just the same way as a variable of type int is used to contain an integer value, a pointer variable is used to contain a memory address, as illustrated in Figure 8.1.

FIGURE 8.1
Visualizing a pointer.

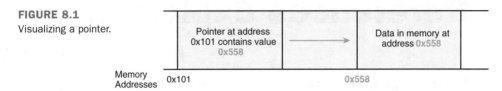

Thus, a pointer is a variable, and like all variables a pointer occupies space in memory (in the case of Figure 8.1, at address 0x101). What's special about pointers is that the value contained in a pointer (in this case, 0x558) is interpreted as a memory address. So, a pointer is a special variable that *points to* a location in memory.

NOTE　Memory locations are typically addressed using *hexadecimal* notation. This is a number system with base 16, that is, one featuring 16 distinct symbols from 0–9 followed by A–F. It is convention to prefix 0x when displaying hexadecimal numbers. Thus, 0xA is hexadecimal for 10 in decimal; 0xF is hexadecimal for 15; and 0x10 is hexadecimal for 16. For more information, see Appendix A, "Working with Numbers: Binary and Hexadecimal."

Declaring a Pointer

A pointer being a variable needs to be declared, too. You normally declare a pointer to point to a specific value type (for example, int). This would mean that the address contained in the pointer points to a location in the memory that holds an integer. You can also specify a pointer to a block of memory (also called a void pointer).

A pointer being a variable needs to be declared like all variables do:

```
PointedType * PointerVariableName;
```

As is the case with most variables, unless you initialize a pointer it will contain a random value. You don't want a random memory address to be accessed so you initialize a pointer to NULL. NULL is a value that can be checked against and one that cannot be a memory address:

```
PointedType * PointerVariableName = NULL; // initializing value
```

Thus, declaring a pointer to an integer would be

```
int *pointsToInt = NULL;
```

CAUTION

> A pointer, like all data types you have learned, contains a junk value unless it has been initialized. This junk value is particularly dangerous in the case of a pointer because the value of the pointer is expected to contain an address. Uninitialized pointers can result in your program accessing invalid memory locations, resulting in a crash.

8

Determining the Address of a Variable Using the Reference Operator (&)

Variables are tools the language provides for you to work with data in memory. This concept is explained in detail in Lesson 3, "Using Variables, Declaring Constants."

If varName is a variable, &varName gives the address in memory where its value is placed.

So, if you have declared an integer, using the syntax that you're well acquainted with, such as

```
int age = 30;
```

&age would be the address in memory where the value (30) is placed. Listing 8.1 demonstrates the concept of the memory address of an integer variable that is used to hold the value it contains.

LISTING 8.1 Determining the Addresses of an int and a double

```
0: #include <iostream>
1: using namespace std;
2:
3: int main()
4: {
5:     int age = 30;
6:     const double Pi = 3.1416;
7:
8:     // Use & to find the address in memory
9:     cout << "Integer age is located at: 0x" << &age << endl;
10:    cout << "Double Pi is located at: 0x" << &Pi << endl;
11:
12:    return 0;
13: }
```

Output ▼

```
Integer age is at: 0x0045FE00
Double Pi is located at: 0x0045FDF8
```

Analysis ▼

Note how referencing operator (&) has been used in Lines 9 and 10 to reveal the addresses of variables age and constant Pi. The text 0x has been appended as a convention that is used when displaying hexadecimal numbers.

> **NOTE**
>
> You know that the amount of memory consumed by a variable is dependent on its type. Listing 3.4 in Lesson 3 uses sizeof() to demonstrate that the size of an integer is 4 bytes (on my system, using my compiler). So, using the preceding output that says that integer age is located at address 0x0045FE00 and using the knowledge that sizeof(int) is 4, you know that the four bytes located in the range 0x0045FE00 to 0x0045FE04 belong to the integer age.

> **NOTE**
>
> The referencing operator (&) is also called the address-of operator.

Using Pointers to Store Addresses

You have learned how to declare pointers and how to determine the address of a variable. You also know that pointers are variables that are used to hold memory addresses. It's time to connect these dots and use pointers to store the addresses obtained using the referencing operator (&).

Assume a variable declaration of the types you already know:

```
// Declaring a variable
Type VariableName = InitialValue;
```

To store the address of this variable in a pointer, you would declare a pointer to the same Type and initialize the pointer to the variable's address using the referencing operator (&):

```
// Declaring a pointer to Type and initializing to address
Type* Pointer = &Variable;
```

Thus, if you have declared an integer, using the syntax that you're well acquainted with, such as

```
int age = 30;
```

You would declare a pointer to the type `int` to hold the actual address where `age` is stored, like this:

```
int* pointsToInt = &age; // Pointer to integer age
```

In Listing 8.2 you see how a pointer can be used to store an address fetched using the referencing operator (&).

LISTING 8.2 Demonstrating the Declaration and Initialization of a Pointer

```
0: #include <iostream>
1: using namespace std;
2:
3: int main()
4: {
5:     int age = 30;
6:     int* pointsToInt = &age;   // pointer initialized to &age
7:
8:     // Displaying the value of pointer
9:     cout << "Integer age is at: 0x" << hex << pointsToInt << endl;
10:
11:     return 0;
12: }
```

Output ▼

```
Integer age is at: 0x0045FE00
```

Analysis ▼

Essentially, the output of this code snippet is the same as the previous one in Listing 8.1 because both the samples are displaying the same thing—the address in memory where integer `age` is stored. The difference here is that the address is first assigned to a pointer at Line 6, and the value of the pointer (now the address) is displayed using `cout` at Line 9.

NOTE

Your output might differ in addresses from those you see in these samples. In fact, the address of a variable might change at every run of the application on the very same computer.

Now that you know how to store an address in a pointer variable, it is easy to imagine that the same pointer variable can be reassigned a different memory address and made to point to a different value, as shown in Listing 8.3.

LISTING 8.3   Pointer Reassignment to Another Variable

```
0: #include <iostream>
1: using namespace std;
2:
3: int main()
4: {
5:    int age = 30;
6:
7:    int* pointsToInt = &age;
8:    cout << "pointsToInt points to age now" << endl;
9:
10:    // Displaying the value of pointer
11:    cout << "pointsToInt = 0x" << hex << pointsToInt << endl;
12:
13:    int dogsAge = 9;
14:    pointsToInt = &dogsAge;
15:    cout << "pointsToInt points to dogsAge now" << endl;
16:
17:    cout << "pointsToInt = 0x" << hex << pointsToInt << endl;
18:
19:    return 0;
20: }
```

Output ▼

```
pointsToInt points to age now
pointsToInt = 0x002EFB34
pointsToInt points to dogsAge now
pointsToInt = 0x002EFB1C
```

Analysis ▼

This program demonstrates that one pointer to an integer, pointsToInt, can point to any integer. In Line 7, it has been initialized to &age, hence containing the address of variable age. In Line 14 the same pointer is assigned &dogsAge, pointing to another location in the memory that contains dogsAge. Correspondingly, the output indicates that the value of the pointer, that is the address being pointed to, changes as the two integers age and dogsAge are, of course, stored in different locations in memory, 0x002EFB34 and 0x002EFB1C, respectively.

Access Pointed Data Using the Dereference Operator (*)

You have a pointer to data, containing a valid address. How do you access that location—that is, get or set data at that location? The answer lies in using the dereferencing operator (*). Essentially, if you have a valid pointer pData, use *pData to access the value stored at the address contained in the pointer. Operator (*) is demonstrated by Listing 8.4.

8

LISTING 8.4 Demonstrating the Use of the Dereference Operator (*) to Access Integer Values

```
0: #include <iostream>
1: using namespace std;
2:
3: int main()
4: {
5:     int age = 30;
6:     int dogsAge = 9;
7:
8:     cout << "Integer age = " << age << endl;
9:     cout << "Integer dogsAge = " << dogsAge << endl;
10:
11:     int* pointsToInt = &age;
12:     cout << "pointsToInt points to age" << endl;
13:
14:     // Displaying the value of pointer
15:     cout << "pointsToInt = 0x" << hex << pointsToInt << endl;
16:
17:     // Displaying the value at the pointed location
18:     cout << "*pointsToInt = " << dec << *pointsToInt << endl;
19:
20:     pointsToInt = &dogsAge;
21:     cout << "pointsToInt points to dogsAge now" << endl;
22:
23:     cout << "pointsToInt = 0x" << hex << pointsToInt << endl;
24:     cout << "*pointsToInt = " << dec << *pointsToInt << endl;
25:
26:     return 0;
27: }
```

Output ▼

```
Integer age = 30
Integer dogsAge = 9
pointsToInt points to age
pointsToInt = 0x0025F788
```

```
*pointsToInt = 30
pointsToInt points to dogsAge now
pointsToInt = 0x0025F77C
*pointsToInt = 9
```

Analysis ▼

In addition to changing the address stored within a pointer as also in the previous sample in Listing 8.3, this one also uses the dereference operator (*) with the same pointer variable pointsToInt to print the different values at these two addresses. Note Lines 18 and 24. In both these lines, the integer pointed to by pointsToInt is accessed using the dereference operator (*). As the address contained in pointsToInt is changed at Line 20, the same pointer after this assignment accesses the variable dogsAge, displaying 9.

When the dereference operator (*) is used, the application essentially uses the address stored in the pointer as a starting point to fetch 4 bytes from the memory that belong to an integer (as this is a pointer to integers and sizeof(int) is 4). Thus, the validity of the address contained in the pointer is absolutely essential. By initializing the pointer to &age in Line 11, you have ensured that the pointer contains a valid address. When you don't initialize the pointer, it can contain any random value (that existed in the memory location where the pointer variable is located) and dereference of that pointer usually results in an Access Violation—that is, accessing a memory location that your application was not authorized to.

NOTE The dereferencing operator (*) is also called the indirection operator.

You have used the pointer in the preceding sample to read (get) values from the pointed memory location. Listing 8.5 shows what happens when *pointsToInt is used as an l-value—that is, assigned to instead of just being accessed.

LISTING 8.5 Manipulating Data Using a Pointer and the Dereference Operator (*)

```
0: #include <iostream>
1: using namespace std;
2:
3: int main()
4: {
5:     int dogsAge = 30;
6:     cout << "Initialized dogsAge = " << dogsAge << endl;
7:
```

```
 8:     int* pointsToAnAge = &dogsAge;
 9:     cout << "pointsToAnAge points to dogsAge" << endl;
10:
11:     cout << "Enter an age for your dog: ";
12:
13:     // store input at the memory pointed to by pointsToAnAge
14:     cin >> *pointsToAnAge;
15:
16:     // Displaying the address where age is stored
17:     cout << "Input stored at 0x" << hex << pointsToAnAge << endl;
18:
19:     cout << "Integer dogsAge = " << dec << dogsAge << endl;
20:
21:     return 0;
22: }
```

Output ▼

```
Initialized dogsAge = 30
pointsToAnAge points to dogsAge
Enter an age for your dog: 10
Input stored at 0x0025FA18
Integer dogsAge = 10
```

Analysis ▼

The key step here is in Line 14 where the age input by the user is saved at the location stored in the pointer pointsToAnAge. Line 19 that displays variable dogsAge shows the value you stored using the pointer. This is because pointsToAnAge points to dogsAge, as initialized in Line 8. Any change to that memory location where dogsAge is stored, and where pointsToAnAge points to, made using one is going to be reflected in the other.

What Is the `sizeof()` of a Pointer?

You have learned that the pointer is just another variable that contains a memory address. Hence, irrespective of the type that is being pointed to, the content of a pointer is an address—a number. The length of an address, that is the number of bytes required to store it, is a constant for a given system. The sizeof() a pointer is hence dependent on the compiler and the operating system the program has been compiled for and is *not* dependent on the nature of the data being pointed to, as Listing 8.6 demonstrates.

LISTING 8.6 Demonstrating That Pointers to Different Types Have the Same Sizes

```
0: #include <iostream>
1: using namespace std;
2:
3: int main()
4: {
5:     cout << "sizeof fundamental types -" << endl;
6:     cout << "sizeof(char) = " << sizeof(char) << endl;
7:     cout << "sizeof(int) = " << sizeof(int) << endl;
8:     cout << "sizeof(double) = " << sizeof(double) << endl;
9:
10:     cout << "sizeof pointers to fundamental types -" << endl;
11:     cout << "sizeof(char*) = " << sizeof(char*) << endl;
12:     cout << "sizeof(int*) = " << sizeof(int*) << endl;
13:     cout << "sizeof(double*) = " << sizeof(double*) << endl;
14:
15:     return 0;
16: }
```

Output ▼

```
sizeof fundamental types -
sizeof(char) = 1
sizeof(int) = 4
sizeof(double) = 8
sizeof pointers to fundamental types -
sizeof(char*) = 4
sizeof(int*) = 4
sizeof(double*) = 4
```

Analysis ▼

The output clearly shows that even though a sizeof(char) is 1 byte and a sizeof(double) is 8 bytes, the sizeof(char*) and sizeof(double*) are both 4 bytes. This is because the amount of memory consumed by a pointer that stores an address is the same, irrespective of whether the memory at the address contains 1 byte or 8 bytes of data.

NOTE

The output for Listing 8.6 that displays that the sizeof a pointer is 4 bytes might be different than what you see on your system. The output was generated when the code was compiled using a 32-bit compiler. If you use a 64-bit compiler and run the program on a 64-bit system, you might see that the sizeof your pointer variable is 64 bits—that is, 8 bytes.

Dynamic Memory Allocation

When you write a program containing an array declaration such as

```
int myNums[100]; // a static array of 100 integers
```

your program has two problems:

1. You are actually limiting the capacity of your program as it cannot store more than 100 numbers.

2. You are reducing the performance of the system in cases where only 1 number needs to be stored, yet space has been reserved for 100.

These problems exist because the memory allocation in an array as declared earlier is static and fixed by the compiler.

To program an application that is able to optimally consume memory resources on the basis of the needs of the user, you need to use dynamic memory allocation. This enables you to allocate more when you need more memory and release memory that you have in excess. C++ supplies you two operators, new and delete, to help you better manage the memory consumption of your application. Pointers being variables that are used to contain memory addresses play a critical role in efficient dynamic memory allocation.

Using Operators new and delete to Allocate and Release Memory Dynamically

You use new to allocate new memory blocks. The most frequently used form of new returns a pointer to the requested memory if successful or else throws an exception. When using new, you need to specify the data type for which the memory is being allocated:

```
Type* Pointer = new Type; // request memory for one element
```

You can also specify the number of elements you want to allocate that memory for (when you need to allocate memory for more than one element):

```
Type* Pointer = new Type[numElements]; // request memory for numElements
```

Thus, if you need to allocate integers, you use the following syntax:

```
int* pointToAnInt = new int;  // get a pointer to an integer
int* pointToNums = new int[10];  // pointer to a block of 10 integers
```

> **NOTE** —————
> Note that new indicates a request for memory. There is no guarantee that a call for allocation always succeeds because this depends on the state of the system and the availability of memory resources.

Every allocation using new needs to be eventually released using an equal and opposite de-allocation via delete:

```
Type* Pointer = new Type; // allocate memory
delete Pointer;  // release memory allocated above
```

This rule also applies when you request memory for multiple elements:

```
Type* Pointer = new Type[numElements]; // allocate a block
delete[] Pointer; // release block allocated above
```

> **NOTE** —————
> Note the usage of delete[] when you allocate a block using new[...] and delete when you allocate just an element using new.

If you don't release allocated memory after you stop using it, this memory remains reserved and allocated for your application. This in turn reduces the amount of system memory available for applications to consume and possibly even makes the execution of your application slower. This is called a *leak* and should be avoided at all costs.

Listing 8.7 demonstrates memory dynamic allocation and deallocation.

LISTING 8.7 Accessing Memory Allocated Using new via Operator (*) and Releasing It Using delete

```
 0: #include <iostream>
 1: using namespace std;
 2:
 3: int main()
 4: {
 5:     // Request for memory space for an int
 6:     int* pointsToAnAge = new int;
 7:
 8:     // Use the allocated memory to store a number
 9:     cout << "Enter your dog's age: ";
10:     cin >> *pointsToAnAge;
```

```
11:
12:    // use indirection operator* to access value
13:    cout << "Age " << *pointsToAnAge << " is stored at 0x" << hex <<
pointsToAnAge << endl;
14:
15:    delete pointsToAnAge; // release memory
16:
17:    return 0;
18: }
```

Output ▼

```
Enter your dog's age: 9
Age 9 is stored at 0x00338120
```

Analysis ▼

Line 6 demonstrates the use of operator new to request space for an integer where you plan to store the dog's age as input by the user. Note that new returns a pointer, and that is the reason it is assigned to one. The age entered by the user is stored in this newly allocated memory using cin and the dereference operator (*) in Line 10. Line 13 displays this stored value using the dereference operator (*) again and also displays the memory address where the value is stored. Note that the address contained in pointsToAnAge in Line 13 still is what was returned by new in Line 6 and hasn't changed since.

CAUTION

> Operator delete cannot be invoked on any address contained in a pointer, rather only those that have been returned by new and only those that have not already been released by a delete.
>
> Thus, the pointers seen in Listing 8.6 contain valid addresses, yet should not be released using delete because the addresses were not returned by a call to new.

Note that when you allocate for a range of elements using new[...], you would de-allocate using delete[] as demonstrated by Listing 8.8.

LISTING 8.8   Allocating Using new[...] and Releasing It Using delete[]

```
0: #include <iostream>
1: #include <string>
2: using namespace std;
3:
```

```
4: int main()
5: {
6:     cout << "How many integers shall I reserve memory for?" << endl;
7:     int numEntries = 0;
8:     cin >> numEntries;
9:
10:    int* myNumbers = new int[numEntries];
11:
12:    cout << "Memory allocated at: 0x" << myNumbers << hex << endl;
13:
14:    // de-allocate before exiting
15:    delete[] myNumbers;
16:
17:    return 0;
18: }
```

Output ▼

```
How many integers shall I reserve memory for?
5001
Memory allocated at: 0x00C71578
```

Analysis ▼

The most important lines in question are the `new[]` and `delete[]` operators used in Lines 10 and 15, respectively. What makes this sample different from Listing 8.7 is the dynamic allocation of a block of memory that can accommodate as many integers as the user requests. During this execution, we requested space for 5001 integers. In another run, it may be 20 or 55000. This program will allocate a different amount of memory required in every execution, depending on user input. Such allocations for an array of elements need to be matched by de-allocation using `delete[]` to free memory when done.

NOTE _____ Operators `new` and `delete` allocate memory from the free store. The free store is a memory abstraction in the form of a pool of memory where your application can allocate (that is, reserve) memory from and de-allocate (that is, release) memory to.

Effect of Incrementing and Decrementing Operators (++ and --) on Pointers

A pointer contains a memory address. For example, the pointer to an integer in Listing 8.3 contains 0x002EFB34—the address where the integer is placed. The integer itself is 4 bytes long and hence occupies four places in memory from 0x002EFB34 to 0x002EFB37. Incrementing this pointer using operator (++) would *not* result in the pointer pointing to 0x002EFB35, for pointing to the middle of an integer would literally be pointless.

An increment or decrement operation on a pointer is interpreted by the compiler as your need to point to the next value in the block of memory, assuming it to be of the same type, and *not* to the next byte (unless the value type is 1 byte large, like a char, for instance).

So, incrementing a pointer such as pointsToInt seen in Listing 8.3 results in it being incremented by 4 bytes, which is the sizeof an int. Using ++ on this pointer is telling the compiler that you want it to point to the next consecutive integer. Hence, after incrementing, the pointer would then point to 0x002EFB38. Similarly, adding 2 to this pointer would result in it moving 2 integers ahead, that is 8 bytes ahead. Later you see a correlation between this behavior displayed by pointers and indexes used in arrays.

Decrementing pointers using operator (--) demonstrates the same effect—the address value contained in the pointer is reduced by the sizeof the data type it is being pointed to.

What Happens When You Increment or Decrement a Pointer?

The address contained in the pointer is incremented or decremented by the sizeof the type being pointed to (and not necessarily a byte). This way, the compiler ensures that the pointer never points to the middle or end of data placed in the memory; it only points to the beginning.

If a pointer has been declared as

```
Type* pType = Address;
```

++pType would mean that pType contains (and hence points to) Address + sizeof(Type).

See Listing 8.9 that explains the effect of incrementing pointers or adding offsets to them.

LISTING 8.9 Using Offset Values and Operators to Increment and Decrement Pointers

```
 0: #include <iostream>
 1: using namespace std;
 2:
 3: int main()
 4: {
 5:     cout << "How many integers you wish to enter? ";
 6:     int numEntries = 0;
 7:     cin >> numEntries;
 8:
 9:     int* pointsToInts = new int [numEntries];
10:
11:     cout << "Allocated for " << numEntries << " integers" << endl;
12:     for(int counter = 0; counter < numEntries; ++counter)
13:     {
14:         cout << "Enter number "<< counter << ": ";
15:         cin >> *(pointsToInts + counter);
16:     }
17:
18:     cout << "Displaying all numbers entered: " << endl;
19:     for(int counter = 0; counter < numEntries; ++counter)
20:         cout << *(pointsToInts++) << " ";
21:
22:     cout << endl;
23:
24:     // return pointer to initial position
25:     pointsToInts -= numEntries;
26:
27:     // done with using memory? release
28:     delete[] pointsToInts;
29:
30:     return 0;
31: }
```

Output ▼

```
How many integers you wish to enter? 2
Allocated for 2 integers
Enter number 0: 8774
Enter number 1: -5
Displaying all numbers entered:
8774 -5
```

Another run:

```
How many integers you wish to enter? 5
How many integers you wish to enter? 5
Allocated for 5 integers
Enter number 0: 543
Enter number 1: 756
Enter number 2: 2017
```

```
Enter number 3: -101
Enter number 4: 101010012
Displaying all numbers entered:
543 756 2017 -101 101010012
```

Analysis ▼

The program asks the user for the number of integers he wants to feed into the system before allocating memory for the same in Line 9. The sample demonstrates two methods of incrementing pointers. One uses an offset value as seen in Line 15, where we store user input directly into the memory location using offset variable `counter`. The other uses operator `++` as seen in Line 20 to increment the address contained in the pointer variable to the next valid integer in the allocated memory. Operators were introduced in Lesson 5, "Working with Expressions, Statements, and Operators."

Lines 12–16 are a `for` loop where the user is asked to enter the numbers that are then stored in consecutive positions in the memory using the expression in Line 15. It is here that the zero-based offset value (`counter`) is added to the pointer, causing the compiler to create instructions that insert the value fed by the user at the next appropriate location for an integer without overwriting the previous value. The `for` loop in Lines 19 and 20 is similarly used to display those values stored by the previous loop.

The original pointer address returned by `new` during allocation needs to be used in the call to `delete[]` during de-allocation. As this value contained in `pointsToInts` has been modified by operator `++` in Line 20, we bring the pointer back to the original position (address) using operator `-=` in Line 25 before invoking `delete[]` on that address in Line 28.

Using the `const` Keyword on Pointers

In Lesson 3, you learned that declaring a variable as `const` effectively ensures that value of the variable is fixed as the initialization value for the life of the variable. The value of a const-variable cannot be changed, and therefore it cannot be used as an l-value.

Pointers are variables, too, and hence the `const` keyword that is relevant to variables is relevant to pointers as well. However, pointers are a special kind of variable as they contain a memory address and are used to modify memory at that address. Thus, when it comes to pointers and constants, you have the following combinations:

- The address contained in the pointer is constant and cannot be changed, yet the data at that address can be changed:

```
int daysInMonth = 30;
int* const pDaysInMonth = &daysInMonth;
*pDaysInMonth = 31; // OK! Data pointed to can be changed
int daysInLunarMonth = 28;
pDaysInMonth = &daysInLunarMonth; // Not OK! Cannot change address!
```

■ Data pointed to is constant and cannot be changed, yet the address contained in the pointer can be changed—that is, the pointer can also point elsewhere:

```
int hoursInDay = 24;
const int* pointsToInt = &hoursInDay;
int monthsInYear = 12;
pointsToInt = &monthsInYear; // OK!
*pointsToInt = 13; // Not OK! Cannot change data being pointed to
int* newPointer = pointsToInt; // Not OK! Cannot assign const to non-const
```

■ Both the address contained in the pointer and the value being pointed to are constant and cannot be changed (most restrictive variant):

```
int hoursInDay = 24;
const int* const pHoursInDay = &hoursInDay;
*pHoursInDay = 25; // Not OK! Cannot change data being pointed to
int daysInMonth = 30;
pHoursInDay = &daysInMonth; // Not OK! Cannot change address
```

These different forms of const are particularly useful when passing pointers to functions. Function parameters need to be declared to support the highest possible (restrictive) level of const-ness, to ensure that a function does not modify the pointed value when it is not supposed to. This will keep programmers of your application from making unwanted changes to pointer values or data.

Passing Pointers to Functions

Pointers are an effective way to pass memory space that contains relevant data for functions to work on. The memory space shared can also return the result of an operation. When using a pointer with functions, it becomes important to ensure that the called function is only allowed to modify parameters that you want to let it modify, but not others. For example, a function that calculates the area of a circle given radius sent as a pointer should not be allowed to modify the radius. This is where you use the keyword const to control what a function is allowed to modify and what it isn't as demonstrated by Listing 8.10.

LISTING 8.10 Use the const Keyword in Calculating the Area of a Circle

```
0: #include <iostream>
1: using namespace std;
2:
3: void CalcArea(const double* const ptrPi, // const pointer to const data
4:               const double* const ptrRadius, // i.e. no changes allowed
5:               double* const ptrArea)  // can change data pointed to
```

8

```
 6: {
 7:    // check pointers for validity before using!
 8:    if (ptrPi && ptrRadius && ptrArea)
 9:       *ptrArea = (*ptrPi) * (*ptrRadius) * (*ptrRadius);
10: }
11:
12: int main()
13: {
14:    const double Pi = 3.1416;
15:
16:    cout << "Enter radius of circle: ";
17:    double radius = 0;
18:    cin >> radius;
19:
20:    double area = 0;
21:    CalcArea (&Pi, &radius, &area);
22:
23:    cout << "Area is = " << area << endl;
24:
25:    return 0;
26: }
```

Output ▼

```
Enter radius of circle: 10.5
Area is = 346.361
```

Analysis ▼

Lines 3–5 demonstrate the two forms of const where both ptrRadius and ptrPi are supplied as "const pointers to const data," so that neither the pointer address nor the data being pointed to can be modified. ptrArea is evidently the parameter meant to store the output, for the value contained in the pointer (address) cannot be modified, but the data being pointed to can be. Line 8 shows how pointer parameters to a function are checked for validity before using them. You don't want the function to calculate the area if the caller inadvertently sends a NULL pointer as any of the three parameters, for that would risk an access violation followed by an application crash.

Similarities between Arrays and Pointers

Don't you think that the sample in Listing 8.9 where the pointer was incremented using zero-based index to access the next integer in the memory has too many similarities to the manner in which arrays are indexed? When you declare an array of integers:

```
int myNumbers[5];
```

You tell the compiler to allocate a fixed amount of memory to hold five integers and give you a pointer to the first element in that array that is identified by the name you assign the array variable. In other words, myNumbers is a pointer to the first element myNumbers[0]. Listing 8.11 highlights this correlation.

LISTING 8.11 Demonstrate That the Array Variable Is a Pointer to the First Element

```
0: #include <iostream>
1: using namespace std;
2:
3: int main()
4: {
5:     // Static array of 5 integers
6:     int myNumbers[5];
7:
8:     // array assigned to pointer to int
9:     int* pointToNums = myNumbers;
10:
11:     // Display address contained in pointer
12:     cout << "pointToNums = 0x" << hex << pointToNums << endl;
13:
14:     // Address of first element of array
15:     cout << "&myNumbers[0] = 0x" << hex << &myNumbers[0] << endl;
16:
17:     return 0;
18: }
```

Output ▼

```
pointToNums = 0x004BFE8C
&myNumbers[0] = 0x004BFE8C
```

Analysis ▼

This simple program demonstrates that an array variable can be assigned to a pointer of the same type as seen in Line 9, essentially confirming that an array is akin to a pointer. Lines 12 and 15 demonstrate that the address stored in the pointer is the same as the address where the first element in the array (at index 0) is placed in memory. This program demonstrates that an array is a pointer to the first element in it.

Should you need to access the second element via the expression myNumbers[1], you can also access the same using the pointer pointToNums with the syntax *(pointToNums + 1). The third element is accessed in the static array using myNumbers[2], whereas the third element is accessed in the dynamic array using the syntax *(pointToNums + 2).

Because array variables are essentially pointers, it should be possible to use the de-reference operator (*) that you have used with pointers to work with arrays. Similarly, it should be possible to use the array operator ([]) to work with pointers as demonstrated by Listing 8.12.

LISTING 8.12 Accessing Elements in an Array Using the Dereference Operator (*) and Using the Array Operator ([]) with a Pointer

```
0: #include <iostream>
1: using namespace std;
2:
3: int main()
4: {
5:     const int ARRAY_LEN = 5;
6:
7:     // Static array of 5 integers, initialized
8:     int myNumbers[ARRAY_LEN] = {24, -1, 365, -999, 2011};
9:
10:     // Pointer initialized to first element in array
11:     int* pointToNums = myNumbers;
12:
13:     cout << "Display array using pointer syntax, operator*" << endl;
14:     for (int index = 0; index < ARRAY_LEN; ++index)
15:         cout << "Element " << index << " = " << *(myNumbers + index) << endl;
16:
17:     cout << "Display array using ptr with array syntax, operator[]" << endl;
18:     for (int index = 0; index < ARRAY_LEN; ++index)
19:         cout << "Element " << index << " = " << pointToNums[index] << endl;
20:
21:     return 0;
22: }
```

Output ▼

```
Display array using pointer syntax, operator*
Element 0 = 24
Element 1 = -1
Element 2 = 365
Element 3 = -999
Element 4 = 2011
Display array using ptr with array syntax, operator[]
Element 0 = 24
Element 1 = -1
Element 2 = 365
Element 3 = -999
Element 4 = 2011
```

Analysis ▼

The application contains a static array of five integers initialized to five initial values in Line 8. The application displays the contents of this array, using two alternative routes—one using the array variable myNumbers with the indirection operator (*) in Line 15 and the other using the pointer variable with the array operator ([]) in Line 19.

Thus, what this program demonstrates is that both array myNumbers and pointer pointToNums actually exhibit pointer behavior. In other words, an array declaration is similar to a pointer that will be created to operate within a fixed range of memory. Note that one can assign an array to a pointer as in Line 11, but one cannot assign a pointer to an array. This is because by its very nature, an array like myNumbers is static and cannot be used as an l-value. myNumbers cannot be modified.

> **CAUTION**
>
> It is important to remember that pointers that are allocated dynamically using operator new still need to be released using operator delete, even if you accessed data using syntax commonly used with static arrays.
>
> If you forget this, your application leaks memory, and that's bad.

Common Programming Mistakes When Using Pointers

C++ enables you to allocate memory dynamically so that you can optimize and control the memory consumption of your application. Unlike newer languages such as C# and Java that are based on a runtime environment, C++ does not feature an automatic garbage collector that cleans up the memory your program has allocated but can't use. This incredible control over managing memory resources using pointers is accompanied by a host of opportunities to make mistakes.

Memory Leaks

This is probably one of the most frequent problems with C++ applications: The longer they run, the larger the amount of memory they consume and the slower the system gets. This typically happens when the programmer did not ensure that his application releases memory allocated dynamically using new with a matching call to delete after the block of memory is no longer required.

It is up to you—the programmer—to ensure that all allocated memory is also released by your application. Something like this should never be allowed to happen:

```
int* pointToNums = new int[5]; // initial allocation
// use pointToNums
...
// forget to release using delete[] pointToNums;
...
// make another allocation and overwrite
pointToNums = new int[10]; // leaks the previously allocated memory
```

8

When Pointers Don't Point to Valid Memory Locations

When you dereference a pointer using operator (*) to access the pointed value, you need to be sure that the pointer contains a valid memory location, or else your program will either crash or misbehave. Logical as this may seem, invalid pointers are quite a common reason for application crashes. Pointers can be invalid for a range of reasons, primarily due to poor programming and memory management. A typical case where a pointer might be invalid is shown in Listing 8.13.

LISTING 8.13 Poor Pointer Hygiene in a Program That Stores a Boolean Value Using Pointers

```
0: #include <iostream>
1: using namespace std;
2:
3: int main()
4: {
5:    // uninitialized pointer (bad)
6:    bool* isSunny;
7:
8:    cout << "Is it sunny (y/n)? ";
9:    char userInput = 'y';
10:   cin >> userInput;
11:
12:   if (userInput == 'y')
13:   {
14:      isSunny = new bool;
15:      *isSunny = true;
16:   }
17:
18:   // isSunny contains invalid value if user entered 'n'
19:   cout << "Boolean flag sunny says: " << *isSunny << endl;
20:
21:   // delete being invoked also when new wasn't
```

```
22:     delete isSunny;
23:
24:     return 0;
25: }
```

Output ▼

```
Is it sunny (y/n)? y
Boolean flag sunny says: 1
```

Second run:

```
Is it sunny (y/n)? n
<CRASH!>
```

Analysis ▼

There are many problems in the program, some already commented in the code. Note how memory is allocated and assigned to the pointer in Line 14, which is conditionally executed when the user presses 'y' for yes. For all other inputs of the user, this `if` block is not executed, and the pointer `isSunny` remains invalid. Thus, when the user presses 'n' in the second run, the application crashes because `isSunny` contains an invalid memory address and dereferencing an invalid pointer in Line 19 causes problems.

Similarly, invoking `delete` on this pointer, which has not been allocated for using `new` as seen in Line 22, is equally wrong. Note that if you have a copy of a pointer, you need to be calling `delete` on only one of them (you also need to avoid having copies of a pointer floating around).

A better (safer, more stable) version of this program would be one where pointers are initialized, used where their values are valid, and released only once but only when valid.

Dangling Pointers (Also Called Stray or Wild Pointers)

Note that any valid pointer is invalid after it has been released using `delete`. In other words, even a valid pointer `isSunny` in Listing 8.13 would be invalid after the call to `delete` at Line 22, and should not be used after this point.

To avoid this problem, some programmers follow the convention of assigning NULL to a pointer when initializing it or after it has been deleted. They also always check a pointer for validity (by comparing against NULL) before dereferencing it using operator (*).

Having learned some typical problems when using pointers, it's time to correct the faulty code in Listing 8.13 as seen in Listing 8.14.

LISTING 8.14 Safer Pointer Programming, a Correction of Listing 8.13

8

```
0: #include <iostream>
1: using namespace std;
2:
3: int main()
4: {
5:     cout << "Is it sunny (y/n)? ";
6:     char userInput = 'y';
7:     cin >> userInput;
8:
9:     // declare pointer and initialize
10:    bool* const isSunny = new bool;
11:    *isSunny = true;
12:
13:    if (userInput == 'n')
14:        *isSunny = false;
15:
16:    cout << "Boolean flag sunny says: " << *isSunny << endl;
17:
18:    // release valid memory
19:    delete isSunny;
20:
21:    return 0;
22: }
```

Output ▼

```
Is it sunny (y/n)? y
Boolean flag sunny says: 1
```

Next run:

```
Is it sunny (y/n)? n
Boolean flag sunny says: 0
```

(Ends without crashing, irrespective of user input.)

Analysis ▼

Minor restructuring has made the code safer for all combinations of user input. Note how the pointer is initialized to a valid memory address during declaration in Line 10. We used `const` to ensure that while the data being pointed to can be modified, the pointer value (address contained) remains fixed and unchangeable. We also initialized the Boolean value being pointed to, to `true` in Line 11. This data initialization doesn't add to the stability of the program but to the reliability of the output. These steps ensure that the pointer is valid for the rest of the program, and it is safely deleted in Line 19, for every combination of user input.

Checking Whether Allocation Request Using `new` Succeeded

In our code to this point, we have assumed that new will return a valid pointer to a block of memory. Indeed, new usually succeeds unless the application asks for an unusually large amount of memory or if the system is in such a critical state that it has no memory to spare. There are applications that need to make requests for large chunks of memory (for example, database applications). Additionally, it is good to not simply assume that memory allocation requests will always be successful. C++ provides you with two possible methods to ensure that your pointer is valid before you use it. The default method—one that we have been using thus far—uses *exceptions* wherein unsuccessful allocations result in an exception of the type `std::bad_alloc` to be *thrown*. An exception results in the execution of your application being disrupted, and unless you have programmed an `exception handler`, your application ends rather unelegantly with an error message "unhandled exception."

Exceptions are explained in detail in Lesson 28, "Exception Handling." Listing 8.15 gives you a sneak peek of how exception handling can be used to check for failed memory allocation requests. Don't be too worried if exception handling seems overwhelming at this stage—it's mentioned here only for the sake of completeness of the topic of memory allocations. You may revisit this sample again, after covering Lesson 28.

LISTING 8.15 Handle Exceptions, Exit Gracefully When `new` Fails

```
 0: #include <iostream>
 1: using namespace std;
 2:
 3: // remove the try-catch block to see this application crash
 4: int main()
 5: {
 6:    try
 7:    {
 8:       // Request a LOT of memory!
 9:       int* pointsToManyNums = new int [0x1fffffff];
10:       // Use the allocated memory
11:
```

```
12:        delete[] pointsToManyNums;
13:    }
14:    catch (bad_alloc)
15:    {
16:        cout << "Memory allocation failed. Ending program" << endl;
17:    }
18:    return 0;
19: }
```

8

Output ▼

```
Memory allocation failed. Ending program
```

Analysis ▼

This program might execute differently on your computer. My environment could not successfully allocate the requested space for 536870911 integers! Had I not programmed an exception handler (the `catch` block you see in Lines 14–17), the program would have ended disgracefully. You may experiment with the behavior of the program in the absence of the exception handler by commenting Lines 6, 7, and 13–17. When using debug mode binaries built using Microsoft Visual Studio, program execution results in output as shown in Figure 8.2.

FIGURE 8.2
Program crash in absence of exception handling in Listing 8.15 (debug build using MSVC compiler).

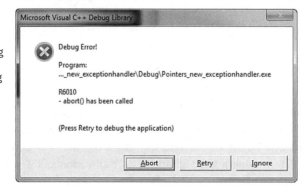

The exception handling `try-catch` construct thus helped the application in making a controlled exit after informing the user that a problem in memory allocation hampers normal execution.

For those who don't want to rely on exceptions, there is a variant of new called new(nothrow). This variant does not throw an exception when allocation requests fail, rather it results in the operator new returning NULL. The pointer being assigned, therefore, can be checked for validity against NULL before it is used. See Listing 8.16.

LISTING 8.16 Using new(nothrow) That Returns NULL When Allocation Fails

```
 0: #include <iostream>
 1: using namespace std;
 2:
 3: int main()
 4: {
 5:     // Request LOTS of memory space, use nothrow
 6:     int* pointsToManyNums = new(nothrow) int [0x1fffffff];
 7:
 8:     if (pointsToManyNums) // check pointsToManyNums != NULL
 9:     {
10:         // Use the allocated memory
11:         delete[] pointsToManyNums;
12:     }
13:     else
14:         cout << "Memory allocation failed. Ending program" << endl;
15:
16:     return 0;
17: }
```

Output ▼

```
Memory allocation failed. Ending program
```

Analysis ▼

Listing 8.16 is the same function as Listing 8.15 with the exception that this uses new(nothrow). As this variant of new returns NULL when memory allocation fails, we check the pointer before using it as seen in Line 8. Both variants of new are good, and the choice is for you to make.

Pointer Programming Best-Practices

There are some basic rules when it comes to using pointers in your application that will make living with them easier.

DO	DON'T
DO always initialize pointer variables, or else they will contain junk values. These junk values are interpreted as address locations—ones your application is not authorized to access. If you cannot initialize a pointer to a valid address returned by `new` during variable declaration, initialize to `NULL`.	**DON'T** access a block of memory or use a pointer after it has been released using `delete`.
	DON'T invoke `delete` on a memory address more than once.
DO ensure that your application is programmed in a way that pointers are used when their validity is assured, or else your program might encounter a crash.	**DON'T** leak memory by forgetting to invoke `delete` when done using an allocated block of memory.
DO remember to release memory allocated using `new` by using `delete`, or else your application will leak memory and reduce system performance.	

What Is a Reference?

A reference is an alias for a variable. When you declare a reference, you need to initialize it to a variable. Thus, the reference variable is just a different way to access the data stored in the variable being referenced.

You would declare a reference using the reference operator (&) as seen in the following statement:

```
VarType original = Value;
VarType& ReferenceVariable = original;
```

To further understand how to declare references and use them, see Listing 8.17.

LISTING 8.17 Demonstrating That References Are Aliases for the Assigned Value

```
0: #include <iostream>
1: using namespace std;
2:
3: int main()
```

```
4: {
5:    int original = 30;
6:    cout << "original = " << original << endl;
7:    cout << "original is at address: " << hex << &original << endl;
8:
9:    int& ref1 = original;
10:   cout << "ref1 is at address: " << hex << &ref1 << endl;
11:
12:   int& ref2 = ref1;
13:   cout << "ref2 is at address: " << hex << &ref2 << endl;
14:   cout << "Therefore, ref2 = " << dec << ref2 << endl;
15:
16:   return 0;
17: }
```

Output ▼

```
original = 30
original is at address: 0099F764
ref1 is at address: 0099F764
ref2 is at address: 0099F764
Therefore, ref2 = 30
```

Analysis ▼

The output demonstrates that references, irrespective of whether they're initialized to the original variable as seen in Line 9 or to a reference as seen in Line 12, address the same location in memory where the original is contained. Thus, references are true aliases—that is, just another name for original. Displaying the value using ref2 in Line 14 gets the same value as the original in Line 6 because ref2 aliases original and is contained in the same location in memory.

What Makes References Useful?

References enable you to work with the memory location they are initialized to. This makes references particularly useful when programming functions. As you learned in Lesson 7, "Organizing Code with Functions," a typical function is declared like this:

```
ReturnType DoSomething(Type parameter);
```

Function DoSomething() is invoked like this:

```
ReturnType Result = DoSomething(argument); // function call
```

The preceding code would result in the argument being copied into `Parameter`, which is then used by the function `DoSomething()`. This copying step can be quite an overhead if the `argument` in question consumes a lot of memory. Similarly, when `DoSomething()` returns a value, it is copied again into `Result`. It would be ideal if we could avoid or eliminate the copy steps, enabling the function to work directly on the data in the caller's stack. References enable you to do just that.

A version of the function without the copy step looks like this:

```
ReturnType DoSomething(Type& parameter); // note the reference&
```

This function would be invoked as the following:

```
ReturnType Result = DoSomething(argument);
```

As the argument is being passed by reference, `Parameter` is not a copy of `argument` rather an alias of the latter, much like `Ref` in Listing 8.17. Additionally, a function that accepts a parameter as a reference can optionally return values using reference parameters. See Listing 8.18 to understand how functions can use references instead of return values.

LISTING 8.18 Function That Calculates Square Returned in a Parameter by Reference

```
 0: #include <iostream>
 1: using namespace std;
 2:
 3: void GetSquare(int& number)
 4: {
 5:     number *= number;
 6: }
 7:
 8: int main()
 9: {
10:     cout << "Enter a number you wish to square: ";
11:     int number = 0;
12:     cin >> number;
13:
14:     GetSquare(number);
15:     cout << "Square is: " << number << endl;
16:
17:     return 0;
18: }
```

Output ▼

```
Enter a number you wish to square: 5
Square is: 25
```

Analysis ▼

The function that performs the operation of squaring is in Lines 3–6. Note how it accepts the number to be squared as a parameter by reference and returns the result in the same. Had you forgotten to mark the parameter `number` as a reference (&), the result would not reach the calling function `main()` as `GetSquare()` would then perform its operations on a local copy of `number` and that would be destroyed when the function exits. Using references, you ensure that `GetSquare()` is operating in the same address space where `number` in `main()` is defined. Thus, the result of the operation is available in `main()` even after the function `GetSquare()` has exited.

In this sample, the input parameter containing the number sent by the user has been modified. If you need both values, the original and the square, you can have the function accept two parameters: one that contains the input and the other that supplies the square.

Using Keyword `const` on References

You might need to have references that are not allowed to change the value of the original variable being aliased. Using `const` when declaring such references is the way to achieve that:

```
int original = 30;
const int& constRef = original;
constRef = 40; // Not allowed: constRef can't change value in original
int& ref2 = constRef; // Not allowed: ref2 is not const
const int& constRef2 = constRef; // OK
```

Passing Arguments by Reference to Functions

One of the major advantages of references is that they allow a called function to work on parameters that have not been copied from the calling function, resulting in significant performance improvements. However, as the called function works using parameters directly on the stack of the calling function, it is often important to ensure that the called function cannot change the value of the variable at the caller's end. References that are defined as `const` help you do just that, as demonstrated by Listing 8.19. A `const` reference parameter cannot be used as an l-value, so any attempt at assigning to it causes a compilation failure.

LISTING 8.19 Using `const` Reference to Ensure That the Calling Function Cannot Modify a Value Sent by Reference

```
0: #include <iostream>
1: using namespace std;
2:
3: void GetSquare(const int& number, int& result)
4: {
5:     result = number*number;
6: }
7:
8: int main()
9: {
10:     cout << "Enter a number you wish to square: ";
11:     int number = 0;
12:     cin >> number;
13:
14:     int square = 0;
15:     GetSquare(number, square);
16:     cout << number << "^2 = " << square << endl;
17:
18:     return 0;
19: }
```

Output ▼

```
Enter a number you wish to square: 27
27^2 = 729
```

Analysis ▼

In contrast to the program in Listing 8.18 where the variable that sent the number to be squared also held the result, this one uses two variables—one to send the number to be squared and the other to hold the result of the operation. To ensure that the number being sent cannot be modified, it has been marked as a `const` reference using the `const` keyword, as shown in Line 3. This automatically makes parameter `number` an input parameter—one whose value cannot be modified.

As an experiment, you may modify Line 5 to return the square using the same logic shown in the Listing 8.18:

```
number *= number;
```

You are certain to face a compilation error that tells you that a `const` value cannot be modified. Thus, `const` references indicate that a parameter is an input parameter and ensure that its value cannot be modified. It might seem trivial at first, but in a multiprogrammer environment where the person writing the first version might be different from the one enhancing it, using `const` references will add to the quality of the program.

Summary

In this lesson you learned about pointers and references. You learned how pointers can be used to access and manipulate memory and how they're a tool that assists in dynamic memory allocation. You learned operators `new` and `delete` that can be used to allocate memory for an element. You learned that their variants `new…[]` and `delete[]` help you allocate memory for an array of data. You were introduced to traps in pointer programming and dynamic allocation and found out that releasing dynamically allocated memory is important to avoiding leaks. References are aliases and are a powerful alternative to using pointers when passing arguments to functions in that references are guaranteed to be valid. You learned of "const correctness" when using pointers and references, and will hopefully henceforth declare functions with the most restrictive level of `const`-ness in parameters as possible.

Q&A

Q Why dynamically allocate when you can do with static arrays where you don't need to worry about deallocation?

A Static arrays have a fixed size and will neither scale upward if your application needs more memory nor will they optimize if your application needs less. This is where dynamic memory allocation makes a difference.

Q I have two pointers:

```
int* pointToAnInt = new int;
int* pCopy = pointToAnInt;
```

Am I not better off calling `delete` using both to ensure that the memory is gone?

A That would be wrong. You are allowed to invoke `delete` only once on the address returned by `new`. Also, you would ideally avoid having two pointers pointing to the same address because performing `delete` on any one would invalidate the other. Your program should also not be written in a way that you have any uncertainty about the validity of pointers used.

Q When should I use `new(nothrow)`?

A If you don't want to handle the exception `std::bad_alloc`, you use the `nothrow` version of operator `new` that returns NULL if the requested allocation fails.

Q I can call a function to calculate area using the following two methods:

```
void CalculateArea (const double* const ptrRadius, double* const
ptrArea);
void CalculateArea (const double& radius, double& area);
```

Which variant should I prefer?

A Use the latter one using references, as references cannot be invalid, whereas pointers can be. Besides, it's simpler, too.

Q I have a pointer:

```
int number = 30;
const int* pointToAnInt = &number;
```

I understand that I cannot change the value of number **using the pointer** pointToAnInt **due to the** const **declaration. Can I assign** pointToAnInt **to a non-**const **pointer and then use it to manipulate the value contained in integer** number?

A No, you cannot change the const-correctness of the pointer:

```
int* pAnother = pointToAnInt; // cannot assign pointer to const to a
non-const
```

Q Why should I bother passing values to a function by reference?

A You don't need to so long as it doesn't affect your program performance much. However, if your function parameters accept objects that are quite heavy (large in bytes), then passing by value would be quite an expensive operation. Your function call would be a lot more efficient in using references. Remember to use const generously, except where the function needs to store a result in a variable.

Q What is the difference between these two declarations:

```
int myNumbers[100];
int* myArrays[100];
```

A myNumbers is an array of integers—that is, myNumbers is a pointer to a memory location that holds 100 integers, pointing to the first at index 0. It is the static alternative of the following:

```
int* myNumbers = new int [100]; // dynamically allocated array
// use myNumbers
delete[] myNumbers;
```

myArrays, on the other hand, is an array of 100 pointers, each pointer being capable of pointing to an integer or an array of integers.

Workshop

The Workshop provides quiz questions to help you solidify your understanding of the material covered and exercises to provide you with experience in using what you've learned. Try to answer the quiz and exercise questions before checking the answers in Appendix E, and be certain you understand the answers before continuing to the next lesson.

Quiz

1. Why can't you assign a const reference to a non-const reference?

2. Are new and delete functions?

3. What is the nature of value contained in a pointer variable?

4. What operator would you use to access the data pointed by a pointer?

Exercises

1. What is the display when these statements are executed:

```
0: int number = 3;
1: int* pNum1 = &number;
2: *pNum1 = 20;
3: int* pNum2 = pNum1;
4: number *= 2;
5: cout << *pNum2;
```

2. What are the similarities and differences between these three overloaded functions:

```
int DoSomething(int num1, int num2);
int DoSomething(int& num1, int& num2);
int DoSomething(int* pNum1, int* pNum2);
```

3. How would you change the declaration of pNum1 in Exercise 1 at Line 1 so as to make the assignment at Line 3 invalid? (*Hint:* It has something to do with ensuring that pNum1 cannot change the data pointed to.)

4. **BUG BUSTERS:** What is wrong with this code?

```
#include <iostream>
using namespace std;
int main()
{
    int *pointToAnInt = new int;
    pointToAnInt = 9;
    cout << "The value at pointToAnInt: " << *pointToAnInt;
    delete pointToAnInt;
    return 0;
}
```

5. BUG BUSTERS: What is wrong with this code?

```
#include <iostream>
using namespace std;
int main()
{
    int pointToAnInt = new int;
    int* pNumberCopy = pointToAnInt;
    *pNumberCopy = 30;
    cout << *pointToAnInt;
    delete pNumberCopy;
    delete pointToAnInt;
    return 0;
}
```

6. What is the output of the above program when corrected?

8

LESSON 9
Classes and Objects

So far you have explored simple programs that start execution at `main()`, comprise local and global variables and constants, and feature execution logic organized into function modules that take parameters and return values. Our programming style thus far has been *procedural*, and we haven't observed an object-oriented approach yet. In other words, you need to now learn the basics of object-oriented programming using C++.

In this lesson, you learn

- What classes and objects are
- How classes help you consolidate data with functions that work on them
- About constructors, copy constructors, and the destructor
- What the move constructor is
- Object-oriented concepts of encapsulation and abstraction
- What the `this` pointer is about
- What a `struct` is and how it differs from `class`

The Concept of Classes and Objects

Imagine you are writing a program that models a human being, like yourself. This human being needs to have an identity: a name, date of birth, place of birth, and gender—information that makes him or her unique. Additionally, the human can perform certain functions, such as talk and introduce him- or herself, among others. Thus, a human being can also be modeled as illustrated by Figure 9.1.

FIGURE 9.1
A broad representation of a human.

Human Being

Data
- Gender
- Date of birth
- Place of birth
- Name

Methods
- IntroduceSelf()
- ...

To model a human in a program, what you now need is a construct that enables you to group within it the attributes that define a human (data) and the activities a human can perform (functions) using the available attributes. This construct is the *class*.

Declaring a Class

You declare a class using the keyword `class` followed by the name of the class, followed by a statement block {...} that encloses a set of member attributes and member functions within curly braces, and finally terminated by a semicolon ';'.

A declaration of a class tells the compiler about the class and its properties. Declaration of a class alone does not make a difference to the execution of a program, as the class needs to be used just the same way as a function would need to be invoked.

A class that models a human looks like the following (ignore syntactic short-comings for the moment):

```
class Human
{
    // Member attributes:
    string name;
    string dateOfBirth;
    string placeOfBirth;
    string gender;

    // Member functions:
    void Talk(string textToTalk);
    void IntroduceSelf();
    ...
};
```

Needless to say, `IntroduceSelf()` uses `Talk()` and some of the data attributes that are grouped within `class Human`. Thus, in keyword `class`, C++ has provided you with a powerful way to create your own data type that allows you to *encapsulate* attributes and functions that work using those. All attributes of a class, in this case `name`, `dateOfBirth`, `placeOfBirth`, and `gender`, and all functions declared within it, namely `Talk()` and `IntroduceSelf()`, are called members of class `Human`.

Encapsulation, which is the ability to logically group data and functions that work using it, is an important property of object-oriented programming.

> **NOTE**
>
> You may often encounter the term *method*—these are essentially functions that are members of a `class`.

An Object as an Instance of a Class

A class is like a blueprint, and declaring a class alone has no effect on the execution of a program. The real-world avatar of a class at program execution time is an *object*. To use the features of a class, you typically create an instance of that class, called an object. You use that object to access its member methods and attributes.

Creating an object of type `class` `Human` is similar to creating an instance of another type, say `double`:

```
double pi= 3.1415;  // a variable of type double
Human  firstMan;  // firstMan: an object of class Human
```

Alternatively, you would dynamically create an instance of `class` `Human` using `new` as you would for another type, say an `int`:

```
int* pointsToNum = new int;  // an integer allocated dynamically
delete pointsToNum;  // de-allocating memory when done using
```

```
Human* firstWoman = new Human(); // dynamically allocated Human
delete firstWoman;  // de-allocating memory
```

Accessing Members Using the Dot Operator (.)

An example of a human would be Adam, male, born in 1970 in Alabama. Instance `firstMan` is an object of `class` `Human`, an avatar of the class that exists in reality, that is at runtime:

```
Human  firstMan;  // an instance i.e. object of Human
```

As the class declaration demonstrates, `firstMan` has attributes such as `dateOfBirth` that can be accessed using the dot operator (.):

```
firstMan.dateOfBirth = "1970";
```

This is because attribute `dateOfBirth` belongs to class `Human`, being a part of its blueprint as seen in the class declaration. This attribute exists in reality—that is, at runtime—only when an object has been instantiated. The dot operator (.) helps you access attributes of an object.

Ditto for methods such as `IntroduceSelf()`:

```
firstMan.IntroduceSelf();
```

If you have a pointer `firstWoman` to an instance of `class` `Human`, you can either use the pointer operator (->) to access members, as explained in the next section, or use the indirection operator (*) to reference the object following the dot operator.

```
Human* firstWoman = new Human();
(*firstWoman).IntroduceSelf();
```

> **NOTE**
>
> Naming conventions continue to apply. A class name and member functions are declared in Pascal case, for example, `IntroduceSelf()`. Class member attributes are in camel case, for example, `dateOfBirth`.
>
> When we instantiate an object of a class, we declare a variable with type as that class. We therefore use camel case, which we have been using for variable names thus far, for example, `firstMan`.

Accessing Members Using the Pointer Operator (->)

If an object has been instantiated on the free store using `new` or if you have a pointer to an object, then you use the pointer operator (->) to access the member attributes and functions:

```
Human* firstWoman = new Human();
firstWoman->dateOfBirth = "1970";
firstWoman->IntroduceSelf();
delete firstWoman;
```

A compile-worthy form of `class` Human featuring a new keyword `public` is demonstrated by Listing 9.1.

LISTING 9.1   A Compile-worthy Class Human

```
0: #include <iostream>
1: #include <string>
2: using namespace std;
3:
4: class Human
5: {
6: public:
7:     string name;
8:     int age;
9:
10:     void IntroduceSelf()
11:     {
12:         cout << "I am " + name << " and am ";
13:        cout << age << " years old" << endl;
14:     }
15: };
16:
17: int main()
18: {
19:     // An object of class Human with attribute name as "Adam"
20:     Human firstMan;
```

```
21:     firstMan.name = "Adam";
22:     firstMan.age = 30;
23:
24:     // An object of class Human with attribute name as "Eve"
25:     Human firstWoman;
26:     firstWoman.name = "Eve";
27:     firstWoman.age = 28;
28:
29:     firstMan.IntroduceSelf();
30:     firstWoman.IntroduceSelf();
31: }
```

Output ▼

```
I am Adam and am 30 years old
I am Eve and am 28 years old
```

Analysis ▼

Lines 4–15 demonstrate a basic C++ `class Human`. Note the structure of `class Human` and how this class has been utilized in `main()`.

This class contains two member variables, one of type `string` called `name` at Line 7 and another of type `int` called `age` at Line 8. It also contains a function (also called method) `IntroduceSelf()` at Lines 10–14. Lines 20 and 25 in `main()` instantiate two objects of class `Human`, named `firstMan` and `firstWoman`, respectively. The lines following this instantiation of objects set the member variables of the objects `firstMan` and `firstWoman` using `operator`, which has been explained shortly before. Note how Lines 29 and 30 invoke the same function `IntroduceSelf()` on the two objects to create two distinct lines in the output. In a way this program demonstrates how objects `firstMan` and `firstWoman` are unique and individually distinct real-world representatives of an abstract type defined by a `class Human`.

Did you notice the keyword `public` in Listing 9.1? It's time you learned features that help you protect attributes your class should keep hidden from those using it.

Keywords `public` **and** `private`

Information can be classified into at least two categories: data that we don't mind the *public* knowing and data that is *private*. Gender, for most people, is an example of information that we may not mind sharing. However, income may be a private matter.

C++ enables you to model class attributes and methods as public or private. Public class members can be used by anyone in possession of an object of the class. Private class members can be used only within the class (or its "friends"). C++ keywords public and private help you as the designer of a class decide what parts of a class can be invoked from outside it, for instance, from main(), and what cannot.

What advantages does this ability to mark attributes or methods as private present you as the programmer? Consider the declaration of class Human ignoring all but the member attribute age:

```cpp
class Human
{
private:
    // Private member data:
    int age;
    string name;

public:
    int GetAge()
    {
        return age;
    }

    void SetAge(int humansAge)
    {
        age = humansAge;
    }

// ...Other members and declarations
};
```

Assume an instance of a Human called Eve:

```cpp
Human eve;
```

When the user of this instance tries to access member age:

```cpp
cout << eve.age; // compile error
```

then this user would get a compile error akin to "Error: Human::age—cannot access private member declared in class Human." The only permissible way to know the age would be to ask for it via public method GetAge() supplied by class Human and implemented in a way the programmer of the class thought was an appropriate way to expose the age:

```cpp
cout << eve.GetAge(); // OK
```

If the programmer of class Human so desires, he could use GetAge() to show Eve as younger than she is! In other words, this means C++ allows the class to control what attributes it wants to expose and how it wants to expose the same. If there were no

GetAge() public member method implemented by `class Human`, the class would effectively have ensured that the user cannot query `age` at all. This feature can be useful in situations that are explained later in this lesson.

Similarly, `Human::age` cannot be assigned directly either:

```
eve.age = 22; // compile error
```

The only permissible way to set the age is via method `SetAge()`:

```
eve.SetAge(22); // OK
```

This has many advantages. The current implementation of `SetAge()` does nothing but directly set the member variable `Human::age`. However, you can use `SetAge()` to verify the `age` being set is non-zero and not negative and thus validate external input:

```
class Human
{
private:
    int age;

public:
    void SetAge(int humansAge)
    {
        if (humansAge > 0)
            age = humansAge;
    }
};
```

Thus, C++ enables the designer of the class to control how data attributes of the class are accessed and manipulated.

Abstraction of Data via Keyword `private`

While allowing you to design a class as a container that encapsulates data and methods that operate on that data, C++ empowers you to decide what information remains unreachable to the outside world (that is, unavailable outside the class) via keyword `private`. At the same time, you have the possibility to allow controlled access to even information declared `private` via methods that you have declared as `public`. Thus your implementation of a class can abstract member information that classes and functions outside this class don't need to have access to.

Going back to the example related to `Human::age` being a private member, you know that even in reality many people don't like to reveal their true age. If `class Human` was required to tell an age two years younger than the current age, it could do so easily via a public function `GetAge()` that uses the `Human::age` parameter, reduces it by two, and supplies the result as demonstrated by Listing 9.2.

LISTING 9.2   A Model of Class Human Where the True age Is Abstracted from the User and a Younger age Is Reported

```
0: #include <iostream>
1: using namespace std;
2:
3: class Human
4: {
5: private:
6:     // Private member data:
7:     int age;
8:
9: public:
10:     void SetAge(int inputAge)
11:     {
12:         age = inputAge;
13:     }
14:
15:     // Human lies about his / her age (if over 30)
16:     int GetAge()
17:     {
18:         if (age > 30)
19:             return (age - 2);
20:         else
21:             return age;
22:     }
23: };
24:
25: int main()
26: {
27:     Human firstMan;
28:     firstMan.SetAge(35);
29:
30:     Human firstWoman;
31:     firstWoman.SetAge(22);
32:
33:     cout << "Age of firstMan " << firstMan.GetAge() << endl;
34:     cout << "Age of firstWoman " << firstWoman.GetAge() << endl;
35:
36:     return 0;
37: }
```

9

Output ▼

```
Age of firstMan 33
Age of firstWoman 22
```

Analysis ▼

Note the public method `Human::GetAge()` at Line 16. As the actual age contained in private integer member `Human::age` is not directly accessible, the only resort external users of this class have toward querying an object of `class Human` for attribute `age` is via method `GetAge()`. Thus, the actual age held in `Human::age` is abstracted from the outside world. Indeed, our `Human` lies about its age, and `GetAge()` returns a reduced value for all humans that are older than 30, as seen in Lines 18–21!

Abstraction is an important concept in object-oriented languages. It empowers programmers to decide what attributes of a class need to remain known only to the class and its members with nobody outside it (with the exception of those declared as its "friends") having access to it.

Constructors

A *constructor* is a special function (or method) invoked during the instantiation of a class to construct an object. Just like functions, constructors can also be overloaded.

Declaring and Implementing a Constructor

A constructor is a special function that takes the name of the class and returns no value. So, `class Human` would have a constructor that is declared like this:

```
class Human
{
public:
    Human(); // declaration of a constructor
};
```

This constructor can be implemented either inline within the class or externally outside the class declaration. An implementation (also called definition) inside the class looks like this:

```
class Human
{
public:
    Human()
    {
        // constructor code here
    }
};
```

A variant enabling you to define the constructor outside the class' declaration looks like this:

```
class Human
{
public:
   Human(); // constructor declaration
};

// constructor implementation (definition)
Human::Human()
{
   // constructor code here
}
```

9

NOTE

> `::` is called the scope resolution operator. For example, `Human::dateOfBirth` is referring to variable `dateOfBirth` declared within the scope of class `Human`. `::dateOfBirth`, on the other hand would refer to another variable `dateOfBirth` in a global scope.

When and How to Use Constructors

A constructor is always invoked during object creation, when an instance of a class is constructed. This makes a constructor a perfect place for you to initialize class member variables such as integers, pointers, and so on to values you choose. Take a look at Listing 9.2 again. Note that if you had forgotten to `SetAge()`, the integer variable `Human::age` may contain an unknown value as that variable has not been initialized (try it by commenting out Lines 28 and 31). Listing 9.3 uses constructors to implement a better version of class `Human`, where variable `age` has been initialized.

LISTING 9.3 Using Constructors to Initialize Class Member Variables

```
0: #include <iostream>
1: #include <string>
2: using namespace std;
3:
4: class Human
5: {
6: private:
7:    string name;
8:    int age;
9:
```

```
10: public:
11:     Human() // constructor
12:     {
13:         age = 1; // initialization
14:         cout << "Constructed an instance of class Human" << endl;
15:     }
16:
17:     void SetName (string humansName)
18:     {
19:         name = humansName;
20:     }
21:
22:     void SetAge(int humansAge)
23:     {
24:         age = humansAge;
25:     }
26:
27:     void IntroduceSelf()
28:     {
29:         cout << "I am " + name << " and am ";
30:         cout << age << " years old" << endl;
31:     }
32: };
33:
34: int main()
35: {
36:     Human firstWoman;
37:     firstWoman.SetName("Eve");
38:     firstWoman.SetAge (28);
39:
40:     firstWoman.IntroduceSelf();
41: }
```

Output ▼

```
Constructed an instance of class Human
I am Eve and am 28 years old
```

Analysis ▼

In the output you see a new line that indicates object construction. Now, take a look at main() defined in Lines 34–41. You see that the first line in output was the result of the creation (construction) of object firstWoman in Line 36. The constructor Human::Human() in Lines 11–15 contains the cout statement that contributes to this output. Note how the constructor initializes integer age to zero. Should you forget to SetAge() on a newly constructed object, you can rest assured that the constructor would have ensured that the value contained in variable age is not a random integer (that might look valid) but instead a zero.

> **NOTE**
>
> A constructor that is invoked without arguments is called the default constructor. Programming a default constructor is optional.
>
> If you don't program any constructor, as seen in Listing 9.1, the compiler creates one for you (that constructs member attributes but does not initialize Plain Old Data types such as `int` to any specific non-zero value).

Overloading Constructors

Constructors can be overloaded just like functions. We can therefore write a constructor that requires Human to be instantiated with a name as a parameter, for example:

```
class Human
{
public:
    Human()
    {
        // default constructor code here
    }

    Human(string humansName)
    {
        // overloaded constructor code here
    }
};
```

The application of overloaded constructors is demonstrated by Listing 9.4 in creating an object of class Human with a name supplied at the time of construction.

LISTING 9.4   A Class Human with Multiple Constructors

```
 0: #include <iostream>
 1: #include <string>
 2: using namespace std;
 3:
 4: class Human
 5: {
 6: private:
 7:     string name;
 8:     int age;
 9:
10: public:
11:     Human() // default constructor
12:     {
```

```
13:        age = 0; // initialized to ensure no junk value
14:        cout << "Default constructor: name and age not set" << endl;
15:    }
16:
17:    Human(string humansName, int humansAge) // overloaded
18:    {
19:        name = humansName;
20:        age = humansAge;
21:        cout << "Overloaded constructor creates ";
22:        cout << name << " of " << age << " years" << endl;
23:    }
24: };
25:
26: int main()
27: {
28:    Human firstMan; // use default constructor
29:    Human firstWoman ("Eve", 20); // use overloaded constructor
30: }
```

Output ▼

```
Default constructor: name and age not set
Overloaded constructor creates Eve of 20 years
```

Analysis ▼

main() in Lines 26–30 is minimalistic and creates two instances of class Human. firstMan uses the default constructor while firstWoman uses the overloaded constructor supplying name and age at instantiation. The output is the result of object construction only! You may appreciate that if class Human had chosen to not support the default constructor, main() would've had no option but to construct every object of Human using the overloaded constructor that takes name and age as a prerequisite—making it impossible to create a Human without supplying a name or age.

TIP
> You can choose to not implement the default constructor to enforce object instantiation with certain minimal parameters as explained in the next section.

Class Without a Default Constructor

In Listing 9.5, see how class Human without the default constructor enforces the creator to supply a name and age as a prerequisite to creating an object.

LISTING 9.5 A Class with Overloaded Constructor(s) and No Default Constructor

```
0: #include <iostream>
1: #include <string>
2: using namespace std;
3:
4: class Human
5: {
6: private:
7:     string name;
8:     int age;
9:
10: public:
11:     Human(string humansName, int humansAge)
12:     {
13:         name = humansName;
14:         age = humansAge;
15:         cout << "Overloaded constructor creates " << name;
16:         cout << " of age " << age << endl;
17:     }
18:
19:     void IntroduceSelf()
20:     {
21:         cout << "I am " + name << " and am.";
22:         cout << age << " years old" << endl;
23:     }
24: };
25:
26: int main()
27: {
28:     Human firstMan("Adam", 25);
29:     Human firstWoman("Eve", 28);
30:
31:     firstMan.IntroduceSelf();
32:     firstWoman.IntroduceSelf();
33: }
```

Output ▼

```
Overloaded constructor creates Adam of age 25
Overloaded constructor creates Eve of age 28
I am Adam and am 25 years old
I am Eve and am 28 years old
```

Analysis ▼

This version of `class Human` has only one constructor that takes a `string` and an `int` as input parameters, as seen in Line 11. There is no default constructor available, and given the presence of an overloaded constructor, the C++ compiler does not generate a default constructor for you. This sample also demonstrates the ability to create an object of `class Human` with `name` and `age` set at instantiation, and no possibility to change it afterward. This is because the name attribute of the `Human` is stored as a `private` variable. `Human::name` cannot be accessed or modified by `main()` or by any entity that is not a member of `class Human`. In other words, the user of `class Human` is forced by the overloaded constructor to specify a name (and age) for every object he creates and is not allowed to change that name. This models a real-world scenario quite well, don't you think? You were named at birth; people are allowed to know your name, but nobody (except you) has the authority to change it.

Constructor Parameters with Default Values

Just the same way as functions can have parameters with default values specified, so can constructors. What you see in the following code is a slightly modified version of the constructor from Listing 9.5 at Line 11 where the `age` parameter has a default value of 25:

```
class Human
{
private:
   string name;
   int age;

public:
   // overloaded constructor (no default constructor)
   Human(string humansName, int humansAge = 25)
   {
      name = humansName;
      age = humansAge;
      cout << "Overloaded constructor creates " << name;
      cout << " of age " << age << endl;
   }

   // ... other members
};
```

Such a class can be instantiated with the syntax:

```
Human adam("Adam"); // adam.age is assigned a default value 25
Human eve("Eve, 18); // eve.age is assigned 18 as specified
```

NOTE

Note that a default constructor is one that can be instantiated without arguments, and not necessarily one that doesn't take parameters. So, this constructor with two parameters, both with default values, is a default constructor:

```cpp
class Human
{
private:
    string name;
    int age;

public:
    // default values for both parameters
    Human(string humansName = "Adam", int humansAge = 25)
    {
        name = humansName;
        age = humansAge;
        cout << "Overloaded constructor creates ";
        cout << name << " of age " << age;
    }
};
```

The reason is that `class Human` can still be instantiated without arguments:

```cpp
Human adam; // Human takes default name "Adam", age 25
```

Constructors with Initialization Lists

You have seen how useful constructors are in initializing member variables. Another way to initialize members is by using *initialization lists*. A variant of the constructor in Listing 9.5 using initialization lists would look like this:

```cpp
class Human
{
private:
    string name;
    int age;
```

```
public:
    // two parameters to initialize members age and name
    Human(string humansName, int humansAge)
        :name(humansName), age(humansAge)
    {
        cout << "Constructed a human called " << name;
        cout << ", " << age << " years old" << endl;
    }
// ... other class members
};
```

Thus, the initialization list is characterized by a colon (:) following the parameter declaration contained in parentheses (...), followed by an individual member variable and the value it is initialized to. This initialization value can be a parameter such as humansName or can even be a fixed value. Initialization lists can also be useful in invoking base class constructors with specific arguments. These are discussed again in Lesson 10, "Implementing Inheritance."

You can see a version of class Human that features a default constructor with parameters, default values, and an initialization list in Listing 9.6.

LISTING 9.6   Default Constructor That Accepts Parameters with Default Values to Set Members Using Initialization Lists

```
 0: #include <iostream>
 1: #include <string>
 2: using namespace std;
 3:
 4: class Human
 5: {
 6: private:
 7:     int age;
 8:     string name;
 9:
10: public:
11:     Human(string humansName = "Adam", int humansAge = 25)
12:          :name(humansName), age(humansAge)
13:     {
14:         cout << "Constructed a human called " << name;
15:         cout << ", " << age << " years old" << endl;
16:     }
17: };
18:
```

```
19: int main()
20: {
21:     Human adam;
22:     Human eve("Eve", 18);
23:
24:     return 0;
25: }
```

Output ▼

```
Constructed a human called Adam, 25 years old
Constructed a human called Eve, 18 years old
```

9

Analysis ▼

The constructor with initialization lists is seen in Lines 11–16, where you can also see that the parameters have been given default values "Adam" for name and 25 for age. Hence, when an instance of class Human called adam is created in Line 21, without arguments, its members are automatically assigned the default values. eve, on the other hand, has been supplied with arguments as shown in Line 22—these arguments become values that are assigned to Human::name and Human::age during construction.

NOTE

> It is possible to define a constructor as a constant expression too, using keyword constexpr. In special cases where such a construct would be useful from a performance point of view, you would use it at the constructor declaration.
>
> ```
> class Sample
> {
> const char* someString;
> public:
>     constexpr Sample(const char* input)
>                     : someString(input)
>     { // constructor code }
> };
> ```

Destructor

A destructor, like a constructor, is a special function, too. A constructor is invoked at object instantiation, and a destructor is automatically invoked when an object is destroyed.

Declaring and Implementing a Destructor

The destructor looks like a function that takes the name of the class, yet has a tilde (~) preceding it. So, `class Human` would have a destructor that is declared like this:

```
class Human
{
    ~Human(); // declaration of a destructor
};
```

This destructor can either be implemented inline in the class or externally outside the class declaration. An implementation or definition inside the class looks like this:

```
class Human
{
public:
    ~Human()
    {
        // destructor code here
    }
};
```

A variant enabling you to define the destructor outside the class's declaration looks like this:

```
class Human
{
public:
    ~Human(); // destructor declaration
};

// destructor definition (implementation)
Human::~Human()
{
    // destructor code here
}
```

As you can see, the declaration of the destructor differs from that of the constructor slightly in that this contains a tilde (~). The role of the destructor is, however, diametrically opposite to that of the constructor.

When and How to Use a Destructor

A destructor is always invoked when an object of a class is destroyed when it goes out of scope or is deleted via `delete`. This property makes a destructor the ideal place to reset variables and release dynamically allocated memory and other resources.

This book has recommended the usage of std::string over a char* buffer, so that you don't need to worry about managing memory allocation and timely deallocation yourself. std::string and other such utilities are nothing but classes themselves that make use of constructors and the destructor (in addition to operators, which you study in Lesson 12, "Operator Types and Operator Overloading") in taking away the work of allocation, deallocation, and memory management from you. Analyze a sample class MyString as shown in Listing 9.7 that allocates memory for a character string in the constructor and releases it in the destructor.

LISTING 9.7 A Simple Class That Encapsulates a Character Buffer to Ensure Deallocation via the Destructor

9

```
0: #include <iostream>
1: #include <string.h>
2: using namespace std;
3: class MyString
4: {
5: private:
6:    char* buffer;
7:
8: public:
9:    MyString(const char* initString)   // constructor
10:    {
11:       if(initString != NULL)
12:       {
13:          buffer = new char [strlen(initString) + 1];
14:          strcpy(buffer, initString);
15:       }
16:       else
17:          buffer = NULL;
18:    }
19:
20:    ~MyString()
21:    {
22:       cout << "Invoking destructor, clearing up" << endl;
23:       if (buffer != NULL)
24:          delete [] buffer;
25:    }
26:
27:    int GetLength()
28:    {
29:       return strlen(buffer);
30:    }
31:
32:    const char* GetString()
33:    {
34:       return buffer;
35:    }
```

```
36: };
37:
38: int main()
39: {
40:     MyString sayHello("Hello from String Class");
41:     cout << "String buffer in sayHello is " << sayHello.GetLength();
42:     cout << " characters long" << endl;
43:
44:     cout << "Buffer contains: " << sayHello.GetString() << endl;
45: }
```

Output ▼

```
String buffer in sayHello is 23 characters long
Buffer contains: Hello from String Class
Invoking destructor, clearing up
```

Analysis ▼

This class basically encapsulates a C-style string in MyString::buffer and relieves you of the task of allocating memory; it deallocates the same every time you need to use a string. The lines of utmost interest to us are the constructor MyString() in Lines 9–18, and the destructor ~MyString() in Lines 20–25. The constructor enforces construction with an input string via a compulsory input parameter and then copies it to the character buffer after allocating memory for it using new and strlen in Line 13. strlen is a function supplied by the standard library that helps determine the length of the input string. strcpy is the standard library function used in Line 14 for copying from source initString into this newly allocated memory pointed by buffer. In case the user of the class has supplied a NULL as initString, MyString::buffer is initialized to NULL as well (to keep this pointer from containing a random value that can be dangerous when used to access a memory location). The destructor code does the job of ensuring that the memory allocated in the constructor is automatically returned to the system. It checks whether MyString::buffer is not NULL, and, if so, it performs a delete[] on it that complements the new in the constructor. Note that nowhere in main() has the programmer ever done a new or a delete. In addition to abstracting the implementation of memory management from the user, class MyString also ensured technical correctness in releasing allocated memory. The destructor ~MyString() is automatically invoked when main ends, and this is demonstrated in the output that executes the cout statements in the destructor.

Classes that handle strings better are one of the many applicable uses of a destructor. Lesson 26, "Understanding Smart Pointers," demonstrates how the destructor play a critical role in working with pointers in a smarter way.

NOTE — A destructor cannot be overloaded. A class can have only one destructor. If you forget to implement a destructor, the compiler creates and invokes a dummy destructor, that is, an empty one (that does no cleanup of dynamically allocated memory).

9

Copy Constructor

In Lesson 7, "Organizing Code with Functions," you learned that arguments passed to a function like `Area()` (shown in Listing 7.1) are copied:

```
double Area(double radius);
```

So, the argument sent as parameter `radius` is copied when `Area()` is invoked. This rule applies to objects, that is, instances of classes as well.

Shallow Copying and Associated Problems

Classes such as `MyString`, shown in Listing 9.7, contain a pointer member `buffer` that points to dynamically allocated memory, allocated in the constructor using `new` and deallocated in the destructor using `delete[]`. When an object of this class is copied, the pointer member is copied, but not the pointed memory, resulting in two objects pointing to the same dynamically allocated buffer in memory. When an object is destructed, `delete[]` deallocates the memory, thereby invalidating the pointer copy held by the other object. Such copies are *shallow* and are a threat to the stability of the program, as Listing 9.8 demonstrates.

LISTING 9.8   The Problem in Passing Objects of a Class Such as `MyString` by Value

```
0: #include <iostream>
1: #include <string.h>
2: using namespace std;
3: class MyString
4: {
5: private:
6:     char* buffer;
7:
8: public:
```

```
 9:    MyString(const char* initString) // Constructor
10:    {
11:       buffer = NULL;
12:       if(initString != NULL)
13:       {
14:          buffer = new char [strlen(initString) + 1];
15:          strcpy(buffer, initString);
16:       }
17:    }
18:
19:    ~MyString() // Destructor
20:    {
21:       cout << "Invoking destructor, clearing up" << endl;
22:       delete [] buffer;
23:    }
24:
25:    int GetLength()
26:    { return strlen(buffer); }
27:
28:    const char* GetString()
29:    { return buffer; }
30: };
31:
32: void UseMyString(MyString str)
33: {
34:    cout << "String buffer in MyString is " << str.GetLength();
35:    cout << " characters long" << endl;
36:
37:    cout << "buffer contains: " << str.GetString() << endl;
38:    return;
39: }
40:
41: int main()
42: {
43:    MyString sayHello("Hello from String Class");
44:    UseMyString(sayHello);
45:
46:    return 0;
47: }
```

Output ▼

```
String buffer in MyString is 23 characters long
buffer contains: Hello from String Class
Invoking destructor, clearing up
Invoking destructor, clearing up
<crash as seen in Figure 9.2>
```

FIGURE 9.2
Screenshot of crash caused by executing Listing 9.8 (in MS Visual Studio debug mode).

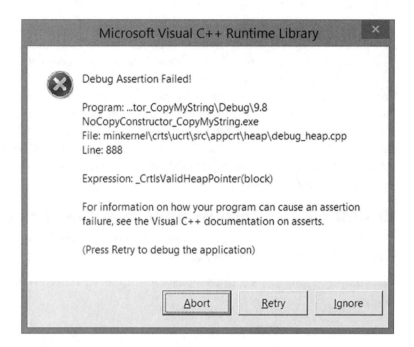

Analysis ▼

Why does class `MyString` that worked just fine in Listing 9.6 cause a crash in Listing 9.7? The only difference between Listing 9.6 and 9.7 is that the job of using the object `sayHello` of class `MyString` created in `main()` has been delegated to function `UseMyString()`, invoked in Line 44. Delegating work to this function has resulted in object `sayHello` in `main()` to be copied into parameter `str` used in `UseMyString()`. This is a copy generated by the compiler as the function has been declared to take `str` as a parameter by value and not by reference. The compiler performs a binary copy of Plain Old Data such as integers, characters, and pointers to the same. So the pointer value contained in `sayHello.buffer` has simply been copied to `str`—that is, `sayHello.buffer` points to the same memory location as `str.buffer`. This is illustrated in Figure 9.3.

FIGURE 9.3
Shallow copy of `sayHello` into `str` when `UseMyString()` is invoked.

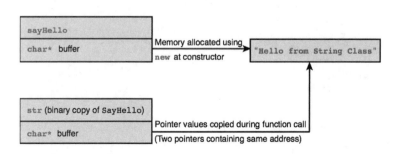

The binary copy did not perform a deep copy of the pointed memory location, and you now have two objects of class MyString pointing to the same location in memory. Thus, when the function UseMyString() ends, variable str goes out of scope and is destroyed. In doing so, the destructor of class MyString is invoked, and the destructor code in Line 22 in Listing 9.8 releases the memory allocated to buffer via delete[]. Note that this call to delete[] invalidates the memory being pointed to in copy say-Hello contained in main(). When main() ends, sayHello goes out of scope and is destroyed. This time, however, Line 22 repeats a call to delete on a memory address that is no longer valid (released and invalidated via the previous destruction of str). This double delete is what results in a crash.

Ensuring Deep Copy Using a Copy Constructor

The copy constructor is an overloaded constructor that you supply. It is invoked by the compiler every time an object of the class is copied.

The declaration syntax of a copy constructor for class MyString is the following:

```
class MyString
{
    MyString(const MyString& copySource); // copy constructor
};

MyString::MyString(const MyString& copySource)
{
    // Copy constructor implementation code
}
```

Thus, a copy constructor takes an object of the same class by reference as a parameter. This parameter is an alias of the source object and is the handle you have in writing your custom copy code. You would use the copy constructor to ensure a deep copy of all buffers in the source, as Listing 9.9 demonstrates.

LISTING 9.9   Define a Copy Constructor to Ensure Deep Copy of Dynamically Allocated Buffers

```
 0: #include <iostream>
 1: #include <string.h>
 2: using namespace std;
 3: class MyString
 4: {
 5: private:
 6:     char* buffer;
 7:
 8: public:
 9:     MyString(const char* initString) // constructor
10:     {
```

```
11:         buffer = NULL;
12:         cout << "Default constructor: creating new MyString" << endl;
13:         if(initString != NULL)
14:         {
15:             buffer = new char [strlen(initString) + 1];
16:             strcpy(buffer, initString);
17:
18:             cout << "buffer points to: 0x" << hex;
19:             cout << (unsigned int*)buffer << endl;
20:         }
21:     }
22:
23:     MyString(const MyString& copySource) // Copy constructor
24:     {
25:         buffer = NULL;
26:         cout << "Copy constructor: copying from MyString" << endl;
27:         if(copySource.buffer != NULL)
28:         {
29:             // allocate own buffer
30:             buffer = new char [strlen(copySource.buffer) + 1];
31:
32:             // deep copy from the source into local buffer
33:             strcpy(buffer, copySource.buffer);
34:
35:             cout << "buffer points to: 0x" << hex;
36:             cout << (unsigned int*)buffer << endl;
37:         }
38:     }
39:
40:     // Destructor
41:     ~MyString()
42:     {
43:         cout << "Invoking destructor, clearing up" << endl;
44:         delete [] buffer;
45:     }
46:
47:     int GetLength()
48:     { return strlen(buffer); }
49:
50:     const char* GetString()
51:     { return buffer; }
52: };
53:
54: void UseMyString(MyString str)
55: {
56:     cout << "String buffer in MyString is " << str.GetLength();
57:     cout << " characters long" << endl;
58:
59:     cout << "buffer contains: " << str.GetString() << endl;
60:     return;
61: }
62:
```

9

```
63: int main()
64: {
65:     MyString sayHello("Hello from String Class");
66:     UseMyString(sayHello);
67:
68:     return 0;
```

Output ▼

```
Default constructor: creating new MyString
buffer points to: 0x01232D90
Copy constructor: copying from MyString
buffer points to: 0x01232DD8
String buffer in MyString is 17 characters long
buffer contains: Hello from String Class
Invoking destructor, clearing up
Invoking destructor, clearing up
```

Analysis ▼

Most of the code is similar to Listing 9.8 save a new copy constructor in Lines 23–38. To start with, let's focus on `main()` that (as before) creates an object `sayHello` in Line 65. Creating `sayHello` results in the first line of output that comes from the constructor of `MyString`, at Line 12. For sake of convenience, the constructor also displays the memory address that `buffer` points to. `main()` then passes `sayHello` by value to function `UseMyString()` in Line 66, which automatically results in the copy constructor being invoked as shown in the output. The code in the copy constructor is similar to that in the constructor. The basic idea is the same, check the length of C-style string `buffer` contained in the copy source at Line 30, allocate proportional memory in one's own instance of `buffer`, and then use `strcpy` to copy from source to destination at Line 33. This is not a shallow copy of pointer values. This is a deep copy where the content being pointed to is copied to a newly allocated buffer that belongs to this object, as illustrated in Figure 9.4.

FIGURE 9.4
Illustration of a deep copy of argument `sayHello` into parameter `str` when function `UseMyString()` is invoked.

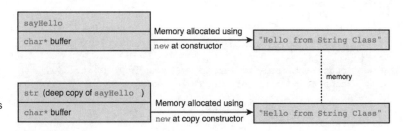

The output in Listing 9.9 indicates that the memory address being pointed to by `buffer` is different in the copy—that is, two objects don't point to the same dynamically allocated memory address. As a result, when function `UseMyString()` returns and parameter `str` is destroyed, the destructor code does a `delete[]` on the memory address that was allocated in the copy constructor and belongs to this object. In doing so, it does not touch memory that is being pointed to by `sayHello` in `main()`. So, both functions end and their respective objects are destroyed successfully and peacefully without the application crashing.

NOTE

The copy constructor has ensured deep copy in cases such as function calls:

```
MyString sayHello("Hello from String Class");
UseMyString(sayHello);
```

However, what if you tried copying via assignment:

```
MyString overwrite("who cares? ");
overwrite = sayHello;
```

This would still be a shallow copy because you still haven't yet supplied a copy assignment `operator=`. In the absence of one, the compiler has supplied a default for you that does a shallow copy.

The copy assignment operator is discussed in length in Lesson 12. Listing 12.8 is an improved `MyString` that implements the same:

```
MyString::operator= (const MyString& copySource)
{
    //... copy assignment operator code
}
```

9

CAUTION

Using `const` in the copy constructor declaration ensures that the copy constructor does not modify the source object being referred to.

Additionally, the parameter in the copy constructor is passed by reference as a necessity. If this weren't a reference, the copy constructor would itself invoke a copy, thus invoking itself again and so on till the system runs out of memory.

DO	DON'T
DO always program a copy constructor and copy assignment operator when your class contains raw pointer members (`char*` and the like).	**DON'T** use raw pointers as class members unless absolutely unavoidable.
DO always program the copy constructor with a `const` reference source parameter.	
DO evaluate avoiding implicit conversions by using keyword `explicit` in declaring constructors.	
DO use string classes such as `std::string` and smart pointer classes as members instead of raw pointers as they implement copy constructors and save you the effort.	

NOTE

The class `MyString` with a raw pointer member, `char* buffer` is used as an example to explain the need for copy constructors.

If you were to program a class that needs to contain string data for storing names and so on, you use `std::string` instead of `char*` and might not even need a copy constructor given the absence of raw pointers. This is because the default copy constructor inserted by the compiler would ensure the invocation of all available copy constructors of member objects such as `std::string`.

Move Constructors Help Improve Performance

There are cases where objects are subjected to copy steps automatically, due to the nature of the language and its needs. Consider the following:

```
class MyString
{
    // pick implementation from Listing 9.9
};
MyString Copy(MyString& source) // function
{
    MyString copyForReturn(source.GetString());  // create copy
    return copyForReturn;  // return by value invokes copy constructor
}
```

```
int main()
{
   MyString sayHello ("Hello World of C++");
   MyString sayHelloAgain(Copy(sayHello)); // invokes 2x copy constructor

   return 0;
}
```

As the comment indicates, in the instantiation of sayHelloAgain, the copy constructor was invoked twice, thus a deep copy was performed twice because of our call to function Copy(sayHello) that returns a MyString by value. However, this value returned is very temporary and is not available outside this expression. So, the copy constructor invoked in good faith by the C++ compiler is a burden on performance. This impact becomes significant if our class were to contain objects of great size.

To avoid this performance bottleneck, versions of C++ starting with C++11 feature a *move constructor* in addition to a copy constructor. The syntax of a move constructor is

```
// move constructor
MyString(MyString&& moveSource)
{
   if(moveSource.buffer != NULL)
   {
      buffer = moveSource.buffer; // take ownership i.e. 'move'
      moveSource.buffer = NULL;   // set the move source to NULL
   }
}
```

When a move constructor is programmed, the compiler automatically opts for the same for "moving" the temporary resource and hence avoiding a deep-copy step. With the move constructor implemented, the comment should be appropriately changed to the following:

```
MyString sayHelloAgain(Copy(sayHello)); // invokes 1x copy, 1x move constructors
```

The move constructor is usually implemented with the move assignment operator, which is discussed in greater detail in Lesson 12. Listing 12.11 is a better version of class MyString that implements the move constructor and the move assignment operator.

Different Uses of Constructors and the Destructor

You have learned a few important and basic concepts in this lesson, such as the concepts of constructors, destructor, and the abstraction of data and methods via keywords such as `public` and `private`. These concepts enable you to create classes that can control how they're created, copied, destroyed, or expose data.

Let's look at a few interesting patterns that help you solve many important design problems.

Class That Does Not Permit Copying

You are asked to model the constitution of your country. Your constitution permits one president. Your `class President` risks the following:

```
President ourPresident;
DoSomething(ourPresident); // duplicate created in passing by value
President clone;
clone = ourPresident; // duplicate via assignment
```

Clearly, you need to avoid this situation. Beyond modeling a certain constitution, you might be programming an operating system and need to model one local area network, one processor, and so on. You need to ensure that certain resources cannot be copied or duplicated. If you don't declare a copy constructor, the C++ compiler inserts a default public copy constructor for you. This ruins your design and threatens your implementation. Yet, the language gives you a solution to this design paradigm.

You would ensure that your class cannot be copied by declaring a `private` copy constructor. This ensures that the function call `DoSomething(ourPresident)` will cause a compile failure. To avoid assignment, you declare a `private` assignment operator.

Thus, the solution is the following:

```
class President
{
private:
    President(const President&); // private copy constructor
    President& operator= (const President&); // private copy assignment operator

    // ... other attributes
};
```

There is no need for implementation of the private copy constructor or assignment operator. Just declaring them as private is adequate and sufficient toward fulfilling your goal of ensuring non-copyable objects of `class President`.

Singleton Class That Permits a Single Instance

`class President` discussed earlier is good, but it has a shortcoming: It cannot help creation of multiple presidents via instantiation of multiple objects:

```
President One, Two, Three;
```

Individually they are non-copyable thanks to the `private` copy constructors, but what you ideally need is a `class President` that has one, and only one, real-world manifestation—that is, there is only one object and creation of additional ones is prohibited. Welcome to the concept of singleton that uses private constructors, a private assignment operator, and a static instance member to create this (controversially) powerful pattern.

9

> **TIP**
>
> When the keyword `static` is used on a class's data member, it ensures that the member is shared across all instances.
>
> When `static` is used on a local variable declared within the scope of a function, it ensures that the variable retains its value between function calls.
>
> When `static` is used on a member function—a method—the method is shared across all instances of the class.

Keyword `static` is an essential ingredient in creating a singleton class as demonstrated by Listing 9.10.

LISTING 9.10   Singleton `class President` That Prohibits Copying, Assignment, and Multiple Instance Creation

```cpp
0: #include <iostream>
1: #include <string>
2: using namespace std;
3:
4: class President
5: {
6: private:
7:     President() {}; // private default constructor
8:     President(const President&); // private copy constructor
9:     const President& operator=(const President&); // assignment operator
10:
11:     string name;
12:
13: public:
14:     static President& GetInstance()
```

```
15:      {
16:          // static objects are constructed only once
17:          static President onlyInstance;
18:          return onlyInstance;
19:      }
20:
21:      string GetName()
22:      { return name; }
23:
24:      void SetName(string InputName)
25:      { name = InputName; }
26: };
27:
28: int main()
29: {
30:      President& onlyPresident = President::GetInstance();
31:      onlyPresident.SetName("Abraham Lincoln");
32:
33:      // uncomment lines to see how compile failures prohibit duplicates
34:      // President second; // cannot access constructor
35:      // President* third= new President(); // cannot access constructor
36:      // President fourth = onlyPresident; // cannot access copy constructor
37:      // onlyPresident = President::GetInstance(); // cannot access operator=
38:
39:      cout << "The name of the President is: ";
40:      cout << President::GetInstance().GetName() << endl;
41:
42:      return 0;
43: }
```

Output ▼

```
The name of the President is: Abraham Lincoln
```

Analysis ▼

Take a quick look at main() in Lines 28–43 that has a host of commented lines that show all the combinations in creating new instances or copies of a class President that won't compile. Let's analyze them one by one:

```
34:      // President second; // cannot access constructor
35:      // President* third= new President(); // cannot access constructor
```

Lines 34 and 35 try object creation on the stack and free store, respectively, using the default constructor, which is unavailable because it's private, as declared in Line 7.

```
36:      // President fourth = onlyPresident; // cannot access copy constructor
```

Line 36 is an attempt at creating a copy of an existing object via the copy constructor (assignment at creation time invokes copy constructor), which is unavailable in `main()` because it is declared `private` in Line 8:

```
37:    // OnlyPresident = President::GetInstance(); // cannot access operator=
```

Line 37 is an attempt at creating a copy via assignment, which does not work as the assignment operator is declared `private` in Line 9. Therefore, `main()` can never create an instance of `class President`, and the only option left is seen in Line 30, where it uses the static function `GetInstance()` to get an instance of `class President`. Because `GetInstance()` is a static member, it is like a global function that can be invoked without having an object as a handle. `GetInstance()`, implemented in Lines 14–19, uses a static variable `onlyInstance` to ensure that there is one and only one instance of `class President` created. To understand that better, imagine that Line 17 is executed only once (static initialization) and hence `GetInstance()` returns the only one available instance of `class President`, irrespective of how often `President::GetInstance()` is invoked.

9

CAUTION

Use the singleton pattern only where absolutely necessary, keeping future growth of the application and its features in perspective. Note that the very feature that it restricts creation of multiple instances can become an architectural bottleneck when a use case comes up that needs multiple instances of the class.

For example, if our project were to change from modeling a nation to modeling the United Nations, which is currently represented by 193 member nations, each with its own president, clearly we would have an architectural problem given a singleton `class President` that would permit the existence of only one instance.

Class That Prohibits Instantiation on the Stack

Space on the stack is often limited. If you are writing a database that may contain terabytes of data in its internal structures, you might want to ensure that a client of this class cannot instantiate it on the stack; instead it is forced to create instances only on the free store. The key to ensuring this is declaring the destructor `private`:

```
class MonsterDB
{
private:
    ~MonsterDB();   // private destructor

    //... members that consume a huge amount of data
};
```

Declaring a private destructor ensures that one is not allowed to create an instance like this:

```
int main()
{
    MonsterDB myDatabase; // compile error
    // … more code
    return 0;
}
```

This instance, if successfully constructed, would be on the stack. All objects on the stack get popped when the stack is unwound and therefore the compiler would need to compile and invoke the destructor ~MonsterDB() at the end of main(). However, this destructor is private and therefore inaccessible, resulting in a compile failure.

A private destructor would not stop you from instantiating on the heap:

```
int main()
{
    MonsterDB* myDatabase = new MonsterDB(); // no error
    // … more code
    return 0;
}
```

If you see a memory leak there, you are not mistaken. As the destructor is not accessible from main, you cannot do a delete, either. What class MonsterDB needs to support is a public static member function that would destroy the instance (a class member would have access to the private destructor). See Listing 9.11.

LISTING 9.11   A Database class MonsterDB That Allows Object Creation Only on the Free Store (Using new)

```
 0: #include <iostream>
 1: using namespace std;
 2:
 3: class MonsterDB
 4: {
 5: private:
 6:     ~MonsterDB() {}; // private destructor prevents instances on stack
 7:
 8: public:
 9:     static void DestroyInstance(MonsterDB* pInstance)
10:     {
11:         delete pInstance; // member can invoke private destructor
12:     }
13:
14:     void DoSomething() {} // sample empty member method
```

```
15: };
16:
17: int main()
18: {
19:     MonsterDB* myDB = new MonsterDB(); // on heap
20:     myDB->DoSomething();
21:
22:     // uncomment next line to see compile failure
23:     // delete myDB; // private destructor cannot be invoked
24:
25:     // use static member to release memory
26:     MonsterDB::DestroyInstance(myDB);
27:
28:     return 0;
29: }
```

9

Output ▼

The code snippet produces no output.

Analysis ▼

The purpose of the code is just to demonstrate the programming of a class that prohibits instance creation on the stack. A `private` destructor, as shown in Line 6, is key. Static function `DestroyInstance()` in Lines 9–12 is required for memory deallocation, because `main()` cannot invoke `delete` on `myDB`. You may test this by uncommenting Line 23.

Using Constructors to Convert Types

Earlier in this lesson, you learned that constructors can be overloaded, that is, they may take one or more parameters. This feature is often used to convert one type to another. Let's consider a `class Human` that features an overloaded constructor that accepts an integer.

```
class Human
{
    int age;
public:
    Human(int humansAge): age(humansAge) {}
};

// Function that takes a Human as a parameter
void DoSomething(Human person)
{
    cout << "Human sent did something" << endl;
    return;
}
```

This constructor allows a conversion:

```
Human kid(10); // convert integer in to a Human
DoSomething(kid);
```

CAUTION

Such *converting constructors* allow implicit conversions:

```
Human anotherKid = 11; // int converted to Human
DoSomething(10); // 10 converted to Human!
```

We declared `DoSomething(Human person)` as a function that accepts a parameter of type `Human` and does not accept an `int`! So, why did that line work? The compiler knows that `class Human` supports a constructor that accepts an integer and performed an *implicit* conversion for you—it created an object of type `Human` using the integer you supplied and sent it as an argument to the function.

To avoid implicit conversions, use keyword `explicit` at the time of declaring the constructor:

```
class Human
{
    int age;
public:
    explicit Human(int humansAge) : age(humansAge) {}
};
```

Using `explicit` is not a prerequisite but in many cases a good programming practice. The following sample in Listing 9.12 demonstrates a version of `class Human` that does not permit implicit conversions.

LISTING 9.12 Use Keyword `explicit` to Block Unintentional Implicit Conversions

```
0: #include<iostream>
1: using namespace std;
2:
3: class Human
4: {
5:     int age;
6: public:
7:     // explicit constructor blocks implicit conversions
```

```
 8:     explicit Human(int humansAge) : age(humansAge) {}
 9: };
10:
11: void DoSomething(Human person)
12: {
13:     cout << "Human sent did something" << endl;
14:     return;
15: }
16:
17: int main()
18: {
19:     Human kid(10);     // explicit conversion is OK
20:     Human anotherKid = Human(11); // explicit, OK
21:     DoSomething(kid); // OK
22:
23:     // Human anotherKid2 = 11; // failure: implicit conversion not OK
24:     // DoSomething(10); // implicit conversion
25:
26:     return 0;
27: }
```

Output ▼

```
Human sent did something
```

Analysis ▼

The lines of code that don't contribute to the output are at least as significant as those that do. main() in Lines 17–27 features variants of object instantiation of class Human that has been declared with an explicit constructor at Line 8. The lines that compile are attempts at explicit conversion where an int has been used to instantiate a Human. Lines 23 and 24 are variants that involve implicit conversion. These lines that are commented out will compile when we remove keyword explicit at Line 8. Thus, this sample demonstrates how keyword explicit protects against implicit conversions.

TIP

> The problem of implicit conversions and avoiding them using keyword explicit applies to operators too. Remember to note the usage of explicit when programming conversion operators introduced to you in Lesson 12.

`this` **Pointer**

An important concept in C++, `this` is a reserved keyword applicable within the scope of a class and contains the address of the object. In other words, the value of `this` is `&object`. Within a class member method, when you invoke another member method, the compiler sends `this` pointer as an implicit, invisible parameter in the function call:

```
class Human
{
private:
    void Talk (string Statement)
    {
        cout << Statement;
    }

public:
    void IntroduceSelf()
    {
        Talk("Bla bla"); // same as Talk(this, "Bla Bla")
    }
};
```

What you see here is the method `IntroduceSelf()` using private member `Talk()` to print a statement on the screen. In reality, the compiler embeds the `this` pointer in calling `Talk`, that is invoked as `Talk(this, "Bla bla")`.

From a programming perspective, `this` does not have too many applications, except those where it is usually optional. For instance, the code to access `age` within `SetAge()`, as shown in Listing 9.2, can have a variant:

```
void SetAge(int humansAge)
{
    this->age = humansAge;    // same as age = humansAge
}
```

NOTE _____

> Note that the `this` pointer is not sent to class methods declared as `static` as static functions are not connected to an instance of the class. Instead they are shared by all instances.
>
> To use an instance variable in a static function, you would explicitly declare a parameter and send `this` pointer as an argument.

sizeof() **a Class**

You have learned the fundamentals of defining your own type using keyword class that enables you to encapsulate data attributes and methods that operate on that data. Operator sizeof(), covered in Lesson 3, "Using Variables, Declaring Constants," is used to determine the memory requirement of a specific type, in bytes. This operator is valid for classes, too, and basically reports the sum of bytes consumed by each data attribute contained within the class declaration. Depending on the compiler you use, sizeof() might or might not include padding for certain attributes on word boundaries. Note that member functions and their local variables do not play a role in defining the sizeof() a class. See Listing 9.13.

LISTING 9.13   The Result of Using sizeof on Classes and Their Instances

```
 0: #include <iostream>
 1: #include <string.h>
 2: using namespace std;
 3: class MyString
 4: {
 5: private:
 6:    char* buffer;
 7:
 8: public:
 9:    MyString(const char* initString) // default constructor
10:    {
11:       buffer = NULL;
12:       if(initString != NULL)
13:       {
14:          buffer = new char [strlen(initString) + 1];
15:          strcpy(buffer, initString);
16:       }
17:    }
18:
19:    MyString(const MyString& copySource) // copy constructor
20:    {
21:       buffer = NULL;
22:       if(copySource.buffer != NULL)
23:       {
24:          buffer = new char [strlen(copySource.buffer) + 1];
25:          strcpy(buffer, copySource.buffer);
26:       }
27:    }
28:
29:    ~MyString()
30:    {
31:       delete [] buffer;
32:    }
```

```
33:
34:     int GetLength()
35:     { return strlen(buffer); }
36:
37:     const char* GetString()
38:     { return buffer; }
39: };
40:
41: class Human
42: {
43: private:
44:     int age;
45:     bool gender;
46:     MyString name;
47:
48: public:
49:     Human(const MyString& InputName, int InputAge, bool gender)
50:         : name(InputName), age (InputAge), gender(gender) {}
51:
52:     int GetAge ()
53:     { return age; }
54: };
55:
56: int main()
57: {
58:     MyString mansName("Adam");
59:     MyString womansName("Eve");
60:
61:     cout << "sizeof(MyString) = " << sizeof(MyString) << endl;
62:     cout << "sizeof(mansName) = " << sizeof(mansName) << endl;
63:     cout << "sizeof(womansName) = " << sizeof(womansName) << endl;
64:
65:     Human firstMan(mansName, 25, true);
66:     Human firstWoman(womansName, 18, false);
67:
68:     cout << "sizeof(Human) = " << sizeof(Human) << endl;
69:     cout << "sizeof(firstMan) = " << sizeof(firstMan) << endl;
70:     cout << "sizeof(firstWoman) = " << sizeof(firstWoman) << endl;
71:
72:     return 0;
73: }
```

Output Using 32-Bit Compiler ▼

```
sizeof(MyString) = 4
sizeof(mansName) = 4
sizeof(womansName) = 4
sizeof(Human) = 12
sizeof(firstMan) = 12
sizeof(firstWoman) = 12
```

Output Using 64-Bit Compiler ▼

```
sizeof(MyString) = 8
sizeof(mansName) = 8
sizeof(womansName) = 8
sizeof(Human) = 16
sizeof(firstMan) = 16
sizeof(firstWoman) = 16
```

Analysis ▼

The sample is admittedly long as it contains class MyString and a variant of class Human that uses type MyString to store name. Human also has an added parameter bool for gender.

Let's start with analyzing the output. What you see is that the result of sizeof() on a class is the same as that of an object of the class. Hence, sizeof(MyString) is the same as sizeof(mansName), because essentially the number of bytes consumed by a class is fixed at compile-time. Don't be surprised that mansName and womansName have the same size in bytes in spite of one containing "Adam" and the other "Eve" because these are stored by MyString::buffer that is a char*, a pointer whose size is fixed at 4 bytes (on my 32-bit system) and is independent of the volume of data being pointed to.

Try calculating the sizeof() a Human manually that is reported as 12. Lines 44, 45, and 46 tell that a Human contains an int, a bool, and a MyString. Referring to Listing 3.4 for a quick refresh on bytes consumed by inbuilt types, you know that an int consumes 4 bytes, a bool 1 byte, and MyString 4 bytes on the system I used for the examples, which do not sum up to 12 as reported by the output. This is because of *word padding* and other factors that influence the result of sizeof().

How struct Differs from class

struct is a keyword from the days of C, and for all practical purposes it is treated by a C++ compiler similarly to a class. The exceptions are applicable to the access specifiers (public and private) when the programmer has not specified any. Unless specified, members in a struct are public by default (private for a class), and unless specified, a struct features public inheritance from a base struct (private for a class). Inheritance is discussed in detail in Lesson 10.

A struct variant of class Human from Listing 9.13 would be the following:

```
struct Human
{
    // constructor, public by default (as no access specified is mentioned)
    Human(const MyString& humansName, int humansAge, bool humansGender)
        : name(humansName), age (humansAge), Gender(humansGender) {}
```

9

```
   int GetAge ()
   {
      return age;
   }

private:
   int age;
   bool gender;
   MyString name;
};
```

As you can see, a `struct` `Human` is similar to `class` `Human`, and instantiation of an object of type `struct` would be similar to type `class` as well:

```
Human firstMan("Adam", 25, true); // an instance of struct Human
```

Declaring a friend of a class

A class does not permit external access to its data members and methods that are declared `private`. This rule is waived for classes and functions that are disclosed as friend classes or functions, using keyword `friend` as seen in Listing 9.14.

LISTING 9.14   Using the `friend` Keyword to Allow an External Function `DisplayAge()` Access to Private Data Members

```
 0: #include <iostream>
 1: #include <string>
 2: using namespace std;
 3:
 4: class Human
 5: {
 6: private:
 7:    friend void DisplayAge(const Human& person);
 8:    string name;
 9:    int age;
10:
11: public:
12:    Human(string humansName, int humansAge)
13:    {
14:       name = humansName;
15:       age = humansAge;
16:    }
17: };
18:
19: void DisplayAge(const Human& person)
20: {
21:    cout << person.age << endl;
22: }
```

```
23:
24: int main()
25: {
26:    Human firstMan("Adam", 25);
27:    cout << "Accessing private member age via friend function: ";
28:    DisplayAge(firstMan);
29:
30:    return 0;
31: }
```

Output ▼

```
Accessing private member age via friend function: 25
```

Analysis ▼

Line 7 contains the declaration that indicates to the compiler that function DisplayAge() in global scope is a friend and therefore is permitted special access to the private members of class Human. You can comment out Line 7 to see a compile failure at Line 22.

Like functions, external classes can also be designated as a trusted friend, as Listing 9.15 demonstrates.

LISTING 9.15 Using the friend Keyword to Allow an External Class Utility Access to Private Data Members

```
0: #include <iostream>
1: #include <string>
2: using namespace std;
3:
4: class Human
5: {
6: private:
7:    friend class Utility;
8:    string name;
9:    int age;
10:
11: public:
12:    Human(string humansName, int humansAge)
13:    {
14:       name = humansName;
15:       age = humansAge;
16:    }
17: };
18:
19: class Utility
```

```
20: {
21: public:
22:     static void DisplayAge(const Human& person)
23:     {
24:         cout << person.age << endl;
25:     }
26: };
27:
28: int main()
29: {
30:     Human firstMan("Adam", 25);
31:     cout << "Accessing private member age via friend class: ";
32:     Utility::DisplayAge(firstMan);
33:
34:     return 0;
35: }
```

Output ▼

```
Accessing private member age via friend class: 25
```

Analysis ▼

Line 7 indicates class Utility is a friend of class Human. This friend declaration allows all methods in class Utility access even to the private data members and methods in class Human.

union: A Special Data Storage Mechanism

A *union* is a special class type where only one of the non-static data members is active at a time. Thus, a union can accommodate multiple data members, just like a class can, with the exception that only one of them can actually be used.

Declaring a Union

A union is declared using keyword union, followed by the name of the union and its data members within braces:

```
union UnionName
{
    Type1 member1;
    Type2 member2;
...
    TypeN memberN;
};
```

You would instantiate and use a union like this:

```
UnionName unionObject;
unionObject.member2 = value; // choose member2 as the active member
```

NOTE

> Similar to the struct, the members of a union are public by default. Unlike a struct, however, unions cannot be used in inheritance hierarchies.
>
> Additionally, the sizeof() a union is always fixed as the size of the largest member contained in the union—even if that member were inactive in an instance of the union.

9

Where Would You Use a union?

Often a union is used as a member of a struct to model a complex data type. In some implementations, the ability of a union to interpret the fixed memory space as another type is used for type conversions or memory reinterpretation—a practice that is controversial and not necessary given alternatives.

Listing 9.16 demonstrates the declaration and usage of unions.

LISTING 9.16   Declaration, Instantiation, and sizeof() Union

```
0: #include <iostream>
1: using namespace std;
2:
3: union SimpleUnion
4: {
5:     int num;
6:     char alphabet;
7: };
8:
9: struct ComplexType
10: {
11:     enum DataType
12:     {
13:         Int,
14:         Char
15:     } Type;
16:
17:     union Value
18:     {
19:         int num;
20:         char alphabet;
21:
22:         Value() {}
```

```
23:          ~Value() {}
24:      }value;
25: };
26:
27: void DisplayComplexType(const ComplexType& obj)
28: {
29:      switch (obj.Type)
30:      {
31:      case ComplexType::Int:
32:          cout << "Union contains number: " << obj.value.num << endl;
33:          break;
34:
35:      case ComplexType::Char:
36:          cout << "Union contains character: " << obj.value.alphabet << endl;
37:          break;
38:      }
39: }
40:
41: int main()
42: {
43:      SimpleUnion u1, u2;
44:      u1.num = 2100;
45:      u2.alphabet = 'C';
46:      cout << "sizeof(u1) containing integer: " << sizeof(u1) << endl;
47:      cout << "sizeof(u2) containing character: " << sizeof(u2) << endl;
48:
49:      ComplexType myData1, myData2;
50:      myData1.Type = ComplexType::Int;
51:      myData1.value.num = 2017;
52:
53:      myData2.Type = ComplexType::Char;
54:      myData2.value.alphabet = 'X';
55:
56:      DisplayComplexType(myData1);
57:      DisplayComplexType(myData2);
58:
59:      return 0;
60: }
```

Output ▼

```
sizeof(u1) containing integer: 4
sizeof(u2) containing character: 4
Union contains number: 2017
Union contains character: X
```

Analysis ▼

The sample demonstrates that `sizeof()` the union objects `u1` and `u2` returns the same amount of memory reserved for both objects, notwithstanding the fact that `u1` is used to hold an integer and `u2` a `char`, `char` being smaller than an `int`. This is because the compiler reserves the amount of memory for a union that is consumed by the largest object it contains. Struct `ComplexType` defined in Lines 9–25, actually contains an enumeration `DataType` that is used to indicate the nature of the object stored in the union, in addition to the data member, which is a `union` called `Value`. This combination of a `struct` comprising an enumeration used to hold type information and a union used to hold value is a popular application of the union. For example, the structure `VARIANT` popularly used in Windows application programming follows a similar approach. This combination is used by function `DisplayComplexType()` defined in Lines 27–39 that uses the enumeration in executing the right case in the supplied switch-case construct. For an example, we have included a constructor and destructor in this union—these are optional in Listing 9.16 given that the union contains Plain-Old-Data types, but may be required if the union comprises another user-defined type such as a `class` or a `struct`.

9

TIP

> C++17 is expected to introduce a typesafe alternative to a union. To learn about the `std::variant`, visit Lesson 29, "Going Forward."

Using Aggregate Initialization on Classes and Structs

The following initialization syntax is called an *aggregate initialization* syntax:

```
Type objectName = {argument1, …, argumentN};
```

Alternatively, since C++11:

```
Type objectName {argument1, …, argumentN};
```

Aggregate initialization can be applied to an aggregate, and therefore it is important to understand what data types fall under this category.

You already saw examples of aggregate initialization in the initialization of arrays in Lesson 4, "Managing Arrays and Strings."

```
int myNums[] = { 9, 5, -1 }; // myNums is int[3]
char hello[6] = { 'h', 'e', 'l', 'l', 'o', ' \0' };
```

The term *aggregate*, however, is not limited to arrays of simple types like integers or characters, but extends also to classes (and therefore structs and unions) too. There are restrictions imposed by the standard on the specification of a `struct` or a `class` that can be called an aggregate. These restrictions get nuanced depending on the version of C++ standard that you refer to. Yet, it can be safely said that classes/structs that comprise public and non-static data members, contain no private or protected data members, contain no virtual member functions, feature none or only public inheritance (that is, no private, protected, or virtual inheritance), and no user-defined constructors are aggregates too and can be initialized as one.

> **TIP**
>
> Inheritance is explained in detail in Lesson 10, "Implementing Inheritance" and in Lesson 11, "Polymorphism."

Thus, the following `struct` fulfills the prerequisites of being an aggregate and hence, can be initialized as one:

```
struct Aggregate1
{
    int num;
    double pi;
};
```

Initialization:

```
Aggregate1 a1{ 2017, 3.14 };
```

Another example:

```
struct Aggregate2
{
    int num;
    char hello[6];
    int impYears[5];
};
```

Initialization:

```
Aggregate2 a2 {42, {'h', 'e', 'l', 'l', 'o'}, {1998, 2003, 2011, 2014, 2017}};
```

Listing 9.17 is a sample demonstrating aggregate initialization applied to classes and structs.

LISTING 9.17 Aggregate Initialization on Class Type

```
 0: #include <iostream>
 1: #include<string>
 2: using namespace std;
 3:
 4: class Aggregate1
 5: {
 6: public:
 7:     int num;
 8:     double pi;
 9: };
10:
11: struct Aggregate2
12: {
13:     char hello[6];
14:     int impYears[3];
15:     string world;
16: };
17:
18: int main()
19: {
20:     int myNums[] = { 9, 5, -1 }; // myNums is int[3]
21:     Aggregate1 a1{ 2017, 3.14 };
22:     cout << "Pi is approximately: " << a1.pi << endl;
23:
24:     Aggregate2 a2{ {'h', 'e', 'l', 'l', 'o'}, {2011, 2014, 2017}, "world"};
25:
26:     // Alternatively
27:     Aggregate2 a2_2{'h', 'e', 'l', 'l', 'o', '\0', 2011, 2014, 2017, "world"};
28:
29:     cout << a2.hello << ' ' << a2.world << endl;
30:     cout << "C++ standard update scheduled in: " << a2.impYears[2] << endl;
31:
32:     return 0;
33: }
```

Output ▼

```
Pi is approximately: 3.14
hello world
C++ standard update scheduled in: 2017
```

Analysis ▼

The sample demonstrates how you can use aggregate initialization in instantiating classes (or structs). `Aggregate1` defined in Lines 4–9 is a class with public data members, and `Aggregate2` defined in Lines 11–16 is a `struct`. Lines 21, 24, and 27 are the ones that demonstrate aggregate initialization on the `class` and `struct`, respectively. We access the members of the class/struct in demonstrating how the compiler placed the initialization values into the respective data members. Note how some members are an array, and how a `std::string` member contained in `Aggregate2` has been initialized using this construct in Line 24.

CAUTION	Aggregate initialization will initialize only the first non-static member of a union. The aggregate initialization of the unions declared in Listing 9.16 would be
	
	 `43:    SimpleUnion u1{ 2100 }, u2{ 'C' };`
	 `// In u2, member num (int) is initialized to 'C'`
	 `(ASCII 67)`
	 `// Although, you wished to initialize member alphabet`
	 `(char)`
	
	 Therefore, for sake of clarity, it may be a good idea to not use aggregate initialization syntax on union, but the one used in Listing 9.16.

`constexpr` **with Classes and Objects**

We were introduced to `constexpr` in Lesson 3, where we learned that it offers a powerful way to improve the performance of your C++ application. By marking functions that operate on constants or `const`-expressions as `constexpr`, we are instructing the compiler to evaluate those functions and insert their result instead of inserting instructions that compute the result when the application is executed. This keyword can also be used with classes and objects that evaluate as constants as demonstrated by Listing 9.18. Note that the compiler would ignore `constexpr` when the function or class is used with entities that are not constant.

LISTING 9.18   Using `constexpr` with class `Human`

```
0: #include <iostream>
1: using namespace std;
2:
3: class Human
4: {
5:     int age;
```

```
 6: public:
 7:     constexpr Human(int humansAge) :age(humansAge) {}
 8:     constexpr int GetAge() const { return age; }
 9: };
10:
11: int main()
12: {
13:     constexpr Human somePerson(15);
14:     const int hisAge = somePerson.GetAge();
15:
16:     Human anotherPerson(45); // not constant expression
17:
18:     return 0;
19: }
```

9

Output ▼

```
<This sample produces no output>
```

Analysis ▼

Note the slight modification in class Human in Lines 3–9. It now uses constexpr in the declaration of its constructor and member function GetAge(). This little addition tells the compiler to evaluate the creation and usage of instances of class Human as a constant expression, where possible. somePerson in Line 13 is declared as a constant instance and used as one in Line 14. Therefore, this instance is likely to be evaluated by the compiler and the code is optimized for performance at execution. Instance another-Person in Line 16 is not declared to be a constant and therefore its instantiation or usage may not be treated by the compiler as a constant expression.

Summary

This lesson taught you one of the most fundamental keywords and concepts in C++, that of a class. You learned how a class encapsulates member data and member functions that operate using the same. You saw how access specifiers such as public and private help you abstract data and functionality that entities external to the class don't need to see. You learned the concept of copy constructors, and move constructors introduced by C++11 that help reduce unwanted copy steps. You saw some special cases where all these elements come together to help you implement design patterns such as the singleton.

Q&A

Q What is the difference between the instance of a class and an object of that class?

A Essentially none. When you instantiate a class, you get an instance that can also be called an object.

Q What is a better way to access members: using the dot operator (.) or using the pointer operator (->)?

A If you have a pointer to an object, the pointer operator would be best suited. If you have instantiated an object as a local variable on the stack, then the dot operator is best suited.

Q Should I always program a copy constructor?

A If your class' data members are well-programmed smart pointers, string classes, or STL containers such as `std::vector`, then the default copy constructor inserted by the compiler ensures that their respective copy constructors are invoked. However, if your class has raw pointer members (such as `int*` for a dynamic array instead of `std::vector<int>`), you need to supply a correctly programmed copy constructor that ensures a deep copy of an array during function calls where an object of the class is passed by value.

Q My class has only one constructor that has been defined with a parameter with a default value. Is this still a default constructor?

A Yes. If an instance of a class can be created without arguments, then the class is said to have a default constructor. A class can have only one default constructor.

Q Why do some samples in this lesson use functions such as `SetAge()` to set integer `Human::age`? Why not make `age` public and assign it as needed?

A From a technical viewpoint, making `Human::age` a `public` member would work as well. However, from a design point of view, keeping member data private is a good idea. Accessor functions such as `GetAge()` or `SetAge()` are a refined and scalable way to access this private data, allowing you to perform error checks for instance before the value of `Human::age` is set or reset.

Q Why is the parameter of a copy constructor one that takes the copy source by reference?

A For one, the copy constructor is expected by the compiler to be that way. The reason behind it is that a copy constructor would invoke itself if it accepted the copy source by value, resulting in an endless copy loop.

Workshop

The Workshop provides quiz questions to help you solidify your understanding of the material covered and exercises to provide you with experience in using what you've learned. Try to answer the quiz and exercise questions before checking the answers in Appendix E, and be certain you understand the answers before continuing to the next lesson.

9

Quiz

1. When I create an instance of a class using `new`, where is the class created?

2. My class has a raw pointer `int*` that contains a dynamically allocated array of integers. Does `sizeof` report different sizes depending on the number of integers in the dynamic array?

3. All my class members are private, and my class does not contain any declared `friend` class or function. Who can access these members?

4. Can one class member method invoke another?

5. What is a constructor good for?

6. What is a destructor good for?

Exercises

1. **BUG BUSTERS:** What is wrong in the following `class` declaration?

```
Class Human
{
    int age;
    string name;

public:
    Human() {}
}
```

2. How would the user of the class in Exercise 1 access member `Human::age`?

3. Write a better version of the class seen in Exercise 1 that initializes all parameters using an initialization list in the constructor.

4. Write a `class Circle` that computes the area and circumference given a radius that is supplied to the class as a parameter at the time of instantiation. Pi should be contained in a constant private member that cannot be accessed from outside the circle.

LESSON 10
Implementing Inheritance

Object-oriented programming is based on four important aspects: encapsulation, abstraction, inheritance, and polymorphism. Inheritance is a powerful way to reuse attributes and is a stepping stone towards polymorphism.

In this lesson, you find out about

- Inheritance in the context of programming
- The C++ syntax of inheritance
- `public`, `private`, and `protected` inheritance
- Multiple inheritance
- Problems caused by hiding base class methods and *slicing*

Basics of Inheritance

What Tom Smith inherits from his forefathers is first and foremost his family name that makes him a Smith. In addition, he inherits certain values that his parents have taught him and a skill at sculpting wood that has been the Smith family occupation for many generations. These attributes collectively identify Tom as an offspring of the Smith family tree.

In programming parlance, you are often faced with situations where components being managed have similar attributes, differing minutely in details or in behavior. One way to solve this problem is to make each component a class where each class implements all attributes and re-implements the common ones. Another solution is using inheritance to allow classes that are similar to derive from a base class that contains common attributes and implements common functionality, overriding this base functionality to implement behavior that makes each class unique. The latter is often the preferred way. Welcome to inheritance in our world of object-oriented programming, as illustrated by Figure 10.1.

FIGURE 10.1
Inheritance between classes.

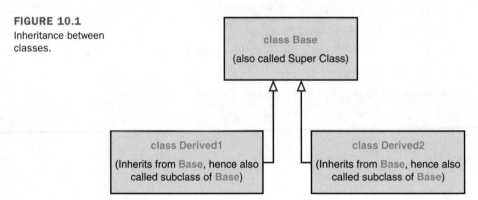

Inheritance and Derivation

Figure 10.1 shows a diagrammatic relationship between a base class and its derived classes. It might not be easy right now to visualize what a base class or a derived class could be. Try to understand that a derived class inherits from the base class and in that sense is a base class (just like Tom is a Smith).

NOTE

The is-a relationship between a derived class and its base is applicable only to `public` inheritance. This lesson starts with public inheritance to understand the concept of inheritance and the most frequent form of inheritance before moving on to `private` or `protected` inheritance.

To make understanding this concept easy, think of a base class Bird. Classes are derived from Bird are class Crow, class Parrot, or class Kiwi. A class Bird would define the most basic attributes of a bird, such as "is feathered," "has wings," "lays eggs," "can fly," and so on. Derived classes such as Crow, Parrot, or Kiwi inherit these attributes and customize them (for example, a class Kiwi that represents a flightless-bird would contain no implementation of Fly()). Table 10.1 demonstrates a few more examples of inheritance.

TABLE 10.1 Examples of Public Inheritance Taken from Daily Life

Base Class	Example Derived Classes
Fish	Goldfish, Carp, Tuna (Tuna "is a" Fish)
Mammal	Human, Elephant, Lion, Platypus (Platypus "is a" Mammal)
Bird	Crow, Parrot, Ostrich, Kiwi, Platypus (Platypus "is a" Bird, too!)
Shape	Circle, Polygon (Polygon "is a" Shape)
Polygon	Triangle, Octagon (Octagon "is a" Polygon, which in turn "is a" Shape)

What these examples show is that when you put on your object-oriented programming glasses, you see examples of inheritance in many objects around yourself. Fish is a base class for a Tuna because a Tuna, like a Carp, is a Fish and presents all fish-like characteristics such as being cold-blooded. However, Tuna differs from a Carp in the way it looks, swims, and in the fact that it is a saltwater fish. Thus, Tuna and Carp inherit common characteristics from a common base class Fish, yet specialize the base class attributes to distinguish themselves from each other. This is illustrated in Figure 10.2.

FIGURE 10.2
Hierarchical relationship between Tuna, Carp, and Fish.

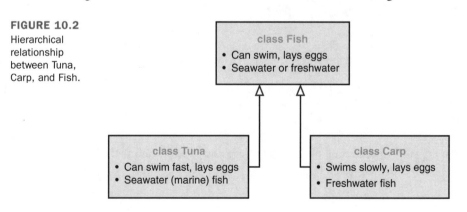

A platypus can swim, yet is a special animal with mammalian characteristics such as feeding its young with milk, avian (bird-like) characteristics as it lays eggs, and reptilian characteristics as it is venomous. Thus, one can imagine a class Platypus inheriting from two base classes, class Mammal and class Bird, to inherit mammalian and avian features. This form of inheritance is called *multiple inheritance*, which is discussed later in this lesson.

C++ Syntax of Derivation

How would you inherit class Carp from class Fish, or in general a class Derived from class Base? C++ syntax for doing this would be the following:

```
class Base
{
    // ... base class members
};

class Derived: access-specifier Base
{
    // ... derived class members
};
```

The access-specifier can be one of public (most frequently used) where a "derived class is a base class" relationship; private or protected for a "derived class has a base class" relationship.

An inheritance hierarchical representation for a class Carp that derives from class Fish would be

```
class Fish // base class
{
    // ... Fish's members
};

class Carp:public Fish // derived class
{
    // ... Carp's members
};
```

A compile-worthy declaration of a class Carp and class Tuna that derive from class Fish is demonstrated by Listing 10.1.

A Note About Terminology

When reading about inheritance, you will come across terms such as *inherits from* or *derives from*, which essentially mean the same.

Similarly, the base class is also called the *super class*. The class that derives from the base, also known as the *derived class*, can be called the *subclass*.

LISTING 10.1   A Simple Inheritance Hierarchy Demonstrated by the Piscean World

```
 0: #include <iostream>
 1: using namespace std;
 2:
 3: class Fish
 4: {
 5: public:
 6:     bool isFreshWaterFish;
 7:
 8:     void Swim()
 9:     {
10:         if (isFreshWaterFish)
11:             cout << "Swims in lake" << endl;
12:         else
13:             cout << "Swims in sea" << endl;
14:     }
15: };
16:
17: class Tuna: public Fish
18: {
19: public:
20:     Tuna()
21:     {
22:         isFreshWaterFish = false;
23:     }
24: };
25:
26: class Carp: public Fish
27: {
28: public:
29:     Carp()
30:     {
31:         isFreshWaterFish = true;
32:     }
33: };
34:
35: int main()
36: {
37:     Carp myLunch;
```

10

```
38:    Tuna myDinner;
39:
40:    cout << "About my food:" << endl;
41:
42:    cout << "Lunch: ";
43:    myLunch.Swim();
44:
45:    cout << "Dinner: ";
46:    myDinner.Swim();
47:
48:    return 0;
49: }
```

Output ▼

```
About my food:
Lunch: Swims in lake
Dinner: Swims in sea
```

Analysis ▼

Note Lines 37 and 38 in main() that create an instance of classes Carp and Tuna, respectively, called myLunch and myDinner. Lines 43 and 46 are where I ask my lunch and dinner to swim by invoking method Swim(). Now, look at the class definitions of Tuna in Lines 17–24 and Carp in Lines 26–33. As you can see, these classes are compact with their constructors setting the Boolean flag Fish::isFreshWaterFish to the appropriate values. This flag is later used in function Fish::Swim(). Neither of the two derived classes seems to define a method Swim() that you have managed to successfully invoke in main(). This is because Swim() is a public member of base class Fish that they inherit from, defined in Lines 3–15. This public inheritance in Lines 17 and 26 automatically exposes the base class's public members, including method Swim(), through instances of the derived classes Carp and Tuna, which we invoke in main().

Access Specifier Keyword `protected`

Listing 10.1 is one where class Fish has a public attribute isFreshWaterFish that is set by the derived classes Tuna and Carp so as to customize (also called *specialize*) the behavior of Fish and adapt it to saltwater and freshwater, respectively. However, Listing 10.1 exhibits a serious flaw: If you want, even main() could tamper with isFreshWater-Fish, which is public and hence open for manipulation from outside class Fish:

```
myDinner.isFreshWaterFish = true; // but Tuna isn't a fresh water fish!
```

Apparently, you need a mechanism that allows derived class members to modify chosen attributes of the base class, while denying access to the same from everyone else. This means that you want Boolean flag `isFreshWaterFish` in class `Fish` to be accessible to class `Tuna` and class `Carp`, but not accessible to `main()` that instantiates classes `Tuna` or `Carp`. This is where keyword `protected` helps you.

> **NOTE**
>
> `protected`, like `public` and `private`, is also an access specifier. When you declare a class attribute or function as `protected`, you are effectively making it accessible to classes that derive (and friends), yet simultaneously making it inaccessible to everyone else outside the class, including `main()`.

`protected` is the access specifier you should use if you want a certain attribute in a base class to be accessible to classes that derive from this base, as demonstrated in Listing 10.2.

10

LISTING 10.2 A Better `class Fish` Using the `protected` Keyword to Expose Its Member Attribute Only to the Derived Classes

```
 0: #include <iostream>
 1: using namespace std;
 2:
 3: class Fish
 4: {
 5: protected:
 6:    bool isFreshWaterFish; // accessible only to derived classes
 7:
 8: public:
 9:    void Swim()
10:    {
11:        if (isFreshWaterFish)
12:           cout << "Swims in lake" << endl;
13:        else
14:           cout << "Swims in sea" << endl;
15:    }
16: };
17:
18: class Tuna: public Fish
19: {
20: public:
21:    Tuna()
22:    {
23:        isFreshWaterFish = false; // set protected member in base
24:    }
25: };
```

```
26:
27: class Carp: public Fish
28: {
29: public:
30:     Carp()
31:     {
32:         isFreshWaterFish = false;
33:     }
34: };
35:
36: int main()
37: {
38:     Carp myLunch;
39:     Tuna myDinner;
40:
41:     cout << "About my food" << endl;
42:
43:     cout << "Lunch: ";
44:     myLunch.Swim();
45:
46:     cout << "Dinner: ";
47:     myDinner.Swim();
48:
49:     // uncomment line below to see that protected members
50:     // are not accessible from outside the class hierarchy
51:     // myLunch.isFreshWaterFish = false;
52:
53:     return 0;
54: }
```

Output ▼

```
About my food
Lunch: Swims in lake
Dinner: Swims in sea
```

Analysis ▼

In spite of the fact that the output of Listing 10.2 is the same as Listing 10.1, there are a good number of fundamental changes to class Fish as defined in Lines 3–16. The first and most evident change is that the Boolean member Fish::isFreshWaterFish is now a protected attribute, and hence, not accessible via main() as shown in Line 51 (uncomment it to see a compiler error). All the same, this member of Fish with access specifier protected is accessible from the derived classes Tuna and Carp as shown in Lines 23 and 32, respectively. What this little program effectively demonstrates is the use of keyword protected in ensuring that base class attributes that need to be inherited are protected from being accessed outside the class hierarchy.

Basics of Inheritance

279

This is an important aspect of object-oriented programming, combining data abstraction and inheritance, in ensuring that derived classes can safely inherit base class attributes that cannot be tampered with by anyone outside this hierarchical system.

Base Class Initialization—Passing Parameters to the Base Class

What if a base class were to contain an overloaded constructor that requires arguments at the time of instantiation? How would such a base class be instantiated when the derived class is being constructed? The clue lies in using initialization lists and in invoking the appropriate base class constructor via the constructor of the derived class as shown in the following code:

```
class Base
{
public:
    Base(int someNumber) // overloaded constructor
    {
        // Use someNumber
    }
};
Class Derived: public Base
{
public:
    Derived(): Base(25)  // instantiate Base with argument 25
    {
        // derived class constructor code
    }
};
```

This mechanism can be quite useful in class Fish wherein, by supplying a Boolean input parameter to the constructor of Fish that initializes Fish::isFreshWaterFish, this base class Fish can ensure that every derived class is forced to mention whether the Fish is a freshwater one or a saltwater one as shown in Listing 10.3.

LISTING 10.3 Derived Class Constructor with Initialization Lists

```
0: #include <iostream>
1: using namespace std;
2:
3: class Fish
4: {
5: protected:
6:     bool isFreshWaterFish; // accessible only to derived classes
7:
8: public:
```

```
 9:      // Fish constructor
10:      Fish(bool isFreshWater) : isFreshWaterFish(isFreshWater){}
11:
12:      void Swim()
13:      {
14:         if (isFreshWaterFish)
15:            cout << "Swims in lake" << endl;
16:         else
17:            cout << "Swims in sea" << endl;
18:      }
19: };
20:
21: class Tuna: public Fish
22: {
23: public:
24:      Tuna(): Fish(false) {} // constructor initializes base
25: };
26:
27: class Carp: public Fish
28: {
29: public:
30:      Carp(): Fish(true) {}
31: };
32:
33: int main()
34: {
35:      Carp myLunch;
36:      Tuna myDinner;
37:
38:      cout << "About my food" << endl;
39:
40:      cout << "Lunch: ";
41:      myLunch.Swim();
42:
43:      cout << "Dinner: ";
44:      myDinner.Swim();
45:
46:      return 0;
47: }
```

Output ▼

```
About my food
Lunch: Swims in lake
Dinner: Swims in sea
```

Analysis ▼

Fish now has a constructor that takes a default parameter initializing Fish::is FreshWaterFish. Thus, the only possibility to create an object of Fish is via providing it a parameter that initialized the protected member. This way class Fish ensures that the protected member doesn't contain a random value, especially if a derived class forgets to set it. Derived classes Tuna and Carp are now forced to define a constructor that instantiates the base class instance of Fish with the right parameter (true or false, indicating freshwater or otherwise), as shown in Lines 24 and 30, respectively.

NOTE

In Listing 10.3 you see that boolean member variable Fish::isFreshWaterFish was never accessed directly by a derived class in spite of it being a protected member, as this variable was set via the constructor of Fish.

To ensure maximum security, if the derived classes don't need to access a base class attribute, remember to mark the attribute private. Therefore, a superior version of Listing 10.3 would feature Fish::isFreshWaterFish as private, for it is consumed only by base class Fish. See Listing 10.4.

10

Derived Class Overriding Base Class's Methods

If a class Derived implements the same functions with the same return values and signatures as in a class Base it inherits from, it effectively overrides that method in class Base as shown in the following code:

```
class Base
{
public:
    void DoSomething()
    {
        // implementation code… Does something
    }
};
class Derived:public Base
{
public:
    void DoSomething()
    {
        // implementation code… Does something else
    }
};
```

Thus, if method DoSomething() were to be invoked using an instance of Derived, then it would not invoke the functionality in class Base.

If classes `Tuna` and `Carp` were to implement their own `Swim()` method that also exists in the base class as `Fish::Swim()`, then a call to `Swim` as shown in `main()` from the following excerpt of Listing 10.3

```
36:    Tuna myDinner;
// ...other lines
44:    myDinner.Swim();
```

would result in the local implementation of `Tuna::Swim()` being invoked, which essentially overrides the base class's `Fish::Swim()` method. This is demonstrated by Listing 10.4.

LISTING 10.4   Derived Classes `Tuna` and `Carp` Overriding Method `Swim()` in Base Class `Fish`

```
0: #include <iostream>
1: using namespace std;
2:
3: class Fish
4: {
5: private:
6:    bool isFreshWaterFish;
7:
8: public:
9:    // Fish constructor
10:    Fish(bool isFreshWater) : isFreshWaterFish(isFreshWater){}
11:
12:    void Swim()
13:    {
14:       if (isFreshWaterFish)
15:          cout << "Swims in lake" << endl;
16:       else
17:          cout << "Swims in sea" << endl;
18:    }
19: };
20:
21: class Tuna: public Fish
22: {
23: public:
24:    Tuna(): Fish(false) {}
25:
26:    void Swim()
27:    {
28:       cout << "Tuna swims real fast" << endl;
29:    }
30: };
31:
32: class Carp: public Fish
33: {
34: public:
```

```
35:      Carp(): Fish(true) {}
36:
37:      void Swim()
38:      {
39:          cout << "Carp swims real slow" << endl;
40:      }
41: };
42:
43: int main()
44: {
45:      Carp myLunch;
46:      Tuna myDinner;
47:
48:      cout << "About my food" << endl;
49:
50:      cout << "Lunch: ";
51:      myLunch.Swim();
52:
53:      cout << "Dinner: ";
54:      myDinner.Swim();
55:
56:      return 0;
57: }
```

Output ▼

```
About my food
Lunch: Carp swims real slow
Dinner: Tuna swims real fast
```

Analysis ▼

The output demonstrates that `myLunch.Swim()` in Line 51 invokes `Carp::Swim()` defined in Lines 37–40. Similarly, `myDinner.Swim()` from Line 54 invokes `Tuna::Swim()` defined in Lines 26–29. In other words, the implementation of `Fish::Swim()` in the base class `Fish`, as shown in Lines 12–18, is overridden by the identical function `Swim()` defined by the classes `Tuna` and `Carp` that derive from `Fish`. The only way to invoke `Fish::Swim()` is by having `main()` use the *scope resolution operator* (::) in explicitly invoking `Fish::Swim()`, as shown later in this lesson.

Invoking Overridden Methods of a Base Class

In Listing 10.4, you saw an example of derived `class Tuna` overriding the `Swim()` function in `Fish` by implementing its version of the same. Essentially:

```
Tuna myDinner;
myDinner.Swim(); // will invoke Tuna::Swim()
```

If you want to be invoke `Fish::Swim()` in Listing 10.4 via `main()`, you need to use the scope resolution operator (::) in the following syntax:

```
myDinner.Fish::Swim(); // invokes Fish::Swim() using instance of Tuna
```

Listing 10.5 that follows shortly demonstrates invoking a base class member using an instance of the derived class.

Invoking Methods of a Base Class in a Derived Class

Typically, `Fish::Swim()` would contain a generic implementation of swimming applicable to all fishes, tunas, and carps included. If your specialized implementations in `Tuna:Swim()` and `Carp::Swim()` need to reuse the base class's generic implementation of `Fish::Swim()`, you use the scope resolution operator (::) as shown in the following code:

```
class Carp: public Fish
{
public:
    Carp(): Fish(true) {}

    void Swim()
    {
        cout << "Carp swims real slow" << endl;
        Fish::Swim();  // invoke base class function using operator::
    }
};
```

This is demonstrated in Listing 10.5.

LISTING 10.5 Using Scope Resolution Operator (::) to Invoke Base Class Functions from Derived Class and `main()`

```
 0: #include <iostream>
 1: using namespace std;
 2:
 3: class Fish
 4: {
 5: private:
 6:     bool isFreshWaterFish;
 7:
 8: public:
 9:     // Fish constructor
10:     Fish(bool isFreshWater) : isFreshWaterFish(isFreshWater){}
11:
12:     void Swim()
13:     {
```

```
14:         if (isFreshWaterFish)
15:             cout << "Swims in lake" << endl;
16:         else
17:             cout << "Swims in sea" << endl;
18:     }
19: };
20:
21: class Tuna: public Fish
22: {
23: public:
24:     Tuna(): Fish(false) {}
25:
26:     void Swim()
27:     {
28:         cout << "Tuna swims real fast" << endl;
29:     }
30: };
31:
32: class Carp: public Fish
33: {
34: public:
35:     Carp(): Fish(true) {}
36:
37:     void Swim()
38:     {
39:         cout << "Carp swims real slow" << endl;
40:         Fish::Swim();
41:     }
42: };
43:
44: int main()
45: {
46:     Carp myLunch;
47:     Tuna myDinner;
48:
49:     cout << "About my food" << endl;
50:
51:     cout << "Lunch: ";
52:     myLunch.Swim();
53:
54:     cout << "Dinner: ";
55:     myDinner.Fish::Swim();
56:
57:     return 0;
58: }
```

Output ▼

```
About my food
Lunch: Carp swims real slow
Swims in lake
Dinner: Swims in sea
```

Analysis ▼

`Carp::Swim()` in Lines 37–41 demonstrates calling the base class function
`Fish::Swim()` using the scope resolution operator (::). Line 55, on the other hand,
shows how you would use the scope resolution operator (::) to invoke base class method
`Fish::Swim()` from `main()` given an instance of derived class `Tuna`.

Derived Class Hiding Base Class's Methods

Overriding can take an extreme form where `Tuna::Swim()` can potentially hide all overloaded versions of `Fish::Swim()` available, even causing compilation failure when the
overloaded ones are used (hence, called hidden), as demonstrated by Listing 10.6.

LISTING 10.6   `Tuna::Swim()` Hides Overloaded Method `Fish::Swim(bool)`

```
0: #include <iostream>
1: using namespace std;
2:
3: class Fish
4: {
5: public:
6:     void Swim()
7:     {
8:         cout << "Fish swims... !" << endl;
9:     }
10:
11:     void Swim(bool isFreshWaterFish) // overloaded version
12:     {
13:         if (isFreshWaterFish)
14:             cout << "Swims in lake" << endl;
15:         else
16:             cout << "Swims in sea" << endl;
17:     }
18: };
19:
20: class Tuna: public Fish
21: {
22: public:
23:     void Swim()
24:     {
25:         cout << "Tuna swims real fast" << endl;
26:     }
27: };
28:
29: int main()
30: {
31:     Tuna myDinner;
32:
```

```
33:     cout << "About my food" << endl;
34:
35:     // myDinner.Swim(false);//failure: Tuna::Swim() hides Fish::Swim(bool)
36:     myDinner.Swim();
37:
38:     return 0;
39: }
```

Output ▼

```
About my food
Tuna swims real fast
```

Analysis ▼

This version of class Fish is a bit different from those that you have seen so far. Apart from being a minimalized version to explain the problem at hand, this version of Fish contains two overloaded methods for Swim(), one that takes no parameters, as shown in Lines 6–9, and another that takes a bool parameter, as shown in Lines 11–17. As Tuna inherits public from Fish as shown in Line 20, one would not be wrong to expect that both versions of method Fish::Swim() would be available via an instance of class Tuna. The fact is, however, that Tuna implementing its own Tuna::Swim(), as shown in Lines 23–26, results in the hiding of Fish::Swim(bool) from the compiler. If you uncomment Line 35, you see a compilation failure.

So, if you want to invoke the Fish::Swim(bool) function via an instance of Tuna, you have the following solutions:

- Solution 1: Use the scope resolution operator in main():

```
myDinner.Fish::Swim();
```

- Solution 2: Use keyword using in class Tuna to unhide Swim() in class Fish:

```
class Tuna: public Fish
{
public:
   using Fish::Swim;   // unhide all Swim() methods in class Fish

   void Swim()
   {
      cout << "Tuna swims real fast" << endl;
   }
};
```

10

■ Solution 3: Override all overloaded variants of `Swim()` in class Tuna (invoke methods of `Fish::Swim(...)` via `Tuna::Fish(...)` if you want):

```
class Tuna: public Fish
{
public:
    void Swim(bool isFreshWaterFish)
    {
        Fish::Swim(isFreshWaterFish);
    }

    void Swim()
    {
        cout << "Tuna swims real fast" << endl;
    }
};
```

Order of Construction

So, when you create an object of `class Tuna` that derives from `class Fish`, was the constructor of `Tuna` invoked before or after the constructor of class `Fish`? Additionally, within the instantiation of objects in the class hierarchy, what respective order do member attributes such as `Fish::isFreshWaterFish` have? Thankfully, the instantiation sequence is standardized. Base class objects are instantiated before the derived class. So, the `Fish` part of `Tuna` is constructed first, so that member attributes—especially the protected and public ones contained in `class Fish`—are ready for consumption when `class Tuna` is instantiated. Within the instantiation of `class Fish` and `class Tuna`, the member attributes (such as `Fish::isFreshWaterFish`) are instantiated before the constructor `Fish::Fish()` is invoked, ensuring that member attributes are ready before the constructor works with them. The same applies to `Tuna::Tuna()`.

Order of Destruction

When an instance of `Tuna` goes out of scope, the sequence of destruction is the opposite to that of construction. Listing 10.7 is a simple example that demonstrates the sequence of construction and destruction.

LISTING 10.7   The Order of Construction and Destruction of the Base Class, Derived Class, and Members Thereof

```
0: #include <iostream>
1: using namespace std;
2:
3: class FishDummyMember
```

```
 4: {
 5: public:
 6:    FishDummyMember()
 7:    {
 8:        cout << "FishDummyMember constructor" << endl;
 9:    }
10:
11:    ~FishDummyMember()
12:    {
13:        cout << "FishDummyMember destructor" << endl;
14:    }
15: };
16:
17: class Fish
18: {
19: protected:
20:    FishDummyMember dummy;
21:
22: public:
23:    // Fish constructor
24:    Fish()
25:    {
26:        cout << "Fish constructor" << endl;
27:    }
28:
29:    ~Fish()
30:    {
31:        cout << "Fish destructor" << endl;
32:    }
33: };
34:
35: class TunaDummyMember
36: {
37: public:
38:    TunaDummyMember()
39:    {
40:        cout << "TunaDummyMember constructor" << endl;
41:    }
42:
43:    ~TunaDummyMember()
44:    {
45:        cout << "TunaDummyMember destructor" << endl;
46:    }
47: };
48:
49:
50: class Tuna: public Fish
51: {
52: private:
53:    TunaDummyMember dummy;
54:
```

10

```
55: public:
56:     Tuna()
57:     {
58:         cout << "Tuna constructor" << endl;
59:     }
60:     ~Tuna()
61:     {
62:         cout << "Tuna destructor" << endl;
63:     }
64:
65: };
66:
67: int main()
68: {
69:     Tuna myDinner;
70: }
```

Output ▼

```
FishDummyMember constructor
Fish constructor
TunaDummyMember constructor
Tuna constructor
Tuna destructor
TunaDummyMember destructor
Fish destructor
FishDummyMember destructor
```

Analysis ▼

main() as shown in Lines 67–70 is pretty short for the volume of output it generates. Instantiation of a Tuna is enough to generate these lines of output because of the cout statements that you have inserted into the constructors and destructors of all objects involved. For the sake of understanding how member variables are instantiated and destroyed, you defined two dummy classes, FishDummyMember, and TunaDummyMember with cout in their constructors and destructors. class Fish and class Tuna contain a member of each of these dummy classes as shown in Lines 20 and 53. The output indicates that when an object of class Tuna is instantiated, instantiation actually starts at the top of the hierarchy. So, the base class Fish part of class Tuna is instantiated first, and in doing so, the members of the Fish—that is, Fish::dummy—are instantiated first. This is then followed by the constructor of the Fish, which is rightfully executed after the member attributes such as dummy have been constructed. After the base class has been constructed, the instantiation of Tuna continues first with instantiation of member Tuna::dummy, finally followed by the execution of the constructor code in Tuna::Tuna(). The output demonstrates that the sequence of destruction is exactly the opposite.

Private Inheritance

Private inheritance differs from public inheritance (which is what you have seen up to now) in that the keyword `private` is used in the line where the derived class declares its inheritance from a base class:

```
class Base
{
   // ... base class members and methods
};

class Derived: private Base      // private inheritance
{
   // ... derived class members and methods
};
```

Private inheritance of the base class means that all public members and attributes of the base class are private (that is, inaccessible) to anyone with an instance of the derived class. In other words, even public members and methods of `class Base` can only be consumed by `class Derived`, but not by anyone else in possession of an instance of `Derived`.

This is in sharp contrast to the examples with `Tuna` and base `Fish` that you have been following since Listing 10.1. `main()` in Listing 10.1 could invoke function `Fish::Swim()` on an instance of `Tuna` because `Fish::Swim()` is a public method and because `class Tuna` derives from `class Fish` using `public` inheritance.

Thus, for the world outside the inheritance hierarchy, `private` inheritance essentially does not imply an "is-a" relationship (imagine a tuna that can't swim!). As private inheritance allows base class attributes and methods to be consumed only by the subclass that derives from it, this relationship is also called a "has-a" relationship. There are a few examples of private inheritance in some things you see around you in daily life (see Table 10.2).

TABLE 10.2 Examples of Private Inheritance Taken from Daily Life

Base Class	Example Derived Class
Motor	Car (Car "has a" Motor)
Heart	Mammal (Mammal "has a" Heart)
Nib	Pen (Pen "has a" Nib)

10

Let's visualize private inheritance in a car's relationship to its motor. See Listing 10.8.

LISTING 10.8 A class Car Related to class Motor via private Inheritance

```
 0: #include <iostream>
 1: using namespace std;
 2:
 3: class Motor
 4: {
 5: public:
 6:     void SwitchIgnition()
 7:     {
 8:         cout << "Ignition ON" << endl;
 9:     }
10:     void PumpFuel()
11:     {
12:         cout << "Fuel in cylinders" << endl;
13:     }
14:     void FireCylinders()
15:     {
16:         cout << "Vroooom" << endl;
17:     }
18: };
19:
20: class Car:private Motor // private inheritance
21: {
22: public:
23:     void Move()
24:     {
25:         SwitchIgnition();
26:         PumpFuel();
27:         FireCylinders();
28:     }
29: };
30:
31: int main()
32: {
33:     Car myDreamCar;
34:     myDreamCar.Move();
35:
36:     return 0;
37: }
```

Output ▼

```
Ignition ON
Fuel in cylinders
Vroooom
```

Analysis ▼

`class Motor` defined in Lines 3–18 is simple with three `public` member functions that switch ignition, pump fuel, and fire the cylinders. `class Car` as Line 20 demonstrates inherits from `Motor`, using keyword `private`. Thus, public function `Car::Move()` invokes members from the base class `Motor`. If you try inserting the following in `main()`:

```
myDreamCar.PumpFuel(); // cannot access base's public member
```

it fails compilation with an error similar to `error C2247: Motor::PumpFuel not accessible` because `'Car' uses 'private' to inherit from 'Motor.'`

NOTE

If another `class RaceCar` had to inherit from `Car`, then irrespective of the nature of inheritance between `RaceCar` and `Car`, `RaceCar` would not have access to any public member or function of base class `Motor`. This is because the relationship between `Car` and `Motor` is one of `private` inheritance, meaning that all entities other than `Car` have `private` access (that is, no access) to `public` and `protected` members of `Base` when using an instance of `Car`.

In other words, the most restrictive access specifier takes dominance in the compiler's calculation of whether one class should have access to a base class's `public` or `protected` members.

10

Protected Inheritance

Protected inheritance differs from public inheritance in that the keyword `protected` is used in the line where the derived class declares its inheritance from a base class:

```
class Base
{
    // ... base class members and methods
};

class Derived: protected Base      // protected inheritance
{
    // ... derived class members and methods
};
```

Protected inheritance is similar to private inheritance in the following ways:

- It also signifies a has-a relationship.
- It also lets the derived class access all public and protected members of Base.
- Those outside the inheritance hierarchy with an instance of Derived cannot access public members of Base.

Yet, protected inheritance is a bit different when it comes to the derived class being inherited from:

```
class Derived2: protected Derived
{
    // can access public & protected members of Base
};
```

Protected inheritance hierarchy allows the subclass of the subclass (that is, Derived2) access to public and protected members of the Base as shown in Listing 10.9. This would not be possible if the inheritance between Derived and Base were private.

LISTING 10.9 class RaceCar That Derives from class Car That Derives from class Motor Using protected Inheritance

```
 0: #include <iostream>
 1: using namespace std;
 2:
 3: class Motor
 4: {
 5: public:
 6:     void SwitchIgnition()
 7:     {
 8:         cout << "Ignition ON" << endl;
 9:     }
10:     void PumpFuel()
11:     {
12:         cout << "Fuel in cylinders" << endl;
13:     }
14:     void FireCylinders()
15:     {
16:         cout << "Vroooom" << endl;
17:     }
18: };
19:
20: class Car:protected Motor
21: {
22: public:
23:     void Move()
24:     {
```

```
25:        SwitchIgnition();
26:        PumpFuel();
27:        FireCylinders();
28:    }
29: };
30:
31: class RaceCar:protected Car
32: {
33: public:
34:    void Move()
35:    {
36:        SwitchIgnition();  // RaceCar has access to members of
37:        PumpFuel();  // base Motor due to "protected" inheritance
38:        FireCylinders(); // between RaceCar & Car, Car & Motor
39:        FireCylinders();
40:        FireCylinders();
41:    }
42: };
43:
44: int main()
45: {
46:    RaceCar myDreamCar;
47:    myDreamCar.Move();
48:
49:    return 0;
50: }
```

10

Output ▼

```
Ignition ON
Fuel in cylinders
Vroooom
Vroooom
Vroooom
```

Analysis ▼

class Car inherits using protected from Motor as shown in Line 20. class RaceCar inherits using protected from class Car using protected as shown in Line 31. As you can see, the implementation of RaceCar::Move() uses public methods defined in base class Motor. This access to the ultimate base class Motor via intermediate base class Car is governed by the relationship between Car and Motor. If this were private instead of protected, SuperClass would have no access to the public members of Motor as the compiler would choose the most restrictive of the relevant access specifiers. Note that the nature of the relationship between the classes Car and RaceCar plays no role in access to base Motor, while the relationship between Car and

`Motor` does. So, even if you change `protected` in Line 31 to `public` or to `private`, the fate of compilation of this program remains unchanged.

CAUTION

Use `private` or `protected` inheritance only when you have to. In most cases where private inheritance is used, such as that of the Car and the Motor, the base class could have as well been a member attribute of the `class Car` instead of being a super-class. By inheriting from `class Motor`, you have essentially restricted your Car to having only one motor, for no significant gain over having an instance of `class Motor` as a `private` member.

Cars have evolved, and hybrid cars, for instance, have a gas motor in addition to an electric one. Our inheritance hierarchy for `class Car` would prove to be a bottleneck in being compatible to such developments.

NOTE

Having an instance of `Motor` as a `private` member instead of inheriting from it is called *composition* or *aggregation*. Such a `class Car` looks like this:

```
class Car
{
private:
    Motor heartOfCar;

public:
    void Move()
    {
        heartOfCar.SwitchIgnition();
        heartOfCar.PumpFuel();
        heartOfCar.FireCylinders();
    }
};
```

This can be good design as it enables you to easily add more motors as member attributes to an existing Car class without changing its inheritance hierarchy or its design with respect to its clients.

The Problem of Slicing

What happens when a programmer does the following?

```
Derived objDerived;
Base objectBase = objDerived;
```

Or, alternatively, what if a programmer does this?

```
void UseBase(Base input);
...
Derived objDerived;
UseBase(objDerived);   // copy of objDerived will be sliced and sent
```

In both cases, an object of type `Derived` is being copied into another of type `Base`, either explicitly via assignment or by passing as an argument. What happens in these cases is that the compiler copies only the `Base` part of `objDerived`—that is, not the complete object. The information contained by the data members belonging to `Derived` is lost in the process. This is not anticipated, and this unwanted reduction of that part of data that makes the `Derived` a specialization of `Base` is called *slicing*.

10

CAUTION

> To avoid slicing problems, don't pass parameters by value. Pass them as pointers to the base class or as a (optionally `const`) reference to the same.

Multiple Inheritance

Earlier in this lesson I mentioned that in some certain cases multiple inheritance might be relevant, such as with the platypus. The platypus is part mammal, part bird, and part reptile. For such cases, C++ allows a class to derive from two or more base classes:

```
class Derived: access-specifier Base1, access-specifier Base2
{
    // class members
};
```

The class diagram for a platypus, as illustrated by Figure 10.3, looks different from the previous ones for `Tuna` and `Carp` (refer to Figure 10.2).

FIGURE 10.3
Relationship of a
`class Platypus`,
to classes
`Mammal`, `Reptile`,
and `Bird`.

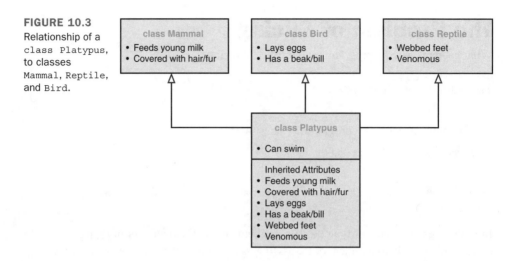

Thus, the C++ representation of `class Platypus` is the following:

```
class Platypus: public Mammal, public Reptile, public Bird
{
    // ... platypus members
};
```

A manifestation of `Platypus` that demonstrates multiple inheritance is demonstrated by Listing 10.10.

LISTING 10.10   Using Multiple Inheritance to Model a Platypus That Is Part Mammal, Part Bird, and Part Reptile

```
0: #include <iostream>
1: using namespace std;
2:
3: class Mammal
4: {
5: public:
6:     void FeedBabyMilk()
7:     {
8:         cout << "Mammal: Baby says glug!" << endl;
9:     }
10: };
11:
12: class Reptile
13: {
```

```
14: public:
15:    void SpitVenom()
16:    {
17:        cout << "Reptile: Shoo enemy! Spits venom!" << endl;
18:    }
19: };
20:
21: class Bird
22: {
23: public:
24:    void LayEggs()
25:    {
26:        cout << "Bird: Laid my eggs, am lighter now!" << endl;
27:    }
28: };
29:
30: class Platypus: public Mammal, public Bird, public Reptile
31: {
32: public:
33:    void Swim()
34:    {
35:        cout << "Platypus: Voila, I can swim!" << endl;
36:    }
37: };
38:
39: int main()
40: {
41:    Platypus realFreak;
42:    realFreak.LayEggs();
43:    realFreak.FeedBabyMilk();
44:    realFreak.SpitVenom();
45:    realFreak.Swim();
46:
47:    return 0;
48: }
```

10

Output ▼

```
Bird: Laid my eggs, am lighter now!
Mammal: Baby says glug!
Reptile: Shoo enemy! Spits venom!
Platypus: Voila, I can swim!
```

Analysis ▼

class Platypus features a really compact definition in Lines 30–37. It essentially does nothing more than inherit from the three classes Mammal, Reptile, and Bird. main()

in Lines 41–44 is able to invoke these three characteristics of the individual base classes using an object of the derived class Platypus that is named realFreak. In addition to invoking the functions inherited from classes Mammal, Bird, and Reptile, main() in Line 45 invokes Platypus::Swim(). This program demonstrates the syntax of multiple inheritance and also how a derived class exposes all the public attributes (in this case public member functions) of its many base classes.

Avoiding Inheritance Using final

Starting with C++11, compilers support specifier final. It is used to ensure that a class declared as final cannot be used as a base class. In Listing 10.10 for instance, class Platypus represents a well-evolved species. You may therefore want to ensure that this class is final, thereby blocking every possibility to inherit from it. A version of class Platypus taken from Listing 10.10 and declared as final would look like this:

```
class Platypus final: public Mammal, public Bird, public Reptile
{
public:
    void Swim()
    {
        cout << "Platypus: Voila, I can swim!" << endl;
    }
};
```

In addition to classes, final can also be used on member functions in controlling polymorphic behavior. This is discussed in Lesson 11, "Polymorphism."

NOTE

Platypus can swim, but it's not a fish. Hence, in Listing 10.10, you did not inherit Platypus from Fish just for the convenience of reusing an existing Fish::Swim() function. When making design decisions, don't forget that public inheritance also should signify an "is-a" relationship. It should not be used indiscriminately with the purpose of fulfilling goals related to code reuse. Those goals can still be achieved differently.

DO	**DON'T**
DO create a `public` inheritance hierarchy to establish an is-a relationship.	**DON'T** create an inheritance hierarchy just to reuse a trivial function.
DO create a `private` or `protected` inheritance hierarchy to establish a has-a relationship.	**DON'T** use private or public inheritance indiscriminately as they can end up being architectural bottlenecks towards the future scalability of your application.
DO remember that public inheritance means that classes deriving from the derived class have access to the `public` and `protected` members of the base class. An object of the derived class can be used to access public members of the base.	**DON'T** program derived class functions that hide those in the base class by having the same name but a different set of input parameters.
DO remember that private inheritance means that even classes deriving from the derived class have no access to any member of the base class.	
DO remember that protected inheritance means that classes deriving from the derived class have access to the `public` and `protected` methods of the base class. Yet, an object of the derived class cannot be used to access public members of the base.	
DO remember that irrespective of the nature of inheritance relationship, `private` members in the base class cannot be accessed by any derived class.	

10

Summary

In this lesson, you learned the basics of inheritance in C++. You learned that public inheritance is an is-a relationship between the derived class and base class, whereas `private` and `protected` inheritances create has-a relationships. You saw the application of access specifier `protected` in exposing attributes of a base class only to the derived class, but keeping them hidden from classes outside the inheritance hierarchy. You learned that `protected` inheritance differs from `private` in that the derived classes of the `derived` class can access `public` and `protected` members of the base class, which is not possible in private inheritance. You learned the basics of overriding methods and hiding them and how to avoid unwanted method hiding via the `using` keyword.

You are now ready to answer some questions and then continue to learning the next major pillar of object-oriented programming, polymorphism.

Q&A

Q I have been asked to model `class Mammal` along with a few mammals such as the `Human`, `Lion`, and `Whale`. Should I use an inheritance hierarchy, and if so which one?

A As `Human`, `Lion`, and `Whale` are all mammals and essentially fulfill an is-a relationship, you should use public inheritance where `class Mammal` is the base class, and others such as `class Human`, `Lion`, and `Whale` inherit from it.

Q What is the difference between the terms derived *class* and *subclass*?

A Essentially none. These are both used to imply a class that derives—that is, specializes—a base class.

Q A derived class uses public inheritance in relating to its base class. Can it access the base class's private members?

A No. The compiler always ensures that the most restrictive of the applicable access specifiers is in force. Irrespective of the nature of inheritance, `private` members of a class are never accessible outside the class. An exception to this rule applies to classes and functions that have been declared as a `friend`.

Workshop

The Workshop provides quiz questions to help you solidify your understanding of the material that was covered and exercises to provide you with experience in using what you've learned. Try to answer the quiz and exercise questions before checking the answers in Appendix E, and be certain you understand the answers before continuing to the next lesson.

Quiz

1. I want some base class members to be accessible to the derived class but not outside the class hierarchy. What access specifier do I use?

2. If I pass an object of the derived class as an argument to a function that takes a parameter of the base class by value, what happens?

3. Which one should I favor? Private inheritance or composition?

4. How does the using keyword help me in an inheritance hierarchy?

5. A class Derived inherits private from class Base. Another class SubDerived inherits public from class Derived. Can SubDerived access public members of class Base?

Exercises

1. In what order are the constructors invoked for class Platypus as shown in Listing 10.10?

2. Show how a class Polygon, class Triangle, and class Shape are related to each other.

3. class D2 inherits from class D1, which inherits from class Base. To keep D2 from accessing the public members in Base, what access specifier would you use and where would you use it?

4. What is the nature of inheritance with this code snippet?

```
class Derived: Base
{
    // ... Derived members
};
```

5. BUG BUSTERS: What is the problem in this code:

```
class Derived: public Base
{
    // ... Derived members
};
void SomeFunc (Base value)
{
    // ...
}
```

LESSON 11
Polymorphism

Having learned the basics of inheritance, creating an inheritance hierarchy, and understanding that public inheritance essentially models an is-a relationship, it's time to move on to consuming this knowledge in learning the holy grail of object-oriented programming: polymorphism.

In this lesson, you find out

- What polymorphism actually means
- What virtual functions do and how to use them
- What abstract base classes are and how to declare them
- What virtual inheritance means and where you need it

Basics of Polymorphism

"Poly" is Greek for *many*, and "morph" means *form*. Polymorphism is that feature of object-oriented languages that allows objects of different types to be treated similarly. This lesson focuses on polymorphic behavior that can be implemented in C++ via the inheritance hierarchy, also known as *subtype polymorphism*.

Need for Polymorphic Behavior

In Lesson 10, "Implementing Inheritance," you found out how Tuna and Carp inherit public method Swim() from Fish as shown in Listing 10.1. It is, however, possible that both Tuna and Carp provide their own Tuna::Swim() and Carp::Swim() methods to make Tuna and Carp different swimmers. Yet, as each of them is also a Fish, if a user with an instance of Tuna uses the base class type to invoke Fish::Swim(), he ends up executing only the generic part Fish::Swim() and not Tuna::Swim(), even though that base class instance Fish is a part of a Tuna. This problem is demonstrated in Listing 11.1.

NOTE	All the code samples in this lesson have been stripped to the bare essentials required to explain the topic in question and to keep the number of lines of code to a minimum to improve readability.
	When you are programming, you should program your classes correctly and create inheritance hierarchies that make sense, keeping the design and purpose of the application in perspective.

LISTING 11.1   Invoking Methods Using an Instance of the Base Class Fish That Belongs to a Tuna

```
 0: #include <iostream>
 1: using namespace std;
 2:
 3: class Fish
 4: {
 5: public:
 6:    void Swim()
 7:    {
 8:       cout << "Fish swims! " << endl;
 9:    }
10: };
11:
```

```
12: class Tuna:public Fish
13: {
14: public:
15:     // override Fish::Swim
16:     void Swim()
17:     {
18:         cout << "Tuna swims!" << endl;
19:     }
20: };
21:
22: void MakeFishSwim(Fish& inputFish)
23: {
24:     // calling Fish::Swim
25:     inputFish.Swim();
26: }
27:
28: int main()
29: {
30:     Tuna myDinner;
31:
32:     // calling Tuna::Swim
33:     myDinner.Swim();
34:
35:     // sending Tuna as Fish
36:     MakeFishSwim(myDinner);
37:
38:     return 0;
39: }
```

11

Output ▼

```
Tuna swims!
Fish swims!
```

Analysis ▼

class Tuna specializes class Fish via public inheritance as shown in Line 12. It also overrides Fish::Swim(). main() makes a direct call to Tuna::Swim() in Line 33 and passes myDinner (of type Tuna) as a parameter to MakeFishSwim() that interprets it as a reference Fish&, as shown in the declaration at Line 22. In other words, MakeFishSwim(Fish&) doesn't care if the object sent was a Tuna, handles it as a Fish, and invokes Fish::Swim(). So, the second line of output indicates that the same object Tuna produced the output of a Fish not indicating any specialization thereof (this could as well be a Carp).

What the user would ideally expect is that an object of type `Tuna` behaves like a tuna even if the method invoked is `Fish::Swim()`. In other words, when `inputFish.Swim()` is invoked in Line 25, he expects it to execute `Tuna::Swim()`. Such polymorphic behavior where an object of known type `class Fish` can behave as its actual type; namely, derived `class Tuna`, can be implemented by making `Fish::Swim()` a virtual function.

Polymorphic Behavior Implemented Using Virtual Functions

You have access to an object of type `Fish`, via pointer `Fish*` or reference `Fish&`. This object could have been instantiated solely as a `Fish`, or be part of a `Tuna` or `Carp` that inherits from `Fish`. You don't know (and don't care). You invoke method `Swim()` using this pointer or reference, like this:

```
pFish->Swim();
myFish.Swim();
```

What you expect is that the object `Fish` swims as a `Tuna` if it is part of a `Tuna`, as a `Carp` if it is part of a `Carp`, or an anonymous `Fish` if it wasn't instantiated as part of a specialized class such as `Tuna` or `Carp`. You can ensure this by declaring function `Swim()` in the base class `Fish` as a virtual function:

```
class Base
{
    virtual ReturnType FunctionName (Parameter List);
};
class Derived
{
    ReturnType FunctionName (Parameter List);
};
```

Use of keyword `virtual` means that the compiler ensures that any overriding variant of the requested base class method is invoked. Thus, if `Swim()` is declared `virtual`, invoking `myFish.Swim()` (myFish being of type `Fish&`) results in `Tuna::Swim()` being executed as demonstrated by Listing 11.2.

LISTING 11.2 The Effect of Declaring `Fish::Swim()` as a `virtual` Method

```
0: #include <iostream>
1: using namespace std;
2:
3: class Fish
4: {
5: public:
```

```
 6:    virtual void Swim()
 7:    {
 8:        cout << "Fish swims!" << endl;
 9:    }
10: };
11:
12: class Tuna:public Fish
13: {
14: public:
15:    // override Fish::Swim
16:    void Swim()
17:    {
18:        cout << "Tuna swims!" << endl;
19:    }
20: };
21:
22: class Carp:public Fish
23: {
24: public:
25:    // override Fish::Swim
26:    void Swim()
27:    {
28:        cout << "Carp swims!" << endl;
29:    }
30: };
31:
32: void MakeFishSwim(Fish& inputFish)
33: {
34:    // calling virtual method Swim()
35:    inputFish.Swim();
36: }
37:
38: int main()
39: {
40:    Tuna myDinner;
41:    Carp myLunch;
42:
43:    // sending Tuna as Fish
44:    MakeFishSwim(myDinner);
45:
46:    // sending Carp as Fish
47:    MakeFishSwim(myLunch);
48:
49:    return 0;
50: }
```

11

Output ▼

```
Tuna swims!
Carp swims!
```

Analysis ▼

The implementation of function `MakeFishSwim(Fish&)` has not changed one bit since Listing 11.1. Yet, the output it produces is dramatically different. For one, `Fish::Swim()` has not been invoked at all because of the presence of overriding variants `Tuna::Swim()` and `Carp::Swim()` that have taken priority over `Fish::Swim()` because the latter has been declared as a `virtual` function. This is a very important development. It implies that even without knowing the exact type of `Fish` being handled, the implementation `MakeFishSwim()` could result in different implementations of `Swim()` defined in different derived classes being invoked, given only a base class instance.

This is polymorphism: treating different fishes as a common type `Fish`, yet ensuring that the right implementation of `Swim()` supplied by the derived types is executed.

Need for Virtual Destructors

There is a more sinister side to the feature demonstrated by Listing 11.1—unintentionally invoking base class functionality of an instance of type derived, when a specialization is available. What happens when a function calls operator `delete` using a pointer of type `Base*` that actually points to an instance of type `Derived`?

Which destructor would be invoked? See Listing 11.3.

LISTING 11.3   A Function That Invokes Operator `delete` on `Base*`

```
0: #include <iostream>
1: using namespace std;
2:
3: class Fish
4: {
5: public:
6:    Fish()
7:    {
8:       cout << "Constructed Fish" << endl;
9:    }
10:    ~Fish()
11:    {
12:       cout << "Destroyed Fish" << endl;
13:    }
14: };
15:
16: class Tuna:public Fish
17: {
18: public:
19:    Tuna()
20:    {
21:       cout << "Constructed Tuna" << endl;
22:    }
```

```
23:     ~Tuna()
24:     {
25:         cout << "Destroyed Tuna" << endl;
26:     }
27: };
28:
29: void DeleteFishMemory(Fish* pFish)
30: {
31:     delete pFish;
32: }
33:
34: int main()
35: {
36:     cout << "Allocating a Tuna on the free store:" << endl;
37:     Tuna* pTuna = new Tuna;
38:     cout << "Deleting the Tuna: " << endl;
39:     DeleteFishMemory(pTuna);
40:
41:     cout << "Instantiating a Tuna on the stack:" << endl;
42:     Tuna myDinner;
43:     cout << "Automatic destruction as it goes out of scope: " << endl;
44:
45:     return 0;
46: }
```

Output ▼

```
Allocating a Tuna on the free store:
Constructed Fish
Constructed Tuna
Deleting the Tuna:
Destroyed Fish
Instantiating a Tuna on the stack:
Constructed Fish
Constructed Tuna
Automatic destruction as it goes out of scope:
Destroyed Tuna
Destroyed Fish
```

Analysis ▼

main() creates an instance of Tuna on the free store using new at Line 37 and then releases the allocated memory immediately after using service function DeleteFishMemory() at Line 39. For the sake of comparison, another instance of Tuna is created as a local variable myDinner on the stack at Line 42 and goes out of scope when main() ends. The output is created by the cout statements in the constructors and destructors of classes Fish and Tuna. Note that while Tuna and Fish were both constructed on the free store due to `new`, the destructor of `Tuna` was not invoked during `delete`, rather only that of the `Fish`. This is in stark contrast to the construction and destruction of local member `myDinner` where all constructors and destructors are invoked. Lesson 10 demonstrated in Listing 10.7 the correct order of construction and destruction of classes in an inheritance hierarchy, showing that all destructors need to be invoked, including `~Tuna()`. Clearly, something is amiss.

This flaw means that the destructor of a deriving class that has been instantiated on the free store using `new` would not be invoked if `delete` is called using a pointer of type `Base*`. This can result in resources not being released, memory leaks, and so on and is a problem that is not to be taken lightly.

To avoid this problem, you use virtual destructors as seen in Listing 11.4.

LISTING 11.4 Using `virtual` Destructors to Ensure That Destructors in Derived Classes Are Invoked When Deleting a Pointer of Type `Base*`

```
 0: #include <iostream>
 1: using namespace std;
 2:
 3: class Fish
 4: {
 5: public:
 6:     Fish()
 7:     {
 8:         cout << "Constructed Fish" << endl;
 9:     }
10:     virtual ~Fish()    // virtual destructor!
11:     {
12:         cout << "Destroyed Fish" << endl;
13:     }
14: };
15:
16: class Tuna:public Fish
17: {
18: public:
19:     Tuna()
20:     {
21:         cout << "Constructed Tuna" << endl;
22:     }
23:     ~Tuna()
24:     {
25:         cout << "Destroyed Tuna" << endl;
26:     }
27: };
28:
```

```
29: void DeleteFishMemory(Fish* pFish)
30: {
31:     delete pFish;
32: }
33:
34: int main()
35: {
36:     cout << "Allocating a Tuna on the free store:" << endl;
37:     Tuna* pTuna = new Tuna;
38:     cout << "Deleting the Tuna: " << endl;
39:     DeleteFishMemory(pTuna);
40:
41:     cout << "Instantiating a Tuna on the stack:" << endl;
42:     Tuna myDinner;
43:     cout << "Automatic destruction as it goes out of scope: " << endl;
44:
45:     return 0;
46: }
```

Output ▼

```
Allocating a Tuna on the free store:
Constructed Fish
Constructed Tuna
Deleting the Tuna:
Destroyed Tuna
Destroyed Fish
Instantiating a Tuna on the stack:
Constructed Fish
Constructed Tuna
Automatic destruction as it goes out of scope:
Destroyed Tuna
Destroyed Fish
```

11

Analysis ▼

The only improvement in Listing 11.4 over Listing 11.3 is the addition of keyword
virtual at Line 10 where the destructor of base class Fish has been declared. Note
that this small change resulted in the compiler essentially executing Tuna::~Tuna() in
addition to Fish::~Fish() when operator delete is invoked on Fish* that actually
points to a Tuna, as shown in Line 31. Now, this output also demonstrates that the
sequence and the invocation of constructors and destructors are the same irrespective of
whether the object of type Tuna is instantiated on the free store using new, as shown in
Line 37, or as a local variable on the stack, as shown in Line 42.

NOTE

> Always declare the base class destructor as `virtual`:
>
> ```
> class Base
> {
> public:
>     virtual ~Base() {};   // virtual destructor
> };
> ```
>
> This ensures that one with a `pointer Base*` cannot invoke `delete` in a way that instances of the deriving classes are not correctly destroyed.

How Do `virtual` Functions Work? Understanding the Virtual Function Table

NOTE

> This section is optional toward learning to use polymorphism. Feel free to skip it or read it to feed your curiosity.

Function `MakeFishSwim(Fish&)` in Listing11.2 ends up invoking `Carp::Swim()` or `Tuna::Swim()` methods in spite of the programmer calling `Fish::Swim()`within it. Clearly, at compile time, the compiler knows nothing about the nature of objects that such a function will encounter to be able to ensure that the same function ends up executing different `Swim()` methods at different points in time. The `Swim()` method that needs to be invoked is evidently a decision made at runtime, using a logic that implements polymorphism, which is supplied by the compiler at compile-time.

Consider a `class Base` that declared *N* virtual functions:

```
class Base
{
public:
    virtual void Func1()
    {
        // Func1 implementation
    }
    virtual void Func2()
    {
        // Func2 implementation
    }
```

```
   // .. so on and so forth
   virtual void FuncN()
   {
       // FuncN implementation
   }
};
```

`class Derived` that inherits from `Base` overrides `Base::Func2()`, exposing the other virtual functions directly from `class Base`:

```
class Derived: public Base
{
public:
   virtual void Func1()
   {
       // Func2 overrides Base::Func2()
   }

   // no implementation for Func2()

   virtual void FuncN()
   {
       // FuncN implementation
   }
};
```

The compiler sees an inheritance hierarchy and understands that the Base defines certain virtual functions that have been overridden in Derived. What the compiler now does is to create a table called the Virtual Function Table (VFT) for every class that implements a virtual function or derived class that overrides it. In other words, classes Base and Derived get an instance of their own Virtual Function Table. When an object of these classes is instantiated, a hidden pointer (let's call it VFT*) is initialized to the respective VFT. The Virtual Function Table can be visualized as a static array containing function pointers, each pointing to the virtual function (or override) of interest, as illustrated in Figure 11.1.

11

FIGURE 11.1
Visualization of a
Virtual Function
Table for classes
Derived and
Base.

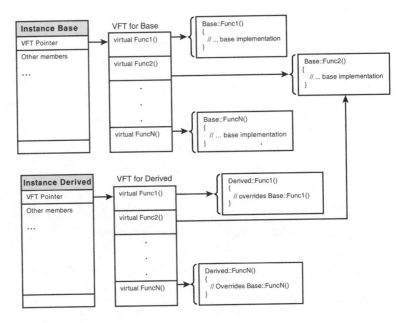

Thus, each table is comprised of function pointers, each pointing to the available implementation of a virtual function. In the case of class Derived, all except one function pointer in its VFT point to local implementations of the virtual method in Derived. Derived has not overridden Base::Func2(), and hence that function pointer points to the implementation in class Base.

This means that when a user of class Derived calls

```
CDerived objDerived;
objDerived.Func2();
```

the compiler ensures a lookup in the VFT of class Derived and ensures that the implementation Base::Func2() is invoked. This also applies to calls that use methods that have been virtually overridden:

```
void DoSomething(Base& objBase)
{
    objBase.Func1();    // invoke Derived::Func1
}
int main()
{
    Derived objDerived;
    DoSomething(objDerived);
};
```

In this case, even though `objDerived` is being interpreted via `objBase` as an instance of class `Base`, the VFT pointer in this instance is still pointing to the same table created for class `Derived`. Thus, `Func1()` executed via this VFT is certainly `Derived::Func1()`.

This is how Virtual Function Tables help the implementation of (subtype) polymorphism in C++.

The proof of existence of a hidden Virtual Function Table pointer is demonstrated by Listing 11.5, which compares the `sizeof` two identical classes—one that has virtual functions and another that doesn't.

LISTING 11.5 Demonstrating the Presence of a Hidden VFT Pointer in Comparing Two Classes Identical but for a Function Declared Virtual

```
 0: #include <iostream>
 1: using namespace std;
 2:
 3: class SimpleClass
 4: {
 5:     int a, b;
 6:
 7: public:
 8:     void DoSomething() {}
 9: };
10:
11: class Base
12: {
13:     int a, b;
14:
15: public:
16:     virtual void DoSomething() {}
17: };
18:
19: int main()
20: {
21:     cout << "sizeof(SimpleClass) = " << sizeof(SimpleClass) << endl;
22:     cout << "sizeof(Base) = " << sizeof(Base) << endl;
23:
24:     return 0;
25: }
```

Output Using 32-Bit Compiler ▼

```
sizeof(SimpleClass) = 8
sizeof(Base) = 12
```

11

Output Using 64-Bit Compiler ▼

```
sizeof(SimpleClass) = 8
sizeof(Base) = 16
```

Analysis ▼

This is a sample that has been stripped to the bare minimum. You see two classes, SimpleClass and Base, that are identical in the types and number of members, yet Base has the function DoSomething() declared as virtual (nonvirtual in SimpleClass). The difference in adding this virtual keyword is that the compiler generates a virtual function table for class Base and a reserved place for a pointer to the same in Base as a hidden member. This pointer consumes the 4 extra bytes in my 32-bit system and is the proof of the pudding.

NOTE

> C++ also allows you to query a pointer Base* if it is of type Derived* using casting operator dynamic_cast and then perform conditional execution on the basis of the result of the query.
>
> This is called runtime type identification (RTTI) and should ideally be avoided even though it is supported by most C++ compilers. This is because needing to know the type of derived class object behind a base class pointer is commonly considered poor programming practice.
>
> RTTI and dynamic_cast are discussed in Lesson 13, "Casting Operators."

Abstract Base Classes and Pure Virtual Functions

A base class that cannot be instantiated is called an *abstract base class*. Such a base class fulfills only one purpose, that of being derived from. C++ allows you to create an abstract base class using pure virtual functions.

A virtual method is said to be *pure virtual* when it has a declaration as shown in the following:

```
class AbstractBase
{
public:
    virtual void DoSomething() = 0;  // pure virtual method
};
```

This declaration essentially tells the compiler that DoSomething() needs to be implemented and by the class that derives from AbstractBase:

```
class Derived: public AbstractBase
{
public:
   void DoSomething()    // pure virtual fn. must be implemented
   {
      cout << "Implemented virtual function" << endl;
   }
};
```

Thus, what class AbstractBase has done is that it has enforced class Derived to supply an implementation for virtual method DoSomething(). This functionality where a base class can enforce support of methods with a specified name and signature in classes that derive from it is that of an interface. Think of a Fish again. Imagine a Tuna that cannot swim fast because Tuna did not override Fish::Swim(). This is a failed implementation and a flaw. Making class Fish an abstract base class with Swim as a pure virtual function ensures that Tuna that derives from Fish implements Tuna::Swim() and swims like a Tuna and not like just any Fish. See Listing 11.6.

LISTING 11.6 class Fish as an Abstract Base Class for Tuna and Carp

11

```
 0: #include <iostream>
 1: using namespace std;
 2:
 3: class Fish
 4: {
 5: public:
 6:    // define a pure virtual function Swim
 7:    virtual void Swim() = 0;
 8: };
 9:
10: class Tuna:public Fish
11: {
12: public:
13:    void Swim()
14:    {
15:       cout << "Tuna swims fast in the sea! " << endl;
16:    }
17: };
18:
19: class Carp:public Fish
20: {
21:    void Swim()
22:    {
23:       cout << "Carp swims slow in the lake!" << endl;
```

```
24:     }
25: };
26:
27: void MakeFishSwim(Fish& inputFish)
28: {
29:     inputFish.Swim();
30: }
31:
32: int main()
33: {
34:     // Fish myFish; // Fails, cannot instantiate an ABC
35:     Carp myLunch;
36:     Tuna myDinner;
37:
38:     MakeFishSwim(myLunch);
39:     MakeFishSwim(myDinner);
40:
41:     return 0;
42: }
```

Output ▼

```
Carp swims slow in the lake!
Tuna swims fast in the sea!
```

Analysis ▼

The first line in `main()` at Line 34 (commented out) is significant. It demonstrates that the compiler does not allow you to create an instance of an abstract base class ('ABC') `Fish`. It expects something concrete, such as a specialization of `Fish`—for example, `Tuna`—which makes sense even in the real-world arrangement of things. Thanks to the pure virtual function `Fish::Swim()` declared in Line 7, both `Tuna` and `Carp` are forced into implementing `Tuna::Swim()` and `Carp::Swim()`. Lines 27–30 that implement `MakeFishSwim(Fish&)` demonstrate that even if an abstract base class cannot be instantiated, you can use it as a reference or a pointer. Abstract base classes are thus a very good mechanism to declare functions that you expect derived classes to implement and fulfill. If a class `Trout` that derived from `Fish` forgets to implement `Trout::Swim()`, the compilation also fails.

NOTE | Abstract Base Classes are often simply called ABCs.

ABCs help enforce certain design constraints on your program.

Using `virtual` **Inheritance to Solve the Diamond Problem**

In Lesson 10 you saw the curious case of a duck-billed platypus that is part mammal, part bird, and part reptile. This is an example where a class `Platypus` needs to inherits from class `Mammal`, class `Bird`, and class `Reptile`. However, each of these in turn inherits from a more generic class `Animal`, as illustrated in Figure 11.2.

FIGURE 11.2
The class diagram of a platypus demonstrating multiple inheritance.

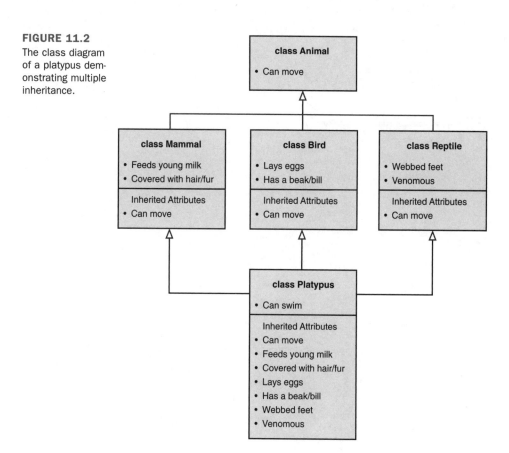

11

So, what happens when you instantiate a `Platypus`? How many instances of class `Animal` are instantiated for one instance of `Platypus`? Listing 11.7 helps answer this question.

LISTING 11.7   Checking for the Number of Base Class `Animal` Instances for One
Instance of `Platypus`

```
0: #include <iostream>
1: using namespace std;
2:
3: class Animal
4: {
5: public:
6:     Animal()
7:     {
8:         cout << "Animal constructor" << endl;
9:     }
10:
11:     // sample member
12:     int age;
13: };
14:
15: class Mammal:public Animal
16: {
17: };
18:
19: class Bird:public Animal
20: {
21: };
22:
23: class Reptile:public Animal
24: {
25: };
26:
27: class Platypus:public Mammal, public Bird, public Reptile
28: {
29: public:
30:     Platypus()
31:     {
32:         cout << "Platypus constructor" << endl;
33:     }
34: };
35:
36: int main()
37: {
38:     Platypus duckBilledP;
39:
40:     // uncomment next line to see compile failure
41:     // age is ambiguous as there are three instances of base Animal
42:     // duckBilledP.age = 25;
43:
44:     return 0;
45: }
```

Output ▼

```
Animal constructor
Animal constructor
Animal constructor
Platypus constructor
```

Analysis ▼

As the output demonstrates, due to multiple inheritance and all three base classes of `Platypus` inheriting in turn from `class Animal`, you have three instances of `Animal` created automatically for every instance of a `Platypus`, as shown in Line 38. This is ridiculous as `Platypus` is still one animal that has inherited certain attributes from `Mammal`, `Bird`, and `Reptile`. The problem in the number of instances of base `Animal` is not limited to memory consumption alone. `Animal` has an integer member `Animal::age` (that has been kept public for explanation purposes). When you want to access `Animal::age` via an instance of `Platypus`, as shown in Line 42, you get a compilation error simply because the compiler doesn't know whether you want to set `Mammal::Animal::age` or `Bird::Animal::age` or `Reptile::Animal::age`. It can get even more ridiculous—if you so wanted you could set all three:

```
duckBilledP.Mammal::Animal::age = 25;
duckBilledP.Bird::Animal::age = 25;
duckBilledP.Reptile::Animal::age = 25;
```

11

Clearly, one duck-billed platypus should have only one `age`. Yet, you want class `Platypus` to be a `Mammal`, `Bird`, and `Reptile`. The solution is in virtual inheritance. If you expect a derived class to be used as a base class, it possibly is a good idea to define its relationship to the base using the keyword virtual:

```
class Derived1: public virtual Base
{
    // ... members and functions
};
class Derived2: public virtual Base
{
    // ... members and functions
};
```

A better class `Platypus` (actually a better class `Mammal`, class `Bird`, and class `Reptile`) is in Listing 11.8.

LISTING 11.8 Demonstrating How `virtual` Keyword in Inheritance Hierarchy Helps Restrict the Number of Instances of Base Class `Animal` to One

```
0: #include <iostream>
1: using namespace std;
2:
3: class Animal
4: {
5: public:
6:    Animal()
7:    {
8:       cout << "Animal constructor" << endl;
9:    }
10:
11:    // sample member
12:    int age;
13: };
14:
15: class Mammal:public virtual Animal
16: {
17: };
18:
19: class Bird:public virtual Animal
20: {
21: };
22:
23: class Reptile:public virtual Animal
24: {
25: };
26:
27: class Platypus final:public Mammal, public Bird, public Reptile
28: {
29: public:
30:    Platypus()
31:    {
32:       cout << "Platypus constructor" << endl;
33:    }
34: };
35:
36: int main()
37: {
38:    Platypus duckBilledP;
39:
40:    // no compile error as there is only one Animal::age
41:    duckBilledP.age = 25;
42:
43:    return 0;
44: }
```

Output ▼

```
Animal constructor
Platypus constructor
```

Analysis ▼

Do a quick comparison against the output of the previous Listing 11.7, and you see that the number of instances of `class Animal` constructed has fallen to one, which is finally reflective of the fact that only one `Platypus` has been constructed as well. This is because of the keyword `virtual` used in the relationship between classes `Mammal`, `Bird`, and `Reptile` ensures that when these classes are grouped together under `Platypus` the common base `Animal` exists only in a single instance. This solves a lot of problems; one among them is Line 41 that now compiles without ambiguity resolution as shown in Listing 11.7. Also note the usage of keyword `final` in Line 27 to ensure that class `Platypus` cannot be used as a base class.

NOTE	Problems caused in an inheritance hierarchy containing two or more base classes that inherit from a common base, which results in the need for ambiguity resolution in the absence of virtual inheritance, is called the Diamond Problem.
	The name "Diamond" is possibly inspired by the shape the class diagram takes (visualize Figure 11.2 with straight and slanted lines relating `Platypus` to `Animal` via `Mammal`, `Bird`, and `Reptile` to see a diamond).

11

NOTE	The `virtual` keyword in C++ often is used in different contexts for different purposes. (My best guess is that someone wanted to save time on inventing an apt keyword.) Here is a summary:
	A function declared *virtual* means that an existing overriding function in a derived class is invoked.
	An inheritance relationship declared using keyword `virtual` between classes `Derived1` and `Derived2` that inherits from class `Base` means that another class `Derived3` that inherits from `Derived1` and `Derived2` still results in the creation of only one instance of `Base` during instantiation of type `Derived3`.
	Thus the same keyword `virtual` is used to implement two different concepts.

Specifier Override to Indicate Intention to Override

Our versions of base class `Fish` have featured a virtual function called `Swim()` as seen in the following code:

```
class Fish
{
public:
   virtual void Swim()
   {
      cout << "Fish swims!" << endl;
   }
};
```

Assume that derived class `Tuna` were to define a function `Swim()` but with a slightly different signature—one using `const` inserted unintentionally by a programmer who wants to override `Fish::Swim()`:

```
class Tuna:public Fish
{
public:
   void Swim() const
   {
      cout << "Tuna swims!" << endl;
   }
};
```

This function `Tuna::Swim()` actually does not override `Fish::Swim()`. The signatures are different thanks to the presence of `const` in `Tuna::Swim()`. Compilation succeeds, however, and the programmer may falsely believe that he has successfully overridden the function `Swim()` in `class Tuna`. C++11 and beyond give the programmer a specifier `override` that is used to verify whether the function being overridden has been declared as virtual by the base class:

```
class Tuna:public Fish
{
public:
   void Swim() const override // Error: no virtual fn with this sig in Fish
   {
      cout << "Tuna swims!" << endl;
   }
};
```

Thus, `override` supplies a powerful way of expressing the explicit intention to override a base class virtual function, thereby getting the compiler to check whether

- The base class function is `virtual`.
- The signature of the base class virtual function exactly matches the signature of the derived class function declared to `override`.

Use `final` to Prevent Function Overriding

Specifier `final`, introduced in C++11, was first presented to you in Lesson 10. A class declared as `final` cannot be used as a base class. Similarly, a `virtual` function declared as `final` cannot be overridden in a derived class.

Thus, a version of `class Tuna` that doesn't allow any further specialization of virtual function `Swim()` would look like this:

```
class Tuna:public Fish
{
public:
    // override Fish::Swim and make this final
    void Swim() override final
    {
        cout << "Tuna swims!" << endl;
    }
};
```

This version of `Tuna` can be inherited from, but `Swim()` cannot be overridden any further:

```
class BluefinTuna final:public Tuna
{
public:
    void Swim() // Error: Swim() was final in Tuna, cannot override
    {
    }
};
```

A demonstration of specifiers `override` and `final` is available in Listing 11.9.

11

NOTE

> We used `final` in the declaration of `class BluefinTuna` as well. This ensures that `class BluefinTuna` cannot be used as a base class. Therefore, the following would result in error:
>
> ```
> class FailedDerivation:public BluefinTuna
> {
> };
> ```

Virtual Copy Constructors?

Well, the question mark at the end of the section title is justified. It is technically impossible in C++ to have virtual copy constructors. Yet, such a feature would help you create a collection (for example, a static array) of type `Base*`, each element being a specialization of that type:

```
// Tuna, Carp and Trout are classes that inherit public from base class Fish
Fish* pFishes[3];
Fishes[0] = new Tuna();
Fishes[1] = new Carp();
Fishes[2] = new Trout();
```

Then assigning it into another array of the same type, where the virtual copy constructor ensures a deep copy of the derived class objects as well, ensures that `Tuna`, `Carp`, and `Trout` are copied as `Tuna`, `Carp`, and `Trout` even though the copy constructor is operating on `type Fish*`.

Well, that's a nice dream.

Virtual copy constructors are not possible because the `virtual` keyword in context of base class methods being overridden by implementations available in the derived class are about polymorphic behavior generated at runtime. Constructors, on the other hand, are not polymorphic in nature as they can construct only a fixed type, and hence C++ does not allow usage of the virtual copy constructors.

Having said that, there is a nice workaround in the form of defining your own clone function that allows you to do just that:

```
class Fish
{
public:
    virtual Fish* Clone() const = 0; // pure virtual function
};

class Tuna:public Fish
{
```

```
// ... other members
public:
   Tuna * Clone() const  // virtual clone function
   {
      return new Tuna(*this);  // return new Tuna that is a copy of this
   }
};
```

Thus, virtual function Clone is a simulated virtual copy constructor that needs to be explicitly invoked, as shown in Listing 11.9.

LISTING 11.9 Tuna and Carp That Support a Clone Function as a Simulated Virtual Copy Constructor

```
0: #include <iostream>
1: using namespace std;
2:
3: class Fish
4: {
5: public:
6:     virtual Fish* Clone() = 0;
7:     virtual void Swim() = 0;
8:     virtual ~Fish() {};
9: };
10:
11: class Tuna: public Fish
12: {
13: public:
14:     Fish* Clone() override
15:     {
16:         return new Tuna (*this);
17:     }
18:
19:     void Swim() override final
20:     {
21:         cout << "Tuna swims fast in the sea" << endl;
22:     }
23: };
24:
25: class BluefinTuna final:public Tuna
26: {
27: public:
28:     Fish* Clone() override
29:     {
30:         return new BluefinTuna(*this);
31:     }
32:
33:     // Cannot override Tuna::Swim as it is "final" in Tuna
34: };
35:
36: class Carp final: public Fish
```

11

```
37: {
38:     Fish* Clone() override
39:     {
40:         return new Carp(*this);
41:     }
42:     void Swim() override final
43:     {
44:         cout << "Carp swims slow in the lake" << endl;
45:     }
46: };
47:
48: int main()
49: {
50:     const int ARRAY_SIZE = 4;
51:
52:     Fish* myFishes[ARRAY_SIZE] = {NULL};
53:     myFishes[0] = new Tuna();
54:     myFishes[1] = new Carp();
55:     myFishes[2] = new BluefinTuna();
56:     myFishes[3] = new Carp();
57:
58:     Fish* myNewFishes[ARRAY_SIZE];
59:     for (int index = 0; index < ARRAY_SIZE; ++index)
60:         myNewFishes[index] = myFishes[index]->Clone();
61:
62:     // invoke a virtual method to check
63:     for (int index = 0; index < ARRAY_SIZE; ++index)
64:         myNewFishes[index]->Swim();
65:
66:     // memory cleanup
67:     for (int index = 0; index < ARRAY_SIZE; ++index)
68:     {
69:         delete myFishes[index];
70:         delete myNewFishes[index];
71:     }
72:
73:     return 0;
74: }
```

Output ▼

```
Tuna swims fast in the sea
Carp swims slow in the lake
Tuna swims fast in the sea
Carp swims slow in the lake
```

Analysis ▼

In addition to demonstrating virtual copy constructors via virtual function
Fish::Clone(), Listing 11.9 also demonstrates the usage of keywords override and

final—the latter being applied to virtual functions and classes alike. It also features a virtual destructor for class Fish in Line 8. Lines 52–56 in main() demonstrate how a static array of pointers to base class Fish* has been declared and individual elements assigned to newly created objects of type Tuna, Carp, Tuna, and Carp, respectively. Note how this array myFishes is able to collect seemingly different types that are all related by a common base type Fish. This is already cool, if you compare it against previous arrays in this book that have mostly been of a simple monotonous type int. If that wasn't cool enough, you were able to copy into a new array of type Fish* called myNewFishes using the virtual function Fish::Clone() within a loop, as shown in Line 60. Note that your array is quite small at only four elements. It could've been a lot longer but wouldn't have made much of a difference to the copy logic that would only need to adjust the loop-ending condition parameter. Line 64 is the actual check where you invoke virtual function Fish::Swim() on each stored element in the new array to verify whether Clone() copied a Tuna as a Tuna and not just a Fish(). The output demonstrates that it genuinely did copy the Tunas and the Carps just as expected. Also note that the output of Swim() used on instance of BluefinTuna was the same as that for a Tuna, because Tuna::Swim() was declared as final. Thus, BluefinTuna was not permitted to override Swim(), and the compiler executed Tuna::Swim() for it.

DO	DON'T
DO remember to mark base class functions that need to be overridden by the derived class as virtual.	**DON'T** forget to supply your base class with a virtual destructor.
DO remember that pure virtual functions make your class an Abstract Base Class, and these functions must be implemented by a deriving class.	**DON'T** forget that the compiler does not allow you to create a standalone instance of an Abstract Base Class.
Do mark functions in derived classes that are intended to override base functionality using keyword override.	**DON'T** forget that virtual inheritance is about ensuring that the common base in a diamond hierarchy has only one instance.
DO use virtual inheritance to solve the Diamond Problem.	**DON'T** confuse the function of keyword virtual when used in creating an inheritance hierarchy with the same when used in declaring base class functions.

11

Summary

In this lesson you learned to tap the power of creating inheritance hierarchies in your C++ code, by using polymorphism. You learned how to declare and program virtual functions—how they ensure that the derived class implementation overrides that in the base class even if an instance of the base class is used to invoke the virtual method. You saw how pure virtual functions were a special type of virtual functions that ensure that the base class alone cannot be instantiated, making it a perfect place to define interfaces that derived classes must fulfill. Finally, you saw the Diamond Problem created by multiple inheritance and how `virtual` inheritance helps you solve it.

Q&A

Q Why use the `virtual` keyword with a base class function when code compiles without it?

A Without the `virtual` keyword, you are not able to ensure that someone calling `objBase.Function()` will be redirected to `Derived::Function()`. Besides, compilation of code is not the only measure of its quality.

Q Why did the compiler create the Virtual Function Table?

A To store function pointers that ensure that the right version of a virtual function is invoked.

Q Should a base class always have a virtual destructor?

A Ideally yes. Only then can you ensure that when someone does a

```
Base* pBase = new Derived();
delete pBase;
```

`delete` on a pointer of type `Base*` results in the destructor `~Derived()` being invoked. This occurs when destructor `~Base()` is declared `virtual`.

Q What is an `Abstract Base Class` good for when I can't even instantiate it standalone?

A The ABC is not meant to be instantiated as a standalone object; rather it is always meant to be derived from. It contains pure virtual functions that define the minimal blueprint of functions that deriving classes need to implement, thus taking the role of an interface.

Q Given an inheritance hierarchy, do I need to use the keyword `virtual` on all declarations of a virtual function or just in the base class?

A It is enough to declare a function as `virtual` once, but that declaration has to be in the base class.

Q Can I define member functions and have member attributes in an ABC?

A Sure you can. Remember that you still cannot instantiate an ABC as it has at least one pure virtual function that needs to be implemented by a deriving class.

Workshop

The Workshop provides quiz questions to help you solidify your understanding of the material covered and exercises to provide you with experience in using what you've learned. Try to answer the quiz and exercise questions before checking the answers in Appendix E, and be certain you understand the answers before continuing to the next lesson.

Quiz

1. You are modeling shapes—circle and triangle—and want every shape to compulsorily implement functions `Area()` and `Print()`. How would you do it?

2. Does a compiler create a Virtual Function Table for all classes?

3. My `class Fish` has two public methods, one pure virtual function, and some member attributes. Is it still an abstract base class?

11

Exercises

1. Demonstrate an inheritance hierarchy that implements the question in Quiz 1 for Circle and Triangle.

2. **BUG BUSTERS:** What is the problem in the following code:
```
class Vehicle
{
public:
    Vehicle() {}
    ~Vehicle(){}
};
class Car: public Vehicle
{
public:
    Car() {}
    ~Car() {}
};
```

3. In the (uncorrected) code in Exercise 2, what is the order of execution of constructors and destructors if an instance of `car` is created and destroyed like this:
```
Vehicle* pMyRacer = new Car;
delete pMyRacer;
```

LESSON 12
Operator Types and Operator Overloading

In addition to encapsulating data and methods, classes can also encapsulate *operators* that make it easy to operate on instances of this class. You can use these operators to perform operations such as assignment or addition on class objects similar to those on integers that you saw in Lesson 5, "Working with Expressions, Statements, and Operators." Just like functions, operators can also be overloaded.

In this lesson, you learn:

- Using the keyword `operator`
- Unary and binary operators
- Conversion operators
- The move assignment operator
- Operators that cannot be redefined

What Are Operators in C++?

On a syntactical level, there is very little that differentiates an operator from a function, save for the use of the keyword `operator`. An operator declaration looks quite like a function declaration:

```
return_type operator operator_symbol (...parameter list...);
```

The `operator_symbol` in this case could be any of the several operator types that the programmer can define. It could be + (addition) or && (logical AND) and so on. The operands help the compiler distinguish one operator from another. So, why does C++ provide operators when functions are also supported?

Consider a utility class `Date` that encapsulates the day, month, and year:

```
Date holiday (12, 25, 2016);  // initialized to Dec 25, 2016
```

Assuming that you want to add a day and get the instance to contain the next day—Dec 26, 2016—which of the following two options would be more intuitive?

- Option 1 (using the increment operator):

  ```
  ++ holiday;
  ```

- Option 2 (using a member function `Increment()`):

  ```
  holiday.Increment();  // Dec 26, 2016
  ```

Clearly, Option 1 scores over method `Increment()`. The operator-based mechanism facilitates consumption by supplying ease of use and intuitiveness. Implementing operator (<) in class `Date` would help you compare two instances of `class Date` like this:

```
if(date1 < date2)
{
   // Do something
}
else
{
   // Do something else
}
```

Operators can be used in more situations than just classes that manage dates. An addition operator (+) in a string utility class such as `MyString` introduced to you in Listing 9.9 in Lesson 9, "Classes and Objects," would facilitate easy concatenation:

```
MyString sayHello ("Hello ");
MyString sayWorld (" world");
MyString sumThem (sayHello + sayWorld); // if operator+ were supported by
MyString
```

NOTE	The effort in implementing relevant operators will be rewarded by the ease of consumption of the class.

On a broad level, operators in C++ can be classified into two types: unary operators and binary operators.

Unary Operators

As the name suggests, operators that function on a single operand are called *unary operators*. A unary operator that is implemented in the global namespace or as a static member function of a class uses the following structure:

```
return_type operator operator_type (parameter_type)
{
    // ... implementation
}
```

A unary operator that is a (non-static) member of a class has a similar structure but is lacking in parameters, because the single parameter that it works upon is the instance of the class itself (*this):

```
return_type operator operator_type ()
{
    // ... implementation
}
```

Types of Unary Operators

The unary operators that can be overloaded (or redefined) are shown in Table 12.1.

TABLE 12.1   Unary Operators

Operator	Name
++	Increment
--	Decrement
*	Pointer dereference
->	Member selection
!	Logical NOT
&	Address-of

12

Operator	Name
~	One's complement
+	Unary plus
-	Unary negation
Conversion operators	Conversion into other types

Programming a Unary Increment/Decrement Operator

A unary prefix increment operator (++) can be programmed using the following syntax within the class declaration:

```
// Unary increment operator (prefix)
Date& operator ++ ()
{
    // operator implementation code
    return *this;
}
```

The postfix increment operator (++), on the other hand, has a different return type and an input parameter (that is not always used):

```
Date operator ++ (int)
{
    // Store a copy of the current state of the object, before incrementing day
    Date copy (*this);

    // increment implementation code

    // Return state before increment (because, postfix)
    return copy;
}
```

The prefix and postfix decrement operators have a similar syntax as the increment operators, just that the declaration would contain a -- where you see a ++. Listing 12.1 shows a simple class Date that allows incrementing days using operator (++).

LISTING 12.1 A Calendar Class That Handles Day, Month, and Year, and Allows
Incrementing and Decrementing Days

```
 0: #include <iostream>
 1: using namespace std;
 2:
 3: class Date
 4: {
 5: private:
 6:     int day, month, year;
 7:
 8: public:
 9:     Date (int inMonth, int inDay, int inYear)
10:            : month (inMonth), day(inDay), year (inYear) {};
11:
12:     Date& operator ++ () // prefix increment
13:     {
14:         ++day;
15:         return *this;
16:     }
17:
18:     Date& operator -- () // prefix decrement
19:     {
20:         --day;
21:         return *this;
22:     }
23:
24:     void DisplayDate()
25:     {
26:         cout << month << " / " << day << " / " << year << endl;
27:     }
28: };
29:
30: int main ()
31: {
32:     Date holiday (12, 25, 2016); // Dec 25, 2016
33:
34:     cout << "The date object is initialized to: ";
35:     holiday.DisplayDate ();
36:
37:     ++holiday; // move date ahead by a day
38:     cout << "Date after prefix-increment is: ";
39:     holiday.DisplayDate ();
40:
41:     --holiday; // move date backwards by a day
42:     cout << "Date after a prefix-decrement is: ";
43:     holiday.DisplayDate ();
44:
45:     return 0;
46: }
```

12

Output ▼

```
The date object is initialized to: 12 / 25 / 2016
Date after prefix-increment is: 12 / 26 / 2016
Date after a prefix-decrement is: 12 / 25 / 2016
```

Analysis ▼

The operators of interest defined in Lines 12 to 22, help in adding or subtracting a day at a time from instances of class Day, as shown in Lines 37 and 41 in main(). Prefix increment operators as demonstrated in this sample need to return a reference to the instance after completing the increment operation.

NOTE This version of a date class has a bare minimum implementation to reduce lines and to explain how prefix operator (++) and operator (--) are to be implemented. A professional version of the same would implement rollover functionalities for month and year and take leap years into consideration as well.

To support postfix increment or decrement, you simply add the following code to class Date:

```
// postfix differs from prefix operator in return-type and parameters
Date operator ++ (int) // postfix increment
{
    Date copy(month, day, year);
    ++day;
    return copy; // copy of instance before increment returned
}

Date operator -- (int) // postfix decrement
{
    Date copy(month, day, year);
    --day;
    return copy; // copy of instance before decrement returned
}
```

When your version of class Date supports both prefix and postfix increment and decrement operators, you will be able to use objects of the class using the following syntax:

```
Date holiday (12, 25, 2016);  // instantiate
++ holiday;  // using prefix increment operator++
holiday ++;  // using postfix increment operator++
-- holiday;  // using prefix decrement operator --
holiday --;  // using postfix decrement operator --
```

> As the implementation of the postfix operators demonstrates, a copy containing the existing state of the object is created before the increment or decrement operation to be returned thereafter.
>
> In other words, if you had the choice between using ++ object; and object ++; to essentially only increment, you should choose the former to avoid the creation of a temporary copy that will not be used.

Programming Conversion Operators

If you use Listing 12.1 and insert the following line in main():

```
cout << holiday;  // error in absence of conversion operator
```

The code would result in the following compile failure: error: binary '<<' : no operator found which takes a right-hand operand of type 'Date' (or there is no acceptable conversion). This error essentially indicates that cout doesn't know how to interpret an instance of Date as class Date does not support the operators that convert its contents into a type that cout would accept.

We know that cout can work well with a const char*:

```
std::cout << "Hello world"; // const char* works!
```

So, getting cout to work with an instance of type Date might be as simple as adding an operator that returns a const char* version:

```
operator const char*()
{
   // operator implementation that returns a char*
}
```

Listing 12.2 is a simple implementation of this conversion operator.

LISTING 12.2 Implementing Conversion operator const char* for class Date

```
0: #include <iostream>
1: #include <sstream> // new include for ostringstream
2: #include <string>
3: using namespace std;
4:
5: class Date
6: {
```

12

```
 7: private:
 8:     int day, month, year;
 9:     string dateInString;
10:
11: public:
12:     Date(int inMonth, int inDay, int inYear)
13:         : month(inMonth), day(inDay), year(inYear) {};
14:
15:     operator const char*()
16:     {
17:         ostringstream formattedDate; // assists string construction
18:         formattedDate << month << " / " << day << " / " << year;
19:
20:         dateInString = formattedDate.str();
21:         return dateInString.c_str();
22:     }
23: };
24:
25: int main ()
26: {
27:     Date Holiday (12, 25, 2016);
28:
29:     cout << "Holiday is on: " << Holiday << endl;
30:
31:     // string strHoliday (Holiday); // OK!
32:     // strHoliday = Date(11, 11, 2016); // also OK!
33:
34:     return 0;
35: }
```

Output ▼

```
Holiday is on: 12 / 25 / 2016
```

Analysis ▼

The benefit of implementing operator `const char*` as shown in Lines 15 to 23 is visible in Line 29 in `main()`. Now, an instance of `class Date` can directly be used in a `cout` statement, taking advantage of the fact that `cout` understands `const char*`. The compiler automatically uses the output of the appropriate (and in this case, the only available) operator in feeding it to `cout` that displays the date on the screen. In your implementation of operator `const char*`, you use `std::ostringstream` to convert the member integers into a `std::string` object as shown in Line 18. You could've directly returned `formattedDate.str()`, yet you store a copy in private member `Date::dateInString` in Line 20 because `formattedDate` being a local variable is destroyed when the operator returns. So, the pointer got via `str()` would be invalidated on function return.

This operator opens up new possibilities toward consuming class Date. It allows you to even assign an instance of a Date directly to a string:

```
string strHoliday (holiday);
strHoliday = Date(11, 11, 2016);
```

CAUTION

Note that such assignments cause implicit conversions, that is, the compiler has used the available conversion operator (in this case const char*) thereby permitting unintended assignments that get compiled without error. To avoid implicit conversions, use keyword explicit at the beginning of an operator declaration, as follows:

```
explicit operator const char*()
{
    // conversion code here
}
```

Using explicit would force the programmer to assert his intention to convert using a cast:

```
string strHoliday(static_cast<const char*>(Holiday));
strHoliday=static_cast<const char*>(Date(11,11,2016));
```

Casting, including static_cast, is discussed in detail in Lesson 13, "Casting Operators."

12

NOTE

Program as many operators as you think your class would be used with. If your application needs an integer representation of a Date, then you may program it as follows:

```
explicit operator int()
{
    return day + month + year;
}
```

This would allow an instance of Date to be used or transacted as an integer:

```
FuncTakesInt(static_cast<int>(Date(12, 25, 2016)));
```

Listing 12.8 later in this lesson also demonstrates conversion operators used with a string class.

Programming Dereference Operator (*) and Member Selection Operator (->)

The dereference operator (*) and member selection operator (->) are most frequently used in the programming of smart pointer classes. *Smart pointers* are utility classes that wrap regular pointers and simplify memory management by resolving ownership and copy issues using operators. In some cases, they can even help improve the performance of the application. Smart pointers are discussed in detail in Lesson 26, "Understanding Smart Pointers." This lesson takes a brief look at how overloading operators helps in making smart pointers work.

Analyze the use of the `std::unique_ptr` in Listing 12.3 and understand how it uses operator (*) and operator (->) to help you use the smart pointer class like any normal pointer.

LISTING 12.3   Using Smart Pointer `unique_ptr` to Manage a Dynamically Allocated Instance of `class Date`

```
 0: #include <iostream>
 1: #include <memory>  // new include to use unique_ptr
 2: using namespace std;
 3:
 4: class Date
 5: {
 6: private:
 7:     int day, month, year;
 8:     string dateInString;
 9:
10: public:
11:     Date(int inMonth, int inDay, int inYear)
12:         : month(inMonth), day(inDay), year(inYear) {};
13:
14:     void DisplayDate()
15:     {
16:         cout << month << " / " << day << " / " << year << endl;
17:     }
18: };
19:
20: int main()
21: {
22:     unique_ptr<int> smartIntPtr(new int);
23:     *smartIntPtr = 42;
24:
25:     // Use smart pointer type like an int*
26:     cout << "Integer value is: " << *smartIntPtr << endl;
27:
```

```
28:      unique_ptr<Date> smartHoliday (new Date(12, 25, 2016));
29:      cout << "The new instance of date contains: ";
30:
31:      // use smartHoliday just as you would a Date*
32:      smartHoliday->DisplayDate();
33:
34:      return 0;
35: }
```

Output ▼

```
Integer value is: 42
The new instance of date contains: 12 / 25 / 2016
```

Analysis ▼

Line 22 is where you declare a smart pointer to type `int`. This line shows template initialization syntax for smart pointer class `unique_ptr`. Similarly, Line 28 declares a smart pointer to an instance of class `Date`. Focus on the pattern, and ignore the details for the moment.

> **NOTE**
> Don't worry if this template syntax looks awkward because templates are introduced later in Lesson 14, "An Introduction to Macros and Templates."

This example demonstrates how a smart pointer allows you to use normal pointer syntax as shown in Lines 23 and 32. In Line 23, you are able to display the value of the `int` using `*smartIntPtr`, whereas in Line 32 you use `smartHoliday->DisplayData()` as if these two variables were an `int*` and `Date*`, respectively. The secret lies in the pointer class `std::unique_ptr` that is smart because it implements operator (`*`) and operator (`->`).

> **NOTE**
> Smart pointer classes can do a lot more than just parade around as normal pointers, or de-allocate memory when they go out of scope. Find out more about this topic in Lesson 26.
>
> To see an implementation of a basic smart pointer class that has overloaded these operators, you may briefly visit Listing 26.1.

12

Binary Operators

Operators that function on two operands are called *binary operators*. The definition of a binary operator implemented as a global function or a static member function is the following:

```
return_type operator_type (parameter1, parameter2);
```

The definition of a binary operator implemented as a class member is

```
return_type operator_type (parameter);
```

The reason the class member version of a binary operator accepts only one parameter is that the second parameter is usually derived from the attributes of the class itself.

Types of Binary Operators

Table 12.2 contains binary operators that can be overloaded or redefined in your C++ application.

TABLE 12.2 Overloadable Binary Operators

Operator	Name
,	Comma
!=	Inequality
%	Modulus
%=	Modulus/assignment
&	Bitwise AND
&&	Logical AND
&=	Bitwise AND/assignment
*	Multiplication
*=	Multiplication/assignment
+	Addition
+=	Addition/assignment
-	Subtraction
-=	Subtraction/assignment

Operator	Name
->*	Pointer-to-member selection
/	Division
/=	Division/assignment
<	Less than
<<	Left shift
<<=	Left shift/assignment
<=	Less than or equal to
=	Assignment, Copy Assignment and Move Assignment
==	Equality
>	Greater than
>=	Greater than or equal to
>>	Right shift
>>=	Right shift/assignment
^	Exclusive OR
^=	Exclusive OR/assignment
|	Bitwise inclusive OR
|=	Bitwise inclusive OR/assignment
||	Logical OR
[]	Subscript operator

12

Programming Binary Addition (a+b) and Subtraction (a-b) Operators

Similar to the increment/decrement operators, the binary plus and minus, when defined, enable you to add or subtract the value of a supported data type from an object of the class that implements these operators. Take a look at your calendar class Date again. Although you have already implemented the capability to increment Date so that it moves the calendar one day forward, you still do not support the capability to move it, say, five days ahead. To do this, you need to implement binary operator (+), as the code in Listing 12.4 demonstrates.

LISTING 12.4   Calendar Class Featuring the Binary Addition Operator

```
0: #include <iostream>
1: using namespace std;
2:
3: class Date
4: {
5: private:
6:     int day, month, year;
7:     string dateInString;
8:
9: public:
10:     Date(int inMonth, int inDay, int inYear)
11:         : month(inMonth), day(inDay), year(inYear) {};
12:
13:     Date operator + (int daysToAdd) // binary addition
14:     {
15:         Date newDate (month, day + daysToAdd, year);
16:         return newDate;
17:     }
18:
19:     Date operator - (int daysToSub) // binary subtraction
20:     {
21:         return Date(month, day - daysToSub, year);
22:     }
23:
24:     void DisplayDate()
25:     {
26:         cout << month << " / " << day << " / " << year << endl;
27:     }
28: };
29:
30: int main()
31: {
32:     Date Holiday (12, 25, 2016);
33:     cout << "Holiday on: ";
34:     Holiday.DisplayDate ();
35:
36:     Date PreviousHoliday (Holiday - 19);
37:     cout << "Previous holiday on: ";
38:     PreviousHoliday.DisplayDate();
39:
40:     Date NextHoliday(Holiday + 6);
41:     cout << "Next holiday on: ";
42:     NextHoliday.DisplayDate ();
43:
44:     return 0;
45: }
```

Output ▼

```
Holiday on: 12 / 25 / 2016
Previous holiday on: 12 / 6 / 2016
Next holiday on: 12 / 31 / 2016
```

Analysis ▼

Lines 13 to 22 contain the implementations of the binary operator (+) and operator (-) that permit the use of simple addition and subtraction syntax as seen in main() in Lines 40 and 36, respectively.

The binary addition operator would also be useful in a string class. In Lesson 9, you analyze a simple string wrapper class MyString that encapsulates memory management, copying, and the like, as shown in Listing 9.9. This class MyString doesn't support the concatenation of two strings using a simple syntax:

```
MyString Hello("Hello ");
MyString World(" World");
MyString HelloWorld(Hello + World);   // error: operator+ not defined
```

Defining this operator (+) makes using MyString extremely easy and is hence worth the effort:

```
MyString operator+ (const MyString& addThis)
{
   MyString newString;

   if (addThis.buffer != NULL)
   {
      newString.buffer = new char[GetLength() + strlen(addThis.buffer) + 1];
      strcpy(newString.buffer, buffer);
      strcat(newString.buffer, addThis.buffer);
   }

   return newString;
}
```

12

Add the preceding code to Listing 9.9 with a private default constructor MyString() with empty implementation to be able to use the addition syntax. You can see a version of class MyString with operator (+) among others in Listing 12.11 later in this lesson.

Implementing Addition Assignment (+=) and Subtraction Assignment (-=) Operators

The addition assignment operators allow syntax such as "a += b;" that allows the programmer to increment the value of an object a by an amount b. In doing this, the utility of the addition assignment operator is that it can be overloaded to accept different types of parameter b. Listing 12.5 that follows allows you to add an integer value to a Date object.

LISTING 12.5 Defining Operator (+=) and Operator (-=) to Add or Subtract Days in the Calendar Given an Integer Input

```
0: #include <iostream>
1: using namespace std;
2:
3: class Date
4: {
5: private:
6:     int day, month, year;
7:
8: public:
9:     Date(int inMonth, int inDay, int inYear)
10:         : month(inMonth), day(inDay), year(inYear) {}
11:
12:     void operator+= (int daysToAdd) // addition assignment
13:     {
14:         day += daysToAdd;
15:     }
16:
17:     void operator-= (int daysToSub) // subtraction assignment
18:     {
19:         day -= daysToSub;
20:     }
21:
22:     void DisplayDate()
23:     {
24:         cout << month << " / " << day << " / " << year << endl;
25:     }
26: };
27:
```

```
28: int main()
29: {
30:     Date holiday (12, 25, 2016);
31:     cout << "holiday is on: ";
32:     holiday.DisplayDate ();
33:
34:     cout << "holiday -= 19 gives: ";
35:     holiday -= 19;
36:     holiday.DisplayDate();
37:
38:     cout << "holiday += 25 gives: ";
39:     holiday += 25;
40:     holiday.DisplayDate ();
41:
42:     return 0;
43: }
```

Output ▼

```
holiday is on: 12 / 25 / 2016
holiday -= 19 gives: 12 / 6 / 2016
holiday += 25 gives: 12 / 31 / 2016
```

Analysis ▼

The addition and subtraction assignment operators of interest are in Lines 12 to 20. These allow adding and subtracting an integer value for days, as seen in `main()`, for instance:

```
35:     holiday -= 19;
39:     holiday += 25;
```

12

Your `class Date` now allows users to add or remove days from it as if they are dealing with integers using addition or subtraction assignment operators that take an `int` as a parameter. You can even provide overloaded versions of the addition assignment operator (`+=`) that work with an instance of a fictitious class `Days`:

```
// operator that adds a Days to an existing Date
void operator += (const Days& daysToAdd)
{
    day += daysToAdd.GetDays();
}
```

NOTE _____

The multiplication assignment *=, division assignment /=, modulus assignment %=, subtraction assignment -=, left-shift assignment <<=, right-shift assignment >>=, XOR assignment ^=, bitwise inclusive OR assignment |=, and bitwise AND assignment &= operators have a syntax similar to the addition assignment operator shown in Listing 12.5.

Although the ultimate objective of overloading operators is making the class easy and intuitive to use, there are many situations where implementing an operator might not make sense. For example, our calendar class Date has absolutely no use for a bitwise AND assignment &= operator. No user of this class should ever expect (or even think of) getting useful results from an operation such as greatDay &= 20;.

Overloading Equality (==) and Inequality (!=) Operators

What do you expect when the user of class Date compares one instance to another:

```
if (date1 == date2)
{
    // Do something
}
else
{
    // Do something else
}
```

In the absence of an equality operator ==, the compiler simply performs a binary comparison of the two objects and returns true when they are exactly identical. This binary comparison will work for instances of classes containing simple data types (like the Date class as of now), but it will not work if the class in question has a non-static string member (char*), such as MyString in Listing 9.9. When two instances of class MyString are compared, a binary comparison of the member attributes would actually compare the member string pointer values (MyString::buffer). These would not be equal even when the strings are identical in content. Comparisons involving two instances of MyString would return false consistently. You solve this problem by defining comparison operators. A generic expression of the equality operator is the following:

```
bool operator== (const ClassType& compareTo)
{
    // comparison code here, return true if equal else false
}
```

The inequality operator can reuse the equality operator:

```
bool operator!= (const ClassType& compareTo)
{
    // comparison code here, return true if inequal else false
}
```

The inequality operator can be the inverse (logical NOT) of the result of the equality operator. Listing 12.6 demonstrates comparison operators defined by our calendar class Date.

LISTING 12.6   Demonstrates Operators == and !=

```
 0: #include <iostream>
 1: using namespace std;
 2:
 3: class Date
 4: {
 5: private:
 6:     int day, month, year;
 7:
 8: public:
 9:     Date(int inMonth, int inDay, int inYear)
10:          : month(inMonth), day(inDay), year(inYear) {}
11:
12:     bool operator== (const Date& compareTo)
13:     {
14:        return ((day == compareTo.day)
15:              && (month == compareTo.month)
16:              && (year == compareTo.year));
17:     }
18:
19:     bool operator!= (const Date& compareTo)
20:     {
21:        return !(this->operator==(compareTo));
22:     }
23:
24:     void DisplayDate()
25:     {
26:        cout << month << " / " << day << " / " << year << endl;
27:     }
28: };
29:
30: int main()
31: {
32:     Date holiday1 (12, 25, 2016);
33:     Date holiday2 (12, 31, 2016);
34:
35:     cout << "holiday 1 is: ";
```

12

```
36:     holiday1.DisplayDate();
37:     cout << "holiday 2 is: ";
38:     holiday2.DisplayDate();
39:
40:     if (holiday1 == holiday2)
41:         cout << "Equality operator: The two are on the same day" << endl;
42:     else
43:         cout << "Equality operator: The two are on different days" << endl;
44:
45:     if (holiday1 != holiday2)
46:         cout << "Inequality operator: The two are on different days" << endl;
47:     else
48:         cout << "Inequality operator: The two are on the same day" << endl;
49:
50:     return 0;
51: }
```

Output ▼

```
holiday 1 is: 12 / 25 / 2016
holiday 2 is: 12 / 31 / 2016
Equality operator: The two are on different days
Inequality operator: The two are on different days
```

Analysis ▼

The equality operator (==) is a simple implementation that returns true if the day, month, and year are all equal, as shown in Lines 12 to 17. The inequality operator (!=) simply reuses the equality operator code as seen in Line 21. The presence of these operators helps compare two Date objects, holiday1 and holiday2, in main() in Lines 40 and 45.

Overloading <, >, <=, and >= Operators

The code in Listing 12.6 made the Date class intelligent enough to be able to tell whether two Date objects are equal or unequal. You need to program the less-than (<), greater-than (>), less-than-equals (<=), and greater-than-equals (>=) operators to enable conditional checking akin to the following:

```
if (date1 < date2) {// do something}
```

or

```
if (date1 <= date2) {// do something}
```

or

```
if (date1 > date2) {// do something}
```

or

```
if (date1 >= date2) {// do something}
```

These operators are demonstrated by the code shown in Listing 12.7.

LISTING 12.7 Demonstrates Implementing `<`, `<=`, `>`, and `>=` Operators

```
0: #include <iostream>
1: using namespace std;
2:
3: class Date
4: {
5: private:
6:     int day, month, year;
7:
8: public:
9:     Date(int inMonth, int inDay, int inYear)
10:         : month(inMonth), day(inDay), year(inYear) {}
11:
12:     bool operator< (const Date& compareTo)
13:     {
14:         if (year < compareTo.year)
15:             return true;
16:         else if (month < compareTo.month)
17:             return true;
18:         else if (day < compareTo.day)
19:             return true;
20:         else
21:             return false;
22:     }
23:
24:     bool operator<= (const Date& compareTo)
25:     {
26:         if (this->operator== (compareTo))
27:             return true;
28:         else
29:             return this->operator< (compareTo);
30:     }
31:
32:     bool operator > (const Date& compareTo)
33:     {
34:         return !(this->operator<= (compareTo));
35:     }
36:
```

12

```
37:     bool operator== (const Date& compareTo)
38:     {
39:        return ((day == compareTo.day)
40:            && (month == compareTo.month)
41:            && (year == compareTo.year));
42:     }
43:
44:     bool operator>= (const Date& compareTo)
45:     {
46:        if(this->operator== (compareTo))
47:            return true;
48:        else
49:            return this->operator> (compareTo);
50:     }
51:
52:     void DisplayDate()
53:     {
54:        cout << month << " / " << day << " / " << year << endl;
55:     }
56: };
57:
58: int main()
59: {
60:     Date holiday1 (12, 25, 2016);
61:     Date holiday2 (12, 31, 2016);
62:
63:     cout << "holiday 1 is: ";
64:     holiday1.DisplayDate();
65:     cout << "holiday 2 is: ";
66:     holiday2.DisplayDate();
67:
68:     if (holiday1 < holiday2)
69:        cout << "operator<: holiday1 happens first" << endl;
70:
71:     if (holiday2 > holiday1)
72:        cout << "operator>: holiday2 happens later" << endl;
73:
74:     if (holiday1 <= holiday2)
75:        cout << "operator<=: holiday1 happens on or before holiday2" << endl;
76:
77:     if (holiday2 >= holiday1)
78:        cout << "operator>=: holiday2 happens on or after holiday1" << endl;
79:
80:     return 0;
81: }
```

Output ▼

```
holiday 1 is: 12 / 25 / 2016
holiday 2 is: 12 / 31 / 2016
operator<: holiday1 happens first
operator>: holiday2 happens later
operator<=: holiday1 happens on or before holiday2
operator>=: holiday2 happens on or after holiday1
```

Analysis ▼

The operators of interest are implemented in Lines 12 to 50 and partially reuse operator (==) that you saw in Listing 12.6. The implementation of operators ==, <, and > has been consumed by the rest.

The operators have been consumed inside `main()` between Lines 68 and 78, which indicate how easy it now is to compare two different dates.

Overloading Copy Assignment Operator (=)

There are times when you want to assign the contents of an instance of a class to another, like this:

```
Date holiday(12, 25, 2016);
Date anotherHoliday(1, 1, 2017);
anotherHoliday = holiday; // uses copy assignment operator
```

This assignment invokes the default copy assignment operator that the compiler has built in to your class when you have not supplied one. Depending on the nature of your class, the default copy assignment operator might be inadequate, especially if your class is managing a resource that will not be copied. This problem with the default copy assignment operator is similar to the one with the default copy constructor discussed in Lesson 9. To ensure deep copies, as with the copy constructor, you need to specify an accompanying copy assignment operator:

```
ClassType& operator= (const ClassType& copySource)
{
    if(this != &copySource)  // protection against copy into self
    {
        // copy assignment operator implementation
    }
    return *this;
}
```

12

Deep copies are important if your class encapsulates a raw pointer, such as `class` `MyString` shown in Listing 9.9. To ensure deep copy during assignments, define a copy assignment operator as shown in Listing 12.8.

LISTING 12.8 A Better `class` `MyString` from Listing 9.9 with a Copy Assignment Operator =

```
0: #include <iostream>
1: using namespace std;
2: #include <string.h>
3: class MyString
4: {
5: private:
6:    char* buffer;
7:
8: public:
9:    MyString(const char* initialInput)
10:    {
11:       if(initialInput != NULL)
12:       {
13:          buffer = new char [strlen(initialInput) + 1];
14:          strcpy(buffer, initialInput);
15:       }
16:       else
17:          buffer = NULL;
18:    }
19:
20:    // Copy assignment operator
21:    MyString& operator= (const MyString& copySource)
22:    {
23:       if ((this != &copySource) && (copySource.buffer != NULL))
24:       {
25:          if (buffer != NULL)
26:           delete[] buffer;
27:
28:          // ensure deep copy by first allocating own buffer
29:          buffer = new char [strlen(copySource.buffer) + 1];
30:
31:          // copy from the source into local buffer
32:          strcpy(buffer, copySource.buffer);
33:       }
34:
35:       return *this;
36:    }
37:
```

```
38:     operator const char*()
39:     {
40:        return buffer;
41:     }
42:
43:     ~MyString()
44:     {
45:        delete[] buffer;
46:     }
47: };
48:
49: int main()
50: {
51:     MyString string1("Hello ");
52:     MyString string2(" World");
53:
54:     cout << "Before assignment: " << endl;
55:     cout << string1 << string2 << endl;
56:     string2 = string1;
57:     cout << "After assignment string2 = string1: " << endl;
58:     cout << string1 << string2 << endl;
59:
60:     return 0;
61: }
```

Output ▼

```
Before assignment:
Hello  World
After assignment string2 = string1:
Hello Hello
```

12

Analysis ▼

I have purposely omitted the copy constructor in this sample to reduce lines of code (but you should be inserting it when programming such a class; refer Listing 9.9 as a reference). The copy assignment operator is implemented in Lines 21 to 36. It is similar in function to a copy constructor and performs a starting check to ensure that the same object is not both the copy source and destination. After the checks return `true`, the copy assignment operator for `MyString` first deallocates its internal `buffer` before reallocating space for the text from the copy source and then uses `strcpy()` to copy, as shown in Line 14.

NOTE ——————

> Another subtle change in Listing 12.8 over Listing 9.9 is that you have replaced function `GetString()` by `operator const char*` as shown in Lines 38 to 41. This operator makes it even easier to use `class MyString,` as shown in Line 55, where one `cout` statement is used to display two instances of `MyString`.

CAUTION ——————

> When implementing a class that manages a dynamically allocated resource such as an array allocated using `new`, always ensure that you have implemented (or evaluated the implementation of) the copy constructor and the copy assignment operator in addition to the constructor and the destructor.
>
> Unless you address the issue of resource ownership when an object of your class is copied, your class is incomplete and endangers the stability of the application when used.

TIP ——————

> To create a class that cannot be copied, declare the copy constructor and copy assignment operator as `private`. Declaration as `private` without implementation is sufficient for the compiler to throw error on all attempts at copying this class via passing to a function by value or assigning one instance into another.

Subscript Operator ([ ])

The operator that allow array-style `[]` access to a class is called *subscript operator.* The typical syntax of a subscript operator is:

```
return_type& operator [] (subscript_type& subscript);
```

So, when creating a class such as `MyString` that encapsulates a dynamic array class of characters in a `char*` buffer, a subscript operator makes it really easy to randomly access individual characters in the buffer:

```
class MyString
{
    // ... other class members
public:
    /*const*/ char& operator [] (int index) /*const*/
    {
```

```
          // return the char at position index in buffer
    }
};
```

The sample in Listing 12.9 demonstrates how the subscript operator ([]) helps the user in iterating through the characters contained in an instance of MyString using normal array semantics.

LISTING 12.9 Implementing Subscript Operator [] in class MyString to Allow Random Access to Characters Contained in MyString::buffer

```
 0: #include <iostream>
 1: #include <string>
 2: #include <string.h>
 3: using namespace std;
 4: class MyString
 5: {
 6: private:
 7:    char* buffer;
 8:
 9:    // private default constructor
10:    MyString() {}
11:
12: public:
13:    // constructor
14:    MyString(const char* initialInput)
15:    {
16:       if(initialInput != NULL)
17:       {
18:          buffer = new char [strlen(initialInput) + 1];
19:          strcpy(buffer, initialInput);
20:       }
21:       else
22:          buffer = NULL;
23:    }
24:
25:    // Copy constructor: insert from Listing 9.9 here
26:    MyString(const MyString& copySource);
27:
28:    // Copy assignment operator: insert from Listing 12.8 here
29:    MyString& operator= (const MyString& copySource);
30:
31:    const char& operator[] (int index) const
32:    {
33:       if (index < GetLength())
34:          return buffer[index];
35:    }
36:
```

12

```
37:    // Destructor
38:    ~MyString()
39:    {
40:       if (buffer != NULL)
41:          delete [] buffer;
42:    }
43:
44:    int GetLength() const
45:    {
46:       return strlen(buffer);
47:    }
48:
49:    operator const char*()
50:    {
51:       return buffer;
52:    }
53: };
54:
55: int main()
56: {
57:    cout << "Type a statement: ";
58:    string strInput;
59:    getline(cin, strInput);
60:
61:    MyString youSaid(strInput.c_str());
62:
63:    cout << "Using operator[] for displaying your input: " << endl;
64:    for(int index = 0; index < youSaid.GetLength(); ++index)
65:       cout << youSaid[index] << " ";
66:    cout << endl;
67:
68:    cout << "Enter index 0 - " << youSaid.GetLength() - 1 << ": ";
69:    int index = 0;
70:    cin >> index;
71:    cout << "Input character at zero-based position: " << index;
72:    cout << " is: "<< youSaid[index] << endl;
73:
74:    return 0;
75: }
```

Output ▼

```
Type a statement: Hey subscript operators[] are fabulous
Using operator[] for displaying your input:
H e y   s u b s c r i p t   o p e r a t o r s [ ]   a r e   f a b u l o u s
Enter index 0 - 37: 2
Input character at zero-based position: 2 is: y
```

Analysis ▼

This is just a fun program that takes a sentence you input, constructs a MyString using it, as shown in Line 61, and then uses a for loop to print the string character by character with the help of the subscript operator ([]) using an array-like syntax, as shown in Lines 64 and 65. The operator ([]) itself is defined in Lines 31 to 35 and supplies direct access to the character at the specified position after ensuring that the requested position is not beyond the end of the char* buffer.

CAUTION

Using keyword const is important even when programming operators. Note how Listing 12.9 has restricted the return value of subscript operator [] to const char&. The program works and compiles even without the const keywords, yet the reason you have it there is to avoid this code:

```
MyString sayHello("Hello World");
sayHello[2] = 'k'; //error: operator[] is const
```

By using const you are protecting internal member MyString::buffer from direct modifications from the outside via operator []. In addition to classifying the return value as const, you even have restricted the operator function type to const to ensure that it cannot modify the class's member attributes.

In general, use the maximum possible const restriction to avoid unintentional data modifications and increase protection of the class's member attributes.

12

When implementing subscript operators, you can improve on the version shown in Listing 12.9. That one is an implementation of a single subscript operator that works for both reading from and writing to the slots in the dynamic array.

You can, however, implement two subscript operators—one as a const function and the other as a non-const one:

```
char& operator [] (int index);   // use to write / change buffer at index
char& operator [] (int index) const; // used only for accessing char at index
```

The compiler will invoke the const function for read operations and the non-const version for operations that write into the MyString object. Thus, you can (if you want to) have separate functionalities in the two subscript operations. There are other binary operators (listed in Table 12.2) that can be redefined or overloaded, but that are not discussed further in this lesson. Their implementation, however, is similar to those that have already been discussed.

Other operators, such as the logical operators and the bitwise operators, need to be programmed if the purpose of the class would be enhanced by having them. Clearly, a calendar class such as Date does not necessarily need to implement logical operators, whereas a class that performs string and numeric functions might need them frequently.

Keep the objective of your class and its use in perspective when overloading operators or writing new ones.

Function Operator ( )

The operator () that make objects behave like a function is called a function operator. They find application in the standard template library (STL) and are typically used in STL algorithms. Their usage can include making decisions; such function objects are typically called *unary* or *binary predicates*, depending on the number of operands they work on. Listing 12.10 analyzes a really simple function object so you can first understand what gives them such an intriguing name!

LISTING 12.10   A Function Object Created Using Operator ()

```
 1: #include <iostream>
 2: #include <string>
 3: using namespace std;
 4:
 5: class Display
 6: {
 7: public:
 8:     void operator () (string input) const
 9:     {
10:        cout << input << endl;
11:     }
12: };
13:
14: int main ()
15: {
16:    Display displayFuncObj;
17:
18:    // equivalent to displayFuncObj.operator () ("Display this string! ");
19:    displayFuncObj ("Display this string! ");
20:
21:    return 0;
22: }
```

Output ▼

```
Display this string!
```

Analysis ▼

Lines 8 to 11 implement `operator()` that is then used inside the function `main()` at Line 19. Note how the compiler allows the use of `object displayFuncObj` as a `function` in Line 19 by implicitly converting what looks like a function call to a call to `operator()`.

Hence, this operator is also called the function operator `()`, and the object of `Display` is also called a function object or *functor*. This topic is discussed exhaustively in Lesson 21, "Understanding Function Objects."

Move Constructor and Move Assignment Operator for High Performance Programming

The move constructor and the move assignment operators are performance optimization features that have become a part of the standard in C++11, ensuring that temporary values (*rvalues* that don't exist beyond the statement) are not wastefully copied. This is particularly useful when handling a class that manages a dynamically allocated resource, such as a dynamic array class or a string class.

The Problem of Unwanted Copy Steps

Take a look at the addition `operator+` as implemented in Listing 12.4. Notice that it actually creates a copy and returns it. If `class MyString` as demonstrated in Listing 12.9 supported the addition `operator+`, the following lines of code would be valid examples of easy string concatenation:

```
MyString Hello("Hello ");
MyString World("World");
MyString CPP(" of C++");
MyString sayHello(Hello + World + CPP);  // operator+, copy constructor
MyString sayHelloAgain ("overwrite this");
sayHelloAgain = Hello + World + CPP;  // operator+, copy constructor, copy
assignment operator=
```

12

This simple construct that makes concatenating three strings easy, uses the binary addition `operator+`:

```
MyString operator+ (const MyString& addThis)
{
    MyString newStr;

    if (addThis.buffer != NULL)
    {
        // copy into newStr
    }
    return newStr;  // return copy by value, invoke copy constructor
}
```

While making it easy to concatenate the strings, the addition `operator+` can cause performance problems. The creation of `sayHello` requires the execution of the addition operator twice. Each execution of `operator+` results in the creation of a temporary copy as a `MyString` is returned by value, thus causing the execution of the copy constructor. The copy constructor executes a deep copy—to a temporary value that does not exist after the expression. Thus, this expression results in temporary copies (rvalues, for the purists) that are not ever required after the statement and hence are a performance bottleneck forced by C++. Well, until recently at least.

This problem has now finally been resolved in C++11 in which the compiler specifically recognizes temporaries and uses move constructors and move assignment operators, where supplied by the programmer.

Declaring a Move Constructor and Move Assignment Operator

The syntax of the move constructor is as follows:

```
class Sample
{
private:
    Type* ptrResource;

public:
    Sample(Sample&& moveSource) // Move constructor, note &&
    {
        ptrResource = moveSource.ptrResource; // take ownership, start move
        moveSource.ptrResource = NULL;
    }

    Sample& operator= (Sample&& moveSource)//move assignment operator, note &&
    {
```

```
        if(this != &moveSource)
        {
            delete [] ptrResource;  // free own resource
            ptrResource = moveSource.ptrResource;  // take ownership, start move
            moveSource.ptrResource = NULL;  // free move source of ownership
        }
    }

    Sample(); // default constructor
    Sample(const Sample& copySource); // copy constructor
    Sample& operator= (const Sample& copySource); // copy assignment
};
```

Thus, the declaration of the move constructor and assignment operator are different from the regular copy constructor and copy assignment operator in that the input parameter is of type `Sample&&`. Additionally, as the input parameter is the move-source, it cannot be a `const` parameter as it is modified. Return values remain the same, as these are overloaded versions of the constructor and the assignment operator, respectively.

C++11 compliant compilers ensure that for rvalue temporaries the move constructor is used instead of the copy constructor and the move assignment operator is invoked instead of the copy assignment operator. In your implementation of these two, you ensure that instead of copying, you are simply moving the resource from the source to the destination. Listing 12.11 demonstrates the effectiveness of these two recent additions in optimizing `class MyString`.

LISTING 12.11 class `MyString` with Move Constructor and Move Assignment Operator in Addition to Copy Constructor and Copy Assignment Operator

12

```
 0: #include <iostream>
 1: #include <string.h>
 2: using namespace std;
 3: class MyString
 4: {
 5: private:
 6:     char* buffer;
 7:
 8:     MyString(): buffer(NULL) // private default constructor
 9:     {
10:         cout << "Default constructor called" << endl;
11:     }
12:
13: public:
14:     MyString(const char* initialInput) // constructor
15:     {
16:         cout << "Constructor called for: " << initialInput << endl;
```

```
17:          if(initialInput != NULL)
18:          {
19:             buffer = new char [strlen(initialInput) + 1];
20:             strcpy(buffer, initialInput);
21:          }
22:          else
23:             buffer = NULL;
24:       }
25:
26:       MyString(MyString&& moveSrc) // move constructor
27:       {
28:          cout << "Move constructor moves: " << moveSrc.buffer << endl;
29:          if(moveSrc.buffer != NULL)
30:          {
31:             buffer = moveSrc.buffer; // take ownership i.e.  'move'
32:             moveSrc.buffer = NULL;   // free move source
33:          }
34:        }
35:
36:       MyString& operator= (MyString&& moveSrc) // move assignment op.
37:       {
38:          cout << "Move assignment op. moves: " << moveSrc.buffer << endl;
39:          if((moveSrc.buffer != NULL) && (this != &moveSrc))
40:          {
41:             delete[] buffer; // release own buffer
42:
43:             buffer = moveSrc.buffer; // take ownership i.e.  'move'
44:             moveSrc.buffer = NULL;   // free move source
45:          }
46:
47:          return *this;
48:       }
49:
50:       MyString(const MyString& copySrc) // copy constructor
51:       {
52:          cout << "Copy constructor copies: " << copySrc.buffer << endl;
53:          if (copySrc.buffer != NULL)
54:          {
55:             buffer = new char[strlen(copySrc.buffer) + 1];
56:             strcpy(buffer, copySrc.buffer);
57:          }
58:          else
59:             buffer = NULL;
60:       }
61:
62:       MyString& operator= (const MyString& copySrc) // Copy assignment op.
63:       {
64:          cout << "Copy assignment op. copies: " << copySrc.buffer << endl;
65:          if ((this != &copySrc) && (copySrc.buffer != NULL))
66:          {
67:             if (buffer != NULL)
```

```
68:                 delete[] buffer;
69:
70:             buffer = new char[strlen(copySrc.buffer) + 1];
71:             strcpy(buffer, copySrc.buffer);
72:         }
73:
74:         return *this;
75:     }
76:
77:     ~MyString() // destructor
78:     {
79:         if (buffer != NULL)
80:             delete[] buffer;
81:     }
82:
83:     int GetLength()
84:     {
85:         return strlen(buffer);
86:     }
87:
88:     operator const char*()
89:     {
90:         return buffer;
91:     }
92:
93:     MyString operator+ (const MyString& addThis)
94:     {
95:         cout << "operator+ called: " << endl;
96:         MyString newStr;
97:
98:         if (addThis.buffer != NULL)
99:         {
100:            newStr.buffer = new char[GetLength()+strlen(addThis.buffer)+1];
101:            strcpy(newStr.buffer, buffer);
102:            strcat(newStr.buffer, addThis.buffer);
103:        }
104:
105:        return newStr;
106:     }
107: };
108:
109: int main()
110: {
111:     MyString Hello("Hello ");
112:     MyString World("World");
113:     MyString CPP(" of C++");
114:
115:     MyString sayHelloAgain ("overwrite this");
116:     sayHelloAgain = Hello + World + CPP;
117:
118:     return 0;
119: }
```

12

Output ▼

Output without the move constructor and move assignment operator (by commenting out Lines 26 to 48):

```
Constructor called for: Hello
Constructor called for: World
Constructor called for:  of C++
Constructor called for: overwrite this
operator+ called:
Default constructor called
Copy constructor copies: Hello World
operator+ called:
Default constructor called
Copy constructor copies: Hello World of C++
Copy assignment op. copies: Hello World of C++
```

Output with the move constructor and move assignment operator enabled:

```
Constructor called for: Hello
Constructor called for: World
Constructor called for:  of C++
Constructor called for: overwrite this
operator+ called:
Default constructor called
Move constructor moves: Hello World
operator+ called:
Default constructor called
Move constructor moves: Hello World of C++
Move assignment op. moves: Hello World of C++
```

Analysis ▼

This might be a really long code sample, but most of it has already been demonstrated in previous examples and lessons. The most important part of this listing is in Lines 26 to 48 that implement the move constructor and the move assignment operator, respectively. Parts of the output that have been influenced by this new addition to C++11 has been marked in bold. Note how the output changes drastically when compared against the same class without these two entities. If you look at the implementation of the move constructor and the move assignment operator again, you see that the move semantic is essentially implemented by taking ownership of the resources from the move source moveSrc as shown in Line 31 in the move constructor and Line 43 in the move assignment operator. This is immediately followed by assigning NULL to the move source pointer as shown in Lines 32 and 44. This assignment to NULL ensures that the destructor of the instance that is the move source essentially does no memory deallocation via delete in Line 80 as the ownership has been moved to the destination object. Note that in the absence of the move constructor, the copy constructor is called that does a deep copy of the pointed string. Thus, the move constructor has saved a good amount of processing time in reducing unwanted memory allocations and copy steps.

Programming the move constructor and the move assignment operator is completely optional. Unlike the copy constructor and the copy assignment operator, the compiler does not add a default implementation for you.

Use this feature to optimize the functioning of classes that point to dynamically allocated resources that would otherwise be deep copied even in scenarios where they're only required temporarily.

User Defined Literals

Literal constants were introduced in Lesson 3, "Using Variables, Declaring Constants." Here are some examples of a few:

```
int bankBalance = 10000;
double pi = 3.14;
char firstAlphabet = 'a';
const char* sayHello = "Hello!";
```

In the preceding code, `10000`, `3.14`, `'a'`, and `"Hello!"` are all literal constants! C++11 extended the standard's support of literals by allowing you to define your own literals. For instance, if you were working on a scientific application that deals with thermodynamics, you may want all your temperatures to be stored and operated using a scale called Kelvin. You may now declare all your temperatures using a syntax similar to the following:

```
Temperature k1 = 32.15_F;
Temperature k2 = 0.0_C;
```

Using literals `_F` and `_C` that you have defined, you have made your application a lot simpler to read and therefore maintain.

To define your own literal, you define `operator ""` like this:

```
ReturnType operator "" YourLiteral(ValueType value)
{
    // conversion code here
}
```

12

NOTE

Depending on the nature of the user defined literal, the `ValueType` parameter would be restricted to one of the following:

`unsigned long long int` for integral literal

`long double` for floating point literal

`char`, `wchar_t`, `char16_t`, and `char32_t` for character literal

`const char*` for raw string literal

`const char*` together with `size_t` for string literal

`const wchar_t*` together with `size_t` for string literal

`const char16_t*` together with `size_t` for string literal

`const char32_t*` together with `size_t` for string literal

Listing 12.12 demonstrates a user defined literal that converts types.

LISTING 12.12   Conversion from Fahrenheit and Centigrade to the Kelvin Scale

```
 0: #include <iostream>
 1: using namespace std;
 2:
 3: struct Temperature
 4: {
 5:     double Kelvin;
 6:     Temperature(long double kelvin) : Kelvin(kelvin) {}
 7: };
 8:
 9: Temperature operator"" _C(long double celcius)
10: {
11:     return Temperature(celcius + 273);
12: }
13:
14: Temperature operator "" _F(long double fahrenheit)
15: {
16:     return Temperature((fahrenheit + 459.67) * 5 / 9);
17: }
18:
19: int main()
20: {
21:     Temperature k1 = 31.73_F;
22:     Temperature k2 = 0.0_C;
23:
```

```
24:      cout << "k1 is " << k1.Kelvin << " Kelvin" << endl;
25:      cout << "k2 is " << k2.Kelvin << " Kelvin" << endl;
26:
27:      return 0;
28: }
```

Output ▼

```
k1 is 273 Kelvin
k2 is 273 Kelvin
```

Analysis ▼

Lines 21 and 22 in the sample above initialize two instances of `Temperature`, one using a user defined literal `_F` to declare an initial value in Fahrenheit and the other using a user defined literal to declare an initial value in Celcius (also called Centigrade). The two literals are defined in Lines 9–17, and do the work of converting the respective units into Kelvin and returning an instance of `Temperature`. Note that `k2` has intentionally been initialized to `0.0_C` and not to `0_C`, because the literal `_C` has been defined (and is required) to take a `long double` as input value and 0 would've interpreted as an integer.

Operators That Cannot Be Overloaded

With all the flexibility that C++ gives you in customizing the behavior of the operators and making your classes easy to use, it still keeps some cards to itself by not allowing you to change or alter the behavior of some operators that are expected to perform consistently. The operators that cannot be redefined are shown in Table 12.3.

TABLE 12.3   Operators That CANNOT Be Overloaded or Redefined

Operator	Name
.	Member selection
.*	Pointer-to-member selection
::	Scope resolution
? :	Conditional ternary operator
sizeof	Gets the size of an object/class type

12

DO	**DON'T**
DO program as many operators as would help making using your class easy, but not more. **DO** mark conversion operators as `explicit` to avoid implicit conversions. **DO** always program a copy assignment operator (with a copy constructor and destructor) for a class that contains raw pointer members. **DO** always program a move assignment operator (and move constructor) for classes that manage dynamically allocated resources, such as an array of data, when using a C++11-compliant compiler.	**DON'T** forget that the compiler provides a default copy assignment operator and copy constructor if you don't supply these, and they won't ensure deep copies of any raw pointers contained within the class. **DON'T** forget that if you don't supply a move assignment operator or move constructor, the compiler does not create these for you, but instead falls back on the regular copy assignment operator and copy constructor.

Summary

You learned how programming operators can make a significant difference to the ease with which your class can be consumed. When programming a class that manages a resource, for example a dynamic array or a string, you need to supply a copy constructor and copy assignment operator for a minimum, in addition to a destructor. A utility class that manages a dynamic array can do very well with a move constructor and a move assignment operator that ensures that the contained resource is not deep-copied for temporary objects. Last but not least, you learned that operators such as ., .*, ::, ?:, and `sizeof` cannot be redefined.

Q&A

Q My class encapsulates a dynamic array of integers. What functions and operators should I implement for a minimum?

A When programming such a class, you need to clearly define the behavior in the scenario where an instance is being copied directly into another via assignment or copied indirectly by being passed to a function by value. You typically implement the copy constructor, copy assignment operator, and the destructor. You also implement the move constructor and move assignment operator if you want to tweak the performance of this class in certain cases. To enable an array-like access to elements stored inside an instance of the class, you would want to overload the subscript `operator[]`.

Q I have an instance `object` of a class. I want to support this syntax: `cout << object;`. What operator do I need to implement?

A You need to implement a conversion operator that allows your class to be interpreted as a type that `std::cout` can handle upfront. One way is to define operator `char*()` as you also did in Listing 12.2.

Q I want to create my own smart pointer class. What functions and operators do I need to implement for a minimum?

A A smart pointer needs to supply the ability of being used as a normal pointer as in `*pSmartPtr` or `pSmartPtr->Func()`. To enable this you implement operator (`*`) and operator (`->`). In addition, for it to be smart, you also take care of automatic resource release/returns by programming the destructor accordingly, and you would clearly define how copy or assignment works by implementing the copy constructor and copy assignment operator or by prohibiting it by declaring these two as `private`.

Workshop

The Workshop contains quiz questions to help solidify your understanding of the material covered and exercises to provide you with experience in using what you've learned. Try to answer the quiz and exercise questions before checking the answers in Appendix E, and be certain you understand the answers before going to the next lesson.

Quiz

1. Can my subscript operator `[]` return `const` and non-`const` variants of return types?

```
const Type& operator[](int index);
Type& operator[](int index); // is this OK?
```

2. Would you ever declare the copy constructor or copy assignment operator as `private`?

3. Would it make sense to define a move constructor and move assignment operator for your `class Date`?

Exercises

1. Program a conversion operator for class `Date` that converts the date it holds into a unique integer.

2. Program a move constructor and move assignment operator for `class DynIntegers` that encapsulates a dynamically allocated array in the form of private member `int*`.

LESSON 13
Casting Operators

Casting is a mechanism by which the programmer can temporarily or permanently change the interpretation of an object by the compiler. Note that this does not imply that the programmer changes the object itself—he simply changes the interpretation thereof. Operators that change the interpretation of an object are called *casting operators*.

In this lesson, you learn

- The need for casting operators
- Why C-style casts are not popular with some C++ programmers
- The four C++ casting operators
- The concepts of upcasting and downcasting
- Why C++ casting operators are not all-time favorites either

The Need for Casting

In a perfectly type-safe and type-strong world comprising well-written C++ applications, there should be no need for casting and for casting operators. However, we live in a real world where modules programmed by a lot of different people and vendors often using different environments have to work together. To make this happen, compilers very often need to be instructed to interpret data in ways that make them compile and the application function correctly.

Let's take a real-world example: Although most C++ compilers might support `bool` as a native type, a lot of libraries are still in use that were programmed years back and in C. These libraries made for C compilers had to rely on the use of an integral type to hold Boolean data. So, a `bool` on these compilers is something akin to

```
typedef unsigned short BOOL;
```

A function that returns Boolean data would be declared as

```
BOOL IsX ();
```

Now, if such a library is to be used with a new application programmed in the latest version of the C++ compiler, the programmer has to find a way to make the `bool` data type as understood by his C++ compiler function with the `BOOL` data type as understood by the library. The way to make this happen is by using casts:

```
bool Result = (bool)IsX ();     // C-Style cast
```

The evolution of C++ saw the emergence of new C++ casting operators and that created a split in the C++ programming community: a group that continued using C-style casts in their C++ applications, and another that religiously converted to casting keywords introduced by C++ compilers. The argument of the former group is that the C++ casts are cumbersome to use, and sometimes differ in functionality to such a small extent that they are of only theoretical value. The latter group, which evidently is comprised of C++ syntax purists, points out at the flaws in the C-style casts to make their case.

Because the real world contains both kinds of code in operation, it would be good to simply read through this lesson, know the advantages and disadvantages of each style, and formulate your own opinion.

Why C-Style Casts Are Not Popular with Some C++ Programmers

Type safety is one of the mantras that C++ programmers swear by when singing praises to the qualities of this programming language. In fact, most C++ compilers won't even let you get away with this:

```
char* staticStr = "Hello World!";
int* intArray = staticStr;     // error: cannot convert char* to int*
```

... and rightfully so!

Now, C++ compilers still do see the need to be backward compliant to keep old and legacy code building, and therefore automatically allow syntax such as:

```
int* intArray = (int*)staticStr; // Cast one problem away, create another
```

This C-style cast actually forces the compiler to interpret the destination as a type that is conveniently of the programmer's choice—a programmer who, in this case, did not bother thinking that the compiler reported an error in the first place for good reason and simply muzzled the compiler and forced it to obey. This, of course, does not go well down the throats of C++ programmers who see their type safety being compromised by casts that force anything through.

The C++ Casting Operators

Despite the disadvantages of casting, the concept of casting itself cannot be discarded. In many situations, casts are legitimate requirements to solve important compatibility issues. C++ additionally supplies a new casting operator specific to inheritance-based scenarios that did not exist with C programming.

The four C++ casting operators are

- `static_cast`
- `dynamic_cast`
- `reinterpret_cast`
- `const_cast`

The usage syntax of the casting operators is consistent:

```
destination_type result = cast_operator<destination_type> (object_to_cast);
```

13

Using `static_cast`

`static_cast` is a mechanism that can be used to convert pointers between related types, and perform explicit type conversions for standard data types that would otherwise happen automatically or implicitly. As far as pointers go, `static_cast` implements a basic compile-time check to ensure that the pointer is being cast to a related type. This is an improvement over a C-style cast that allows a pointer to one object to be cast to an absolutely unrelated type without any complaint. Using `static_cast`, a pointer can be upcasted to the base type, or can be downcasted to the derived type, as the following code-sample indicates.

```
Base* objBase = new Derived ();
Derived* objDer = static_cast<Derived*>(objBase);  // ok!

// class Unrelated is not related to Base
Unrelated* notRelated = static_cast<Unrelated*>(objBase); // Error
// The cast is not permitted as types are unrelated
```

NOTE _____

Casting a `Derived*` to a `Base*` is called *upcasting* and can be done without any explicit casting operator:

```
Derived objDerived;
Base* objBase = &objDerived;  // ok!
```

Casting a `Base*` to a `Derived*` is called *downcasting* and cannot be done without usage of explicit casting operators:

```
Derived objDerived;
Base* objBase = &objDerived; // Upcast -> ok!
Derived* objDer = objBase; // Error: Downcast needs
explicit cast
```

However, note that `static_cast` verifies only that the pointer types are related. It does *not* perform any runtime checks. So, with `static_cast`, a programmer could still get away with this bug:

```
Base* objBase = new Base();
Derived* objDer = static_cast<Derived*>(objBase); // Still no errors!
```

Here, `objDer` actually points to a partial Derived object because the object being pointed to is actually a `Base()` type. Because `static_cast` performs only a compile-time check of verifying that the types in question are related and does not perform a runtime check, a call to `objDer->DerivedFunction()` would get compiled, but probably result in unexpected behavior during runtime.

Apart from helping in upcasting or downcasting, `static_cast` can, in many cases, help make implicit casts explicit and bring them to the attention of the programmer or reader:

```
double Pi = 3.14159265;
int num = static_cast<int>(Pi); // Making an otherwise implicit cast, explicit
```

In the preceding code, num = Pi would have worked as well and to the same effect. However, using a `static_cast` brings the nature of conversion to the attention of the reader and indicates (to someone who knows `static_cast`) that the compiler has performed the necessary adjustments based on the information available at compile-time to perform the required type conversion. You would also need to use `static_cast` when using conversion operators or constructors that have been declared using keyword `explicit`. Avoiding implicit conversions via keyword `explicit` is discussed in Lesson 9, "Classes and Objects," and Lesson 12, "Operator Types and Operator Overloading."

Using `dynamic_cast` and Runtime Type Identification

Dynamic casting, as the name suggests, is the opposite of static casting and actually executes the cast at runtime—that is, at application execution time. The result of a `dynamic_cast` operation can be checked to see whether the attempt at casting succeeded. The typical usage syntax of the `dynamic_cast` operator is

```
destination_type* Dest = dynamic_cast<class_type*>(Source);

if(Dest)      // Check for success of the casting operation
    Dest->CallFunc ();
```

For example:

```
Base* objBase = new Derived();

// Perform a downcast
Derived* objDer = dynamic_cast<Derived*>(objBase);

if(objDer)      // Check for success of the cast
    objDer->CallDerivedFunction ();
```

As shown in the preceding short example, given a pointer to a base-class object, the programmer can resort to `dynamic_cast` to verify the type of the destination object being pointed to before proceeding to use the pointer as such. Note that in the code snippet it is apparent that the destination object is a `Derived` type. So, the sample is of demonstrative value only. Yet, this is not always the case—for example, when a pointer of type `Derived*` is passed to a function that accepts type `Base*`. The function can

13

use `dynamic_cast` given a base-class pointer type to detected type and then perform operations specific to the types detected. Thus, `dynamic_cast` helps determine the type at runtime and use a casted pointer when it is safe to do so. See Listing 13.1, which uses a familiar hierarchy of `class Tuna` and `class Carp` related to base `class Fish`, where the function `DetectFishType()` dynamically detects whether a `Fish*` is a `Tuna*` or a `Carp*`.

NOTE _____ | Therefore, this mechanism of identifying the type of the object at runtime is called _runtime type identification (RTTI)_.

LISTING 13.1   Using Dynamic Casting to Tell Whether a Fish Object Is a Tuna or a Carp

```
 0: #include <iostream>
 1: using namespace std;
 2:
 3: class Fish
 4: {
 5: public:
 6:    virtual void Swim()
 7:    {
 8:       cout << "Fish swims in water" << endl;
 9:    }
10:
11:    // base class should always have virtual destructor
12:    virtual ~Fish() {}
13: };
14:
15: class Tuna: public Fish
16: {
17: public:
18:    void Swim()
19:    {
20:       cout << "Tuna swims real fast in the sea" << endl;
21:    }
22:
23:    void BecomeDinner()
24:    {
25:       cout << "Tuna became dinner in Sushi" << endl;
26:    }
27: };
28:
29: class Carp: public Fish
30: {
31: public:
32:    void Swim()
```

```
33:    {
34:        cout << "Carp swims real slow in the lake" << endl;
35:    }
36:
37:    void Talk()
38:    {
39:        cout << "Carp talked Carp!" << endl;
40:    }
41: };
42:
43: void DetectFishType(Fish* objFish)
44: {
45:    Tuna* objTuna = dynamic_cast <Tuna*>(objFish);
46:    if (objTuna) // check success of cast
47:    {
48:        cout << "Detected Tuna. Making Tuna dinner: " << endl;
49:        objTuna->BecomeDinner();
50:    }
51:
52:    Carp* objCarp = dynamic_cast <Carp*>(objFish);
53:    if(objCarp)
54:    {
55:        cout << "Detected Carp. Making carp talk: " << endl;
56:        objCarp->Talk();
57:    }
58:
59:    cout << "Verifying type using virtual Fish::Swim: " << endl;
60:    objFish->Swim(); // calling virtual function Swim
61: }
62:
63: int main()
64: {
65:    Carp myLunch;
66:    Tuna myDinner;
67:
68:    DetectFishType(&myDinner);
69:    cout << endl;
70:    DetectFishType(&myLunch);
71:
72:    return 0;
73:}
```

13

Output ▼

```
Detected Tuna. Making Tuna dinner:
Tuna became dinner in Sushi
Verifying type using virtual Fish::Swim:
Tuna swims real fast in the sea
```

```
Detected Carp. Making carp talk:
Carp talked Carp!
Verifying type using virtual Fish::Swim:
Carp swims real slow in the lake
```

Analysis ▼

This sample uses a hierarchy where classes `Tuna` and `Carp` inherit from `Fish`. For sake of explanation, not only do the two derived classes implement the virtual function `Swim()`, but they contain a function each that is specific to their types, namely `Tuna::BecomeDinner()` and `Carp::Talk()`. What is special in this sample is that given an instance of the base class `Fish*`, you are able to dynamically detect whether that pointer points to a `Tuna` or a `Carp`. This dynamic detection or runtime type identification happens in function `DetectFishType()` defined in Lines 43–61. In Line 45, `dynamic_cast` is used to test the nature of the input base class pointer of type `Fish*` for type `Tuna*`. If this `Fish*` points to a `Tuna`, the operator returns a valid address, else it returns NULL. Hence, the result of a `dynamic_cast` always needs to be checked for validity. After the check in Line 46 succeeds, you know that the pointer `objTuna` points to a valid `Tuna`, and you are able to call function `Tuna::BecomeDinner()` using it, as shown in Line 49. With the Carp, you use the pointer to invoke function `Carp::Talk()` as shown in Line 56. Before returning, `DetectFishType()` does a verification on the type by invoking `Fish::Swim()`, which being virtual redirects the call to the `Swim()` method implemented in `Tuna` or `Carp`, as applicable.

CAUTION	The return value of a `dynamic_cast` operation should always be checked for validity. It is NULL when the cast fails.

Using `reinterpret_cast`

`reinterpret_cast` is the closest a C++ casting operator gets to the C-style cast. It really does allow the programmer to cast one object type to another, regardless of whether or not the types are related; that is, it forces a reinterpretation of type using a syntax as seen in the following sample:

```
Base* objBase = new Base ();
Unrelated* notRelated = reinterpret_cast<Unrelated*>(objBase);
// The code above compiles, but is not good programming!
```

This cast actually forces the compiler to accept situations that `static_cast` would normally not permit. It finds usage in certain low-level applications (such as drivers, for example) where data needs to be converted to a simple type that an API—Application Program Interface—can accept (for example, some OS-level APIs require data to be sent as a BYTE array, that is, `unsigned char*`):

```
SomeClass* object = new SomeClass();
// Need to send the object as a byte-stream...
unsigned char* bytesFoAPI = reinterpret_cast<unsigned char*>(object);
```

The cast used in the preceding code has not changed the binary representation of the source object and has effectively cheated the compiler into allowing the programmer to peek into individual bytes contained by an object of type `SomeClass`. Because no other C++ casting operator would allow such a conversion that compromises type safety, `reinterpret_cast` is a last resort in performing an otherwise unsafe (and nonportable) conversion.

CAUTION

> As far as possible, you should refrain from using `reinterpret_cast` in your applications because it allows you to instruct the compiler to treat type X as an unrelated type Y, which does not look like good design or implementation.

Using `const_cast`

`const_cast` enables you to turn off the `const` access modifier to an object. If you are wondering why this cast is necessary at all, you are probably right in doing so. In an ideal situation where programmers write their classes correctly, they remember to use the `const` keyword frequently and in the right places. The practical world is unfortunately way too different, and code like following is prevalent:

```
class SomeClass
{
public:
    // ...
    void DisplayMembers(); //problem - display function isn't const
};
```

13

So, when you program a function such as

```
void DisplayAllData (const SomeClass& object)
{
    object.DisplayMembers ();  // Compile failure
    // reason: call to a non-const member using a const reference
}
```

You are evidently correct in passing `object` as a const reference. After all, a display function should be read-only and should not be allowed to call non-const member functions—that is, should not be allowed to call a function that can change the state of the object. However, the implementation of `DisplayMembers()`, which also ought to be `const`, unfortunately is not. Now, so long as `SomeClass` belongs to you and the source code is in your control, you can make corrective changes to `DisplayMembers()`. In many cases, however, it might belong to a third-party library, and making changes to it is not possible. In situations such as these, `const_cast` is your savior.

The syntax for invoking `DisplayMembers()` in such a scenario is

```
void DisplayAllData (const SomeClass& object)
{
    SomeClass& refData = const_cast<SomeClass&>(object);
    refData.DisplayMembers ();    // Allowed!
}
```

Note that using `const_cast` to invoke non-const functions should be a last resort. In general, keep in mind that using `const_cast` to modify a `const` object can also result in undefined behavior.

Note that `const_cast` can also be used with pointers:

```
void DisplayAllData (const SomeClass* data)
{
    // data->DisplayMembers (); Error: attempt to invoke a non-const function!
    SomeClass* pCastedData = const_cast<SomeClass*>(data);
    pCastedData->DisplayMembers ();    // Allowed!
}
```

Problems with the C++ Casting Operators

Not everyone is happy with all C++ casting operators—not even those who swear by C++. Their reasons range from the syntax being cumbersome and non-intuitive to being redundant.

Let's simply compare this code:

```
double Pi = 3.14159265;

// C++ style cast: static_cast
int num = static_cast <int>(Pi);    // result: Num is 3

// C-style cast
int num2 = (int)Pi;                 // result: num2 is 3

// leave casting to the compiler
int num3 = Pi;                      // result: num3 is 3. No errors!
```

In all three cases, the programmer achieved the same result. In practical scenarios, the second option is probably the most prevalent, followed by the third. Few people might use the first option. In any case, the compiler is intelligent enough to convert such types correctly. This gives the cast syntax an impression that it makes the code more difficult to read.

Similarly, other uses of static_cast are also handled well by C-style casts that are admittedly simpler looking:

```
// using static_cast
Derived* objDer = static_cast <Derived*>(objBase);

// But, this works just as well...
Derived* objDerSimple = (Derived*)objBase;
```

Thus, the advantage of using static_cast is often overshadowed by the clumsiness of its syntax.

Looking at other operators, reinterpret_cast is for forcing your way through when static_cast does not work; ditto for const_cast with respect to modifying the const access modifiers. Thus, C++ casting operators other than dynamic_cast are avoidable in modern C++ applications. Only when addressing the needs of legacy applications might other casting operators become relevant. In such cases, preferring C-style casts to C++ casting operators is often a matter of taste. What's important is that you avoid casting as far as possible, and when you do use it, you know what happens behind the scenes.

13

DO	DON'T
DO remember that casting a `Derived*` to a `Base*` is called upcasting and this is safe.	**DON'T** forget to check the pointer for validity after using `dynamic_cast`.
DO remember that casting a `Base*` directly to a `Derived*` is called downcasting, and this can be unsafe unless you use `dynamic_cast`, and check for success.	**DON'T** design your application around RTTI using `dynamic_cast`.
DO remember that the objective of creating an inheritance hierarchy is typically in having virtual functions that when invoked using base class pointers ensure that the available derived class versions are invoked.	

Summary

In this lesson, you learned the different C++ casting operators, the arguments for and against using them. You also learned that in general you should avoid the usage of casts.

Q&A

Q Is it okay to modify the contents of a const-object by casting a pointer or reference to it using `const_cast`?

A Most definitely not. The result of such an operation is not defined and is definitely not desired.

Q I need a `Bird*`, but have a `Dog*` at hand. The compiler does not allow me to use the pointer to the `Dog` object as a `Bird*`. However, when I use `reinterpret_cast` to cast the `Dog*` to `Bird*`, the compiler does not complain and it seems I can use this pointer to call `Bird`'s member function, `Fly()`. Is this okay?

A Again, definitely not. `reinterpret_cast` changed only the interpretation of the pointer, and did not change the object being pointed to (that is still a `Dog`). Calling a `Fly()` function on a `Dog` object will not give the results you are looking for, and could possibly cause an application failure.

Q I have a `Derived` object being pointed to by a `objBase` that is a `Base*`. I am sure that `objBase` points to a `Derived` object, so do I really need to use `dynamic_cast`?

A Because you are sure that the object being pointed to is a `Derived` type, you can save on runtime performance by using `static_cast`.

Q C++ provides casting operators, and yet I am advised to not use them as much as possible. Why is that?

A You keep aspirin at home, but you don't make it your staple diet just because it's available, right? Use casts only when you need them.

Workshop

The workshop contains quiz questions to help solidify your understanding of the material covered and exercises to provide you with experience in using what you've learned. Try to answer the quiz and exercise questions before checking the answers in Appendix E, and be certain you understand the answers before going to the next lesson.

Quiz

1. You have a base class object pointer `objBase`. What cast would you use to determine whether it is a `Derived1` type or a `Derived2` type?

2. You have a `const` reference to an object and tried calling a public member function, written by you. The compiler does not allow this because the function in question is not a `const` member. Would you correct the function or would you use `const_cast`?

3. `reinterpret_cast` should be used only when `static_cast` does not work, and the cast is known to be required and safe. True or false?

4. Is it true that many instances of `static_cast`-based conversions, especially between simple data types, would be performed automatically by a good C++ compiler?

13

Exercises

1. **BUG BUSTERS:** What is the problem in the following code?

```
void DoSomething(Base* objBase)
{
    Derived* objDer = dynamic_cast <Derived*>(objBase);
    objDer->DerivedClassMethod();
}
```

2. You have pointer `objFish*` that points to object of class `Tuna`.

```
Fish* objFish = new Tuna;
Tuna* pTuna = <what cast?>objFish;
```

What cast would you use to get a pointer `Tuna*` point to this object of type `Tuna`? Demonstrate using code.

LESSON 14
An Introduction to Macros and Templates

By now, you should have a solid understanding of basic C++ syntax. Programs written in C++ should be understandable and you are poised to learn language features that help you write applications efficiently.

In this lesson, you learn

- An introduction to the preprocessor
- The `#define` keyword and macros
- An introduction to templates
- How to write templates functions and classes
- The difference between macros and templates
- How to use `static_assert` introduced in C++11 to perform compile-time checks

The Preprocessor and the Compiler

Lesson 2, "The Anatomy of a C++ Program," introduced the preprocessor. The preprocessor, as the name indicates, is what runs before the compiler starts. In other words, the preprocessor actually decides what is compiled on the basis of how you instruct it. Preprocessor directives are characterized by the fact that they all start with a # sign. For example:

```
// instruct preprocessor to insert contents of iostream here
#include <iostream>

// define a macro constant
#define ARRAY_LENGTH 25
int numbers[ARRAY_LENGTH]; // array of 25 integers

// define a macro function
#define SQUARE(x) ((x) * (x))
int TwentyFive = SQUARE(5);
```

This lesson focuses on two types of preprocessor directives seen in the code snippet above, one using #define to define a constant and another using #define to define a macro function. Both these directives, irrespective of what role they play, actually tell the preprocessor to replace every instance of the macro (ARRAY_LENGTH or SQUARE) with the value they define.

NOTE	Macros are also about text substitution. The preprocessor does nothing intelligent beyond replacing in-place the identifier by another text.

Using Macro #define to Define Constants

The syntax of using #define to compose a constant is simple:

```
#define identifier value
```

For example, a constant ARRAY_LENGTH that is substituted by 25 would hence be the following:

```
#define ARRAY_LENGTH 25
```

This identifier is now replaced by 25 wherever the preprocessor encounters the text
ARRAY_LENGTH:

```
int numbers [ARRAY_LENGTH] = {0};
double radiuses [ARRAY_LENGTH] = {0.0};
std::string names [ARRAY_LENGTH];
```

After the preprocessor runs, the three are visible to the compiler as follows:

```
int numbers [25] = {0};   // an array of 25 integers
double radiuses [25] = {0.0};   // an array of 25 doubles
std::string names [25];   // an array of 25 std::strings
```

The replacement is applicable to every section of your code, including a for loop such
as this one:

```
for(int index = 0; index < ARRAY_LENGTH; ++index)
   numbers[index] = index;
```

This for loop is visible to the compiler as

```
for(int index = 0; index < 25; ++index)
   numbers[index] = index;
```

To see exactly how such a macro works, review Listing 14.1.

LISTING 14.1   Declaring and Using Macros That Define Constants

```
0: #include <iostream>
1: #include<string>
2: using namespace std;
3:
4: #define ARRAY_LENGTH 25
5: #define PI 3.1416
6: #define MY_DOUBLE double
7: #define FAV_WHISKY "Jack Daniels"
8:
9: int main()
10: {
11:    int numbers [ARRAY_LENGTH] = {0};
12:    cout << "Array's length: " << sizeof(numbers) / sizeof(int) << endl;
13:
14:    cout << "Enter a radius: ";
15:    MY_DOUBLE radius = 0;
16:    cin >> radius;
17:    cout << "Area is: " << PI * radius * radius << endl;
18:
```

14

```
19:     string favoriteWhisky (FAV_WHISKY);
20:     cout << "My favorite drink is: " << FAV_WHISKY << endl;
21:
22:     return 0;
23: }
```

Output ▼

```
Array's length: 25
Enter a radius: 2.1569
Area is: 14.7154
My favorite drink is: Jack Daniels
```

Analysis ▼

ARRAY_LENGTH, PI, MY_DOUBLE, and FAV_WHISKY are the four macro constants defined in Lines 4 to 7, respectively. As you can see, ARRAY_LENGTH is used in defining the length of an array at Line 11, which has been confirmed indirectly by using operator sizeof() in Line 12. MY_DOUBLE is used to declare a variable radius of type double in Line 15, whereas PI is used to calculate the area of the circle in Line 17. Finally, FAV_WHISKY is used to initialize a std::string object in Line 19 and is directly used in the cout statement in Line 20. All these instances show how the preprocessor simply makes a text replacement.

This "dumb" text replacement that seems to have found a ubiquitous application in Listing 14.1 has its drawbacks, too.

> **TIP**
>
> As the preprocessor makes dumb text substitutions, it does not check for correctness of the substitution (but the compiler always does). You could define FAV_WHISKY in Line 7 in Listing 14.1 like this:
>
> ```
> #define FAV_WHISKY 42 // "Jack Daniels"
> ```
>
> which would result in a compilation error in Line 19 for the std::string instantiation, but in the absence of it, the compiler would go ahead and print the following:
>
> ```
> My favorite drink is: 42
> ```
>
> This, of course, wouldn't make sense, and most importantly went through undetected. Additionally, you don't have much control on the macro defined constant PI: was it a double or a float? The answer is neither. PI to the preprocessor was just a text substitution element "3.1416". It never was a defined data type.

Constants are better defined using the const keyword with data types instead. So, this is much better:

```
const int ARRAY_LENGTH = 25;
const double PI = 3.1416;
const char* FAV_WHISKY = "Jack Daniels";
typedef double MY_DOUBLE;  // typedef aliases a type
```

Using Macros for Protection against Multiple Inclusion

C++ programmers typically declare their classes and functions in .H files called header files. The respective functions are defined in .CPP files that include the header files using the #include<header> preprocessor directive. If one header file—let's call it class1.h—declares a class that has another class declared in class2.h as a member, then class1.h needs to include class2.h. If the design were complicated, and the other class required the former as well, then class2.h would include class1.h, too!

For the preprocessor however, two header files that include each other is a problem of recursive nature. To avoid this problem, you can use macros in conjunction with preprocessor directives #ifndef and #endif.

header1.h that includes <header2.h> looks like the following:

```
#ifndef HEADER1_H _//multiple inclusion guard:
#define HEADER1_H_ // preprocessor will read this and following lines once
#include <header2.h>

class Class1
{
   // class members
};
#endif  // end of header1.h
```

header2.h looks similar, but with a different macro definition and includes <header1.h>:

```
#ifndef HEADER2_H_//multiple inclusion guard
#define HEADER2_H_
#include <header1.h>

class Class2
{
   // class members
};
#endif // end of header2.h
```

14

NOTE

> `#ifndef` can be read as if-not-defined. It is a conditional processing command, instructing the preprocessor to continue only if the identifier has not been defined.
>
> `#endif` marks the end of this conditional processing instruction for the preprocessor.

Thus, when the preprocessor enters `header1.h` in the first run and encounters `#ifndef` statement, it notices that the macro `HEADER1_H_` has not been defined and proceeds. The first line following `#ifndef` defines the macro `HEADER1_H_` ensuring that a second preprocessor run of this file terminates at the first line containing `#ifndef`, as that condition now evaluates to `false`. The same stands true for `header2.h`. This simple mechanism is arguably one of the most frequently used macro-based functionalities in the world of C++ programming.

Using `#define` to Write Macro Functions

The capability of the preprocessor to simply replace text elements identified by a macro often results it in being used to write simple functions, for example:

```
#define SQUARE(x) ((x) * (x))
```

This helps determine the square of a number. Similarly, a macro that calculates the area of a circle looks like this:

```
#define PI 3.1416
#define AREA_CIRCLE(r) (PI*(r)*(r))
```

Macro functions are often used for such very simple calculations. They provide the advantage of normal function calls in that these are expanded inline before compilations and hence can help improve code performance in certain cases. Listing 14.2 demonstrates the use of these macro functions.

LISTING 14.2   Using Macro Functions That Calculate the Square of a Number, Area of a Circle, and Min and Max of Two Numbers

```
0: #include <iostream>
1: #include<string>
2: using namespace std;
3:
```

```
 4: #define SQUARE(x) ((x) * (x))
 5: #define PI 3.1416
 6: #define AREA_CIRCLE(r) (PI*(r)*(r))
 7: #define MAX(a, b) (((a) > (b)) ? (a) : (b))
 8: #define MIN(a, b) (((a) < (b)) ? (a) : (b))
 9:
10: int main()
11: {
12:     cout << "Enter an integer: ";
13:     int num = 0;
14:     cin >> num;
15:
16:     cout << "SQUARE(" << num << ") = " << SQUARE(num) << endl;
17:     cout << "Area of a circle with radius " << num << " is: ";
18:     cout << AREA_CIRCLE(num) << endl;
19:
20:     cout << "Enter another integer: ";
21:     int num2 = 0;
22:     cin >> num2;
23:
24:     cout << "MIN(" << num << ", " << num2 << ") = ";
25:     cout << MIN (num, num2) << endl;
26:
27:     cout << "MAX(" << num << ", " << num2 << ") = ";
28:     cout << MAX (num, num2) << endl;
29:
30:     return 0;
31: }
```

Output ▼

```
Enter an integer: 36
SQUARE(36) = 1296
Area of a circle with radius 36 is: 4071.51
Enter another integer: -101
MIN(36, -101) = -101
MAX(36, -101) = 36
```

Analysis ▼

Lines 4 to 8 contain a few utility macro functions that return the square of a number, area of a circle, and min and max of two numbers, respectively. Note how AREA_CIRCLE in Line 6 evaluates the area using a macro constant PI, thus indicating that one macro can reuse another. After all, these are just plain text replacement commands for the preprocessor. Let's analyze Line 25, which uses the macro MIN:

```
cout << MIN (num, num2) << endl;
```

14

This line is essentially fed to the compiler in the following format where the macro is expanded in-place:

```
cout << (((num) < (num2)) ? (num) : (num2)) << endl;
```

CAUTION

> Note that macros are not type sensitive and macro functions can therefore cause problems. AREA_CIRCLE, for instance, should ideally be a function that returns double so that you are certain of the return value resolution of the area calculated, and its independence to the nature of the input radius was.

Why All the Parentheses?

Take a look at the macro to calculate the circle's area again:

```
#define AREA_CIRCLE(r) (PI*(r)*(r))
```

This calculation has curious syntax in the number of brackets used. In comparison, refer to the function `Area()` programmed in Listing 7.1 of Lesson 7, "Organizing Code with Functions."

```
// Function definitions (implementations)
double Area(double radius)
{
    return Pi * radius * radius;  // look, no brackets?
}
```

So, why did you overdo the brackets for the macro while the same formula in a function looks a lot different. The reason lies in the way the macro is evaluated—as a text substitution mechanism supported by the preprocessor.

Consider the macro without most of the brackets:

```
#define AREA_CIRCLE(r) (PI*r*r)
```

What would happen when you invoke this macro using a statement like this:

```
cout << AREA_CIRCLE (4+6);
```

This would be expanded by the compiler into

```
cout << (PI*4+6*4+6);  // not the same as PI*10*10
```

Thus, following the rules of operator precedence where multiplication happens before addition, the compiler actually evaluates the area like this:

```
cout << (PI*4+24+6);    // 42.5664 (which is incorrect)
```

In the absence of parenthesis, plain-text conversion played havoc on our programming logic! Parenthesis help avoid this problem:

```
#define AREA_CIRCLE(r) (PI*(r)*(r))
cout << AREA_CIRCLE (4+6);
```

The expression after substitution is viewed by the compiler as the following:

```
cout << (PI*(4+6)*(4+6));   // PI*10*10, as expected
```

These brackets automatically result in the calculation of an accurate area, making your macro code independent of operator precedence and the effects thereof.

Using Macro `assert` to Validate Expressions

Although it is good to test every code path immediately after programming, it might be physically impossible for very large applications. What is possible, though, is to check for valid expressions or variable values.

The `assert` macro enables you to do just that. To use `assert` you include `<assert.h>` and the syntax is as follows:

```
assert (expression that evaluates to true or false);
```

A sample use of `assert()` that validates the contents of a pointer is

```
#include <assert.h>
int main()
{
   char* sayHello = new char [25];
   assert(sayHello != NULL); // throws a message if pointer is NULL

   // other code

   delete [] sayHello;
   return 0;
}
```

`assert()` ensures that you are notified if the pointer is invalid. For demonstration purposes, I initialized `sayHello` to NULL, and on execution in debug mode Visual Studio immediately popped up the screen you see in Figure 14.1.

14

FIGURE 14.1
What happens when an assert checking validity of the pointer fails.

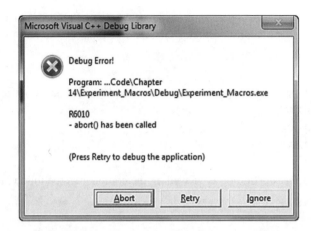

Thus, `assert()`, as implemented in Microsoft Visual Studio, enables you to click the Retry button that brings you back into your application, and the call stack indicates which line failed the assertion test. This makes `assert()` a handy debugging feature; for instance, you can validate input parameters of functions using `assert`. This is highly recommended and helps you improve the quality of your code over the long term.

NOTE

`assert()` is typically disabled in release modes and provides you with an error message or information only in the debug build of most development environments.

Additionally, some environments have implemented this as a function, not as a macro.

CAUTION

As assert does not make it to the release build, it is important to ensure that checks that are critical to the functioning of your application (for example, the return value of a `dynamic_cast` operation) are still performed using an `if`-statement. An assert assists you in problem detection; it's not something to replace pointer checks necessary in the code.

Advantages and Disadvantages of Using Macro Functions

Macros enable you to reuse certain utility functions irrespective of the type of variables you are dealing with. Consider the following line from Listing 14.2 again:

```
#define MIN(a, b) (((a) < (b)) ? (a) : (b))
```

You can use this macro function `MIN` on integers:

```
cout << MIN(25, 101) << endl;
```

But you can reuse the same on `double`, too:

```
cout << MIN(0.1, 0.2) << endl;
```

Note that if `MIN()` were to be a normal function, you would program two variants of it: `MIN_INT()` that accepted int parameters and returned an int and `MIN_DOUBLE()` that does the same with type double instead. This optimization in reducing lines of code is a slight advantage and entices some programmers into using macros for defining simple utility functions. These macro functions get expanded inline before compilation and hence the performance of a simple macro is superior to that of an ordinary function call doing the same task. This is because the function call requires the creation of a call stack, passing arguments, and so on—administrative overload that often takes more CPU time than the calculation of `MIN` itself.

Yet, macros do not support any form of type safety, and that is a major disadvantage. Additionally, debugging a complicated macro is not easy either.

If you need the ability to program generic functions that are type independent, yet type safe, you program a template function instead of a macro function. These are explained in the next section. If you need to boost performance, you call that function `inline`.

You have already been introduced to programming inline functions using keyword `inline` in Listing 7.10 in Lesson 7.

DO	DON'T
DO program your own macro functions as infrequently as possibly.	**DON'T** forget to envelop every variable in a macro function definition with brackets.
DO use `const` variables where you can instead of macros.	**DON'T** forget to insert multiple inclusion guards using `#ifndef`, `#define`, and `#endif` in your header files.
DO remember that macros are not type safe and the preprocessor performs no type checking.	**DON'T** forget to sprinkle your code with generous number of `assert()` statements—these don't make it to the release version and are good at improving the quality of your code.

14

It's time to learn generic programming practices using templates!

An Introduction to Templates

Templates are arguably one of the most powerful features of the C++ language that often are the least approached, or understood. Before we tackle with this matter, let's first look at the definition of a template as supplied by Webster's Dictionary:

> Pronunciation: \'tem-plét\
>
> Function: noun
>
> Etymology: Probably from French *templet,* diminutive of *temple,* part of a loom, probably from Latin *templum*
>
> Date: 1677
>
> 1: a short piece or block placed horizontally in a wall under a beam to distribute its weight or pressure (as over a door)
>
> 2: (1): a gauge, pattern, or mold (as a thin plate or board) used as a guide to the form of a piece being made (2): a molecule (as of DNA) that serves as a pattern for the generation of another macromolecule (as messenger RNA) b: overlay
>
> 3: something that establishes or serves as a pattern

The last definition probably comes closest to the interpretation of the word *template* as used in the C++ parlance. Templates in C++ enable you to define a behavior that you can apply to objects of varying types. This sounds ominously close to what macros let you do (refer to the simple macro MAX that determined the greater of two numbers), save for the fact that macros are type unsafe and templates are type safe.

Template Declaration Syntax

You begin the declaration of a template using the `template` keyword followed by a type parameter list. The format of this declaration is

```
template <parameter list>
template function / class declaration..
```

The keyword `template` marks the start of a template declaration and is followed by the template parameter list. This parameter list contains the keyword `typename` that defines the template parameter `objType`, making it a placeholder for the `type` of the object that the template is being instantiated for.

```
template <typename T1, typename T2 = T1>
bool TemplateFunction(const T1& param1, const T2& param2);

// A template class
template <typename T1, typename T2 = T1>
```

```
class MyTemplate
{
private:
    T1 member1;
    T2 member2;

public:
    T1 GetObj1() {return member1; }
    // ... other members
};
```

What you see is a template function and a template class, each taking two template parameters T1 and T2, where T2 has been given the default type as that of T1.

The Different Types of Template Declarations

A template declaration can be

- A declaration or definition of a function
- A declaration or definition of a class
- A definition of a member function or a member class of a class template
- A definition of a static data member of a class template
- A definition of a static data member of a class nested within a class template
- A definition of a member template of a class or class template

Template Functions

Imagine a function that would adapt itself to suit parameters of different types. Such a function is possible using template syntax! Let's analyze a sample template declaration that is the equivalent of the previously discussed macro MAX that returns the greater of two supplied parameters:

```
template <typename objType>
const objType& GetMax(const objType& value1, const objType& value2)
{
    if (value1 > value2)
        return value1;
    else
        return value2;
}
```

Sample usage:

```
int num1 = 25;
int num2 = 40;
```

14

```
int maxVal = GetMax <int> (num1, num2);
double double1 = 1.1;
double double2 = 1.001;
double maxVal = GetMax <double>(double1, double2);
```

Note the detail <int> used in the call to GetMax. It effectively defines the template parameter objType as int. The preceding code leads to the compiler generating two versions of the template function GetMax, which can be visualized as the following:

```
const int& GetMax(const int& value1, const int& value2)
{
    //...
}
const double& GetMax(const double& value1, const double& value2)
{
    // ...
}
```

In reality, however, template functions don't necessarily need an accompanying type specifier. So, the following function call works perfectly well:

```
int maxVal = GetMax(num1, num2);
```

Compilers in this case are intelligent enough to understand that the template function is being invoked for the integer type. With template classes, however, you need to explicitly specify type, as shown in Listing 14.3.

LISTING 14.3　A Template Function GetMax That Helps Evaluate the Higher of Two Supplied Values

```
 0: #include<iostream>
 1: #include<string>
 2: using namespace std;
 3:
 4: template <typename Type>
 5: const Type& GetMax(const Type& value1, const Type& value2)
 6: {
 7:     if (value1 > value2)
 8:         return value1;
 9:     else
10:         return value2;
11: }
12:
13: template <typename Type>
14: void DisplayComparison(const Type& value1, const Type& value2)
15: {
16:     cout << "GetMax(" << value1 << ", " << value2 << ") = ";
```

```
17:     cout << GetMax(value1, value2) << endl;
18: }
19:
20: int main()
21: {
22:     int num1 = -101, num2 = 2011;
23:     DisplayComparison(num1, num2);
24:
25:     double d1 = 3.14, d2 = 3.1416;
26:     DisplayComparison(d1, d2);
27:
28:     string name1("Jack"), name2("John");
29:     DisplayComparison(name1, name2);
30:
31:     return 0;
32: }
```

Output ▼

```
GetMax(-101, 2011) = 2011
GetMax(3.14, 3.1416) = 3.1416
GetMax(Jack, John) = John
```

Analysis ▼

This sample features two template functions: GetMax() in Lines 4 to 11, which is used by DisplayComparison() in Lines 13 to 18. main() demonstrates in Lines 23, 26, and 29 how the same template function has been reused for very different data types: integer, double, and std::string. Not only are these template functions reusable (just like their macro counterparts), but they're easier to program and maintain and are type-safe!

Note that you could've also invoked DisplayComparison with the explicit type:

```
23:     DisplayComparison<int>(num1, num2);
```

However, this is unnecessary when calling template functions. You don't need to specify the template parameter type(s) because the compiler is able to infer it automatically. When programming template classes, though, you need to do it.

Templates and Type Safety

14

Template functions DisplayComparison() and GetMax() shown in Listing 14.3 are type safe. This means that they would not allow a meaningless call like this one:

```
DisplayComparison(num1, name1);
```

This would immediately result in a compile failure.

Template Classes

Lesson 9, "Classes and Objects," taught you that classes are programming units that encapsulate certain attributes and methods that operate on those attributes. Attributes typically are private members, such as int Age in a class Human. Classes are design blueprints, and the real-world representation of a class is an object of the class. So, "Tom" can be thought of as an object of class Human with attribute Age containing value 15, for example. Apparently, we mean years. If you were required to store age as the number of seconds since birth for a certain reason unique to your application, then int might be insufficient. To be on the safe side, you might want to use a long long instead. This is where template classes could be handy. Template classes are the templatized versions of C++ classes. These are blueprints of blueprints. When using a template class, you are given the option to specify the "type" you are specializing the class for. This enables you to create some humans with template parameter Age as a long long, some with int, and some with Age as an integer of type short.

A simple template class that uses a single parameter T to hold a member variable can be written as the following:

```
template <typename T>
class HoldVarTypeT
{
private:
    T value;

public:
    void SetValue   (const T& newValue) { value = newValue; }
    T& GetValue() {return value;}
};
```

The type of the variable value is T, and that is assigned at the time the template is used, that is, *instantiated*. So, let's look at a sample usage of this template class:

```
HoldVarTypeT <int> holdInt;  // template instantiation for int
holdInt.SetValue(5);
cout << "The value stored is: " << holdInt.GetValue() << endl;
```

You have used this template class to hold and retrieve an object of type int; that is, the Template class is instantiated for a template parameter of type int. Similarly, you can use the same class to deal with character strings in a similar manner:

```
HoldVarTypeT <char*> holdStr;
holdStr.SetValue("Sample string");
cout << "The value stored is: " << holdStr.GetValue() << endl;
```

Thus, the template class defines a pattern for classes and helps implement that pattern on different data types that the template may be instantiated with.

TIP

Template classes can be instantiated with types other than simple ones like `int` or classes supplied by the standard library. You may instantiate a template using a class defined by you. For example, when you add the code that defines template class `HoldVarTypeT` to Listing 9.1 in Lesson 9, you will be able to instantiate the template for `class Human` by appending the following code to `main()`:

```
HoldVarTypeT<Human> holdHuman;
holdHuman.SetValue(firstMan);
holdHuman.GetValue().IntroduceSelf();
```

Declaring Templates with Multiple Parameters

The template parameter list can be expanded to declare multiple parameters separated by a comma. So, if you want to declare a generic class that holds a pair of objects that can be of differing types, you can do so using the construct as shown in the following sample (that displays a template class with two template parameters):

```
template <typename T1, typename T2>
class HoldsPair
{
private:
    T1 value1;
    T2 value2;
public:
    // Constructor that initializes member variables
    HoldsPair (const T1& val1, const T2& val2)
    {
        value1 = val1;
        value2 = val2;
    };
    // ... Other member functions
};
```

In this example, `class HoldsPair` accepts two template parameters named `T1` and `T2`. We can use this class to hold two objects of the same type or of different types as you can see here:

```
// A template instantiation that pairs an int with a double
HoldsPair <int, double> pairIntDouble (6, 1.99);

// A template instantiation that pairs an int with an int
HoldsPair <int, int> pairIntDouble (6, 500);
```

14

Declaring Templates with Default Parameters

We could modify the previous version of HoldsPair <...> to declare int as the default template parameter type.

```
template <typename T1=int, typename T2=int>
class HoldsPair
{
    // ... method declarations
};
```

This is similar in construction to functions that define default input parameter values except for the fact that, in this case, we define default *types*.

The second usage of HoldsPair can thus be compacted to

```
// Pair an int with an int (default type)
HoldsPair <> pairInts (6, 500);
```

Sample Template class<> HoldsPair

It's time to develop further on the template version of HoldsPair that has been covered so far. Have a look at Listing 14.4.

LISTING 14.4 A Template Class with a Pair of Member Attributes

```
 0: #include <iostream>
 1: using namespace std;
 2:
 3: // template with default params: int & double
 4: template <typename T1=int, typename T2=double>
 5: class HoldsPair
 6: {
 7: private:
 8:     T1 value1;
 9:     T2 value2;
10: public:
11:     HoldsPair(const T1& val1, const T2& val2) // constructor
12:         : value1(val1), value2(val2) {}
13:
14:     // Accessor functions
15:     const T1 & GetFirstValue () const
16:     {
17:         return value1;
18:     }
19:
20:     const T2& GetSecondValue () const
```

```
21:    {
22:        return value2;
23:    }
24: };
25:
26: int main ()
27: {
28:    HoldsPair<> pairIntDbl (300, 10.09);
29:    HoldsPair<short,const char*>pairShortStr(25,"Learn templates, love C++");
30:
31:    cout << "The first object contains -" << endl;
32:    cout << "Value 1: " << pairIntDbl.GetFirstValue () <<   endl;
33:    cout << "Value 2: " << pairIntDbl.GetSecondValue () << endl;
34:
35:    cout << "The second object contains -" << endl;
36:    cout << "Value 1: " << pairShortStr.GetFirstValue () <<   endl;
37:    cout << "Value 2: " << pairShortStr.GetSecondValue () << endl;
38:
39:    return 0;
40: }
```

Output ▼

```
The first object contains -
Value 1: 300
Value 2: 10.09
The second object contains -
Value 1: 25
Value 2: Learn templates, love C++
```

Analysis ▼

This simple program illustrates how to declare the template class HoldsPair to hold a pair of values of types that are dependent on the template's parameter list. Line 1 contains a template parameter list that defines two template parameters T1 and T2 with default types as int and double, respectively. Accessor functions GetFirstValue() and GetSecondValue() can be used to query the values held by the object. Note how GetFirstValue and GetSecondValue get adapted on the basis of the template instantiation syntax to return the appropriate object types. You have managed to define a pattern in HoldsPair that you can reuse to deliver the same logic for different variable types. Thus, templates increase code reusability.

14

Template Instantiation and Specialization

A template class is a blueprint of a class, and therefore doesn't truly exist for the compiler before it has been used in one form or another. That is, as far as the compiler is concerned, a template class you define but don't consume is code that is simply ignored. However, once you *instantiate* a template class, like `HoldsPair`, by supplying template arguments like this:

```
HoldsPair<int, double> pairIntDbl;
```

You are instructing the compiler to create a class for you using the template and instantiate it for the types specified as template arguments (`int` and `double` in this case). Thus, in the case of templates, *instantiation* is the act or process of creating a specific type using one or more template arguments.

On the other hand, there may be situations that require you to explicitly define a (different) behavior of a template when instantiated with a specific type. This is where you specialize a template (or behavior thereof) for that type. A specialization of template class `HoldsPair` when instantiated with template parameters both of type `int` would look like this:

```
template<> class HoldsPair<int, int>
{
    // implementation code here
};
```

Needless to say, code that specializes a template must follow the template definition. Listing 14.5 is an example of a template specialization that demonstrates how different a specialized version can be from the template it specializes.

LISTING 14.5   Demonstrates Template Specialization

```
0: #include <iostream>
1: using namespace std;
2:
3: template <typename T1 = int, typename T2 = double>
4: class HoldsPair
5: {
6: private:
7:     T1 value1;
8:     T2 value2;
9: public:
10:     HoldsPair(const T1& val1, const T2& val2) // constructor
11:         : value1(val1), value2(val2) {}
12:
```

```
13:     // Accessor functions
14:     const T1 & GetFirstValue() const;
15:     const T2& GetSecondValue() const;
16: };
17:
18: // specialization of HoldsPair for types int & int here
19: template<> class HoldsPair<int, int>
20: {
21: private:
22:     int value1;
23:     int value2;
24:     string strFun;
25: public:
26:     HoldsPair(const int& val1, const int& val2) // constructor
27:         : value1(val1), value2(val2) {}
28:
29:     const int & GetFirstValue() const
30:     {
31:         cout << "Returning integer " << value1 << endl;
32:         return value1;
33:     }
34: };
35:
36: int main()
37: {
38:     HoldsPair<int, int> pairIntInt(222, 333);
39:     pairIntInt.GetFirstValue();
40:
41:     return 0;
42: }
```

Output ▼

```
Returning integer 222
```

Analysis ▼

Clearly, when you compare the behavior of the class HoldsPair in Listing 14.4 to that in this one, you notice that the template is behaving remarkably different. In fact, the function GetFirstValue() has been modified in the template instantiation for HoldsPair<int,int> to also display output. A closer look at the specialization code in Lines 18 to 34 shows that this version also has a string member declared in Line 24—a member that is missing in the original template definition of HoldsPair<> seen in Lines 3–16. In fact, the original template definition doesn't even supply an implementation of the accessor functions GetFirstValue() and GetSecondValue(), and the program still compiles. This is because the compiler was only required to consider the template instantiation for <int, int>—for which we have supplied a

14

specialized implementation that was complete enough. Thus, this sample has not only demonstrated template specialization but also how template code is considered or even ignored by the compiler depending on its usage.

Template Classes and `static` Members

We learned how code in templates begins to exist for the compiler when used and not otherwise. So, how would `static` member attributes function within a template class? You learned in Lesson 9 that declaring a class member `static` results in the member being shared across all instances of a class. It's similar with a template class, too, save for the fact that a `static` member is shared across all objects of a template class with the same template instantiation. So a `static` member X within a template class is static within all instances of the class instantiated for `int`. Similarly, X is also static within all instances of the class specialized for `double`, independent of the other template instantiation for `int`. In other words, you can visualize it as the compiler creating two versions of the static member variable in a template class: X_int for template instantiation as `int` and X_double for template instantiations as `double`. Listing 14.6 demonstrates this.

LISTING 14.6   The Effect of Static Variables on Template Class and Instances Thereof

```
0: #include <iostream>
1: using namespace std;
2:
3: template <typename T>
4: class TestStatic
5: {
6: public:
7:     static int staticVal;
8: };
9:
10: // static member initialization
11: template<typename T> int TestStatic<T>::staticVal;
12:
13: int main()
14: {
15:     TestStatic<int> intInstance;
16:     cout << "Setting staticVal for intInstance to 2011" << endl;
17:     intInstance.staticVal = 2011;
18:
19:     TestStatic<double> dblInstance;
20:     cout << "Setting staticVal for Double_2 to 1011" << endl;
21:     dblInstance.staticVal = 1011;
22:
23:     cout << "intInstance.staticVal = " << intInstance.staticVal << endl;
24:     cout << "dblInstance.staticVal = " << dblInstance.staticVal <<   endl;
25:
26:     return 0;
27: }
```

Output ▼

```
Setting staticVal for intInstance to 2011
Setting staticVal for Double_2 to 1011
intInstance.staticVal = 2011
dblnstance.staticVal = 1011
```

Analysis ▼

In Lines 17 and 21, you set member staticVal for an instantiation of the template for type int and type double, respectively. The output demonstrates that the compiler has stored two distinct values in two different static members though both are called staticVal. Thus, the compiler ensured that the behavior of the static variable remains intact for the instantiation of the template class for a particular type.

NOTE

> Static member instantiation syntax for a template class is not to be missed in Line 11 in Listing 14.6.
>
> ```
> template<typename T> int TestStatic<T>::staticVal;
> ```
>
> This follows the pattern:
>
> ```
> template<template parameters> StaticType
> ClassName<Template   Arguments>::StaticVarName;
> ```

Variable Templates, Also Called Variadic Templates

Let's assume that you want to write a generic function that adds two values. Template function Sum() achieves just that:

```
template <typename T1, typename T2, typename T3>
void Sum(T1& result, T2 num1, T3 num2)
{
   result = num1 + num2;
   return;
}
```

This is simple. However, if you were required to write one single function that would be capable of adding any number of values, each passed as an argument, you would need to make use of *variable templates* in defining such a function. Variable templates or variadic templates have been part of C++ since C++14, released in 2014. Listing 14.7 demonstrates the use of variable templates in defining such a function.

14

LISTING 14.7   Function Using Variadic Templates Demonstrates Variable Arguments

```
0: #include <iostream>
1: using namespace std;
2:
3: template <typename Res, typename ValType>
4: void Sum(Res& result, ValType& val)
5: {
6:     result = result + val;
7: }
8:
9: template <typename Res, typename First, typename... Rest>
10: void Sum(Res& result, First val1, Rest... valN)
11: {
12:     result = result + val1;
13:     return Sum(result, valN ...);
14: }
15:
16: int main()
17: {
18:     double dResult = 0;
19:     Sum (dResult, 3.14, 4.56, 1.1111);
20:     cout << "dResult = " << dResult << endl;
21:
22:     string strResult;
23:     Sum (strResult, "Hello ", "World");
24:     cout << "strResult = " << strResult.c_str() << endl;
25:
26:     return 0;
27: }
```

Output ▼

```
dResult = 8.8111
strResult = Hello World
```

Analysis ▼

The sample demonstrates that the function Sum() we defined using variable templates not only processed completely different argument types as seen in Lines 19 and 23, but also processed a varying number of arguments. Sum() invoked by Line 19 uses four arguments, while that in Line 23 uses three arguments of which one is a std::string and the following two are const char*. During compilation, the compiler actually creates code for the right kind of Sum() that would suit the call, doing so recursively until all arguments have been processed.

> **NOTE**
>
> You may have noticed the use of the ellipsis mark . . . in the preceding code sample. Ellipses in C++ used with templates tell the compiler that the template class or function may accept an arbitrary number of template arguments of any type.

Variable templates are a powerful addition to C++ that finds application in mathematical processing as well as in the accomplishment of certain simple tasks. Programmers using variable templates save themselves the repetitive effort of implementing functions that perform a task in various overloaded versions, creating code that is shorter and simpler to maintain.

> **NOTE**
>
> C++14 supplies you with an operator that would tell the number of template arguments passed in a call to a variable template. In Listing 14.7, you could use this operator inside a function like `Sum()`, like this:
>
> ```
> int arrNums[sizeof...(Rest)];
> // length of array evaluated using sizeof...()
> at compile time
> ```
>
> You must not confuse `sizeof...()` with `sizeof(Type)`. The latter returns the size of a type, while the former returns the number of template arguments sent to a variadic template.

The support of variable templates has also ushered in standard support for *tuples*. `std::tuple` is the class template that implements the tuple. It may be instantiated with a varying number of member elements and types thereof. These may be individually accessed using standard library function `std::get`. Listing 14.8 demonstrates the instantiation and use of a `std::tuple`.

LISTING 14.8   Instantiating and Using a `std::tuple`

```
0: #include <iostream>
1: #include <tuple>
2: #include <string>
3: using namespace std;
4:
5: template <typename tupleType>
6: void DisplayTupleInfo(tupleType& tup)
7: {
8:     const int numMembers = tuple_size<tupleType>::value;
9:     cout << "Num elements in tuple: " << numMembers << endl;
```

14

```
10:     cout << "Last element value: " << get<numMembers - 1>(tup) << endl;
11: }
12:
13: int main()
14: {
15:     tuple<int, char, string> tup1(make_tuple(101, 's', "Hello Tuple!"));
16:     DisplayTupleInfo(tup1);
17:
18:     auto tup2(make_tuple(3.14, false));
19:     DisplayTupleInfo(tup2);
20:
21:     auto concatTup(tuple_cat(tup2, tup1)); // contains tup2, tup1 members
22:     DisplayTupleInfo(concatTup);
23:
24:     double pi;
25:     string sentence;
26:     tie(pi, ignore, ignore, ignore, sentence) = concatTup;
27:     cout << "Unpacked! Pi: " << pi << " and \"" << sentence << "\"" << endl;
28:
29:     return 0;
30: }
```

Output ▼

```
Num elements in tuple: 3
Last element value: Hello Tuple!
Num elements in tuple: 2
Last element value: 0
Num elements in tuple: 5
Last element value: Hello Tuple!
Unpacked! Pi: 3.14 and "Hello Tuple!"
```

Analysis ▼

First and foremost, if the code in Listing 14.8 overwhelms you, then do not worry! Tuples are an advanced concept and typically find application in generic template programming. The topic has nevertheless been introduced in this book to give you a broad idea about what this concept, which is still under evolution, is all about. Lines 15, 18, and 21 contain three different instantiations of a `std::tuple`. `tup1` contains three members: an `int`, a `char`, and a `std::string`. `tup2` contains a `double` and a `bool` and also uses the compiler's automatic type deduction feature via keyword the `auto`. `tup3` is actually a tuple with five members: `double`, `bool`, `int`, `char`, and `string`—a result of concatenation using template function `std::tuple_cat`.

Template function `DisplayTupleInfo()` in Lines 5–14 demonstrates the usage of `tuple_size` that resolves to the number of elements contained by that specific instantiation of `std::tuple` during compilation. `std::get` used in Line 10 is the mechanism to access individual values stored in a tuple using their zero-based indices. Finally, `std::tie` in Line 26 demonstrates how the contents of a tuple can be unpacked or copied into individual objects. We use `std::ignore` to instruct `tie` to ignore the tuple members that were not of any interest to the application.

Using `static_assert` to Perform Compile-Time Checks

This is a feature introduced since C++11 that enables you to block compilation if certain checks are not fulfilled. Weird as this might sound, it's useful with template classes. For example, you might want to ensure that your template class is not instantiated for an integer! `static_assert` is a compile-time assert that can display a custom message on your development environment (or console):

```
static_assert(expression being validated, "Error message when check fails");
```

To ensure that your template class cannot be instantiated for type `int`, you can use `static_assert()` with `sizeof(T)`, comparing it against `sizeof(int)` and displaying an error message if the inequality check fails:

```
static_assert(sizeof(T) != sizeof(int), "No int please!");
```

Such a template class that uses `static_assert` to block compilation for certain instantiation types is seen in Listing 14.9.

LISTING 14.9   A Finicky Template Class That Protests Using `static_assert` When Instantiated for Type `int`

```
0: template <typename T>
1: class EverythingButInt
2: {
3: public:
4:     EverythingButInt()
5:     {
6:         static_assert(sizeof(T) != sizeof(int), "No int please!");
7:     }
8: };
9:
10: int main()
11: {
12:     EverythingButInt<int> test;  // template instantiation with int.
13:     return 0;
14: }
```

14

Output ▼

There is no output as compile fails, providing you with the note you supplied:

```
error: No int please!
```

Analysis ▼

The protest registered by the compiler is programmed in Line 6. Thus, `static_assert` is a way C++11 helps you protect your template code against unwanted instantiation.

Using Templates in Practical C++ Programming

An important and powerful application of templates is in the Standard Template Library (STL). STL is comprised of a collection of template classes and functions containing generic utility classes and algorithms. These STL template classes enable you to implement dynamic arrays, lists, and key-value pair containers, whereas algorithms, such as sort, work on those containers and process the data they contain.

The knowledge of template syntax you gained earlier greatly assists you in using STL containers and functions that are presented in great detail in the following lessons of this book. A better understanding of STL containers and algorithms in turn helps you write efficient C++ applications that use STL's tested and reliable implementation and helps you avoid spending time in boilerplate details.

DO	DON'T
DO use templates for the implementation of generic concepts. **DO** choose templates over macros.	**DON'T** forget to use the principles of `const` correctness when programming template functions and classes. **DON'T** forget that a static member contained within a template class is static for every type-specialization of the class.

Summary

In this lesson, you learned more details about working with the preprocessor. Each time you run the compiler, the preprocessor runs first and translates directives such as `#define`.

The preprocessor does text substitution, although with the use of macros these can be somewhat complex. Macro functions provide complex text substitution based on arguments passed at compile time to the macro. It is important to put parentheses around every argument in the macro to ensure that the correct substitution takes place.

Templates help you write reusable code that supplies the developer with a pattern that can be used for a variety of data types. They also make for a type-safe replacement of macros. With the knowledge of templates gained in this lesson, you are now poised to learn to use the STL!

Q&A

Q Why should I use inclusion guards in my header files?

A Inclusion guards using `#ifndef`, `#define`, and `#endif` protect your header from multiple or recursive inclusion errors, and in some cases they even speed up compilation.

Q When should I favor macro functions over templates if the functionality in question can be implemented in both?

A Ideally, you should always favor templates as the templates allow for generic implementation that is also type safe. Macros don't allow for type-safe implementations and are best avoided.

Q Do I need to specify template arguments when invoking a template function?

A Normally not as the compiler can infer this for you, given the arguments used in the function call.

Q How many instances of static variables exist for a given template class?

A This is entirely dependent on the number of types for which the template class has been instantiated. So, if your class has been instantiated for an `int`, a `string`, and a custom type `X`, you can expect three instances of your static variable to be available—one per template instantiation.

Workshop

The Workshop provides quiz questions to help you solidify your understanding of the material covered and exercises to provide you with experience in using what you've learned. Try to answer the quiz and exercise questions before checking the answers in Appendix E, and be certain you understand the answers.

14

Quiz

1. What is an inclusion guard?

2. Consider the following macro:

```
#define SPLIT(x) x / 5
```

What is the result if this is called with 20?

3. What is the result if the SPLIT macro in Question 2 is called with 10+10?

4. How would you modify the SPLIT macro to avoid erroneous results?

Exercises

1. Write a macro that multiplies two numbers.

2. Write a template version of the macro in Exercise 1.

3. Implement a template function for swap that exchanges two variables.

4. **BUG BUSTERS**: How would you improve the following macro that computes the quarter of an input value?

```
#define QUARTER(x) (x / 4)
```

5. Write a simple template class that holds two arrays of types that are defined via the class's template parameter list. The size of the array is 10, and the template class should have accessor functions that allow for the manipulation of array elements.

6. Write a template function Display() that can be invoked with a varying number and type of arguments, and would display each of them.

LESSON 15

An Introduction to the Standard Template Library

Put in simple terms, the standard template library (STL) is a set of template classes and functions that supply the programmer with

- Containers for storing information
- Iterators for accessing the information stored
- Algorithms for manipulating the content of the containers

In this lesson, you get an overview of these three pillars of STL.

STL Containers

Containers are STL classes that are used to store data. STL supplies two types of container classes:

- Sequential containers
- Associative containers

In addition to these STL also provides classes called *container adapters* that are variants of the same with reduced functionality to support a specific purpose.

Sequential Containers

As the name suggests, these are containers used to hold data in a sequential fashion, such as arrays and lists. Sequential containers are characterized by a fast insertion time, but are relatively slow in `find` operations.

The STL sequential containers are

- **std::vector**—Operates like a dynamic array and grows at the end. Think of a vector like a shelf of books to which you can add or remove books on one end
- **std::deque**—Similar to `std::vector` except that it allows for new elements to be inserted or removed at the beginning, too
- **std::list**—Operates like a doubly linked list. Think of this like a chain where an object is a link in the chain. You can add or remove links—that is, objects—at any position
- **std::forward_list**—Similar to a `std::list` except that it is a singly linked list of elements that allows you to iterate only in one direction

The STL `vector` class is akin to an array and allows for random access of an element; that is, you can directly access or manipulate an element in the `vector` given its position (index) using the subscript operator (`[]`). In addition to this, the STL `vector` is a dynamic array and therefore can resize itself to suit the application's runtime requirements. To keep the property of being able to randomly access an element in the array when given a position, most implementations of the STL `vector` keep all elements in contiguous locations. Therefore, a `vector` that needs to resize itself often can reduce the performance of the application, depending on the type of the object it contains. Lesson 4, "Managing Arrays and Strings," introduced you to the vector briefly in Listing 4.4. This container is discussed extensively in Lesson 17, "STL Dynamic Array Classes."

You can think of the STL `list` as STL's implementation of a regular linked list. Although elements in a `list` cannot be randomly accessed, as they can be in the STL `vector`, a `list` can organize elements in noncontiguous sections of memory. Therefore, the `std::list` does not have the performance issues that are applicable to a `vector` when the `vector` needs to reallocate its internal array. STL list class is discussed extensively in Lesson 18, "STL `list` and `forward_list`."

Associative Containers

Associative containers are those that store data in a sorted fashion—akin to a dictionary. This results in slower insertion times, but presents significant advantages when it comes to searching.

The associative containers supplied by STL are

- `std::set`—Stores unique values sorted on insertion in a container featuring logarithmic complexity

- `std::unordered_set`—Stores unique values sorted on insertion in a container featuring near constant complexity. Available starting C++11

- `std::map`—Stores key-value pairs sorted by their unique keys in a container with logarithmic complexity

- `std::unordered_map`—Stores key-value pairs sorted by their unique keys in a container with near constant complexity. Available starting C++11

- `std::multiset`—Akin to a `set`. Additionally, supports the ability to store multiple items having the same value; that is, the value doesn't need to be unique

- `std::unordered_multiset`—Akin to a `unordered_set`. Additionally, supports the ability to store multiple items having the same value; that is, the value doesn't need to be unique. Available starting C++11.

- `std::multimap`—Akin to a `map`. Additionally, supports the ability to store key-value pairs where keys don't need to be unique.

- `std::unordered_multimap`—Akin to a `unordered_map`. Additionally, supports the ability to store key-value pairs where keys don't need to be unique. Available starting C++11.

NOTE

> *Complexity* in this case is an indication of the performance of the container with relation to the number of elements contained by it. Therefore, when we speak of *constant complexity*, as in the case of `std::unordered_map`, we mean that the performance of the container is unrelated to the number of elements contained by it. Such a container would need as much time to perform on a thousand elements as it would on a million.
>
> *Logarithmic complexity* as is the case with `std::map` indicates that the performance is proportional to the logarithm of the number of elements contained in it. Such a container would take twice as long in processing a million elements as it would in processing a thousand.
>
> *Linear complexity* means that the performance is proportional to the number of elements. Such a container would be a thousand times slower in processing a million elements than it would be in processing a thousand.
>
> For a given container, the complexities may be different for differing operations. That is, the element insertion complexity may be constant but search complexity linear. Therefore, an understanding of how a container may perform in addition to the functionality it will be used with is key to choosing the right container.

The sort criteria of STL containers can be customized by programming predicate functions.

TIP

> Some implementations of STL also feature associative containers such as `hash_set`, `hash_multiset`, `hash_map`, and `hash_multimap`. These are similar to the `unordered_*` containers, which are supported by the standard. In some scenarios, `hash_*` and the `unordered_*` variants can be better at searching for an element as they offer constant time operations (independent of the number of elements in the container). Typically, these containers also supply public methods that are identical to those supplied by their standard counterparts and hence are as easy to use.
>
> Using the standard-compliant variants will result in code that is easier to port across platforms and compilers, and should hence be preferred. It is also possible that the logarithmic reduction in performance of a standard-compliant container might not significantly affect your application.

Container Adapters

Container adapters are variants of sequential and associative containers that have limited functionality and are intended to fulfill a particular purpose. The main adapter classes are

- `std::stack`—Stores elements in a LIFO (last-in-first-out) fashion, allowing elements to be inserted (pushed) and removed (popped) at the top.

- `std::queue`—Stores elements in FIFO (first-in-first-out) fashion, allowing the first element to be removed in the order they're inserted.

- `std::priority_queue`—Stores elements in a sorted order, such that the one whose value is evaluated to be the highest is always first in the queue.

These containers are discussed in detail in Lesson 24, "Adaptive Containers: Stack and Queue."

STL Iterators

The simplest example of an iterator is a pointer. Given a pointer to the first element in an array, you can increment it and point to the next element or, in many cases, manipulate the element at that location.

Iterators in STL are template classes that in some ways are a generalization of pointers. These are template classes that give the programmer a handle by which he can work with and manipulate STL containers and perform operations on them. Note that operations could as well be STL algorithms that are template functions, Iterators are the bridge that allows these template functions to work with containers, which are template classes, in a consistent and seamless manner.

Iterators supplied by STL can be broadly classified into the following:

- **Input iterator**—One that can be dereferenced to reference an object. The object can be in a collection, for instance. Input iterators of the purest kinds guarantee read access only.

- **Output iterator**—One that allows the programmer to write to the collection. Output iterators of the strictest types guarantee write access only.

The basic iterator types mentioned in the preceding list are further refined into the following:

- **Forward iterator**—A refinement of the input and output iterators allowing both input and output. Forward iterators may be constant, allowing for read-only access to the object the iterator points to, and otherwise allow for both read and write operations, making it mutable. A forward iterator would typically find use in a singly linked list.

- **Bidirectional iterator**—A refinement of the forward iterator in that it can be decremented to move backward as well. A bidirectional iterator would typically find use in a doubly linked list.

- **Random access iterators**—In general, a refinement over the concept of bidirectional iterators that allow addition and subtraction of offsets or allow one iterator to be subtracted from another to find the relative separation or distance between the two objects in a collection. A random iterator would typically find use in an array.

NOTE   At an implementation level, a *refinement* can be thought of as an *inheritance* or a *specialization*.

STL Algorithms

Finding, sorting, reversing, and the like are standard programming requirements that should not require the programmer to reinvent implementation to support. This is precisely why STL supplies these functions in the form of STL algorithms that work well with containers using iterators to help the programmer with some of the most common requirements.

Some of the most used STL algorithms are

- `std::find`—Helps find a value in a collection
- `std::find_if`—Helps find a value in a collection on the basis of a specific user-defined predicate
- `std::reverse`—Reverses a collection
- `std::remove_if`—Helps remove an item from a collection on the basis of a user-defined predicate
- `std::transform`—Helps apply a user-defined transformation function to elements in a container

These algorithms are template functions in the `std` namespace and require that the standard header `<algorithm>` be included.

The Interaction between Containers and Algorithms Using Iterators

Let's examine how iterators seamlessly connect containers and the STL algorithms using an example. The program shown in Listing 15.1 uses the STL sequential container `std::vector`, which is akin to a dynamic array, to store some integers and then find one in the collection using the algorithm `std::find`. Note how iterators form the bridge connecting the two. Don't worry about the complexity of the syntax or functionality. Containers such as `std::vector` and algorithms such as `std::find` are discussed in detail in Lesson 17, "STL Dynamic Array Classes," and Lesson 23, "STL Algorithms," respectively. If you find this part complicated, you can skip the section for the moment.

15

LISTING 15.1   Find an Element and Its Position in a Vector

```
 1: #include <iostream>
 2: #include <vector>
 3: #include <algorithm>
 4: using namespace std;
 5:
 6: int main ()
 7: {
 8:     // A dynamic array of integers
 9:     vector <int> intArray;
10:
11:     // Insert sample integers into the array
12:     intArray.push_back (50);
13:     intArray.push_back (2991);
14:     intArray.push_back (23);
15:     intArray.push_back (9999);
16:
17:     cout << "The contents of the vector are: " << endl;
18:
19:     // Walk the vector and read values using an iterator
20:     vector <int>::iterator arrIterator = intArray.begin ();
21:
22:     while (arrIterator != intArray.end ())
23:     {
24:         // Write the value to the screen
25:         cout << *arrIterator << endl;
26:
27:         // Increment the iterator to access the next element
28:         ++ arrIterator;
29:     }
30:
31:     // Find an element (say 2991) using the 'find' algorithm
32:     vector <int>::iterator elFound = find (intArray.begin ()
33:                            ,intArray.end (), 2991);
```

```
34:
35:    // Check if value was found
36:    if (elFound != intArray.end ())
37:    {
38:        // Determine position of element using std::distance
39:        int elPos = distance (intArray.begin (), elFound);
40:        cout << "Value "<< *elFound;
41:        cout << " found in the vector at position: " << elPos << endl;
42:    }
43:
44:    return 0;
45: }
```

Output ▼

```
The contents of the vector are:
50
2991
23
9999
Value 2991 found in the vector at position: 1
```

Analysis ▼

Listing 15.1 displays the use of iterators in walking through the vector and as interfaces that help connect algorithms such as find to containers like vector that contains the data on which the algorithm is meant to operate. The iterator object arrIterator is declared in Line 20 and is initialized to the beginning of the container; that is, the vector using the return value of the member function begin(). Lines 22 to 29 demonstrate how this iterator is used in a loop to locate and display the elements contained in the vector, in a manner that is quite similar to how one can display the contents of a static array. The usage of the iterator is consistent across all STL containers. They all feature a function begin() that points to the first element, and a function end() that points to the end of the container after the last element. This also explains why the while loop in Line 22 stops at the element before end() and not with end(). Line 32 demonstrates how find is used to locate a value in the vector. The result of the find operation is an iterator as well, and the success of the find is tested by comparing the iterator against the end of the container, as seen in Line 36. If an element is found, it can be displayed by dereferencing that iterator (such as how one would dereference a pointer). The algorithm distance is applied by computing the offset position of the element found.

If you blindly replace all instances of "vector" with "deque" in Listing 15.1, your code would still compile and work perfectly. That's how easy iterators make working with algorithms and containers.

Using Keyword `auto` to Let Compiler Define Type

Listing 15.1 shows a number of iterator declarations. They look similar to this:

```
20:    vector <int>::iterator arrIterator = intArray.begin ();
```

This iterator type definition might look intimidating. If you are using a C++11-compliant compiler, you can simplify this line to the following:

```
20:    auto arrIterator = intArray.begin (); // compiler detects type
```

Note that a variable defined as type `auto` needs initialization (so the compiler can detect type depending on that of the value it is being initialized to).

Choosing the Right Container

Clearly, your application might have requirements that can be satisfied by more than one STL container. There is a selection to be made, and this selection is important because a wrong choice could result in performance issues and scalability bottlenecks.

Therefore, it is important to evaluate the advantages and disadvantages of the containers before selecting one. See Table 15.1 for more details.

TABLE 15.1 Properties of STL's Container Classes

Container	Advantages	Disadvantages
`std::vector` (Sequential Container)	Quick (constant time) insertion at the end.	Resizing can result in performance loss.
	Array-like access.	Search time is proportional to the number of elements in the container.
		Insertion only at the end.
`std::deque` (Sequential Container)	All advantages of the `vector`. Additionally, offers constant-time insertion at the beginning of the container too.	Disadvantages of the `vector` with respect to performance and search are applicable to the `deque`.

Container	Advantages	Disadvantages
		Unlike the `vector`, the `deque` by specification does not need to feature the `reserve()` function that allows the programmer to reserve memory space to be used—a feature that avoids frequent resizing to improve performance.
`std::list` (Sequential Container)	Constant time insertion at the front, middle, or end of the list.	Elements cannot be accessed randomly given an index as in an array.
	Removal of elements from a `list` is a constant-time activity regardless of the position of the element.	Accessing elements can be slower than the `vector` because elements are not stored in adjacent memory locations.
	Insertion or removal of elements does not invalidate iterators that point to other elements in the `list`.	Search time is proportional to the number of elements in the container.
`std::forward_list` (Sequential Container)	Singly linked list class that allows iteration only in one direction.	Allows insertion only at the front of the list via `push_front()`.
`std::set` (Associative Container)	Search is not directly proportional to the number of elements in the container, rather to the logarithm thereof and hence is often significantly faster than sequential containers.	Insertion of elements is slower than in sequential counterparts, as elements are sorted at insertion.
`std::unordered set` (Associative Container)	Search, insertion, and removal in this type of container are nearly independent of the number of elements in the container.	As elements are weakly ordered, one cannot rely on their relative position within the container.
`std::multiset` (Associative Container)	Should be used when a set needs to contain nonunique values too.	Insertions may be slower than in a sequential container as elements (pairs) are sorted on insertion.

Container	Advantages	Disadvantages
`std::unordered_ multiset` (Associative Container)	Should be preferred over an `unordered_set` when you need to contain nonunique values too. Performance is similar to `unordered_set`, namely, constant average time for search, insertion, and removal of elements, independent of size of container.	Elements are weakly ordered, so one cannot rely on their relative position within the container.
`std::map` (Associative Container)	Key-value pairs container that offers search performance proportional to the logarithm of number of elements in the container and hence often significantly faster than sequential containers.	Elements (pairs) are sorted on insertion, hence insertion will be slower than in a sequential container of pairs.
`std::unordered_map.` (Associative Container)	Offers advantage of near constant time search, insertion, and removal of elements independent of the size of the container.	Elements are weakly ordered and hence not suited to cases where order is important.
`std::multimap.` (Associative Container)	To be selected over `std::map` when requirements necessitate the need of a key-value pairs container that holds elements with nonunique keys.	Insertion of elements will be slower than in a sequential equivalent as elements are sorted on insertion.
`std::unordered_ multimap` (Associative Container)	To be selected over `multimap` when you need a key-value pairs container where keys can be nonunique. Allows constant average time insertion, search, and removal of elements, independent of the size of the container.	Is a weakly ordered container, so you cannot use it when you need to rely on the relative order of elements.

STL String Classes

STL supplies a template class that has been specially designed for string operations. `std::basic_string<T>` is used popularly in its two template specializations:

- **std::string**—A char-based specialization of `std::basic_string` used for the manipulation of simple character strings.

- **std::wstring**— A wchar_t-based specialization of `std::basic_string` used for the manipulation of wide character strings typically used to store Unicode characters that support symbols from different languages.

This utility class is extensively discussed in Lesson 16, "The STL String Class," where you see how it makes working with and manipulating strings really simple.

Summary

In this lesson, you learned the concepts on which STL containers, iterators, and algorithms are based. You were introduced to the `basic_string<T>`, which is discussed in detailed in the upcoming lesson. Containers, iterators, and algorithms are one of the most important concepts in STL, and a thorough understanding of these will help you efficiently use STL in your application. Lessons 17 through 25 explain the implementation of these concepts and their application in greater detail.

Q&A

Q I need to use an array. I don't know the number of elements it needs to contain. What STL container should I use?

A A `std::vector` or a `std::deque` is perfectly suited to this requirement. Both manage memory and can dynamically scale themselves to an application's increasing requirements.

Q My application has a requirement that involves frequent searches. What kind of container should I choose?

A An associative container like `std::map` or `std::set` or the unordered variants thereof are most suited to requirements that involve frequent searches.

Q I need to store key-value pairs for quick lookup. However, the use-case can result in multiple keys that are not unique. What container should I choose?

A An associative container of type `std::multimap` is suited to this requirement. A `multimap` can hold nonunique key-value pairs and can offer a quick lookup that is characteristic of associative containers.

Q An application needs to be ported across platforms and compilers. There is a requirement for a container that helps in a quick lookup based on a key. Should I use `std::map` or `std::hash_map`?

A Portability is an important constraint and using standard-compliant containers is necessary. `hash_map` is not part of the C++ standard and therefore may not be supported across all platforms relevant to your application. You may use `std::unordered_map` if you are using C++11-compliant compilers for all the platforms concerned.

Workshop

The Workshop contains quiz questions to help solidify your understanding of the material covered. Try to answer the quiz questions before checking the answers in Appendix E, and be certain you understand the answers before going to the next lesson.

Quiz

1. What would be your choice of a container that has to contain an array of objects with insertion possible at the top and at the bottom?

2. You need to store elements for quick lookup. What container would you choose?

3. You need to store elements in a `std::set` but still have the storage and lookup criteria altered, based on conditions that are not necessarily the value of the elements. Is this possible?

4. What feature in STL is used to connect algorithms to containers?

5. Would you choose to use container `hash_set` in an application that needs to be ported to different platforms and built using different C++ compilers?

LESSON 16
The STL String Class

The standard template library (STL) supplies the programmer with a container class that aids in string operations and manipulations. The `string` class not only dynamically resizes itself to cater to the application's requirement but also supplies useful helper functions or methods that help manipulate the string and work using it. Thus, it helps programmers make use of standard, portable, and tested functionality in their applications and focus time on developing features that are critical to it.

In this lesson, you learn

- Why string manipulation classes are necessary
- How to work with the STL `string` class
- How STL helps you concatenate, append, find, and perform other string operations with ease
- How to use template-based implementation of the STL `string`
- The `operator ""`s supported by STL `string` since C++14

The Need for String Manipulation Classes

In C++, a `string` is an array of characters. As you saw in Lesson 4, "Managing Arrays and Strings," the simplest character array can be defined as following:

```
char staticName [20];
```

`staticName` is the declaration of a character array (also called a string) of a fixed (hence static) length of 20 elements. As you see, this buffer can hold a string of limited length and would soon be overrun if you tried to hold a greater number of characters in it. Resizing this statically allocated array is not possible. To overcome this constraint, C++ supplies dynamic allocation of data. Therefore, a more dynamic representation of a `string array` is

```
char* dynamicName = new char [arrayLen];
```

`dynamicName` is a dynamically allocated character array that can be instantiated to the length as stored in the value `arrayLen`, determinable at runtime, and hence can be allocated to hold a data of variable length. However, should you want to change the length of the array at runtime, you would first have to deallocate the allocated memory and then reallocate to hold the required data.

Things get complicated if these `char*` strings are used as member attributes of a class. In situations where an object of this class is assigned to another, in the absence of a correctly programmed copy constructor and assignment operator, the two objects contain copies of a pointer, essentially pointing to the same `char` buffer. The result is two string pointers in two objects, each holding the same address and hence pointing to the same location in memory. The destruction of the first object results in the pointer in the other object being invalidated, and an impending crash looms on the horizon.

String classes solve these problems for you. The STL string classes `std::string` that models a character string and `std::wstring` that models a wide character string helps you in the following ways:

- Reduces the effort of string creation and manipulation
- Increases the stability of the application being programmed by internally managing memory allocation details
- Features copy constructor and assignment operators that automatically ensure that member strings get correctly copied

- Supplies useful utility functions that help in truncating, finding, and erasing to name a few

- Provides operators that help in comparisons

- Lets you focus efforts on your application's primary requirements rather than on string manipulation details

NOTE _____

> Both `std::string` and `std::wstring` are actually template specializations of the same class, namely `std::basic_string<T>` for types `char` and `wchar_t`, respectively. When you have learned using one, you can use the same methods and operators on the other.

16

You will soon learn some useful helper functions that STL string classes supply using `std::string` as an example.

Working with the STL String Class

The most commonly used string functions are

- Copying

- Concatenating

- Finding characters and substrings

- Truncating

- String reversal and case conversions, which are achieved using algorithms provided by the standard library

To use the STL string class, you must include the header `<string>`.

Instantiating the STL String and Making Copies

The `string` class features many overloaded constructors and therefore can be instantiated and initialized in many different ways. For example, you can simply initialize or assign a constant character string literal to a regular STL `std::string` object:

```
const char* constCStyleString = "Hello String!";
std::string strFromConst (constCStyleString);
```

or

```
std::string strFromConst = constCStyleString;
```

The preceding is similar to

```
std::string str2 ("Hello String!");
```

As is apparent, instantiating a string object and initializing it to a value did not require supplying the length of the string or the memory allocation details—the constructor of the STL string class automatically did this.

Similarly, it is possible to use one `string` object to initialize another:

```
std::string str2Copy (str2);
```

You can also instruct the constructor of `string` to accept only the first n characters of the supplied input string:

```
// Initialize a string to the first 5 characters of another
std::string strPartialCopy (constCStyleString, 5);
```

You can also initialize a string to contain a specific number of instances of a particular character:

```
// Initialize a string object to contain 10 'a's
std::string strRepeatChars (10, 'a');
```

Listing 16.1 analyzes some popularly used `std::string` instantiation and string copy techniques.

LISTING 16.1   STL String Instantiation and Copy Techniques

```
0: #include <string>
1: #include <iostream>
2:
3: int main ()
4: {
5:    using namespace std;
6:    const char* constCStyleString = "Hello String!";
7:    cout << "Constant string is: " << constCStyleString << endl;
8:
9:    std::string strFromConst (constCStyleString);  // constructor
```

```
10:     cout << "strFromConst is: " << strFromConst << endl;
11:
12:     std::string str2 ("Hello String!");
13:     std::string str2Copy (str2);
14:     cout << "str2Copy is: " << str2Copy << endl;
15:
16:     // Initialize a string to the first 5 characters of another
17:     std::string strPartialCopy (constCStyleString, 5);
18:     cout << "strPartialCopy is: " << strPartialCopy << endl;
19:
20:     // Initialize a string object to contain 10 'a's
21:     std::string strRepeatChars (10, 'a');
22:     cout << "strRepeatChars is: " << strRepeatChars << endl;
23:
24:     return 0;
25: }
```

Output ▼

```
Constant string is: Hello String!
strFromConst is: Hello String!
str2Copy is: Hello String!
strPartialCopy is: Hello
strRepeatChars is: aaaaaaaaaa
```

Analysis ▼

The preceding code sample displays how you can instantiate an STL string object and initialize it to another string, creating a partial copy or initializing your STL string object to a set of recurring characters. constCStyleString is a C-style character string that contains a sample value, initialized in Line 6. Line 9 displays how easy std::string makes it to create a copy using the constructor. Line 12 copies another constant string into a std::string object str2, and Line 13 demonstrates how std::string has another overloaded constructor that allows you to copy a std::string object, to get str2Copy. Line 17 demonstrates how partial copies can be achieved and Line 21 how a std::string can be instantiated and initialized to contain repeating occurrences of the same character. This code sample was just a small demonstration of how std::string and its numerous copy constructors make it easy for a programmer to create strings, copy them, and display them.

16

NOTE

> If you were to use character strings to copy from another of the same kind, the equivalent of Line 9 in Listing 16.1 would be this:
>
> ```
> const char* constCStyleString = "Hello World!";
>
> // To create a copy, first allocate memory for one...
> char* copy = new char [strlen (constCStyleString) + 1];
> strcpy (copy, constCStyleString);   // The copy step
>
> // deallocate memory after using copy
> delete [] copy;
> ```
>
> As you can see, the result is many more lines of code and higher probability of introducing errors, and you need to worry about memory management and deallocations. STL `string` does all this for you, and more!

Accessing Character Contents of a `std::string`

The character contents of an STL `string` can be accessed via iterators or via an array-like syntax where the offset is supplied, using the subscript operator [].
A C-style representation of the `string` can be obtained via member function `c_str ()`.
See Listing 16.2.

LISTING 16.2 Two Ways of Accessing Character Clements of an STL `string::Operator[]` and Iterators

```
0: #include <string>
1: #include <iostream>
2:
3: int main ()
4: {
5:    using namespace std;
6:
7:    string stlString ("Hello String"); // sample
8:
9:     // Access the contents of the string using array syntax
10:    cout << "Display elements in string using array-syntax: " << endl;
11:    for (size_t charCounter = 0;
12:        charCounter < stlString.length();
13:        ++ charCounter)
14:    {
15:        cout << "Character [" << charCounter << "] is: ";
16:        cout << stlString [charCounter] << endl;
```

```
17:      }
18:      cout << endl;
19:
20:      // Access the contents of a string using iterators
21:      cout << "Display elements in string using iterators: " << endl;
22:      int charOffset = 0;
23:      string::const_iterator charLocator;
24:      for (auto charLocator = stlString.cbegin();
25:          charLocator != stlString.cend ();
26:          ++ charLocator)
27:      {
28:          cout << "Character [" << charOffset ++ << "] is: ";
29:          cout << *charLocator << endl;
30:      }
31:      cout << endl;
32:
33:      // Access contents as a const char*
34:      cout << "The char* representation of the string is: ";
35:      cout << stlString.c_str () << endl;
36:
37:      return 0;
38: }
```

16

Output ▼

```
Display elements in string using array-syntax:
Character [0] is: H
Character [1] is: e
Character [2] is: l
Character [3] is: l
Character [4] is: o
Character [5] is:
Character [6] is: S
Character [7] is: t
Character [8] is: r
Character [9] is: i
Character [10] is: n
Character [11] is: g

Display elements in string using iterators:
Character [0] is: H
Character [1] is: e
Character [2] is: l
Character [3] is: l
Character [4] is: o
Character [5] is:
Character [6] is: S
Character [7] is: t
Character [8] is: r
Character [9] is: i
```

```
Character [10] is: n
Character [11] is: g

The char* representation of the string is: Hello String
```

Analysis ▼

The code displays the multiple ways of accessing the contents of a string. Iterators are important in the sense that many of the string's member function return their results in the form of iterators. Lines 11–17 display the characters in the string using array-like semantics via the subscript operator [], implemented by the std::string class. Note that this operator needs you to supply the offset as seen in Line 16. Therefore, it is important that you do not cross the bounds of the string; that is, you do not read a character at an offset beyond the length of the string. Lines 24–30 also print the content of the string character by character, but using iterators.

TIP

You may avoid the tedious iterator declaration seen in Line 24 by using keyword auto, thereby telling the compiler to determine the type of charLocator using the return value of std::string::cbegin(), as seen here:

```
24: // delete line: string::const_iterator charLocator;

25: for (auto charLocator = stlString.cbegin();

26:      charLocator != stlString.cend();

27:      ++ charLocator )

28: {

29:   cout << "Character ["<<charOffset++ <<"] is: ";

30:   cout << *charLocator << endl;

31: }
```

Concatenating One String to Another

String concatenation can be achieved by using either the += operator or the append() member function:

```
string sampleStr1 ("Hello");
string sampleStr2 (" String! ");
sampleStr1 += sampleStr2;   // use std::string::operator+=
// alternatively use std::string::append()
sampleStr1.append (sampleStr2);  // (overloaded for char* too)
```

Listing 16.3 demonstrates the usage of these two variants.

LISTING 16.3   Concatenate Strings Using Addition Assignment Operator (`+=`) or `append()`

```
 0: #include <string>
 1: #include <iostream>
 2:
 3: int main ()
 4: {
 5:     using namespace std;
 6:
 7:     string sampleStr1 ("Hello");
 8:     string sampleStr2 (" String!");
 9:
10:     // Concatenate
11:     sampleStr1 += sampleStr2;
12:     cout << sampleStr1 << endl << endl;
13:
14:     string sampleStr3 (" Fun is not needing to use pointers!");
15:     sampleStr1.append (sampleStr3);
16:     cout << sampleStr1 << endl << endl;
17:
18:     const char* constCStyleString = " You however still can!";
19:     sampleStr1.append (constCStyleString);
20:     cout << sampleStr1 << endl;
21:
22:     return 0;
23: }
```

Output ▼

```
Hello String!

Hello String! Fun is not needing to use pointers!

Hello String! Fun is not needing to use pointers! You however still can!
```

Analysis ▼

Lines 11, 15, and 19 display different methods of concatenating to an STL `string`. Note the use of the `+=` operator and the capability of the `append` function, which has many overloads, to accept another `string` object (as shown in Line 11) and to accept a C-style character string.

16

Finding a Character or Substring in a String

The STL `string` supplies a `find()` member function with a few overloaded versions that help find a character or a substring in a given `string` object.

```
// Find substring "day" in sampleStr, starting at position 0
size_t charPos = sampleStr.find ("day", 0);

// Check if the substring was found, compare against string::npos
if (charPos != string::npos)
    cout << "First instance of \"day\" was found at position " << charPos;
else
    cout << "Substring not found." << endl;
```

Listing 16.4 demonstrates the utility of `std::string::find()`.

LISTING 16.4   Using `string::find()` to Locate a Substring or `char`

```
0: #include <string>
1: #include <iostream>
2:
3: int main ()
4: {
5:    using namespace std;
6:
7:    string sampleStr ("Good day String! Today is beautiful!");
8:    cout << "Sample string is:" << endl << sampleStr << endl << endl;
9:
10:    // Find substring "day" - find() returns position
11:    size_t charPos = sampleStr.find ("day", 0);
12:
13:    // Check if the substring was found...
14:    if (charPos != string::npos)
15:       cout << "First instance \"day\" at pos. " << charPos << endl;
16:    else
17:       cout << "Substring not found." << endl;
18:
19:    cout << "Locating all instances of substring \"day\"" << endl;
20:    size_t subStrPos = sampleStr.find ("day", 0);
21:
22:    while (subStrPos != string::npos)
23:    {
24:       cout << "\"day\" found at position " << subStrPos << endl;
25:
26:       // Make find() search forward from the next character onwards
27:       size_t searchOffset = subStrPos + 1;
28:
29:       subStrPos = sampleStr.find ("day", searchOffset);
30:    }
```

```
31:
32:    return 0;
33: }
```

Output ▼

```
Sample string is:
Good day String! Today is beautiful!

First instance "day" at pos. 5
Locating all instances of substring "day"
"day" found at position 5
"day" found at position 19
```

16

Analysis ▼

Lines 11–17 display the simplest usage of the `find()` function where it ascertains whether a particular substring is found in a `string`. This is done by comparing the result of the `find()` operation against `std::string::npos` (that is actually –1) and indicates that the element searched for has not been found. When the `find()` function does not return `npos`, it returns the offset that indicates the position of the substring or character in the `string`. The code thereafter indicates how `find()` can be used in a `while` loop to locate all instances of a substring in an STL `string`. The overloaded version of the `find()` function used here accepts two parameters: the substring or character to search for and the search offset that indicates the point from which `find()` should search. We manipulate the search using this offset to get `find()` to search for the next occurrence of the substring as seen in Line 29.

NOTE

> The STL `string` also features find functions such as `find_first_of()`, `find_first_not_of()`, `find_last_of()`, and `find_last_not_of()` that assist the programmer in working with strings.

Truncating an STL `string`

The STL `string` features a function called `erase()` that can erase

- A number of characters when given an offset position and count

```
string sampleStr ("Hello String! Wake up to a beautiful day!");
sampleStr.erase (13, 28);  // Hello String!
```

- A character when supplied with an iterator pointing to it

  ```
  sampleStr.erase (iCharS); // iterator points to a specific character
  ```

- A number of characters given a range supplied by two iterators that bind the same

  ```
  sampleStr.erase (sampleStr.begin (), sampleStr.end ()); // erase from begin
  to end
  ```

The sample that follows in Listing 16.5 demonstrates different applications of the overloaded versions of `string::erase()` function.

LISTING 16.5 Using `string::erase()` to Truncate a String Starting an Offset Position or Given an Iterator

```cpp
0: #include <string>
1: #include <algorithm>
2: #include <iostream>
3:
4: int main ()
5: {
6:     using namespace std;
7:
8:     string sampleStr ("Hello String! Wake up to a beautiful day!");
9:     cout << "The original sample string is: " << endl;
10:    cout << sampleStr << endl << endl;
11:
12:    // Delete characters given position and count
13:    cout << "Truncating the second sentence: " << endl;
14:    sampleStr.erase (13, 28);
15:    cout << sampleStr << endl << endl;
16:
17:    // Find character 'S' using find() algorithm
18:    string::iterator iCharS = find (sampleStr.begin (),
19:                                    sampleStr.end (), 'S');
20:
21:    // If character found, 'erase' to deletes a character
22:    cout << "Erasing character 'S' from the sample string:" << endl;
23:    if (iCharS != sampleStr.end ())
24:        sampleStr.erase (iCharS);
25:
26:    cout << sampleStr << endl << endl;
27:
28:    // Erase a range of characters using an overloaded version of erase()
29:    cout << "Erasing a range between begin() and end(): " << endl;
30:    sampleStr.erase (sampleStr.begin (), sampleStr.end ());
31:
32:    // Verify the length after the erase() operation above
33:    if (sampleStr.length () == 0)
34:        cout << "The string is empty" << endl;
35:
36:    return 0;
37: }
```

Output ▼

```
The original sample string is:
Hello String! Wake up to a beautiful day!

Truncating the second sentence:
Hello String!

Erasing character 'S' from the sample string:
Hello tring!

Erasing a range between begin() and end():
The string is empty
```

Analysis ▼

The listing indicates the three versions of the erase() function. One version erases a set of characters when supplied a staring offset and count, as shown in Line 14. Another version erases a specific character given an iterator that points to it, as shown in Line 24. The final version erases a range of characters given a couple of iterators that supply the bounds of this range, as shown in Line 30. As the bounds of this range are supplied by begin() and end() member functions of the string that effectively include all the contents of the string, calling an erase() on this range clears the string object of its contents. Note that the string class also supplies a clear() function that effectively clears the internal buffer and resets the string object.

TIP

C++11 helps simplify wordy iterator declarations as shown in Listing 16.5:

```
string::iterator iCharS = find (sampleStr.begin(),
                                sampleStr.end (), 'S');
```

To reduce this, use keyword auto as introduced in Lesson 3, "Using Variables, Declaring Constants":

```
auto iCharS = find (sampleStr.begin(),
                    sampleStr.end (), 'S');
```

The compiler automatically deducts type of variable iCharS given return value type information from std::find().

String Reversal

Sometimes it is important to reverse the contents of a string. Say you want to determine whether the string input by the user is a palindrome. One way to do it would be to reverse a copy of the same and then compare the two. STL strings can be reversed easily using the generic algorithm `std::reverse()`:

```
string sampleStr ("Hello String! We will reverse you!");
reverse (sampleStr.begin (), sampleStr.end ());
```

Listing 16.6 demonstrates the application of algorithm `std::reverse()` to a `std::string`.

LISTING 16.6   Reversing an STL String Using `std::reverse`

```
 0: #include <string>
 1: #include <iostream>
 2: #include <algorithm>
 3:
 4: int main ()
 5: {
 6:    using namespace std;
 7:
 8:    string sampleStr ("Hello String! We will reverse you!");
 9:    cout << "The original sample string is: " << endl;
10:    cout << sampleStr << endl << endl;
11:
12:    reverse (sampleStr.begin (), sampleStr.end ());
13:
14:    cout << "After applying the std::reverse algorithm: " << endl;
15:    cout << sampleStr << endl;
16:
17:    return 0;
18: }
```

Output ▼

```
The original sample string is:
Hello String! We will reverse you!

After applying the std::reverse algorithm:
!uoy esrever lliw eW !gnirtS olleH
```

Analysis ▼

The `std::reverse()` algorithm used in Line 12 works on the bounds of the container that are supplied to it using the two input parameters. In this case, these bounds are the starting and the ending bounds of the `string` object, reversing the contents of the entire string. It would also be possible to reverse a string in parts by supplying the appropriate bounds as input. Note that the bounds should never exceed `end()`.

String Case Conversion

String case conversion can be effected using the algorithm `std::transform()`, which applies a user-specified function to every element of a collection. In this case, the collection is the `string` object itself. The sample in Listing 16.7 shows how to switch the case of characters in a `string`.

16

LISTING 16.7 Converting an STL String Using `std::transform()` to Uppercase

```
 0: #include <string>
 1: #include <iostream>
 2: #include <algorithm>
 3:
 4: int main ()
 5: {
 6:    using namespace std;
 7:
 8:    cout << "Please enter a string for case-convertion:" << endl;
 9:    cout << "> ";
10:
11:    string inStr;
12:    getline (cin, inStr);
13:    cout << endl;
14:
15:    transform(inStr.begin(), inStr.end(), inStr.begin(), ::toupper);
16:    cout << "The string converted to upper case is: " << endl;
17:    cout << inStr << endl << endl;
18:
19:    transform(inStr.begin(), inStr.end(), inStr.begin(), ::tolower);
20:    cout << "The string converted to lower case is: " << endl;
21:    cout << inStr << endl << endl;
22:
23:    return 0;
24: }
```

Output ▼

```
Please enter a string for case-convertion:
> ConverT thIS StrINg!

The string converted to upper case is:
CONVERT THIS STRING!

The string converted to lower case is:
convert this string!
```

Analysis ▼

Lines 15 and 19 demonstrate how efficiently `std::transform()` can be used to change the case of the contents of an STL string.

Template-Based Implementation of an STL String

The `std::string` class, as you have learned, is actually a specialization of the STL template class `std::basic_string <T>`. The template declaration of container class `basic_string` is as follows:

```
template<class _Elem,
    class _Traits,
    class _Ax>
    class basic_string
```

In this template definition, the parameter of utmost importance is the first one: `_Elem`. This is the type collected by the `basic_string` object. The `std::string` is therefore the template specialization of `basic_string` for `_Elem=char`, whereas the wstring is the template specialization of `basic_string` for `_Elem=wchar_t`.

In other words, the STL `string` class is defined as

```
typedef basic_string<char, char_traits<char>, allocator<char> >
    string;
```

and the STL `wstring` class is defined as

```
typedef basic_string<wchar_t, char_traits<wchar_t>, allocator<wchar_t> >
    string;
```

So, all string features and functions studied so far are actually those supplied by `basic_string`, and are therefore also applicable to the STL `wstring` class.

> **TIP**
>
> You would use the `std::wstring` when programming an application that needs to better support non-Latin characters such as those in Japanese or Chinese.

C++14 `operator ""s` **in** `std::string`

16

C++14 compliant versions of the standard library support `operator ""s` that convert the string contained within the quotes, in entirety, to a `std::basic_string<t>`. This makes certain string operations intuitive and simple as Listing 16.8 demonstrates.

LISTING 16.8 Using `operator ""s` Introduced by C++14

```
0: #include<string>
1: #include<iostream>
2: using namespace std;
3:
4: int main()
5: {
6:     string str1("Traditional string \0 initialization");
7:     cout << "Str1: " << str1 << " Length: " << str1.length() <<  endl;
8:
9:     string str2("C++14 \0 initialization using literals"s);
10:     cout << "Str2: " << str2 << " Length: " << str2.length() <<  endl;
11:
12:     return 0;
13: }
```

Output ▼

```
Str1: Traditional string  Length: 19
Str2: C++14    initialization using literals Length: 37
```

Analysis ▼

Line 6 initializes an instance of `std::string` from a regular character string literal. Note the null character placed in the middle of the string that results in the word "initialization" to be completely missed by `str1`. Line 9 uses the `operator ""s` introduced by C++14 to demonstrate how the instance `str2` can now be used to contain (and therefore also manipulate) character buffers containing null characters too, for instance.

CAUTION

> C++14 introduces a literal `operator ""s` in `std::chrono`, as seen here:
>
> `std::chrono::seconds timeInSec(100s); // 100 seconds`
> `std::string timeinText = "100"s; // string "100"`
>
> The former indicates time in seconds and is an integer literal, while the latter gives a string.

TIP

> C++17 is expected to introduce `std::string_view`, which promises to improve performance by avoiding unnecessary memory allocation. Visit Lesson 29, "Going Forward," to learn of this and other features expected in C++17.

Summary

In this lesson, you learned that the STL `string` class is a container supplied by the standard template library that helps the programmer with many string manipulation requirements. The advantage of using this class is apparent in that the need for the programmer to implement memory management, string comparison, and string manipulation functions is taken care of by a container class supplied by the STL framework.

Q&A

Q I need to reverse a string using `std::reverse()`. What header has to be included for me to be able to use this function?

A `<algorithm>` is the header that needs to be included for `std::reverse()` to be available.

Q What role does `std::transform()` play in converting a string to lowercase using the `tolower ()` function?

A `std::transform()` invokes `tolower ()` for the characters in the `string` object that are within the bounds supplied to the transform function.

Q Why do `std::wstring` and `std::string` feature exactly the same behavior and member functions?

A They do so because they are both template specializations of the template class `std::basic_string`.

Q Does the comparison operator `<` of the STL `string` class produce results that are case sensitive or not case sensitive?

A The results are based on a case-sensitive comparison.

Workshop

The Workshop contains quiz questions to help solidify your understanding of the material covered and exercises to provide you with experience in using what you've learned. Try to answer the quiz and exercise questions before checking the answers in Appendix E, and be certain you understand the answers before going to the next lesson.

Quiz

1. What STL template class does the `std::string` specialize?

2. If you were to perform a case-insensitive comparison of two strings, how would you do it?

3. Are the STL string and a C-style string similar?

Exercises

1. Write a program to verify whether the word input by the user is a palindrome. For example: ATOYOTA is a palindrome, as the word does not change when reversed.

2. Write a program that tells the user the number of vowels in a sentence.

3. Convert every alternate character of a string into uppercase.

4. Your program should have four string objects that are initialized to "I," "Love," "STL," and "String." Append them with a space in between and display the sentence.

5. Write a program that displays the position of every occurrence of character `'a'` in the string `"Good day String! Today is beautiful!"`.

LESSON 17
STL Dynamic Array Classes

Unlike static arrays, dynamic arrays supply the programmer with the flexibility of storing data without needing to know the exact volume thereof at the time of programming the application. Naturally, this is a frequently needed requirement, and the Standard Template Library (STL) supplies a ready-to-use solution in the form of the `std::vector` class.

In this lesson, you learn

- The characteristics of `std::vector`
- Typical `vector` operations
- The concept of a vector's size and capacity
- The STL `deque` class

The Characteristics of `std::vector`

`vector` is a template class that supplies generic functionality of a dynamic array and features the following characteristics:

- Addition of elements to the end of the array in constant time; that is, the time needed to insert at the end is not dependent on the size of the array. Ditto for removal of an element at the end.

- The time required for the insertion or removal of elements at the middle is directly proportional to the number of elements behind the element being removed.

- The number of elements held is dynamic, and the `vector` class manages the memory usage.

A *vector* is a dynamic array that can be visualized as seen in Figure 17.1.

FIGURE 17.1
The internals of a vector.

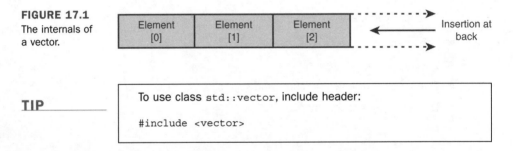

| Element [0] | Element [1] | Element [2] | Insertion at back |

TIP

To use class `std::vector`, include header:

```
#include <vector>
```

Typical Vector Operations

The behavioral specifications and public members of the `std::vector` class are defined by the C++ standard. Consequently, operations on the `vector` that you will learn in this lesson are supported by a variety of C++ programming platforms that are standard compliant.

Instantiating a Vector

A `vector` is a template class that needs to be instantiated in accordance with template instantiation techniques that are covered in Lesson 14, "An introduction to Macros and Templates." The template instantiation of `vector` needs to specify the type of object that you want to collect in this dynamic array.

```
std::vector<int> dynIntArray;    // vector containing integers
std::vector<float> dynFloatArray;    // vector containing floats
std::vector<Tuna> dynTunaArray;    // vector containing Tunas
```

To declare an iterator that points to an element in the list, you would use

```
std::vector<int>::const_iterator elementInVec;
```

If you need an iterator that can be used to modify values or invoke non-`const` functions, you use `iterator` instead of `const_iterator`.

Given that `std::vector` has a few overloaded constructors, you also have an option of instantiating a vector telling the number of elements it should start with and their initial values, or you can use a part of whole of one vector in instantiating another.

Listing 17.1 demonstrates a few vector instantiations

LISTING 17.1   Different Forms of Instantiating `std::vector`: Specify Size, Initial Value, and Copying Values from Another

```
0: #include <vector>
1:
2: int main ()
3: {
4:    // vector of integers
5:    std::vector<int> integers;
6:
7:    // vector initialized using C++11 list initialization
8:    std::vector<int> initVector{ 202, 2017, -1 };
9:
10:    // Instantiate a vector with 10 elements (it can still grow)
11:    std::vector<int> tenElements (10);
12:
13:    // Instantiate a vector with 10 elements, each initialized to 90
14:    std::vector<int> tenElemInit (10, 90);
15:
16:    // Initialize vector to the contents of another
17:    std::vector<int> copyVector (tenElemInit);
18:
19:    // Vector initialized to 5 elements from another using iterators
20:    std::vector<int> partialCopy (tenElements.cbegin(),
21:                     tenElements.cbegin() + 5);
22:
23:    return 0;
24: }
```

17

Analysis ▼

The preceding code features a template specialization of the `vector` class for type `integer`; in other words, it instantiates a `vector` of integers. This `vector`, named `integers`, uses the default constructor in Line 5 that is useful when you do not know the minimal size requirements of the container—that is, when you do not know how many integers you want to hold in it. The second form of instantiation seen in Line 8 uses the concept of list initialization introduced by C++11 to initialize initVector with three elements containing values 202, 2017, and –1, respectively. The vector instantiation as seen in Lines 11 and 14 are ones where the programmer knows that he needs a vector that contains at least 10 elements. Note that this does not limit the ultimate size of the container, rather just sets the initializing size. Finally, Lines 17 and 20 demonstrate how a vector can be used to instantiate the contents of another—in other words, to create one vector object that is the copy of another, or a part thereof. This is also a construct that works for all STL containers. The last form is the one that uses iterators. partialCopy contains the first five elements from vecWithTenElements.

NOTE

The fourth construct can work only with objects of like types. So, you could instantiate a vecArrayCopy—a vector of integer objects using another vector of integer objects. If one of them were to be a vector of, say, type float, the code would not compile.

Inserting Elements at the End Using push_back()

Having instantiated a vector of integers, the obvious next task is to insert elements (integers) into it. Insertion in a vector happens at the end of the array, and elements are "pushed" into its back using the member function push_back():

```
vector <int> integers;   // declare a vector of type int

// Insert sample integers into the vector:
integers.push_back (50);
integers.push_back (1);
```

Listing 17.2 demonstrates the use of push_back() in the dynamic addition of elements to a std::vector.

LISTING 17.2   Inserting Elements in a Vector Using push_back()

```
0: #include <iostream>
1: #include <vector>
2: using namespace std;
3:
4: int main ()
5: {
6:    vector <int> integers;
7:
```

```
 8:     // Insert sample integers into the vector:
 9:     integers.push_back (50);
10:     integers.push_back (1);
11:     integers.push_back (987);
12:     integers.push_back (1001);
13:
14:     cout << "The vector contains ";
15:     cout << integers.size () << " Elements" << endl;
16:
17:     return 0;
18: }
```

Output ▼

```
The vector contains 4 Elements
```

Analysis ▼

17

push_back(), as seen in Lines 9–12 is the vector class's public member function that inserts objects at the end of the dynamic array. Note the usage of function size(), which returns the number of elements held in the vector.

List Initialization

C++11 features initializer lists via class std::initialize_list<> that, when supported, enables you to instantiate and initialize elements in a container like you would in a static array. std::vector, like most containers, supports List Initialization allowing you to instantiate a vector with elements in one line:

```
vector<int> integers = {50, 1, 987, 1001};
// alternatively:
vector<int> vecMoreIntegers {50, 1, 987, 1001};
```

This syntax reduces three lines in Listing 17.2.

Inserting Elements at a Given Position Using insert()

You use push_back() to insert elements at the end of a vector. What if you want to insert in the middle? Many STL containers, including std::vector, feature an insert() function with many overloads.

In one, you can specify the position at which an element can be inserted into the sequence:

```
// insert an element at the beginning
integers.insert (integers.begin (), 25);
```

In another, you can specify the position as well as the number of elements with a value that need to be inserted:

```
// Insert 2 elements of value 45 at the end
integers.insert (integers.end (), 2, 45);
```

You can also insert the contents of one vector into another at a chosen position:

```
// Another vector containing 2 elements of value 30
vector <int> another (2, 30);

// Insert two elements from another container in position [1]
integers.insert (integers.begin () + 1,
                  another.begin (), another.end ());
```

You use an iterator, often returned by `begin()` or `end()`, to tell the `insert()` function the position where you want the new elements to be placed.

TIP

> Note that this iterator can also be the return value of an STL algorithm, for example the `std::find()` function, which can be used to find an element and then insert another at that position (insertion will shift the element found). Algorithms like `find()` and more are discussed in detail in Lesson 23, "STL Algorithms."

These forms of `vector::insert()` are demonstrated in Listing 17.3.

LISTING 17.3 Using the `vector::insert` Function to Insert Elements at a Set Position

```
0: #include <vector>
1: #include <iostream>
2: using namespace std;
3:
4: void DisplayVector(const vector<int>& inVec)
5: {
6:    for (auto element = inVec.cbegin();
7:          element != inVec.cend();
```

```
 8:            ++ element )
 9:        cout << *element << ' ';
10:
11:    cout << endl;
12: }
13:
14: int main ()
15: {
16: // Instantiate a vector with 4 elements, each initialized to 90
17:    vector <int> integers (4, 90);
18:
19:    cout << "The initial contents of the vector: ";
20:    DisplayVector(integers);
21:
22:    // Insert 25 at the beginning
23:    integers.insert (integers.begin (), 25);
24:
25:    // Insert 2 numbers of value 45 at the end
26:    integers.insert (integers.end (), 2, 45);
27:
28:    cout << "Vector after inserting elements at beginning and end: ";
29:    DisplayVector(integers);
30:
31:    // Another vector containing 2 elements of value 30
32:    vector <int> another (2, 30);
33:
34:    // Insert two elements from another container in position [1]
35:    integers.insert (integers.begin () + 1,
36:        another.begin (), another.end ());
37:
38:    cout << "Vector after inserting contents from another vector: ";
39:    cout << "in the middle:" << endl;
40:    DisplayVector(integers);
41:
42:    return 0;
43: }
```

17

Output ▼

```
The initial contents of the vector: 90 90 90 90
Vector after inserting elements at beginning and end: 25 90 90 90 90 45 45
Vector after inserting contents from another vector: in the middle:
25 30 30 90 90 90 90 45 45
```

Analysis ▼

This code demonstrates the power of the insert() function by enabling you to put values in the middle of the container. vector in Line 17 contains four elements, all initialized to 90. Taking this vector as a starting point, we use various overloaded forms of the `vector::insert()` member function. In Line 23 you add one element at the beginning. Line 26 adds two elements of value 45 at the end. Line 35 demonstrates how elements can be inserted from one vector into the middle (in this example, the second position at offset 1) of another.

Although `vector::insert()` is a versatile function, `push_back()` should be your preferred way of adding elements to a vector. This is because `insert()` is an inefficient way to add elements to the `vector` (when adding in a position that is not the end of the sequence) because adding elements in the beginning or the middle makes the `vector` class shift all subsequent elements backward (after making space for the last ones at the end). Thus, depending on the type of the objects contained in the sequence, the cost of this shift operation can be significant in terms of the copy constructor or copy assignment operator invoked. In our little sample, the `vector` contains objects of type `int` that are relatively inexpensive to move around. This might not be the case in many other uses of the `vector` class.

| TIP | If your container needs to have very frequent insertions in the middle, you should ideally choose the `std::list`, explained in Lesson 18, "STL `list` and `forward_list`." |

Accessing Elements in a Vector Using Array Semantics

Elements in a `vector` can be accessed using the following methods: via array semantics using the subscript operator (`[]`), using the member function `at()`, or using iterators.

Listing 17.1 showed how an instance of `vector` can be created that is initialized for 10 elements:

```
std::vector <int> tenElements (10);
```

You can access and set individual elements using an array-like syntax:

```
tenElements[3] = 2011; // set 4th element
```

Listing 17.4 demonstrates how elements in a vector can be accessed using the subscript operator (`[]`).

LISTING 17.4 Accessing Elements in a `vector` Using Array Semantics

```
0: #include <iostream>
1: #include <vector>
2:
3: int main ()
4: {
5:     using namespace std;
6:     vector <int> integers{ 50, 1, 987, 1001 };
7:
8:     for (size_t index = 0; index < integers.size (); ++index)
9:     {
10:         cout << "Element[" << index << "] = " ;
11:         cout << integers[index] << endl;
12:     }
13:
14:     integers[2] = 2011; // change value of 3rd element
15:     cout << "After replacement: " << endl;
16:     cout << "Element[2] = " << integers[2] << endl;
17:
18:     return 0;
19: }
```

17

Output ▼

```
Element[0] = 50
Element[1] = 1
Element[2] = 987
Element[3] = 1001
After replacement:
Element[2] = 2011
```

Analysis ▼

At Lines 11, 14, and 16 the `vector` has been used to access and assign elements the same way you might use a static array using `vector`'s subscript operator (`[]`). This subscript operator accepts an element-index that is zero-based just as in a static array. Note how the `for` loop has been programmed in Line 15 to ensure that the index doesn't cross the bounds of the vector by comparing it against `vector::size()`.

CAUTION

> Accessing elements in a `vector` using `[]` is fraught with the same dangers as accessing elements in an array; that is, you should not cross the bounds of the container. If you use the subscript operator (`[]`) to access elements in a `vector` at a position that is beyond its bounds, the result of the operation will be undefined (anything could happen, possibly an access violation).
>
> A safer alternative is to use the `at()` member function:
>
> ```
> // gets element at position 2
> cout < < integers.at (2);
> // the vector::at() version of the code above in
> Listing   17.4, line 11:
> cout < < integers.at(index);
> ```
>
> `at()` performs a runtime check against the `size()` of the container and throws an exception if you cross the boundaries (which you shouldn't anyway).
>
> Subscript operator (`[]`) is safe when used in a manner that ensures bound integrity, as in the earlier example.

Accessing Elements in a Vector Using Pointer Semantics

You can also access elements in a `vector` using pointer-like semantics by the use of iterators, as shown in Listing 17.5.

LISTING 17.5   Accessing Elements in a Vector Using Pointer Semantics (Iterators)

```
0: #include <iostream>
1: #include <vector>
2:
3: int main ()
4: {
5:    using namespace std;
6:    vector <int> integers{ 50, 1, 987, 1001 };
7:
8:    vector <int>::const_iterator element = integers.cbegin ();
9:    // auto element = integers.cbegin (); // auto type deduction
10:
11:    while (element != integers.end ())
12:    {
13:       size_t index = distance (integers.cbegin (), element);
14:
```

```
15:         cout << "Element at position ";
16:         cout << index << " is: " << *element << endl;
17:
18:         // move to the next element
19:         ++ element;
20:     }
21:
22:     return 0;
23: }
```

Output ▼

```
Element at position 0 is: 50
Element at position 1 is: 1
Element at position 2 is: 987
Element at position 3 is: 1001
```

Analysis ▼

The iterator in this example behaves more or less like a pointer, and the nature of its usage in the preceding application is like pointer arithmetic, as seen in Line 16 where the value stored in the vector is accessed using the dereference operator (*) and Line 19 where the iterator, when incremented using operator (++), points to the next element. Notice how std::distance() is used in Line 21 to evaluate the zero-based offset position of the element in the vector (that is, position relative to the beginning), given cbegin() and the iterator pointing to the element. Line 9 presents a simpler alternative to the iterator declaration seen in Line 8 using automatic type deduction capabilities of the compiler, introduced in Lesson 3, "Using Variables, Declaring Constants."

Removing Elements from a Vector

Just the same way as the vector features insertion at the end via the push_back() function, it also features the removal of an element at the end via the pop_back() function. Removal of an element from the vector using pop_back() takes constant time—that is, the time required is independent of the number of elements stored in the vector. The code that follows in Listing 17.6 demonstrates the use of function pop_back() to delete elements at the end of the vector.

LISTING 17.6 Using pop_back() to Delete the Last Element

```
0: #include <iostream>
1: #include <vector>
2: using namespace std;
3:
```

```
 4: template <typename T>
 5: void DisplayVector(const vector<T>& inVec)
 6: {
 7:    for (auto element = inVec.cbegin(); // auto and cbegin(): C++11
 8:          element != inVec.cend();   // cend() is new in C++11
 9:          ++ element )
10:       cout << *element << ' ';
11:
12:    cout << endl;
13: }
14:
15: int main ()
16: {
17:    vector <int> integers;
18:
19:    // Insert sample integers into the vector:
20:    integers.push_back (50);
21:    integers.push_back (1);
22:    integers.push_back (987);
23:    integers.push_back (1001);
24:
25:    cout << "Vector contains " << integers.size () << " elements: ";
26:    DisplayVector(integers);
27:
28:    // Erase one element at the end
29:    integers.pop_back ();
30:
31:    cout << "After a call to pop_back()" << endl;
32:    cout << "Vector contains " << integers.size () << " elements: ";
33:    DisplayVector(integers);
34:
35:    return 0;
36: }
```

Output ▼

```
Vector contains 4 elements: 50 1 987 1001
After a call to pop_back()
Vector contains 3 elements: 50 1 987
```

Analysis ▼

The output indicates that the pop_back() function used at Line 29 has reduced the elements in the vector by erasing the last element inserted into it. Line 32 calls size() again to demonstrate that the number of elements in the vector has reduced by one, as indicated in the output.

NOTE

Function `DisplayVector()` in Lines 4–13 has taken a template form in Listing 17.6 as compared to Listing 17.3 where it accepted only a `vector` for integers. This helps us reuse this template function for a vector of type `float` (instead of `int`):

```
vector <float> vecFloats;
DisplayVector(vecFloats); // works, as a generic
function
```

This generic form of `DisplayVector()` would also support a `vector` of any class that features an operator that returns a value `cout` would understand.

Understanding the Concepts of Size and Capacity

17

The *size* of a `vector` is the number of elements stored in a `vector`. The *capacity* of a `vector` is the total number of elements that can potentially be stored in the `vector` before it reallocates memory to accommodate more elements. Therefore, a `vector`'s size is less than or equal to its capacity.

You can query a `vector` for the number of elements by calling `size()`:

```
cout << "Size: " << integers.size ();
```

or query it for its capacity by calling `capacity()`:

```
cout << "Capacity: " <<  integers.capacity () << endl;
```

A `vector` can cause some amount of performance problems when it needs to frequently reallocate the memory of the internal dynamic array. To a great extent, this problem can be addressed by using the member function `reserve(number)`. What `reserve()` essentially does is increase the amount of memory allocated for the vector's internal array so as to accommodate the `number` of elements without needing to reallocate. Depending on the type of the objects stored in the vector, reducing the number of reallocations also reduces the number of times the objects are copied and saves on performance. The code sample in Listing 17.7 demonstrates the difference between `size()` and `capacity()`.

LISTING 17.7   Demonstration of `size()` and `capacity()`

```
0: #include <iostream>
1: #include <vector>
2:
3: int main ()
4: {
5:    using namespace std;
6:
7:    // instantiate a vector object that holds 5 integers of default value
8:    vector <int> integers (5);
9:
10:    cout << "Vector of integers was instantiated with " << endl;
11:    cout << "Size: " << integers.size ();
12:    cout << ", Capacity: " << integers.capacity () << endl;
13:
14:    // Inserting a 6th element in to the vector
15:    integers.push_back (666);
16:
17:    cout << "After inserting an additional element... " << endl;
18:    cout << "Size: " << integers.size ();
19:    cout << ", Capacity: " <<  integers.capacity () << endl;
20:
21:    // Inserting another element
22:    integers.push_back (777);
23:
24:    cout << "After inserting yet another element... " << endl;
25:    cout << "Size: " << integers.size ();
26:    cout << ", Capacity: " <<  integers.capacity () << endl;
27:
28:    return 0;
29: }
```

Output ▼

```
Vector of integers was instantiated with
Size: 5, Capacity: 5
After inserting an additional element...
Size: 6, Capacity: 7
After inserting yet another element...
Size: 7, Capacity: 7
```

Analysis ▼

Line 8 shows the instantiation of a `vector` of integers containing five integers at default value (0). Lines 11 and 12, which display the size and the capacity of the `vector`, respectively, display that both are equal at instantiation time. Line 9 inserts a sixth element in the vector. Given that the capacity of the vector was five prior to the insertion, there isn't adequate memory in the internal buffer of the vector to support this new sixth element. In other words, for the vector class to scale itself and store six elements, it needs to reallocate the internal buffer. The implementation of the reallocation logic is smart—to avoid another reallocation on insertion of another element, it preemptively allocates a capacity greater than the requirements of the immediate scenario.

The output shows that on insertion of a sixth element in a vector that has the capacity for five, the reallocation involved increases the capacity to seven elements. size() always reflects the number of elements in the vector and has a value of six at this stage. The addition of a seventh element in Line 22 results in no increase in capacity—the existing allocated memory meets the demand sufficiently. Both size and capacity display an equal value at this stage, indicating that the vector is used to its full capacity, and insertion of the next element will cause the vector to reallocate its internal buffer, copying existing values before it inserts the new value.

17

NOTE

> The preemptive increase in the capacity of the vector when the internal buffer is reallocated is not regulated by any clause in the C++ standard. This level of performance optimization may vary depending on the provider of STL library in use.

The STL deque Class

deque (pronunciation rhymes with *deck*) is an STL dynamic array class quite similar in properties to that of the vector except that it allows for the insertion and removal of elements at the front and back of the array. You would instantiate a deque of integers like this:

```
// Define a deque of integers
std::deque <int> intDeque;
```

TIP

> To use a std::deque, include header <deque>:
>
> ```
> #include<deque>
> ```

A deque can be visualized as shown in Figure 17.2.

FIGURE 17.2
Internals of a deque.

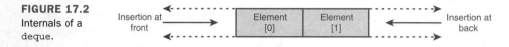

The deque is similar to the vector in that it supports element insertions and deletions at the back via the push_back() and pop_back() functions. Just like the vector, the deque also allows you to access it using array semantics via operator ([]). deque is different from the vector in that it also enables you to insert elements at the front using push_front() and remove from the front using pop_front(), as demonstrated by Listing 17.8.

LISTING 17.8 Instantiating an STL deque and Using push_front() and pop_front() Functions to Insert and Delete Elements at the Front

```
 0: #include <deque>
 1: #include <iostream>
 2: #include <algorithm>
 3:
 4: int main ()
 5: {
 6:     using namespace std;
 7:
 8:     // Define a deque of integers
 9:     deque<int> intDeque;
10:
11:     // Insert integers at the bottom of the array
12:     intDeque.push_back (3);
13:     intDeque.push_back (4);
14:     intDeque.push_back (5);
15:
16:     // Insert integers at the top of the array
17:     intDeque.push_front (2);
18:     intDeque.push_front (1);
19:     intDeque.push_front (0);
20:
21:     cout << "The contents of the deque after inserting elements ";
22:     cout << "at the top and bottom are:" << endl;
23:
24:     // Display contents on the screen
25:     for (size_t count = 0;
26:         count < intDeque.size ();
27:         ++ count )
28:     {
29:         cout << "Element [" << count << "] = ";
```

```
30:          cout << intDeque [count] << endl;
31:      }
32:
33:      cout << endl;
34:
35:      // Erase an element at the top
36:      intDeque.pop_front ();
37:
38:      // Erase an element at the bottom
39:      intDeque.pop_back ();
40:
41:      cout << "The contents of the deque after erasing an element ";
42:      cout << "from the top and bottom are:" << endl;
43:
44:      // Display contents again: this time using iterators
45:      // if on older compilers, remove auto and uncomment next line
46:      // deque <int>::iterator element;
47:      for (auto element = intDeque.begin ();
48:           element != intDeque.end ();
49:           ++ element )
50:      {
51:          size_t Offset = distance (intDeque.begin (), element);
52:          cout << "Element [" << Offset << "] = " << *element << endl;
53:      }
54:
55:      return 0;
56: }
```

Output ▼

```
The contents of the deque after inserting elements at the top and bottom are:
Element [0] = 0
Element [1] = 1
Element [2] = 2
Element [3] = 3
Element [4] = 4
Element [5] = 5

The contents of the deque after erasing an element from the top and bottom are:
Element [0] = 1
Element [1] = 2
Element [2] = 3
Element [3] = 4
```

Analysis ▼

Line 9 is where you instantiate a deque of integers. Note how similar this syntax is to the instantiation of a vector of integers. Lines 12–14 display the usage of the deque member function push_back() followed by push_front() in Lines 17–19. The latter

17

makes the deque unique in comparison to the vector. Ditto for the usage of pop_front(), as shown in Line 36. The first mechanism of displaying the contents of deque as seen in Lines 25–31 uses the array-like syntax to access elements, whereas Lines 47–53 demonstrate the usage of iterators. Algorithm std::distance() is used in Line 51 to evaluate the offset position of the element in the deque in the same manner that you have already seen work with the vector in Listing 17.5.

TIP

When you need to empty an STL container such as a vector or a deque, that is, delete all elements contained in it, you would use member function clear().

The following code deletes all elements in vector integers from Listing 17.7:

```
integers.clear();
```

To delete all elements in deque intDeque from Listing 17.8, add code:

```
intDeque.clear();
```

Note that both vector and deque also feature a member function called empty() that returns true when the container is empty. It doesn't actually delete existing elements—the way clear() does.

```
intDeque.clear();
if (intDeque.empty())
    cout << "The container is now empty" << endl;
```

DO	**DON'T**
DO use the dynamic arrays vector or deque when you don't know the number of elements you need to store.	**DON'T** forget that the function pop_back() deletes the last element from the collection.
DO remember that a vector can grow only at one end via the function push_back().	**DON'T** forget that the function pop_front() deletes the first element from a deque.
DO remember that a deque can grow on both ends via the functions push_back() and push_front().	**DON'T** access a dynamic array beyond its bounds.

Summary

In this lesson, you learned the basics of using the `vector` and the `deque` as dynamic arrays. The concepts of size and capacity were explained, and you saw how the usage of the `vector` can be optimized to reduce the number of reallocations of its internal buffer, which copies the objects contained and potentially reduces performance. The `vector` is the simplest of the STL's containers, yet the most used and, arguably, the most efficient one.

Q&A

Q Does the `vector` change the order of the elements stored in it?

A The `vector` is a sequential container, and elements are stored and accessed in the very order that they are inserted.

Q What function is used to insert items in a `vector`, and where is the object inserted?

A The member function `push_back()` inserts elements at the end of the `vector`.

Q What function gets the number of elements stored in a `vector`?

A The member function `size()` returns the number of elements stored in a `vector`. Incidentally, this is true for all STL containers.

Q Does the insertion or removal of elements at the end of the `vector` take more time if the `vector` contains more elements?

A No. Insertion and removal of elements at the end of a `vector` are constant-time activities.

Q What is the advantage of using the `reserve()` member function?

A `reserve()` allocates space in the internal buffer of the `vector`, and insertion of elements does not need the `vector` to reallocate the buffer and copy existing contents. Depending on the nature of the objects stored in the `vector`, reserving space in a `vector` can result in performance improvements.

Q Are the properties of the deque any different than the vector when it comes to insertion of elements?

A No, the properties of the deque are similar to that of the vector when it comes to insertion, which is a constant-time activity for elements added at the end of sequence and a linear-time activity for elements inserted in the middle. However, the vector allows insertion at only one end (the bottom), whereas the `deque` allows for insertion at both ends (the top and the bottom).

17

Workshop

The Workshop contains quiz questions to help solidify your understanding of the material covered and exercises to provide you with experience in using what you've learned. Try to answer the quiz and exercise questions before checking the answers in Appendix E, and be certain you understand the answers before going to the next lesson.

Quiz

1. Can elements be inserted at the middle or the beginning of a vector in constant time?

2. My vector returns size() as 10 and capacity() as 20. How many more elements can I insert in it without needing the vector class to trigger a buffer reallocation?

3. What does the pop_back() function do?

4. If vector <int> is a dynamic array of integers, a vector <Mammal> is a dynamic array of what type?

5. Can elements in a vector be randomly accessed? If so, how?

6. What iterator type allows random access of elements in a vector?

Exercises

1. Write an interactive program that accepts integer input from the user and saves it in the vector. The user should be able to query a value stored in the vector at any time, given an index.

2. Extend the program from Exercise 1 to be able to tell the user whether a value he queries for already exists in the vector.

3. Jack sells jars on eBay. To help him with packaging and shipment, write a program in which he can enter the dimensions of each of these articles, store them in a vector, and have them printed on the screen.

4. Write an application that initializes a deque to the following three strings: "Hello", "Containers are cool!", and "C++ is evolving!". You must display them using a generic function that would work for a deque of all kinds. Your application needs to demonstrate the usage of List Initialization introduced by C++11 and the operator ""s introduced by C++14.

LESSON 18
STL `list` **and**
`forward_list`

The Standard Template Library (STL) supplies the programmer with a doubly linked list in the form of template class `std::list`. The main advantage of a linked list is in fast and constant time insertion and removal of elements. Starting with C++11, you can also use a singly linked list in the form of `std::forward_list` that can be traversed only in one direction.

In this lesson, you learn

- How to instantiate `list` and `forward_list`
- How to use the STL list classes, including insertion and removal
- How to reverse and sort elements

The Characteristics of a `std::list`

A `linked list` is a collection of nodes in which each node, in addition to containing a value or object of interest, also points to the next node; that is, each node links to the next one and previous one as shown in Figure 18.1.

FIGURE 18.1
Visual representation
of a doubly linked
list.

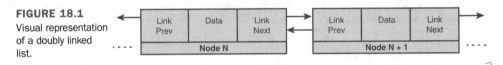

The STL implementation of the `list` class allows for constant-time insertions in the top, bottom, or middle of the `list`.

TIP	To use class `std::list`, include header: `#include <list>`

Basic `list` Operations

To use STL's `list` class, include header file `<list>`. The template class `list` that exists in the `std` namespace is a generic implementation that needs to be template-instantiated before you can use any of its useful member functions.

Instantiating a `std::list` Object

The template instantiation of `list` needs to specify the type of object that you want to collect in the list. So, the initialization of a list would look like the following:

```
std::list<int> linkInts;   // list containing integers
std::list<float> listFloats;  // list containing floats
std::list<Tuna> listTunas;  // list containing objects of type Tuna
```

To declare an iterator that points to an element in the list, you would use

```
std::list<int>::const_iterator elementInList;
```

If you need an iterator that can be used to modify values or invoke non-`const` functions, you use `iterator` instead of `const_iterator`.

Given that implementations of the `std::list` do provide you with a set of overloaded constructors, you can even create lists that are initialized to contain a number of elements of your choosing, each initialized to a value, as demonstrated by Listing 18.1.

LISTING 18.1   Different Forms of Instantiating std::list, Specifying Number of Elements and Initial Values

```
 0: #include <list>
 1: #include <vector>
 2:
 3: int main ()
 4: {
 5:    using namespace std;
 6:
 7:    // instantiate an empty list
 8:    list <int> linkInts;
 9:
10:    // instantiate a list with 10 integers
11:    list<int> listWith10Integers(10);
12:
13:    // instantiate a list with 4 integers, each value 99
14:    list<int> listWith4IntegerEach99 (10, 99);
15:
16:    // create an exact copy of an existing list
17:    list<int> listCopyAnother(listWith4IntegerEach99);
18:
19:    // a vector with 10 integers, each 2017
20:    vector<int> vecIntegers(10, 2017);
21:
22:    // instantiate a list using values from another container
23:    list<int> listContainsCopyOfAnother(vecIntegers.cbegin(),
24:                                        vecIntegers.cend());
25:
26:    return 0;
27: }
```

18

Analysis ▼

This program produces no output and demonstrates the application of the various overloaded constructors in creating a list of integers. In Line 8 you create an empty list, whereas in Line 11 you create a list containing 10 integers. Line 14 is a list, called listWith4IntegersEach99, that contains 4 integers that are each initialized to value 99. Line 17 demonstrates creating a list that is an exact copy of the contents of another. Lines 20–24 are surprising and curious! You instantiate a vector that contains 10 integers, each containing value 2017, and then instantiate a list in Line 23 that contains elements copied from the vector, using const iterators returned by vector::cbegin() and vector::cend() (new in C++11). Listing 18.1 is also a demonstration of how iterators help decouple the implementation of one container from another, enabling you to use their generic functionality to instantiate a list using values taken from a vector, as shown in Lines 23 and 24.

NOTE

On comparing Listing 18.1 against Listing 17.1 in Lesson 17, "STL Dynamic Array Classes," you will note a remarkable pattern and similarity in the way containers of different types have been instantiated. The more you program using STL containers, the more reusable patterns you will see and the easier it will get.

Inserting Elements at the Front or Back of the List

Similar to a `deque`, insertion at the front (or top, depending on your perspective) is effected using the `list` member method `push_front()`. Insertion at the end is done using member method `push_back()`. These two methods take one input parameter, which is the value to be inserted:

```
linkInts.push_back (-1);
linkInts.push_front (2001);
```

Listing 18.2 demonstrates the effect of using these two methods on a `list` of integers.

LISTING 18.2   Inserting Elements in the List Using `push_front()` and `push_back()`

```
0: #include <list>
1: #include <iostream>
2: using namespace std;
3:
4: template <typename T>
5: void DisplayContents (const T& container)
6: {
7:    for (auto element = container.cbegin();
8:          element != container.cend();
9:          ++ element )
10:       cout << *element << ' ';
11:
12:    cout << endl;
13: }
14:
15: int main ()
16: {
17:    std::list <int> linkInts{ -101, 42 };
18:
19:    linkInts.push_front (10);
20:    linkInts.push_front (2011);
21:    linkInts.push_back (-1);
22:    linkInts.push_back (9999);
23:
```

```
24:     DisplayContents(linkInts);
25:
26:     return 0;
27: }
```

Output ▼

```
2011 10 -101 42 -1 9999
```

Analysis ▼

Line 17 features the template instantiation of a `list` for type int and uses C++11 List Initialization syntax {...} to ensure that `linkInts` is constructed with two integers (-101 and 42) linked within it. Lines 19–22 demonstrate the usage of `push_front()` and `push_back()`. The value being supplied as an argument to `push_front()` takes the first position in the list, whereas that sent via `push_back()` takes the last position. The output displays the content of the list via generic template function `DisplayContents()` demonstrating the order of the inserted elements (and that they aren't stored in order of insertion).

NOTE

> DisplayContents() in Listing 18.2, Lines 4–13 is a more generic version of the method `DisplayVector()` in Listing 17.6 (note the changed parameter list). Although the latter worked only for the `vector`, generalizing the type of elements stored in one, this version is truly generic even across container types.
>
> You can invoke the version of `DisplayContents()` in Listing 18.2 with a `vector`, a `list`, or a `deque` as an argument, and it will work just fine.

18

Inserting at the Middle of the List

`std::list` is characterized by its capability to insert elements at the middle of the collection in constant time. This is done using the member function `insert()`.

The `list::insert()` member function is available in three forms:

- **Form 1**

```
iterator insert(iterator pos, const T& x)
```

Here the insert function accepts the position of insertion as the first parameter and the value to insert as the second. This function returns an iterator pointing to the recently inserted element in the list.

- **Form 2**

  ```
  void insert(iterator pos, size_type n, const T& x)
  ```

  This function accepts the position of insertion as the first parameter, the value to insert as the last parameter, and the number of elements in variable n.

- **Form 3**

  ```
  template <class InputIterator>
  void insert(iterator pos, InputIterator f, InputIterator l)
  ```

  This overloaded variant is a template function that accepts, in addition to the position, two input iterators that mark the bounds of the collection to insert into the list. Note that the input type `InputIterator` is a template-parameterized type and therefore can point to the bounds of any collection—be it an array, a `vector`, or just another `list`.

Listing 18.3 demonstrates the use of these overloaded variants of the `list::insert()` function.

LISTING 18.3 Various Methods of Inserting Elements in a List

```cpp
 0: #include <list>
 1: #include <iostream>
 2: using namespace std;
 3:
 4: template <typename T>
 5: void DisplayContents (const T& container)
 6: {
 7:     for (auto element = container.cbegin();
 8:           element != container.cend();
 9:           ++ element )
10:        cout << *element << ' ';
11:
12:     cout << endl;
13: }
14:
15: int main ()
16: {
17:     list <int> linkInts1;
18:
19:     // Inserting elements at the beginning...
20:     linkInts1.insert (linkInts1.begin (), 2);
21:     linkInts1.insert (linkInts1.begin (), 1);
22:
23:     // Inserting an element at the end...
24:     linkInts1.insert (linkInts1.end (), 3);
25:
26:     cout << "The contents of list 1 after inserting elements:" << endl;
27:     DisplayContents (linkInts1);
```

```
28:
29:     list <int> linkInts2;
30:
31:     // Inserting 4 elements of the same value 0...
32:     linkInts2.insert (linkInts2.begin (), 4, 0);
33:
34:     cout << "The contents of list 2 after inserting '";
35:     cout << linkInts2.size () << "' elements of a value:" << endl;
36:     DisplayContents (linkInts2);
37:
38:     list <int> linkInts3;
39:
40:     // Inserting elements from another list at the beginning...
41:     linkInts3.insert (linkInts3.begin (),
42:                       linkInts1.begin (), linkInts1.end ());
43:
44:     cout << "The contents of list 3 after inserting the contents of ";
45:     cout << "list 1 at the beginning:" << endl;
46:     DisplayContents (linkInts3);
47:
48:     // Inserting elements from another list at the end...
49:     linkInts3.insert (linkInts3.end (),
50:                       linkInts2.begin (), linkInts2.end ());
51:
52:     cout << "The contents of list 3 after inserting ";
53:     cout << "the contents of list 2 at the end:" << endl;
54:     DisplayContents (linkInts3);
55:
56:     return 0;
57: }
```

18

Output ▼

```
The contents of list 1 after inserting elements:
1 2 3
The contents of list 2 after inserting '4' elements of a value:
0 0 0 0
The contents of list 3 after inserting the contents of list 1 at the beginning:
1 2 3
The contents of list 3 after inserting the contents of list 2 at the end:
1 2 3 0 0 0 0
```

Analysis ▼

begin() and end() are member functions that return iterators pointing to the beginning and the end of the `list`, respectively. This is generally true for all STL containers, including the std::list. The list::insert() function accepts an iterator that marks the position before which items are to be inserted. The iterator returned by the end()

function, as used in Line 24, points to after the last element in the `list`. Therefore, that line inserts integer value 3 before the end as the last value. Line 32 indicates the initialization of a `list` with four elements placed at the beginning—that is, at the front—each with value 0. Lines 41 and 42 demonstrate the usage of the `list::insert()` function to insert elements from one list at the end of another. Although this example inserts a `list` of integers into another `list`, the range inserted could as well have been within the limits of a `vector`, supplied by `begin()` and `end()` as also seen in Listing 18.1, or a regular static array.

Erasing Elements from the List

The `list` member function `erase()` comes in two overloaded forms: one that erases one element given an iterator that points to it and another that accepts a range and therefore erases a range of elements from the `list`. You can see the `list::erase()` function in action in Listing 18.4, which demonstrates how you erase an element or a range of elements from a list.

LISTING 18.4   Erasing Elements from a List

```
 0: #include <list>
 1: #include <iostream>
 2: using namespace std;
 3:
 4: template <typename T>
 5: void DisplayContents(const T& container)
 6: {
 7:     for(auto element = container.cbegin();
 8:          element != container.cend();
 9:         ++ element )
10:        cout << *element << ' ';
11:
12:     cout << endl;
13: }
14:
15: int main()
16: {
17:     std::list <int> linkInts{ 4, 3, 5, -1, 2017 };
18:
19:     // Store an iterator obtained in using insert()
20:     auto val2 = linkInts.insert(linkInts.begin(), 2);
21:
22:     cout << "Initial contents of the list:" << endl;
23:     DisplayContents(linkInts);
24:
25:     cout << "After erasing element '"<< *val2 << "':" << endl;
26:     linkInts.erase(val2);
27:     DisplayContents(linkInts);
28:
```

```
29:    linkInts.erase(linkInts.begin(), linkInts.end());
30:    cout << "Number of elements after erasing range: ";
31:    cout << linkInts.size() << endl;
32:
33:    return 0;
34: }
```

Output ▼

```
Initial contents of the list:
2 4 3 5 -1 2017
After erasing element '2':
4 3 5 -1 2017
Number of elements after erasing range: 0
```

Analysis ▼

When `insert()` is used to insert a value as seen in Line 20, it returns an iterator to the newly inserted element. This iterator pointing to an element with value 2 is stored in a variable `val2`, to be used later in a call to `erase()` at Line 26 to delete this very element from the `list`. Line 29 demonstrates the usage of `erase()` to delete a range of elements. You clear a range from `begin()` to `end()`, effectively erasing the entire list.

18

TIP

> The shortest and simplest way to empty an STL container, such as a `std::list`, is to call member function `clear()`.
>
> A simpler Line 29 in Listing 18.4 would therefore be
>
> ```
> linkInts.clear();
> ```

NOTE

> Listing 18.4 demonstrates at Line 31 that the number of elements in a `std::list` can be determined using list method `size()`, very similar to that of a vector. This is a pattern applicable to all STL container classes.

Reversing and Sorting Elements in a List

`list` has a special property that iterators pointing to the elements in a `list` remain valid in spite of rearrangement of the elements or insertion of new elements and so on. To keep this important property intact, the `list` function features `sort()` and `reverse()` as member methods even though the STL supplies these as algorithms that will and do work on the `list` class. The member versions of these algorithms ensure that iterators pointing to elements in the `list` are not invalidated when the relative position of an element is disturbed.

Reversing Elements Using `list::reverse()`

`list` features a member function `reverse()` that takes no parameters and reverses the order of contents in a `list` for the programmer:

```
linkInts.reverse();   // reverse order of elements
```

The usage of `reverse()` is demonstrated in Listing 18.5.

LISTING 18.5   Reversing Elements in a List

```
 0: #include <list>
 1: #include <iostream>
 2: using namespace std;
 3:
 4: template <typename T>
 5: void DisplayContents(const T& container)
 6: {
 7:    for (auto element = container.cbegin();
 8:          element != container.cend();
 9:          ++ element )
10:      cout << *element << ' ';
11:
12:    cout << endl;
13: }
14:
15: int main()
16: {
17:    std::list<int> linkInts{ 0, 1, 2, 3, 4, 5 };
18:
19:    cout << "Initial contents of list:" << endl;
20:    DisplayContents(linkInts);
21:
22:    linkInts.reverse();
23:
24:    cout << "Contents of list after using reverse():" << endl;
25:    DisplayContents(linkInts);
26:
27:    return 0;
28: }
```

Output ▼

```
Initial contents of list:
0 1 2 3 4 5
Contents of list after using reverse():
5 4 3 2 1 0
```

Analysis ▼

As shown in Line 22, `reverse()` simply reverses the order of elements in the `list`. It is a simple call without parameters that ensures that iterators pointing to elements in the `list`, if kept by the programmer, remain valid even after the reversal.

Sorting Elements

The `list` member function `sort()` is available in a version that takes no parameters:

```
linkInts.sort();  // sort in ascending order
```

Another version allows you to define your own sort priorities via a binary predicate function as a parameter:

```
bool SortPredicate_Descending (const int& lhs, const int& rhs)
{
    // define criteria for list::sort: return true for desired order
    return (lhs > rhs);
}
// Use predicate to sort a list:
linkInts.sort (SortPredicate_Descending);
```

These two variants are demonstrated in Listing 18.6.

LISTING 18.6 Sorting a List of Integers in Ascending and Descending Order Using `list::sort()`

```
0: #include <list>
1: #include <iostream>
2: using namespace std;
3:
4: bool SortPredicate_Descending (const int& lhs, const int& rhs)
5: {
6:     // define criteria for list::sort: return true for desired order
7:     return (lhs > rhs);
8: }
9:
```

18

```
10: template <typename T>
11: void DisplayContents (const T& container)
12: {
13:     for (auto element = container.cbegin();
14:           element != container.cend();
15:           ++ element )
16:        cout << *element << ' ';
17:
18:     cout << endl;
19: }
20:
21: int main ()
22: {
23:     list <int> linkInts{ 0, -1, 2011, 444, -5 };
24:
25:     cout << "Initial contents of the list are - " << endl;
26:     DisplayContents (linkInts);
27:
28:     linkInts.sort ();
29:
30:     cout << "Order after sort():" << endl;
31:     DisplayContents (linkInts);
32:
33:     linkInts.sort (SortPredicate_Descending);
34:     cout << "Order after sort() with a predicate:" << endl;
35:     DisplayContents (linkInts);
36:
37:     return 0;
38: }
```

Output ▼

```
Initial contents of the list are -
0 -1 2011 444 -5
Order after sort():
-5 -1 0 444 2011
Order after sort() with a predicate:
2011 444 0 -1 -5
```

Analysis ▼

This sample demonstrates the `sort()` member function on a `list` of integers. Line 28 displays the usage of a `sort()` function without parameters that sorts elements in ascending order by default, comparing integers using `operator <` (which, in the case of integers, is implemented by the compiler). However, if the programmer wants to override this default behavior, he must supply the `sort()` with a binary predicate as seen in Line 33. The function `SortPredicate_Descending()`, defined in Lines 4–8, is a binary predicate that helps the `list`'s `sort()` function decide whether one element is less than the other. If not, it swaps their positions. In other words, you tell the list what's to be interpreted as less (which, in this case, is the first parameter being greater than the second). The predicate returns `true` only if the first value is greater than the second. That is, `sort()` that uses the predicate interprets the first value (`lhs`) to be logically less than the second (`rhs`) only if the numeric value of the former is greater than that of the latter. On the basis of this interpretation, it swaps position to fulfill the criteria specified by the predicate.

Sorting and Removing Elements from a `list` That Contains Instances of a `class`

What if you had a `list` of a class type, and not a simple built-in type such as `int`? Say a list of address book entries where each entry is a class that contains name, address, and so on. How would you ensure that this list is sorted on name?

The answer is one of the following:

- Implement `operator <` within the class type that the `list` contains.
- Supply a sort *binary predicate*—a function that takes two values as input and returns a Boolean value indicating whether the first value is smaller than the second.

18

Most practical applications involving STL containers rarely collect integers; instead, they collect user-defined types such as `classes` or `structs`. Listing 18.7 demonstrates one using the example of a contacts `list`. It seems rather long at first sight but is mostly full of simple code.

LISTING 18.7   A List of Class Objects: Creating a Contacts List

```
0: #include <list>
1: #include <string>
2: #include <iostream>
3: using namespace std;
4:
5: template <typename T>
6: void displayAsContents (const T& container)
7: {
8:    for (auto element = container.cbegin();
9:          element != container.cend();
10:          ++ element )
11:      cout << *element << endl;
12:
13:    cout << endl;
14: }
15:
```

```
16: struct ContactItem
17: {
18:     string name;
19:     string phone;
20:     string displayAs;
21:
22:     ContactItem (const string& conName, const string & conNum)
23:     {
24:         name = conName;
25:         phone = conNum;
26:         displayAs = (name + ": " + phone);
27:     }
28:
29:     // used by list::remove() given contact list item
30:     bool operator == (const ContactItem& itemToCompare) const
31:     {
32:         return (itemToCompare.name == this->name);
33:     }
34:
35:     // used by list::sort() without parameters
36:     bool operator < (const ContactItem& itemToCompare) const
37:     {
38:         return (this->name < itemToCompare.name);
39:     }
40:
41:     // Used in displayAsContents via cout
42:     operator const char*() const
43:     {
44:         return displayAs.c_str();
45:     }
46: };
47:
48: bool SortOnphoneNumber (const ContactItem& item1,
49:                         const ContactItem& item2)
50: {
51:     return (item1.phone < item2.phone);
52: }
53:
54: int main ()
55: {
56:     list <ContactItem> contacts;
57:     contacts.push_back(ContactItem("Jack Welsch", "+1 7889879879"));
58:     contacts.push_back(ContactItem("Bill Gates", "+1 97789787998"));
59:     contacts.push_back(ContactItem("Angi Merkel", "+49 234565466"));
60:     contacts.push_back(ContactItem("Vlad Putin", "+7 66454564797"));
61:     contacts.push_back(ContactItem("Ben Affleck", "+1 745641314"));
62:     contacts.push_back(ContactItem("Dan Craig", "+44 123641976"));
63:
64:     cout << "List in initial order: " << endl;
65:     displayAsContents(contacts);
66:
```

```
67:     contacts.sort();
68:     cout << "Sorting in alphabetical order via operator<:" << endl;
69:     displayAsContents(contacts);
70:
71:     contacts.sort(SortOnphoneNumber);
72:     cout << "Sorting in order of phone numbers via predicate:" << endl;
73:     displayAsContents(contacts);
74:
75:     cout << "Erasing Putin from the list: " << endl;
76:     contacts.remove(ContactItem("Vlad Putin", ""));
77:     displayAsContents(contacts);
78:
79:     return 0;
80: }
```

Output ▼

```
List in initial order:
Jack Welsch: +1 7889879879
Bill Gates: +1 97 789787998
Angi Merkel: +49 234565466
Vlad Putin: +7 66454564797
Ben Affleck: +1 745641314
Dan Craig: +44 123641976

Sorting in alphabetical order via operator<:
Angi Merkel: +49 234565466
Ben Affleck: +1 745641314
Bill Gates: +1 97 789787998
Dan Craig: +44 123641976
Jack Welsch: +1 7889879879
Vlad Putin: +7 66454564797

Sorting in order of phone numbers via predicate:
Ben Affleck: +1 745641314
Jack Welsch: +1 7889879879
Bill Gates: +1 97 789787998
Dan Craig: +44 123641976
Angi Merkel: +49 234565466
Vlad Putin: +7 66454564797

After erasing Putin from the list:
Ben Affleck: +1 745641314
Jack Welsch: +1 7889879879
Bill Gates: +1 97 789787998
Dan Craig: +44 123641976
Angi Merkel: +49 234565466
```

18

Analysis ▼

For a start, focus on `main()` in Lines 54–80. You have instantiated a list of address book items of type `ContactItem` in Line 56. In Lines 57–62, you populate this list with names and (fake) telephone numbers of celebrity technologists and politicians, and display this initial order in Line 65. Line 67 uses `list::sort()` without a predicate function. In the absence of a predicate, this sort function seeks the presence of `operator<` in `ContactItem` that has been defined in Lines 36–39. `ContactItem::operator<` helps `list::sort()` sort its elements in alphabetical order of the stored names (and not telephone numbers or a random logic). To sort the same list in the order of phone numbers, you use `list::sort()` supplying a binary predicate function `SortOnPhoneNumber()` as an argument in Line 71. This function implemented in Lines 48–52 ensures that the input arguments of type `ContactItem` are compared to each other on the basis of the phone numbers and not the names. Thus, it helps `list::sort()` sort the list of celebrities on the basis of their phone numbers as the output indicates. Finally, Line 76 is where you use `list::remove()` to remove a celebrity contact from the list. You supply an object with the celebrity's name as a parameter. `list::remove()` compares this object to other elements in the list, using `ContactItem::operator=` implemented in Lines 30–33. This operator returns `true` if the names match, helping `list::remove()` decide what the criteria of a match should be.

This example not only demonstrates how STL's template version of the linked `list` can be used to create a `list` of any object type, but also the importance of operators and predicates.

`std::forward_list` **Introduced in C++11**

Starting with C++11, you have the option of using a `forward_list` instead of a doubly linked list in `std::list`. `std::forward_list` is a singly linked list—that is, it allows iteration in only one direction as shown in Figure 18.2.

FIGURE 18.2
A visual representation of a singly linked list.

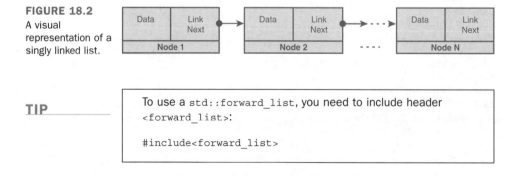

TIP

> To use a `std::forward_list`, you need to include header `<forward_list>`:
>
> ```
> #include<forward_list>
> ```

The usage of the `forward_list` is similar to `list`, save for the fact that you can move iterators only in one direction and that you have a `push_front()` function to insert elements but no `push_back()`. Of course, you can always use `insert()` and its overloaded functions to insert an element at a given position.

Listing 18.8 demonstrates some functions of a `forward_list` class.

LISTING 18.8   Basic Insertion and Removal Operations on a `forward_list`

```
0: #include<forward_list>
1: #include<iostream>
2: using namespace std;
3:
4: template <typename T>
5: void DisplayContents (const T& container)
6: {
7:     for (auto element = container.cbegin();
8:             element != container.cend ();
9:             ++ element)
10:         cout << *element << ' ';
11:
12:     cout << endl;
13: }
14:
15: int main()
16: {
17:     forward_list<int> flistIntegers{ 3, 4, 2, 2, 0 };
18:     flistIntegers.push_front(1);
19:
20:     cout << "Contents of forward_list: " << endl;
21:     DisplayContents(flistIntegers);
22:
23:     flistIntegers.remove(2);
24:     flistIntegers.sort();
25:     cout << "Contents after removing 2 and sorting: " << endl;
26:     DisplayContents(flistIntegers);
27:
28:     return 0;
29: }
```

18

Output ▼

```
Contents of forward_list:
1 3 4 2 2 0
Contents after removing 2 and sorting:
0  1  3  4
```

Analysis ▼

As the sample shows, the `forward_list` is similar in function to a `list`. As the `forward_list` doesn't support bidirectional iteration, you can use `operator++` on an iterator, but not `operator--`. This sample demonstrates the usage of function `remove(2)` in Line 23 to remove all elements with value 2. Line 29 demonstrates `sort()` using the default sort predicate that uses `std::less<T>`.

The advantage of the `forward_list` is that in being a singly linked list, its memory consumption is slightly lower than that of a `list` (as an element needs to know only the next element but not the previous one).

DO	DON'T
DO choose a `std::list` over `std::vector` where you frequently insert or delete elements, especially in the middle—a vector needs to resize its internal buffer to allow array semantics and causes expensive copy operations, but a list just links or unlinks elements.	**DON'T** use a list when you have infrequent insertions or deletions at the ends and no insertions or deletions in the middle; `vector` or `deque` can be significantly faster in these cases.
DO remember that you can insert in the beginning or end of a list using the `push_front()` or `push_back()` member methods, respectively.	**DON'T** forget to supply a predicate function if you want the list to `sort()` or `remove()` using non-default criteria.
DO remember to program `operator<` and `operator==` in a class that will be collected in a STL container such as `list` to supply the default sort or remove predicate.	
DO remember that you can always determine the number of elements in the `list` using the `list::size()` method, as with any other STL container class.	
DO remember that you can empty a `list` using `list::clear()` method, as with any other STL container class.	

Summary

This lesson taught you the properties of the list and the different list operations. You now know some of the most useful list functions and can create a list of any object type.

Q&A

Q Why does the list provide member functions such as sort() and remove()?

A The STL list class is bound to respect the property that iterators pointing to elements in the list should remain valid irrespective of the position of the elements in the list itself. Although STL algorithms work on list too, the list's member functions ensure that the aforementioned property of the list is withheld and iterators pointing to elements in the list before the sort was done continue to point to the same elements even after the sort.

Q You are using a list of type CAnimal, which is a class. What operators should CAnimal define for list member functions to be able to work on it accurately?

A You must provide the default comparison operator == and the default < operator to any class that can be used in STL containers.

Q How would you replace keyword auto by an explicit type declaration in the following line:

```
list<int> linkInts(10);  // list of 10 integers
auto firstElement = linkInts.begin();
```

A You would replace auto by the following explicit type declaration:

```
list<int> linkInts(10);  // list of 10 integers
list<int>::iterator firstElement = linkInts.begin();
```

18

Workshop

The Workshop contains quiz questions to help solidify your understanding of the material covered and exercises to provide you with experience in using what you've learned. Try to answer the quiz and exercise questions before checking the answers in Appendix E, and be certain you understand the answers before going to the next lesson.

Quiz

1. Is there any loss in performance when inserting items in the middle of the STL `list` as compared to the beginning or the end?

2. Two iterators are pointing to two elements in an STL `list` object, and then an element is inserted between them. Are these iterators invalidated by the insert action?

3. How can the contents of a `std::list` be cleared?

4. Is it possible to insert multiple elements in a `list`?

Exercises

1. Write a short program that accepts numbers from the user and inserts them at the top of the `list`.

2. Using a short program, demonstrate that an iterator pointing to an element in a `list` continues to remain valid even after another element has been inserted before it, thus changing the relative position of the former element.

3. Write a program that inserts the contents of a vector into an STL `list` using the `list`'s `insert()` function.

4. Write a program that sorts and reverses a `list` of strings.

LESSON 19
STL Set Classes

The Standard Template Library (STL) supplies the programmer with container classes that help with applications requiring frequent and quick searches. The `std::set` and `std::multiset` are used to contain a sorted set of elements and offer you the ability to find elements given a logarithmic complexity. Their unordered counterparts offer constant-time insertion and search capabilities.

This lesson includes

- How STL `set` and `multiset`, `unordered_set`, and `unordered_multiset` containers can be of use to you
- Insertion, removal, and search of elements
- Advantages and disadvantages in using these containers

An Introduction to STL Set Classes

The set and multiset are containers that facilitate a quick lookup of keys in a container that stores them; that is, the keys are the values stored in the one-dimensional container. The difference between the set and the multiset is that the latter allows for duplicates whereas the former can store only unique values.

Figure 19.1 is only demonstrative and indicates that a set of names contains unique names, whereas a multiset permits duplicates.

FIGURE 19.1
Visual
representation
of a set and a
multiset of
names.

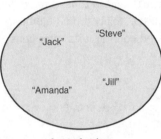

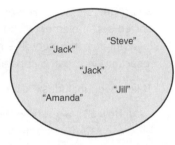

A set of strings   **A multiset of strings**

To facilitate quick searching, STL implementations of the set and multiset internally look like a binary tree. This means that elements inserted in a set or a multiset are sorted on insertion for quicker lookups. It also means that, unlike in a vector where elements at a position can be replaced by another, an element at a given position in a set cannot be replaced by a new element of a different value. This enables the set to place the new element in a possible different location in accordance with its value relative to those in the internal tree.

TIP

> To use class std::set or std::multiset, include header:
>
> #include <set>

Basic STL set and multiset Operations

STL set and multiset are template classes that need to be instantiated before you can use any of their member functions.

Instantiating a std::set **Object**

Instantiating a set or multiset of a type requires a specialization of the template class std::set or std::multiset for that type:

```
std::set <int> setInts;
std::multiset <int> msetInts;
```

To define a set or multiset that contains objects of class Tuna, you would program the following:

```
std::set <Tuna> tunaSet;
std::multiset <Tuna> tunaMSet;
```

To declare an iterator that points to an element in the set or multiset, you would use this:

```
std::set<int>::const_iterator element;
std::multiset<int>::const_iterator element;
```

If you need an iterator that can be used to modify values or invoke non-const functions, you would use iterator instead of const_iterator.

Given that both set and multiset are containers that sort elements on insertion, they use a default predicate std::less when you don't supply a sort criteria. This ensures that your set contains elements sorted in ascending order.

You create a binary sort predicate by defining a class with operator() that takes two values of the type contained in the set as input and returns true depending on your criteria. One such sort predicate that sorts in descending order is the following:

```
// used as a template parameter in set / multiset instantiation
template <typename T>
struct SortDescending
{
    bool operator()(const T& lhs, const T& rhs) const
    {
        return (lhs > rhs);
    }
};
```

You then supply this predicate in the set or multiset instantiation as follows:

```
// a set and multiset of integers (using sort predicate)
set <int, SortDescending<int>> setInts;
multiset <int, SortDescending<int>> msetInts;
```

In addition to these variants, you can always create a set or a multiset that copies from another or copies via a supplied range, as demonstrated in Listing 19.1.

19

LISTING 19.1   Different Instantiation Techniques of `set` and `multiset`

```
 0: #include <set>
 1:
 2: // used as a template parameter in set / multiset instantiation
 3: template <typename T>
 4: struct SortDescending
 5: {
 6:    bool operator()(const T& lhs, const T& rhs) const
 7:    {
 8:       return (lhs > rhs);
 9:    }
10: };
11:
12: int main ()
13: {
14:    using namespace std;
15:
16:    // a simple set or multiset of integers (using default sort predicate)
17:    set<int> setInts1;
18:    multiset<int> msetInts1;
19:
20:    // set and multiset instantiated given a user-defined sort predicate
21:    set<int, SortDescending<int>> setInts2;
22:    multiset<int, SortDescending<int>> msetInts2;
23:
24:    // creating one set from another, or part of another container
25:    set<int> setInts3(setInts1);
26:    multiset<int> msetInts3(setInts1.cbegin(), setInts1.cend());
27:
28:    return 0;
29: }
```

Analysis ▼

This program produces no output but demonstrates the various instantiation techniques for `set` and `multiset`, specialized to contain type `int`. In Lines 17 and 18, you see the simplest form where the template parameters other than type have been ignored, resulting in the default sort predicate being taken, as implemented in `struct` (or class) `std::less<T>`. If you want to override the default sort, you need to specify a predicate like the ones defined in Lines 3–10 and used in `main()` in Lines 21 and 22. This predicate ensures that the sort is descending (default ascending). Finally, Lines 25 and 26 show instantiation techniques where one set is a copy of another and a `multiset` instantiates from a range of values taken from a set (but could be a `vector` or a `list` or any STL container class that returns iterators that describe bounds via `cbegin()` and `cend()`).

Inserting Elements in a set or multiset

Most functions in a set and multiset work in a similar fashion. They accept similar parameters and return similar value types. For instance, inserting elements in both kinds of containers can be done using the member insert(), which accepts the value to be inserted or a range taken from another container:

```
setInts.insert (-1);
msetInts.insert (setInts.begin (), setInts.end ());
```

Listing 19.2 demonstrates inserting elements in these containers.

LISTING 19.2   Inserting Elements in an STL set and multiset

```
 0: #include <set>
 1: #include <iostream>
 2: using namespace std;
 3:
 4: template <typename T>
 5: void DisplayContents(const T& container)
 6: {
 7:    for (auto element = container.cbegin();
 8:          element != container.cend();
 9:          ++element)
10:       cout << *element << ' ';
11:
12:    cout << endl;
13: }
14:
15: int main()
16: {
17:    set <int> setInts{ 202, 151, -999, -1 };
18:    setInts.insert(-1); // duplicate
19:    cout << "Contents of the set: " << endl;
20:    DisplayContents(setInts);
21:
22:    multiset <int> msetInts;
23:    msetInts.insert(setInts.begin(), setInts.end());
24:    msetInts.insert(-1); // duplicate
25:
26:    cout << "Contents of the multiset: " << endl;
27:    DisplayContents(msetInts);
28:
29:    cout << "Number of instances of '-1' in the multiset are: '";
30:    cout << msetInts.count(-1) << "'" << endl;
31:
32:    return 0;
33: }
```

19

Output ▼

```
Contents of the set:
-999 -1 151 202
Contents of the multiset:
-999 -1 -1 151 202
Number of instances of '-1' in the multiset are: '2'
```

Analysis ▼

Lines 4–13 contain the generic template function `DisplayContents()`, which you have also seen in Lesson 17, "STL Dynamic Array Classes," and Lesson 18, "STL list and `forward_list`," and writes the contents of an STL container to the console or screen. Lines 17 and 22, as you already know, instantiate a `set` and a `multiset`, respectively, with the former using C++11 List Initialization syntax. In Lines 18 and 24 we attempt inserting a duplicate value in the `set` and `multiset`. Line 23 demonstrates how `insert()`can be used to insert the contents of a `set` into a `multiset`, inserting in this case the contents of `setInts` into `msetInts`. The output demonstrates that the `multiset` is able to hold multiple values, while `set` isn't. Line 30 demonstrates the `multiset::count()` member function, which returns the number of elements in the `multiset` that hold that particular value.

TIP

> Use `multiset::count()` to find the number of elements in the `multiset` that have the same value as that supplied as an argument to this function.

Finding Elements in an STL `set` or `multiset`

Associative containers like `set` and `multiset` or `map` and `multimap` feature `find()`—a member function that enables you to find a value given a key:

```
auto elementFound = setInts.find (-1);

// Check if found...
if (elementFound != setInts.end ())
    cout << "Element " << *elementFound << " found!" << endl;
else
    cout << "Element not found in set!" << endl;
```

The use of `find()` is demonstrated in Listing 19.3. In case of a `multiset` that allows multiple elements with the same value, this function finds the first value that matches the supplied key.

LISTING 19.3 Using the `find` Member Function

```
0: #include <set>
1: #include <iostream>
2: using namespace std;
3:
4: int main ()
5: {
6:     set<int> setInts{ 43, 78, -1, 124 };
7:
8:     // Display contents of the set to the screen
9:     for (auto element = setInts.cbegin();
10:            element != setInts.cend ();
11:            ++ element )
12:         cout << *element << endl;
13:
14:     // Try finding an element
15:     auto elementFound = setInts.find (-1);
16:
17:     // Check if found...
18:     if (elementFound != setInts.end ())
19:         cout << "Element " << *elementFound << " found!" << endl;
20:     else
21:         cout << "Element not found in set!" << endl;
22:
23:     // finding another
24:     auto anotherFind = setInts.find (12345);
25:
26:     // Check if found...
27:     if (anotherFind != setInts.end ())
28:         cout << "Element " << *anotherFind << " found!" << endl;
29:     else
30:         cout << "Element 12345 not found in set!" << endl;
31:
32:     return 0;
33: }
```

19

Output ▼

```
-1
43
78
124
Element -1 found!
Element 12345 not found in set!
```

Analysis ▼

Lines 15–21 display the usage of the `find()` member function. `find()` returns an iterator that needs to be compared against `end()`, as shown in Line 18, to verify whether

an element was found. If the iterator is valid, you can access the value pointed by it using
`*elementFound`.

NOTE

The example in Listing 19.3 works correctly for a `multiset`, too;
that is, if Line 6 is a `multiset` instead of a `set`, it does not
change the way the application works. Given that a `multiset`
may hold multiple elements of the same value at contiguous
locations, you may access them using the iterator returned by
`find()` and advancing it (`count()` - 1) number of times to
access all elements of a value. Member function `count()` was
demonstrated in Listing 19.2.

Erasing Elements in an STL `set` or `multiset`

Associative containers such as `set` and `multiset` or `map` and `multimap` feature
`erase()`—a member function that allows you to delete a value given a key:

```
setObject.erase (key);
```

Another form of the `erase()` function allows the deletion of a particular element given
an iterator that points to it:

```
setObject.erase (element);
```

You can erase a range of elements from a set or a `multiset` using iterators that supply
the bounds:

```
setObject.erase (iLowerBound, iUpperBound);
```

The sample in Listing 19.4 demonstrates the use of `erase()` in removing elements from
the `set` or `multiset`.

LISTING 19.4   Using the `erase` Member Function on a `multiset`

```
0: #include <set>
1: #include <iostream>
2: using namespace std;
3:
4: template <typename T>
5: void DisplayContents (const T& Input)
6: {
7:     for (auto element = Input.cbegin();
```

```
 8:                element != Input.cend ();
 9:                 ++ element )
10:            cout << *element << ' ';
11:
12:        cout << endl;
13: }
14:
15: typedef multiset <int> MSETINT;
16:
17: int main ()
18: {
19:     MSETINT msetInts{ 43, 78, 78, -1, 124 };
20:
21:     cout << "multiset contains " << msetInts.size () << " elements: ";
22:     DisplayContents(msetInts);
23:
24:     cout << "Enter a number to erase from the set: ";
25:     int input = 0;
26:     cin >> input;
27:
28:     cout << "Erasing " << msetInts.count (input);
29:     cout << " instances of value " << input << endl;
30:
31:     msetInts.erase (input);
32:
33:     cout << "multiset now contains " << msetInts.size () << " elements: ";
34:     DisplayContents(msetInts);
35:
36:     return 0;
37: }
```

Output ▼

19

```
multiset contains 5 elements: -1 43 78 78 124
Enter a number to erase from the set: 78
Erasing 2 instances of value 78
multiset now contains 3 elements: -1 43 124
```

Analysis ▼

Note the usage of typedef in Line 15. Line 28 demonstrates the usage of count() to tell the number of elements with a specific value. The actual erase happens in Line 31, which deletes all elements that match the particular number input by the user.

TIP

Member function `erase()` is overloaded. Invoked with a value as seen in Listing 19.4, it will delete all elements that evaluate to it. Invoked using an iterator, say one returned by a `find()` operation, it will delete that one element, as seen here:

```
MSETINT::iterator elementFound = msetInts.find
(numberToErase);
if (elementFound != msetInts.end ())
    msetInts.erase (elementFound);
else
    cout << "Element not found!" << endl;
```

You can also use `erase()` to delete a range of values from the `multiset`:

```
MSETINT::iterator elementFound = msetInts.find
(valueToErase);

if (elementFound != msetInts.end ())
    msetInts.erase (msetInts.begin (), elementFound);
```

The preceding snippet removes all elements from the start to the element of value `valueToErase`, not including the latter. Both `set` and `multiset` can be emptied of their contents using member function `clear()`.

Now that you have an overview of the basic `set` and `multiset` functions, it's time to review a sample that features a practical application made using this container class. The sample in Listing 19.5 is the simplest implementation of a menu-based telephone directory that enables the user to insert names and telephone numbers, find them, erase them, and display them all.

LISTING 19.5 A Telephone Directory Featuring STL `set`, `find`, and `erase`

```
0: #include <set>
1: #include <iostream>
2: #include <string>
3: using namespace std;
4:
5: template <typename T>
6: void DisplayContents (const T& container)
7: {
8:     for (auto iElement = container.cbegin();
9:          iElement != container.cend();
10:         ++ iElement )
11:      cout << *iElement << endl;
```

```
12:
13:     cout << endl;
14: }
15:
16: struct ContactItem
17: {
18:     string name;
19:     string phoneNum;
20:     string displayAs;
21:
22:     ContactItem (const string& nameInit, const string & phone)
23:     {
24:         name = nameInit;
25:         phoneNum = phone;
26:         displayAs = (name + ": " + phoneNum);
27:     }
28:
29:     // used by set::find() given contact list item
30:     bool operator == (const ContactItem& itemToCompare) const
31:     {
32:         return (itemToCompare.name == this->name);
33:     }
34:
35:     // used to sort
36:     bool operator < (const ContactItem& itemToCompare) const
37:     {
38:         return (this->name < itemToCompare.name);
39:     }
40:
41:     // Used in DisplayContents via cout
42:     operator const char*() const
43:     {
44:         return displayAs.c_str();
45:     }
46: };
47:
48: int main ()
49: {
50:     set<ContactItem> setContacts;
51:     setContacts.insert(ContactItem("Jack Welsch", "+1 7889 879 879"));
52:     setContacts.insert(ContactItem("Bill Gates", "+1 97 7897 8799 8"));
53:     setContacts.insert(ContactItem("Angi Merkel", "+49 23456 5466"));
54:     setContacts.insert(ContactItem("Vlad Putin", "+7 6645 4564 797"));
55:     setContacts.insert(ContactItem("John Travolta", "91 234 4564 789"));
56:     setContacts.insert(ContactItem("Ben Affleck", "+1 745 641 314"));
57:     DisplayContents(setContacts);
58:
59:     cout << "Enter a name you wish to delete: ";
60:     string inputName;
61:     getline(cin, inputName);
62:
63:     auto contactFound = setContacts.find(ContactItem(inputName, ""));
64:     if(contactFound != setContacts.end())
```

19

```
65:    {
66:        setContacts.erase(contactFound);
67:        cout << "Displaying contents after erasing " << inputName << endl;
68:        DisplayContents(setContacts);
69:    }
70:    else
71:        cout << "Contact not found" << endl;
72:
73:    return 0;
74: }
```

Output ▼

```
Angi Merkel: +49 23456 5466
Ben Affleck: +1 745 641 314
Bill Gates: +1 97 7897 8799 8
Jack Welsch: +1 7889 879 879
John Travolta: 91 234 4564 789
Vlad Putin: +7 6645 4564 797

Enter a name you wish to delete: John Travolta
Displaying contents after erasing John Travolta
Angi Merkel: +49 23456 5466
Ben Affleck: +1 745 641 314
Bill Gates: +1 97 7897 8799 8
Jack Welsch: +1 7889 879 879
Vlad Putin: +7 6645 4564 797
```

Analysis ▼

This is similar to Listing 18.7 that sorted a `std::list` in alphabetical order, the difference being that in the case of `std::set`, sort happens on insertion. As the output indicates, you didn't need to invoke any function to ensure that elements in the `set` are sorted because they're sorted on insertion, using `operator<` that you implemented in Lines 36–39. You give the user the choice to delete an entry, and Line 63 demonstrates the call to `find()` to locate that entry that is deleted in Line 66 using `erase()`.

TIP

This implementation of the telephone directory is based on the STL `set` and therefore does not allow for multiple entries containing the same value. If you need your implementation of the directory to allow two people with the same name to be stored, you would choose the STL `multiset`. The preceding code would still work correctly if `setContacts` were to be a `multiset`. To make further use of the `multiset`'s capability to store multiple entries of the same value, you use the `count()` member function to know the number of items that hold a particular value.

Pros and Cons of Using STL set and multiset

The STL set and multiset provide significant advantages in applications that need frequent lookups because their contents are sorted and therefore quicker to locate. However, to provide this advantage, the container needs to sort elements at insertion time. Thus, there is an overhead in inserting elements because elements are sorted—an overhead that might be a worthwhile compromise if you need to use features and functions such as find() often.

find() makes use of the internal binary tree structure. This sorted binary tree structure results in another implicit disadvantage over sequential containers such as the vector. In a vector, the element pointed to by an iterator (say, one returned by a std::find() operation) can be overwritten by a new value. In case of a set, however, elements are sorted by the set class according to their respective values, and therefore overwriting an element using an iterator should never be done, even if that were programmatically possible.

STL Hash Set Implementation std::unordered_set and std::unordered_multiset

The STL std::set and STL std::multiset sort elements (that are simultaneously the keys) on the basis of std::less<T> or a supplied predicate. Searching in a sorted container is faster than searching in an unsorted container such as a vector, and std::sort() offers logarithmic complexity. This means that the time spent finding an element in a set is not directly proportional to the number of elements in the set, rather to the LOG thereof. So, on average it takes twice as long to search in a set of 10,000 elements as it would take in a set of 100 (as $100^2 = 10000$, or $\log(10000) = 2 \times \log(100)$).

19

Yet, this dramatic improvement of performance over an unsorted container (where search is directly proportional to the number of elements) is not enough at times. Programmers and mathematicians alike seek constant-time insertions and sort possibilities, and one of them uses a hash-based implementation, where a hash function is used to determine the sorting index. Elements inserted into a hash set are first evaluated by a hash function that generates a unique index, which is the index of the *bucket* they're placed in.

The hash set variant provided by STL since C++11 is the container class std::unordered_set.

TIP

> To use STL containers std::unordered_set or std::unordered_multiset, include
>
> #include<unordered_set>

The usage of this class doesn't change too much in comparison to a `std::set`:

```
// instantiation:
unordered_set<int> usetInt;

// insertion of an element
usetInt.insert(1000);

// find():
auto elementFound = usetInt.find(1000);

if (elementFound != usetInt.end())
   cout << *elementFound << endl;
```

Yet, one very important feature of an `unordered_set` is the availability of a hash function that is responsible for deciding the sorting order:

```
unordered_set<int>::hasher HFn = usetInt.hash_function();
```

The decision to use a `std::unordered_set` or a `std::set` is best taken after the performance of the respective containers is measured in simulations involving operations and data volumes that closely resemble real-world usage. Listing 19.6 demonstrates the usage of some of the common methods supplied by `std::hash_set`.

LISTING 19.6   `std::unordered_set` and the Use of `insert()`, `find()`, `size()`, `max_bucket_count()`, `load_factor()`, and `max_load_factor()`

```
 0: #include<unordered_set>
 1: #include <iostream>
 2: using namespace std;
 3:
 4: template <typename T>
 5: void DisplayContents(const T& cont)
 6: {
 7:    cout << "Unordered set contains: ";
 8:    for (auto element = cont.cbegin();
 9:         element != cont.cend();
10:         ++ element )
11:       cout<< *element << ' ';
12:
13:    cout << endl;
14:
15:    cout << "Number of elements, size() = " << cont.size() << endl;
16:    cout << "Bucket count = " << cont.bucket_count() << endl;
17:    cout << "Max load factor = " << cont.max_load_factor() << endl;
18:    cout << "Load factor: " << cont.load_factor() << endl << endl;
19: }
20:
21: int main()
```

```
22: {
23:     unordered_set<int> usetInt{ 1, -3, 2017, 300, -1, 989, -300, 9 };
24:     DisplayContents(usetInt);
25:     usetInt.insert(999);
26:     DisplayContents(usetInt);
27:
28:     cout << "Enter int you want to check for existence in set: ";
29:     int input = 0;
30:     cin >> input;
31:     auto elementFound = usetInt.find(input);
32:
33:     if (elementFound != usetInt.end())
34:         cout << *elementFound << " found in set" << endl;
35:     else
36:         cout << input << " not available in set" << endl;
37:
38:     return 0;
39: }
```

Output ▼

```
Unordered set contains: 9 1 -3 989 -1 2017 300 -300
Number of elements, size() = 8
Bucket count = 8
Max load factor = 1
Load factor: 1

Unordered set contains: 9 1 -3 989 -1 2017 300 -300 999
Number of elements, size() = 9
Bucket count = 64
Max load factor = 1
Load factor: 0.140625

Enter int you want to check for existence in set: -300
-300 found in set
```

Analysis ▼

The sample creates an `unordered_set` of integers; inserts values into it using List Initialization at Line 23; and then displays contents, including statistics supplied by methods `max_bucket_count()`, `load_factor()`, and `max_load_factor()` as shown in Lines 15–18. The output tells that the bucket count is initially at eight, with eight elements in the container, resulting in a load factor of 1, which is the same as the maximum load factor. When a ninth element is inserted into the `unordered_set`, it reorganizes itself, creates 64 buckets, and re-creates the hash table and the load factor reduces. The rest of the code in `main()` demonstrates how the syntax for finding elements in an `unordered_set` is similar to that in a set. `find()` returns an iterator that needs to be checked for success of `find()` as shown in Line 33 before it can be used.

19

NOTE

> As hashes are typically used in a hash table to look up a value given a key, see the section on `std::unordered_map` in Lesson 20, "STL Map Classes."
>
> `std::unordered_map` is an implementation of a hash table that was new in C++11.

DO	DON'T
DO remember that STL `set` and `multiset` containers are optimized for situations that involve frequent search.	**DON'T** forget to program `operator<` and `operator==` for classes that can be collected in containers such as `set` or `multiset`. The former becomes the sort predicate, whereas the latter is used for functions such as `set::find()`.
DO remember that a `std::multiset` allows multiple elements (keys) of the same value whereas `std::set` permits only unique values.	**DON'T** use `std::set` or `std::multiset` in scenarios with frequent insertions and infrequent searches. `std::vector` or `std::list` is usually better suited to such cases.
DO use `multiset::count(value)` to find the number of elements of a particular `value`.	
DO remember that `set::size()` or `multiset::size()` gives you the number of elements in the container.	

Summary

In this lesson, you learned about using the STL `set` and `multiset`, their significant member functions, and their characteristics. You also saw their application in the programming of a simple menu-based telephone directory that also features search and erase functions.

Q&A

Q How would I declare a `set` of integers to be sorted and stored in order of descending magnitude?

A `set <int>` is a set of integers. This takes the default sort predicate `std::less <T>` to sort items in order of ascending magnitude and can also be expressed as `set <int, less <int>>`. To sort in order of descending magnitude, define the `set` as `set <int, greater <int>>`.

Q What would happen if, in a `set` of strings, I inserted the string `"Jack"` twice?

A A `set` is not meant to be used to contain non-unique values. The set of strings would contain only one instance of `"Jack"`.

Q In the preceding example, if I wanted to have two instances of `"Jack"`, what would I change?

A By design, a `set` holds only unique values. You would need to change your selection of container to a `multiset`.

Q What `multiset` member function returns the count of items of a particular value in the container?

A `count(value)` is the function of interest.

Q I have found an element in the `set` using the `find()` function and have an iterator pointing to it. Would I use this iterator to change the value being pointed to?

A No. Some STL implementations might allow the user to change the value of an element inside a `set` via an iterator returned by, for example, `find`. However, this is not the correct thing to do. An iterator to an element in the `set` should be used as a `const` iterator—even when the STL implementation has not enforced it as such.

Workshop

The Workshop contains quiz questions to help solidify your understanding of the material covered and exercises to provide you with experience in using what you've learned. Try to answer the quiz and exercise questions before checking the answers in Appendix E, and be certain you understand the answers before going to the next lesson.

19

Quiz

1. You declare a set of integers as `set <int>`. What function supplies the sort criteria?

2. Where would you find duplicate elements in a `multiset`?

3. What `set` or `multiset` function supplies the number of elements in the container?

Exercises

1. Extend the telephone directory example in this lesson to find a person's name given a phone number. (Hint: Adjust operators < and == and ensure that items are sorted and compared according to phone numbers.)

2. Define a `multiset` to store entered words and their meanings; that is, make a `multiset` work as a dictionary. (Hint: The `multiset` should be one of a structure that contains two strings: the word and its meaning.)

3. Demonstrate via a simple program that a `set` cannot accept duplicate entries, whereas a `multiset` can.

LESSON 20
STL Map Classes

The Standard Template Library (STL) supplies the programmer with container classes that help with applications that require frequent and quick searches.

This lesson covers

- How STL `map` and `multimap`, `unordered_map`, and `unordered_multimap` containers can be of use to you
- Insertion, removal, and search of elements
- Supplying a custom sort predicate
- Basics of how hash tables work

An Introduction to STL Map Classes

The `map` and `multimap` are key-value pair containers that allow for a lookup on the basis of a key as shown in Figure 20.1.

FIGURE 20.1
Visual illustration of a container for pairs, each holding a key and a value.

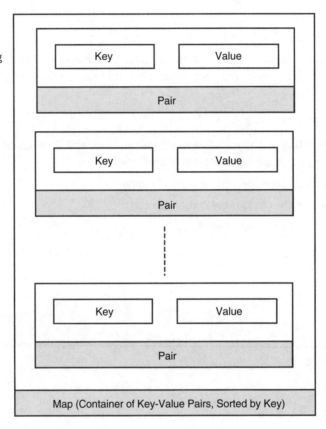

The difference between the `map` and the `multimap` is that only the latter allows for duplicates, whereas the former can store only unique keys.

To facilitate quick searching, STL implementations of the `map` and `multimap` internally look like binary trees. This means that elements inserted in a `map` or a `multimap` are sorted on insertion. It also means that, unlike in a vector where elements at a position can be replaced by another, elements in a `map` at a given position cannot be replaced by a new element of a different value. This is because the `map` would ideally like to have it placed in a possible different location in accordance with its value relative to those in the internal tree.

<table>
<tr><td>TIP</td><td>To use class `std::map` or `std::multimap`, include header:

`#include<map>`</td></tr>
</table>

Basic `std::map` and `std::multimap` Operations

STL map and `multimap` are template classes that need to be instantiated before you can use any of their member functions.

Instantiating a `std::map` or `std::multimap`

Instantiating a map or `multimap` of an integer as key and a string as value requires a specialization of the template class `std::map` or `std::multimap`. The template instantiation of the map class needs the programmer to specify the key type, the value type, and optionally a predicate that helps the map class to sort the elements on insertion. Therefore, typical map instantiation syntax looks like this:

```
#include <map>
using namespace std;
...
map <keyType, valueType, Predicate=std::less <keyType>> mapObj;
multimap <keyType, valueType, Predicate=std::less <keyType>> mmapObj;
```

Thus, the third template parameter is optional. When you supply only the key type and the value type, ignoring the third template parameter, `std::map` and `std::multimap` default to `class std::less<>` to define the sort criteria. Thus, a map or `multimap` that maps an integer to a string looks like this:

```
std::map<int, string> mapIntToStr;
std::multimap<int, string> mmapIntToStr;
```

Listing 20.1 illustrates instantiation techniques in greater detail.

20

LISTING 20.1 Instantiating map and `multimap` Objects That Map an int Key to a string Value

```
0: #include<map>
1: #include<string>
2:
3: template<typename keyType>
4: struct ReverseSort
```

```
 5: {
 6:     bool operator()(const keyType& key1, const keyType& key2)
 7:     {
 8:         return (key1 > key2);
 9:     }
10: };
11:
12: int main ()
13: {
14:     using namespace std;
15:
16:     // map and multimap key of type int to value of type string
17:     map<int, string> mapIntToStr1;
18:     multimap<int, string> mmapIntToStr1;
19:
20:     // map and multimap constructed as a copy of another
21:     map<int, string> mapIntToStr2(mapIntToStr1);
22:     multimap<int, string> mmapIntToStr2(mmapIntToStr1);
23:
24:     // map and multimap constructed given a part of another map or multimap
25:     map<int, string> mapIntToStr3(mapIntToStr1.cbegin(),
26:                                     mapIntToStr1.cend());
27:
28:     multimap<int, string> mmapIntToStr3(mmapIntToStr1.cbegin(),
29:                                         mmapIntToStr1.cend());
30:
31:     // map and multimap with a predicate that inverses sort order
32:     map<int, string, ReverseSort<int>> mapIntToStr4
33:         (mapIntToStr1.cbegin(), mapIntToStr1.cend());
34:
35:     multimap<int, string, ReverseSort<int>> mmapIntToStr4
36:         (mapIntToStr1.cbegin(), mapIntToStr1.cend());
37:
38:     return 0;
39: }
```

Analysis ▼

For a start, focus on `main()` in Lines 12–39. The simplest `map` and `multimap` of an integer key to a string value can be seen in Lines 17 and 18. Lines 25–28 demonstrate the creation of a `map` or a `multimap` initialized to a range of values from another as input. Lines 31–36 demonstrate how you instantiate a `map` or `multimap` with your own custom sort criteria. Note that the default sort (in the previous instantiations) uses `std::less<T>` that would sort elements in the increasing order. If you want to change this behavior, you supply a predicate that is a `class` or a `struct` that implements `operator()`. Such a predicate `struct ReverseSort` is in Lines 3–10 and has been used in the instantiation of a `map` at Line 32 and a `multimap` at Line 35.

Inserting Elements in an STL `map` or `multimap`

Most functions in a map and `multimap` work in a similar fashion. They accept similar parameters and return similar value types. You can insert elements in both kinds of containers by using the `insert` member function:

```
std::map<int, std::string> mapIntToStr1;
// insert pair of key and value using make_pair function
mapIntToStr.insert (make_pair (-1, "Minus One"));
```

As these two containers maintain elements in key-value pairs, you can also directly supply a `std::pair` initialized to the key and value to be inserted:

```
mapIntToStr.insert (pair <int, string>(1000, "One Thousand"));
```

Alternatively, you can use an array-like syntax to insert, which does appear quite user friendly and is supported via subscript `operator[]`:

```
mapIntToStr [1000000] = "One Million";
```

You can also instantiate a `multimap` as a copy of a `map`:

```
std::multimap<int, std::string> mmapIntToStr(mapIntToStr.cbegin(),
                                             mapIntToStr.cend());
```

Listing 20.2 demonstrates the various instantiation methods.

LISTING 20.2 Inserting Elements in a `map` and `multimap` Using Overloads of `insert()` and Array Semantics via `operator[]`

```
 0: #include <map>
 1: #include <iostream>
 2: #include<string>
 3:
 4: using namespace std;
 5:
 6: // Type-define the map and multimap definition for easy readability
 7: typedef map <int, string> MAP_INT_STRING;
 8: typedef multimap <int, string> MMAP_INT_STRING;
 9:
10: template <typename T>
11: void DisplayContents (const T& cont)
12: {
13:     for (auto element = cont.cbegin();
14:            element != cont.cend();
15:          ++ element )
16:        cout << element->first << " -> " << element->second << endl;
17:
18:     cout << endl;
19: }
```

20

```
20:
21: int main ()
22: {
23:     MAP_INT_STRING mapIntToStr;
24:
25:     // Insert key-value pairs into the map using value_type
26:     mapIntToStr.insert (MAP_INT_STRING::value_type (3, "Three"));
27:
28:     // Insert a pair using function make_pair
29:     mapIntToStr.insert (make_pair (-1, "Minus One"));
30:
31:     // Insert a pair object directly
32:     mapIntToStr.insert (pair <int, string>(1000, "One Thousand"));
33:
34:     // Use an array-like syntax for inserting key-value pairs
35:     mapIntToStr [1000000] = "One Million";
36:
37:     cout << "The map contains " << mapIntToStr.size ();
38:     cout << " key-value pairs. They are: " << endl;
39:     DisplayContents(mapIntToStr);
40:
41:     // instantiate a multimap that is a copy of a map
42:     MMAP_INT_STRING mmapIntToStr(mapIntToStr.cbegin(),
43:                                 mapIntToStr.cend());
44:
45:     // The insert function works the same way for multimap too
46:     // A multimap can store duplicates - insert a duplicate
47:     mmapIntToStr.insert (make_pair (1000, "Thousand"));
48:
49:     cout << endl << "The multimap contains " << mmapIntToStr.size();
50:     cout << " key-value pairs. They are: " << endl;
51:     cout << "The elements in the multimap are: " << endl;
52:     DisplayContents(mmapIntToStr);
53:
54:     // The multimap can return number of pairs with same key
55:     cout << "The number of pairs in the multimap with 1000 as their key: "
56:          << mmapIntToStr.count (1000) << endl;
57:
58:     return 0;
59: }
```

Output ▼

```
The map contains 4 key-value pairs. They are:
-1 -> Minus One
3 -> Three
1000 -> One Thousand
1000000 -> One Million
```

```
The multimap contains 5 key-value pairs. They are:
The elements in the multimap are:
-1 -> Minus One
3 -> Three
1000 -> One Thousand
1000 -> Thousand
1000000 -> One Million

The number of pairs in the multimap with 1000 as their key: 2
```

Analysis ▼

Note how we `typedef` the template instantiation of the `map` and `multimap` in Lines 7 and 8. You can do this to make your code look a bit simpler (and reduce clutter caused by template syntax). Lines 10–19 are a form of `DisplayContents()` adapted for `map` and `multimap` in which the iterator is used to access `first`, which indicates the key, and `second`, which indicates the value. Lines 26–32 demonstrate the different ways of inserting a key-value pair into a `map` using overloaded variants of method `insert()`. Line 35 demonstrates how you can use array-semantics via `operator[]` to insert elements in a `map`. Note that these insert mechanisms work as well for a `multimap`, which is demonstrated in Line 47, where you insert a duplicate into a `multimap`. Interestingly, the `multimap` is initialized as a copy of the `map`, as shown in Lines 42 and 43. The output demonstrates how the two containers have automatically sorted the input key-value pairs in ascending order of keys. The output also demonstrates that the `multimap` can store two pairs with the same key (in this case `1000`). Line 56 demonstrates the usage of `multimap::count()` to tell the number of elements with a supplied key in the container.

Finding Elements in an STL `map`

Associative containers, such as `map` and `multimap`, feature a member function called `find()` that enables you to find a value given a key. The result of a `find()` operation is always an iterator:

```
multimap <int, string>::const_iterator pairFound = mapIntToStr.find(key);
```

You would first check this iterator for the success of `find()` and then use it to access the found value:

```
if (pairFound != mapIntToStr.end())
{
   cout << "Key " << pairFound->first << " points to Value: ";
   cout << pairFound->second << endl;
}
else
   cout << "Sorry, pair with key " << key << " not in map" << endl;
```

TIP

If you are using C++11-compliant compilers, the iterator declaration can be simplified using keyword `auto`:

```
auto pairFound = mapIntToStr.find(key);
```

The compiler determines the type of the iterator automatically by inferring it from the declared return value of `map::find()`.

The example in Listing 20.3 demonstrates the usage of `multimap::find()`.

LISTING 20.3 Using `find()` Member Function to Locate a Key-Value Pair in a `map`

```
0: #include <map>
1: #include <iostream>
2: #include <string>
3: using namespace std;
4:
5: template <typename T>
6: void DisplayContents (const T& cont)
7: {
8:     for (auto element = cont.cbegin();
9:            element != cont.cend();
10:           ++ element )
11:       cout << element->first << " -> " << element->second << endl;
12:
13:     cout << endl;
14: }
15:
16: int main()
17: {
18:     map<int, string> mapIntToStr;
19:
20:     mapIntToStr.insert(make_pair(3, "Three"));
21:     mapIntToStr.insert(make_pair(45, "Forty Five"));
22:     mapIntToStr.insert(make_pair(-1, "Minus One"));
23:     mapIntToStr.insert(make_pair(1000, "Thousand"));
24:
25:     cout << "The multimap contains " << mapIntToStr.size();
26:     cout << " key-value pairs. They are: " << endl;
27:
28:     // Print the contents of the map to the screen
29:     DisplayContents(mapIntToStr);
30:
31:     cout << "Enter the key you wish to find: ";
32:     int key = 0;
33:     cin >> key;
34:
```

```
35:     auto pairFound = mapIntToStr.find(key);
36:     if (pairFound != mapIntToStr.end())
37:     {
38:         cout << "Key " << pairFound->first << " points to Value: ";
39:         cout << pairFound->second << endl;
40:     }
41:     else
42:         cout << "Sorry, pair with key " << key << " not in map" << endl;
43:
44:      return 0;
45: }
```

Output ▼

```
The multimap contains 4 key-value pairs. They are:
-1 -> Minus One
3 -> Three
45 -> Forty Five
1000 -> Thousand

Enter the key you wish to find: 45
Key 45 points to Value: Forty Five
```

Next, run (where `find()` locates no matching key):

```
The multimap contains 4 key-value pairs. They are:
-1 -> Minus One
3 -> Three
45 -> Forty Five
1000 -> Thousand

Enter the key you wish to find: 2011
Sorry, pair with key 2011 not in map
```

Analysis ▼

Lines 20–23 in `main()` populate a `map` with sample pairs, each mapping an integer key to a string value. When the user supplies a key to be used in finding in the `map`, Line 35 uses the `find()` function to look up the supplied key in the map. `map::find()` always returns an iterator, and it is always wise to check for the success of the `find()` operation by comparing this iterator to `end()`, as shown in Line 36. If the iterator is indeed valid, use member `second` to access the value, as shown in Line 39. In the second run, you input a key `2011` that is not represented in the map, and an error message is displayed to the user.

20

<table>
<tr><td>CAUTION</td><td>Never use the result of a find() operation directly without checking the iterator returned for success.</td></tr>
</table>

Finding Elements in an STL `multimap`

If Listing 20.3 were a `multimap`, opening the possibility that the container contains multiple pairs with the same key, you would need to find the values that correspond to the repeating key. Hence, in the case of a `multiset` you would use `multiset::count()` to find the number of values corresponding to a key and increment the iterator to access those consequently placed values.

```
auto pairFound = mmapIntToStr.find(key);

// Check if find() succeeded
if(pairFound != mmapIntToStr.end())
{
    // Find the number of pairs that have the same supplied key
    size_t numPairsInMap = mmapIntToStr.count(1000);

    for(size_t counter = 0;
        counter < numPairsInMap;   // stay within bounds
        ++ counter )
    {
        cout << "Key: " << pairFound->first;   // key
        cout << ", Value [" << counter << "] = ";
        cout << pairFound->second << endl;     // value

        ++ pairFound;
    }
}
else
    cout << "Element not found in the multimap";
```

Erasing Elements from an STL `map` or `multimap`

The `map` and `multimap` feature a member function, `erase()`, which deletes an element from the container. The `erase()` is invoked with the key as the parameter to delete all pairs with a certain key:

```
mapObject.erase (key);
```

Another form of the `erase()` function allows the deletion of a particular element given an iterator that points to it:

```
mapObject.erase(element);
```

You can erase a range of elements from a `map` or a `multimap` using iterators that supply the bounds:

```
mapObject.erase (lowerBound, upperBound);
```

Listing 20.4 illustrates the usage of the `erase()` functions.

LISTING 20.4   Erasing Elements from a `multimap`

```
0: #include<map>
1: #include<iostream>
2: #include<string>
3: using namespace std;
4:
5: template<typename T>
6: void DisplayContents(const T& cont)
7: {
8:     for (auto element = cont.cbegin();
9:             element != cont.cend();
10:            ++ element)
11:       cout<< element->first<< " -> "<< element->second<< endl;
12:
13:     cout<< endl;
14: }
15:
16: int main()
17: {
18:     multimap<int, string> mmapIntToStr;
19:
20:     // Insert key-value pairs into the multimap
21:     mmapIntToStr.insert(make_pair(3, "Three"));
22:     mmapIntToStr.insert(make_pair(45, "Forty Five"));
23:     mmapIntToStr.insert(make_pair(-1, "Minus One"));
24:     mmapIntToStr.insert(make_pair(1000, "Thousand"));
25:
26:     // Insert duplicates into the multimap
27:     mmapIntToStr.insert(make_pair(-1, "Minus One"));
28:     mmapIntToStr.insert(make_pair(1000, "Thousand"));
29:
30:     cout<< "The multimap contains "<< mmapIntToStr.size();
31:     cout<< " key-value pairs. "<< "They are: "<< endl;
32:     DisplayContents(mmapIntToStr);
33:
34:     // Erasing an element with key as -1 from the multimap
35:     auto numPairsErased = mmapIntToStr.erase(-1);
36:     cout<< "Erased " << numPairsErased << " pairs with -1 as key."<< endl;
37:
38:     // Erase an element given an iterator from the multimap
39:     auto pair = mmapIntToStr.find(45);
```

20

```
40:     if(pair != mmapIntToStr.end())
41:     {
42:        mmapIntToStr.erase(pair);
43:        cout<< "Erased a pair with 45 as key using an iterator"<< endl;
44:     }
45:
46:     // Erase a range from the multimap...
47:     cout << "Erasing the range of pairs with 1000 as key." << endl;
48:     mmapIntToStr.erase(mmapIntToStr.lower_bound(1000),
48:                             mmapIntToStr.upper_bound(1000) );
50:
51:     cout<< "The multimap now contains "<< mmapIntToStr.size();
52:     cout<< " key-value pair(s)."<< "They are: "<< endl;
53:     DisplayContents(mmapIntToStr);
54:
55:     return 0;
56: }
```

Output ▼

```
The multimap contains 6 key-value pairs. They are:
-1 -> Minus One
-1 -> Minus One
3 -> Three
45 -> Forty Five
1000 -> Thousand
1000 -> Thousand

Erased 2 pairs with -1 as key.
Erased a pair with 45 as key using an iterator
Erasing the range of pairs with 1000 as key.
The multimap now contains 1 key-value pair(s).They are:
3 -> Three
```

Analysis ▼

Lines 21–28 insert sample values into the multimap, some of them being duplicates (because a multimap, unlike a map, does support the insertion of pairs with duplicate keys). After pairs have been inserted into the multimap, the code erases items by using the version of the erase function that accepts a key and erases all items with that key (–1) as shown in Line 35. The return value of map::erase(key) is the number of elements erased, which is displayed on the screen. In Line 39, you use the iterator returned by find(45) to erase a pair from the map with key 45. Lines 48 and 49 demonstrate how pairs with a key can be deleted given a range specified by lower_bound() and upper_bound().

Supplying a Custom Sort Predicate

The `map` and `multimap` template definition includes a third parameter that accepts the sort predicate for the `map` to function correctly. This third parameter, when not supplied (as in the preceding examples), is substituted with the default sort criterion provided by `std::less <>`, which essentially compares two objects using `operator <`.

To supply a different sort criterion than what the key-type supports, you would typically program a binary predicate in the form of a class or a struct using `operator()`:

```
template<typename keyType>
struct Predicate
{
    bool operator()(const keyType& key1, const keyType& key2)
    {
        // your sort priority logic here
    }
};
```

A map that holds a `std::string` type as the key has a default sort criterion based on the `operator <` defined by the `std::string` class, triggered via default sort predicate `std::less<T>` and therefore is case sensitive. For many applications, such as a telephone directory, it is important to feature an insertion and search operation that is not case sensitive. One way of solving this requirement is to supply the `map` with a sort predicate that returns either true or false on the basis of a comparison that is not case sensitive:

```
map <keyType, valueType, Predicate> mapObject;
```

Listing 20.5 explains this in detail.

LISTING 20.5   Supplying a Custom Sort Predicate—A Telephone Directory

```
0: #include<map>
1: #include<algorithm>
2: #include<string>
3: #include<iostream>
4: using namespace std;
5:
6: template <typename T>
7: void DisplayContents (const T& cont)
8: {
9:     for (auto element = cont.cbegin();
10:            element != cont.cend();
11:            ++ element )
12:        cout << element->first << " -> " << element->second << endl;
13:
```

20

```
14:    cout << endl;
15: }
16:
17: struct PredIgnoreCase
18: {
19:     bool operator()(const string& str1, const string& str2) const
20:     {
21:         string str1NoCase(str1), str2NoCase(str2);
22:          transform(str1.begin(), str1.end(), str1NoCase.begin(), ::tolower);
23:          transform(str2.begin(), str2.end(), str2NoCase.begin(), ::tolower);
24:
25:         return(str1NoCase< str2NoCase);
26:     };
27: };
28:
29: typedef map<string, string> DIR_WITH_CASE;
30: typedef map<string, string, PredIgnoreCase> DIR_NOCASE;
31:
32: int main()
33: {
34:     // Case-sensitive directorycase of string-key plays no role
35:     DIR_WITH_CASE dirWithCase;
36:
37:     dirWithCase.insert(make_pair("John", "2345764"));
38:     dirWithCase.insert(make_pair("JOHN", "2345764"));
39:     dirWithCase.insert(make_pair("Sara", "42367236"));
40:     dirWithCase.insert(make_pair("Jack", "32435348"));
41:
42:     cout << "Displaying contents of the case-sensitive map:"<< endl;
43:     DisplayContents(dirWithCase);
44:
45:     // Case-insensitive mapcase of string-key affects insertion & search
46:     DIR_NOCASE dirNoCase(dirWithCase.begin(), dirWithCase.end());
47:
48:     cout << "Displaying contents of the case-insensitive map:"<< endl;
49:     DisplayContents(dirNoCase);
50:
51:     // Search for a name in the two maps and display result
52:     cout << "Please enter a name to search"<< endl<< "> ";
53:     string name;
54:     cin >> name;
55:
56:     auto pairWithCase = dirWithCase.find(name);
57:     if(pairWithCase != dirWithCase.end())
58:        cout << "Num in case-sens. dir: " << pairWithCase->second << endl;
59:     else
60:        cout << "Num not found in case-sensitive dir" << endl;
61:
62:     auto pairNoCase = dirNoCase.find(name);
63:     if (pairNoCase != dirNoCase.end())
64:        cout << "Num found in CI dir: " << pairNoCase->second << endl;
```

```
65:      else
66:          cout << "Num not found in the case-insensitive directory" << endl;
67:
68:      return 0;
69: }
```

Output ▼

```
Displaying contents of the case-sensitive map:
JOHN -> 2345764
Jack -> 32435348
John -> 2345764
Sara -> 42367236

Displaying contents of the case-insensitive map:
Jack -> 32435348
JOHN -> 2345764
Sara -> 42367236

Please enter a name to search
> jack
Num not found in case-sensitive dir
Num found in CI dir: 32435348
```

Analysis ▼

The code in question contains two directories with equal content, one that has been instantiated with the default sort predicate, using `std::less<T>` and case-sensitive `std::string::operator<`, and another that has been instantiated with a predicate struct `PredIgnoreCase` defined in Lines 17–27. This predicate compares two strings after reducing them to lowercase, thereby ensuring a "case-insensitive" comparison that will evaluate `"John"` and `"JOHN"` as equals. The output indicates that when you search the two maps for `"jack"` the map with the case-insensitive instantiation is able to locate `"Jack"` in its records, whereas the map with default instantiation is unable to find this entry. Also note how the case-sensitive map has two entries for John, one of them being `"JOHN"`, while the case-insensitive map that identified `"John"` and `"JOHN"` as duplicate elements with an identical key has only one element with the same.

20

NOTE

In Listing 20.5, struct `PredIgnoreCase` can also be a class if you add the keyword `public` for `operator()`. For a C++ compiler, a `struct` is akin to a class with members that are `public` by default and inherit `public` by default.

This sample demonstrated how you can use predicates to customize the behavior of a map. It also implies that the key could potentially be of any type, and that the programmer can supply a predicate that defines the behavior of the map for that type. Note that the predicate was a `struct` that implemented `operator()`. Such objects that double as functions are called *function objects* or *functors*. This topic is addressed in further detail in Lesson 21, "Understanding Function Objects."

NOTE _____

> The `std::map` is well suited for storing key-value pairs where you can look up a value given a key. `map` does probably deliver better performance than an STL `vector` or `list` when it comes to searching. Yet, it does slow down when the number of elements increases. The operational performance of a `map` is said to be logarithmic in nature—that is, proportional to the LOG of the number of elements placed in the map.
>
> In simple words, logarithmic complexity means that a container such as `std::map` or `std::set` needs twice as long in finding an element when it contains 10,000 elements as it would need if it contained 100 ($100^2 = 10000$).
>
> An unsorted `vector` presents linear complexity when it comes to search, which means that it would be a 100 times slower if it contained 10,000 elements instead of 100.

So, while logarithmic complexity already looks good, one should remember that insertions in a map (or `multimap` or `set` or `multiset`) get slower, too, as these containers sort on insertion. Thus, the search for faster containers continues, and mathematicians and programmers alike seek the holy grail of containers featuring constant-time insertions and searches. The Hash Table is one such container that promises constant-time insertions and near-constant–time searches (in most cases), given a key, independent of the size of the container.

STL's Hash Table-Based Key-Value Container

Starting with C++11, the STL supports a hash map in the form of class `std::unordered_map`. To use this template container class include

```
#include<unordered_map>
```

The `unordered_map` promises average constant-time insertion and the removal and lookup of arbitrary elements in the container.

How Hash Tables Work

Although it is not within the scope of this book to discuss this topic in detail (for it has been the subject of one PhD thesis too many), let's just try to grasp the basics of what makes hash tables work.

A hash table can be viewed as a collection of key-value pairs, where given a key, the table can find a value. The difference between the hash table and a simple map is that a hash table stores key-value pairs in buckets, each bucket having an index that defines its relative position in the table (akin to an array). This index is decided by a hash-function that uses the key as input:

```
Index = HashFunction(key, TableSize);
```

When performing a `find()` given a key, `HashFunction()` is used once again to determine the position of the element and the table returns the value at the position, like an array would return an element stored within it. In cases where `HashFunction()` is not optimally programmed, more than one element would have the same Index, landing in the same bucket—that internally would be a list of elements. In such cases, called *collisions*, a search would be slower and not a constant any more.

Using `unordered_map` and `unordered_multimap`

Introduced starting in C++11, these two containers that implement hash tables are not too different from `std::map` and `std::multimap`, respectively. Instantiation, insertion, and find follow similar patterns:

```cpp
// instantiate unordered_map of int to string:
unordered_map<int, string> umapIntToStr;

// insert()
umapIntToStr.insert(make_pair(1000, "Thousand"));

// find():
auto pairFound = umapIntToStr.find(1000);
cout << pairFound->first << " - " << pairFound->second << endl;

// find value using array semantics:
cout << "umapIntToStr[1000] = " << umapIntToStr[1000] << endl;
```

20

Yet, one important feature of an `unordered_map` is the availability of a hash function that is responsible for deciding the sorting order:

```
unordered_map<int, string>::hasher hFn =
        umapIntToStr.hash_function();
```

You can view the priority assigned to a key by invoking the hash function for a key:

```
size_t hashingVal = hFn(1000);
```

As an `unordered_map` stores key-value pairs in buckets, it does an automatic load balancing when the number of elements in the map reach or tend to reach the number of buckets in the same:

```
cout << "Load factor: " << umapIntToStr.load_factor() << endl;
cout << "Max load factor = " << umapIntToStr.max_load_factor() << endl;
cout << "Max bucket count = " << umapIntToStr.max_bucket_count() << endl;
```

`load_factor()` is an indicator of the extent to which buckets in the `unordered_map` have been filled. When `load_factor()` exceeds `max_load_factor()` due to an insertion, the `map` reorganizes itself to increase the number of available buckets and rebuilds the hash table, as demonstrated by Listing 20.6.

TIP ────────
> `std::unordered_multimap` is similar to `unordered_map` except that it supports multiple pairs with the same key.

LISTING 20.6 Instantiating STL Hash Table Implementation `unordered_map`, Using `insert()`, `find()`, `size()`, `max_bucket_count()`, `load_factor()`, and `max_load_factor()`

```
0: #include<iostream>
1: #include<string>
2: #include<unordered_map>
3: using namespace std;
4:
5: template <typename T1, typename T2>
6: void DisplayUnorderedMap(unordered_map<T1, T2>& cont)
7: {
8:     cout << "Unordered Map contains: " << endl;
9:     for (auto element = cont.cbegin();
10:        element != cont.cend();
11:        ++ element )
12:        cout << element->first << " -> "<< element->second<< endl;
13:
```

```
14:        cout << "Number of pairs, size(): " << cont.size() << endl;
15:        cout << "Bucket count = " << cont.bucket_count() << endl;
16:        cout << "Current load factor: " << cont.load_factor() << endl;
17:        cout << "Max load factor = " << cont.max_load_factor() << endl;
18: }
19:
20: int main()
21: {
22:        unordered_map<int, string> umapIntToStr;
23:        umapIntToStr.insert(make_pair(1, "One"));
24:        umapIntToStr.insert(make_pair(45, "Forty Five"));
25:        umapIntToStr.insert(make_pair(1001, "Thousand One"));
26:        umapIntToStr.insert(make_pair(-2, "Minus Two"));
27:        umapIntToStr.insert(make_pair(-1000, "Minus One Thousand"));
28:        umapIntToStr.insert(make_pair(100, "One Hundred"));
29:        umapIntToStr.insert(make_pair(12, "Twelve"));
30:        umapIntToStr.insert(make_pair(-100, "Minus One Hundred"));
31:
32:        DisplayUnorderedMap<int, string>(umapIntToStr);
33:
34:        cout << "Inserting one more element" << endl;
35:        umapIntToStr.insert(make_pair(300, "Three Hundred"));
36:        DisplayUnorderedMap<int, string>(umapIntToStr);
37:
38:        cout << "Enter key to find for: ";
39:        int Key = 0;
40:        cin >> Key;
41:
42:        auto element = umapIntToStr.find(Key);
43:        if (element != umapIntToStr.end())
44:           cout << "Found! Key pairs with value " << element->second << endl;
45:        else
46:           cout << "Key has no corresponding pair value!" << endl;
47:
48:        return 0;
49: }
```

Output ▼

```
Unordered Map contains:
1 -> One
-2 -> Minus Two
45 -> Forty Five
1001 -> Thousand One
-1000 -> Minus One Thousand
12 -> Twelve
100 -> One Hundred
-100 -> Minus One Hundred
```

```
Number of pairs, size(): 8
Bucket count = 8
Current load factor: 1
Max load factor = 1
Inserting one more element
Unordered Map contains:
1 -> One
-2 -> Minus Two
45 -> Forty Five
1001 -> Thousand One
-1000 -> Minus One Thousand
12 -> Twelve
100 -> One Hundred
-100 -> Minus One Hundred
300 -> Three Hundred
Number of pairs, size(): 9
Bucket count = 64
Current load factor: 0.140625
Max load factor = 1
Enter key to find for: 300
Found! Key pairs with value Three Hundred
```

Analysis ▼

Observe the output and note how `unordered_map` that starts with an initial bucket count of eight, populated with eight pairs, resizes itself when a ninth pair has been inserted. This is when the bucket count is increased to 64. Note the usage of methods `bucket_count()`, `load_factor()`, and `max_load_factor()` in Lines 14–17. Apart from these, note that the rest of code really doesn't distinguish heavily compared to a `std::map`. This includes the usage of `find()` in Line 42, which returns an iterator as with a `std::map` that needs to be checked against `end()` to confirm success of the operation.

CAUTION	Don't rely on the order of elements in an `unordered_map` (hence the name) irrespective of the key. The order of an element relative to other elements in a map depends on many factors, including its key, order of insertion, and number of buckets to name a few.
	These containers are optimized for search performance and are not for you to rely on the order of elements when you iterate through them.

<table>
<tr><td>NOTE</td><td>

std::unordered_map supplies insertions and searches (in event of no collisions) that are almost constant time, independent of the number of elements contained. This, however, doesn't necessarily make the std::unordered_map superior to the std::map that provides logarithmic complexity in all situations. The constant could be a lot longer, making the former slow in cases where the number of elements contained is small.

It is important to base one's decision on the type of container after performing certain benchmark tests that simulate usage in a real scenario.

</td></tr>
</table>

DO	DON'T
DO use a map in those situations where you need a key-value pair where keys are unique.	**DON'T** forget that multimap::count(key) can tell you the number of pairs indexed using key available in the container.
DO use a multimap in those situations where you need a key-value pair where keys can repeat (for example, a telephone directory).	**DON'T** forget to check the result of a find() operation by comparing it against the end() of a container.
DO remember that both map and multimap, like other STL containers, feature member method size() that tells you the number of pairs they contain.	
DO use an unordered_map or unordered_multimap when constant-time insertions and searches are absolutely essential (typically when the number of elements is very high).	

20

Summary

In this lesson, you learned about using the STL map and multimap, their significant member functions, and their characteristics. You also learned that these containers have a logarithmic complexity and that STL supplies your hash table containers in the form of unordered_map and unordered_multimap. These feature performance in insert() and find() operations that is independent of container size. You also learned the importance of being able to customize the sort criterion using a predicate, as demonstrated in the Directory application of Listing 20.5.

Q&A

Q How would I declare a `map` of integers to be sorted or stored in order of descending magnitude?

A `map <int>` defines a `map` of integers. This takes the default sort predicate `std::less <T>` to sort items in order of ascending magnitude and can also be expressed as `map <int, less <int>>`. To sort in order of descending magnitude, define the `map` as `map <int, greater <int>>`.

Q What would happen if in a `map` of strings I inserted the string `"Jack"` twice?

A A `map` is not meant to be used to insert non-unique values. So, the map would still contain only one pair having a key called `"Jack"`.

Q In the preceding example, what would I change if I wanted to have two instances of `"Jack"`?

A By design a `map` holds only unique values. You need to change your selection of container to a `multimap`.

Q What `multimap` member function returns the count of items of a particular value in the container?

A `count(value)` is the function of interest.

Q I have found an element in the `map` using the `find()` function and have an iterator pointing to it. Would I use this iterator to change the value being pointed to?

A No. Some STL implementations might allow the user to change the value of an element inside a `map` via an iterator returned by `find()`. This, however, is not the correct thing to do. An iterator to an element in the `map` should be used as a `const` iterator—even when your implementation of STL has not enforced it as such.

Q I am using an older compiler that doesn't support keyword `auto`. How should I declare a variable that holds the return value of a `map::find()`?

A An iterator is always defined using this syntax:

```
container<Type>::iterator variableName;
```

So the iterator declaration for a map of integers would be the following:

```
std::map<int>::iterator pairFound = mapIntegers.find(1000);
if (pairFound != mapIntegers.end())
{ // Do Something }
```

Workshop

The Workshop contains quiz questions to help solidify your understanding of the material covered and exercises to provide you with experience in using what you've learned. Try to answer the quiz and exercise questions before checking the answers in Appendix E, and be certain you understand the answers before going to the next lesson.

Quiz

1. You declare a map of integers as `map<int>`. What function supplies the sort criteria?

2. Where would you find duplicate elements in a `multimap`?

3. What `map` or `multimap` function supplies the number of elements in the container?

4. Where would you find duplicate elements in a `map`?

Exercises

1. You need to write an application that works as a telephone directory where the names of the people need not be unique. What container would you choose? Write a definition of the container.

2. The following is a `map` template definition in your dictionary application:

```
map <wordProperty, string, fPredicate> mapWordDefinition;
```

where `WordProperty` is a structure:

```
struct WordProperty
{
    string word;
    bool isLatinBase;
};
```

Define the binary predicate `fPredicate` that helps the map sort a key of type `WordProperty` according to the string attribute it contains.

3. Demonstrate via a simple program that a `map` cannot accept duplicate entries, whereas a `multimap` can.

20

LESSON 21
Understanding Function Objects

Function objects or *functors* might sound exotic or intimidating, but they are entities of C++ that you have probably seen, if not also used, without having realized it. In this lesson, you learn

- The concept of function objects
- The usage of function objects as predicates
- How unary and binary predicates are implemented using function objects

The Concept of Function Objects and Predicates

On a conceptual level, function objects are objects that work as functions. On an implementation level, however, function objects are objects of a class that implement `operator()`. Although functions and function-pointers can also be classified as function objects, it is the capability of an object of a class that implements `operator()` to carry `state` (that is, values in member attributes of the class) that makes it useful with Standard Template Library (STL) algorithms.

Function objects as typically used by a C++ programmer working with STL are classifiable into the following types:

- **Unary function**—A function called with one argument; for example, `f(x)`. When a unary function returns a `bool`, it is called a *predicate*.

- **Binary function**—A function called with two arguments; for example, `f(x, y)`. A binary function that returns a `bool` is called a *binary predicate*.

Function objects that return a `boolean` type are naturally suited for use in algorithms that help in decision making. `find()` and `sort()` are two such algorithms that you learned about in previous lessons. A function object that combines two function objects is called an *adaptive function object*.

Typical Applications of Function Objects

It is possible to explain function objects over pages and pages of theoretical explanations. It is also possible to understand how they look and work via tiny sample applications. Let's take the practical approach and dive straight into the world of C++ programming with function objects or functors!

Unary Functions

Functions that operate on a single parameter are unary functions. A unary function can do something very simple—for example, display an element on the screen. This can be programmed as the following:

```
// A unary function
template <typename elementType>
void FuncDisplayElement (const elementType& element)
{
    cout << element << ' ';
};
```

The function `FuncDisplayElement` accepts one parameter of templatized type `elementType` that it displays using console output statement `std::cout`. The same function can also have another representation in which the implementation of the function is actually contained by the `operator()` of a `class` or a `struct`:

```cpp
// Struct that can behave as a unary function
template <typename elementType>
struct DisplayElement
{
    void operator () (const elementType& element) const
    {
        cout << element << ' ';
    }
};
```

TIP

> Note that `DisplayElement` is a `struct`. If it were a class, `operator()` would need to be given a `public` access modifier. A struct is akin to a class where members are `public` by default.

Either of these implementations can be used with the STL algorithm `for_each()` to print the contents of a collection to the screen, an element at a time, as shown in Listing 21.1.

LISTING 21.1 Displaying the Contents of a Collection on the Screen Using a Unary Function

```cpp
 0: #include <algorithm>
 1: #include <iostream>
 2: #include <vector>
 3: #include <list>
 4: using namespace std;
 5:
 6: // struct that behaves as a unary function
 7: template <typename elementType>
 8: struct DisplayElement
 9: {
10:     void operator () (const elementType& element) const
11:     {
12:         cout << element << ' ';
13:     }
14: };
15:
16: int main ()
17: {
18:     vector <int> numsInVec{ 0, 1, 2, 3, -1, -9, 0, -999 };
19:     cout << "Vector of integers contains: " << endl;
```

21

```
20:
21:    for_each (numsInVec.begin (),      // Start of range
22:              numsInVec.end (),        // End of range
23:              DisplayElement<int> () ); // Unary function object
24:
25:     // Display the list of characters
26:     list <char> charsInList{ 'a', 'z', 'k', 'd' };
27:     cout << endl << "List of characters contains: " << endl;
28:
29:     for_each (charsInList.begin(),
30:               charsInList.end(),
31:               DisplayElement<char> () );
32:
33:     return 0;
34: }
```

Output ▼

```
Vector of integers contains:
0 1 2 3 -1 -9 0 -999
List of characters contains:
a z k d
```

Analysis ▼

Lines 8–14 contain the function object `DisplayElement`, which implements `operator()`. The usage of this function object is seen with STL algorithm `std::for_each()` in Lines 21–23. `for_each()` accepts three parameters: The first is the starting point of the range, the second is the end of the range, and the third parameter is the function that is called for every element in the specified range. In other words, that code invokes `DisplayElement::operator()` for every element in the `vector numsInVec`. Lines 29–31 demonstrate the same functionality with a `list` of `characters`.

NOTE

In Listing 21.1, you may optionally use `FuncDisplayElement` instead of `struct DisplayElement` to the same effect:

```
for_each (charsInList.begin(),
          charsInList.end(),
          FuncDisplayElement<char>);
```

TIP

C++11 introduced lambda expressions that are unnamed function objects.

A lambda expression version of `struct DisplayElement<T>` from Listing 21.1 compacts the entire code, including the definition of the `struct` and its usage, in three lines within `main()`, replacing Lines 21–24:

```
// Display elements using lambda expression
for_each (numsInVec.begin(), // Start of range
            numsInVec.end(),   // End of range
    [] (int& Element) {cout << element << ' '; });
    // Lambda expression
```

Thus, lambdas are a fantastic improvement to C++, and you should not miss learning them in Lesson 22, "Lambda Expressions." Listing 22.1 demonstrates using lambda functions in a `for_each()` to display the contents of a container, instead of the function object as seen in Listing 21.1.

The real advantage of using a function object implemented in a `struct` becomes apparent when you are able to use the object of the `struct` to store information. This is something `FuncDisplayElement` cannot do the way a `struct` can because a `struct` can have member attributes in addition to `operator()`. A slightly modified version that makes use of member attributes is the following:

```
template <typename elementType>
struct DisplayElementKeepCount
{
    int count;

    DisplayElementKeepCount ()  // constructor
    {
        count = 0;
    }

    void operator () (const elementType& element)
    {
        ++ count;
        cout << element << ' ';
    }
};
```

21

In the preceding snippet, `DisplayElementKeepCount` is a slight modification over the previous version. `operator()` is not a const member function anymore as it increments (hence, changes) member `count` to keep a count of the number of times it was called to display data. This count is made available via the public member attribute `count`. The advantage of using such function objects that can also store `state` is shown in Listing 21.2.

LISTING 21.2 Function Object That Holds State

```
0: #include<algorithm>
1: #include<iostream>
2: #include<vector>
3: using namespace std;
4:
5: template<typename elementType>
6: struct DisplayElementKeepCount
7: {
8:     int count;
9:
10:     DisplayElementKeepCount() : count(0) {} // constructor
11:
12:     void operator()(const elementType& element)
13:     {
14:         ++ count;
15:         cout << element<< ' ';
16:     }
17: };
18:
19: int main()
20: {
21:     vector<int> numsInVec{ 22, 2017, -1, 999, 43, 901 };
22:     cout << "Displaying the vector of integers: "<< endl;
23:
24:     DisplayElementKeepCount<int> result;
25:     result = for_each (numsInVec.begin(),
26:                        numsInVec.end(),
27:                        DisplayElementKeepCount<int>() );
28:
29:     cout << endl << "Functor invoked " << result.count << " times";
30:
31:     return 0;
32: }
```

Output ▼

```
Displaying the vector of integers:
22 2017 -1 999 43 901
Functor invoked 6 times
```

Analysis ▼

The biggest difference between this sample and the one in Listing 21.1 is the usage of `DisplayElementKeepCount()` as the return value of `for_each()`. `operator()` implemented in `struct DisplayElementKeepCount` is invoked by algorithm `for_each()` for every element in the container. It displays the element and increments the internal counter stored in member attribute `count`. After `for_each()` is done, you use the object in Line 29 to display the number of times elements were displayed. Note that a regular function used in this scenario instead of the function implemented in a `struct` would not be able to supply this feature in such a direct way.

Unary Predicate

A unary function that returns a `bool` is a `predicate`. Such functions help make decisions for STL algorithms. Listing 21.3 is a sample predicate that determines whether an input element is a multiple of an initial value.

LISTING 21.3   A Unary Predicate That Determines Whether a Number Is a Multiple of Another

```
0: // A structure as a unary predicate
1: template <typename numberType>
2: struct IsMultiple
3: {
4:     numberType Divisor;
5:
6:     IsMultiple (const numberType& divisor)
7:     {
8:         Divisor = divisor;
9:     }
10:
11:    bool operator () (const numberType& element) const
12:    {
13:        // Check if the divisor is a multiple of the divisor
14:        return ((element % Divisor) == 0);
15:    }
16: };
```

Analysis ▼

Here the `operator()` returns `bool` and can work as a unary predicate. The structure has a constructor and is initialized to the value of the divisor in Line 8. This value stored in the object is then used to determine whether the elements sent for comparison are divisible by it, as you can see in the implementation of `operator()`, using the math operation modulus `%` that returns the remainder of a division operation in Line 14. The predicate compares that remainder to zero to determine whether the number is a multiple.

21

In Listing 21.4, we make use of the predicate as seen previously in Listing 21.3 to determine whether numbers in a collection are multiples of a divisor input by the user.

LISTING 21.4   Unary Predicate `IsMultiple` Used with `std::find_if()` to Find an Element in a `vector` That Is a Multiple of a User-Supplied Divisor

```
0: #include <algorithm>
1: #include <vector>
2: #include <iostream>
3: using namespace std;
4: // insert code from Listing 21.3 here
5:
6: int main ()
7: {
8:    vector <int> numsInVec{ 25, 26, 27, 28, 29, 30, 31 };
9:    cout << "The vector contains: 25, 26, 27, 28, 29, 30, 31" << endl;
10:
11:    cout << "Enter divisor (> 0): ";
12:    int divisor = 2;
13:    cin >> divisor;
14:
15:    // Find the first element that is a multiple of divisor
16:    auto element = find_if (numsInVec.begin (),
17:                            numsInVec.end (),
18:                            IsMultiple<int>(divisor) );
19:
20:    if (element != numsInVec.end ())
21:    {
22:       cout << "First element in vector divisible by " << divisor;
23:       cout << ": " << *element << endl;
24:    }
25:
26:    return 0;
27: }
```

Output ▼

```
The vector contains: 25, 26, 27, 28, 29, 30, 31
Enter divisor (> 0): 4
First element in vector divisible by 4: 28
```

Analysis ▼

The sample starts with a sample container that is a vector of integers. The usage of the unary predicate is in `find_if()` as shown in Line 16. In here, the function object `IsMultiple()` is initialized to a divisor value supplied by the user and stored in variable `Divisor`. `find_if()` works by invoking the unary predicate `IsMultiple::operator()` for every element in the specified range. When the `operator()` returns `true` for an element (which happens when that element is divided by 4 and does not produce a remainder), `find_if()` returns an iterator `element` to that element. The result of the `find_if()` operation is compared against the `end()` of the container to verify that an element was found, as shown in Line 20, and the iterator `element` is then used to display the value, as shown in Line 23.

TIP ————

> To see how using lambda expressions compact the program shown in Listing 21.4, take a look at Listing 22.3 in Lesson 22.

Unary predicates find application in a lot of STL algorithms such as `std::partition()` that can partition a range using the predicate, `stable_partition()` that does the same while keeping relative order of the elements partitioned, find functions such as `std::find_if()`, and functions that help erase elements such as `std::remove_if()` that erases elements in a range that satisfy the predicate.

Binary Functions

Functions of type `f(x, y)` are particularly useful when they return a value based on the input supplied. Such binary functions can be used for a host of arithmetic activity that involves two operands, such as addition, multiplication, subtraction, and so on. A sample binary function that returns the multiple of input arguments can be written as follows:

```cpp
template <typename elementType>
class Multiply
{
public:
    elementType operator () (const elementType& elem1,
                             const elementType& elem2)
    {
        return (elem1 * elem2);
    }
};
```

The implementation of interest is again in `operator()` that accepts two arguments and returns their multiple. Such binary functions are used in algorithms such as `std::transform()` where you can use it to multiply the contents of two containers. Listing 21.5 demonstrates the usage of such binary functions in `std::transform()`.

21

LISTING 21.5 Using a Binary Function to Multiply Two Ranges

```
0: #include <vector>
1: #include <iostream>
2: #include <algorithm>
3:
4: template <typename elementType>
5: class Multiply
6: {
7: public:
8:     elementType operator () (const elementType& elem1,
9:                              const elementType& elem2)
10:     {
11:         return (elem1 * elem2);
12:     }
13: };
14:
15: int main ()
16: {
17:     using namespace std;
18:
19:     vector <int> multiplicands{ 0, 1, 2, 3, 4 };
20:     vector <int> multipliers{ 100, 101, 102, 103, 104 };
21:
22:     // A third container that holds the result of multiplication
23:     vector <int> vecResult;
24:
25:     // Make space for the result of the multiplication
26:     vecResult.resize (multipliers.size());
27:     transform (multiplicands.begin (), // range of multiplicands
28:                multiplicands.end (), // end of range
29:                multipliers.begin (),  // multiplier values
30:                vecResult.begin (), // holds result
31:                Multiply <int> () );     // multiplies
32:
33:     cout << "The contents of the first vector are: " << endl;
34:     for (size_t index = 0; index < multiplicands.size (); ++ index)
35:         cout << multiplicands [index] << ' ';
36:     cout << endl;
37:
38:     cout << "The contents of the second vector are: " << endl;
39:     for (size_t index = 0; index < multipliers.size (); ++index)
40:         cout << multipliers [index] << ' ';
41:     cout << endl;
42:
43:     cout << "The result of the multiplication is: " << endl;
44:     for (size_t index = 0; index < vecResult.size (); ++ index)
45:         cout << vecResult [index] << ' ';
46:
47:     return 0;
48: }
```

Output ▼

```
The contents of the first vector are:
0  1  2  3  4
The contents of the second vector are:
100  101  102  103  104
The result of the multiplication is:
0  101  204  309  416
```

Analysis ▼

Lines 4–13 contain the class `Multiply`, as shown in the preceding code snippet. In this sample, you use the algorithm `std::transform()` to multiply the contents of two ranges and store in a third. In this case, the ranges in question are held in `std::vector` as `multiplicands`, `multipliers`, and `vecResult`. You use `std::transform()` in Lines 27–31 to multiply every element in `multiplicands` by its corresponding element in `multipliers` and store the result of the multiplication in `vecResult`. The multiplication itself is done by the binary function `Multiply::operator()` that is invoked for every element in the vectors that make the source and destination ranges. The return value of the `operator()` is held in `vecResult`.

This sample thus demonstrates the application of binary functions in performing arithmetic operations on elements in STL containers. The next sample also uses `std::transform()` but to convert a string to lowercase using function `tolower()`.

Binary Predicate

A function that accepts two arguments and returns a `bool` is a binary predicate. Such functions find application in STL functions such as `std::sort()`. Listing 21.6 demonstrates the usage of a binary predicate that compares two strings after reducing them both to lowercase. Such a predicate can be used in performing a case-insensitive sort on a `vector` of `string`, for instance.

LISTING 21.6   A Binary Predicate for Case-Insensitive String Sort

```
0: #include <algorithm>
1: #include <string>
2: using namespace std;
3:
4: class CompareStringNoCase
5: {
6: public:
7:    bool operator () (const string& str1, const string& str2) const
8:    {
9:        string str1LowerCase;
```

21

```
10:
11:        // Assign space
12:        str1LowerCase.resize (str1.size ());
13:
14:        // Convert every character to the lower case
15:        transform (str1.begin (), str1.end (), str1LowerCase.begin (),
16:                      ::tolower);
17:
18:        string str2LowerCase;
19:        str2LowerCase.resize (str2.size ());
20:        transform (str2.begin (), str2.end (), str2LowerCase.begin (),
21:                      ::tolower);
22:
23:        return (str1LowerCase < str2LowerCase);
24:    }
25: };
```

Analysis ▼

The binary predicate implemented in `operator()` first brings the input strings down to lowercase using algorithm `std::transform()` as shown in Lines 15 and 20 before using the string's comparison operator, `operator <`, to return the result of comparison.

You can use this binary-predicate with algorithm `std::sort()` to sort a dynamic array contained in a `vector` of `string` as demonstrated by Listing 21.7.

LISTING 21.7 Using Function Object class `CompareStringNoCase` to Perform a Case-Insensitive Sort on a `vector<string>`

```
0: // Insert class CompareStringNoCase from Listing 21.6 here
1: #include <vector>
2: #include <iostream>
3:
4: template <typename T>
5: void DisplayContents (const T& container)
6: {
7:    for (auto element = container.cbegin();
8:        element != container.cend ();
9:        ++ element )
10:        cout << *element << endl;
11: }
12:
13: int main ()
14: {
15:    // Define a vector of string to hold names
16:    vector <string> names;
17:
18:    // Insert some sample names in to the vector
```

```
19:     names.push_back ("jim");
20:     names.push_back ("Jack");
21:     names.push_back ("Sam");
22:     names.push_back ("Anna");
23:
24:     cout << "The names in vector in order of insertion: " << endl;
25:     DisplayContents(names);
26:
27:     cout << "Names after sorting using default std::less<>: " << endl;
28:     sort(names.begin(), names.end());
29:     DisplayContents(names);
30:
31:     cout << "Sorting using predicate that ignores case:" << endl;
32:     sort(names.begin(), names.end(), CompareStringNoCase());
33:     DisplayContents(names);
34:
35:     return 0;
36: }
```

Output ▼

```
The names in vector in order of insertion:
jim
Jack
Sam
Anna
Names after sorting using default std::less<>:
Anna
Jack
Sam
jim
Sorting using predicate that ignores case:
Anna
Jack
jim
Sam
```

Analysis ▼

Output displays the contents of the vector in three stages. The first displays contents in order of insertion. The second after a sort() at Line 28 reorders using default sort predicate less<T>, the output demonstrates that jim is not placed after Jack because this is a case-sensitive sort via string::operator<. The last version uses the sort predicate class CompareStringNoCase<> in Line 32 (implemented in Listing 21.6) that ensures that jim comes after Jack notwithstanding the difference in case.

21

Binary predicates are required in a variety of STL algorithms. For example, `std::unique()` that erases duplicate neighboring elements, `std::sort()` that sorts, `std::stable_sort()` that sorts while maintaining relative order, and `std::transform()` that can perform an operation on two ranges are some of the STL algorithms that need a binary predicate.

Summary

In this lesson, you gained an insight into the world of functors (or function objects). You learned how function objects are more useful when implemented in a structure or a class than those that are simple functions because the former can also be used to hold state-related information. You got an insight into predicates, which are a special class of function objects, and saw some practical examples that display their utility.

Q&A

Q A predicate is a special category of a function object. What makes it special?

A Predicates always return `boolean`.

Q What kind of a function object should I use in a call to a function such as `remove_if()`?

A You should use a unary predicate that would take the value to be processed as the initial state via the constructor.

Q What kind of a function object should I use for a `map`?

A You should use a binary predicate.

Q Is it possible that a simple function with no return value can be used as a predicate?

A Yes. A function with no return values can still do something useful. For example, it can display input data.

Workshop

The Workshop provides quiz questions to help you solidify your understanding of the material covered and exercises to provide you with experience in using what you've learned. Try to answer the quiz and exercise questions before checking the answers in Appendix E, and be certain you understand the answers before going to the next lesson.

Quiz

1. What is the term used for a unary function that returns a `bool` result?

2. What would be the utility of a function object that neither modifies data nor returns `bool`? Can you explain using an example?

3. What is the definition of the term *function objects*?

Exercises

1. Write a unary function that can be used with `std::for_each()` to display the double of the input parameter.

2. Extend this predicate to indicate the number of times it was used.

3. Write a binary predicate that helps sort in ascending order.

LESSON 22
Lambda Expressions

Lambda expressions are a compact way to define and construct function objects without a name. These expressions were introduced in C++11. In this lesson, you find out

- How to program a lambda expression
- How to use lambda expressions as predicates
- What are C++14 generic lambda expressions
- How to program lambda expressions that can hold and manipulate a state

What Is a Lambda Expression?

A lambda expression can be visualized as a compact version of an unnamed `struct` (or `class`) with a public `operator()`. In that sense, a lambda expression is a function object like those in Lesson 21, "Understanding Function Objects." Before jumping into analyzing the programming of lambda functions, take a function object from Listing 21.1 (from Lesson 21) as an example:

```
// struct that behaves as a unary function
template <typename elementType>
struct DisplayElement
{
    void operator () (const elementType& element) const
    {
        cout << element << ' ';
    }
};
```

This function object displays an object `element` on the screen using `cout` and is typically used in algorithms such as `std::for_each()`:

```
// Display every integer contained in a vector
for_each (numsInVec.cbegin (),      // Start of range
          numsInVec.cend (),        // End of range
          DisplayElement <int> ()); // Unary function object
```

A lambda expression compacts the entire code including the definition of the function object into three lines:

```
// Display every integer contained in a vector using lambda exp.
for_each (numsInVec.cbegin (),      // Start of range
          numsInVec.cend (),        // End of range
          [](const int& element) {cout << element << ' '; } );
```

When the compiler sees the lambda expression, in this case

```
[](const int& element) {cout << element << ' '; }
```

it automatically expands this expression into a representation that is similar to struct `DisplayElement<int>`:

```
struct NoName
{
    void operator () (const int& element) const
    {
```

```
        cout << element << ' ';
    }
};
```

> **TIP**
>
> Lambda Expressions are also called Lambda Functions.

How to Define a Lambda Expression

The definition of a lambda expression has to start with square brackets`[]`. These brackets essentially tell the compiler that the lambda expression has started. They are followed by the parameter list, which is the same as the parameter list you would supply your implementation of `operator()` if you were not using a lambda expression.

Lambda Expression for a Unary Function

The lambda version of a unary `operator(Type)` that takes one parameter would be the following:

```
[](Type paramName) {   // lambda expression code here;   }
```

Note that you can pass the parameter by reference if you so wish:

```
[](Type& paramName) {   // lambda expression code here;   }
```

Use Listing 22.1 to study the usage of a lambda function in displaying the contents of a Standard Template Library (STL) container using algorithm `for_each()`.

LISTING 22.1   Displaying Elements in a Container via Algorithm `for_each()` That Is Invoked with a Lambda Expression Instead of a Function Object

```
0: #include <algorithm>
1: #include <iostream>
2: #include <vector>
3: #include <list>
4:
5: using namespace std;
6:
```

```
7: int main ()
8: {
9:     vector <int> numsInVec{ 101, -4, 500, 21, 42, -1 };
10:
11:    list <char> charsInList{ 'a', 'h', 'z', 'k', 'l' };
12:    cout << "Display elements in a vector using a lambda: " << endl;
13:
14:    // Display the array of integers
15:    for_each (numsInVec.cbegin (),     // Start of range
16:             numsInVec.cend (),         // End of range
17:             [](const int& element) {cout << element << ' '; } ); // lambda
18:
19:    cout << endl;
20:    cout << "Display elements in a list using a lambda: " << endl;
21:
22:    // Display the list of characters
23:    for_each (charsInList.cbegin (),    // Start of range
24:             charsInList.cend (),       // End of range
25:             [](auto& element) {cout << element << ' '; } ); // lambda
26:
27:    return 0;
28: }
```

Output ▼

```
Display elements in a vector using a lambda:
101 -4 500 21 42 -1
Display elements in a list using a lambda:
a h z k l
```

Analysis ▼

There are two lambda expressions of interest in Lines 17 and 25. They are similar, save for the type of the input parameter, as they have been customized to the nature of the elements within the two containers. The first takes one parameter that is an int, as it is used to print one element at a time from a vector of integers, whereas the second accepts a char (automatically deduced by the compiler) as it is used to display elements of type char stored in a std::list.

TIP

> You may have noticed that the second lambda expression in Listing 22.1 is slightly different:
>
> ```
> for_each (charsInList.cbegin (),    // Start of range
>           charsInList.cend (),      // End of range
> [](auto& element) {cout << element << ' '; } ); // lambda
> ```
>
> This lambda uses the compiler's automatic type deduction capabilities invoked using keyword `auto`. This is an improvement to lambda expressions that are supported by compilers that are C++14 compliant. The compiler would interpret this lambda expression as
>
> ```
> for_each (charsInList.cbegin (),    // Start of range
>           charsInList.cend (),      // End of range
> [](const char& element) {cout << element << ' '; } );
> ```

NOTE

> The code in Listing 22.1 is similar to that in Listing 21.1 with the exception that the latter uses function objects. In fact, Listing 22.1 is a lambda version of function object `DisplayElement<T>`.
>
> Comparing the two, you realize how lambda functions have the potential to make C++ code simpler and more compact.

Lambda Expression for a Unary Predicate

A predicate helps make decisions. A unary predicate is a unary expression that returns a `bool`, conveying `true` or `false`. Lambda expressions can return values, too. For example, the following code is a lambda expression that returns `true` for numbers that are even:

```
[](int& num) {return ((num % 2) == 0); }
```

The nature of the return value in this case tells the compiler that the lambda expression returns a `bool`.

You can use a lambda expression that is a unary predicate in algorithms, such as `std::find_if()`, to find even numbers in a collection. See Listing 22.2 for an example.

LISTING 22.2 Find an Even Number in a Collection Using a Lambda Expression for a Unary Predicate and Algorithm `std::find_if()`

```
 0: #include<algorithm>
 1: #include<vector>
 2: #include<iostream>
 3: using namespace std;
 4:
 5: int main()
 6: {
 7:     vector<int> numsInVec{ 25, 101, 2017, -50 };
 8:
 9:     auto evenNum = find_if(numsInVec.cbegin(),
10:                       numsInVec.cend(),  // range to find in
11:                  [](const int& num){return ((num % 2) == 0); } );
12:
13:     if (evenNum != numsInVec.cend())
14:        cout << "Even number in collection is: " << *evenNum << endl;
15:
16:     return 0;
17: }
```

Output ▼

```
Even number in collection is: -50
```

Analysis ▼

The lambda function that works as a unary predicate is shown in Line 11. Algorithm `find_if()` invokes the unary predicate for every element in the range. When the predicate returns `true`, `find_if()` reports a find by returning an iterator `evenNum` to that element. The predicate in this case is the lambda expression that returns `true` when `find_if()` invokes it with an integer that is even (that is, the result of modulus operation with 2 is zero).

NOTE	Listing 22.2 not only demonstrates a lambda expression as a unary predicate, but also the use of `const` within a lambda expression.
	Remember to use `const` for input parameters, especially when they're a reference to avoid unintentional changes to the value of elements in a container.

Lambda Expression with State via Capture Lists [...]

In Listing 22.2, you created a unary predicate that returned true if an integer was divisible by 2—that is, the integer is an even number. What if you want a more generic function that returns `true` when the number is divisible by a divisor of the user's choosing? You need to maintain that "state"—the divisor—in the expression:

```
int divisor = 2; // initial value
...
auto element = find_if (begin of a range,
                        end of a range,
        [divisor](int dividend){return (dividend % divisor) == 0; } );
```

A list of arguments transferred as state variables [...] is also called the lambda's capture list.

> **NOTE**
>
> Such a lambda expression is a one-line equivalent of the 16 lines of code seen in Listing 21.3 that defines unary predicate `struct IsMultiple<>`.
>
> Thus, lambdas introduced in C++11 improve programming efficiency by leaps and bounds!

Listing 22.3 demonstrates the application of a unary predicate given a state variable in finding a number in the collection that is a multiple of a divisor supplied by the user.

LISTING 22.3 Demonstrating the Use of Lambda Expressions That Hold State to Check Whether One Number Is Divisible by Another

```
0: #include <algorithm>
1: #include <vector>
2: #include <iostream>
3: using namespace std;
4:
5: int main()
6: {
7:     vector <int> numsInVec{25, 26, 27, 28, 29, 30, 31};
8:     cout << "The vector contains: {25, 26, 27, 28, 29, 30, 31}";
9:
10:    cout << endl << "Enter divisor (> 0): ";
11:    int divisor = 2;
12:    cin >> divisor;
13:
```

```
14:     // Find the first element that is a multiple of divisor
15:     vector <int>::iterator element;
16:     element = find_if (numsInVec.begin ()
17:                       , numsInVec.end ()
18:           , [divisor] (int dividend){return (dividend % divisor) == 0; } );
19:
20:     if (element != numsInVec.end ())
21:     {
22:         cout << "First element in vector divisible by " << divisor;
23:         cout << ": " << *element << endl;
24:     }
25:
26:     return 0;
27: }
```

Output ▼

```
The vector contains: {25, 26, 27, 28, 29, 30, 31}
Enter divisor (> 0): 4
First element in vector divisible by 4: 28
```

Analysis ▼

The lambda expression that contains state and works as a predicate is shown in Line 18. divisor is the state-variable, comparable to IsMultiple::Divisor that you saw in Listing 21.3. Hence, state variables are akin to members in a function object class that you would have composed in days prior to C++11. You are now able to pass states on to your lambda function and customize its usage on the basis of the same.

> **NOTE** ———— Listing 22.3 features the lambda expression equivalent of Listing 21.4, without the function object class IsMultiple. Lambda expressions introduced in C++11 have served a reduction in 16 lines of code!

The Generic Syntax of Lambda Expressions

A lambda expression always starts with square brackets and can be configured to take multiple state variables separated using commas in a capture list [...]:

```
[stateVar1, stateVar2](Type& param) { // lambda code here; }
```

If you want to ensure that these state variables are modified within a lambda, you add keyword `mutable`:

```
[stateVar1, stateVar2](Type& param) mutable { // lambda code here; }
```

Note that here, the variables supplied in the capture list [] are modifiable within the lambda, but changes do not take effect outside it. If you want to ensure that modifications made to the state variables within the lambda are valid outside it, too, then you use references:

```
[&stateVar1, &stateVar2](Type& param) { // lambda code here; }
```

Lambdas can take multiple input parameters, separated by commas:

```
[stateVar1, stateVar2](Type1& var1, Type2& var2) { // lambda code here; }
```

If you want to mention the return type and not leave the disambiguation to the compiler, you use -> as in the following:

```
[stateVar1, stateVar2](Type1 var1, Type2 var2) -> ReturnType
{ return (value or expression ); }
```

Finally, the compound statement {} can hold multiple statements, each separated by a ; as shown here:

```
[stateVar1, stateVar2](Type1 var1, Type2 var2) -> ReturnType
{
    Statement 1;
    Statement 2;
    return (value or expression);
}
```

NOTE

If your lambda expression spans multiple lines, you are required to supply an explicit return type.

Listing 22.5 later in this lesson demonstrates a lambda function that specifies a return type and spans multiple lines.

Thus, a lambda function is a compact, fully functional replacement of a function object such as the following:

```
template<typename Type1, typename Type2>
struct IsNowTooLong
{
    // State variables
    Type1 var1;
    Type2 var2;
```

```
// Constructor
IsNowTooLong(const Type1& in1, Type2& in2): var1(in1), var2(in2) {};

// the actual purpose
ReturnType operator()
{
    Statement 1;
    Statement 2;
    return (value or expression);
}
};
```

Lambda Expression for a Binary Function

A binary function takes two parameters and optionally returns a value. A lambda expression equivalent of the same would be

```
[...](Type1& param1Name, Type2& param2Name) {  // lambda code here;  }
```

A lambda function that multiplies two equal-sized vectors element by element using std::transform() and stores the result in a third vector is shown in Listing 22.4.

LISTING 22.4 Lambda Expression as a Binary Function to Multiply Elements from Two Containers and Store in a Third

```
0: #include <vector>
1: #include <iostream>
2: #include <algorithm>
3:
4: int main ()
5: {
6:     using namespace std;
7:
8:     vector <int> vecMultiplicand{ 0, 1, 2, 3, 4 };
9:     vector <int> vecMultiplier{ 100, 101, 102, 103, 104 };
10:
11:     // Holds the result of multiplication
12:     vector <int> vecResult;
13:
14:     // Make space for the result of the multiplication
15:     vecResult.resize(vecMultiplier.size());
16:
17:     transform (vecMultiplicand.begin (), // range of multiplicands
18:                vecMultiplicand.end (), // end of range
19:                vecMultiplier.begin (),  // multiplier values
```

```
20:                    vecResult.begin (), // range that holds result
21:                    [](int a, int b) {return a * b; } );  // lambda
22:
23:    cout << "The contents of the first vector are: " << endl;
24:    for (size_t index = 0; index < vecMultiplicand.size(); ++index)
25:    cout << vecMultiplicand[index] << ' ';
26:    cout << endl;
27:
28:    cout << "The contents of the second vector are: " << endl;
29:    for (size_t index = 0; index < vecMultiplier.size(); ++index)
30:    cout << vecMultiplier[index] << ' ';
31:    cout << endl;
32:
33:    cout << "The result of the multiplication is: " << endl;
34:    for (size_t index = 0; index < vecResult.size(); ++index)
35:    cout << vecResult[index] << ' ';
36:
37:    return 0;
38:  }
```

22

Output ▼

```
The contents of the first vector are:
0 1 2 3 4
The contents of the second vector are:
100 101 102 103 104
The result of the multiplication is:
0 101 204 309 416
```

Analysis ▼

The lambda expression in question is shown in Line 17 as a parameter to std::transform(). This algorithm takes two ranges as input and applies a transformation algorithm that is contained in a binary function. The return value of the binary function is stored in a target container. This binary function is a lambda expression that takes two integers as input and returns the result of the multiplication via the return value. This return value is stored by std::transform() in vecResult. The output demonstrates the contents of the two containers and the result of multiplying them element by element.

NOTE

Listing 22.4 was the demonstration of the lambda equivalent of function object class Multiply<> in Listing 21.5.

Lambda Expression for a Binary Predicate

A binary function that returns `true` or `false` to help make a decision is called a *binary predicate*. These predicates find use in sort algorithms, such as `std::sort()`, that invoke the binary predicate for any two values in a container to know which one should be placed after the other. The generic syntax of a binary predicate is

```
[...](Type1& param1Name, Type2& param2Name) {  // return bool expression; }
```

Listing 22.5 demonstrates a lambda expression used in a sort.

LISTING 22.5   Lambda Expression as a Binary Predicate in `std::sort()` to Enable Case-Insensitive Sort

```
0: #include <algorithm>
1: #include <string>
2: #include <vector>
3: #include <iostream>
4: using namespace std;
5:
6: template <typename T>
7: void DisplayContents (const T& input)
8: {
9:    for (auto element = input.cbegin();
10:          element != input.cend ();
11:          ++ element )
12:       cout << *element << endl;
13: }
14:
15: int main ()
16: {
17:    vector <string> namesInVec{ "jim", "Jack", "Sam", "Anna" };
18:
19:    cout << "The names in vector in order of insertion: " << endl;
20:    DisplayContents(namesInVec);
21:
22:    cout << "Order after case sensitive sort: " << endl;
23:    sort(namesInVec.begin(), namesInVec.end());
24:    DisplayContents(namesInVec);
25:
26:    cout << "Order after sort ignoring case:" << endl;
27:    sort(namesInVec.begin(), namesInVec.end(),
28:       [](const string& str1, const string& str2) -> bool // lambda
29:       {
30:          string str1LC; // LC = lowercase
31:
```

```
32:             // Assign space
33:             str1LC.resize (str1.size ());
34:
35:             // Convert every character to the lower case
36:             transform(str1.begin(), str1.end(), str1LC.begin(),::tolower);
37:
38:             string str2LC;
39:             str2LC.resize (str2.size ());
40:             transform(str2.begin(), str2.end(), str2LC.begin(),::tolower);
41:
42:             return (str1LC < str2LC);
43:          } // end of lambda
44:       ); // end of sort
45:
46:    DisplayContents(namesInVec);
47:
48:    return 0;
49: }
```

Output ▼

```
The names in vector in order of insertion:
jim
Jack
Sam
Anna
Order after case sensitive sort:
Anna
Jack
Sam
jim
Order after sort ignoring case:
Anna
Jack
jim
Sam
```

Analysis ▼

This demonstrates a genuinely large lambda function spanning Lines 28–43 as the third parameter of std::sort()! What this lambda function demonstrates is that a lambda can span multiple statements, the prerequisite being that the return value type is explicitly specified as shown in Line 28 (bool). The output demonstrates the content of the vector as inserted, where "jim" is before "Jack". The content of the vector after a sort without a supplied lambda or predicate as shown in Line 23 sorts "jim" after "Sam", as this is a case-sensitive via std::less<> executed using string::operator<. Finally, a case-insensitive `sort()` that uses a lambda expression to first convert the string to low-ercase and then compares them is seen in Lines 28–43 that places `"jim"` after `"Jack"` as the user typically would expect.

NOTE	This extraordinarily large lambda in Listing 22.5 is a lambda version of Listing 21.6, `class CompareStringNoCase`, used in Listing 21.7. Clearly, this example also demonstrates that a function object as seen in Listing 21.6 is reusable in multiple `std::sort()` statements, if required, and also in other algorithms that need a binary predicate, while a lambda would need to be rewritten every time it needs to be used. So, you need to use lambdas when they're short, sweet, and effective.

DO	**DON'T**
DO remember that lambda expressions always start with `[]` or `[state1, state2, ..]`. **DO** remember that unless specified, state variables supplied within a capture list `[]` are not modifiable unless you use the keyword `mutable`.	**DON'T** forget that lambda expressions are unnamed representations of a class or a struct with `operator()`. **DON'T** forget to use `const` correct parameter types when writing your lambda expressions `[](const T& value) { // lambda expression ; }`. **DON'T** forget to explicitly mention return type when the lambda expression includes multiple statements within the statement block `{}`. **DON'T** choose lambda expressions over a function object when the lambda gets extremely long and spans multiple statements, for these are redefined in every use and do not assist code reusability.

Summary

In this lesson, you learned about an important feature introduced in C++11: lambda expressions. You saw how lambdas are basically unnamed function objects that can take parameters, have state, return values, and be multiple lined. You learned how to use lambdas instead of function objects in STL algorithms, helping `find()`, `sort()`, or `transform()`. Lambdas make programming in C++ fast and efficient, and you should try to use them where applicable.

Q&A

Q Should I always prefer a lambda over a function object?

A Lambdas that span multiple lines as shown in Listing 22.5 might not help increase programming efficiency over function objects that are easily reused.

Q How are the state parameters of a lambda transferred, by value or by reference?

A When a lambda is programmed with a capture list as this:

```
[Var1, Var2, ... N](Type& Param1, ... ) { ...expression ;}
```

the state parameters Var1 and Var2 are copied (not supplied as a reference). If you want to have them as reference parameters, you use this syntax:

```
[&Var1, &Var2, ... &N](Type& Param1, ... ) { ...expression ;}
```

In this case, you need to exercise caution as modifications to the state variables supplied within the capture list continue outside the lambda.

Q Can I use the local variables in a function in a lambda?

A You can pass the local variables in a capture list:

```
[Var1, Var2, ... N](Type& Param1, ... ) { ...expression ;}
```

If you want to capture all variables, you use this syntax:

```
[=](Type& Param1, ... ) { ...expression ;}
```

Workshop

The Workshop provides quiz questions to help you solidify your understanding of the material covered and exercises to provide you with experience in using what you've learned. Try to answer the quiz and exercise questions before checking the answers in Appendix E, and be certain you understand the answers before going to the next lesson.

Quiz

1. How does a compiler recognize the start of a lambda expression?

2. How would you pass state variables to a lambda function?

3. If you need to supply a return value in a lambda, how would you do it?

Exercises

1. Write a lambda binary predicate that would help sort elements in a container in descending order.

2. Write a lambda function that, when used in `for_each()`, adds a user-specified value to that in a container such as vector.

LESSON 23
STL Algorithms

An important part of the Standard Template Library (STL) is a set of generic functions, supplied by the header `<algorithm>`, that help manipulate or work with the contents of a container. In this lesson, you learn the usage of algorithms that reduce boilerplate code in helping you:

- Count, search, find, copy, and remove elements from a container
- Set values in a range of elements to the return value of a generator function or a predefined constant
- Sort or partition elements in a range
- Insert elements at the correct position in a sorted range

What Are STL Algorithms?

Finding, searching, removing, and counting are some generic algorithmic activities that find application in a broad range of programs. STL solves these and many other requirements in the form of generic template functions that work on containers using iterators. To use STL algorithms, the programmer first has to include the header <algorithm>.

NOTE　Although most algorithms work via iterators on containers, not all algorithms necessarily work on containers and hence not all algorithms need iterators. Some, such as swap(), simply accept a pair of values to swap them. Similarly, min() and max() work directly on values, too.

Classification of STL Algorithms

STL algorithms can be broadly classified into two types: non-mutating and mutating algorithms.

Non-Mutating Algorithms

Algorithms that change neither the order nor the contents of a container are called *non-mutating algorithms*. Some of the prominent non-mutating algorithms are shown in Table 23.1.

TABLE 23.1　Quick Reference of Non-Mutating Algorithms

Algorithm	Description
Counting Algorithms	
count()	Finds all elements in a range whose values match a supplied value
count_if()	Finds all elements in a range whose values satisfy a supplied condition
Search Algorithms	
search()	Searches for the first occurrence of a given sequence within a target range either on the basis of element equality (that is, the operator ==) or using a specified binary predicate
search_n()	Searches a specified target range for the first occurrence of *n* number of elements of a given value or those that satisfy a given predicate

Algorithm	Description
find()	Searches for the first element in the range that matches the specified value
find_if()	Searches for the first element in a range that satisfies the specified condition
find_end()	Searches for the last occurrence of a particular subrange in a supplied range
find_first_of()	Searches for the first occurrence of any element supplied in one range within a target range; or, in an overloaded version, searches for the first occurrence of an element that satisfies a supplied find criterion
adjacent_find()	Searches for two elements in a collection that are either equal or satisfy a supplied condition
Comparison Algorithms	
equal()	Compares two elements for equality or uses a specified binary predicate to determine the same
mismatch()	Locates the first difference position in two ranges of elements using a specified binary predicate
lexicographical_ compare()	Compares the elements between two sequences to determine which is the lesser of the two

Mutating Algorithms

Mutating algorithms are those that change the contents or the order of the sequence they are operating on. Some of the most useful mutating algorithms supplied by STL are shown in Table 23.2.

TABLE 23.2   A Quick Reference of Mutating Algorithms

Algorithm	Description
Initialization Algorithms	
fill()	Assigns the specified value to every element in the specified range.
fill_n()	Assigns the specified value to the first *n* elements in the specified range.
generate()	Assigns the return value of a specified function object to each element in the supplied range.
generate_n()	Assigns the value generated by a function to a specified count of values in a specified range.

Algorithm	Description
Modifying Algorithms	
`for_each()`	Performs an operation on every element in a range. When the specified argument modifies the range, `for_each` becomes a mutating algorithm.
`transform()`	Applies a specified unary function on every element in the specified range.
Copy Algorithms	
`copy()`	Copies one range into another.
`copy_backward()`	Copies one range into another, arranging elements in the destination range in the reverse order.
Removal Algorithms	
`remove()`	Removes an element of a specified value from a specified range.
`remove_if()`	Removes an element that satisfies a specified unary predicate from a specified range.
`remove_copy()`	Copies all elements from a source range to a destination range, except those of a specified value.
`remove_copy_if()`	Copies all elements from a source range to a destination range except those that satisfy a specified unary predicate.
`unique()`	Compares adjacent elements in a range and removes the following duplicates. An overloaded version works using a binary predicate.
`unique_copy()`	Copies all but adjacent duplicate elements from a specified source range to a specified destination range.
Replacement Algorithms	
`replace()`	Replaces every element in a specified range that matches a specified value by a replacement value.
`replace_if()`	Replaces every element in a specified range that matches a specified value by a replacement value.
Sort Algorithms	
`sort()`	Sorts elements in a range using a specified sort criterion, which is a binary predicate that supplies a strict-weak–ordering. `sort` might change relative positions of equivalent elements.
`stable_sort()`	Stable sort is similar to `sort` but preserves order, too.
`partial_sort()`	Sorts a specified number of elements in a range.

Algorithm	Description
`partial_sort_copy()`	Copies elements from a specified source range to a destination range that holds them in a sort order.
Partitioning Algorithms	
`partition()`	Given a specified range, splits elements into two sets within it: those that satisfy a unary predicate come first and the rest after. Might not maintain the relative order of elements in a set.
`stable_partition()`	Partitions an input range into two sets as in `partition` but maintains relative ordering.
Algorithms That Work on Sorted Containers	
`binary_search()`	Used to determine whether an element exists in a sorted collection.
`lower_bound()`	Returns an iterator pointing to the first position where an element can potentially be inserted in a sorted collection based on its value or on a supplied binary predicate.
`upper_bound()`	Returns an iterator pointing to the last position where an element can potentially be inserted into a sorted collection based on its value or on a supplied binary predicate.

23

Usage of STL Algorithms

The usage of the STL algorithms mentioned in Tables 23.1 and 23.2 is best learned in a hands-on coding session. To that end, practice using the code examples that follow and start applying them to your programs.

Finding Elements Given a Value or a Condition

Given a container such as a `vector`, STL algorithms `find()` and `find_if()` help you find an element that matches a value or fulfills a condition, respectively. The usage of `find()` follows this pattern:

```
auto element = find (numsInVec.cbegin(), // Start of range
                     numsInVec.cend(),   // End of range
                     numToFind);         // Element to find

// Check if find() succeeded
if (element != numsInVec.cend ())
   cout << "Result: Value found!" << endl;
```

find_if() is similar and requires you to supply a unary predicate (a unary function that returns true or false) as the third parameter.

```
auto evenNum = find_if (numsInVec.cbegin(), // Start of range
                        numsInVec.cend(),   // End of range
               [](int element) { return (element % 2) == 0; } );

if (evenNum != numsInVec.cend())
    cout << "Result: Value found!" << endl;
```

Thus, both find functions return an iterator, which you need to compare against the end() or cend() of the container to verify the success of the find operation. If this check is successful, you can use this iterator further. Listing 23.1 demonstrates the usage of find() to locate a value in a vector, and find_if() to locate the first even value.

LISTING 23.1 Using find() to Locate an Integer Value in a vector, find_if to Locate the First Even Number Given an Unary Predicate in a Lambda Expression

```
 0: #include <iostream>
 1: #include <algorithm>
 2: #include <vector>
 3:
 4: int main()
 5: {
 6:     using namespace std;
 7:     vector<int> numsInVec{ 2017, 0, -1, 42, 10101, 25 };
 8:
 9:     cout << "Enter number to find in collection: ";
10:     int numToFind = 0;
11:     cin >> numToFind;
12:
13:     auto element = find (numsInVec.cbegin (), // Start of range
14:                          numsInVec.cend (),   // End of range
15:                          numToFind);          // Element to find
16:
17:     // Check if find succeeded
18:     if (element != numsInVec.cend ())
19:        cout << "Value " << *element << " found!" << endl;
20:     else
21:        cout << "No element contains value " << numToFind << endl;
22:
23:     cout << "Finding the first even number using find_if: " << endl;
24:
25:     auto evenNum = find_if (numsInVec.cbegin(), // Start range
26:                             numsInVec.cend(),   // End range
27:                    [](int element) { return (element % 2) == 0; } );
28:
```

```
29:     if (evenNum != numsInVec.cend ())
30:     {
31:         cout << "Number '" << *evenNum << "' found at position [";
32:         cout << distance (numsInVec.cbegin (), evenNum) << "]" << endl;
33:     }
34:
35:     return 0;
36: }
```

Output ▼

23

```
Enter number to find in collection: 42
Value 42 found!
Finding the first even number using find_if:
Number '0' found at position [1]
```

Next run:

```
Enter number to find in collection: 2016
No element contains value 2016
Finding the first even number using find_if:
Number '0' found at position [1]
```

Analysis ▼

main() starts with initializing a vector of integers to sample values in Line 7. You use find() in Lines 13–15 to find the number entered by the user. The use of find_if() to locate the first even number given the range is shown in Lines 25–27. Line 27 is the unary predicate supplied to find_if() as a lambda expression. This lambda expression returns true when element is divisible by 2, thereby indicating to the algorithm that the element satisfies the criteria being checked for. Note the usage of algorithm std::distance() in Line 32 to find the relative position of an element found against the start of the container.

CAUTION

Note how Listing 23.1 always checks the iterator returned by find() or find_if() for validity against cend(). This check should never be skipped, as it indicates the success of the find() operation, which should not be taken for granted.

Counting Elements Given a Value or a Condition

`std::count()` and `count_if()` are algorithms that help in counting elements given a range. `std::count()` helps you count the number of elements that match a value (tested via equality `operator==`):

```
size_t numZeroes = count (numsInVec.cbegin (), numsInVec.cend (), 0);
cout << "Number of instances of '0': " << numZeroes << endl;
```

`std::count_if()` helps you count the number of elements that fulfill a unary predicate supplied as a parameter (which can be a function object or a lambda expression):

```
// Unary predicate:
template <typename elementType>
bool IsEven (const elementType& number)
{
    return ((number % 2) == 0); // true, if even
}
...
// Use the count_if algorithm with the unary predicate IsEven:
size_t numEvenNums = count_if (numsInVec.cbegin (),
                                numsInVec.cend (), IsEven <int> );
cout << "Number of even elements: " << numEvenNums << endl;
```

The code in Listing 23.2 demonstrates the usage of these functions.

LISTING 23.2 Demonstrates the Usage of `std::count()` to Determine Number of Elements with a Value and `count_if()` to Determine Number of Elements That Fulfill a Condition

```
 0: #include <algorithm>
 1: #include <vector>
 2: #include <iostream>
 3:
 4: // unary predicate for *_if functions
 5: template <typename elementType>
 6: bool IsEven (const elementType& number)
 7: {
 8:     return ((number % 2) == 0); // true, if even
 9: }
10:
11: int main ()
12: {
13:     using namespace std;
14:     vector <int> numsInVec{ 2017, 0, -1, 42, 10101, 25 };
15:
16:     size_t numZeroes = count (numsInVec.cbegin(), numsInVec.cend(), 0);
17:     cout << "Number of instances of '0': " << numZeroes << endl << endl;
```

```
18:
19:     size_t numEvenNums = count_if (numsInVec.cbegin(),
20:                          numsInVec.cend(), IsEven <int> );
21:
22:     cout << "Number of even elements: " << numEvenNums << endl;
23:     cout << "Number of odd elements: ";
24:     cout << numsInVec.size () - numEvenNums << endl;
25:
26:     return 0;
27: }
```

Output ▼

23

```
Number of instances of '0': 1
Number of even elements: 2
Number of odd elements: 4
```

Analysis ▼

Line 16 uses `count()` to determine the number of instances of 0 in the `vector`. Similarly, Line 19 uses `count_if()` to determine the number of even elements in the vector. Note the third parameter, which is a unary predicate `IsEven()` defined in Lines 5–9. The number of elements in the vector that are odd is calculated by subtracting the return of `count_if()` with the total number of elements contained in the vector returned by `size()`.

NOTE _____

> Listing 23.2 uses predicate function `IsEven()` in `count_if()`, whereas Listing 23.1 used a lambda function doing the work of `IsEven()` in `find_if()`.
>
> The lambda version saves lines of code, but you should remember that if the two samples were merged, `IsEven()` could be used in both `find_if()` and `count_if()`, increasing opportunities for reuse.

Searching for an Element or a Range in a Collection

Listing 23.1 demonstrated how you can find an element in a container. Sometimes, you need to find a range of values or a pattern. In such situations, you should use `search()` or `search_n()`. `search()` can be used to check if one range is contained in another:

```
auto range = search (numsInVec.cbegin(), // Start range to search in
                     numsInVec.cend(),    // End range to search in
                     numsInList.cbegin(), // start range to search
                     numsInList.cend() ); // End range to search for
```

`search_n()` can be used to check if *n* instances of a value placed consequently are to be found in a container:

```
auto partialRange = search_n (numsInVec.cbegin(), // Start range
                              numsInVec.cend(),   // End range
                              3,   // num items to be searched for
                              9);    // value to search for
```

Both functions return an iterator to the first instance of the pattern found, and this iterator needs to be checked against `end()` before it can be used. Listing 23.3 demonstrates the usage of `search()` and `search_n()`.

LISTING 23.3 Finding a Range in a Collection Using `search()` and `search_n()`

```
 0: #include <algorithm>
 1: #include <vector>
 2: #include <list>
 3: #include <iostream>
 4: using namespace std;
 5:
 6: template <typename T>
 7: void DisplayContents (const T& container)
 8: {
 9:    for(auto element = container.cbegin();
10:        element != container.cend();
11:        ++ element)
12:      cout << *element << ' ';
13:
14:    cout << endl;
15: }
16:
17: int main()
18: {
19:    vector <int> numsInVec{ 2017, 0, -1, 42, 10101, 25, 9, 9, 9 };
20:    list <int> numsInList{ -1, 42, 10101 };
21:
22:    cout << "The contents of the sample vector are: " << endl;
23:    DisplayContents (numsInVec);
24:
25:    cout << "The contents of the sample list are: " << endl;
26:    DisplayContents (numsInList);
27:
28:    cout << "search() for the contents of list in vector:" << endl;
29:    auto range = search (numsInVec.cbegin(), // Start range to search in
30:                         numsInVec.cend(), // End range to search in
31:                         numsInList.cbegin(), // Start range to search for
32:                         numsInList.cend()); // End range to search for
33:
34:    // Check if search found a match
```

```
35:     if (range != numsInVec.end())
36:     {
37:         cout << "Sequence in list found in vector at position: ";
38:         cout << distance (numsInVec.cbegin(), range) << endl;
39:     }
40:
41:     cout << "Searching {9, 9, 9} in vector using search_n(): " << endl;
42:     auto partialRange = search_n (numsInVec.cbegin(), // Start range
43:                                   numsInVec.cend(),    // End range
44:                                   3,   // Count of item to be searched for
45:                                   9 );   // Item to search for
46:
47:     if (partialRange != numsInVec.end())
48:     {
49:         cout << "Sequence {9, 9, 9} found in vector at position: ";
50:         cout << distance (numsInVec.cbegin(), partialRange) << endl;
51:     }
52:
53:     return 0;
54: }
```

Output ▼

```
The contents of the sample vector are:
2017 0 -1 42 10101 25 9 9 9
The contents of the sample list are:
-1 42 10101
search() for the contents of list in vector:
Sequence in list found in vector at position: 2
Searching {9, 9, 9} in vector using search_n():
Sequence {9, 9, 9} found in vector at position: 6
```

Analysis ▼

The sample starts with two sample containers, a vector and a list that are initially populated with sample integer values. search() is used to find the presence of the contents of the list in vector, as shown in Line 29. As you want to search in the entire vector for the contents of the entire list, you supply a range as returned by the iterators corresponding to cbegin() and cend() member methods of the two container classes. This actually demonstrates how well iterators connect the algorithms to the containers. The physical characteristics of the containers that supply those iterators are of no significance to algorithms, which search the contents of a list in a vector seamlessly as they only work with iterators. search_n() is used in Line 42 to find the first occurrence of series {9, 9, 9}in the vector.

Initializing Elements in a Container to a Specific Value

fill() and fill_n() are the STL algorithms that help set the contents of a given range to a specified value. fill() is used to overwrite the elements in a range given the bounds of the range and the value to be inserted:

```
vector <int> numsInVec (3);

// fill all elements in the container with value 9
fill (numsInVec.begin (), numsInVec.end (), 9);
```

As the name suggests, fill_n() resets a specified n number of values. It needs a starting position, a count, and the value to fill:

```
fill_n (numsInVec.begin () + 3, /*count*/ 3, /*fill value*/ -9);
```

Listing 23.4 demonstrates how these algorithms make initializing elements in a vector<int> easy.

LISTING 23.4   Using fill() and fill_n() to Set Initial Values in a Container

```
 0: #include <algorithm>
 1: #include <vector>
 2: #include <iostream>
 3:
 4: int main ()
 5: {
 6:     using namespace std;
 7:
 8:     // Initialize a sample vector with 3 elements
 9:     vector <int> numsInVec (3);
10:
11:     // fill all elements in the container with value 9
12:     fill (numsInVec.begin (), numsInVec.end (), 9);
13:
14:     // Increase the size of the vector to hold 6 elements
15:     numsInVec.resize (6);
16:
17:     // Fill the three elements starting at offset position 3 with value -9
18:     fill_n (numsInVec.begin () + 3, 3, -9);
19:
20:     cout << "Contents of the vector are: " << endl;
```

```
21:      for (size_t index = 0; index < numsInVec.size (); ++ index)
22:      {
23:          cout << "Element [" << index << "] = ";
24:          cout << numsInVec [index] << endl;
25:      }
26:
27:      return 0;
28: }
```

Output ▼

```
Contents of the vector are:
Element [0] = 9
Element [1] = 9
Element [2] = 9
Element [3] = -9
Element [4] = -9
Element [5] = -9
```

23

Analysis ▼

Listing 23.4 uses the `fill()` and `fill_n()` functions to initialize the contents of the container to two separate sets of values, as shown in Lines 12 and 18. Note the usage of the `resize()` function in Line 15 where the vector is asked to create space for a total number of 6 elements. The three new elements are later filled with the value -9 using `fill_n()` in Line 18. The `fill()` algorithm works on a complete range, whereas `fill_n()` has the potential to work on a partial range.

TIP

You may have noticed that code in Listings 23.1, 23.2, and 23.3 use the constant versions of the iterators; that is, `cbegin()` and `cend()` are used in defining the bounds of elements accessed in a container. However, Listing 23.4 is a deviation in that it uses `begin()` and `end()`. This is simply because the purpose of the algorithm `fill()` is to modify the elements in the container, and this cannot be achieved using constant iterators that don't allow changes to the element they point to.

Using constant iterators is a good practice, and you may deviate from it when you are certain about the need to modify the elements they point to.

Using `std::generate()` to Initialize Elements to a Value Generated at Runtime

Just as `fill()` and `fill_n()` functions fill the collection with a specific value, STL algorithms, such as `generate()` and `generate_n()`, are used to initialize collections using values returned by a unary function.

You can use `generate()` to fill a range using the return value of a generator function:

```
generate (numsInVec.begin (), numsInVec.end (),    // range
          rand);    // generator function
```

`generate_n()` is similar to `generate()` except that you supply the number of elements to be assigned instead of the closing bound of a range:

```
generate_n (numsInList.begin (), 5, rand);
```

Thus, you can use these two algorithms to initialize the contents of a container to the contents of a file, for example, or to random values, as shown in Listing 23.5.

LISTING 23.5   Using `generate()` and `generate_n()` to Initialize Collections to Random Values

```
0: #include <algorithm>
1: #include <vector>
2: #include <list>
3: #include <iostream>
4: #include <ctime>
5:
6: int main ()
7: {
8:     using namespace std;
9:     srand(time(NULL)); // seed random generator using time
10:
11:     vector <int> numsInVec (5);
12:     generate (numsInVec.begin (), numsInVec.end (),    // range
13:                 rand);    // generator function
14:
15:     cout << "Elements in the vector are: ";
16:     for (size_t index = 0; index < numsInVec.size (); ++ index)
17:         cout << numsInVec [index] << " ";
18:     cout << endl;
19:
20:     list <int> numsInList (5);
21:     generate_n (numsInList.begin (), 3, rand);
22:
23:     cout << "Elements in the list are: ";
24:     for (auto element = numsInList.begin ();
```

```
25:            element != numsInList.end();
26:            ++ element )
27:            cout << *element << ' ';
28:
29:      return 0;
30: }
```

Output ▼

```
Elements in the vector are: 41 18467 6334 26500 19169
Elements in the list are: 15724 11478 29358 0 0
```

Analysis ▼

The usage of a random number generator seeded using the current time as seen in Line 9 means that the output is likely to be different on every run of the application. Listing 23.5 uses the generate() in Line 12 to populate all elements in the vector and uses generate_n() in Line 21 to populate the first three elements in the list with random values supplied by the generator function rand(). Note that the generate() function accepts a range as an input and consequently calls the specified function object rand() for every element in the range. generate_n(), in comparison, accepts only the starting position. It then invokes the specified function object, rand(), the number of times specified by the count parameter to overwrite the contents of that many elements. The elements in the container that are beyond the specified offset go untouched.

Processing Elements in a Range Using for_each()

The for_each() algorithm applies a specified unary function object to every element in the supplied range. The usage of for_each() is

```
fnObjType retValue = for_each (start_of_range,
                               end_of_range,
                               unaryFunctionObject);
```

This unary function object can also be a lambda expression that accepts one parameter.

The return value indicates that for_each() returns the function object (also called functor) used to process every element in the supplied range. The implication of this specification is that using a struct or a class as a function object can help in storing state information, which you can later query when for_each() is done. This is demonstrated by Listing 23.6, which uses the function object to display elements in a range and also uses it to count the number of elements displayed.

LISTING 23.6   Displaying the Contents of Sequences Using `for_each()`

```cpp
0: #include <algorithm>
1: #include <iostream>
2: #include <vector>
3: #include <string>
4: using namespace std;
5:
6: template <typename elementType>
7: struct DisplayElementKeepcount
8: {
9:     int count;
10:     DisplayElementKeepcount (): count (0) {}
11:
12:     void operator () (const elementType& element)
13:     {
14:         ++ count;
15:         cout << element << ' ';
16:     }
17: };
18:
19: int main ()
20: {
21:     vector <int> numsInVec{ 2017, 0, -1, 42, 10101, 25 };
22:
23:     cout << "Elements in vector are: " << endl;
24:     DisplayElementKeepcount<int> functor =
25:         for_each (numsInVec.cbegin(),    // Start of range
26:                   numsInVec.cend (),        // End of range
27:                   DisplayElementKeepcount<int> ());// functor
28:     cout << endl;
29:
30:     // Use the state stored in the return value of for_each!
31:     cout << "'" << functor.count << "' elements displayed" << endl;
32:
33:     string str ("for_each and strings!");
34:     cout << "Sample string: " << str << endl;
35:
36:     cout << "Characters displayed using lambda:" << endl;
37:     int numChars = 0;
38:     for_each (str.cbegin(),
39:               str.cend (),
40:               [&numChars](char c) { cout << c << ' '; ++numChars; } );
41:
42:     cout << endl;
43:     cout << "'" << numChars << "' characters displayed" << endl;
44:
45:     return 0;
46: }
```

Output ▼

```
Elements in vector are:
2017 0 -1 42 10101 25
'6' elements displayed
Sample string: for_each and strings!
Characters displayed using lambda:
f o r _ e a c h   a n d   s t r i n g s !
'21' characters displayed
```

Analysis ▼

The code sample demonstrates the utility of `for_each()` invoked in Lines 25 and 38, and the function object `functor` returned by `for_each()` that is programmed to hold the number of times it was invoked in member `count`. The code features two sample ranges, one contained in a vector of integers, `numsInVec`, and the other a `std::string` object `str`. The first call to `for_each()` uses `DisplayElementKeepCount` as the unary predicate, and the second uses a lambda expression. `for_each()` invokes `operator()` for every element in the supplied range, which in turn prints the element on the screen and increments an internal counter. The function object is returned when `for_each()` is done, and the member `count` tells the number of times the object was used. This facility of storing information (or state) in the object that is returned by the algorithm can be useful in practical programming situations. `for_each()` in Line 38 does exactly the same as its previous counterpart in Line 25 for a `std::string`, using a lambda expression instead of a function object.

Performing Transformations on a Range Using `std::transform()`

`std::for_each()` and `std::transform()` are similar in that they both invoke a function object for every element in a source range. However, `std::transform()` has two versions. The first version accepts a unary function and is popularly used to convert a string to upper- or lowercase using functions `toupper()` or `tolower()`:

```cpp
string str ("THIS is a TEst string!");
transform (str.cbegin(), // start source range
           str.cend(), // end source range
           strLowerCaseCopy.begin(), // start destination range
           ::tolower);              // unary function
```

The second version accepts a binary function allowing `transform()` to process a pair of elements taken from two different ranges:

```
// sum elements from two vectors and store result in a deque
transform (numsInVec1.cbegin(),     // start of source range 1
           numsInVec1.cend(),        // end of source range 1
           numsInVec2.cbegin(),      // start of source range 2
           sumInDeque.begin(),  // store result in a deque
           plus<int>());             // binary function plus
```

Both versions of the `transform()` always assign the result of the specified transformation function to a supplied destination range, unlike `for_each()`, which works on only a single range. The usage of `std::transform()` is demonstrated in Listing 23.7.

LISTING 23.7 Using `std::transform()` with Unary and Binary Functions

```
0: #include <algorithm>
1: #include <string>
2: #include <vector>
3: #include <deque>
4: #include <iostream>
5: #include <functional>
6:
7: int main()
8: {
9:     using namespace std;
10:
11:     string str ("THIS is a TEst string!");
12:     cout << "The sample string is: " << str << endl;
13:
14:     string strLowerCaseCopy;
15:     strLowerCaseCopy.resize (str.size());
16:
17:     transform (str.cbegin(), // start source range
18:                str.cend(),    // end source range
19:                strLowerCaseCopy.begin(), // start dest range
20:                ::tolower);          // unary function
21:
22:     cout << "Result of 'transform' on the string with 'tolower':" << endl;
23:     cout << "\"" << strLowerCaseCopy << "\"" << endl << endl;
24:
25:     // Two sample vectors of integers...
26:     vector<int> numsInVec1{ 2017, 0, -1, 42, 10101, 25 };
27:     vector<int> numsInVec2 (numsInVec1.size(), -1);
28:
29:     // A destination range for holding the result of addition
30:     deque <int> sumInDeque (numsInVec1.size());
31:
```

```
32:      transform (numsInVec1.cbegin(),   // start of source range 1
33:                 numsInVec1.cend(),      // end of source range 1
34:                 numsInVec2.cbegin(),    // start of source range 2
35:                 sumInDeque.begin(),     // start of dest range
36:                 plus<int>());           // binary function
37:
38:      cout << "Result of 'transform' using binary function 'plus': " << endl;
39:      cout << "Index    Vector1 + Vector2 = Result (in Deque)" << endl;
40:      for (size_t index = 0; index < numsInVec1.size(); ++ index)
41:      {
42:          cout << index << "     \t " << numsInVec1 [index]    << "\t+    ";
43:          cout << numsInVec2 [index]  << " \t  =    ";
44:          cout << sumInDeque [index] << endl;
45:      }
46:
47:      return 0;
48: }
```

23

Output ▼

```
The sample string is: THIS is a TEst string!
Result of 'transform' on the string with 'tolower':
"this is a test string!"

Result of 'transform' using binary function 'plus':
Index    Vector1 + Vector2 = Result (in Deque)
0        2017    +   -1    =    2016
1        0       +   -1    =    -1
2        -1      +   -1    =    -2
3        42      +   -1    =    41
4        10101   +   -1    =    10100
5        25      +   -1    =    24
```

Analysis ▼

The sample demonstrates both versions of std::transform(), one that works on a single range using a unary function tolower(), as shown in Line 20, and another that works on two ranges and uses a binary function plus(), as shown in Line 36. The first changes the case of a string, character by character, to lowercase. If you use toupper() instead of tolower(), you effect a case conversion to uppercase. The other version of std::transform(), shown in Lines 32–36, acts on elements taken from two input ranges (two vectors in this case) and uses a binary predicate in the form of the STL function plus() (supplied by the header <functional>) to add them. std::transform() takes one pair at a time, supplies it to the binary function plus, and assigns the result to an element in the destination range—one that happens to belong to an std::deque.

Note that the change in container used to hold the result is purely for demonstration purposes. It only displays how well iterators are used to abstract containers and their implementation from STL algorithms; `transform()`, being an algorithm, deals with ranges and really does not need to know details on the containers that implement these ranges. So, the input ranges happened to be in `vector`, and the output ranges happened to be a `deque`, and it all works fine—so long as the bounds that define the range (supplied as input parameters to `transform`) are valid.

Copy and Remove Operations

STL supplies three prominent copy functions: `copy()`, `copy_if()`, and `copy_backward()`. `copy()` can assign the contents of a source range into a destination range in the forward direction:

```
auto lastElement = copy (numsInList.cbegin(), // start source range
                         numsInList.cend(),    // end source range
                         numsInVec.begin());   // start dest range
```

`copy_if()` is an addition to the standard library starting with C++11 and copies an element when a unary predicate supplied by you returns `true`:

```
// copy odd numbers from list into vector
copy_if (numsInList.cbegin(), numsInList.cend(),
         lastElement, // copy position in dest range
         [](int element){return ((element % 2) == 1);});
```

`copy_backward()` assigns the contents to the destination range in the backward direction:

```
copy_backward (numsInList.cbegin (),
               numsInList.cend (),
               numsInVec.end ());
```

`remove()`, on the other hand, deletes elements in a container that matches a specified value:

```
// Remove all instances of '0', resize vector using erase()
auto newEnd = remove (numsInVec.begin (), numsInVec.end (), 0);
numsInVec.erase (newEnd, numsInVec.end ());
```

`remove_if()` uses a unary predicate and removes from the container those elements for which the predicate evaluates to true:

```
// Remove all odd numbers from the vector using remove_if
newEnd = remove_if (numsInVec.begin (), numsInVec.end (),
         [](int num) {return ((num % 2) == 1);} ); //predicate

numsInVec.erase (newEnd, numsInVec.end ());  // resizing
```

Listing 23.8 demonstrates the usage of the copy and removal functions.

LISTING 23.8 A Sample That Demonstrates `copy()`, `copy_if()`, `remove()`, and `remove_if()` to Copy a `list` into a `vector`, Remove 0s and Even Numbers

```
 0: #include <algorithm>
 1: #include <vector>
 2: #include <list>
 3: #include <iostream>
 4: using namespace std;
 5:
 6: template <typename T>
 7: void DisplayContents(const T& container)
 8: {
 9:     for (auto element = container.cbegin();
10:            element != container.cend();
11:            ++ element)
12:        cout << *element << ' ';
13:
14:     cout << "| Number of elements: " << container.size() << endl;
15: }
16:
17: int main()
18: {
19:     list <int> numsInList{ 2017, 0, -1, 42, 10101, 25 };
20:
21:     cout << "Source (list) contains:" << endl;
22:     DisplayContents(numsInList);
23:
24:     // Initialize vector to hold 2x elements as the list
25:     vector <int> numsInVec (numsInList.size() * 2);
26:
27:     auto lastElement = copy (numsInList.cbegin(),  // start source range
28:                              numsInList.cend(),    // end source range
29:                              numsInVec.begin() );// start dest range
30:
31:     // copy odd numbers from list into vector
32:     copy_if (numsInList.cbegin(), numsInList.cend(),
33:            lastElement,
34:            [] (int element){return ((element % 2) != 0);});
35:
36:     cout << "Destination (vector) after copy and copy_if:" << endl;
37:     DisplayContents(numsInVec);
38:
39:     // Remove all instances of '0', resize vector using erase()
40:     auto newEnd = remove (numsInVec.begin(), numsInVec.end(), 0);
41:     numsInVec.erase (newEnd, numsInVec.end());
42:
43:     // Remove all odd numbers from the vector using remove_if
44:     newEnd = remove_if (numsInVec.begin(), numsInVec.end(),
45:                [] (int element) {return ((element % 2) != 0);} );
```

23

```
46:    numsInVec.erase (newEnd , numsInVec.end()); // resizing
47:
48:    cout << "Destination (vector) after remove, remove_if, erase:" << endl;
49:    DisplayContents(numsInVec);
50:
51:    return 0;
52: }
```

Output ▼

```
Source (list) contains:
2017 0 -1 42 10101 25 | Number of elements: 6
Destination (vector) after copy and copy_if:
2017 0 -1 42 10101 25 2017 -1 10101 25 0 0 | Number of elements: 12
Destination (vector) after remove, remove_if, erase:
42 | Number of elements: 1
```

Analysis ▼

The usage of `copy()` is shown in Line 27, where you copy the contents of the `list` into the `vector`. `copy_if()` is used in Line 32 and copies all but even numbers from the source range `numsInList` into the destination range `numsInVec` starting at the iterator position `lastElement` returned by `copy()`. `remove()` in Line 40 is used to rid `numsInVec` of all instances of 0. `remove_if()` in Line 44 removes all odd numbers.

CAUTION	Listing 23.8 demonstrates that both `remove()` and `remove_if()` return an iterator that points to the new end of the container. Yet the container `numsInVec` has not been resized yet. Elements have been deleted by the remove algorithms and other elements have been shifted forward, but the `size()` has remained unaltered, meaning there are values at the end of the vector. To resize the container (and this is important, else it has unwanted values at the end), you need to use the iterator returned by `remove()` or `remove_if()` in a subsequent call to `erase()`, as shown in Lines 41 and 46.

Replacing Values and Replacing Element Given a Condition

`replace()` and `replace_if()` are the STL algorithms that can replace elements in a collection that are equivalent to a supplied value or satisfy a given condition, respectively. `replace()` replaces elements based on the return value of the comparison operator (==):

```
cout << "Using 'std::replace' to replace value 5 by 8" << endl;
replace (numsInVec.begin (), numsInVec.end (), 5, 8);
```

`replace_if()` expects a user-specified unary predicate that returns true for every value that needs to be replaced:

```
cout << "Using 'std::replace_if' to replace even values by -1" << endl;
replace_if (numsInVec.begin (), numsInVec.end (),
   [](int element) {return ((element % 2) == 0); }, -1);
```

The usage of these functions is demonstrated by Listing 23.9.

LISTING 23.9 Using `replace()` and `replace_if()` to Replace Values in a Specified Range

```
0: #include <iostream>
1: #include <algorithm>
2: #include <vector>
3: using namespace std;
4:
5: template <typename T>
6: void DisplayContents(const T& container)
7: {
8:    for (auto element = container.cbegin();
9:         element != container.cend();
10:        ++ element)
11:       cout << *element << ' ';
12:
13:    cout << "| Number of elements: " << container.size() << endl;
14: }
15:
16: int main ()
17: {
18:    vector <int> numsInVec (6);
19:
20:    // fill first 3 elements with value 8, last 3 with 5
21:    fill (numsInVec.begin (), numsInVec.begin () + 3, 8);
22:    fill_n (numsInVec.begin () + 3, 3, 5);
23:
24:    // shuffle the container
25:    random_shuffle (numsInVec.begin (), numsInVec.end ());
26:
27:    cout << "The initial contents of vector: " << endl;
28:    DisplayContents(numsInVec);
29:
30:    cout << endl << "'std::replace' value 5 by 8" << endl;
31:    replace (numsInVec.begin (), numsInVec.end (), 5, 8);
32:
33:    cout << "'std::replace_if' even values by -1" << endl;
34:    replace_if (numsInVec.begin (), numsInVec.end (),
35:       [](int element) {return ((element % 2) == 0); }, -1);
36:
```

```
37:    cout << endl << "Vector after replacements:" << endl;
38:    DisplayContents(numsInVec);
39:
40:    return 0;
41: }
```

Output ▼

```
The initial contents of vector:
5 8 5 8 8 5 | Number of elements: 6

'std::replace' value 5 by 8
'std::replace_if' even values by -1

Vector after replacements:
-1 -1 -1 -1 -1 -1 | Number of elements: 6
```

Analysis ▼

The sample fills a `vector<int>` with sample values and then shuffles it using the STL algorithm `std::random_shuffle()` as shown in Line 25. Line 31 demonstrates the usage of `replace()` to replace all 5s by 8s. Hence, when `replace_if()`, in Line 34, replaces all even numbers with –1, the end result is that the collection has six elements, all containing an identical value of –1, as shown in the output.

Sorting and Searching in a Sorted Collection and Erasing Duplicates

Sorting and searching a sorted range (for sake of performance) are requirements that come up in practical applications. Very often you have an array of information that needs to be sorted, say for presentation's sake. You can use STL's `sort()` algorithm to sort a container:

```
sort (numsInVec.begin (), numsInVec.end ()); // ascending order
```

This version of `sort()` uses `std::less<>` as a binary predicate that uses `operator<` implemented by the type in the vector. You can supply your own predicate to change the sort order using an overloaded version:

```
sort (numsInVec.begin (), numsInVec.end (),
      [](int lhs, int rhs) {return (lhs > rhs);} ); // descending order
```

Similarly, duplicates need to be deleted before the collection is displayed. To remove adjacently placed repeating values, use algorithm unique():

```
auto newEnd = unique (numsInVec.begin (), numsInVec.end ());
numsInVec.erase (newEnd, numsInVec.end ());  // to resize
```

To search fast, STL provides you with binary_search() that is effective only on a sorted container:

```
bool elementFound = binary_search (numsInVec.begin (), numsInVec.end (), 2011);

if (elementFound)
    cout << "Element found in the vector!" << endl;
```

23

Listing 23.10 demonstrates STL algorithms std::sort() that can sort a range, std::binary_search() that can search a sorted range, and std::unique() that eliminates duplicate neighboring elements (that become neighbors after a sort() operation).

LISTING 23.10 Using sort(), binary_search(), and unique()

```
 0: #include <algorithm>
 1: #include <vector>
 2: #include <string>
 3: #include <iostream>
 4: using namespace std;
 5:
 6: template <typename T>
 7: void DisplayContents(const T& container)
 8: {
 9:     for (auto element = container.cbegin();
10:             element != container.cend();
11:             ++ element)
12:         cout << *element << endl;
13: }
14:
15: int main ()
16: {
17:     vector<string> vecNames{"John", "jack", "sean", "Anna"};
18:
19:     // insert a duplicate
20:     vecNames.push_back ("jack");
21:
22:     cout << "The initial contents of the vector are: " << endl;
23:     DisplayContents(vecNames);
24:
25:     cout << "The sorted vector contains names in the order:" << endl;
26:     sort (vecNames.begin (), vecNames.end ());
```

```
27:    DisplayContents(vecNames);
28:
29:    cout << "Searching for \"John\" using 'binary_search':" << endl;
30:    bool elementFound = binary_search (vecNames.begin (), vecNames.end (),
31:                                          "John");
32:
33:    if (elementFound)
34:        cout << "Result: \"John\" was found in the vector!" << endl;
35:    else
36:        cout << "Element not found " << endl;
37:
38:    // Erase adjacent duplicates
39:    auto newEnd = unique (vecNames.begin (), vecNames.end ());
40:    vecNames.erase (newEnd, vecNames.end ());
41:
42:    cout << "The contents of the vector after using 'unique':" << endl;
43:    DisplayContents(vecNames);
44:
45:    return 0;
46: }
```

Output ▼

```
The initial contents of the vector are:
John
jack
sean
Anna
jack
The sorted vector contains names in the order:
Anna
John
jack
jack
sean
Searching for "John" using 'binary_search':
Result: "John" was found in the vector!
The contents of the vector after using 'unique':
Anna
John
jack
sean
```

Analysis ▼

The preceding code first sorts the sample vector, vecNames in Line 26, before using binary_search() in Line 30 to find "John" in it. Similarly, std::unique() is used in Line 39 to delete the second occurrence of an adjacent duplicate. Note that unique(), like `remove()`, does not resize the container. It results in values being shifted but not a reduction in the total number of elements. To ensure that you don't have unwanted or unknown values at the tail end of the container, always follow a call to `unique()` with `vector::erase()` using the iterator returned by `unique()`, as demonstrated by Line 40.

CAUTION

> Algorithms such as `binary_search()` are effective only in sorted containers. Use of this algorithm on an unsorted vector can have undesirable consequences.

NOTE

> The usage of `stable_sort()` is the same as that of `sort()`, which you saw earlier. `stable_sort()` ensures that the relative order of the sorted elements is maintained. Maintaining relative order comes at the cost of performance—a factor that needs to be kept in mind, especially if the relative ordering of elements is not essential.

Partitioning a Range

`std::partition()` helps partition an input range into two sections: one that satisfies a unary predicate and another that doesn't:

```
bool IsEven (const int& num)   // unary predicate
{
    return ((num % 2) == 0);
}
...
partition (numsInVec.begin(), numsInVec.end(), IsEven);
```

`std::partition()`, however, does not guarantee the relative order of elements within each partition. To maintain relative order, when that is important, you should use `std::stable_partition()`:

```
stable_partition (numsInVec.begin(), numsInVec.end(), IsEven);
```

Listing 23.11 demonstrates the usage of these algorithms.

LISTING 23.11 Using `partition()` and `stable_partition()` to Partition a Range of Integers into Even and Odd Values

```
0: #include <algorithm>
1: #include <vector>
2: #include <iostream>
```

```
 3: using namespace std;
 4:
 5: bool IsEven (const int& num) // unary predicate
 6: {
 7:     return ((num % 2) == 0);
 8: }
 9:
10: template <typename T>
11: void DisplayContents(const T& container)
12: {
13:     for (auto element = container.cbegin();
14:           element != container.cend();
15:           ++ element)
16:       cout << *element << ' ';
17:
18:     cout << "| Number of elements: " << container.size() << endl;
19: }
20:
21: int main ()
22: {
23:     vector <int> numsInVec{ 2017, 0, -1, 42, 10101, 25 };
24:
25:     cout << "The initial contents: " << endl;
26:     DisplayContents(numsInVec);
27:
28:     vector <int> vecCopy (numsInVec);
29:
30:     cout << "The effect of using partition():" << endl;
31:     partition (numsInVec.begin (), numsInVec.end (), IsEven);
32:     DisplayContents(numsInVec);
33:
34:     cout << "The effect of using stable_partition():" << endl;
35:     stable_partition (vecCopy.begin (), vecCopy.end (), IsEven);
36:     DisplayContents(vecCopy);
37:
38:     return 0;
39: }
```

Output ▼

```
The initial contents:
2017 0 -1 42 10101 25 | Number of elements: 6
The effect of using partition():
42 0 -1 2017 10101 25 | Number of elements: 6
The effect of using stable_partition():
0 42 2017 -1 10101 25 | Number of elements: 6
```

Analysis ▼

The code partitions a range of integers, as contained inside vector `numsInVec`, into even and odd values. This partitioning is first done using `std::partition()`, as shown in Line 31, and is repeated on a copy using `stable_partition()` in Line 35. For the sake of being able to compare, you copy the sample range `numsInVec` into `vecCopy`, the former partitioned using `partition()`, and the latter using `stable_partition()`. The effect of using `stable_partition()` rather than partition is apparent in the output. `stable_partition()` maintains the relative order of elements in each partition. Note that maintaining this order comes at the price of performance that might be small, as in this case, or significant depending on the type of object contained in the range.

23

> **NOTE**
>
> `stable_partition()` is slower than `partition()`, and therefore you should use it only when the relative order of elements in the container is important.

Inserting Elements in a Sorted Collection

It is important that elements inserted in a sorted collection be inserted at the correct positions. STL supplies functions, such as `lower_bound()` and `upper_bound()`, to assist in meeting that need:

```
auto minInsertPos = lower_bound (names.begin(), names.end(),
                                 "Brad Pitt");
// alternatively:
auto maxInsertPos = upper_bound (names.begin(), names.end(),
                                 "Brad Pitt");
```

Hence, `lower_bound()` and `upper_bound()` return iterators pointing to the minimal and the maximal positions in a sorted range where an element can be inserted without breaking the order of the sort.

Listing 23.12 demonstrates the usage of `lower_bound()` in inserting an element at the minimal position in a sorted `list` of names.

LISTING 23.12   Using `lower_bound()` and `upper_bound()` to Insert in a Sorted Collection

```
0: #include <algorithm>
1: #include <list>
2: #include <string>
3: #include <iostream>
4: using namespace std;
5:
```

```
 6: template <typename T>
 7: void DisplayContents(const T& container)
 8: {
 9:    for (auto element = container.cbegin();
10:          element != container.cend();
11:          ++ element)
12:       cout << *element << endl;
13: }
14:
15: int main ()
16: {
17:    list<string> names{ "John", "Brad", "jack", "sean", "Anna" };
18:
19:    cout << "Sorted contents of the list are: " << endl;
20:    names.sort ();
21:    DisplayContents(names);
22:
23:    cout << "Lowest index where \"Brad\" can be inserted is: ";
24:    auto minPos = lower_bound (names.begin (), names.end (), "Brad");
25:    cout << distance (names.begin (), minPos) << endl;
26:
27:    cout << "The highest index where \"Brad\" can be inserted is: ";
28:    auto maxPos = upper_bound (names.begin (), names.end (), "Brad");
29:    cout << distance (names.begin (), maxPos) << endl;
30:
31:    cout << endl;
32:
33:    cout << "List after inserting Brad in sorted order: " << endl;
34:    names.insert (minPos, "Brad");
35:    DisplayContents(names);
36:
37:    return 0;
38: }
```

Output ▼

```
Sorted contents of the list are:
Anna
Brad
John
jack
sean
Lowest index where "Brad" can be inserted is: 1
The highest index where "Brad" can be inserted is: 2

List after inserting Brad in sorted order:
Anna
Brad
Brad
John
jack
sean
```

Analysis ▼

An element can be inserted into a sorted collection at two potential positions: one is returned by `lower_bound()` and is the lowest (the closest to the beginning of the collection) and another is the iterator returned by `upper_bound()` that is the highest (the farthest away from the beginning of the collection). In the case of Listing 23.12, where the string `"Brad"` that is inserted into the sorted collection already exists in it, the lower and upper bounds are different (else, they would've been identical). The usage of these functions is shown in Lines 24 and 29, respectively. As the output demonstrates, the iterator returned by `lower_bound()`, when used in inserting the string into the `list` as shown in Line 35, results in the list keeping its sorted state. Thus, these algorithms help you make an insertion at a point in the collection without breaking the sorted nature of the contents. Using the iterator returned by `upper_bound()` would have worked fine as well.

23

DO	DON'T
DO remember to use the container's `erase()` member method after using algorithms `remove()`, `remove_if()`, or `unique()` to resize the container.	**DON'T** forget sorting a container using `sort()` before calling `unique()` to remove repeating adjacent values. `sort()` will ensure that all elements of a value are aligned adjacent to each other, making `unique()` effective.
DO always check the iterator returned by `find()`, `find_if()`, `search()`, or `search_n()` functions for validity before using it by comparing against the `end()` of the container.	**DON'T** insert elements into a sorted container at randomly chosen positions, rather insert them using positions returned by `lower_bound()` or `upper_bound()` to ensure that the sorted order of elements remains undisturbed.
DO choose `stable_partition()` over `partition()` and `stable_sort()` over `sort()` only when the relative ordering of sorted elements is important as the `stable_*` versions can reduce the performance of the application.	**DON'T** forget that `binary_search()` is used only on a sorted container.

Summary

In this lesson, you learned one of the most important and powerful aspects of STL: algorithms. You gained an insight into the different types of algorithms, and the samples should have given you a clearer understanding of the algorithms application.

Q&A

Q Would I use a mutating algorithm, such as `std::transform()`, on an associative container, such as `std::set`?

A Even if it were possible, this should not be done. The contents of an associative container should be treated as constants. This is because associative containers sort their elements on insertion, and the relative positions of the elements play an important role in functions such as `find()` and also in the efficiency of the container. For this reason, mutating algorithms, such as `std::transform()`, should not be used on STL sets.

Q I need to set the content of every element of a sequential container to a particular value. Would I use `std::transform()` for this activity?

A Although `std::transform()` could be used for this activity, `fill()` or `fill_n()` is more suited to the task.

Q Does `copy_backward()` reverse the contents of the elements in the destination container?

A No, it doesn't. The STL algorithm `copy_backward()` reverses the order in which elements are copied but not the order in which elements are stored; that is, it starts with the end of the range and reaches the top. To reverse the contents of a collection, you should use `std::reverse()`.

Q Should I use `std::sort()` on a list?

A `std::sort()` can be used on a list in the same way it can be used on any sequential container. However, the list needs to maintain a special property that an operation on the list does not invalidate existing iterators—a property that `std::sort()` cannot guarantee to upkeep. So, for this reason, STL `list` supplies the `sort()` algorithm in the form of the member function `list::sort()`, which should be used because it guarantees that iterators to elements in the list are not invalidated even if their relative positions in the list have changed.

Q Why is it important to use functions such as `lower_bound()` or `upper_bound()` while inserting into a sorted range?

A These functions supply the first and the last positions, respectively, where an element can be inserted into a sorted collection without disturbing the sort.

Workshop

The Workshop contains quiz questions to help solidify your understanding of the material covered and exercises to provide you with experience in using what you've learned. Try to answer the quiz and exercise questions before checking the answers in Appendix E, and be certain you understand the answers before going to the next lesson.

Quiz

1. You need to remove items that meet a specific condition from a list. Would you use `std::remove_if()` or `list::remove_if()`?

2. You have a list of a class type `ContactItem`. How does the `list::sort()` function sort items of this type in the absence of an explicitly specified binary predicate?

3. How often does the `generate()` STL algorithm invoke the `generator()` function?

4. What differentiates `std::transform()` from `std::for_each()`?

Exercises

1. Write a binary predicate that accepts strings as input arguments and returns a value based on case-insensitive comparison.

2. Demonstrate how STL algorithms such as `copy()` use iterators to do their functions without needing to know the nature of the destination collections by copying between two sequences held in two dissimilar containers.

3. You are writing an application that records the characteristics of stars that come up on the horizon in the order in which they rise. In astronomy, the size of the star—as well as information on their relative rise and set sequences—is important. If you're sorting this collection of stars on the basis of their sizes, would you use `std::sort` or `std::stable_sort`?

LESSON 24
Adaptive Containers: Stack and Queue

The Standard Template Library (STL) features containers that adapt others to simulate stack and queue behavior. Such containers that internally use another and present a distinct behavior are called *adaptive containers*.

In this lesson, you learn

- The behavioral characteristics of stacks and queues
- Using the STL `stack`
- Using the STL `queue`
- Using the STL `priority_queue`

The Behavioral Characteristics of Stacks and Queues

Stacks and queues are like arrays or lists but present a restriction on how elements are inserted, accessed, and removed. Their behavioral characteristics are decided exactly by the placement of elements on insertion or the position of the element that can be erased from the container.

Stacks

Stacks are LIFO (last-in-first-out) systems where elements can be inserted or removed at the top of the container. A stack can be visualized as a stack of plates. The last plate added to the stack is going to be the first one taken off. Plates in the middle and at the bottom cannot be inspected. This method of organizing elements involving "addition and removal at the top" is illustrated in Figure 24.1.

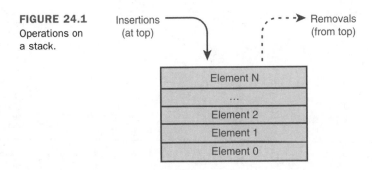

FIGURE 24.1
Operations on a stack.

Insertions (at top)

Removals (from top)

| Element N |
| ... |
| Element 2 |
| Element 1 |
| Element 0 |

This behavior of a stack of plates is simulated in the generic STL container `std::stack`.

TIP

To use class `std::stack`, include header

`#include <stack>`

Queues

Queues are FIFO (first-in-first-out) systems where elements can be inserted behind the previous one, and the one inserted first gets removed first. A queue can be visualized as a queue of people waiting for stamps at the post office—those who join the queue earlier, leave earlier. This method of organizing elements involving "addition at the back but removal at the front" is illustrated in Figure 24.2.

FIGURE 24.2
Operations on a queue.

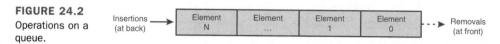

This behavior of a queue is simulated in the generic STL container std::queue.

TIP

> To use class std::queue, include header
>
> ```
> #include <queue>
> ```

Using the STL stack Class

24

The STL stack is a template class that needs the inclusion of header <stack>. It is a generic class that allows insertions and removal of elements at the top and does not permit any access or inspection of elements at the middle. In that sense, the std::stack is quite similar in behavior to a stack of plates.

Instantiating the Stack

std::stack is defined by some implementations of STL as

```
template <
   class elementType,
   class Container=deque<Type>
> class stack;
```

The parameter *elementType* is the type of object that is collected by the stack. The second template parameter Container is the stack's default underlying container implementation class. std::deque is the default for the stack's internal data storage and can be replaced by std::vector or the std::list. Thus, the instantiation of a stack of integers will look like

```
std::stack <int> numsInStack;
```

If you want to create a stack of objects of any type, for instance class Tuna, you would use the following:

```
std::stack <Tuna> tunasInStack;
```

To create a stack that uses a different underlying container, use

```
std::stack <double, vector <double>> doublesStackedInVec;
```

Listing 24.1 demonstrates different instantiation techniques.

LISTING 24.1   Instantiation of an STL Stack

```
0: #include <stack>
1: #include <vector>
2:
3: int main ()
4: {
5:     using namespace std;
6:
7:     // A stack of integers
8:     stack <int> numsInStack;
9:
10:    // A stack of doubles
11:    stack <double> dblsInStack;
12:
13:    // A stack of doubles contained in a vector
14:    stack <double, vector <double>> doublesStackedInVec;
15:
16:    // initializing one stack to be a copy of another
17:    stack <int> numsInStackCopy(numsInStack);
18:
19:    return 0;
20: }
```

Analysis ▼

The sample produces no output but demonstrates the template instantiation of the STL
stack. Lines 8 and 11 instantiate two stack objects to hold elements of type int and
double, respectively. Line 14 also instantiates a stack of doubles but specifies a
second template parameter—the type of collection class that the stack should use internally, a vector. If this second template parameter is not supplied, the stack automatically defaults to using a std::deque instead. Finally, Line 17 demonstrates that one
stack object can be constructed as a copy of another.

Stack Member Functions

The stack, which adapts another container, such as the deque, list, or vector,
implements its functionality by restricting the manner in which elements can be inserted
or removed to supply a behavior that is expected strictly from a stack-like mechanism.
Table 24.1 explains the public member functions of the stack class and demonstrates
their usage for a stack of integers.

TABLE 24.1 Member Function of a `std::stack`

Function	Description
`push()`	Inserts an element at the top of the stack
	`numsInStack.push(25);`
`pop()`	Removes the element at the top of the stack
	`numsInStack.pop();`
`empty()`	Tests whether the stack is empty; returns `bool`
	`if (numsInStack.empty ())`
	`    DoSomething ();`
`size()`	Returns the number of elements in the stack
	`size_t numElements = numsInStack.size ();`
`top()`	Gets a reference to the topmost element in the stack
	`cout << "Element at the top = " << numsInStack.top ();`

24

As the table indicates, the public member functions of the stack expose only those methods that allow insertion and removal at positions that are compliant with a stack's behavior. That is, even though the underlying container might be a `deque`, a `vector`, or a `list`, the functionality of that container has not been revealed to enforce the behavioral characteristics of a stack.

Insertion and Removal at Top Using `push()` and `pop()`

Insertion of elements is done using member method `stack<T>::push()`:

```
numsInStack.push(25); // 25 is atop the stack
```

The stack by definition allows access of elements typically at the top using member `top()`:

```
cout << numsInStack.top() << endl;
```

If you want to remove an element at the top, you can use function `pop()` to help you with the same:

```
numsInStack.pop (); // pop: removes topmost element
```

Listing 24.2 demonstrates inserting elements in a stack using push() and removing elements using pop().

LISTING 24.2   Working with a Stack of Integers

```cpp
0: #include <stack>
1: #include <iostream>
2:
3: int main ()
4: {
5:    using namespace std;
6:    stack <int> numsInStack;
7:
8:    // push: insert values at top of the stack
9:    cout << "Pushing {25, 10, -1, 5} on stack in that order:" << endl;
10:   numsInStack.push (25);
11:   numsInStack.push (10);
12:   numsInStack.push (-1);
13:   numsInStack.push (5);
14:
15:   cout << "Stack contains " << numsInStack.size () << " elements" << endl;
16:   while (numsInStack.size () != 0)
17:   {
18:      cout << "Popping topmost element: " << numsInStack.top() << endl;
19:      numsInStack.pop (); // pop: removes topmost element
20:   }
21:
22:   if (numsInStack.empty ())  // true: due to previous pop()s
23:      cout << "Popping all elements empties stack!" << endl;
24:
25:   return 0;
26: }
```

Output ▼

```
Pushing {25, 10, -1, 5} on stack in that order:
Stack contains 4 elements
Popping topmost element: 5
Popping topmost element: -1
Popping topmost element: 10
Popping topmost element: 25
Popping all elements empties stack!
```

Analysis ▼

The sample first inserts numbers into a stack of integers, numsInStack, using the stack::push() function in Lines 9–13. It then proceeds to delete elements using stack::pop(). As stack permits access to only the topmost element, an element at the top can be accessed using member stack::top() as shown in Line 18. Elements can be deleted from the stack one at a time using stack::pop(), as shown in Line 19. The while loop around it ensures that the pop() operation is repeated until the stack is empty. As is visible from the order of the elements that were popped, the element inserted last was popped first, demonstrating the typical LIFO behavior of a stack.

Listing 24.2 demonstrates all five member functions of the stack. Note that push_back() and insert(), which are available with all STL sequential containers, used as underlying containers by the stack class, are not available as public member functions of the stack. Ditto for iterators that help you peek at elements that are not at the top of the container. All that the stack exposes is the element at the top, nothing else.

Using the STL queue Class

The STL queue is a template class that requires the inclusion of the header <queue>. It is a generic class that allows insertion only at the end and removal of elements only at the front. A queue does not permit any access or inspection of elements at the middle; however, elements at the beginning and the end can be accessed. In a sense, the std::queue is quite similar in behavior to a queue of people at the cashier in a supermarket!

Instantiating the Queue

std::queue is defined as

```
template <
    class elementType,
    class Container = deque<Type>
> class queue;
```

Here, elementType is the type of elements collected by the queue object. Container is the type of collection that the std::queue class uses to maintain its data. The std::list, vector, and deque are possible candidates for this template parameter, and the deque is the default.

The simplest instantiation of a queue of integers would be the following:

```
std::queue <int> numsInQ;
```

If you want to create a queue containing elements of type double inside a std::list (instead of a deque, which is default), use the following:

```
std::queue <double, list <double>> dblsInQInList;
```

Just like a stack, a queue can also be instantiated as a copy of another queue:

```
std::queue<int> copyQ(numsInQ);
```

Listing 24.3 demonstrates the various instantiation techniques of `std::queue`.

LISTING 24.3   Instantiating an STL Queue

```
0: #include <queue>
1: #include <list>
2:
3: int main ()
4: {
5:     using namespace std;
6:
7:     // A queue of integers
8:     queue <int> numsInQ;
9:
10:     // A queue of doubles
11:     queue <double> dblsInQ;
12:
13:     // A queue of doubles stored internally in a list
14:     queue <double, list <double>> dblsInQInList;
15:
16:     // one queue created as a copy of another
17:     queue<int> copyQ(numsInQ);
18:
19:     return 0;
20: }
```

Analysis ▼

The sample demonstrates how the generic STL class `queue` can be instantiated to create a queue of integers, as shown in Line 8, or a queue for objects of type `double`, as shown in Line 11. `dblsInQInList`, as instantiated in Line 14, is a `queue` in which you have explicitly specified that the underlying container adapted by the `queue` to manage its internals be a `std::list`, as specified by the second template parameter. In the absence of the second template parameter, as in the first two queues, the `std::deque` is used as the default underlying container for the contents of the `queue`.

Member Functions of a `queue`

The `std::queue`, like `std::stack`, also bases its implementation on an STL container such as the `vector`, `list`, or `deque`. The `queue` exposes only those member functions that implement the behavioral characteristics of a queue. Table 24.2 explains the member functions using `numsInQ`, which Listing 24.3 demonstrates is a `queue` of integers.

TABLE 24.2 Member Functions of a `std::queue`

Function	Description
push()	Inserts an element at the back of the queue; that is, at the last position `numsInQ.push (10);`
pop()	Removes the element at the front of the queue; that is, at the first position `numsInQ.pop ();`
front()	Returns a reference to the element at the front of the queue `cout << "Element at front: " << numsInQ.front ();`
back()	Returns a reference to the element at the back of the queue; that is, the last inserted element `cout << "Element at back: " << numsInQ.back ();`

empty	Tests whether the queue is empty; returns a `boolean` value
	`if (numsInQ.empty ())`
	`    cout << "Queue is empty!";`

size()	Returns the number of elements in the queue `size_t numElements = numsInQ.size ();`

STL queue does not feature functions such as begin() and end(), which are supplied by most STL containers, including the underlying deque, vector, or list, as used by the queue class. This is by intention so that the only permissible operations on the queue are those in compliance with the queue's behavioral characteristics.

Insertion at End and Removal at the Beginning of queue via push() and pop()

Insertion of elements in a queue happens at the end and is done using member method push():

```
numsInQ.push (5);  // elements pushed are inserted at the end
```

Removal, on the other hand, happens at the beginning and via pop():

```
numsInQ.pop ();  // removes element at front
```

Unlike the `stack`, the `queue` allows elements at both ends—that is, front and back of the container—to be inspected:

```
cout << "Element at front: " << numsInQ.front() << endl;
cout << "Element at back: " << numsInQ.back () << endl;
```

Insertion, removal, and inspection is demonstrated in Listing 24.4.

LISTING 24.4　Inserting, Removing, and Inspecting Elements in a `queue` of Integers

```
0: #include <queue>
1: #include <iostream>
2:
3: int main ()
4: {
5:     using namespace std;
6:     queue <int> numsInQ;
7:
8:     cout << "Inserting {10, 5, -1, 20} into queue" << endl;
9:     numsInQ.push (10);
10:    numsInQ.push (5);  // elements are inserted at the end
11:    numsInQ.push (-1);
12:    numsInQ.push (20);
13:
14:    cout << "Queue contains " << numsInQ.size () << " elements" << endl;
15:    cout << "Element at front: " << numsInQ.front() << endl;
16:    cout << "Element at back: " << numsInQ.back () << endl;
17:
18:    while (numsInQ.size () != 0)
19:    {
20:        cout << "Deleting element: " << numsInQ.front () << endl;
21:        numsInQ.pop ();  // removes element at front
22:    }
23:
24:    if (numsInQ.empty ())
25:        cout << "The queue is now empty!" << endl;
26:
27:    return 0;
28: }
```

Output ▼

```
Inserting {10, 5, -1, 20} into queue
Queue contains 4 elements
Element at front: 10
Element at back: 20
Deleting element: 10
Deleting element: 5
```

```
Deleting element: -1
Deleting element: 20
The queue is now empty!
```

Analysis ▼

Elements were added to numsInQ using push() that inserts them at the end (or back) of the queue in Lines 9–12. Methods front() and back() are used to reference elements at the beginning and the end positions of the queue, as shown in Lines 15 and 16. The while loop in Lines 18–22 displays the element at the beginning of the queue, before removing it using a pop() operation at Line 21. It continues doing this until the queue is empty. The output demonstrates that elements were erased from the queue in the same order in which they were inserted because elements are inserted at the rear of the queue but deleted from the front.

Using the STL Priority Queue

24

The STL priority_queue is a template class that also requires the inclusion of the header <queue>. The priority_queue is different from the queue in that the element of the highest value (or the value deemed as highest by a binary predicate) is available at the front of the queue and queue operations are restricted to the front.

Instantiating the priority_queue Class

std::priority_queue class is defined as

```
template <
    class elementType,
    class Container=vector<Type>,
        class Compare=less<typename Container::value_type>
>
class priority_queue
```

Here, elementType is the template parameter that conveys the type of elements to be collected in the priority queue. The second template parameter tells the collection class to be internally used by priority_queue for holding data, whereas the third parameter allows the programmer to specify a binary predicate that helps the queue determine the element that is at the top. In the absence of a specified binary predicate, the priority_queue class uses the default in std::less, which compares two objects using operator<.

The simplest instantiation of a priority_queue of integers would be

```
std::priority_queue <int> numsInPrioQ;
```

If you want to create a `priority` queue containing elements of type `double` inside a `std::deque`:

```
priority_queue <int, deque <int>, greater <int>> numsInDescendingQ;
```

Just like a stack, a queue can also be instantiated as a copy of another queue:

```
std::priority_queue <int>  copyQ(numsInPrioQ);
```

The instantiation of a `priority_queue` object is demonstrated by Listing 24.5.

LISTING 24.5 Instantiating an STL `priority_queue`

```
0: #include <queue>
1: #include <functional>
2:
3: int main ()
4: {
5:     using namespace std;
6:
7:     // Priority queue of int sorted using std::less <> (default)
8:     priority_queue <int> numsInPrioQ;
9:
10:     // A priority queue of doubles
11:     priority_queue <double> dblsInPrioQ;
12:
13:     // A priority queue of integers sorted using std::greater <>
14:     priority_queue <int, deque <int>, greater<int>> numsInDescendingQ;
15:
16:     // a priority queue created as a copy of another
17:     priority_queue <int> copyQ(numsInPrioQ);
18:
19:     return 0;
20: }
```

Analysis ▼

Lines 8 and 11 demonstrate the instantiation of two `priority_queues` for objects of type `int` and `double`, respectively. The absence of any other template parameter results in the usage of `std::vector` as the internal container of data, and the default comparison criterion is provided by `std::less`. These queues are therefore so prioritized that the integer of the highest value is available at the front of the priority queue. `numsInDescendingQ`, however, supplies a `deque` for the second parameter as the internal container and `std::greater` as the predicate. This predicate results in a queue where the smallest number is available at the front.

The effect of using predicate `std::greater<T>` is explained in Listing 24.7 later in this lesson.

NOTE

> Listing 24.5 includes standard header `<functional>` to use `std::greater<>`.

Member Functions of `priority_queue`

The member functions `front()` and `back()`, available in the `queue`, are not available in the `priority_queue`. Table 24.3 introduces the member functions of a `priority_queue`.

TABLE 24.3   Member Functions of a `std::priority_queue`

Function	Description
push()	Inserts an element into the priority queue
	`numsInPrioQ.push (10);`
pop()	Removes the element at the top of the queue; that is, the largest element in the queue
	`numsInPrioQ.pop ();`
top()	Returns a reference to the largest element in the queue (which also holds the topmost position)
	`cout << "The largest element in the priority queue is: " << numsInPrioQ.top ();`
empty()	Tests whether the priority queue is empty; returns a `boolean` value
	`if (numsInPrioQ.empty ())`
	`cout << "The queue is empty!";`
size()	Returns the number of elements in the priority queue
	`size_t numElements = numsInPrioQ.size ();`

As the table indicates, `queue` members can only be accessed using `top()`, which returns the element of the highest value, evaluated using the user-defined `predicate` or by `std::less` in the absence of one.

Insertion at the End and Removal at the Beginning of `priority_queue` via `push()` and `pop()`

Insertion of elements in a `priority_queue` is done using member method `push()`:

```
numsInPrioQ.push (5);  // elements are organized in sorted order
```

Removal, on the other hand, happens at the beginning via `pop()`:

```
numsInPrioQ.pop ();  // removes element at front
```

The usage of `priority_queue` members is demonstrated by Listing 24.6.

LISTING 24.6 Working with a `priority_queue` Using `push()`, `top()`, and `pop()`

```
 0: #include <queue>
 1: #include <iostream>
 2:
 3: int main ()
 4: {
 5:    using namespace std;
 6:
 7:    priority_queue <int> numsInPrioQ;
 8:    cout << "Inserting {10, 5, -1, 20} into the priority_queue" << endl;
 9:    numsInPrioQ.push (10);
10:    numsInPrioQ.push (5);
11:    numsInPrioQ.push (-1);
12:    numsInPrioQ.push (20);
13:
14:    cout << "Deleting the " << numsInPrioQ.size () << " elements" << endl;
15:    while (!numsInPrioQ.empty ())
16:    {
17:       cout << "Deleting topmost element: " << numsInPrioQ.top () << endl;
18:       numsInPrioQ.pop ();
19:    }
20:
21:    return 0;
22: }
```

Output ▼

```
Inserting {10, 5, -1, 20} into the priority_queue
Deleting the 4 elements
Deleting topmost element: 20
Deleting topmost element: 10
Deleting topmost element: 5
Deleting topmost element: -1
```

Analysis ▼

Listing 24.6 inserts sample integers into a `priority_queue`, as shown in Lines 9–12, and then erases the element on the top/front using `pop()`, as shown in Line 18. The output indicates that the element of greatest value is available at the top of the queue. Usage of `priority_queue::pop()` therefore effectively deletes the element that evaluates to having the greatest value among all elements in the container, which is also exposed as the value at the top, via method `top()` shown in Line 17. Given that you have not supplied a prioritization predicate, the queue has automatically resorted to sorting elements in the descending order (highest value at the top).

The next sample, in Listing 24.7, demonstrates the instantiation of a `priority_queue` with `std::greater <int>` as the predicate. This predicate results in the `queue` evaluating the smallest number as the element with greatest value, which is then available at the `front` of the priority queue.

24

LISTING 24.7   Instantiating a Priority Queue That Holds the Smallest Value at the Top

```
0: #include <queue>
1: #include <iostream>
2: #include <functional>
3: int main ()
4: {
5:     using namespace std;
6:
7:     // Define a priority_queue object with greater <int> as predicate
8:     priority_queue <int, vector <int>, greater <int>> numsInPrioQ;
9:
10:    cout << "Inserting {10, 5, -1, 20} into the priority queue" << endl;
11:    numsInPrioQ.push (10);
12:    numsInPrioQ.push (5);
13:    numsInPrioQ.push (-1);
14:    numsInPrioQ.push (20);
15:
16:    cout << "Deleting " << numsInPrioQ.size () << " elements" << endl;
17:    while (!numsInPrioQ.empty ())
18:    {
19:        cout << "Deleting topmost element " << numsInPrioQ.top () << endl;
20:        numsInPrioQ.pop ();
21:    }
22:
23:    return 0;
24: }
```

Output ▼

```
Inserting {10, 5, -1, 20} into the priority queue
Deleting 4 elements
Deleting topmost element -1
Deleting topmost element 5
Deleting topmost element 10
Deleting topmost element 20
```

Analysis ▼

Most of the code and all the values supplied to the `priority_queue` in this sample are intentionally the same as those in the previous sample, Listing 24.6. Yet the output displays how the two queues behave differently. This `priority_queue` compares the elements in it using the predicate `greater <int>` as shown in Line 8. As a result of this predicate, the integer with the lowest magnitude is evaluated as greater than others and is therefore placed at the top position. So, function `top()` used in Line 19 always displays the smallest integer number in the `priority_queue`, one that is deleted soon after using a `pop()` operation in Line 20.

Thus, when elements are popped, this `priority_queue` pops the integers in order of increasing magnitude.

Summary

This lesson explained the usage of the three key adaptive containers—the STL `stack`, queue, and the `priority_queue`. These adapt sequential containers for their internal storage requirements, yet via their member functions they present the behavioral characteristics that make stacks and queues so unique.

Q&A

Q Can an element in the middle of a stack be modified?

A No, for this would contradict the purpose of a `stack`, which is supposed to be a last-in-first-out container.

Q Can I iterate through all the elements of a queue?

A The queue does not feature iterators, and elements in a queue can be accessed only at its ends.

Q Can STL algorithms work with adaptive containers?

A STL algorithms work using iterators. Because neither the `stack` nor the `queue` class supplies iterators that mark the end of the ranges, the use of STL algorithms with these containers would not be possible.

Workshop

The Workshop contains quiz questions to help solidify your understanding of the material covered and exercises to provide you with experience in using what you've learned. Try to answer the quiz and exercise questions before checking the answers in Appendix E, and be certain you understand the answers before going to the next lesson.

Quiz

1. Can you change the behavior of the `priority_queue` for a certain element, such that the one with the greatest value is popped last?

2. You have a `priority_queue` of `class Coin`. What member operator do you need to define for the `priority_queue` class to present the coin with the greater value at the top position?

3. You have a stack of class `Coin` and have pushed six objects into it. Can you access or delete the first coin inserted?

Exercises

1. A queue of people (class `Person`) are lining up at the post office. `Person` contains member attributes that hold age and gender and are defined as

```
class Person
{
    public:
        int age;
        bool isFemale;
};
```

Amend this class such that a `priority_queue` containing objects of it would offer the elderly and women (in that order) priority service.

2. Write a program that reverses the user's string input using the `stack` class.

LESSON 25
Working with Bit Flags Using STL

Bits can be an efficient way of storing settings and flags. The Standard Template Library (STL) supplies classes that help organize and manipulate bitwise information. This lesson introduces you to

- The `bitset` class
- The `vector<bool>`

The `bitset` Class

`std::bitset` is the STL class designed for handling information in bits and bit flags. `std::bitset` is not an STL container class because it cannot resize itself. This is a utility class that is optimized for working with a sequence of bits whose length is known at compile time.

TIP

> To use class `std::bitset`, include header:
>
> `#include <bitset>`

Instantiating the `std::bitset`

This template class requires you to supply one template parameter that contains the number of bits the instance of the class has to manage:

```
bitset <4> fourBits;  // 4 bits initialized to 0000
```

You can also initialize the bitset to a bit sequence represented in a `char*` string literal:

```
bitset <5> fiveBits("10101"); // 5 bits 10101
```

Copying from one bitset while instantiating another is quite simple:

```
bitset <8> fiveBitsCopy(fiveBits);
```

Some instantiation techniques of the bitset class are demonstrated by Listing 25.1.

LISTING 25.1   Instantiating a `std::bitset`

```
 0: #include <bitset>
 1: #include <iostream>
 2: #include <string>
 3:
 4: int main ()
 5: {
 6:    using namespace std;
 7:
 8:    bitset <4> fourBits;  // 4 bits initialized to 0000
 9:    cout << "Initial contents of fourBits: " << fourBits << endl;
10:
11:    bitset <5> fiveBits ("10101"); // 5 bits 10101
12:    cout << "Initial contents of fiveBits: " << fiveBits << endl;
13:
14:    bitset <6> sixBits(0b100001); // C++14 binary literal
```

```
15:       cout << "Initial contents of sixBits: " << sixBits << endl;
16:
17:       bitset <8> eightBits (255); // 8 bits initialized to long int 255
18:       cout << "Initial contents of eightBits: " << eightBits << endl;
19:
20:       // instantiate one bitset as a copy of another
21:       bitset <8> eightBitsCopy(eightBits);
21:
23:       return 0;
24: }
```

Output ▼

```
Initial contents of fourBits: 0000
Initial contents of fiveBits: 10101
Initial contents of sixBits: 100001
Initial contents of eightBits: 11111111
```

Analysis ▼

The sample demonstrates four different ways of constructing a `bitset` object. The default constructor initializes the bit sequence to 0, as shown in Line 9. A C-style string that contains the string representation of the desired bit sequence is used in Line 11. An `unsigned long` that holds the decimal value of the binary sequence is used in Lines 14 and 17, and the copy constructor is used in Line 21. Note that in each of these instances, you had to supply the number of bits that the `bitset` is supposed to contain as a template parameter. This number is fixed at compile time; it isn't dynamic. You can't insert more bits into a `bitset` than what you specified in your code the way you can insert more elements in a vector than the `size()` planned at compile time.

25

TIP

> Note the usage of binary literal `0b100001` in Line 14. The prefix `0b` or `0B` tells the compiler that the following digits are a binary representation of an integer. This literal is new to C++ and introduced in C++14.

Using `std::bitset` and Its Members

The `bitset` class supplies member functions that help perform insertions into the `bitset`, set or reset contents, read the bits, or write them into a stream. It also supplies operators that help display the contents of a `bitset` and perform bitwise logical operations among others.

Useful Operators Featured in `std::bitset`

You learned operators in Lesson 12, "Operator Types and Operator Overloading," and you also learned that the most important role played by operators is in increasing the usability of a class. `std::bitset` provides some very useful operators, as shown in Table 25.1, that make using it really easy. The operators are explained using the sample `bitset` you learned in Listing 25.1, `fourBits`.

TABLE 25.1 Operators Supported by std::bitset

Operator	Description
operator<<	Inserts a text representation of the bit sequence into the output stream
	`cout << fourBits;`
operator>>	Inserts a string into the bitset object
	`"0101" >> fourBits;`
operator&	Performs a bitwise AND operation
	`bitset <4> result (fourBits1 & fourBits2);`
operator|	Performs a bitwise OR operation
	`bitwise <4> result (fourBits1 | fourBits2);`
operator^	Performs a bitwise XOR operation
	`bitwise <4> result (fourBits1 ^ fourBits2);`
operator~	Performs a bitwise NOT operation
	`bitwise <4> result (~fourBits1);`
operator>>=	Performs a bitwise right shift
	`fourBits >>= (2); // Shift two bits to the right`
operator<<=	Performs a bitwise left shift
	`fourBits <<= (2); // Shift two bits to the left`
operator[N]	Returns a reference to the nth bit in the sequence
	`fourBits [2] = 0;   // sets the third bit to 0`
	`bool bNum = fourBits [2]; // reads the third bit`

In addition to these, `std::bitset` also features operators such as `|=`, `&=`, `^=`, and `~=` that help perform bitwise operations on a `bitset` object.

`std::bitset` **Member Methods**

Bits can hold two states—they are either set (1) or reset (0). To help manipulate the contents of a `bitset`, you can use the member functions as listed in Table 25.2 that can help you work with a `bit`, or with all the `bits` in a `bitset`.

TABLE 25.2 Member Methods of a `std::bitset`

Function	Description
`set()`	Sets all bits in the sequence to 1
	`fourBits.set (); // sequence now contains: '1111'`
`set(N, val=1)`	Sets the *N*th bit with the value as specified in `val` (default 1)
	`fourBits.set (2, 0); // sets third bit to 0`
`reset()`	Resets all bits in the sequence to 0
	`fourBits.reset (); // sequence contains: '0000'`
`reset(N)`	Clears the *N*th bit
	`fourBits.reset (2); // the third bit is now 0`
`flip()`	Toggles all bits in the sequence
	`fourBits.flip (); // 0101 changes to 1010`
`size()`	Returns the number of bits in the sequence
	`size_t numBits = fourBits.size (); // returns 4`
`count()`	Returns the number of bits that are set
	`size_t numBitsSet = fourBits.count();`
	`size_t numBitsReset = fourBits.size() - fourBits.` `count();`

The usage of these member methods and operators is demonstrated in Listing 25.2.

LISTING 25.2 Performing Logical Operations Using a Bitset

```
0: #include <bitset>
1: #include <string>
2: #include <iostream>
3:
4: int main ()
5: {
6:    using namespace std;
```

25

```
 7:     bitset <8> inputBits;
 8:     cout << "Enter a 8-bit sequence: ";
 9:
10:     cin >> inputBits;   // store user input in bitset
11:
12:     cout << "Num 1s you supplied: " << inputBits.count () << endl;
13:     cout << "Num 0s you supplied: ";
14:     cout << inputBits.size () - inputBits.count () << endl;
15:
16:     bitset <8> inputFlipped (inputBits);   // copy
17:     inputFlipped.flip ();   // toggle the bits
18:
19:     cout << "Flipped version is: " << inputFlipped << endl;
20:
21:     cout << "Result of AND, OR and XOR between the two:" << endl;
22:     cout << inputBits << " & " << inputFlipped << " = ";
23:     cout << (inputBits & inputFlipped) << endl;   // bitwise AND
24:
25:     cout << inputBits << " | " << inputFlipped << " = ";
26:     cout << (inputBits | inputFlipped) << endl;   // bitwise OR
27:
28:     cout << inputBits << " ^ " << inputFlipped << " = ";
29:     cout << (inputBits ^ inputFlipped) << endl;   // bitwise XOR
30:
31:     return 0;
32: }
```

Output ▼

```
Enter a 8-bit sequence: 10110101
Num 1s you supplied: 5
Num 0s you supplied: 3
Flipped version is: 01001010
Result of AND, OR and XOR between the two:
10110101 & 01001010 = 00000000
10110101 | 01001010 = 11111111
10110101 ^ 01001010 = 11111111
```

Analysis ▼

This interactive program demonstrates not only how easy performing bitwise operations between two-bit sequences using std::bitset is, but also the utility of its stream operators. Shift operators (>> and <<) implemented by std::bitset made writing a bit sequence to the screen and reading a bit sequence from the user in string format a simple task. inputBits contains a user-supplied sequence that is fed into it in Line 10. count() used in Line 12 tells the number of ones in the sequence, and the number of zeroes is evaluated as the difference between size() that returns the number of bits in the bitset and `count()`, as shown in Line 14. `inputFlipped` is at the beginning a copy of `inputBits`, and then flipped using `flip()`, as shown in Line 17. It now contains the sequence with individual bits flipped—that is, toggled (0s become 1s and vice versa). The rest of the program demonstrates the result of bitwise AND, OR, and XOR operations between the two bitsets.

NOTE

One disadvantage of STL `bitset<>` is its inability to resize itself dynamically. You can use the `bitset` only where the number of bits to be stored in the sequence is known at compile time.

STL supplies the programmer with a class `vector<bool>` (also called `bit_vector` in some implementations of STL) that overcomes this shortcoming.

The `vector<bool>`

The `vector<bool>` is a partial specialization of the `std::vector` and is intended for storing `boolean` data. This class is able to dynamically size itself. Therefore, the programmer does not need to know the number of `boolean` flags to be stored at compile time.

25

TIP

To use class `std::vector<bool>`, include header:

```
#include <vector>
```

Instantiating `vector<bool>`

Instantiating a `vector<bool>` is similar to a vector, with some convenient overloads:

```
vector <bool> boolFlags1;
```

For instance, you can create a vector with 10 boolean values to start with, each initialized to 1 (that is, true):

```
vector <bool> boolFlags2 (10, true);
```

You can also create an object as a copy of another:

```
vector <bool> boolFlags2Copy (boolFlags2);
```

Some of the instantiation techniques of a `vector<bool>` are demonstrated by Listing 25.3.

LISTING 25.3   The Instantiation of `vector<bool>`

```
0: #include <vector>
1:
2: int main ()
3: {
4:      using namespace std;
5:
6:      // Instantiate an object using the default constructor
7:      vector <bool> boolFlags1;
8:
9:      // Initialize a vector with 10 elements with value true
10:      vector <bool> boolFlags2 (10, true);
11:
12:      // Instantiate one object as a copy of another
13:      vector <bool> boolFlags2Copy (boolFlags2);
14:
15:      return 0;
16: }
```

Analysis ▼

This sample presents some of the ways in which a `vector<bool>` object can be constructed. Line 7 is one that uses the default constructor. Line 10 demonstrates the creation of an object that is initialized to contain 10 `boolean` flags, each holding the value `true`. Line 13 demonstrates how one `vector<bool>` can be constructed as a copy of another.

`vector<bool>` **Functions and Operators**

The `vector<bool>` features the function `flip()` that toggles the state of the Boolean values in the sequence, similar to the function of `bitset<>::flip()`.

Otherwise, this class is quite similar to the `std::vector` in the sense that you can, for example, even `push_back` flags into the sequence. The example in Listing 25.4 demonstrates the usage of this class in further detail.

LISTING 25.4   Using the `vector<bool>`

```
0: #include <vector>
1: #include <iostream>
2: using namespace std;
3:
4: int main ()
5: {
6:    vector <bool> boolFlags(3);   // instantiated to hold 3 bool flags
7:    boolFlags [0] = true;
8:    boolFlags [1] = true;
```

```
 9:     boolFlags [2] = false;
10:
11:     boolFlags.push_back (true); // insert a fourth bool at the end
12:
13:     cout << "The contents of the vector are: " << endl;
14:     for (size_t index = 0; index < boolFlags.size (); ++ index)
15:         cout << boolFlags [index] << ' ';
16:
17:     cout << endl;
18:     boolFlags.flip ();
19:
20:     cout << "The contents of the vector are: " << endl;
21:     for (size_t index = 0; index < boolFlags.size (); ++ index)
22:         cout << boolFlags [index] << ' ';
23:
24:     cout << endl;
25:
26:     return 0;
27: }
```

Output ▼

```
The contents of the vector are:
1 1 0 1
The contents of the vector are:
0 0 1 0
```

Analysis ▼

In this sample, the Boolean flags in the vector have been accessed using the operator[], as shown in Lines 7–9, just like you would access a regular vector. The function flip() used in Line 18 toggles individual bit flags, essentially converting all 0s to 1s and vice versa. Note the usage of push_back() in Line 11. Even though you initialized boolFlags to contain three flags in Line 6, you were able to add more to it dynamically at Line 11. Adding more flags than the number specified at compile time is what you cannot do with a std::bitset.

TIP

Since C++11, you may instantiate boolFlags in Listing 25.4 with initial values using List Initialization:

```
vector <bool> boolFlags{ true, true, false };
```

25

Summary

In this lesson, you learned about the most effective tool in handling bit sequences and bit flags: the `std::bitset` class. You also gained knowledge on the `vector<bool>` class that allows you to store Boolean flags—the number of which does not need to be known at compile time.

Q&A

Q Given a situation where `std::bitset` and `vector<bool>` can both be used, which of the two classes would you prefer to hold your binary flags?

A The bitset, as it is most suited to this requirement.

Q I have a `std::bitset` object called `myBitSet` that contains a certain number of stored bits. How would I determine the number of bits that are at value 0 (or false)?

A `bitset::count()` supplies the number of bits at value 1. This number, when subtracted from `bitset::size()` (which indicates the total number of bits stored), would give you the number of 0s in the sequence.

Q Can I use iterators to access the individual elements in a `vector<bool>`?

A Yes. Because the `vector<bool>` is a partial specialization of the `std::vector`, iterators are supported.

Q Can I specify the number of elements to be held in a `vector<bool>` at compile time?

A Yes, by either specifying the number in the overloaded constructor or using `vector<bool>::resize()` function at a later instance.

Workshop

The Workshop contains quiz questions to help solidify your understanding of the material covered and exercises to provide you with experience in using what you've learned. Try to answer the quiz and exercise questions before checking the answers in Appendix E, and be certain you understand the answers before going to the next lesson.

Quiz

1. Can the `bitset` expand its internal buffer to hold a variable number of elements?

2. Why is the `bitset` not classified as an STL container class?

3. Would you use the `std::vector` to hold a number of bits that is fixed and known at compile time?

Exercises

1. Write a `bitset` class that contains four bits. Initialize it to a number, display the result, and add it to another bitset object. (The catch: Bitsets don't allow bitsetA = bitsetX + bitsetY.)

2. Demonstrate how you would toggle (that is, switch) the bits in a bitset.

25

LESSON 26
Understanding Smart Pointers

C++ programmers do not necessarily need to use plain pointer types when managing memory on the heap (or the free store); they can make use of smart pointers.

In this lesson, you learn

- What smart pointers are and why you need them
- How smart pointers are implemented
- Different smart pointer types
- Why you should not use the deprecated `std::auto_ptr`
- The Standard Library smart pointer `std::unique_ptr`
- Popular smart pointer libraries

What Are Smart Pointers?

Very simply, a smart pointer in C++ is a class with overloaded operators, which behaves like a conventional pointer. Yet, it supplies additional value by ensuring proper and timely destruction of dynamically allocated data and facilitates a well-defined object lifecycle.

The Problem with Using Conventional (Raw) Pointers

Unlike other modern programming languages, C++ supplies full flexibility to the programmer in memory allocation, deallocation, and management. Unfortunately, this flexibility is a double-edged sword. On one side it makes C++ a powerful language, but on the other it allows the programmer to create memory-related problems, such as memory leaks, when dynamically allocated objects are not correctly released.

For example:

```
SomeClass* ptrData = anObject.GetData ();
/*
    Questions: Is object pointed by ptrData dynamically allocated using new?
    If so, who calls delete? Caller or the called?
    Answer: No idea!
*/
ptrData->DoSomething();
```

In the preceding code, there is no obvious way to tell whether the memory pointed to by ptrData

- Was allocated on the heap, and therefore eventually needs to be deallocated
- Is the responsibility of the caller to deallocate
- Will automatically be destroyed by the object's destructor

Although such ambiguities can be partially solved by inserting comments and enforcing coding practices, these mechanisms are much too loose to efficiently avoid all errors caused by abuse of dynamically allocated data and pointers.

How Do Smart Pointers Help?

Given the problems with using conventional pointer and conventional memory management techniques, it should be noted that the C++ programmer is not forced to use them when he needs to manage data on the heap/free store. The programmer can choose a smarter way to allocate and manage dynamic data by adopting the use of smart pointers in his programs:

```
smart_pointer<SomeClass> spData = anObject.GetData ();

// Use a smart pointer like a conventional pointer!
spData->Display ();
(*spData).Display ();

// Don't have to worry about de-allocation
// (the smart pointer's destructor does it for you)
```

Thus, smart pointers behave like conventional pointers (let's call those *raw pointers* now) but supply useful features via their *overloaded operators* and *destructors* to ensure that dynamically allocated data is destroyed in a timely manner.

How Are Smart Pointers Implemented?

This question can for the moment be simplified to "How did the smart pointer `spData` function like a conventional pointer?" The answer is this: Smart pointer classes overload derefencing operator (*) and member selection operator (->) to make the programmer use them as conventional pointers. Operator overloading was discussed previously in Lesson 12, "Operator Types and Operator Overloading."

Additionally, to allow you to manage a type of your choice on the heap, almost all good smart pointer classes are template classes that contain a generic implementation of their functionality. Being templates, they are versatile and can be specialized to manage an object of a type of your choice.

Listing 26.1 is a sample implementation of a simple smart pointer class.

LISTING 26.1 The Minimal Essential Components of a Smart Pointer Class

```
 0: template <typename T>
 1: class smart_pointer
 2: {
 3: private:
 4:     T* rawPtr;
 5: public:
 6:     smart_pointer (T* pData) : rawPtr(pData) {}  // constructor
 7:     ~smart_pointer () {delete rawPtr;};             // destructor
 8:
 9:     // copy constructor
10:     smart_pointer (const smart_pointer & anotherSP);
11:     // copy assignment operator
12:     smart_pointer& operator= (const smart_pointer& anotherSP);
13:
14:     T& operator* () const   // dereferencing operator
```

26

```
15:      {
16:           return *(rawPtr);
17:      }
18:
19:      T* operator-> () const    // member selection operator
20:      {
21:           return rawPtr;
22:      }
23: };
```

Analysis ▼

The preceding smart pointer class displays the implementation of the two operators
* and ->, as declared in Lines 14–17 and 19–22, that help this class to function as a
"pointer" in the conventional sense. For instance, to use the smart pointer on an object
of type `class Tuna`, you would instantiate it like this:

```
smart_pointer <Tuna> smartTuna (new Tuna);
smartTuna->Swim();
// Alternatively:
(*smartTuna).Swim ();
```

This class `smart_pointer` still doesn't display or implement any functionality that
would make this pointer class very smart and make using it an advantage over using a
conventional pointer. The constructor, as shown in Line 7, accepts a pointer that is saved
as the internal pointer object in the smart pointer class. The destructor frees this pointer,
allowing for automatic memory release.

 NOTE

The implementation that makes a smart pointer really "smart"
is the implementation of the copy constructor, the assignment
operator, and the destructor. They determine the behavior of the
smart pointer object when it is passed across functions, when it
is assigned, or when it goes out of scope (that is, gets destructed).
So, before looking at a complete smart pointer implementation,
you should understand some smart pointer types.

Types of Smart Pointers

The management of the memory resource (that is, the ownership model implemented)
is what sets smart pointer classes apart. Smart pointers decide what they do with the
resource when they are copied and assigned to. The simplest implementations often result

in performance issues, whereas the fastest ones might not suit all applications. In the end, it is for the programmer to understand how a smart pointer functions before she decides to use it in her application.

Classification of smart pointers is actually a classification of their memory resource management strategies. These are

- Deep copy
- Copy on Write (COW)
- Reference counted
- Reference linked
- Destructive copy

Let's take a brief look into each of these strategies before studying the smart pointer supplied by the C++ standard library—the `std::unique_ptr`

Deep Copy

In a smart pointer that implements deep copy, every smart pointer instance holds a complete copy of the object that is being managed. Whenever the smart pointer is copied, the object pointed to is also copied (thus, deep copy). When the smart pointer goes out of scope, it releases the memory it points to (via the destructor).

Although the deep-copy–based smart pointer does not seem to render any value over passing objects by value, its advantage becomes apparent in the treatment of polymorphic objects, as seen in the following, where it can avoid slicing:

```
// Example of Slicing When Passing Polymorphic Objects by Value
// Fish is a base class for Tuna and Carp, Fish::Swim() is virtual
void MakeFishSwim (Fish aFish)     // note parameter type
{
    aFish.Swim(); // virtual function
}

// ... Some function
Carp freshWaterFish;
MakeFishSwim (freshWaterFish);  // Carp will be 'sliced' to Fish
// Slicing: only the Fish part of Carp is sent to MakeFishSwim()

Tuna marineFish;
MakeFishSwim(marineFish); // Slicing again
```

26

Slicing issues are resolved when the programmer chooses a deep-copy smart pointer, as shown in Listing 26.2.

LISTING 26.2   Using a Deep-Copy–Based Smart Pointer to Pass Polymorphic Objects by Their Base Types

```
0: template <typename T>
1: class deepcopy_smart_ptr
2: {
3: private:
4:     T* object;
5: public:
6:     //... other functions
7:
8:     // copy constructor of the deepcopy pointer
9:     deepcopy_smart_ptr (const deepcopy_smart_ptr& source)
10:    {
11:        // Clone() is virtual: ensures deep copy of Derived class object
12:        object = source->Clone ();
13:    }
14:
15:    // copy assignment operator
16:    deepcopy_smart_ptr& operator= (const deepcopy_smart_ptr& source)
17:    {
18:      if (object)
19:         delete object;
20:
21:       object = source->Clone ();
22:    }
23: };
```

Analysis ▼

As you can see, `deepcopy_smart_ptr` implements a copy constructor in Lines 9–13 that allows a deep copy of the polymorphic object via a `Clone()` function that the class needs to implement. Similarly, it also implements a copy assignment operator in Lines 16–22. For the sake of simplicity, it is taken for granted in this example that the virtual function implemented by the base class `Fish` is called `Clone()`. Typically, smart pointers that implement deep-copy models have this function supplied as either a template parameter or a function object.

Thus, when the smart pointer itself is passed as a pointer to base class type `Fish`:

```
deepcopy_smart_ptr<Carp> freshWaterFish(new Carp);
MakeFishSwim (freshWaterFish);   // Carp will not be 'sliced'
```

The deep copy implemented in the smart pointer's constructor kicks in to ensure that the object being passed is not sliced, even though syntactically only the base part of it is required by the destination function `MakeFishSwim()`.

The disadvantage of the deep-copy–based mechanism is performance. This might not be a factor for some applications, but for many others it might inhibit the programmer from using a smart pointer for his application. Instead, he might simply pass a base type pointer (conventional pointer, `Fish*`) to functions such as `MakeFishSwim()`. Other pointer types try to address this performance issue in various ways.

Copy on Write Mechanism

Copy on Write (*COW* as it is popularly called) attempts to optimize the performance of deep-copy smart pointers by sharing pointers until the first attempt at writing to the object is made. On the first attempt at invoking a non-`const` function, a COW pointer typically creates a copy of the object on which the non-`const` function is invoked, whereas other instances of the pointer continue sharing the source object.

COW has its fair share of fans. For those that swear by COW, implementing operators (`*`) and (`->`) in their `const` and non-`const` versions is key to the functionality of the COW pointer. The latter creates a copy.

The point is that when you chose a pointer implementation that follows the COW philosophy, be sure that you understand the implementation details before you proceed to use such an implementation. Otherwise, you might land in situations where you have a copy too few or a copy too many.

Reference-Counted Smart Pointers

26

Reference counting in general is a mechanism that keeps a count of the number of users of an object. When the count reduces to zero, the object is released. So, reference counting makes a very good mechanism for sharing objects without having to copy them. If you have ever worked with a Microsoft technology called COM, the concept of reference counting would have definitely crossed your path on at least one occasion.

Such smart pointers, when copied, need to have the reference count of the object in question incremented. There are at least two popular ways to keep this count:

- Reference count maintained in the object being pointed to
- Reference count maintained by the pointer class in a shared object

The first variant where the reference count is maintained in the object is called *intrusive reference counting* because the object needs to be modified. The object in this case maintains, increments, and supplies the reference count to any smart pointer class that manages it. Incidentally, this is the approach chosen by COM. The second variant where the reference count is maintained in a shared object is a mechanism where the smart pointer class can keep the reference count on the free store (a dynamically allocated integer, for example) and when copied, the copy constructor increments this value.

Therefore, the reference-counting mechanism makes it pertinent that the programmer works with the smart pointers only when using the object. A smart pointer managing the object and a raw pointer pointing to it is a bad idea because the smart pointer (smartly) releases the object when the count maintained by it goes down to zero, but the raw pointer continues pointing to the part of the memory that no longer belongs to your application. Similarly, reference counting can cause issues peculiar to their situation: Two objects that hold a pointer to each other are never released because their cyclic dependency holds their reference counts at a minimum of 1.

Reference-Linked Smart Pointers

Reference-linked smart pointers are ones that don't proactively count the number of references using the object; rather, they just need to know when the number comes down to zero so that the object can be released.

They are called *reference-linked* because their implementation is based on a double-linked list. When a new smart pointer is created by copying an existing one, it is appended to the list. When a smart pointer goes out of scope or is destroyed, the destructor de-indexes the smart pointer from this list. Reference linking also suffers from the problem caused by cyclic dependency, as applicable to reference-counted pointers.

Destructive Copy

Destructive copy is a mechanism where a smart pointer, when copied, transfers complete ownership of the object being handled to the destination and resets itself:

```
destructive_copy_smartptr <SampleClass> smartPtr (new SampleClass ());

SomeFunc (smartPtr);    // Ownership transferred to SomeFunc
// Don't use smartPtr in the caller any more!
```

Although this mechanism is obviously not intuitive to use, the advantage supplied by destructive copy smart pointers is that they ensure that at any point in time, only one active pointer points to an object. So, they make good mechanisms for returning pointers from functions, and are of use in scenarios where you can use their "destructive" properties to your advantage.

The implementation of destructive copy pointers deviates from standard, recommended C++ programming techniques, as shown in Listing 26.3.

CAUTION

`std::auto_ptr` is by far the most popular (or notorious, depending on how you look at it) pointer that follows the principles of destructive copy. Such a smart pointer is useless after it has been passed to a function or copied into another.

`std::auto_ptr` has been deprecated in C++11. Instead, you should use `std::unique_ptr`, which cannot be passed by value due to its private copy constructor and copy assignment operator. It can only be passed as a reference argument.

LISTING 26.3 A Sample Destructive Copy Smart Pointer

```
0: template <typename T>
1: class destructivecopy_ptr
2: {
3: private:
4:     T* object;
5: public:
6:     destructivecopy_ptr(T* input):object(input) {}
7:     ~destructivecopy_ptr() { delete object; }
8:
9:     // copy constructor
10:    destructivecopy_ptr(destructivecopy_ptr& source)
11:    {
12:        // Take ownership on copy
13:        object = source.object;
14:
15:        // destroy source
16:        source.object = 0;
17:    }
18:
19:    // copy assignment operator
20:    destructivecopy_ptr& operator= (destructivecopy_ptr& source)
21:    {
22:        if (object != source.object)
23:        {
24:            delete object;
25:            object = source.object;
26:            source.object = 0;
27:        }
```

26

```
28:    }
29: };
30:
31: int main()
32: {
33:     destructivecopy_ptr<int> num (new int);
34:     destructivecopy_ptr<int> copy = num;
35:
36:     // num is now invalid
37:     return 0;
38: }
```

Analysis ▼

Listing 26.3 demonstrates the implementation of a destructive-copy–based smart pointer. Lines 10–17 and 20–28 contain the copy constructor and the copy assignment operator, respectively. These functions invalidate the source when making a copy; that is, the copy constructor sets the pointer contained by the source to NULL, after copying it, therefore justifying the name "destructive copy". The assignment operator does the same thing. Thus, num is actually invalidated in Line 34 when it is assigned to another pointer. This behavior is counterintuitive to the act of assignment.

CAUTION
> The copy constructor and copy assignment operators that are critical to the implementation of destructive copy smart pointers as shown in Listing 26.3 also attract maximum criticism. Unlike most C++ classes, this smart pointer class cannot have the copy constructor and assignment operator accept const references, as it needs to invalidate the source after copying it. This is not only a deviation from traditional copy-constructor and assignment-operator semantics, but also makes using the smart pointer class counter intuitive. Few expect the copy source or the assignment source to be damaged after a copy or assignment step. The fact that such smart pointers destroy the source also makes them unsuitable for use in STL containers, such as the std::vector, or any other dynamic collection class that you might use. These containers need to copy your content internally and end up invalidating the pointers.
>
> So, for more than one reason, you are advised to avoid using destructive copy smart pointers in your programs.

Using the `std::unique_ptr`

`std::unique_ptr` was introduced to C++ starting with C++11, and it is slightly different from `auto_ptr` in the sense that it does not allow copy or assignment.

The `unique_ptr` is a simple smart pointer similar to what's shown in Listing 26.1, but with a private copy constructor and assignment operator to disallow copy via passing as an argument to a function by value, or copy via assignment. Listing 26.4 demonstrates using one.

LISTING 26.4   Using `std::unique_ptr`

```
0: #include <iostream>
1: #include <memory>  // include this to use std::unique_ptr
2: using namespace std;
3:
4: class Fish
5: {
6: public:
7:     Fish() {cout << "Fish: Constructed!" << endl;}
8:     ~Fish() {cout << "Fish: Destructed!" << endl;}
9:
10:     void Swim() const {cout << "Fish swims in water" << endl;}
11: };
12:
13: void MakeFishSwim(const unique_ptr<Fish>& inFish)
14: {
15:     inFish->Swim();
16: }
17:
```

26

```
18: int main()
19: {
20:     unique_ptr<Fish> smartFish (new Fish);
21:
22:     smartFish->Swim();
23:     MakeFishSwim(smartFish); // OK, as MakeFishSwim accepts reference
24:
25:     unique_ptr<Fish> copySmartFish;
26:     // copySmartFish = smartFish; // error: operator= is private
27:
28:     return 0;
29: }
```

Output ▼

```
Fish: Constructed!
Fish swims in water
Fish swims in water
Fish: Destructed!
```

Analysis ▼

Follow the construction and destruction sequence, as visible in the output. Note that even though the object pointed to by smartFish was constructed in main(), as expected, it was destroyed (and automatically so) even without you having invoked operator delete. This is the behavior of unique_ptr where the pointer that goes out of scope releases the object it owns via the destructor. Note how you are able to pass smartFish as an argument to MakeFishSwim() in Line 23. This is not a copy step as MakeFishSwim() accepts the parameter by reference, as shown in Line 13. If you were to remove the reference symbol & from Line 13, you would immediately encounter a compile error caused by the private copy constructor. Similarly, assignment of one unique_ptr object to another, as shown in Line 26, is also not permitted due to a private copy assignment operator.

In a nutshell, the unique_ptr is safer than the auto_ptr (that was deprecated in C++11) as it does not invalidate the source smart pointer object during a copy or assignment. Yet, it allows simple memory management by releasing the object at time of destruction.

TIP

Listing 26.4 demonstrated that the `unique_ptr` doesn't support copy:

```
copySmartFish = smartFish; // error: operator= is
private
```

It however does support move semantics. Therefore, an option that would work is

```
unique_ptr<Fish> sameFish (std::move(smartFish));
// smartFish is empty henceforth
```

If you were ever to write a lambda expression that would need to capture an `unique_ptr`, then you would use `std::move()` in your lambda capture as supported by C++14.

```
std::unique_ptr<char> alphabet(new char);
*alphabet = 's';
auto lambda = [capture = std::move(alphabet)]()
{ std::cout << *capture << endl; };


// alphabet is empty henceforth as contents have been
'moved'


lambda();
```

Don't be frustrated if the preceding code seems too exotic—it is admittedly complicated and covers a use case that most professional programmers would possibly never come across.

26

NOTE

When writing applications using multiple threads, evaluate using `std::shared_ptr` and `std::weak_ptr` supplied by C++11-compliant libraries. These facilitate thread-safe and reference-counted object sharing.

Popular Smart Pointer Libraries

It's pretty apparent that the version of the smart pointer shipped with the C++ Standard Library is not going to meet every programmer's requirements. This is precisely why there are many smart pointer libraries out there.

Boost (www.boost.org) supplies you with some well-tested and well-documented smart pointer classes, among many other useful utility classes. You can find further information on Boost smart pointers and downloads at http://www.boost.org/libs/smart_ptr/smart_ptr.htm.

Summary

In this lesson, you learned how using the right smart pointers can help write code that uses pointers, yet helps reduce allocation and object ownership–related problems. You also learned of the different smart pointer types and that it is important to know the behavior of a smart pointer class before adopting it in your application. You now know that you should not use `std::auto_ptr` as it invalidates the source during a copy or assignment. You learned about smart pointer classes available starting with C++11, the `std::unique_ptr`.

Q&A

Q I need a vector of pointers. Should I choose `auto_ptr` as the object type to be held in the vector?

A As a rule, you should never use `std::auto_ptr`. It is deprecated. A single copy or assignment operation can render the source object unusable.

Q What two operators does a class always need to load to be called a smart pointer class?

A The following: `operator*` and `operator->`. They help use objects of the class with regular pointer semantics.

Q I have an application in which `Class1` and `Class2` hold member attributes that point to objects of the other's type. Should I use a reference-counted pointer in this scenario?

A Probably you wouldn't because of the cyclic dependency that will keep the reference count from going down to zero and will consequently keep objects of the two classes permanently in the heap.

Q A string class also dynamically manages character arrays on the free store. Is a string class therefore a smart pointer, too?

A No, it isn't. These classes typically don't implement both `operator*` and `operator->` and are therefore not classifiable as smart pointers.

Workshop

The Workshop contains quiz questions to help solidify your understanding of the material covered and exercises to provide you with experience in using what you've learned. Try to answer the quiz and exercise questions before checking the answers in Appendix E, and be certain you understand the answers before going to the next lesson.

Quiz

1. Where would you look before writing your own smart pointer for your application?

2. Would a smart pointer slow down your application significantly?

3. Where can reference-counted smart pointers hold the reference count data?

4. Should the linked list mechanism used by reference-linked pointers be singly or doubly linked?

Exercises

1. **BUG BUSTER:** Point out the bug in this code:

```
std::auto_ptr<SampleClass> object (new SampleClass ());
std::auto_ptr<SampleClass> anotherObject (object);
object->DoSomething ();
anotherObject->DoSomething();
```

2. Use the `unique_ptr` class to instantiate a `Carp` that inherits from `Fish`. Pass the object as a `Fish` pointer and comment on slicing, if any.

3. **BUG BUSTER:** Point out the bug in this code:

```
std::unique_ptr<Tuna> myTuna (new Tuna);
unique_ptr<Tuna> copyTuna;
copyTuna = myTuna;
```

26

LESSON 27
Using Streams for Input and Output

You have actually been using streams all through this book, starting with Lesson 1, "Getting Started," in which you displayed "Hello World" on the screen using std::cout. It's time to give this part of C++ its due attention and learn streams from a practical point of view. In this lesson, you find out

- What streams are and how they are used
- How to write to and read from files using streams
- Useful C++ stream operations

Concept of Streams

You are developing a program that reads from the disk, writes data to the display, reads user input from the keyboard, and saves data on the disk. Wouldn't it be useful if you could treat all read activities and write activities using similar patterns irrespective of what device or location the data is coming from or going to? This is exactly what C++ streams offer you!

C++ streams are a generic implementation of read and write (in other words, input and output) logic that enables you to use certain consistent patterns toward reading or writing data. These patterns are consistent irrespective of whether you are reading data from the disk or the keyboard or whether you are writing to the display or back to the disk. You just need to use the right stream class, and the implementation within the class takes care of device- and OS-specific details.

Let's refer to one relevant line taken from your first C++ program, Listing 1.1 in Lesson 1, again:

```
std::cout << "Hello World!" << std::endl;
```

That's right: `std::cout` is a stream object of `class ostream` for console output. To use `std::cout`, you included header `<iostream>` that supplies this and other functionality such as `std::cin` that allows you to read from a stream.

So, what do I mean when I say that streams allow consistent and device-specific access? If you were to write `"Hello World"` to a text file, you would use this syntax on a file stream object `fsHello`:

```
fsHello << "Hello World!" << endl;  // "Hello World!" into a file stream
```

As you can see, after you've chosen the right stream class, writing "Hello World" to a file isn't too different in C++ than writing it to the display.

> **TIP**
>
> `operator<<` used when writing into a stream is called the stream insertion operator. You use it when writing to the display, file, and so on.
>
> `operator>>` used when writing a stream into a variable is called the stream extraction operator. You use it when reading input from the keyboard, file, and so on.

Going ahead, this lesson studies streams from a practical point of view.

Important C++ Stream Classes and Objects

C++ provides you with a set of standard classes and headers that help you perform some important and frequent I/O operations. Table 27.1 is a list of classes that you use frequently.

TABLE 27.1   Popularly Used C++ Stream Classes in the `std` Namespace

Class/Object	Purpose
cout	Standard output stream, typically redirected to the console
cin	Standard input stream, typically used to read data into variables
cerr	Standard output stream for errors
fstream	Input and output stream class for file operations; inherits from `ofstream` and `ifstream`
ofstream	Output stream class for file operations—that is, used to create files
ifstream	Input stream class for file operations—that is, used to read files
stringsstream	Input and output stream class for string operations; inherits from `istringstream` and `ostringstream`; typically used to perform conversions from (or to) string and other types

NOTE

cout, cin, and cerr are global objects of stream classes ostream, istream, and ostream, respectively. Being global objects, they're initialized before main() starts.

When using a stream class, you have the option of specifying manipulators that perform specific actions for you. `std::endl` is one such manipulator that you have been using thus far to insert a newline character:

```
std::cout  << "This lines ends here" << std::endl;
```

27

Table 27.2 demonstrates a few other such manipulator functions and flags.

TABLE 27.2 Frequently Used Manipulators in the `std` Namespace for Working with Streams

Output Manipulators	Purpose
endl	Inserts a newline character
ends	Inserts a null character
Radix Manipulators	**Purpose**
dec	Instructs stream to interpret input or display output in decimal
hex	Instructs stream to interpret input or display output in hexadecimal
oct	Instructs stream to interpret input or display output in octal
Floating Point	**Representation Manipulators Purpose**
fixed	Instructs stream to display in fixed point notation
scientific	Instructs stream to display in scientific notation
`<iomanip>`	
Manipulators	**Purpose**
setprecision	Set decimal point precision as a parameter
setw	Set field width as a parameter
setfill	Set fill character as a parameter
setbase	Set the radix/base, akin to using dec, hex, or oct as a parameter
setiosflag	Set flags via a mask input parameter of type `std::ios_base::fmtflags`
resetiosflag	Restore defaults for a particular type specified by that contained in `std::ios_base::fmtflags`

Using `std::cout` for Writing Formatted Data to Console

`std::cout` used for writing to the standard output stream is possibly the most used stream in this book thus far. Yet, it's time to revisit `cout` and use some of the manipulators in changing the way we are able to align and display data.

Changing Display Number Formats Using `std::cout`

It is possible to ask cout to display an integer in hexadecimal or in octal notations. Listing 27.1 demonstrates using cout to display an input number in various formats.

LISTING 27.1   Displaying an Integer in Decimal, Octal, and Hexadecimal Formats Using cout and `<iomanip>` Flags

```
0: #include <iostream>
1: #include <iomanip>
2: using namespace std;
3:
4: int main()
5: {
6:     cout << "Enter an integer: ";
7:     int input = 0;
8:     cin >> input;
9:
10:     cout << "Integer in octal: " << oct << input << endl;
11:     cout << "Integer in hexadecimal: " << hex << input << endl;
12:
13:     cout << "Integer in hex using base notation: ";
14:     cout<<setiosflags(ios_base::hex|ios_base::showbase|ios_base::uppercase);
15:     cout << input << endl;
16:
17:     cout << "Integer after resetting I/O flags: ";
18:     cout<<resetiosflags(ios_base::hex|ios_base::showbase|ios_base::uppercase);
19:     cout << input << endl;
20:
21:     return 0;
22: }
```

Output ▼

```
Enter an integer: 253
Integer in octal: 375
Integer in hexadecimal: fd
Integer in hex using base notation: 0XFD
Integer after resetting I/O flags: 253
```

27

Analysis ▼

The code sample uses the manipulators presented in Table 27.2 to change the way cout displays the same integer object input, supplied by the user. Note how manipulators oct and hex are used in Lines 10 and 11. In Line 14 you use setiosflags() telling it to display the numbers in hex using uppercase letters, resulting in cout displaying integer input 253 as 0XFD. The effect of `resetioflags()` used in Line 18 is demonstrated by the integer being displayed by `cout` using decimal notation again. Another way to change the radix used in displaying integer to decimal would be the following:

```
cout << dec << input << endl;   // displays in decimal
```

It is also possible to format the manner in which cout displays numbers such as Pi in that you can specify the precision, which in a fixed-point notation specifies the number of places after decimal to be shown, or you can have a number displayed using scientific notation. This and more is demonstrated by Listing 27.2.

LISTING 27.2   Using `cout` to Display `Pi` and a Circle's Area Using Fixed-Point and Scientific Notations

```
0: #include <iostream>
1: #include <iomanip>
2: using namespace std;
3:
4: int main()
5: {
6:     const double Pi = (double)22.0 / 7;
7:     cout << "Pi = " << Pi << endl;
8:
9:     cout << endl << "Setting precision to 7: " << endl;
10:    cout << setprecision(7);
11:    cout << "Pi = " << Pi << endl;
12:    cout << fixed << "Fixed Pi = " << Pi << endl;
13:    cout << scientific << "Scientific Pi = " << Pi << endl;
14:
15:    cout << endl << "Setting precision to 10: " << endl;
16:    cout << setprecision(10);
17:    cout << "Pi = " << Pi << endl;
18:    cout << fixed << "Fixed Pi = " << Pi << endl;
19:    cout << scientific << "Scientific Pi = " << Pi << endl;
20:
21:    cout << endl << "Enter a radius: ";
22:    double radius = 0.0;
23:    cin >> radius;
24:    cout << "Area of circle: " << 2*Pi*radius*radius << endl;
25:
26:    return 0;
27: }
```

Output ▼

```
Pi = 3.14286

Setting precision to 7:
Pi = 3.142857
Fixed Pi = 3.1428571
Scientific Pi = 3.1428571e+000

Setting precision to 10:
Pi = 3.1428571429e+000
Fixed Pi = 3.1428571429
Scientific Pi = 3.1428571429e+000

Enter a radius: 9.99
Area of circle: 6.2731491429e+002
```

Analysis ▼

The output demonstrates how increasing the precision to 7 in Line 10 and to 10 in Line 16 changes the display of the value of `Pi`. Also note how the manipulator `scientific` results in the calculated area of the circle being displayed as `6.2731491429e+002`.

Aligning Text and Setting Field Width Using `std::cout`

One can use manipulators such as `setw()` to set the width of the field in characters. Any insertion made to the stream is right aligned in this specified width. Similarly, `setfill()` can be used to determine what character fills the empty area in such a situation, as demonstrated by Listing 27.3.

LISTING 27.3 Set the Width of a Field via `setw()` and the Fill Characters Using `setfill()` Manipulators

```
 0: #include <iostream>
 1: #include <iomanip>
 2: using namespace std;
 3:
 4: int main()
 5: {
 6:    cout << "Hey - default!" << endl;
 7:
 8:    cout << setw(35);   // set field width to 25 columns
 9:    cout << "Hey - right aligned!" << endl;
10:
11:    cout << setw(35) << setfill('*');
```

27

```
12:     cout << "Hey - right aligned!" << endl;
13:
14:     cout << "Hey - back to default!" << endl;
15:
16:     return 0;
17: }
```

Output ▼

```
Hey - default!
              Hey - right aligned!
***************Hey - right aligned!
Hey - back to default!
```

Analysis ▼

The output demonstrates the effect of setw(35) supplied to cout in Line 8 and set-fill('*') supplied together with setw(35) in Line 11. You see that the latter results in the free space preceding the text to be displayed to be filled with asterisks, as specified in setfill().

Using `std::cin` for Input

std::cin is versatile and enables you to read input into the plain old data types, such as the int, double, and char*, and you can also read lines or characters from the screen using methods such as getline().

Using `std::cin` for Input into a Plain Old Data Type

You can feed integers, doubles, and chars directly from the standard input via cin. Listing 27.4 demonstrates the usage of cin in reading simple data types from the user.

LISTING 27.4   Using `cin` to Read Input into an `int`, a Floating-Point Number Using Scientific Notation into a `double`, and Three Letters into a `char`

```
0: #include<iostream>
1: using namespace std;
2:
3: int main()
4: {
5:     cout << "Enter an integer: ";
6:     int inputNum = 0;
7:     cin >> inputNum;
8:
9:     cout << "Enter the value of Pi: ";
10:    double Pi = 0.0;
```

```
11:     cin >> Pi;
12:
13:     cout << "Enter three characters separated by space: " << endl;
14:     char char1 = '\0', char2 = '\0', char3 = '\0';
15:     cin >> char1 >> char2 >> char3;
16:
17:     cout << "The recorded variable values are: " << endl;
18:     cout << "inputNum: " << inputNum << endl;
19:     cout << "Pi: " << Pi << endl;
20:     cout << "The three characters: " << char1 << char2 << char3 << endl;
21:
22:     return 0;
23: }
```

Output ▼

```
Enter an integer: 32
Enter the value of Pi: 0.314159265e1
Enter three characters separated by space:
c + +
The recorded variable values are:
inputNum: 32
Pi: 3.14159
The three characters: c++
```

Analysis ▼

The most interesting part about Listing 27.4 is that you entered the value of Pi using exponential notation, and `cin` filled that data into `double Pi`. Note how you are able to fill three-character variables within a single line as shown in Line 15.

Using `std::cin::get` for Input into `char*` Buffer

Just like `cin` allows you to write directly into an `int`, you can do the same with a C-style `char` array, too:

```
cout << "Enter a line: " << endl;
char charBuf [10] = {0};  // can contain max 10 chars
cin >> charBuf;  // Danger: user may enter more than 10 chars
```

When writing into a C-style string buffer, it is very important that you don't exceed the bounds of the buffer to avoid a crash or a security vulnerability. So, a better way of reading into a C-style char buffer is this:

```
cout << "Enter a line: " << endl;
char charBuf[10] = {0};
cin.get(charBuf, 9);  // stop inserting at the 9th character
```

27

This safer way of inserting text into a C-style buffer is demonstrated by Listing 27.5.

LISTING 27.5   Inserting into a `char` Buffer Without Exceeding Its Bounds

```
0: #include<iostream>
1: #include<string>
2: using namespace std;
3:
4: int main()
5: {
6:     cout << "Enter a line: " << endl;
7:     char charBuf[10] = {0};
8:     cin.get(charBuf, 9);
9:     cout << "charBuf: " << charBuf << endl;
10:
11:     return 0;
12: }
```

Output ▼

```
Enter a line:
Testing if I can cross the bounds of the buffer
charBuf: Testing i
```

Analysis ▼

As the output indicates, you have only taken the first nine characters input by the user into the `char` buffer due to the use of `cin::get` as used in Line 8. This is the safest way to deal with buffers given a length.

TIP

> As far as possible, don't use `char` arrays. Use `std::string` instead of `char*` wherever possible.

Using `std::cin` for Input into a `std::string`

`cin` is a versatile tool, and you can even use it to scan a string from the user directly into a `std::string`:

```
std::string input;
cin >> input;   // stops insertion at the first space
```

Listing 27.6 demonstrates input using `cin` into a `std::string`.

LISTING 27.6 Inserting Text into a `std::string` Using `cin`

```
0: #include<iostream>
1: #include<string>
2: using namespace std;
3:
4: int main()
5: {
6:    cout << "Enter your name: ";
7:    string name;
8:    cin >> name;
9:    cout << "Hi " << name << endl;
10:
11:    return 0;
12: }
```

Output ▼

```
Enter your name: Siddhartha Rao
Hi Siddhartha
```

Analysis ▼

The output perhaps surprises you as it displays only my first name and not the entire input string. So what happened? Apparently, `cin` stops insertion when it encounters the first white space.

To allow the user to enter a complete line, including spaces, you need to use `getline()`:

```
string name;
getline(cin, name);
```

This usage of `getline()` with `cin` is demonstrated in Listing 27.7.

27

LISTING 27.7 Reading a Complete Line Input by User Using `getline()` and `cin`

```
0: #include<iostream>
1: #include<string>
2: using namespace std;
3:
4: int main()
5: {
6:    cout << "Enter your name: ";
7:    string name;
```

```
 8:     getline(cin, name);
 9:     cout << "Hi " << name << endl;
10:
11:     return 0;
12: }
```

Output ▼

```
Enter your name: Siddhartha Rao
Hi Siddhartha Rao
```

Analysis ▼

getline() as shown in Line 8 did the job of ensuring that white space characters are not skipped. The output now contains the complete line fed by the user.

Using `std::fstream` for File Handling

std:fstream is a class that C++ provides for (relatively) platform-independent file access. `std::fstream` inherits from `std::ofstream` for writing a file and `std::ifstream` for reading one.

In other words, `std::fstream` provides you with both read and write functionality.

TIP

To use class `std::fstream` or its base classes, include header:

`#include <fstream>`

Opening and Closing a File Using `open()` and `close()`

To use an `fstream`, `ofstream`, or `ifstream` class, you need to open a file using method `open()`:

```
fstream myFile;
myFile.open("HelloFile.txt",ios_base::in|ios_base::out|ios_base::trunc);

if (myFile.is_open()) // check if open() succeeded
{
    // do reading or writing here

    myFile.close();
}
```

open() takes two arguments: The first is the path and name of the file being opened (if you don't supply a path, it assumes the current directory settings for the application), whereas the second is the mode in which the file is being opened. The modes chosen allow the file to be created even if one exists (ios_base::trunc) and allow you to read and write into the file (in | out).

Note the usage of is_open() to test whether open() succeeded.

CAUTION

> Closing the stream using close() is essential to saving the file.

There is an alternative way of opening a file stream, which is via the constructor:

```
fstream myFile("HelloFile.txt",ios_base::in|ios_base::out|ios_base::trunc);
```

Alternatively, if you want to open a file for writing only, use the following:

```
ofstream myFile("HelloFile.txt", ios_base::out);
```

If you want to open a file for reading, use this:

```
ifstream myFile("HelloFile.txt", ios_base::in);
```

TIP

> Irrespective of whether you use the constructor or the member method open(), it is recommended that you check for the successful opening of the file via is_open() before continuing to use the corresponding file stream object.

The various modes in which a file stream can be opened are the following:

27

- **ios_base::app**—Appends to the end of existing files rather than truncating them
- **ios_base::ate**—Places you at the end of the file, but you can write data anywhere in the file
- **ios_base::trunc**—Causes existing files to be truncated; the default
- **ios_base::binary**—Creates a binary file (default is text)
- **ios_base::in**—Opens file for read operations only
- **ios_base::out**—Opens file for write operations only

Creating and Writing a Text File Using `open()` and `operator<<`

After you have opened a file stream, you can write to it using `operator <<`, as Listing 27.8 demonstrates.

LISTING 27.8 Creating a New Text File and Writing Text into It Using `ofstream`

```
0: #include<fstream>
1: #include<iostream>
2: using namespace std;
3:
4: int main()
5: {
6:     ofstream myFile;
7:     myFile.open("HelloFile.txt", ios_base::out);
8:
9:     if (myFile.is_open())
10:     {
11:         cout << "File open successful" << endl;
12:
13:         myFile << "My first text file!" << endl;
14:         myFile << "Hello file!";
15:
16:         cout << "Finished writing to file, will close now" << endl;
17:         myFile.close();
18:     }
19:
20:     return 0;
21: }
```

Output ▼

```
File open successful
Finished writing to file, will close now
```

Content of file HelloFile.txt:

```
My first text file!
Hello file!
```

Analysis ▼

Line 7 opens the file in mode `ios_base::out`—that is, exclusively for writing. In Line 9 you test if `open()` succeeded and then proceed to write to the file stream using the insertion `operator <<` as shown in Lines 13 and 14. Finally, you close at Line 17 and return.

Listing 27.8 demonstrates how you are able to write into a file stream the same way as you would write to the standard output (console) using `cout`.

This indicates how streams in C++ allow for a similar way of handling different devices, writing text to the display via `cout` in the same way one would write to a file via `ofstream`.

Reading a Text File Using `open()` and `operator>>`

To read a file, one can use `fstream` and open it using flag `ios_base::in` or use `ifstream`. Listing 27.9 demonstrates reading the file `HelloFile.txt` created in Listing 27.8.

LISTING 27.9   Reading Text from File `HelloFile.txt` Created in Listing 27.8

```
0: #include<fstream>
1: #include<iostream>
2: #include<string>
3: using namespace std;
4:
5: int main()
6: {
7:     ifstream myFile;
8:     myFile.open("HelloFile.txt", ios_base::in);
9:
10:    if (myFile.is_open())
11:    {
12:       cout << "File open successful. It contains: " << endl;
13:       string fileContents;
14:
15:       while (myFile.good())
16:       {
17:          getline (myFile, fileContents);
18:          cout << fileContents << endl;
19:       }
20:
21:       cout << "Finished reading file, will close now" << endl;
22:       myFile.close();
23:    }
24:    else
25:       cout << "open() failed: check if file is in right folder" << endl;
26:
27:    return 0;
28: }
```

27

Output ▼

```
File open successful. It contains:
My first text file!
Hello file!
Finished reading file, will close now
```

NOTE — As Listing 27.9 reads the text file `"HelloFile.txt"` created using Listing 27.8, you either need to move that file to this project's working directory or merge this code into the previous one.

Analysis ▼

As always, you perform check `is_open()` to verify if the call to `open()` in Line 8 succeeded. Note the usage of the extraction `operator >>` in reading the contents of the file directly into a `string` that is then displayed on using `cout` in Line 18. We use `getline()` in this sample for reading input from a file stream in an exactly identical way as you used it in Listing 27.7 to read input from the user, one complete line at a time.

Writing to and Reading from a Binary File

The actual process of writing to a binary file is not too different from what you have learned thus far. It is important to use `ios_base::binary` flag as a mask when opening the file. You typically use `ofstream::write` or `ifstream::read` as Listing 27.10 demonstrates.

LISTING 27.10 Writing a `struct` to a Binary File and Reconstructing It from the Same

```
0: #include<fstream>
1: #include<iomanip>
2: #include<string>
3: #include<iostream>
4: using namespace std;
5:
6: struct Human
7: {
8:     Human() {};
9:     Human(const char* inName, int inAge, const char* inDOB) : age(inAge)
10:    {
11:        strcpy(name, inName);
12:        strcpy(DOB, inDOB);
13:    }
14:
15:    char name[30];
```

```
16:      int age;
17:      char DOB[20];
18: };
19:
20: int main()
21: {
22:      Human Input("Siddhartha Rao", 101, "May 1916");
23:
24:      ofstream fsOut ("MyBinary.bin", ios_base::out | ios_base::binary);
25:
26:      if (fsOut.is_open())
27:      {
28:        cout << "Writing one object of Human to a binary file" << endl;
29:        fsOut.write(reinterpret_cast<const char*>(&Input), sizeof(Input));
30:        fsOut.close();
31:      }
32:
33:      ifstream fsIn ("MyBinary.bin", ios_base::in | ios_base::binary);
34:
35:      if(fsIn.is_open())
36:      {
37:         Human somePerson;
38:         fsIn.read((char*)&somePerson, sizeof(somePerson));
39:
40:         cout << "Reading information from binary file: " << endl;
41:         cout << "Name = " << somePerson.name << endl;
42:         cout << "Age = " << somePerson.age << endl;
43:         cout << "Date of Birth = " << somePerson.DOB << endl;
44:      }
45:
46:      return 0;
47: }
```

Output ▼

```
Writing one object of Human to a binary file
Reading information from binary file:
Name = Siddhartha Rao
Age = 101
Date of Birth = May 1916
```

27

Analysis ▼

In Lines 22–31, you create an instance of `struct` `Human` that contains a `name`, `age`, and `DOB` and persist it to the disk in a binary file `MyBinary.bin` using `ofstream`. This information is then read using another stream object of type `ifstream` in Lines 33–44. The output of attributes such as `name` and so on is via the information that has been read from the binary file. This sample also demonstrates the usage of `ifstream` and `ofstream` for reading and writing a file using `ifstream::read` and `ofstream::write`, respectively. Note the usage of `reinterpret_cast` in Line 29 to essentially force the compiler to interpret the `struct` as `char*`. In Line 38, you use the C-style cast version of what is used in Line 29.

NOTE

> If it were not for explanation purposes, I would've rather persisted `struct Human` with all its attributes in an XML file. XML is a text- and markup-based storage format that allows flexibility and scalability in the manner in which information can be persisted.
>
> If `struct Human` were to be delivered in this version and after delivery if you were to add new attributes to it (like `numChildren`, for instance), you would need to worry about `ifstream::read` functionality being able to correctly read binary data created using the older versions.

Using `std::stringstream` for String Conversions

You have a string. It contains a string value 45 in it. How do you convert this string value into an integer with value 45? And vice versa? One of the most useful utilities provided by C++ is `class stringstream` that enables you to perform a host of conversion activities.

TIP

> To use class `std::stringstream`, include header:
>
> `#include <sstream>`

Listing 27.11 demonstrates some simple `stringstream` operations.

LISTING 27.11   Converting an Integer Value into a String Representation and Vice Versa Using `std::stringstream`

```
0: #include<fstream>
1: #include<sstream>
2: #include<iostream>
3: using namespace std;
4:
```

```
 5: int main()
 6: {
 7:     cout << "Enter an integer: ";
 8:     int input = 0;
 9:     cin >> input;
10:
11:     stringstream converterStream;
12:     converterStream << input;
13:     string inputAsStr;
14:     converterStream >> inputAsStr;
15:
16:     cout << "Integer Input = " << input << endl;
17:     cout << "String gained from integer = " << inputAsStr << endl;
18:
19:     stringstream anotherStream;
20:     anotherStream << inputAsStr;
21:     int Copy = 0;
22:     anotherStream >> Copy;
23:
24:     cout << "Integer gained from string, Copy = " << Copy << endl;
25:
26:     return 0;
27: }
```

Output ▼

```
Enter an integer: 45
Integer Input = 45
String gained from integer = 45
Integer gained from string, Copy = 45
```

Analysis ▼

You ask the user to enter an integer value. You first insert this integer into the `string-stream` object, as shown in Line 12, using `operator<<`. Then, you use the extraction `operator>>` in Line 14 to convert this integer into a `string`. After that, you use this string as a starting point and get an integer representation `Copy` of the numeric value held in string `inputAsStr`.

27

DO	DON'T
DO use `ifstream` when you only intend to read from a file. **DO** use `ofstream` when you only intend to write a file. **DO** remember to check if a file stream has opened successfully via `is_open()` before inserting or extracting from the stream.	**DON'T** forget to close a file stream using method `close()` after you are done using it. **DON'T** forget that extracting from `cin` to a `string` via `cin >> strData;` typically results in the `strData` containing text until the first white space and not the entire line. **DON'T** forget that function `getline(cin, strData);` fetches you an entire line from the input stream, including white spaces.

Summary

This lesson taught you C++ streams from a practical perspective. You learned that you have been using streams such as I/O streams `cout` and `cin` since the very beginning of the book. You now know how to create simple text files and how to read or write from them. You learned how `stringstream` can help you convert simple types such as integers into strings, and vice versa.

Q&A

Q I see that I can use `fstream` for both writing and reading to a file, so when should I use `ofstream` and `ifstream`?

A If your code or module needs to only be reading from a file, you should instead use `ifstream`. Similarly, if it needs to only write to a file use `ofstream`. In both cases `fstream` would work fine, but for the sake of ensuring data and code integrity, it is better to have a restrictive policy similar to using `const`, which is not compulsory either.

Q When should I use `cin.get()`, and when should I use `cin.getline()`?

A `cin.getline()` ensures that you capture the entire line including white spaces entered by the user. `cin.get()` helps you capture user input one character at a time.

Q When should I use `stringstream`?

A `stringstream` supplies a convenient way of converting integers and other simple types into a string and vice versa, as also demonstrated by Listing 27.11.

Workshop

The Workshop contains quiz questions to help solidify your understanding of the material covered and exercises to provide you with experience in using what you've learned. Try to answer the quiz and exercise questions before checking the answers in Appendix E, and be certain you understand the answers before going to the next lesson.

Quiz

1. You need to only write to a file. What stream would you use?

2. How would you use `cin` to get a complete line from the input stream?

3. You need to write `std::string` objects to a file. Would you choose `ios_base::binary` mode?

4. You opened a stream using `open()`. Why bother using `is_open()`?

Exercises

1. BUG BUSTER: Find the error in the following code:

```
fstream myFile;
myFile.open("HelloFile.txt", ios_base::out);
myFile << "Hello file!";
myFile.close();
```

2. BUG BUSTER: Find the error in the following code:

```
ifstream myFile("SomeFile.txt");
if(myFile.is_open())
{
    myFile << "This is some text" << endl;
    myFile.close();
}
```

27

LESSON 28
Exception Handling

The title says it all: dealing with extraordinary situations that disrupt the flow of your program. The lessons thus far have mostly taken an exceedingly positive approach, assuming that memory allocations will succeed, files will be found, and so on. Reality is often different.

In this lesson, you learn

- What is an exception
- How to handle exceptions
- How exception handling helps you deliver stable C++ applications

What Is an Exception?

Your program allocates memory, reads and writes data, saves to a file—the works. All this executes flawlessly on your awesome development environment, and you are even proud of the fact that your application doesn't leak a byte, though it manages a gigabyte! You ship your application and the customer deploys it on his landscape of a thousand workstations. Some of his computers are ten years old. It doesn't take much time for the first complaint to reach your inbox. Some complaints will be about an "Access Violation," whereas some others will quote an "Unhandled Exception."

There you go—"unhandled" and "exception." Clearly, your application was doing well inside your environment, so why all the fuss?

The fact is that the world out there is very heterogeneous. No two computers, even with the same hardware configuration, are alike. This is because the software running on each computer and the state the machine is in decide the amount of resources that are available at a particular time. It is therefore probable that memory allocation that worked perfectly in your environment fails in another environment.

These failures result in "exceptions."

Exceptions disrupt the normal flow of your application. After all, if there is no memory available, there is possibly no way your application can achieve what it set out to do. Yet, your application can handle that exception and display a friendly error message to the user, perform any minimal rescue operation if needed, and exit gracefully.

Handling exceptions helps you avoid those "Access Violation" or "Unhandled Exception" screens or emails. Let's see what tools C++ provides you for dealing with the unexpected.

What Causes Exceptions?

Exceptions can be caused by external factors, such as a system with insufficient resources, or by factors internal to your application, such as a pointer that is used in spite of it containing an invalid value or a divide-by-zero error. Some modules are designed to communicate errors by throwing exceptions to the caller.

NOTE _____ To protect your code against exceptions, you "handle" exceptions thereby making your code "exception safe."

Implementing Exception Safety via `try` and `catch`

`try` and `catch` are the most important keywords in C++ as far as implementing exception safety goes. To make statements exception safe, you enclose them within a `try` block and handle the exceptions that emerge out of the `try` block in the `catch` block:

```
void SomeFunc()
{
   try
   {
      int* numPtr = new int;
      *numPtr = 999;
      delete numPtr;
   }
   catch(...)  // ... catches all exceptions
   {
      cout << "Exception in SomeFunc(), quitting" << endl;
   }
}
```

Using `catch(...)` to Handle All Exceptions

Remember in Lesson 8, "Pointers and References Explained," that I mentioned that the default form of `new` returns a valid pointer to a location in memory when it succeeds but throws an exception when it fails. Listing 28.1 demonstrates how you can make memory allocations exception safe using `new` and handle situations where the computer is not able to allocate the memory you requested.

LISTING 28.1   Using `try` and `catch` in Ensuring Exception Safety in Memory Allocations

```
0: #include <iostream>
1: using namespace std;
2:
3: int main()
4: {
5:    cout << "Enter number of integers you wish to reserve: ";
6:    try
7:    {
8:       int input = 0;
9:       cin >> input;
10:
11:       // Request memory space and then return it
12:       int* numArray = new int [input];
13:       delete[] numArray;
14:    }
```

28

```
15:    catch (...)
16:    {
17:        cout << "Exception occurred. Got to end, sorry!" << endl;
18:    }
19:    return 0;
20: }
```

Output ▼

```
Enter number of integers you wish to reserve: -1
Exception occurred. Got to end, sorry!
```

Analysis ▼

For this example, I used -1 as the number of integers that I wanted to reserve. This input is ridiculous, but users do ridiculous things all the time. In the absence of the exception handler, the program would encounter a very ugly end. But thanks to the exception handler, you see that the output displays a decent message: Got to end, sorry!

Listing 28.1 demonstrates the usage of try and catch blocks. catch() takes parameters, just like a function does, and ... means that this catch block accepts all kinds of exceptions. In this case, however, we might want to specifically isolate exceptions of type std::bad_alloc as these are thrown when new fails. Catching a specific type will help you handle that type of problem in particular, for instance, show the user a message telling what exactly went wrong.

Catching Exception of a Type

The exception in Listing 28.1 was thrown from the C++ Standard Library. Such exceptions are of a known type, and catching a particular type is better for you as you can pinpoint the reason for the exception, do better cleanup, or at least show a precise message to the user, as Listing 28.2 does.

LISTING 28.2　Catching Exceptions of Type std::bad_alloc

```
0: #include <iostream>
1: #include<exception>  // include this to catch exception bad_alloc
2: using namespace std;
3:
4: int main()
5: {
6:     cout << "Enter number of integers you wish to reserve: ";
7:     try
8:     {
```

```
 9:        int input = 0;
10:        cin >> input;
11:
12:        // Request memory space and then return it
13:        int* numArray = new int [input];
14:        delete[] numArray;
15:    }
16:    catch (std::bad_alloc& exp)
17:    {
18:        cout << "Exception encountered: " << exp.what() << endl;
19:        cout << "Got to end, sorry!" << endl;
20:    }
21:    catch(...)
22:    {
23:        cout << "Exception encountered. Got to end, sorry!" << endl;
24:    }
25:    return 0;
26: }
```

Output ▼

```
Enter number of integers you wish to reserve: -1
Exception encountered: bad array new length
Got to end, sorry!
```

Analysis ▼

Compare the output of Listing 28.2 to that of Listing 28.1. You see that you are now able to supply a more precise reason for the abrupt ending of the application, namely, "bad array new length." This is because you have an additional `catch` block (yes, two `catch` blocks), one that traps exceptions of the type `catch(bad_alloc&)` shown in Lines 16–20, which is thrown by `new`.

TIP

In general, you can insert as many `catch()` blocks as you like, one after another, depending on the exceptions you expect and those that would help.

`catch(...)` as demonstrated in Listing 28.2 catches all those exception types that have not been explicitly caught by other `catch` statements.

28

Throwing Exception of a Type Using `throw`

When you caught `std::bad_alloc` in Listing 28.2, you actually caught an object of class `std::bad_alloc` thrown by `new`. It is possible for you to throw an exception of your own choosing. All you need is the keyword `throw`:

```
void DoSomething()
{
   if(something_unwanted)
      throw object;
}
```

Let's study the usage of throw in a custom-defined exception as demonstrated by Listing 28.3 that divides two numbers.

LISTING 28.3 Throwing a Custom Exception at an Attempt to Divide by Zero

```
 0: #include<iostream>
 1: using namespace std;
 2:
 3: double Divide(double dividend, double divisor)
 4: {
 5:    if(divisor == 0)
 6:       throw "Dividing by 0 is a crime";
 7:
 8:    return (dividend / divisor);
 9: }
10:
11: int main()
12: {
13:    cout << "Enter dividend: ";
14:    double dividend = 0;
15:    cin >> dividend;
16:    cout << "Enter divisor: ";
17:    double divisor = 0;
18:    cin >> divisor;
19:
20:    try
21:    {
22:       cout << "Result is: " << Divide(dividend, divisor);
23:    }
24:    catch(const char* exp)
25:    {
26:       cout << "Exception: " << exp << endl;
27:       cout << "Sorry, can't continue!" << endl;
28:    }
29:
30:    return 0;
31: }
```

Output ▼

```
Enter dividend: 2011
Enter divisor: 0
Exception: Dividing by 0 is a crime
Sorry, can't continue!
```

Analysis ▼

The code not only demonstrates that you are also able to catch exceptions of type char*, as shown in Line 24, but also that you caught an exception thrown in a called function Divide() at Line 6. Also note that you did not include all of main() within try {}; you only include the part of it that you expect to throw. This is generally a good practice, as exception handling can also reduce the execution performance of your code.

How Exception Handling Works

In Listing 28.3, you threw an exception of type char* in function Divide() that was caught in the catch(char*) handler in calling function main().

Where an exception is thrown, using throw, the compiler inserts a dynamic lookup for a compatible catch(Type) that can handle this exception. The exception handling logic first checks if the line throwing the exception is within a try block. If so, it seeks the catch(Type) that can handle the exception of this Type. If the throw statement is not within a try block or if there is no compatible catch() for the exception type, the exception handling logic seeks the same in the calling function. So, the exception handling logic climbs the stack, one calling function after another, seeking a suitable catch(Type) that can handle the exception. At each step in the stack unwinding procedure, the variables local to that function are destroyed in reverse sequence of their construction. This is demonstrated by Listing 28.4.

LISTING 28.4   The Destruction Order of Local Objects in Event of an Exception

```
0: #include <iostream>
1: using namespace std;
2:
3: struct StructA
4: {
5:     StructA() {cout << "StructA constructor" << endl; }
6:     ~StructA() {cout << "StructA destructor" << endl;  }
7: };
8:
9: struct StructB
```

28

```
10: {
11:     StructB() {cout << "StructB constructor" << endl; }
12:     ~StructB() {cout << "StructB destructor" << endl; }
13: };
14:
15: void FuncB()  // throws
16: {
17:     cout << "In Func B" << endl;
18:     StructA objA;
19:     StructB objB;
20:     cout << "About to throw up!" << endl;
21:     throw "Throwing for the heck of it";
22: }
23:
24: void FuncA()
25: {
26:     try
27:     {
28:         cout << "In Func A" << endl;
29:         StructA objA;
30:         StructB objB;
31:         FuncB();
32:         cout << "FuncA: returning to caller" << endl;
33:     }
34:     catch(const char* exp)
35:     {
36:         cout << "FuncA: Caught exception: " << exp << endl;
37:         cout << "Handled it, will not throw to caller" << endl;
38:         // throw;  // uncomment this line to throw to main()
39:     }
40: }
41:
42: int main()
43: {
44:     cout << "main(): Started execution" << endl;
45:     try
46:     {
47:         FuncA();
48:     }
49:     catch(const char* exp)
50:     {
51:         cout << "Exception: " << exp << endl;
52:     }
53:     cout << "main(): exiting gracefully" << endl;
54:     return 0;
55: }
```

Output ▼

```
main(): Started execution
In Func A
StructA constructor
StructB constructor
In Func B
StructA constructor
StructB constructor
About to throw up!
StructB destructor
StructA destructor
StructB destructor
StructA destructor
FuncA: Caught exception: Throwing for the heck of it
Handled it, will not throw to caller
main(): exiting gracefully
```

Analysis ▼

In Listing 28.4, `main()` invokes `FuncA()` that invokes `FuncB()`, which throws in Line 21. Both calling functions `FuncA()` and `main()` are exception safe as they both have a `catch(const char*)` block implemented. `FuncB()` that throws the exception has no `catch()` blocks, and hence the catch block within `FuncA()` at Lines 34–39 is the first handler to the thrown exception from `FuncB()`, as `FuncA()` is the caller of `FuncB()`. Note that `FuncA()` decided that this exception is not of a serious nature and did not propagate it to `main()`. Hence, `main()` continues as if no problem happened. If you uncomment Line 38, the exception is thrown to the caller of `FuncB()`—that is, `main()` receives it, too.

The output also indicates the order in which objects are created (the same order as you coded their instantiations) and the order in which they're destroyed as soon as an exception is thrown (in the reverse order of instantiations). This happens not only in `FuncB()` that threw the exception, but also in `FuncA()` that invoked `FuncB()` and handled the thrown exception.

CAUTION

Listing 28.4 demonstrates how destructors of local objects are invoked when an exception is thrown.

Should the destructor of an object invoked due to an exception also throw an exception, it results in an abnormal termination of your application.

28

Class `std::exception`

In catching `std::bad_alloc` in Listing 28.2, you actually caught an object of class `std::bad_alloc` thrown by `new`. `std::bad_alloc` is a class that inherits from C++ standard class `std::exception`, declared in header `<exception>`.

`std::exception` is the base class for the following important exceptions:

- **`bad_alloc`**—Thrown when a request for memory using `new` fails
- **`bad_cast`**—Thrown by `dynamic_cast` when you try to cast a wrong type (a type that has no inheritance relation)
- **`ios_base::failure`**—Thrown by the functions and methods in the `iostream` library

Class `std::exception` that is the base class supports a very useful and important virtual method `what()` that gives a more descriptive reason on the nature of the problem causing the exception. In Listing 28.2, `exp.what()` in Line 18 gives the information, "bad array new length," telling you what went wrong. You can make use of `std::exception` being a base class for many exceptions types and create one `catch(const exception&)` that can catch all exceptions that have `std::exception` as base:

```
void SomeFunc()
{
   try
   {
      // code made exception safe
   }
   catch (const std::exception& exp) // catch bad_alloc, bad_cast, etc
   {
      cout << "Exception encountered: " << exp.what() << endl;
   }
}
```

Your Custom Exception Class Derived from `std::exception`

You can throw an exception of whatever type you want. However, there is a benefit in inheriting from `std::exception`—all existing exception handlers that `catch(const std::exception&)` and work for `bad_alloc`, `bad_cast` and the like will automatically scale up to catch your new exception class as well because it has the base class in common with them. This is demonstrated in Listing 28.5.

LISTING 28.5   class `CustomException` That Inherits from `std::exception`

```
0: #include <exception>
1: #include <iostream>
2: #include <string>
3: using namespace std;
4:
5: class CustomException: public std::exception
6: {
7:     string reason;
8: public:
9:     // constructor, needs reason
10:     CustomException(const char* why):reason(why) {}
11:
12:     // redefining virtual function to return 'reason'
13:     virtual const char* what() const throw()
14:     {
15:         return reason.c_str();
16:     }
17: };
18:
19: double Divide(double dividend, double divisor)
20: {
21:     if(divisor == 0)
22:         throw CustomException("CustomException: Dividing by 0 is a crime");
23:
24:     return (dividend / divisor);
25: }
26:
27: int main()
28: {
29:     cout << "Enter dividend: ";
30:     double dividend = 0;
31:     cin >> dividend;
32:     cout << "Enter divisor: ";
33:     double divisor = 0;
34:     cin >> divisor;
35:     try
36:     {
37:         cout << "Result is: " << Divide(dividend, divisor);
38:     }
39:     catch(exception& exp)// catch CustomException, bad_alloc, etc
40:     {
41:         cout << exp.what() << endl;
42:         cout << "Sorry, can't continue!" << endl;
43:     }
44:
45:     return 0;
46: }
```

28

Output ▼

```
Enter dividend: 2011
Enter divisor: 0
CustomException: Dividing by 0 is a crime
Sorry, can't continue!
```

Analysis ▼

This is the version of Listing 28.3 that threw a simple char* exception on divide by zero. This one, however, instantiates an object of class CustomException defined in Lines 5– 17 that inherits from std::exception. Note how our custom exception class implements virtual function what() in Lines 13–16, essentially returning the reason why the exception was thrown. The catch(exception&) logic in main() in Lines 39–43 handles not only class CustomException, but also other exceptions of type bad_alloc that have the same base class exception.

NOTE

> Note the declaration of virtual method CustomException::what() in Line 13 in Listing 28.5:
>
> ```
> virtual const char* what() const throw()
> ```
>
> It ends with throw(), which means that this function itself is not expected to throw an exception—a very important and relevant restriction on a class that is used as an exception object. If you still insert a throw within this function, you can expect a compiler warning.
>
> If a function ends with throw(int), it means that the function is expected to throw an exception of type int.

DO	DON'T
DO remember to catch exceptions of type std::exception.	**DON'T** throw exceptions from destructors.
DO remember to inherit your custom exception class (if any) from std::exception.	**DON'T** take memory allocations for granted; code that does new should always be exception safe and within a try block with a catch(std::exception&).
DO throw exceptions but with discretion. They're not a substitute for return values such as true or false.	**DON'T** insert any heavy logic or resource allocations inside a catch() block. You don't want to be causing exceptions when you're handling one.

Summary

In this lesson you learned an important part of practical C++ programming. Making your applications stable beyond your own development environment is important for customer satisfaction and intuitive user experiences, and this is exactly what exceptions help you do. You found out that code that allocates resources or memory can fail and hence needs to be made exception safe. You learned about the C++ exception class `std::exception` and that if you need to be programming a custom exception class, you ideally would be inheriting from this one.

Q&A

Q Why raise exceptions instead of returning an error?

A You may not always have the privilege of returning an error. If a call to `new` fails, you need to handle exceptions thrown by `new` to prevent your application from crashing. Additionally, if an error is very severe and makes the future functioning of your application impossible, you should consider throwing an exception.

Q Why should my exception class inherit from `std::exception`?

A This is, of course, not compulsory, but it helps you reuse all those `catch()` blocks that already catch exceptions of type `std::exception`. You can write your own exception class that doesn't inherit from anything else, but then you have to insert new `catch(MyNewExceptionType&)` statements at all the relevant points.

Q I have a function that throws an exception. Does it need to be caught at the very same function?

A Not at all. Just ensure that the exception type thrown is caught at one of the calling functions in the call stack.

Q Can a constructor throw an exception?

A Constructors actually have no choice! They don't have return values, and throwing an exception is the best way to demonstrate disagreement.

Q Can a destructor throw an exception?

A Technically, yes. However, this is a bad practice as destructors are also called when the stack is unwound due to an exception. So, a destructor invoked due to an exception throwing an exception itself can clearly result in quite an ugly situation for the state of an already unstable application trying to make a clean exit.

28

Workshop

The Workshop contains quiz questions to help solidify your understanding of the material covered and exercises to provide you with experience in using what you've learned. Try to answer the quiz and exercise questions before checking the answers in Appendix E, and be certain you understand the answers before going to the following lesson.

Quiz

1. What is `std::exception`?

2. What type of exception is thrown when an allocation using `new` fails?

3. Is it alright to allocate a million integers in an exception handler (`catch` block) to back up existing data for instance?

4. How would you catch an exception object of type `class MyException` that inherits from `std::exception`?

Exercises

1. **BUG BUSTER:** What is wrong with the following code?

```cpp
class SomeIntelligentStuff
{
    bool isStuffGoneBad;
public:
    ~SomeIntelligentStuff()
    {
        if(isStuffGoneBad)
            throw "Big problem in this class, just FYI";
    }
};
```

2. **BUG BUSTER:** What is wrong with the following code?

```cpp
int main()
{
    int* millionNums = new int [1000000];
    // do something with the million integers

    delete []millionNums;
}
```

3. BUG BUSTER: What is wrong with the following code?

```
int main()
{
    try
    {
        int* millionNums = new int [1000000];
        // do something with the million integers

        delete []millionNums;
    }
    catch(exception& exp)
    {
        int* anotherMillion = new int [1000000];
        // take back up of millionNums and save it to disk
    }
}
```

28

LESSON 29
Going Forward

You have learned the basics of C++ programming. In fact, you have gone beyond theoretical boundaries in understanding how using the Standard Template Library (STL), templates, and the Standard Library can help you write efficient and compact code. It is time to give performance a look and gain a perspective on programming best practices.

In this lesson, you learn

- How your C++ application can best utilize the processor's capabilities
- Threads and multithreading
- Best practices in programming in C++
- New Features expected in C++17
- Improving your C++ skills beyond this book

What's Different in Today's Processors?

Until recently, computers got faster by using processors that featured faster processing speeds, measured in hertz (Hz), megahertz (Mhz), or gigahertz (GHz). For instance, Intel 8086 (see Figure 29.1) was a 16-bit microprocessor launched in 1978 with a clock speed of about 10MHz.

FIGURE 29.1
The Intel 8086
microprocessor.

Those were the days when processors got significantly faster at regular intervals and so did your C++ application. It was easy to rely on a waiting game to make use of improved hardware performance and improving your software's responsiveness through it. Although today's processors are getting faster, the true innovation is in the number of cores they deploy. At the time of writing this book, even popular smartphones feature 64-bit processors with four cores and more processing capacity than a desktop computer from a decade ago.

You can think of a multicore processor as a single chip with multiple processors running in parallel within it. Each processor has its own L1 cache and can work independently of the other.

A faster processor increasing the speed of your application is logical. How do multiple cores in a processor help? Each core is evidently capable of running an application in parallel, but this doesn't necessarily make your application run any faster unless you have programmed it to consume this new capability. Single-threaded C++ applications of the types you have seen this far are possibly missing the bus as far as using multicore processing capabilities go. The applications run in one thread, and hence on only one core, as shown in Figure 29.2.

FIGURE 29.2
A single-threaded application in a multiple-core processor.

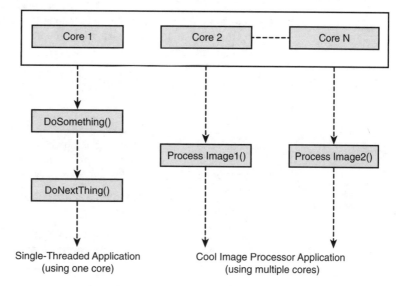

29

If your application executes all use cases in a serial order, the operating system (OS) will possibly give it only as much time as other applications in the queue and it will occupy only one core on the processor. In other words, your application is running on a multicore processor in the same way as it would do in those years gone by.

How to Better Use Multiple Cores

The key is in creating applications that are multithreaded. Each thread runs in parallel, allowing the OS to let the threads run on multiple cores. Although it is beyond the scope of this book to discuss threads and multithreading in great detail, I can just touch this topic and give you a head start toward high-performance computing.

What Is a Thread?

Your application code always runs in a thread. A thread is a synchronous execution entity where statements in a thread run one after another. The code inside `main()` is considered to execute the main thread of the application. In this main thread, you can create new threads that can run in parallel. Such applications that are comprised of one or more threads running in parallel in addition to the main thread are called multithreaded applications.

The OS dictates how threads are to be created, and you can create threads directly by calling those APIs supplied by the OS.

TIP

C++ since C++11 specifies thread functions that take care of calling the OS APIs for you, making your multithreaded application a little more portable.

If you plan to be writing your application for only one OS, check your OS's APIs on creating multithreaded applications.

NOTE

The actual act of creating a thread is an OS-specific functionality. C++ tries to supply you with a platform-independent abstraction in the form of `std::thread` in header `<thread>`.

If you are writing for one platform, you are better off just using the OS-specific thread functions.

Should you need portable threads in your C++ application, do look up Boost Thread Libraries at www.boost.org.

Why Program Multithreaded Applications?

Multithreading is used in applications that need to do multiple sessions of a certain activity in parallel. Imagine that you are one of 10,000 other users making a purchase on Amazon's web portal at a particular moment. Amazon's web server can of course not keep 9,999 users waiting at a time. What the web server does is create multiple threads, servicing multiple users at the same time. If the web server is running on a multiple-core processor or a multiple processor cloud, the threads can extract the best out of the available infrastructure and provide optimal performance to the user.

Another common example of multithreading is an application that does some work in addition to interacting with the user, for instance via a progress bar. Such applications are often divided into a User Interface Thread that displays and updates the user interface and accepts user input, and the Worker Thread that does the work in the background. A tool that defragments your disk is one such application. After you press the start button, a Worker Thread is created that starts with the scan and defragmenting activity. At the same time, the User Interface Thread displays progress and also gives you the option to cancel the defragmentation. Note that for the User Interface Thread to show progress, the Worker Thread that does the defragmentation needs to regularly communicate the same. Similarly, for the Worker Thread to stop working when you cancel, the User Interface Thread needs to communicate the same.

NOTE

Multithreaded applications often need threads to "talk" to each other so that the application can function as a unit (and not a collection of runaway threads that do their stuff irrespective of the other).

Sequence is important, too. You don't want the User Interface Thread to end before the defragmenting Worker Thread has ended. There are situations where one thread needs to wait on another. For instance, a thread that reads from a database should wait until the thread that writes is done.

The act of making threads wait on another is called *thread synchronization*.

How Can Threads Transact Data?

Threads can share variables. Threads have access to globally placed data. Threads can be created with a pointer to a shared object (`struct` or `class`) with data in it, shown in Figure 29.3.

FIGURE 29.3
Worker and user interface threads sharing data.

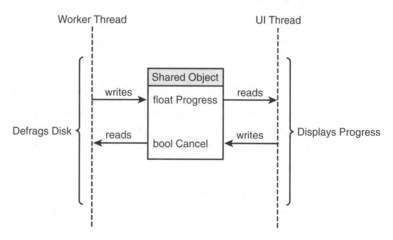

Different threads can communicate by accessing or writing data that is stored in a location in memory that can be accessed by them all and is hence shared. In the example of the defragmenter where the Worker Thread knows the progress and the User Interface Thread needs to be informed of it, the Worker Thread can constantly store the progress in percentage at an integer that the User Interface Thread uses to display the progress.

This is a simple case, though—one thread creates information and the other consumes it. What would happen if multiple threads wrote and read from the same location? Some threads might start reading data when some other threads have not finished writing them. The integrity of the data in question would be compromised.

This is why threads need to be synchronized.

Using Mutexes and Semaphores to Synchronize Threads

Threads are OS-level entities, and the objects that you use to synchronize them are supplied by the OS, too. Most operating systems provide you with *semaphores* and *mutexes* for performing thread synchronization activity.

You use a mutex, a mutual exclusion synchronization object, to ensure that one thread has access to a piece of code at a time. In other words, a mutex is used to bracket a section of code where a thread has to wait until another thread that is currently executing it is done and releases the mutex. The next thread acquires the mutex, does its job, and releases the same. C++ starting with C++11 supplies you with an implementation of a mutex in class `std::mutex` available via header `<mutex>`.

Using semaphores, you can control the number of threads that execute a section of code. A semaphore that allows access to only one thread at a time is also called a binary semaphore.

Problems Caused by Multithreading

Multithreading with its need for good synchronization across threads can also cause a good number of sleepless nights when this synchronization is not effective (read: buggy). Two of the most frequent issues that multithreaded applications face are the following:

- **Race conditions**—Two or more threads trying to write to the same data. Who wins? What is the state of that object?
- **Deadlock**—Two threads waiting on each other to finish resulting in both being in a "wait" state. Your application is hung.

You can avoid race conditions with good synchronization. In general, when threads are allowed to write to a shared object, you must take extra care to ensure that

- Only one thread writes at a time.
- No thread is allowed to read that object until the writing thread is done.

You can avoid deadlocks by ensuring that in no situation do two threads wait on each other. You can either have a master thread that synchronizes worker threads or program in a way such that tasks are distributed between threads and result in clear workload distribution. A thread A can wait on B, but B should never need to wait on A.

Programming multithreaded applications is a specialization in itself. Hence, it is beyond the scope of this book to explain this interesting and exciting topic to you in detail. You should either refer to the plenty of online documentation available on the topic or learn multithreading by hands-on programming. Once you master it, you will automatically position your C++ applications optimally as far as using multicore processors being released in the future goes.

Writing Great C++ Code

C++ has not only evolved significantly since the days it was first conceived, but standardization efforts made by major compiler manufacturers and the availability of utilities and functions help you write compact and clean C++ code. It is indeed easy to program readable and reliable C++ applications.

Here is a short list of best practices that help you create good C++ applications:

- Give your variables names that make sense (to others as well as to you). It is worth spending a second more to give variables better names.
- Always initialize variables such as `int`, `float`, and the like.
- Always initialize pointer values to either NULL or a valid address—for instance, that returned by operator `new`.
- When using arrays, never cross the bounds of the array buffer. This is called a buffer overflow and can be exploited as a security vulnerability.
- Don't use `char*` string buffers or functions such as `strlen()` and `strcpy()`. `std::string` is safer and provides many useful utility methods including ones that help you find the length, copy, and append.
- Use a static array only when you are certain of the number of elements it will contain. If you are not certain of it, choose a dynamic array such as `std::vector`.
- When declaring and defining functions that take non-POD (plain old data) types as input, consider declaring parameters as reference parameters to avoid the unnecessary copy step when the function is called.
- If your class contains a raw pointer member (or members), give thought to how memory resource ownership needs to be managed in the event of a copy or assignment. That is, consider programming copy constructor and copy assignment operator.

- When writing a utility class that manages a dynamic array or the like, remember to program the move constructor and the move assignment operator for better performance.

- Remember to make your code `const`-correct. A `get()` function should ideally not be able to modify the class's members and hence should be a `const`. Similarly, function parameters should be `const`-references, unless you want to change the values they contain.

- Avoid using raw pointers. Choose the appropriate smart pointers where possible.

- When programming a utility class, take effort in supporting all those operators that will make consuming and using the class easy.

- Given an option, choose a template version over a macro. Templates are typesafe and generic.

- When programming a class that will be collected in a container, such as a vector or a list, or used as a key element in a map, remember to support `operator<` that will help define the default sort criteria.

- If your lambda function gets too large, you should possibly consider making a function object of it—that is, a class with `operator()` as the functor is reusable and a single point of maintenance.

- Never take the success of operator `new` for granted. Code that performs resource allocation should always be made exception safe—bracketed within `try` with corresponding `catch()` blocks.

- Never `throw` from the destructor of a class.

This is not an exhaustive list, but it covers some of the most important points that will help you in writing good and maintainable C++ code.

C++17: Expected Features

One of the great things about C++ is that the Standards Committee is active and constantly improving the language. Just like its predecessor, C++11, C++17 is expected to usher in the next wave of major new features to the language. Let us study some features that are most likely to make it to C++ when the new standard is officially ratified in 2017.

NOTE

> The features discussed in the following pages are likely to make it to the standard but aren't currently part of it—it is likely that your favorite compiler partially supports some features and doesn't support all.
>
> Additionally, it is unlikely but not impossible that the final version of C++17 will not support all the features introduced here, even though at the time of writing this book it is expected to.

`if` **and** `switch` **Support Initializers**

This is a small but significant extension to the `if` and `switch` statement syntax, and can be expressed as

```
if (initializer; condition)
{
    // statements to execute if condition evaluates true
}
```

Or

```
switch(initializer; condition)
{
    // cases here
}
```

The variable declared in the `initializer` statement is destroyed at the end of the `if` statement. When used on the following code taken from Listing 20.3:

```
auto pairFound = mapIntToStr.find(key);
if (pairFound != mapIntToStr.end())
{
    cout << "Key " << pairFound->first << " points to Value: ";
    cout << pairFound->second << endl;
}
```

This feature improves it to

```
if (auto pairFound = mapIntToStr.find(key); pairFound != mapIntToStr.end())
{
    cout << "Key " << pairFound->first << " points to Value: ";
    cout << pairFound->second << endl;
}
```

This is more than a reduction of a line of code. It ensures that the variable `pairFound` that is needed only in the `if` block isn't available outside it, restricting scope to the minimum required. Additionally, if you were to copy and paste this improved `if` block, you would have taken the required logic in full.

Copy Elision Guarantee

When you initialize a variable to the return value of a function, it is possible that your compiler will create a temporary copy of the integer returned by the function `ReturnInt()` before initializing variable `num` to it:

```
int num = ReturnInt();
```

C++17 requires the compiler to elide this temporary copy; that is, to avoid one.

`std::string_view` Avoids Allocation Overheads

Consider a function that accepts a `std::string` as a parameter:

```
void DisplayString (const std::string& strIn)
{
    cout << strIn << endl;
}
```

When invoked using a string literal, the string literal "Hello World!" is first converted into a temporary `std::string` that is consumed by the function `DisplayString()`:

```
DisplayString("Hello World!");
```

This temporary conversion is a performance overhead that can be avoided by using `std::string_view` instead:

```
void DisplayString (std::string_view& strIn)
{
    cout << strIn << endl;
}
```

A string literal will not incur allocation overhead when being passed to a function that accepts a `std::string_view` as argument.

std::variant **As a Typesafe Alternative to a** union

Unions are explained in Lesson 9, "Classes and Objects." One of the problems with the union is that it enables its content to be interpreted as any other data type supported by the union; for example:

```
union SimpleUnion
{
    int num;
    double preciseNum;
};
```

You may instantiate this union for a double, yet use it as an integer:

```
SimpleUnion u1;
u1.preciseNum = 3.14; // union stores a double
int num2 = u1.num; // works, but u1 contained a double!
```

C++17 provides the programmer with the std::variant, a typesafe alternative to the union:

```
variant<int, double> varSafe;
varSafe = 3.14; // variant stores double
double pi = get<double>(varSafe); // 3.14
double pi2 = get<1>(varsafe); // 3.14
get<char>(varSafe); // compile fails: no char in variant
get<2>(varSafe); // compile fails: variant with two types, not three
try
{
    get<int>(varSafe); // throws exception as variant stores double
}
catch (bad_variant_access&) { // exception handler code }
```

Conditional Code Compilation Using if constexpr

This feature is similar to an if-else construct with the exception that the if condition is evaluated at compile time and the code in the if block (or the accompanying else) is compiled only if the condition is satisfied at compile time.

```
#include <type_traits>
#include <iostream>
#include <iomanip>

using namespace std;

template <typename T>
void DisplayData(const T& data)
```

```
{
    if constexpr (is_integral<T>::value)
        cout << "Integral data: " << data << endl;
    else if constexpr (is_floating_point<T>::value)
        cout << setprecision(15) << "Floating point data: " << data << endl;
    else
        cout << "Unidentified data: " << data << endl;
}
```

Given `DisplayData(15)`, the C++17-compliant compiler would compile only the following line:

```
cout << "Integral data: " << data << endl;
```

Given `DisplayData("Hello World!")`, the compiler would compile only the following, as the function has been invoked with a type that triggers the else block:

```
cout << "Unidentified data: " << data << endl;
```

Combined with automatic return type deduction, introduced in Lesson 7, "Organizing Code with Functions," this is a powerful feature that can potentially allow a function to return values of different types depending on the path the compiler executes.

Improved Lambda Expressions

Lambda functions are expected to see the following improvements:

- They will be supported inside `constexpr` functions.
- They will be allowed to capture a copy of `*this` using the syntax `[*this]`.

Automatic Type Deduction for Constructors

As of C++14, you would declare a pair combining an integer and a floating point type, like this:

```
std::pair<int, double> pairIntToDb (3, 3.14159265359);
```

C++17 will allow a simplification of the line to

```
std::pair pairIntToDb (3, 3.14159265359);
```

The type deduction of the template arguments for constructors will be automatic.

`template<auto>`

This extends a less-used feature that a template argument may contain a value that is used at compile time. For example, the `std::array` is a container that models fixed-size arrays available starting with C++11. It would be used to model an array of 10 integers, like this:

```
std::array<int, 10> myTenNums;
```

The template declaration of `class std::array` is similar to the following:

```
template <class T, std::size_t N> struct array;
```

C++17 will allow a simplification of the template parameter type that accepts array size to `auto`, such that the following would be a perfectly valid and usable array:

```
template <class T, auto N> struct array;
```

Learning C++ Doesn't Stop Here!

Congratulations, you have made great progress in learning C++. The best way to continue is to code and code more! C++ is a sophisticated language. The more you program, the higher will be your level of understanding of how it all works behind the scenes.

Online Documentation

You are encouraged to learn more about the signatures of STL containers, their methods, their algorithms, and their functional details using online resources and documents. One popular site with structured resources is http://www.cppreference.com/.

Communities for Guidance and Help

C++ has rich and vibrant online communities. Enroll yourself at sites such as StackOverflow (www.StackOverflow.com), CodeGuru (www.CodeGuru.com), or CodeProject (www.CodeProject.com) to have your technical queries inspected and answered by the community.

When you feel confident, feel free to contribute to these communities. You will find yourself answering challenging questions and learning a lot in the process.

29

Summary

This concluding lesson is actually an opening page in your quest to learn C++! Having come this far, you have learned the basics and the advanced concepts of the language. In this lesson, you learned the theoretical basics of multithreaded programming. You learned that the only way you can extract the best from multicore processors is to organize your logic in threads and allow parallel processing. You know that there are pitfalls in multithreaded applications and ways to avoid them. Last but not the least, you learned some basic C++ programming best practices. You know that writing good C++ code is not only about using advanced concepts, but also about giving variable names that others understand, handling exceptions to take care of the unexpected, and using utility classes such as smart pointers instead of raw ones. You are now ready to take a leap into the world of professional C++ programming.

Q&A

Q I am quite happy with the performance of my application. Should I still implement multithreaded capabilities?

A Not at all. Not all applications need to be multithreaded. Rather only those that need to perform a task concurrently or that serve many users in parallel.

Q Why should I bother about C++11 and C++14, instead of simply using the old style of programming?

A C++11 and C++14 bring changes that make programming in C++ simple. Keywords such as `auto` save you long and tedious iterator declarations, and lambda functions make your `for_each()` construct compact without the need for a function object. So, the benefits in programming C++14 are already significant, and well-written programs are shorter and easier to maintain than those compliant with older versions of the C++ standard.

Workshop

The Workshop contains quiz questions to help solidify your understanding of the material covered. Try to answer the questions before checking the answers in Appendix E.

Quiz

1. My image processing application doesn't respond when it is correcting the contrast. What should I do?

2. My multithreaded application allows for extremely fast access to the database. Yet, sometimes I see that the data fetched is garbled. What am I doing wrong?

APPENDIX A

Working with Numbers: Binary and Hexadecimal

Understanding how the binary and hexadecimal number systems work is not critical to programming better applications in C++, but it helps you to better understand what happens under the hood.

Decimal Numeral System

Numbers that we use on a daily basis are in the range of 0–9. This set of numbers is called the Decimal Numeral System. As the system is comprised of 10 unique digits, it's a system with base of 10.

Hence, as the base is 10, the zero-based position of each digit denotes the power of 10 that the digit is multiplied with. So

```
957 = 9 x 10² + 5 x 10¹ + 7 x 10⁰ = 9 x 100 + 5 x 10 + 7
```

In the number 957, the zero-based position of 7 is 0, that of 5 is 1, and that of 9 is 2. These position indexes become powers of the base 10, as shown in the example. Remember that any number to the power 0 is 1 (so, 10^0 is the same as 1000^0 as both evaluate to 1).

NOTE ———— The decimal system is one in which powers of 10 are the most important. Digits in a number are multiplied by 10, 100, 1000, and so on to determine the magnitude of the number.

Binary Numeral System

A system with a base of 2 is called a binary system. As the system allows only two states, it is represented by the numbers 0 and 1. These numbers in C++ typically evaluate to `false` and `true` (`true` being non-zero).

Just as numbers in a decimal system are evaluated to powers of base 10, those in binary are evaluated as powers of their base 2:

```
101 (binary) = 1 x 2² + 0 x 2¹ + 1 x 2⁰ = 4 + 0 + 1 = 5 (decimal)
```

So, the decimal equivalent of binary 101 is 5.

NOTE ———— Digits in a binary number are multiplied by powers of 2 such as 4, 8, 16, 32, and so on to determine the magnitude of the number. The power is decided by the zero-based place the digit in question has.

To understand the binary numeral system better, let's examine Table A.1 that enlists the various powers of two.

TABLE A.1 Powers of 2

Power	Value	Binary Representation
0	$2^0 = 1$	1
1	$2^1 = 2$	10
2	$2^2 = 4$	100
3	$2^3 = 8$	1000
4	$2^4 = 16$	10000
5	$2^5 = 32$	100000
6	$2^6 = 64$	1000000
7	$2^7 = 128$	10000000

Why Do Computers Use Binary?

Widespread usage of the binary system is relatively new in comparison to the period of time number systems have been discovered. Its usage has been accelerated by the development of electronics and computers. The evolution of electronics and electronic components resulted in a system that detected states of a component as being ON (under a significant potential difference or voltage) or OFF (no or low potential difference).

These ON and OFF states were conveniently interpreted as 1 and 0, completely representing the binary number set and making it the method of choice for performing arithmetic calculations. Logical operations, such as NOT, AND, OR, and XOR, as covered in Lesson 5, "Working with Expressions, Statements, and Operators" (in Tables 5.2–5.5), were easily supported by the development of electronic gates, resulting in the binary system being whole-heartedly adopted as conditional processing became easy.

What Are Bits and Bytes?

A *bit* is a basic unit in a computational system that contains a binary state. Thus, a bit is said to be "set" if it contains state 1 or "reset" if it contains state 0. A collection of bits is a *byte*. The number of bits in a byte is theoretically not fixed and is a hardware-dependent number.

However, most computational systems go with the assumption of 8 bits in a byte, for the simple, convenient reason that 8 is a power of 2. Eight bits in a byte also allows the transmission of up to 2^8 different values, allowing for 255 distinct values. These 255 distinct values are enough for the display or transaction of all characters in the ASCII character set, and more.

How Many Bytes Make a Kilobyte?

1024 bytes (210 bytes) make a kilobyte. Similarly, 1024 kilobytes make a megabyte. 1024 megabytes make a gigabyte. 1024 gigabytes make a terabyte.

Hexadecimal Numeral System

Hexadecimal is a number system with base 16. A digit in the hexadecimal system can be in the range of 0–9 and A–F. So, 10 in decimal is A in hexadecimal, and 15 in decimal is F in hexadecimal:

Decimal	Hexadecimal	Decimal (continued)	Hexadecimal (continued)
0	0	8	8
1	1	9	9
2	2	10	A
3	3	11	B
4	4	12	C
5	5	13	D
6	6	14	E
7	7	15	F

Just as numbers in a decimal system are evaluated to powers of base 10, in binary as powers of their base 2, those in hexadecimal are evaluated to powers of base 16:

```
0x31F = 3 x 16² + 1 x 16¹ + F x 16⁰ = 3 x 256 + 16 + 15 (in decimal) = 799
```

NOTE — It is convention that hexadecimal numbers be represented with a prefix "0x".

Why Do We Need Hexadecimal?

Computers work on binary. The state of each unit of memory in a computer is a 0 or a 1. However, if we as human beings were to interact on computer- or programming-specific information in 0s and 1s, we would need a lot of space to transact small pieces of information. So, instead of writing 1111 in binary, you are a lot more efficient writing F in hexadecimal.

So, a hexadecimal representation can very efficiently represent the state of 4 bits in a digit, using a maximum of two hexadecimal digits to represent the state of a byte.

NOTE

> A less-used number system is the Octal Numeral System. This is a system with base 8, comprising of numbers from 0 to 7.

Converting to a Different Base

When dealing with numbers, you might see the need to view the same number in a different base—for instance, the value of a binary number in decimal or that of a decimal number in hexadecimal.

A

In the previous examples, you saw how numbers can be converted from binary or hexadecimal into decimal. Take a look at converting binary and hexadecimal numbers into decimal.

The Generic Conversion Process

When converting a number in one system to another, you successively divide with the base, starting with the number being converted. Each remainder fills places in the destination numeral system, starting with the lowest place. The next division uses the quotient of the previous division operation with the base as the divisor.

This continues until the remainder is within the destination numeral system and the quotient is 0.

This process is also called the *breakdown method*.

Converting Decimal to Binary

To convert decimal 33 into binary, you subtract the highest power of 2 possible (32):

Place 1: 33 / 2 = quotient 16, remainder 1

Place 2: 16 / 2 = quotient 8, remainder 0

Place 3: 8 / 2 = quotient 4, remainder 0

Place 4: 4 / 2 = quotient 2, remainder 0

Place 5: 2 / 2 = quotient 1, remainder 0

Place 6: 1 / 2 = quotient 0, remainder 1

Binary equivalent of 33 (reading places): 100001

Similarly, the binary equivalent of 156 is

Place 1: 156 / 2 = quotient 78, remainder 0

Place 2:   78 / 2 = quotient 39, remainder 0

Place 3:   39 / 2 = quotient 19, remainder 1

Place 4:   19 / 2 = quotient 9, remainder 1

Place 5:   9 / 2 = quotient 4, remainder 1

Place 6:   4 / 2 = quotient 2, remainder 0

Place 7:   2 / 2 = quotient 1, remainder 0

Place 9:   1 / 0 = quotient 0, remainder 1

Binary equivalent of 156: 10011100

Converting Decimal to Hexadecimal

The process is the same as for binary; you divide by base 16 instead of 2.

So, to convert decimal 5211 to hex:

Place 1: 5211 / 16 = quotient 325, remainder B_{16} (11_{10} is B_{16})

Place 2:   325 / 16 = quotient 20, remainder 5

Place 3:   20 / 16 = quotient 1, remainder 4

Place 4:   1 / 16 = quotient 0, remainder 1

$5211_{10} = 145B_{16}$

TIP

> To understand better how different number systems work, you can write a simple C++ program similar to Listing 27.1 in Lesson 27, "Using Streams for Input and Output." It uses `std::cout` with manipulators for displaying an integer in hex, decimal, and octal notations.
>
> To display an integer in binary, use `std::bitset` that has been explained in Lesson 25, "Working with Bit Flags Using STL," deriving inspiration from Listing 25.1.

APPENDIX B
C++ Keywords

Keywords are reserved to the compiler for use by the language. You cannot define classes, variables, or functions that have these keywords as their names.

alignas	enum	return
alignof	explicit	short
and	export	signed
and_eq	extern	sizeof
asm	false	static
auto	float	static_assert
bitand	for	static_cast
bitor	friend	struct
bool	goto	switch
break	if	template
case	inline	this
catch	int	thread_local
char	long	throw
char16_t	mutable	true
char32_t	namespace	try
class	new	typedef
compl	noexcept	typeid
const	not	typename
constexpr	not_eq	union
const_cast	nullptr	unsigned
continue	operator	using
decltype	or	virtual
default	or_eq	void
delete	private	volatile
do	protected	wchar_t
double	public	while
dynamic_cast	register	xor
else	reinterpret_cast	xor_eq

NOTE

Lesson 10, "Implementing Inheritance," and Lesson 11, "Polymorphism," introduced to two interesting terms—final and override. These are not reserved C++ keywords for you may name your objects and functions after them. However, they carry a special meaning when accompanying certain constructs as explained in the lessons.

APPENDIX C
Operator Precedence

It is a good practice to use parentheses that explicitly compartmentalize your operations. In absence of those parentheses, the compiler resorts to a predefined order of precedence in which the operators are used. This operator precedence, as listed in Table C.1, is what the C++ compiler adheres to in event of ambiguity.

TABLE C.1   The Precedence of Operators

Rank	Name	Operator
1	Scope resolution	`::`

2	Member selection, subscripting, function calls, postfix increment, and decrement	`. ->`
		 `[]`
		 `()`
		 `++ --`

3	`sizeof`, prefix increment and decrement, complement, and, not, unary minus and plus, address-of and dereference, `new, new[]`, `delete, delete[]`, `casting, sizeof()`	`++ --`
		 `^ !`
		 `- +`
		 `& *`
		 `sizeof`
		 `new`
		 `new[]`
		 `delete`
		 `delete[]`
		 `()`

4	Member selection for pointer	`.* ->*`
5	Multiply, divide, modulo	`* / %`
6	Add, subtract	`+ -`
7	Bitwise shift	`<< >>`
8	Inequality relational	`<< = >>=`
9	Equality, inequality	`== !=`
10	Bitwise AND	`&`
11	Bitwise exclusive OR	`^`
12	Bitwise OR	`|`
13	Logical AND	`&&`
14	Logical OR	`||`

15	Ternary conditional, throw, assignment and compound assignment	`?:`
		 `throw`
		 `= *= /= %=`
		 `+= -= <<=`
		 `>>=`
		 `&= |= ^=`

16	Comma	`,`

APPENDIX D
ASCII Codes

Computers work using bits and bytes, essentially numbers. To represent character data in this numeric system, a standard established by the American Standard Code for Information Interchange (ASCII) is prevalently used. ASCII assigns 7-bit numeric codes to Latin characters A–Z, a–z, numbers 0–9, some special keystrokes (for example, DEL), and special characters (such as backspace).

7 bits allow for 128 combinations of which the first 32 (0–31) are reserved as control characters used to interface with peripherals such as printers.

ASCII Table of Printable Characters

ASCII codes 32–127 are used for printable characters such as 0–9, A–Z, and a–z and a few others such as space. The table below shows the decimal and the hexadecimal values reserved for these symbols.

Symbol	DEC	HEX	Description
	32	20	Space
!	33	21	Exclamation mark
"	34	22	Double quotes (or speech marks)
#	35	23	Number
$	36	24	Dollar
%	37	25	Percent sign
&	38	26	Ampersand
'	39	27	Single quote
(	40	28	Open parenthesis (or open bracket)
)	41	29	Close parenthesis (or close bracket)
*	42	2A	Asterisk
+	43	2B	Plus
,	44	2C	Comma
-	45	2D	Hyphen
.	46	2E	Period, dot or full stop
/	47	2F	Slash or divide
0	48	30	Zero
1	49	31	One
2	50	32	Two
3	51	33	Three
4	52	34	Four
5	53	35	Five
6	54	36	Six
7	55	37	Seven
8	56	38	Eight
9	57	39	Nine

Symbol	DEC	HEX	Description
:	58	3A	Colon
;	59	3B	Semicolon
<	60	3C	Less than (or open angled bracket)
=	61	3D	Equals
>	62	3E	Greater than (or close angled bracket)
?	63	3F	Question mark
@	64	40	At symbol
A	65	41	Uppercase A
B	66	42	Uppercase B
C	67	43	Uppercase C
D	68	44	Uppercase D
E	69	45	Uppercase E
F	70	46	Uppercase F
G	71	47	Uppercase G
H	72	48	Uppercase H
I	73	49	Uppercase I
J	74	4A	Uppercase J
K	75	4B	Uppercase K
L	76	4C	Uppercase L
M	77	4D	Uppercase M
N	78	4E	Uppercase N
O	79	4F	Uppercase O
P	80	50	Uppercase P
Q	81	51	Uppercase Q
R	82	52	Uppercase R
S	83	53	Uppercase S
T	84	54	Uppercase T
U	85	55	Uppercase U
V	86	56	Uppercase V
W	87	57	Uppercase W

D

Symbol	DEC	HEX	Description
X	88	58	Uppercase X
Y	89	59	Uppercase Y
Z	90	5A	Uppercase Z
[	91	5B	Opening bracket
\	92	5C	Backslash
]	93	5D	Closing bracket
^	94	5E	Caret—circumflex
_	95	5F	Underscore
`	96	60	Grave accent
a	97	61	Lowercase a
b	98	62	Lowercase b
c	99	63	Lowercase c
d	100	64	Lowercase d
e	101	65	Lowercase e
f	102	66	Lowercase f
g	103	67	Lowercase g
h	104	68	Lowercase h
i	105	69	Lowercase i
j	106	6A	Lowercase j
k	107	6B	Lowercase k
l	108	6C	Lowercase l
m	109	6D	Lowercase m
n	110	6E	Lowercase n
o	111	6F	Lowercase o
p	112	70	Lowercase p
q	113	71	Lowercase q
r	114	72	Lowercase r
s	115	73	Lowercase s
t	116	74	Lowercase t
u	117	75	Lowercase u

Symbol	DEC	HEX	Description
v	118	76	Lowercase v
w	119	77	Lowercase w
x	120	78	Lowercase x
y	121	79	Lowercase y
z	122	7A	Lowercase z
{	123	7B	Opening brace
|	124	7C	Vertical bar
}	125	7D	Closing brace
~	126	7E	Equivalency sign—tilde
	127	7F	Delete

D

APPENDIX E
Answers

Answers for Lesson 1

Quiz

1. An interpreter is a tool that interprets what you code (or an intermediate byte code) and performs certain actions. A compiler is one that takes your code as an input and generates an object file. In the case of C++, after compiling and linking you have an executable that can run directly by the processor without need for any further interpretation.

2. A compiler takes a C++ code file as input and generates an object file in machine language. Often your code has dependencies on libraries and functions in other code files. Creating these links and generating an executable that integrates all dependencies directly and indirectly coded by you is the job of the linker.

3. Code. Compile to create object file. Link to create executable. Execute to test. Debug. Fix errors in code and repeat the steps.

   In many cases, compilation and linking is one step.

Exercises

1. Display the result of subtracting y from x, multiplying the two, and adding the two.

2. Output should be

   ```
   2 48 14
   ```

3. A preprocessor command to include iostream as seen in Line 1 should start with #.

4. It displays the following:

   ```
   Hello Buggy World
   ```

Answers for Lesson 2

Quiz

1. Code in C++ is case sensitive. Int is not acceptable to the compiler as an integer type `int`.

2. Yes.

```
/*  if you comment using this C-style syntax
then you can span your comment over multiple lines */
```

Exercises

1. It fails because case-sensitive C++ compilers don't know what `std::Cout` is or why the string following it doesn't start with an opening quote. Additionally, the declaration of `main` should always return an `int`.

2. Here is the corrected version:

```
#include <iostream>
int main()
{
    std::cout << "Is there a bug here?"; // no bug anymore
    return 0;
}
```

3. This program derived from Listing 2.4 demonstrates subtraction and multiplication:

```
##include <iostream>
#using namespace std;
u
// Function declaration
iint DemoConsoleOutput();
{
 int main()
 {
   // Call i.e. invoke the function
   DemoConsoleOutput();

   return 0;
}

 // Function definition
 int DemoConsoleOutput()
 {
   cout << "Performing subtraction 10 - 5 = " << 10 - 5 << endl;
   cout << "Performing multiplication 10 * 5 = " << 10 * 5 << endl;

   return 0;
}
```

Output ▼

```
Performing subtraction 10 - 5 = 5
Performing multiplication 10 * 5 = 50
```

Answers for Lesson 3

Quiz

1. A signed integer is one in which the most-significant-bit (MSB) functions as the sign-bit and indicates if the value of the integer is positive or negative. An unsigned integer in comparison is used to contain only positive integer values.

2. #define is a preprocessor directive that directs the compiler to do a text replacement wherever the defined value is seen. However, it is not type safe and is a primitive way of defining constants. Therefore, it is to be avoided.

3. To ensure that it contains a definite, non-random value.

4. 2.

5. The name is nondescriptive and repeats the type. Though this compiles, such code becomes difficult for humans to read and maintain and should be avoided. An integer is better declared using a name that reveals its purpose. For example:

```
int age = 0;
```

Exercises

1. Many ways of achieving this:
```
enum YourCards {Ace = 43, Jack, Queen, King};
// Ace is 43, Jack is 44, Queen is 45, King is 46
// Alternatively..
enum YourCards {Ace, Jack, Queen = 45, King};
// Ace is 0, Jack is 1, Queen is 45 and King is 46
```

2. See Listing 3.4 and adapt it (reduce it) to get the answer to this question.

3. Here is a program that asks you to enter radius of a circle and calculates the area and circumference for you:
```
#include <iostream>
using namespace std;

int main()
{
    const double Pi = 3.1416;
```

E

```
        cout << "Enter circle's radius: ";
        double radius = 0;
        cin >> radius;

        cout << "Area = " << Pi * radius * radius << endl;
        cout << "Circumference = " << 2 * Pi * radius << endl;

        return 0;
}
```

Output ▼

```
Enter circle's radius: 4
Area = 50.2656
Circumference = 25.1328
```

4. You get a compilation warning (not error) if you store the result of calculating area and circumference in an integer and the output looks like this:

Output ▼

```
Enter circle's radius: 4
Area = 50
Circumference = 25
```

5. auto is a construct where the compiler automatically deduces the type the variable can take depending on the value it is being initialized to. The code in question does not initialize and hence causes a compilation failure.

Answers for Lesson 4

Quiz

1. 0 and 4 are the zero-based indexes of the first and last elements of an array with five elements.

2. No, as they are proven to be unsafe especially in handling user input, giving the user an opportunity to enter a string longer than the length of the array.

3. One null terminating character.

4. Depending on how you use it. If you use it in a cout statement, for instance, the display logic reads successive characters seeking a terminating null and crosses the bounds of the array, possibly causing your application to crash.

5. That would simply replace the `int` in the vector's declaration by `char`.

```
vector<char> dynArrChars (3);
```

Exercises

1. Here you go. The application initializes for ROOKs, but it's enough for you to get an idea:

```
int main()
{
  enum Square
  {
    Empty = 0,
    Pawn,
    Rook,
    Knight,
    Bishop,
    King,
    Queen
  };

  Square chessBoard[8][8];

  // Initialize the squares containing rooks
  chessBoard[0][0] = chessBoard[0][7] = Rook;
  chessBoard[7][0] = chessBoard[7][7] = Rook;

  return 0;
}
```

2. To set the fifth element of an array, you need to access element `myNums[4]` as this is a zero-based index.

3. The fourth element of the array is being accessed without ever being initialized or assigned. The resulting output is unpredictable. Always initialize variables and also arrays; otherwise, they contain the last value stored in the memory location they're created in.

E

Answers for Lesson 5

Quiz

1. Integer types cannot contain decimal values that are possibly relevant for the user who wants to divide two numbers. So, you would use `float`.

2. As the compiler interprets them to be an integer, it is 4.

3. As the numerator is 32.0 and not 32, the compiler interprets this to be a floating-point operation, creating a result in a `float` that is akin to 4.571.

4. No, `sizeof` is an operator, and one that cannot be overloaded.

5. It does not work as intended because the addition operator has priority over shift, resulting in a shift of 1 + 5 = 6 bits instead of just one.

6. The result of XOR is `false` as also indicated by Table 5.5.

Exercises

1. Here is a correct solution:

```
int result = ((number << 1) + 5) << 1;
```

2. The result contains number shifted 7 bits left, as `operator` + takes priority over `operator` <<.

3. Here is a program that stores two Boolean values entered by the user and demonstrates the result of using bitwise operators on them:

```
#include <iostream>
using namespace std;

int main()
{
    cout << "Enter a boolean value true(1) or false(0): ";
    bool value1 = false;
    cin >> value1;

    cout << "Enter another boolean value true(1) or false(0): ";
    bool value2 = false;
    cin >> value2;

    cout << "Result of bitwise operators on these operands: " << endl;
    cout << "Bitwise AND: " << (value1 & value2) << endl;
    cout << "Bitwise OR: " << (value1 | value2) << endl;
    cout << "Bitwise XOR: " << (value1 ^ value2) << endl;

    return 0;
}
```

Output ▼

```
Enter a boolean value true(1) or false(0): 1
Enter another boolean value true(1) or false(0): 0
Result of bitwise operators on these operands:
Bitwise AND: 0
Bitwise OR: 1
Bitwise XOR: 1
```

Answers for Lesson 6

Quiz

1. You indent not for sake of the compiler, but for the sake of other programmers (humans) who might need to read or understand your code.

2. You avoid it to keep your code from getting unintuitive and expensive to maintain.

3. See the code in the solution to Exercise 1 that uses the decrement operator.

4. As the condition in the `for` statement is not satisfied, the loop won't execute even once and the `cout` statement it contains is never executed.

Exercises

1. You need to be aware that array indexes are zero-based and the last element is at index Length − 1:

```cpp
#include <iostream>
using namespace std;

int main()
{
    const int ARRAY_LEN = 5;
    int myNums[ARRAY_LEN] = {-55, 45, 9889, 0, 45};

    for (int index = ARRAY_LEN - 1; index >= 0; --index)
        cout<<"myNums[" << index << "] = "<<myNums[index]<<endl;

    return 0;
}
```

Output ▼

```
myNums[4] = 45
myNums[3] = 0
myNums[2] = 9889
myNums[1] = 45
myNums[0] = -55
```

E

2. One nested loop equivalent of Listing 6.13 that adds elements in two arrays in the reverse order is demonstrated below:

```cpp
#include <iostream>
using namespace std;
```

```
int main()
{
    const int ARRAY1_LEN = 3;
    const int ARRAY2_LEN = 2;

    int myNums1[ARRAY1_LEN] = {35, -3, 0};
    int MyInts2[ARRAY2_LEN] = {20, -1};

    cout << "Adding each int in myNums1 by each in MyInts2:" << endl;

    for(int index1 = ARRAY1_LEN - 1; index1 >= 0; --index1)
        for(int index2 = ARRAY2_LEN - 1; index2 >= 0; --index2)
            cout << myNums1[index1] << " + " << MyInts2[index2] \
                << " = " << myNums1[index1] + MyInts2[index2] << endl;

    return 0;
}
```

Output ▼

```
Adding each int in myNums1 by each in myNums2:
0 + -1 = -1
0 + 20 = 20
-3 + -1 = -4
-3 + 20 = 17
35 + -1 = 34
35 + 20 = 55
```

3. You need to replace the constant integer numsToCalculate with a value fixed at 5 with code that asks the user the following:

```
cout << "How many Fibonacci numbers you wish to calculate: ";
int numsToCalculate = 0; // no const
cin >> numsToCalculate;
```

4. The switch-case construct using enumerated constants that tells if a color is in the rainbow is as below:

```
#include <iostream>
using namespace std;

int main()
{
    enum Colors
    {
        Violet = 0,
        Indigo,
        Blue,
```

```cpp
        Green,
        Yellow,
        Orange,
        Red,
        Crimson,
        Beige,
        Brown,
        Peach,
        Pink,
        White,
    };

    cout << "Here are the available colors: " << endl;
    cout << "Violet: " << Violet << endl;
    cout << "Indigo: " << Indigo << endl;
    cout << "Blue: " << Blue << endl;
    cout << "Green: " << Green << endl;
    cout << "Yellow: " << Yellow << endl;
    cout << "Orange: " << Orange << endl;
    cout << "Red: " << Red << endl;
    cout << "Crimson: " << Crimson << endl;
    cout << "Beige: " << Beige << endl;
    cout << "Brown: " << Brown << endl;
    cout << "Peach: " << Peach << endl;
    cout << "Pink: " << Pink << endl;
    cout << "White: " << White << endl;

    cout << "Choose one by entering code: ";
    int YourChoice = Blue; // initial
    cin >> YourChoice;

    switch (YourChoice)
    {
    case Violet:
    case Indigo:
    case Blue:
    case Green:
    case Yellow:
    case Orange:
    case Red:
        cout << "Bingo, your choice is a Rainbow color!" << endl;
        break;

    default:
        cout << "The color you chose is not in the rainbow" << endl;
        break;
    }

    return 0;
}
```

Output ▼

```
Here are the available colors:
Violet: 0
Indigo: 1
Blue: 2
Green: 3
Yellow: 4
Orange: 5
RED: 6
Crimson: 7
Beige: 8
Brown: 9
Peach: 10
Pink: 11
White: 12
Choose one by entering code: 4
Bingo, your choice is a Rainbow color!
```

5. The programmer unintentionally makes an assignment to 10 in the `for` loop condition statement.

6. The `while` statement is followed by a null statement `';'` on the same line. Thus, the intended loop following the `while` is never reached and because `loopCounter` that governs the `while` is never incremented, the `while` does not end and the statements following it are never executed.

7. Missing `break` statement (that is, the `default` case always executes).

Answers for Lesson 7

Quiz

1. The scope of these variables is the life of the function.

2. `someNumber` is a reference to the variable in the calling function. It does not hold a copy.

3. A recursive function.

4. Overloaded functions.

5. Top! Visualize a stack of plates; the one at the top is available for withdrawal, and that is what the stack pointer points to.

Exercises

1. The function prototypes would look like this:

```
double Area (double radius); // circle
double Area (double radius, double height); // cylinder
```

The function implementations (definitions) use the respective formulas supplied in the question and return the area to the caller as a return value.

2. Let Listing 7.8 inspire you. The function prototype would be the following:

```
void ProcessArray(double numbers[], int length);
```

3. The parameter `result` ought to be a reference for the function `Area()` to be effective:

```
void Area(double radius, double &result)
```

4. The default parameter should be listed at the end, or else you will have a compile error. Alternatively, all parameters should have default values specified.

5. The function needs to return its output data by reference to the caller:

```
void Calculate (double radius, double &Area, double &Circumference)
{
    Area = 3.14 * radius * radius;
    Circumference = 2 * 3.14 * radius;
}
```

Answers for Lesson 8

Quiz

1. If the compiler let you do that, it would be an easy way to break exactly what `const` references were meant to protect: the data being referred to that cannot be changed.

2. They're operators.

3. A memory address.

4. `operator *`.

E

Exercises

1. 40.

2. In the first overloaded variant, the arguments are copied to the called function. In the second, they're not copied as they're references to the variables in the caller and the function can change them. The third variant uses pointers, which unlike references can be NULL or invalid, and validity needs to be ensured in such a system.

3. Use the const keyword:

```
1: const int* pNum1 = &number;
```

4. You are assigning an integer to a pointer directly (that is, overwriting the contained memory address by an integer value). Correct version:

```
*pointToAnInt = 9; // previously: pointToAnInt = 9;
```

5. There is a double delete on the same memory address returned by new to pNumber and duplicated in pNumberCopy. Remove one.

6. 30.

Answers for Lesson 9

Quiz

1. On the free store. This is the same as it would be if you allocated for an int using new.

2. sizeof() calculates the size of a class on the basis of the declared data members. As the sizeof(pointer) is constant and independent of the mass of data being pointed to, the sizeof(Class) containing one such pointer member remains constant as well.

3. None except member methods of the same class.

4. Yes, it can.

5. A constructor is typically used to initialize data members and resources.

6. Destructors are typically used for releasing resources and deallocating memory.

Exercises

1. C++ is case sensitive. A class declaration should start with class, not Class. It should end with a semicolon (;) as shown below:

```
class Human
```

```
{
    int Age;
    string Name;

public:
    Human() {}
};
```

2. As `Human::Age` is a private member (remember members of a `class` are private by default as opposed to those in a `struct`) and as there is no public accessor function, there is no way that the user of this class can access `Age`.

3. Here is a version of `class Human` with an initialization list in the constructor:

```
class Human
{
    int Age;
    string Name;

public:
    Human(string InputName, int InputAge)
           : Name(InputName), Age(InputAge) {}
};
```

4. Note how Pi has not been exposed outside the class as required:

```
#include <iostream>
using namespace std;

class Circle
{
    const double Pi;
    double radius;

public:
    Circle(double InputRadius) : radius(InputRadius), Pi(3.1416) {}

    double GetCircumference()
    {
        return 2*Pi*radius;
    }

    double GetArea()
    {
        return Pi*radius*radius;
    }
};

int main()
{
```

E

```
    cout << "Enter a radius: ";
    double radius = 0;
    cin >> radius;

    Circle MyCircle(radius);

    cout << "Circumference = " << MyCircle.GetCircumference() << endl;
    cout << "Area = " << MyCircle.GetArea() << endl;

    return 0;
}
```

Answers for Lesson 10

Quiz

1. Use access specifier `protected` to ensure that a member of the base class is visible to the derived class, but not to one with an instance of the same.

2. The base part of the derived class object gets copied and passed as an argument. The resulting behavior due to "slicing" can be unpredictable.

3. Composition for design flexibility.

4. Use it to unhide base class methods.

5. No, because the first class that specializes `Base`—that is, class `Derived`—has a private inheritance relationship with `Base`. Thus, public members of class `Base` are private to class `SubDerived`, hence are not accessible.

Exercises

1. Construction in order mentioned in the class declaration: `Mammal - Bird - Reptile - Platypus`. Destruction in reverse order.

2. Like this:
```
class Shape
{
    // ... Shape members
};

class Polygon: public Shape
{
    // ... Polygon members
}

class Triangle: public Polygon
{
    // ... Triangle members
}
```

3. The inheritance relationship between class `D1` and `Base` should be `private` to restrict `class D2` from accessing the public members of `Base`.

4. Classes inherit `private` by default. If `Derived` had been a `struct`, that inheritance would've been `public`.

5. `SomeFunc` is taking the parameter of `type Base` by value. This means that a call of this type using an instance of `Derived` is subject to slicing, which leads to instability and unpredictable output:

```
Derived objectDerived;
SomeFunc(objectDerived); // slicing problems
```

Answers for Lesson 11

Quiz

1. Declare an abstract base class `Shape` with `Area()` and `Print()` as pure virtual functions, thereby forcing `Circle` and `Triangle` to implement the same. They're forced to comply with your criteria of requiring to support `Area()` and `Print()`.

2. No. It creates a VFT only for those classes that contain virtual functions.

3. Yes, as it still cannot be instantiated. As long as a class has at least one pure virtual function, it remains an ABC irrespective of the presence or absence of other fully defined functions or parameters.

Exercises

1. The inheritance hierarchy using an abstract base class `Shape` for classes `Circle` and `Triangle` is as below:

```
#include<iostream>
using namespace std;

class Shape
{
public:
   virtual double Area() = 0;
   virtual void Print() = 0;
};

class Circle
```

E

```cpp
{
    double radius;
public:
    Circle(double inputRadius) : radius(inputRadius) {}

    double Area()
    {
        return 3.1415 * radius * radius;
    }

    void Print()
    {
        cout << "Circle says hello!" << endl;
    }
};

class Triangle
{
    double base, height;
public:
    Triangle(double inputBase, double inputHeight) : base(inputBase),
    height(inputHeight) {}

    double Area()
    {
        return 0.5 * base * height;
    }

    void Print()
    {
        cout << "Triangle says hello!" << endl;
    }
};

int main()
{
    Circle myRing(5);
    Triangle myWarningTriangle(6.6, 2);

    cout << "Area of circle: " << myRing.Area() << endl;
    cout << "Area of triangle: " << myWarningTriangle.Area() << endl;

    myRing.Print();
    myWarningTriangle.Print();

    return 0;
}
```

2. Missing virtual destructor!

3. Without a virtual destructor, the constructor sequence would be `Vehicle()` followed by `Car()`, whereas the nonvirtual destructor would result only in `~Vehicle()` being invoked.

Answers for Lesson 12

Quiz

1. No, C++ does not allow two functions with the same name to have different return values. You can program two implementations of operator `[]` with identical return types, one defined as a `const` function and the other not. In this case, C++ compiler picks the non-`const` version for assignment-related activities and the `const` version otherwise:

```
Type& operator[](int Index) const;
Type& operator[](int Index);
```

2. Yes, but only if I don't want my class to allow copying or assignment. Such a restriction would be necessity when programming a singleton—a class that permits the existence of only one instance. Listing 9.10 in Lesson 9, "Classes and Objects," contains a demonstration of a singleton class.

3. As there are no dynamically allocated resources contained within `class Date` that cause unnecessary memory allocation and deallocation cycles within the copy constructor or copy assignment operator, this class is not a good candidate for a move constructor or move assignment operator.

Exercises

1. The conversion operator `int()` is as below:

```
class Date
{
    int day, month, year;
public:
    explicit operator int()
    {
        return ((year * 10000) + (month * 100) + day);
    }

    // constructor etc
};
```

E

2. The move constructor and move assignment operators are seen below:

```cpp
class DynIntegers
{
private:
    int* arrayNums;

public:
    // move constructor
    DynIntegers(DynIntegers&& moveSrc)
    {
        arrayNums = moveSrc.arrayNums;   // take ownership
        moveSrc.arrayNums = NULL;   // release ownership from source
    }

    // move assignment operator
    DynIntegers& operator= (DynIntegers&& moveSrc)
    {
        if(this != &moveSrc)
        {
            delete [] arrayNums;   // release own resources
            arrayNums = moveSrc.arrayNums;
            moveSrc.arrayNums = NULL;
        }
        return *this;
    }

    ~DynIntegers() {delete[] arrayNums;}   // destructor

    // implement default constructor, copy constructor, assignment operator
};
```

Answers for Lesson 13

Quiz

1. dynamic_cast.

2. Correct the function, of course. const_cast and casting operators in general should be a last resort.

3. True.

4. Yes, true.

Exercises

1. The result of a `dynamic_cast` operation should always be checked for validity:

```
void DoSomething(base* pBase)
{
    Derived* objDerived = dynamic_cast <Derived*>(pBase);

    if(objDerived) // check for validity
        objDerived->DerivedClassMethod();
}
```

2. Use `static_cast` as you know that the object being pointed to is of type `Tuna`. Using Listing 13.1 as a base, here is what `main()` would look like:

```
int main()
{
    Fish* pFish = new Tuna;
    Tuna* pTuna = static_cast<Tuna*>(pFish);

    // Tuna::BecomeDinner will work only using valid Tuna*
    pTuna->BecomeDinner();

    // virtual destructor in Fish ensures invocation of ~Tuna()
    delete pFish;

    return 0;
}
```

Answers for Lesson 14

Quiz

1. A preprocessor construct that keeps you from multiplying or recursively including header files.

2. 4.

3. 10 + 10 / 5 = 10 + 2 = 12.

4. Use brackets:

```
#define SPLIT(x) ((x) / 5)
```

E

Exercises

1. Here it is:

```
#define MULTIPLY(a,b) ((a)*(b))
```

2. This is the template version of the macro seen in the answer to quiz question 4:

```
template<typename T> T Split(const T& input)
{
    return (input / 5);
}
```

3. The template version of swap would be

```
template <typename T>
void Swap (T& x, T& y)
{
    T temp = x;
    x = y;
    y = temp;
}
```

4. #define QUARTER(x) ((x)/ 4)

5. The `template` class definition would look like the following:

```
template <typename Array1Type, typename Array2Type>
class TwoArrays
{
private:
        Array1Type Array1 [10];
        Array2Type Array2 [10];
public:
        Array1Type& GetArray1Element(int Index){return Array1[Index];}
        Array2Type& GetArray2Element(int Index){return Array2[Index];}
};
```

6. Here is a full sample containing a `Display()` function that features variable templates and usage of the same:

```
#include <iostream>
using namespace std;

void   Display()
{
}

template <typename First, typename ...Last> void Display(First a, Last... U)
```

```
{
    cout << a << endl;
    Display(U...);
}

int main()
{
    Display('a');
    Display(3.14);
    Display('a', 3.14);
    Display('z', 3.14567, "The power of variadic templates!");

    return 0;
}
```

Output ▼

```
a
3.14
a
3.14
z
3.14567
The power of variadic templates!
```

Answers for Lesson 15

Quiz

1. A `std::deque`. Only a `deque` simulates a dynamic array and also allows constant-time insertions at the front and at the back of the container. A `std::vector` does not allow insertions at the beginning and is therefore unsuited.

2. A `std::set` or a `std::map` if you have key-value pairs. If the elements need to be available in duplicates, too, you would choose `std::multiset` or `std::multimap`.

3. Yes. When you instantiate a `std::set` template, you can optionally supply a second template parameter that is a binary predicate that the `set` class uses as the sort criterion. Program this binary predicate to criteria that are relevant to your requirements. It needs to be strict-weak ordering compliant.

4. Iterators form the bridge between algorithms and containers so that the former (which are generic) can work on the latter without having to know (be customized for) every container type possible.

5. `hash_set` is not a C++ standard-compliant container. So, you should not use it in any application that has portability listed as one of its requirements. Use `std::map` instead.

E

Answers for Lesson 16

Quiz

1. `std::basic_string <T>`

2. Copy the two strings into two copy objects. Convert each copied string into either lowercase or uppercase. Return the result of comparison of the converted copied strings.

3. No, they are not. C-style strings are actually raw pointers akin to a character array, whereas STL `string` is a class that implements various operators and member functions to make string manipulation and handling as simple as possible.

Exercises

1. The program needs to use `std::reverse()`:

```
#include <string>
#include <iostream>
#include <algorithm>

int main ()
{
    using namespace std;

    cout << "Please enter a word for palindrome-check:" << endl;
    string strInput;
    cin >> strInput;

    string strCopy (strInput);
    reverse (strCopy.begin (), strCopy.end ());

    if (strCopy == strInput)
        cout << strInput << " is a palindrome!" << endl;
    else
        cout << strInput << " is not a palindrome." << endl;

    return 0;
}
```

2. Use `std::find()`:

```
#include <string>
#include <iostream>

using namespace std;
```

```cpp
// Find the number of character 'chToFind' in string "strInput"
int GetNumCharacters (string& strInput, char chToFind)
{
    int nNumCharactersFound = 0;

    size_t nCharOffset = strInput.find (chToFind);
    while (nCharOffset != string::npos)
    {
        ++ nNumCharactersFound;

        nCharOffset = strInput.find (chToFind, nCharOffset + 1);
    }

    return nNumCharactersFound;
}

int main ()
{

    cout << "Please enter a string:" << endl << "> ";
    string strInput;
    getline (cin, strInput);

    int nNumVowels = GetNumCharacters (strInput, 'a');
    nNumVowels += GetNumCharacters (strInput, 'e');
    nNumVowels += GetNumCharacters (strInput, 'i');
    nNumVowels += GetNumCharacters (strInput, 'o');
    nNumVowels += GetNumCharacters (strInput, 'u');

    // DIY: handle capitals too..

    cout << "The number of vowels in that sentence is:" << nNumVowels;

    return 0;
}
```

3. Use function `toupper()`:

```cpp
#include <string>
#include <iostream>
#include <algorithm>

int main ()
{
    using namespace std;
```

E

```
            cout << "Please enter a string for case-conversion:" << endl;
            cout << "> ";

            string strInput;
            getline (cin, strInput);
            cout << endl;

            for (size_t nCharIndex = 0
                ; nCharIndex < strInput.length ()
                ; nCharIndex += 2)
                strInput [nCharIndex] = toupper (strInput [nCharIndex]);

            cout << "The string converted to upper case is: " << endl;
            cout << strInput << endl << endl;

            return 0;
        }
```

4. This can be simply programmed as

```
    #include <string>
    #include <iostream>

    int main ()
    {
        using namespace std;

        const string str1 = "I";
        const string str2 = "Love";
        const string str3 = "STL";
        const string str4 = "String.";

        string strResult = str1 + " " + str2 + " " + str3 + " " + str4;

        cout << "The sentence reads:" << endl;
        cout << strResult;

        return 0;
    }
```

5. Use `std::string::find()`:

```
    #include <iostream>
    #include <string>

    int main()
    {
        using namespace std;
```

```
        string sampleStr("Good day String! Today is beautiful!");
        cout << "Sample string is: " << sampleStr << endl;
        cout << "Locating all instances of character 'a'" << endl;

        auto charPos = sampleStr.find('a', 0);

        while (charPos != string::npos)
        {
            cout << "'" << 'a' << "' found";
            cout << " at position: " << charPos << endl;

            // Make the 'find' function search forward from the next character
    onwards
            size_t charSearchPos = charPos + 1;

            charPos = sampleStr.find('a', charSearchPos);
        }

        return 0;
    }
```

Output ▼

```
Sample string is: Good day String! Today is beautiful!
Locating all instances of character 'a'
'a' found at position: 6
'a' found at position: 20
'a' found at position: 28
```

Answers for Lesson 17

Quiz

1. No, they can't. Elements can only be added at the back (that is, the end) of a vector sequence in constant time.

2. 10 more. At the 11th insertion, you trigger a reallocation.

3. Deletes the last element; that is, removes the element at the back.

4. Of type `Mammal`.

5. Via (a) the subscript operator ([]) (b) Function `at()`.

6. Random-access iterator.

E

Exercises

1. One solution is

```cpp
#include <vector>
#include <iostream>

using namespace std;

char DisplayOptions ()
{
    cout << "What would you like to do?" << endl;
    cout << "Select 1: To enter an integer" << endl;
    cout << "Select 2: Query a value given an index" << endl;
    cout << "Select 3: To display the vector" << endl << "> ";
    cout << "Select 4: To quit!" << endl << "> ";

    char ch;
    cin >> ch;

    return ch;
}

int main ()
{
    vector <int> vecData;

    char chUserChoice = '\0';
    while ((chUserChoice = DisplayOptions ()) != '4')
    {
        if (chUserChoice == '1')
        {
            cout << "Please enter an integer to be inserted: ";
            int nDataInput = 0;
            cin >> nDataInput;

            vecData.push_back (nDataInput);
        }
        else if (chUserChoice == '2')
        {
            cout << "Please enter an index between 0 and ";
            cout << (vecData.size () - 1) << ": ";
            size_t index = 0;
            cin >> index;

            if (index < (vecData.size ()))
            {
                cout<<"Element ["<<index<<"] = "<<vecData[index];
                cout << endl;
            }
        }
        else if (chUserChoice == '3')
```

```
            {
                cout << "The contents of the vector are: ";
                for (size_t index = 0; index < vecData.size (); ++ index)
                    cout << vecData [index] << ' ';
                cout << endl;
            }
        }
        return 0;
}
```

2. Use the `std::find()` algorithm:

```
vector <int>::iterator elementFound = std::find (vecData.begin (),
                                       vecData.end (), value);
if (elementFound != vecData.end())
    cout << "Element found!" << endl;
```

3. Here is a possible solution. Note the usage of a `vector` to store instances of a `class Dimensions`. Also note how `Dimensions` implements operator `const char*` so that `std::cout` can directly work on instances of it.

```
#include <vector>
#include <iostream>
#include <string>
#include <sstream>

using namespace std;

char DisplayOptions()
{
    cout << "What would you like to do?" << endl;
    cout << "Select 1: To enter length & breadth " << endl;
    cout << "Select 2: Query a value given an index" << endl;
    cout << "Select 3: To display dimensions of all packages" << endl;
    cout << "Select 4: To quit!" << endl << "> ";

    char ch;
    cin >> ch;

    return ch;
}

class Dimensions
{
    int length, breadth;
    string strOut;
public:
    Dimensions(int inL, int inB) : length(inL), breadth(inB) {}

    operator const char* ()
```

E

```
        {
            stringstream os;
            os << "Length "s << length << ", Breadth: "s << breadth << endl;
            strOut = os.str();
            return strOut.c_str();
        }
    };

    int main()
    {
        vector <Dimensions> vecData;

        char chUserChoice = '\0';
        while ((chUserChoice = DisplayOptions()) != '4')
        {
            if (chUserChoice == '1')
            {
                cout << "Please enter length and breadth: " << endl;
                int length = 0, breadth = 0;
                cin >> length;
              cin >> breadth;

                vecData.push_back(Dimensions(length, breadth));
            }
            else if (chUserChoice == '2')
            {
                cout << "Please enter an index between 0 and ";
                cout << (vecData.size() - 1) << ": ";
                size_t index = 0;
                cin >> index;

                if (index < (vecData.size()))
                {
                    cout << "Element [" << index << "] = " << vecData[index];
                    cout << endl;
                }
            }
            else if (chUserChoice == '3')
            {
                cout << "The contents of the vector are: ";
                for (size_t index = 0; index < vecData.size(); ++index)
                    cout << vecData[index] << ' ';
                cout << endl;
            }
        }
        return 0;
    }
```

4. List Initializations introduced in C++11 make the code compact:

```
#include <deque>
#include <string>
#include <iostream>
using namespace std;

template<typename T>
void DisplayDeque(deque<T> inDQ)
{
    for (auto element = inDQ.cbegin();
    element != inDQ.cend();
        ++element)
        cout << *element << endl;
}

int main()
{
    deque<string> strDq{ "Hello"s, "Containers are cool"s, "C++ is
evolving!"s };
    DisplayDeque(strDq);

    return 0;
}
```

Answers for Lesson 18

Quiz

1. Elements can be inserted in the middle of the list as they can be at either end. There is no gain or loss in performance due to position.

2. The specialty of the list is that operations such as these don't invalidate existing iterators.

3. `theList.clear ();`

   or

   `theList.erase (theList.begin(), theList.end());`

4. Yes, an overloaded version of the `insert()` function enables you to insert a range from a source collection.

Exercises

1. This is like Exercise solution 1 for the `vector` in Lesson 17, "STL Dynamic Array Classes." The only change is that you would use the `list::insert()` function as

   `List.insert (List.begin(),nDataInput);`

E

2. Store iterators to two elements in a list. Insert an element in the middle using the list's insert function. Use the iterators to demonstrate that they are still able to fetch the values they pointed to before the insertion.

3. A possible solution is

```cpp
#include <vector>
#include <list>
#include <iostream>

using namespace std;

int main()
{
    vector <int> vecData{ 0, 10, 20, 30 };

    list <int> linkInts;

    // Insert contents of vector into beginning of list
    linkInts.insert(linkInts.begin(),
        vecData.begin(), vecData.end());

    cout << "The contents of the list are: ";

    list <int>::const_iterator element;
    for (element = linkInts.begin();
        element != linkInts.end();
        ++element)
        cout << *element << " ";

    return 0;
}
```

4. A possible solution is

```cpp
#include <list>
#include <string>
#include <iostream>

using namespace std;

int main()
{
    list <string> names;
    names.push_back("Jack");
    names.push_back("John");
    names.push_back("Anna");
    names.push_back("Skate");

    cout << "The contents of the list are: ";
```

```
    list <string>::const_iterator element;
    for (element = names.begin(); element != names.end(); ++element)
        cout << *element << " ";
    cout << endl;

    cout << "The contents after reversing are: ";
    names.reverse();
    for (element = names.begin(); element != names.end(); ++element)
        cout << *element << " ";
    cout << endl;

    cout << "The contents after sorting are: ";
    names.sort();
    for (element = names.begin(); element != names.end(); ++element)
        cout << *element << " ";
    cout << endl;

    return 0;
}
```

Answers for Lesson 19

Quiz

1. The default sort criterion is specified by `std::less<>`, which effectively uses `operator<` to compare two integers and returns true if the first is less than the second.

2. Given that a `multiset` sorts elements on insertion, you would find the two elements of equal value together, one after another.

3. `size()`, as is the case with all STL containers.

Exercises

1. One solution is

```
#include <set>
#include <iostream>
#include <string>
using namespace std;

template <typename T>
void DisplayContents(const T& container)
{
    for (auto iElement = container.cbegin();
    iElement != container.cend();
```

E

```
            ++iElement)
            cout << *iElement << endl;

        cout << endl;
    }

struct ContactItem
{
    string name;
    string phoneNum;
    string displayAs;

    ContactItem(const string& nameInit, const string & phone)
    {
        name = nameInit;
        phoneNum = phone;
        displayAs = (name + ": " + phoneNum);
    }

    // used by set::find() given contact list item
    bool operator == (const ContactItem& itemToCompare) const
    {
        return (itemToCompare.phoneNum == this->phoneNum);
    }

    // used to sort
    bool operator < (const ContactItem& itemToCompare) const
    {
        return (this->phoneNum < itemToCompare.phoneNum);
    }

    // Used in DisplayContents via cout
    operator const char*() const
    {
        return displayAs.c_str();
    }
};

int main()
{
    set<ContactItem> setContacts;
    setContacts.insert(ContactItem("Jack Welsch", "+1 7889 879 879"));
    setContacts.insert(ContactItem("Bill Gates", "+1 97 7897 8799 8"));
    setContacts.insert(ContactItem("Angi Merkel", "+49 23456 5466"));
    setContacts.insert(ContactItem("Vlad Putin", "+7 6645 4564 797"));
    setContacts.insert(ContactItem("John Travolta", "+1 234 4564 789"));
    setContacts.insert(ContactItem("Ben Affleck", "+1 745 641 314"));
    DisplayContents(setContacts);

    cout << "Enter a number you wish to search: ";
    string input;
```

```
        getline(cin, input);

        auto contactFound = setContacts.find(ContactItem("", input));
        if (contactFound != setContacts.end())
        {
            cout << "The number belongs to " << (*contactFound).name << endl;
            DisplayContents(setContacts);
        }
        else
            cout << "Contact not found" << endl;

        return 0;
    }
```

2. The structure and the `multiset` definition would be

```
    #include <set>
    #include <iostream>
    #include <string>

    using namespace std;

    struct PAIR_WORD_MEANING
    {
        string word;
        string meaning;

        PAIR_WORD_MEANING(const string& sWord, const string& sMeaning)
            : word(sWord), meaning(sMeaning) {}

        bool operator< (const PAIR_WORD_MEANING& pairAnotherWord) const
        {
            return (word < pairAnotherWord.word);
        }

        bool operator== (const string& key)
        {
            return (key == this->word);
        }
    };

    int main()
    {
        multiset <PAIR_WORD_MEANING> msetDictionary;
        PAIR_WORD_MEANING word1("C++", "A programming language");
        PAIR_WORD_MEANING word2("Programmer", "A geek!");

        msetDictionary.insert(word1);
        msetDictionary.insert(word2);

        cout << "Enter a word you wish to find the meaning off" << endl;
```

E

```
        string input;
        getline(cin, input);
        auto element = msetDictionary.find(PAIR_WORD_MEANING(input, ""));
        if (element != msetDictionary.end())
            cout << "Meaning is: " << (*element).meaning << endl;

        return 0;
    }
```

3. One solution is

```
    #include <set>
    #include <iostream>

    using namespace std;

    template <typename T>
    void DisplayContent(const T& cont)
    {
        T::const_iterator element;

        for (element = cont.begin(); element != cont.end(); ++element)
            cout << *element << " ";
    }

    int main()
    {
        multiset <int> msetIntegers;

        msetIntegers.insert(5);
        msetIntegers.insert(5);
        msetIntegers.insert(5);

        set <int> setIntegers;
        setIntegers.insert(5);
        setIntegers.insert(5);
        setIntegers.insert(5);

        cout << "Displaying the contents of the multiset: ";
        DisplayContent(msetIntegers);
        cout << endl;

        cout << "Displaying the contents of the set: ";
        DisplayContent(setIntegers);
        cout << endl;

        return 0;
    }
```

Answers for Lesson 20

Quiz

1. The default sort criterion is specified by `std::less<>`.

2. Next to each other.

3. `size()`. In fact, this member function would tell you the number of elements in every container supplied by STL.

4. You would not find duplicate elements in a `map`!

Exercises

1. An associative container that allows duplicate entries. For example, a `std::multimap`:

```
std::multimap <string, string> mapNamesToNumbers;
```

2. An associative container that allows duplicate entries.

```
struct fPredicate
{
    bool operator< (const WordProperty& lsh, const WordProperty& rsh) const
    {
        return (lsh.word < rsh.word);
    }
};
```

3. Take a hint from the similarly solved Exercise 3 in Lesson 19, "STL Set Classes."

Answers for Lesson 21

Quiz

1. A unary predicate.

2. It can display data, for example, or simply count elements. See usage of `std::transform()` in Listing 21.6 with predicate `tolower()`.

3. All entities that exist during the runtime of an application are objects. In this case, even structures and classes can be made to work as functions, hence the term *function objects*. Note that functions can also be available via function pointers—these are function objects, too.

E

Exercises

1. A solution is

```
template <typename elementType=int>
struct Double
{
    void operator () (const elementType element) const
    {
            cout << element * 2 << ' ';
    }
};
```

This unary predicate can be used as

```
#include<vector>
#include<iostream>
#include<algorithm>
using namespace std;

int main()
{
    vector <int> numsInVec;

    for (int count = 0; count < 10; ++count)
        numsInVec.push_back(count);

    cout << "Displaying the vector of integers: " << endl;

    // Display the array of integers
    for_each(numsInVec.begin(),  // Start of range
            numsInVec.end(), // End of range
            Double <>()); // Unary function object

    return 0;
}
```

2. Add a member integer that is incremented every time the `operator()` is used:

```
template <typename elementType=int>
struct Double
{
    int usageCount;

    // Constructor
    Double () : usageCount (0) {};

    void operator () (const elementType element) const
    {
        ++ usageCount;
        cout << element * 2 << ' ';
    }
};
```

3. The binary predicate is the following:

```
template <typename elementType>
template <typename elementType>
class SortAscending
{
public:
   bool operator () (const elementType& num1,
       const elementType& num2) const
   {
       return (num1 < num2);
   }
};
```

This predicate can be used as

```
#include<iostream>
#include<vector>
#include<algorithm>
int main()
{
   std::vector <int> numsInVec;

   // Insert sample numbers: 100, 90... 20, 10
   for (int sample = 10; sample > 0; --sample)
      numsInVec.push_back(sample * 10);

   std::sort(numsInVec.begin(), numsInVec.end(),
      SortAscending<int>());

   for (size_t index = 0; index < numsInVec.size(); ++index)
      cout << numsInVec[index] << ' ';

   return 0;
}
```

Answers for Lesson 22

E

Quiz

1. A lambda always starts with `[]`.

2. Via a capture list `[Var1, Var2, …](Type& param) { ...; }`

3. Like this:

```
[Var1, Var2, ...](Type& param) -> ReturnType { ...; }
```

Exercises

1. One solution for the lambda is

```
sort(container.begin(),container.end(),
    [](auto el1, auto el2) {return (el1 > el2); });
```

It has also been demonstrated in the code supplied in the solution to Exercise 2.

2. This is what the lambda would look like:

```
cout << "Number you wish to add to all elements: ";
int numInput = 0;
cin >> numInput;

for_each(vecNumbers.begin(), vecNumbers.end(),
        [=](int& element) {element += numInput;});
```

The sample that demonstrates the solutions in Exercise 1 and 2 is

```
#include<iostream>
#include<algorithm>
#include<vector>
using namespace std;

template <typename T>
void DisplayContents(const T& container)
{
    for (auto element = container.cbegin();
         element != container.cend();
         ++element)
        cout << *element << ' ';
    cout << endl;
}

int main()
{
    vector<int> vecNumbers{ 25, -5, 122, 2011, -10001 };
    DisplayContents(vecNumbers);

    sort(vecNumbers.begin(), vecNumbers.end());
    DisplayContents(vecNumbers);

    sort(vecNumbers.begin(), vecNumbers.end(),
        [](int Num1, int Num2) {return (Num1 > Num2); });
    DisplayContents(vecNumbers);

    cout << "Number you wish to add to all elements: ";
    int numcontainer = 0;
    cin >> numcontainer;
```

```
    for_each(vecNumbers.begin(), vecNumbers.end(),
        [=](int& element) {element += numcontainer; });

    DisplayContents(vecNumbers);

    return 0;
}
```

Output ▼

```
25 -5 122 2011 -10001
-10001 -5 25 122 2011
2011 122 25 -5 -10001
Number you wish to add to all elements: 5
2016 127 30 0 -9996
```

Answers for Lesson 23

Quiz

1. Use the `std::list::remove_if()` function because it ensures that existing iterators to elements in the list (that were not removed) still remain valid.

2. `list::sort()` (or even `std::sort()`) in the absence of an explicitly supplied predicate resorts to a sort using `std::less<>`, which employs the `operator<` to sort objects in a collection.

3. Once per element in the range supplied.

4. `for_each()` accepts a unary predicate and returns the function object that can be used to contain state information. `std::transform()` can work with unary or binary predicates and features an overloaded version that can therefore work on two input ranges.

E

Exercises

1. Here is one solution:

```
struct CaseInsensitiveCompare
{
    bool operator() (const string& str1, const string& str2) const
    {
        string str1Copy (str1), str2Copy (str2);

        transform (str1Copy.begin (),
```

```
                      str1Copy.end (), str1Copy.begin (), tolower);
         transform (str2Copy.begin (),
                      str2Copy.end (), str2Copy.begin (), tolower);

         return (str1Copy < str2Copy);
      }
   };
```

2. Here is the demonstration. Note how `std::copy()` works without knowing the nature of the collections. It works using the iterator classes only:

```cpp
#include <vector>
#include <algorithm>
#include <list>
#include <string>
#include <iostream>

using namespace std;

int main ()
{
    list <string> listNames;
    listNames.push_back ("Jack");
    listNames.push_back ("John");
    listNames.push_back ("Anna");
    listNames.push_back ("Skate");

    vector <string> vecNames (4);
    copy (listNames.begin (), listNames.end (), vecNames.begin ());

    vector <string> ::const_iterator iNames;
    for (iNames = vecNames.begin (); iNames != vecNames.end (); ++ iNames)
        cout << *iNames << ' ';

    return 0;
}
```

3. The difference between `std::sort()` and `std::stable_sort()` is that the latter, when sorting, ensures the relative positions of the objects remain maintained. Because the application needs to store data in the sequence it happened, you should choose `stable_sort()` to keep the relative ordering between the celestial events intact.

Answers for Lesson 24

Quiz

1. Yes, by supplying a binary predicate.

2. class `Coin` needs to implement `operator<`.

3. No, you can only work on the top of the stack. So you can't access the coin at the bottom, which is the first coin inserted.

Exercises

1. The binary predicate could be `operator<`:

```
class Person
{
public:
    int age;
    bool isFemale;

    bool operator<  (const Person& anotherPerson) const
    {
        bool bRet = false;
        if (age > anotherPerson.age)
            bRet = true;
        else if (isFemale && anotherPerson.isFemale)
            bRet = true;

        return bRet;
    }
};
```

2. Push individual characters into a `stack`. As you pop data, you effectively reverse contents because a stack is a LIFO type of container.

Answers for Lesson 25

Quiz

1. No. The number of bits a bitset can hold is fixed at compile time.

2. Because `bitset` isn't a container class. It can't scale itself dynamically as other containers do; it doesn't support iterators in the way containers need to.

3. No. `std::bitset` is best suited for this purpose.

Exercises

1. `std::bitset` featuring instantiation, initialization, display, and addition is demonstrated here:

```
#include <bitset>
#include <iostream>
```

```
int main()
{
    // Initialize the bitset to 1001
    std::bitset <4> fourBits (9);

    std::cout << "fourBits: " << fourBits << std::endl;

    // Initialize another bitset to 0010
    std::bitset <4> fourMoreBits (2);

    std::cout << "fourMoreBits: " << fourMoreBits << std::endl;

    std::bitset<4>addResult(fourBits.to_ulong()+fourMoreBits.to_ulong());
    std::cout << "The result of the addition is: " << addResult;

    return 0;
}
```

2. Call the `flip()` function on any of the bitset objects in the preceding sample:

```
addResult.flip ();
std::cout << "The result of the flip is: " << addResult << std::endl;
```

Answers for Lesson 26

Quiz

1. I would look at www.boost.org. I hope you would, too!

2. No, typically well-programmed (and correctly chosen) smart pointers would not.

3. When intrusive, objects that they own need to hold it; otherwise, they can hold this information in a shared object on the free store.

4. The list needs to be traversed in both directions, so it needs to be doubly linked.

Exercises

1. `object->DoSomething ();` is faulty because the pointer lost ownership of the object during the previous copy step. This will crash (or do something very unpleasant).

2. The code would look like this:

```cpp
#include <memory>
#include <iostream>
using namespace std;

class Fish
{
public:
    Fish() {cout << "Fish: Constructed!" << endl;}
    ~Fish() {cout << "Fish: Destructed!" << endl;}

    void Swim() const {cout << "Fish swims in water" << endl;}
};

class Carp: public Fish
{
};

void MakeFishSwim(const unique_ptr<Fish>& inFish)
{
    inFish->Swim();
}

int main ()
{
    unique_ptr<Fish> myCarp (new Carp); // note this
    MakeFishSwim(myCarp);

    return 0;
}
```

As there is no copy step involved, given that `MakeFishSwim()` accepts the argument as a reference, there is no question of slicing. Also, note the instantiation syntax of variable `myCarp`.

3. A `unique_ptr` does not allow copy or assignment as the copy constructor and copy assignment operator are both private.

E

Answers for Lesson 27

Quiz

1. Use `ofstream` to only write to a file.

2. You would use `cin.getline()`. See Listing 27.7.

3. You wouldn't because `std::string` contains text information and you can stay with the default mode, which is text (no need for binary).

4. To check whether `open()` succeeded. If it fails, you may want to show an error and suspend file processing.

Exercises

1. You opened the file but didn't check for success of `open()` using `is_open()` before using the stream or closing it.

2. You cannot insert into an `ifstream`, which is designed for input, not output, and hence does not support stream insertion `operator<<`.

Answers for Lesson 28

Quiz

1. A class just like any other, but created expressly as a base class for some other exception classes such as `bad_alloc`.

2. `std::bad_alloc`

3. That's a bad idea for it's also possible that the exception was thrown in the first place because of a lack of memory.

4. Using the same `catch(std::exception& exp)` that you can also use for type `bad_alloc`.

Exercises

1. Never throw in a destructor.

2. You forgot to make the code exception safe (missing `try... catch` block).

3. Don't allocate in a catch block! Assume the data allocated in `try` is lost and continue with damage control.

Answers for Lesson 29

Quiz

1. It seems that your application does all the activity within one thread. So, if the image processing itself (contrast correction) is processor intensive, the UI is unre-

sponsive. You ought to split these two activities into two threads so that the OS switches the two threads, giving processor time to both the UI and the worker that does the correction.

2. Your threads are possibly poorly synchronized. You are writing to and reading from an object at the same time, resulting in inconsistent or garbled data recovery. Insert a binary semaphore and ensure that the table cannot be accessed when it is being modified.

E

Index

Symbols

+ (addition) operator, 88–89, 347–349

+= (addition assignment) operator, 442–443

<> (angle brackets), 19

= (assignment) operator, 87, 357–360

\ (backslash), 76–78, 86

& (bitwise AND) operator, 100–102, 624

>> (bitwise right shift) operator, 102–104

~ (bitwise NOT) operator, 100–102

| (bitwise OR) operator, 100–102, 624

^ (bitwise XOR) operator, 100–102, 624

{ } (braces), 48, 87

: (colon), 10, 232

// comment syntax, 23, 28

/* */ comment syntax, 23, 28

?: (conditional) operator, 126–127

-- (decrement) operator, 89, 190–193, 338–341

* (dereferencing) operator, 183–185, 344–345, 635, 639

. (dot) operator, 218–219

/ (division) operator, 88–89

... (ellipses), 415

== (equality) operator, 92, 352

>> (extraction) operator, 27, 624, 649, 663–664

> (greater than) operator, 92–94, 354–357

>= (greater than or equal to) operator, 354–357

!= (inequality) operator, 92, 352

++ (increment) operator, 89, 191–193, 338–341, 26, 624, 649, 662, 624

< (less than) operator, 92–94, 354–357

<= (less than or equal to) operator, 92–94, 354–357

&& (logical AND) operator, 95–100

|| (logical OR) operator, 95–100

! (logical NOT) operator, 95–100

-> (member selection) operator, 219–220, 344–345, 635, 639

% (modulo) operator, 88–89

* (multiplication) operator, 88–89

( ) (parentheses), 364–365, 398–399

& (referencing) operator, 179–180

>>= (right shift) operator, 624

[ ] (subscript) operator, 197–198, 360–364, 462, 555